773

||||||||||||||||||||||||||||||||||||||||||

✓ **W9-ALH-557**

A step-by-step guide to using your County Atlas

1 To locate any street in your County Atlas, first select the specific city, town or township from the alphabetical listing below. At the right of the listing, note the section or sections.

2 Turn to the end of the color coded section to find the complete street index for that section. Under the specific city, town or township heading, locate the street you wish to find and note both its page number and grid coordinates.

3 Turn to the map and locate the alpha coordinate along the side of the page and the numeric coordinate along the top of the page. The street will be located on the map where the coordinates intersect.

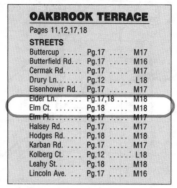

Naperville Twp. Sec.3
New Lenox Sec.8
New Lenox Twp. Sec.8
North Aurora Sec.4
Oak Brook Sec.3
Oakbrook Terrace Sec.3
Pingree Grove Sec.4
Plainfield Sec.8
Plainfield Twp. Sec.8
Plato Center Sec.4
Plato Twp. Sec.4
Richardson Sec.4
Ridgewood Sec.8
Rockdale Sec.8
Romeoville Sec.8
Roselle Sec.3
Rutland Twp. Sec.4
Schaumburg Sec.5
Scraper-Moecherville Sec.4

OAKBROOK TERRACE
Pages 11,12,17,18
STREETS
Buttercup ..... Pg.17 ..... M17
Butterfield Rd... Pg.17 ..... M16
Cermak Rd. .... Pg.17 ..... M17
Drury Ln....... Pg.12 ..... L18
Eisenhower Rd.. Pg.17 ..... M17
Elder Ln. ...... Pg.17,18 ..... M18
Elm Ct. .... Pg.18 ..... M18
Elm Pl. .... Pg.17 ..... M17
Halsey Rd...... Pg.17 ..... M17
Hodges Rd. .... Pg.18 ..... M18
Karban Rd. .... Pg.17 ..... M17
Kolberg Ct. .... Pg.12 ..... L18
Leahy St. ...... Pg.18 ..... M18
Lincoln Ave. ... Pg.17 ..... M16

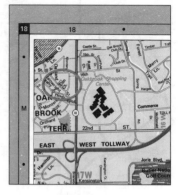

Index to cities, towns and townships
Unincorporated areas indexed under respective townships

City • Town • Twp	Section
Alsip	Sec.1
Arlington Heights	Sec.2
Barrington	Sec.2,5
Barrington Hills	Sec.2,5
Barrington Twp.	Sec.2,5
Bedford Park	Sec.1
Bellwood	Sec.1
Berkeley	Sec.1
Berwyn	Sec.1
Bloom Twp.	Sec.2
Blue Island	Sec.1
Bowes	Sec.5
Bremen Twp.	Sec.2
Bridgeview	Sec.1
Broadview	Sec.1
Brookfield	Sec.1
Buffalo Grove	Sec.2
Burbank	Sec.1
Burnham	Sec.1
Calumet City	Sec.1
Calumet Park	Sec.1
Carpentersville	Sec.5
Chicago	Sec.1
Chicago Heights	Sec.2
Chicago Ridge	Sec.2
Cicero	Sec.1
Country Club Hills	Sec.2
Countryside	Sec.1
Crestwood	Sec.1
Deerfield	Sec.2
Des Plaines	Sec.2
Dixmoor	Sec.1
Dolton	Sec.1
Dundee Twp.	Sec.5
East Chicago	Sec.1
East Dundee	Sec.5
East Hazel Crest	Sec.2
Elgin	Sec.5
Elgin Twp.	Sec.5

City • Town • Twp	Section
Elk Grove Twp.	Sec.2
Elk Grove Village	Sec.2
Elmwood Park	Sec.1
Evanston	Sec.2
Evanston Twp.	Sec.2
Evergreen Park	Sec.1
Flossmoor	Sec.2
Ford Heights	Sec.2
Forest Park	Sec.1
Forest View	Sec.1
Franklin Park	Sec.1
Gilberts	Sec.5
Glencoe	Sec.2
Glenview	Sec.2
Glenwood	Sec.2
Golf	Sec.2
Hammond	Sec.1
Hanover Park	Sec.2,5
Harvey	Sec.1
Harwood Heights	Sec.1
Hazel Crest	Sec.2
Hickory Hills	Sec.2
Hillside	Sec.1
Hodgkins	Sec.1
Hoffman Estates	Sec.2,5
Hometown	Sec.1
Homewood	Sec.2
Indian Head Park	Sec.1
Inverness	Sec.2
Justice	Sec.2
Kenilworth	Sec.2
LaGrange	Sec.1
LaGrange Park	Sec.1
Lansing	Sec.2
Leyden Twp.	Sec.1
Lincolnwood	Sec.1
Lynwood	Sec.2
Lyons	Sec.1
Lyons Twp.	Sec.1,2

City • Town • Twp	Section
Maine Twp.	Sec.2
Markham	Sec.1
Matteson	Sec.2
Maywood	Sec.1
McCook	Sec.1
McQueens	Sec.5
Melrose Park	Sec.1
Merrionette Park	Sec.1
Midlothian	Sec.1
Morton Grove	Sec.2
Mount Prospect	Sec.2
New Trier Twp.	Sec.2
Niles	Sec.2
Niles Twp.	Sec.2
Norridge	Sec.1
North Riverside	Sec.1
Northbrook	Sec.2
Northfield	Sec.2
Northfield Twp.	Sec.2
Northlake	Sec.1
Oak Forest	Sec.2
Oak Lawn	Sec.1
Oak Park	Sec.1
Olympia Fields	Sec.2
Orland Hills	Sec.2
Orland Park	Sec.2
Orland Twp.	Sec.2
Palatine	Sec.2
Palatine Twp.	Sec.2
Palos Heights	Sec.2
Palos Hills	Sec.2
Palos Park	Sec.2
Palos Twp.	Sec.2
Park Forest	Sec.2
Park Ridge	Sec.1,2
Phoenix	Sec.1
Posen	Sec.1
Prospect Heights	Sec.2
Proviso Twp.	Sec.1

City • Town • Twp	Section
Rich Twp.	Sec.2
Richton Park	Sec.2
River Forest	Sec.1
River Grove	Sec.1
Riverdale	Sec.1
Riverside	Sec.1
Robbins	Sec.1
Rolling Meadows	Sec.2
Roselle	Sec.2
Rosemont	Sec.1
Sauk Village	Sec.2
Schaumburg	Sec.2,5
Schaumburg Twp.	Sec.2
Schiller Park	Sec.1
Skokie	Sec.2
Sleepy Hollow	Sec.5
South Barrington	Sec.2,5
South Chicago Heights	Sec.2
South Elgin	Sec.5
South Holland	Sec.1
Steger	Sec.2
Stickney	Sec.1
Stone Park	Sec.1
Streamwood	Sec.2,5
Summit	Sec.1
Thornton	Sec.2
Thornton Twp.	Sec.2
Tinley Park	Sec.2
Udina	Sec.5
West Dundee	Sec.5
Westchester	Sec.1
Western Springs	Sec.1
Wheeling	Sec.2
Wheeling Twp.	Sec.2
Willow Springs	Sec.2
Wilmette	Sec.2
Winnetka	Sec.2
Worth	Sec.2
Worth Twp.	Sec.2

CITY OF CHICAGO
SECTION 1

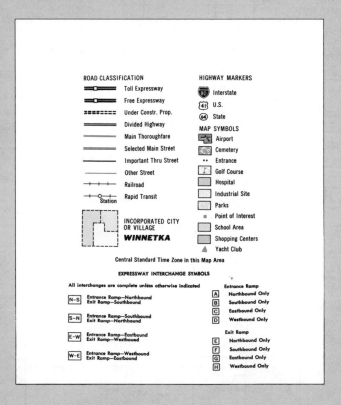

ROAD CLASSIFICATION

- Toll Expressway
- Free Expressway
- Under Constr. Prop.
- Divided Highway
- Main Thoroughfare
- Selected Main Street
- Important Thru Street
- Other Street
- Railroad
- Rapid Transit
  Station

INCORPORATED CITY OR VILLAGE
WINNETKA

Central Standard Time Zone in this Map Area

HIGHWAY MARKERS

- Interstate
- U.S.
- State

MAP SYMBOLS

- Airport
- Cemetery
- Entrance
- Golf Course
- Hospital
- Industrial Site
- Parks
- Point of Interest
- School Area
- Shopping Centers
- Yacht Club

EXPRESSWAY INTERCHANGE SYMBOLS

All interchanges are complete unless otherwise indicated

N-S Entrance Ramp—Northbound / Exit Ramp—Southbound

S-N Entrance Ramp—Southbound / Exit Ramp—Northbound

E-W Entrance Ramp—Eastbound / Exit Ramp—Westbound

W-E Entrance Ramp—Westbound / Exit Ramp—Eastbound

Entrance Ramp
A Northbound Only
B Southbound Only
C Eastbound Only
D Westbound Only

Exit Ramp
E Northbound Only
F Southbound Only
G Eastbound Only
H Westbound Only

TURN PAGE FOR ORIENTATION MAP

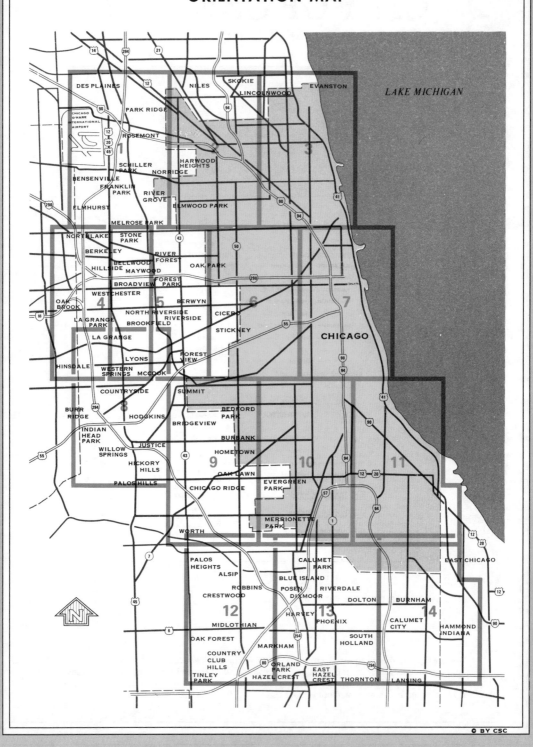

SECTION 1
ORIENTATION MAP

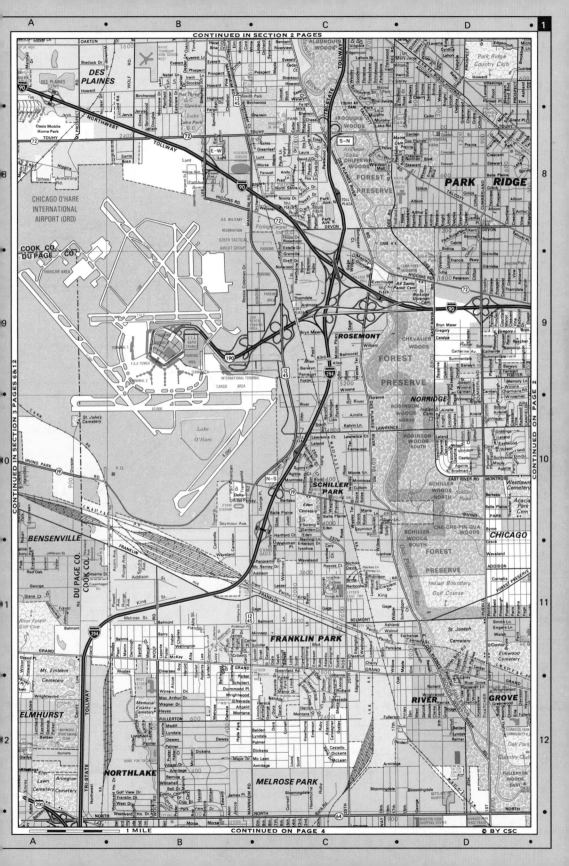

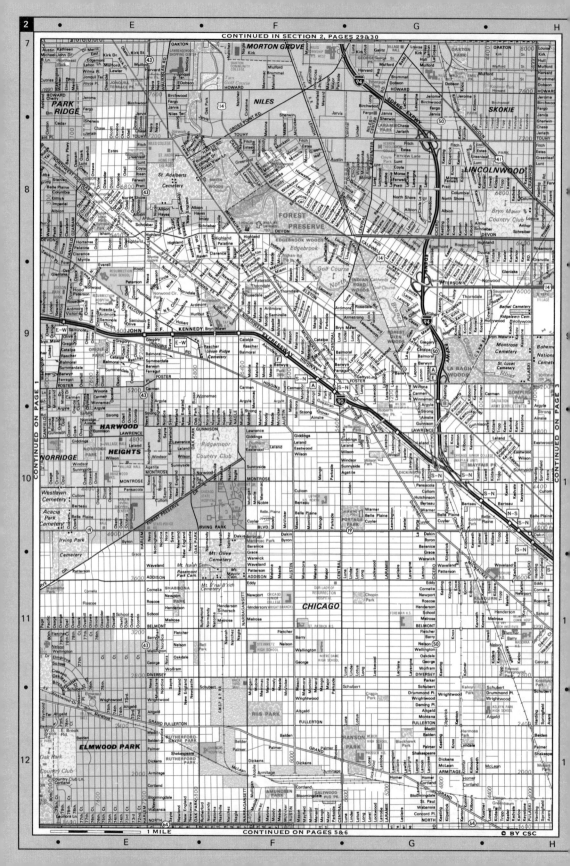

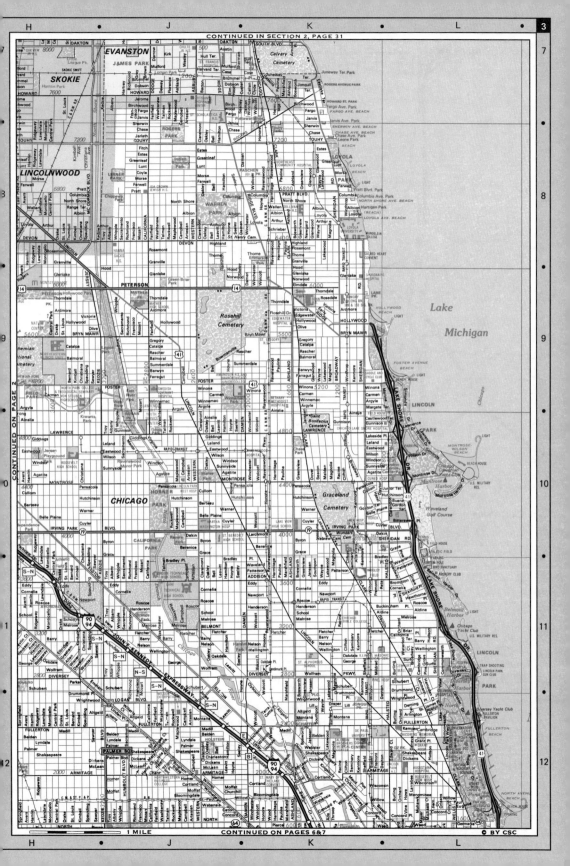

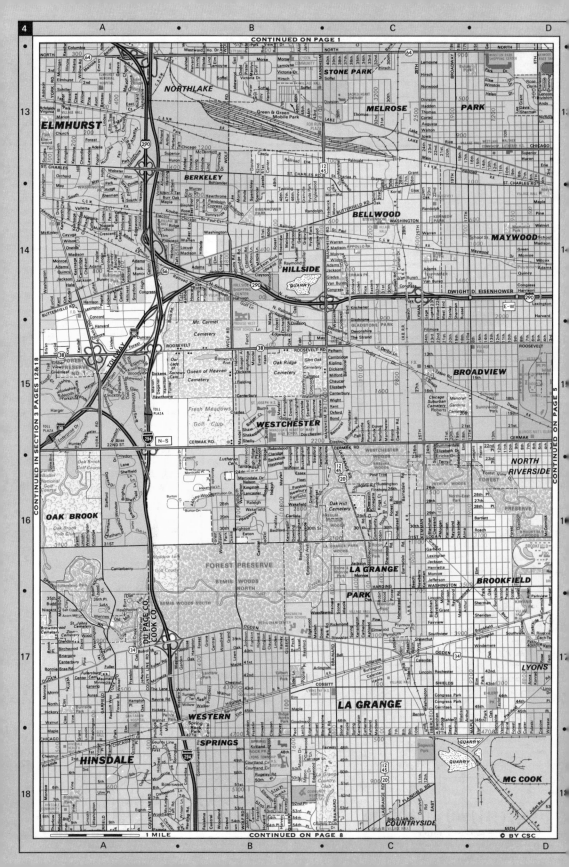

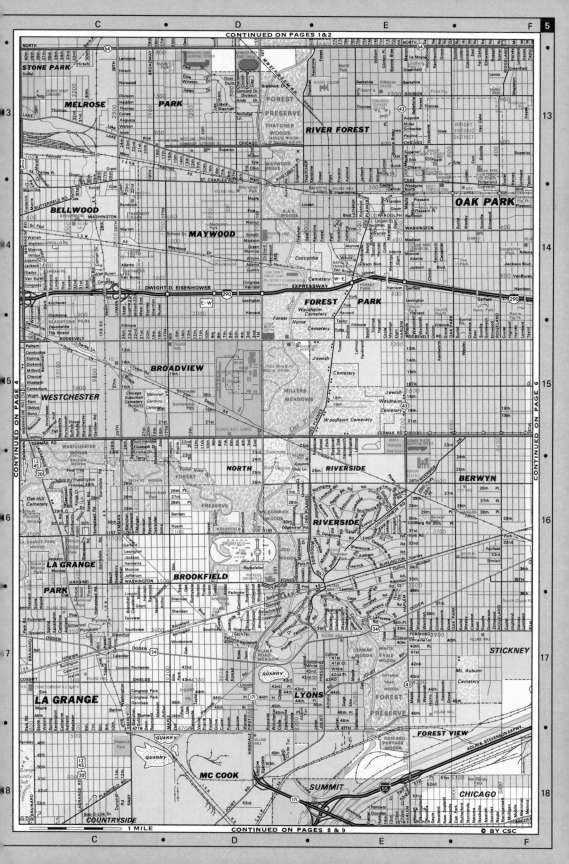

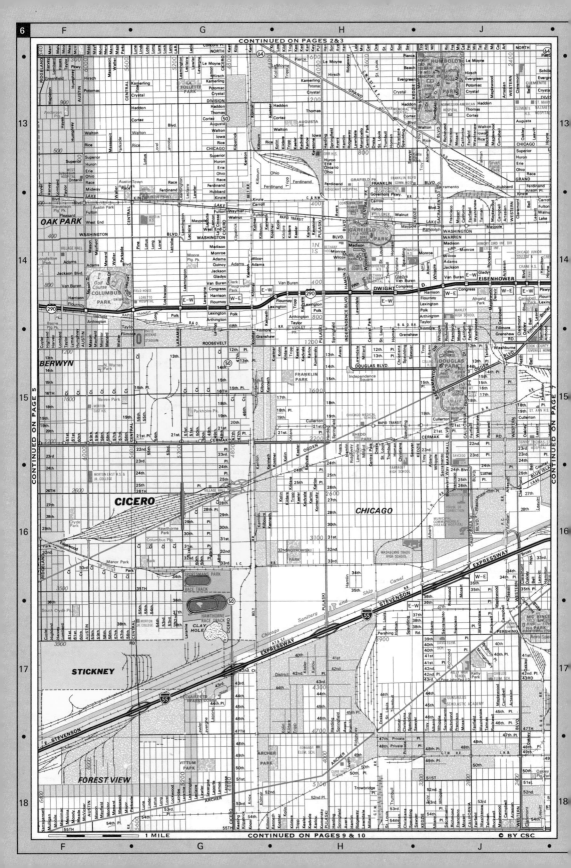

CHICAGO

Lake

Michigan

NAVY PIER

CONTINUED ON PAGE 6

1 MILE

© BY CSC

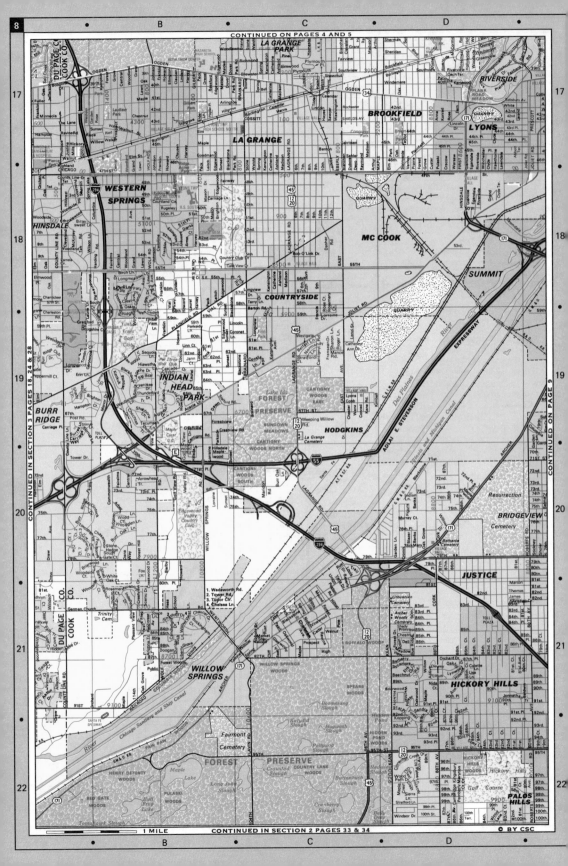

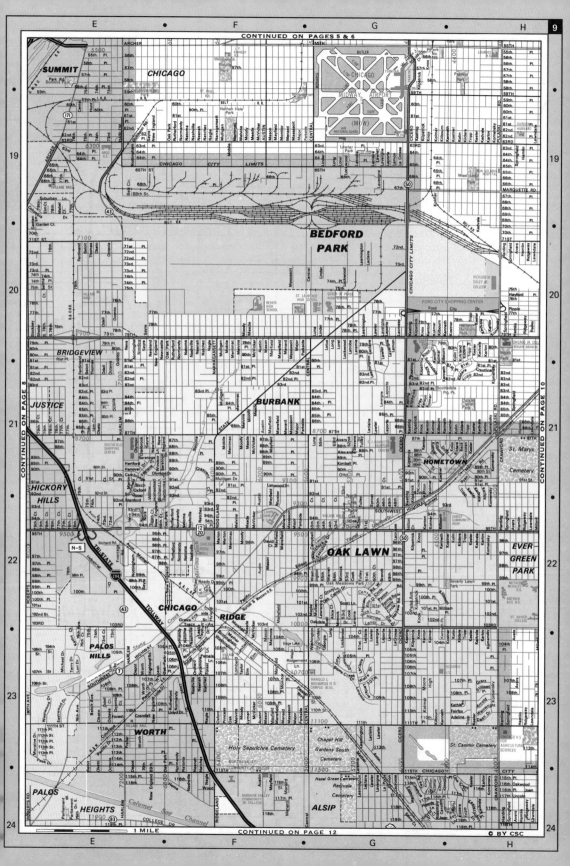

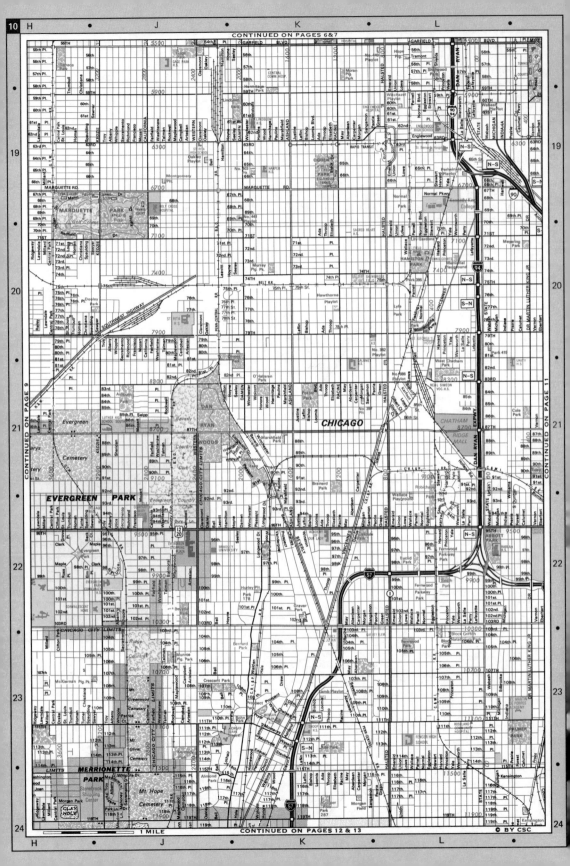

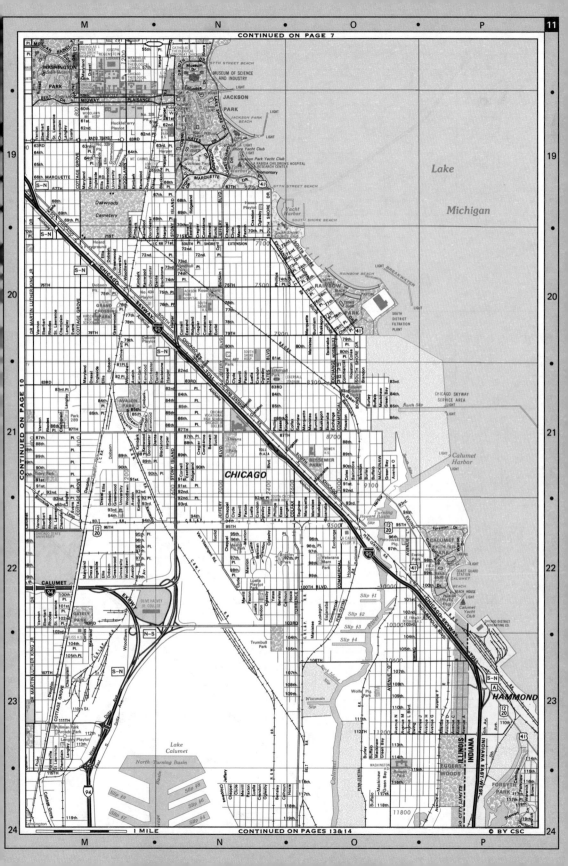

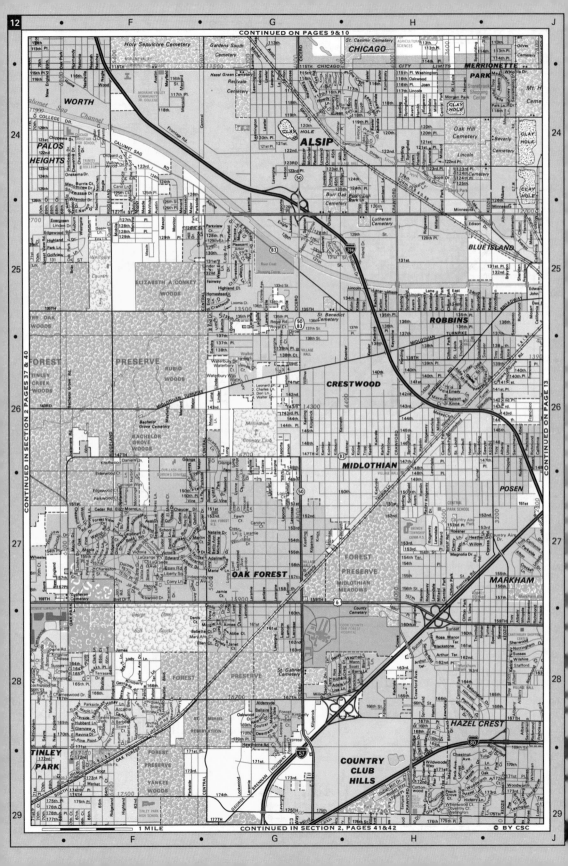

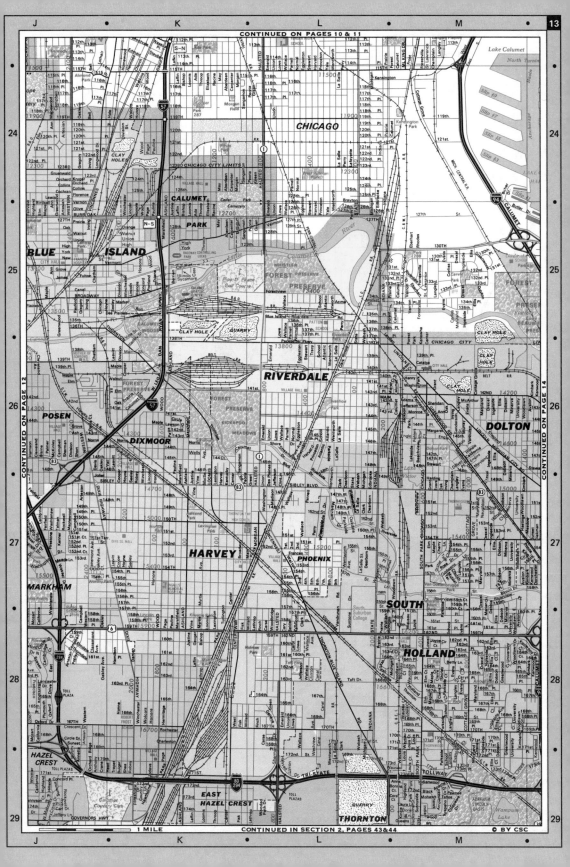

CONTINUED ON PAGE 12

CONTINUED ON PAGE 14

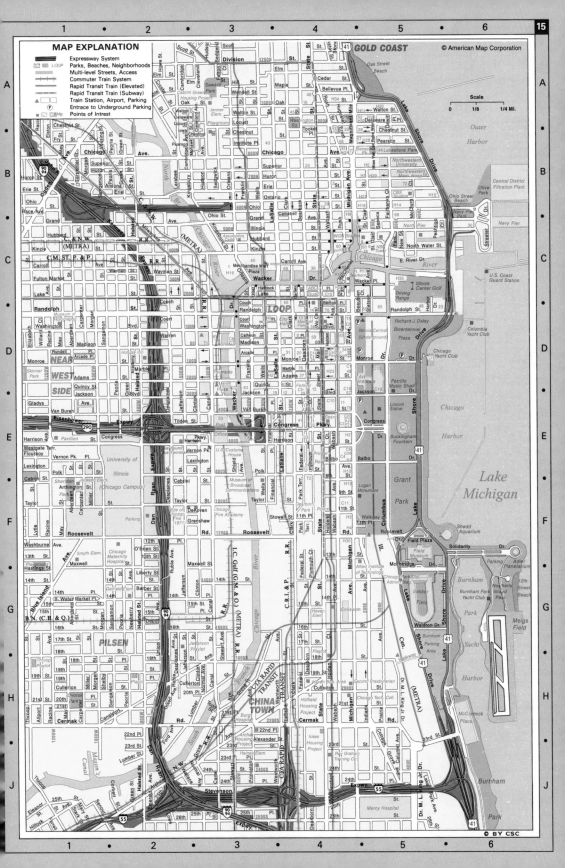

DOWNTOWN INDEX

See Map Page 15

STREETS

Aberdeen St. D,G1
Academy Pl. D2
Adams D1,4
Adlai Stevenson Expwy. . . J3,5
Alexander St. H3
Allport St. H1
Ancona St. B2
Arcade Pl. D1
Archer Ave. J2,H3
Arthington St. F1
Astor St. A4
Balbo Ave. E4
Balbo Dr. E5
Barber St. G2
Beaubien Ct. D4
Bellevue Pl. A4
Benton Pl. C4
Blanchard St. J4
Blue Island Ave. G1
Cabrini St. F1,2
Calhoun Pl. D3
Calumet Ave. J5
Cambridge Ave. B2
Campbell St. B4
Canal St. E,J3
Canalport Ave. H1,3
Carpenter St. B,F,H1
Carroll Ave. C1,4
Cedar St. A4
Cermak Rd. H1,4
Chestnut St. B3,5
Chicago Ave. B1,3
Clark St. B,D,H4
Cleveland Ave. A3
Clinton St. E,H3
Columbus Dr. F5
Congress Dr. E5
Congress Pkwy. E1,4
Congress Plaza Dr. E5
Corbett St. J2
Cottage Grove Ave. . . . H,J5
Couch Pl. C2
Court Pl. D2
Cullerton St. H1,5
Dan Ryan Expwy. . . . F,G,H2
Dearborn St. B,E,J4
Delaware Pl. A2,5
Depot St. G2,3
Des Plaines St. E,H2
DeWitt Pl. A5
Division St. A3,4
E. River Dr. C5
Eisenhower Expwy. E1,3
Eleanor St. J1
Elizabeth St. D1
Elm St. A3,4
Emerald Ave. J2
Erie St. B1,3
Ernst Ct. B4
Fairbanks Ct. B5
Federal St. E,H4
Felton Ct. A3
Field Blvd. C5
Field Plaza Dr. F5
Financial Pl. E,F3
Flournoy St. E1
Ford Ave. H2
Franklin B,D3
Fulton Market C1
Garland Ave. D4
Garvey St. C4
Gladys Ave. E1
Grand Ave. C1,3
Green St. B,E,J2
Grenshaw St. F3
Grove St. H,J3
Haddock Pl. C3
Halstead St. C,G,J2
Harbor Dr. C5
Harrison St. E1,4
Hastings St. G1
Hill St. A3

Hillock Ave. J1
Holden Ct. D,F,H4
Hubbard St. C1,3
Hudson Ave. A,B3
Huguelet Pl. A4
Huron St. B1,3
Illinois St. C3
Indiana Ave. H5
Institute Pl. B3
Iowa St. B2
Jackson Blvd. E1,3
Jackson Dr. E5
Jefferson St. E,H2
John F. Kennedy Expwy. . . B1,C2
King, M.L. Jr. Dr. H,J5
Kingsbury St. B,C3
Kinzie St. C1,3
LaSalle St. B3,E,H4
Lake Park Ave. J5
Lake Shore Drive A,E,G5
Lake St. C1,3
Larabee St. B2
Lexington St. E1,3
Liberty St. G2
Locust St. A4
Lowe Ave. J2
Lumber St. H3,J2
Lytle St. F1
MacChesney Ct. C4
Madison St. D1,3
Magnificent Mile A,B4
Maple St. A4
Marble Pl. D2
Mary St. J1
Maxwell St. F1,3
May St. D,F,H1
McClurg St. B5
McFetridge Dr. G5
Merchandise Mart Plaza . . . C3
Michigan Ave. A,F,H4
Mies Van Der Rohe Way . . B5
Miller St. F,H1
Milwaukee Ave. C2
Mohawk St. B3
Monroe St. D5
Monroe St. D1,4
Morgan St. B,D,H1
New St. C5
Newberry Ave. G2
Normal Ave. H,J3
North Water St. B5
O'Brien St. F2
Oak St. A2,4
Ogden Ave. B1
Ohio St. B1,3
Ontario St. B3
Orleans St. B3
Park Terr. F4
Pearson St. B2,5
Peoria St. B,D,H2
Peshtigo Ct. C5
Plymouth Ct. E,G4
Polk St. E1,3
Post Pl. C3
Prairie Ave. H5
Princeton Ave. J3
Quincy St. D1,3
Race Ave. B1
Racine Ave. D,F,H1
Randolph St. D1,5
Roosevelt Ct. F5
Roosevelt Rd. F1,3
Ruble Ave. G,H2
Rundell Pl. D1
Sangamon St. B,D1,G2
Scott St. A2,3
Sedgwick St. A,B3
Seneca St. C5
Senour Ave. J1
Shelby St. H1
Shield Ave. E3
Solidarity Dr. F6
South Water Market Pl. . . . G1

St. Clair St. B,C5
Stark St. J1
State St. A,F,H4
Stetson Ave. C,D5
Stewart Ave. G-J3
Stone St. A4
Stowell St. F4
Streeter Dr. C6
Superior St. B1,3
Taylor St. F1,3
Throop St. H,J1
Tilden St. E2
Todd St. H3
Tooker Pl. B4
Union Ave. H2
Van Buren St. E1,3
Vernon Pk. Pl. E1,3
Wabash Ave. B,E,H4
Wacker Dr. C3,5,E3
Wacker Pl. C5
Waldron Dr. G5
Wallace St. J2
Walton St. A2,5
Warren Ave. C2
Washburne Ave. F1
Washington Blvd. D1,3
Water St. C5
Wayman St. C2
Wells St. B,F3
Wendell St. A3
Wentworth Ave. H,J4
Westgate Terr. E1
Willard Ct. F1
8th St. E4
9th St. F4
11th Pl. F4,5
11th St. F4
12th Pl. F2
13th St. F1,4
14th Pl. G1,4
14th St. G1,4
15th Pl. G2,3
15th St. G1,4
16th St. G1,4
17th St. G1,4
18th Pl. H1,2
18th St. G1,H4
19th Pl. H1,2
19th St. H1,4
20th Pl. H1,3
21st Pl. H3
21st St. H1,4
22nd Pl. H2,3
23rd Pl. J3
23rd St. H5,6,J2
24th Pl. J3,5
24th St. J3,4
25th Pl. J2,3
25th St. J1
26th St. J2,5

CULTURAL FACILITIES

Adler Planetarium F6
American Conservatory of
Music,C1 . . . . D4
ArchiCenter,C2 . . . . E4
Art Institute D5
Auditorium Theatre,C3 . . . . E4
Blackstone Theatre,C4 . . . . E4
Chicago Public Library & Cultural
Center,C5 . . . . D4
Chicago Theatre,C6 . . . . . . C4
Civic Opera House,C7 . . . . D3
Civic Theatre,C8 . . . . D3
Drury Lane Theatre at Water Tower
Place,17 . . . . B5
Eleventh (11th) Street Theatre,C11 . E4
Field Museum of Natural History . F6
Fine Arts Building,C12 . . . . E4
Goodman Theatre,C13 . . . . D5
HOT TIX Booth,C14 . . . . . . D4
Harold Washington Library . . E4

Museum of Contemporary Art,44 . B5
Newberry Library,45 . . . . . . A4
Orchestra Hall,C16 . . . . . . D4
Petrillo Music Shell D5
Shedd Aquarium F6
Shubert Theatre,C19 . . . . . D4
Spertus College & Museum of
Judaica,C20 . . . . E4
Studebaker Theatre,C21 . . . . E4
World Playhouse,C22 . . . . . E4

DRAINAGE

Burnham Park Yacht Harbor . G,H6
Chicago Harbor E6
Chicago River C3,5
Lake Michigan F6
Mason's Canal J1
North Branch Chicago River . B2,C3
Ogden Slip C5
Outer Harbor (Lake Michigan) .
. . . . A5,6,B6
South Branch Chicago River .
. . . . D,F3,J1
Turning Basin (Chicago River) . C3
Turning Basin (Lake Michigan) . C6

HOTELS

Allerton,H1 . . . . B5
Americana Congress,H2 . . . . E4
Ascot House,H3 . . . . F4
Avenue Hotel,H4 . . . . F4
Barclay Chicago,H5 . . . . . . B5
Bismarck,H6 . . . . D3
Blackstone,H7 . . . . E4
Chicago Hilton,H10 . . . . . . E4
Chicago Lakeshore,H8 . . . . B5
Chicago Marriot,H9 . . . . . . B4
Drake,H11 . . . . A5
Essex Inn,H12 . . . . F4
Executive House,H13 . . . . . C4
Holiday Inn D2
Holiday Inn Chicago City
Centre,H14 . . . . B5
Holiday Inn Lake Shore Drive,H15 .
. . . . B5
Holiday Inn Mart Plaza,H16 . . C3
Hotel Nikko,H34 . . . . C4
Hyatt Regency Chicago,H17 . . C5
Inn of Chicago,H18 . . . . . . B5
Knickerbocker Chicago,H19 . . A5
Mayfair Regent,H20 . . . . . . A5
McCormick Inn J5
Midland,H21 . . . . D3
Oxford House,H22 . . . . . . C4
Palmer House,H23 . . . . . . D4
Park Hyatt on Water Tower
Square,H24 . . . . B4
Radisson Chicago,H25 . . . . C5
Raphael,H26 . . . . B5
Richmont,H27 . . . . B5
Ritz-Carlton,H28 . . . . B5
Sheraton-Plaza,H29 . . . . . . B5
Travelodge Downtown,H30 . . F4
Tremont,H31 . . . . B4
Westin Chicago,H32 . . . . . . A5
Whitehall,H33 . . . . B4

POINTS OF INTEREST

ABC Studios C4
Apparel Center,1 . . . . C3
Archer Housing Project H3
Assumption Roman Catholic
Church C3
Bloomingdale's,75 . . . . A5
Buckingham Fountain E5
Burg Hospital H3
Burnham Park Yacht Club . . . G6
CBS Studios B5
CNA Plaza,11 . . . . E4
Carbide & Carbon Bldg.,2 . . . C4
Carson Pirie Scott D4
Cathedral of St. James,3 . . . B4
Central District Filtration Plant . B6

Chicago Board of Trade,4 . . . . E4
Chicago Building,5 . . . . D4
Chicago Maternity Hospital . . . F1
Chicago Park District
Administration Building . G5,6
Chicago Sun Times Building,7 . C4
Chicago Temple,8 . . . . D4
Chicago Tribune Tower,9 . . . . C5
Chicago Yacht Club D5
China Town H3
City Hall/County Building,10 . . D4
Coliseum G4
Columbia Yacht Club D6
Continental Illinois National
Bank,12 . . . . D4
Daley Center (New Civic
Center),13 . . . . D4
Daley Plaza D5
Delaware Building,14 . . . . . D4
Dirksen Federal Building,15 . . D4
Equitable Building,18 . . . . . C5
Federal Center D4
Federal Reserve Bank,19 . . . . E3
First National Plaza,20 . . . . D4
First Presbyterian Church,22 . . B4
Fisher Building,21 . . . . E4
Fourth Presbyterian Church . . A5
Gold Coast A5
Harbor Point,23 . . . . D5
Hillfield Housing Project H4
Holy Name Cathedral,24 . . . . B4
IBM Building,27 . . . . C4
Inland Steel Building,26 . . . . D4
John Hancock Center,28 . . . . B5
Kluczynski Federal Building,29 . E4
Lake Point Tower,30 . . . . . . C6
Lincoln Statue E5
Logan Monument F5
Loop D3,4
Loop Synagogue,31 . . . . . . D4
Main Post Office,33 . . . . . . E3
Mallers Building,34 . . . . . . D4
Manhattan Building,35 . . . . . E4
Marina City,36 . . . . C4
Marquette Building,37 . . . . . D4
Marshall Field D4
McCarthy Building,38 . . . . . D4
McCormick Place H6
Medinah Temple,39 . . . . . . B4
Meigs Field G6
Merchandise Mart,40 . . . . . C3
Mercy Hospital J5
Metropolitan Correctional
Center,41 . . . . E4
Monadnock Building,42 . . . . E4
Moody Bible Institute,43 . . . . B3
Navy Pier C6
Near West Side D1
Neiman Marcus,76 . . . . B5
Newberry Plaza,46 . . . . A4
North Pier C5
Northwestern Mem. Hosp. . . . B5
Old Colony Building,47 . . . . E4
Original Site of Fort Dearborn . C5
Outer Drive East,48 . . . . . . D5
Pavilion E1
Peoples Gas Building,49 . . . . D4
Pilsen G1,2
Pioneer Court,50 . . . . C5
Pittsfield Building,51 . . . . . D4
Playboy Building,52 . . . . . . A5
Pontiac Building,53 . . . . . . E4
Printer's Row E4
Printer's Row Printing Museum,54 . E4
Prudential Building,55 . . . . . D5
Quigley Seminary North,56 . . . B4
Railway Exchange Building,57 . E4
Rehabilitation Institute of
Chicago,58 . . . . B5
Reliance Building,59 . . . . . . D4
River Plaza,60 . . . . C4
Riverside Plaza,61 . . . . D3
Rookery,62 . . . . D4

Sears E4
Sears Tower,63 . . . . D3
Second Presbyterian H4
Seventeenth Church of Christ
Scientist,64 . . . . C4
Site of Chicago Fire in 1871 . . F2
Soldier Field G5
Standard Oil Building,65 . . . . D5
State of Illinois Building,66 . . . C4
Stone Container Building,67 . . C4
Time-Life Building,68 . . . . . C5
Traffic Court,69 . . . . C4
Tree Studios,70 . . . . B4
U.S. Coast Guard Station C6
U.S. Custom's House E3
Unity Building,71 . . . . D4
V.A. Lakeside Medical Center,72B5
WGN Studios C5
WMAQ Studios C3
Walkway F,H5
Water Tower Visitors Center,73 . B4
Wrigley Building,74 . . . . . . C4
Xerox Centre,75 . . . . D4

PARKS

Beach at 12th Street G6
Burnham Park G,J6
Dvorak Park H1
Grant Park E,F5
Illinois Center Park C5
Jefferson Playlot G3
Lakeshore Park B5
Navy Pier Park B6
Northerly Island Park G6
Oak Street Beach A5
Ohio Street Beach B6
Olive Park B6
Playground A3,F1
Playlot J3
Seneca Park B5
Seward Park A3
Sheridan Park A1
Skinner Park D1
Throop Playlot H1
Washington Square A4

SCHOOLS

Allied Institute of Technology . F4,
. . . . G5
Chicago Fire Academy F3
Chicago Technical College . H4,5
Columbia College,C9 . . . . . E4
DePaul University (Loop
Campus),C10 . . . . E4
Dr. Scholl College of Podiatric
Medicine,16 . . . . A4
Loop College,C15 . . . . C4
Loyola University (Water Twr.
Campus),32 . . . . B4
Moody Bible Institute,43 . . . . B3
Northwestern University B5
Quigley Seminary North,56 . . B4
Ray Graham Training Center . . J4
Roosevelt University,C17 . . . . E4
School of the Art Institute of
Chicago,C18 . . . . D5
Spertus College & Museum of
Judaica,C20 . . . . E4
University of Illinois (Chicago
Campus) E2

TRANSPORTATION

Burnham Parking Area G,H5
Chicago & North Western
Station,T1 . . . . D3
Dearborn Street Station,T2 . . . E4
Greyhound Terminal D4
Ill. Central Commuter Station . D,E
LaSalle Street Station,T4 . . . . E4
Parking D4,5,E4
Randolph Street Station,T5 . . . E4
Trailways Terminal,T6 . . . . . D4
Union Station,T7 . . . . D3
Van Buren Street Station,T8 . . E4

INDEX TO CHICAGO AND SURROUNDING CITIES

See Map Pages 1-14

ALSIP
Pages 9,12
STREETS
Alpine ..... Pg.12 .... G25
Apple Ln. ... Pg.12 .... G25
Austin ...... Pg.12 .... F24
Avers .... Pg.12 .... H24
Avon .... Pg.9 ..... G23
Benck Dr. ... Pg.12 .... H24
Blossom Dr. . Pg.12 .... H25
Carolyn ..... Pg.12 .... G24
Central ...... Pg.12 .... G24
Central Park Ave. ....
.... Pg.12 .. H24,25
Crawford .... Pg.12 .. H24,25
Eastview .... Pg.12 .... G24
Engel Rd. ... Pg.12 .... G25
Fey Ln. ..... Pg.12 .... H24
Frontage Rd. . Pg.12 .... F24
Hamlin ...... Pg.12 .... H24
Harding ..... Pg.12 .... H24
Holmburg Ct. . Pg.12 .... H24
Howdy Ln. ... Pg.12 .... H24
Inland Dr. ... Pg.12 .... H25
Jean .... Pg.12 .... G24
Joalyce Ct. .. Pg.12 .... G24
Joalyce Dr. .. Pg.12 .... G24
Jobey Ln. ... Pg.12 .... H24
Karlov ...... Pg.12 .... H24
Kedvale ..... Pg.12 .... H24
Kedzie ...... Pg.12 .... J25
Keeler ...... Pg.12 .. H24,25
Kenneth ..... Pg.12 .... G24
Kenton ...... Pg.12 .... G24
Kilbourne ... Pg.12 .... G24
Kildare ..... Pg.12 .... G24
Knox .... Pg.12 .... G24
Kolmar ...... Pg.12 .... G24
Komensky ... Pg.12 .... H24
Kostner Ave. . Pg.12 .... H24
Kostner Pl. .. Pg.12 .... G24
La Porte .... Pg.12 .... G24
Lacrosse .... Pg.12 .. G24,25
Lamon ...... Pg.12 .... G24
Laramie ..... Pg.9,12 ... G25
Lavergne .... Pg.12 .... H24
Lawler ...... Pg.9,12 . G23,24
Lawndale .... Pg.12 .... H24
Leamington .. Pg.9,12 . G23,24
Leclaire ..... Pg.9,12 . G23,24
Line Crest Dr. . Pg.12 .... H24
Lombard Ln. . Pg.12 .... G24
Loveland Ave. . Pg.12 .... G25
Loveland St. .. Pg.12 .... G25
Mather ...... Pg.9 ..... G23
Mayfield .... Pg.12 .... F24
McDaniel Ct. . Pg.12 .... G24
McDaniel St. . Pg.12 .... G24
Menard ..... Pg.12 .... G24
Millard ...... Pg.12 .. H24,25
Orchard Ln. .. Pg.12 .... G25
Orchard St. .. Pg.12 .... G24
Park Lane Dr. . Pg.12 .... H24
Prairie Dr. ... Pg.12 .... H24
Rexford ..... Pg.12 .... G24
Ridgeland ... Pg.12 .... F24
Ridgeway ... Pg.12 .. H24,25
Rosemary ... Pg.12 .... G24
Scott Dr. .... Pg.12 .... H24
Shirley Ln. .. Pg.12 .... H24
Spencer Ct. .. Pg.12 .... G24
Spencer St. .. Pg.12 .... G25
Springfield ... Pg.12 .... G24
Stony Ct. .... Pg.12 .... G24
Termunde Dr. . Pg.12 .... H24
Tripp .... Pg.12 .. H24,25
Trumbull .... Pg.12 .... H24
Walter Ln. ... Pg.12 .... H24
44th Pl. ..... Pg.12 .... G24
45th St. ..... Pg.12 .... G24
113th St. .... Pg.12 .... G23
115th Pl. .... Pg.12 .. G,H24
115th St. .... Pg.12 .. F,H24
116th Pl. .... Pg.12 .. F,H24
116th St. .... Pg.12 .. F,H24
117th Pl. .... Pg.12 .. F,G24
117th St. .... Pg.12 .. G,H24
118th St. .... Pg.12 .. F,H24
119th Pl. .... Pg.12 .. G,H24
119th St. .... Pg.12 .. G,H24
120th Pl. .... Pg.12 .. G,H24
120th St. .... Pg.12 .. G,H24
121st Pl. .... Pg.12 .. G,H24
121st St. .... Pg.12 .. G,H24
122nd St. .... Pg.12 .. G,H24
123rd Pl. .... Pg.12 .. G,H24
123rd St. .... Pg.12 .... G24
124th Pl. .... Pg.12 .. G,H24
124th St. .... Pg.12 .. F,H24
125th St. .... Pg.12 .. F,H24
126th Pl. .... Pg.12 .. F,H25
126th St. .... Pg.12 .. G,H24
128th Pl. .... Pg.12 .... G25
128th St. .... Pg.12 .... G25
129th St. .... Pg.12 ... G,H25
130th Ct. .... Pg.12 .... G25
131st St. .... Pg.12 ... G,H25
CEMETERIES
Burr Oak Cem. . Pg.12 .... G24
Chapel Hill Gardens South Cem.
.... Pg.9 ..... G23
Hazel Green Cem. ....
.... Pg.12 .... G24
Holy Sepulchre Cem. ....
.... Pg.9 ..... F23
Lincoln Cem. . Pg.12 .... H24
Lutheran Cem. Pg.12 .... H25
Oak Hill Cem. . Pg.12 .... H24
Restvale Cem. . Pg.12 .... G24
SCHOOLS
Moraine Valley Comm. Jr. College
.... Pg.12 .... F24
MISCELLANEOUS
Village Hall .. Pg.12 .... G24

BEDFORD PARK
Page 9
STREETS
Archer E19
Austin F19
Belt Cir. E19
Central G19,20
Harlem Ave. E19
Lavergne G19
Leamington G20
Leclaire G20
Linder G20
Lockwood G20
Major F19
Massasoit F20
Melvina F19
Menard F19
Narragansett F19
Nashville F19
Natchez F19
Oak Park F19
State G20
64th Pl. E19
64th St. E19
65th Pl. E19
65th St. E-G19
66th Pl. E-G19
66th St. E-G19
67th St. E19
68th St. E19
71st St. E20
72nd St. G20
73rd St. F,G20
74th Pl. G20
75th St. E,G20
77th Ave. E19
78th Ave. E19
MISCELLANEOUS
Village Hall E19

BELLWOOD
Pages 4,5
STREETS
Adams C14
Bellwood C13,14
Bohland C13,14
Butterfield Rd. C14
Castle Dr. B13
Center Ave. B13
Cernan Dr. C14
Congress C14
Davis Dr. B13
Eastern C13,14
Englewood Ave. . B13,14
Erie St. B13
Frederick C14
Gardner Rd. C14
Geneva Ave. B14
Gladys C14
Glos C14
Grant C13
Granville Ave. B14
Hyde Park Ave. ... C14
Jackson C14
Korrel C14
Linden C13,14
Madison C14
Mannheim Rd. .. C13,14
Marik Dr. C14
Marshall Ave. C13
Marshall Ct. C14
Miami Rd. C13
Monroe C14
Morris C13,14
Oak St. B,C14
Park Ct. C14
Railroad Ave. ... B,C13
Randolph B,C14
Rice C13,14
St. Charles Pl. C13
St. Charles Rd. B13

St. Paul C14
Twining B14
Van Buren C14
Warren C14
Washington Blvd. .. C14
Wilcox C14
Zuelke Dr. C13
22nd Ave. C13,14
23rd Ave. C13,14
24th Ave. C13,14
25th St. C13,14
26th Ave. C13
27th Ave. C13
28th Ave. C13
29th Ave. C13
30th Ave. C13,14
31st Ave. C14
32nd Ave. C14
46th Ave. B13,14
47th Ave. B14
48th Ave. B14
49th Ave. B13
50th Ave. B14
51st Ave. B13
52nd Ave. B13
PARKS
Playground C14
MISCELLANEOUS
Village Hall C14

BERKELEY
Page 4
STREETS
Albin Terr. A14
Arthur A13,14
Ashbel B13
Atwood A13,14
Birch Ct. B14
Bohlander B13
Burr Oak A14
Calvin A14
Chicago B13
Coolidge A14
Electric A14
Elm A14
Harding A13
Hawthorne B14
Herbert A13,14
Hillside B13
Howard B13
Huron A13
Irving B13
Jerele B14
King Dr. B14
Kouba A14
Lee B14
Lind B13
Maple A14
McDermott B13
Morris B14
Murray Dr. B14
Park A13
Prospect A14
Richard A13
Ridge A14
Rohde B14
Rose B14
School A14
Spencer B14
Spenchley B14
St. Charles Rd. B13
Sunnyside Dr. B13
Superior A13
Taft A13,14
Victoria A14
Wolf Rd. B13
SCHOOLS
MacArthur Senior H.S. . B13
Sunnyside Elem. Sch. .. B13
MISCELLANEOUS
City Hall A14

BERWYN
Pages 5,6
STREETS
Cermak Rd. E15
Clarence F15-17
Clinton E15-17
Cuyler F15-17
East F15-17
Elmwood F15-17
Euclid F15-17
Fairfield F16
Grove F15-17
Gunderson F15-17
Harvey F15-17
Highland F15-17
Home F15-17
Kenilworth F15-17
Lombard F15-17
Maple F15-17
Oak Park E15-17

Ogden E17
Park F16
Ridgeland F15-17
Riverside Dr. E16
Roosevelt Rd. E15
Scoville F15-17
Sinclair F16
Stanley E16
Wenonah F15-17
Wesley F15-17
Windsor E16
Wisconsin E15-17
13th St. E15
14th St. E15
15th St. E15
16th St. E15
18th St. E15
19th St. E15
21st St. E15
23rd St. E15
24th St. F16
25th St. F16
26th Pkwy. E16
26th Pl. F16
26th St. F16
27th Pl. F16
27th St. E16
28th Pl. F16
28th St. F16
29th Pl. E16
29th St. E,F16
30th Pl. E16
30th St. E16
31st St. E16
32nd St. E,F16
33rd St. F16
34th St. E16
35th St. E16
36th St. E16
37th St. E17
38th St. E17
39th St. E17
PARKS
Berwyn Park E16
SCHOOLS
Morton West H.S. ... E16
SHOPPING CENTERS
Cermak Plaza E15
MISCELLANEOUS
City Hall F16
MacNeal Hosp. F16

BLUE ISLAND
Pages 12,13
STREETS
Ann J24,25
Artesian J24,25
Berrien K25
Birdsall J25
Broadway J25
Burr Oak J25
California J25,26
Calumet K25
Canal J25
Cass K25
Central Park H25
Chatham J25,26
Chicago J25
Clinton J25
Cochran J24
Collins J24
Concord K25
Coopers Grove Rd. . J26
Des Plaines J,K25
Division K24-26
Duane K25
Edison Dr. H25
Edward J25
Elm Dr. J24
Elm St. J24,25
Everett J25
Fairview J25
Florence J24
Francisco J25,26
Fulton J25
Greenwood ... J24,25
Gregory J24,25
Grove J24,25
Gruenwald J24
Hadley K25
High J,K25
Highland J25
Homan H25
Honore K25
Hoyne K25
Illinois K25
Irving J24,25
James J25
John J25
Kruger J24
Lewis J24
Lincoln K25

Longwood Dr. J24
Main St. K26
Maple J24,25
Market K25
Minnesota H,J25
Mozart J25
New J25
Oak J25
Olive J25
Orange K25
Orchard J24
Portland K25
Prairie J25
Rexford J25
Sacramento J25
Sanders St. J25
Seeley K25
Shamrock Ln. J26
Sheridan J25
Sycamore K25
Thornton K25
Union J,K25
Vermont K25
Vernon J25
Vincennes J25
Vine St. K25
Walnut J,K25
Western J25
Whipple J26
Winchester K25
Wireton J25
Wood K24,25
York J25
119th St. J24
120th Pl. J24
120th St. J24
121st Pl. J24
121st St. J24
122nd Pl. J24
122nd St. J24
123rd Pl. J24
123rd St. J24
127th St. J25
135th Pl. J25
135th St. J25
136th St. J25
138th Pl. J26
138th St. J26
139th Pl. J26
139th St. J26
140th Pl. J25
140th St. J26
141st Pl. J26
141st St. J26
142nd Pl. J26
142nd St. J26
143rd St. J26
PARKS
Central Park J25
Memorial Park J25
SCHOOLS
Eisenhower H.S. (New) . J25
Mother of Sorrows H.S. . J26
MISCELLANEOUS
St. Francis Hosp. ... J25

BRIDGEVIEW
Pages 8,9
STREETS
Beloit E20,21
Birch E21
Cambridge E21
Columbia Dr. E19
Cranbrook E21
Dover E21
Elm Ct. E19
Fairlane E21
Ferdinand E20,21
Frontage Rd. E22
Garden Ct. E20
Garden Ln. E20
Hanover E21
Harlem Ave. E21
Hartford E21
Homestead E22
Industrial Dr. E22
Mabel Ct. E19
Marin E21
Oak Park E21
Oconto E20,21
Octavia Ave. ... E20,21
Odell E20,21
Oketo E20,21
Olympic Dr. E21
Orchard Ln. E21
Oxford E21
Pembroke Ln. E21
Richard Rd. E22
Roberts Rd. E21
Saratoga Dr. E21
Sayre E20
Selma Pl. E20
Sholer E20
Southfield Dr. E21
Stanford Dr. E21

Stanford Dr. E21
Stickney E20
Suburban Ln. E19
Thomas E20,21
Willow E21
Windsor E21
70th St. E20
71st St. E20
72nd St. E20
73rd Ave. E21,22
73rd Ct. E20-22
73rd Pl. E20
73rd St. E20
74th St. E20-22
74th St. E20
74th St. E20
75th St. E22
75th St. E21
75th St. E20
76th Ave. E20
76th St. E20
77th Pl. E20
77th Ct. E20
77th St. E20
78th Ave. E19-21
78th St. E20
79th Pl. E19
79th Pl. E20
79th St. E20
80th Pl. E20
80th St. E20
81st Pl. E21
81st St. E20
82nd Pl. E20
82nd St. E20
83rd Pl. E20
83rd St. E20
84th Pl. E21
84th St. E21
85th Pl. E21
85th St. E20
86th Pl. E21
86th St. E21
87th Pl. E20
87th St. E21
88th St. E21
89th St. E21
90th Pl. E21
90th St. E20
91st St. E20
92nd Pl. E22
92nd St. E21
93rd St. E22
95th St. E22
98th Pl. E22
100th Pl. E22
103rd St. E22
SHOPPING CENTERS
Southfield Shopping Ctr. . E21
MISCELLANEOUS
City Hall E20

BROADVIEW
Pages 4,5
STREETS
Beach C14
Braga Dr. C15
Cermak Rd. C15
Depot D15
Elizabeth Dr. C15
Ericka Dr. C15
Filmore C15
Gardner Rd. C14,15
Harvard D14
Lexington D14
Lyman C14
Roberts Dr. C15
Roosevelt Rd. C15
Summerdale C15
Sunnydale C15
Terry C16
Tyson Rd. C15
York C14
9th Ave. D15
10th Ave. D15
11th Ave. D15
12th Ave. D15
13th Ave. D15
13th St. C,D15
14th Ave. D15
14th St. C15
15th Ave. D15
15th St. C15
16th Ave. D15
16th St. C15
17th Ave. D15
18th Ave. D15
18th St. C15
19th Ave. D15
19th St. D15
20th Ave. C15

BROADVIEW

20th St. ... D15
21st Ave. ... C15
21st St. ... D15
22nd Ave. ... C15
23rd Ave. ... C15
23rd St. ... C15
24th Ave. ... C15
25th Ave. ... C15
26th Ave. ... C15
27th Ave. ... C15

PARKS
Schroeder Park ... D15
Sunnywood Park ... D15

MISCELLANEOUS
Village Hall ... D15

BROOKFIELD

Page 5

STREETS
Arden ... D17
Arthur ... C17
Bartlett ... D16
Blanchan ... C17,C18
Broadway ... C17
Brookfield ... D17
Burlington ... D17
Cleveland ... C17
Congress Park ... C17
Cossit ... C17
Custer ... D17,18
Deye ... C18
Division ... D16
Dubois ... C17,18
Elm ... D16,17
Fairview ... C17
Forest ... D17,18
Garfield ... C16
Gerritsen ... C17
Golf View Rd. ... D16
Grand Blvd. ... C16,D17
Grant ... C17
Grove ... D17,18
Harrison ... C17
Henrietta ... C16
Hollywood ... D17
Jackson ... C16
Jefferson ... C16
Lexington ... C16
Lincoln ... C17
Madison ... C17
Maple ... D18
McCormick ... D16,17
Monroe ... C16
Morton ... C17
Oak ... D17
Ogden Blvd. ... C17
Park ... D16,17
Parkview ... D17
Plainfield Rd. ... D17
Prairie ... D17,18
Quincy ... D17
Raymond ... C17,18
Ridgewood ... D16
Riverside ... D17
Riverview Terr. ... D17
Roach ... D16
Rochester ... C17
Rockefeller ... D16
Rosemear ... D17
Sahler ... C17
Sheridan ... D17
Sherman ... D17
Southview ... C,D17
Sunnyside ... D17,18
Taylor ... D17
Vernon ... D17,18
Washington ... C16
Waubansee ... D17
Windmere ... D17
Woodside ... D17
26th Pl. ... D16
26th St. ... D16
27th St. ... D16
28th Pl. ... D16
31st St. ... D16
42nd St. ... D17
43rd St. ... D17
44th Pl. ... D17
44th St. ... D17
45th Pl. ... D17
45th St. ... D17
46th St. ... D17
47th St. ... C18

SCHOOLS
Riverside Brookfield H.S. ... D16

MISCELLANEOUS
Brookfield Woods ... D16
Brookfield Zoo ... D16
Village Hall ... D17

BURBANK

Page 9

STREETS
Austin ... F20,21
Central ... G21
Cicero Ave. ... G20,21
Harlem Ave. ... E21
Lacrosse ... G20
Lamon ... G20
Laporte ... G20,21
Laramie ... G20
Latrobe ... G20
Lavergne ... G20,21
Lawler ... G20,21
Leamington ... G20,21
Leclaire ... G20,21
Linder ... G20
Lockwood ... G20
Long ... G20
Lorel ... G20
Lotus ... G20
Luna ... G20
Major ... F20,21
Mansfield ... F20,21
Mason ... F20
Massasoit ... F20,21
Mayfield ... F20,21
McVicker ... F20
Meade ... F20,21
Melvina ... F20,21
Menard ... F20,21
Merrimac ... F20,21
Mobile ... F20
Moody ... F20,21
Mulligan ... F20,21
Nagle ... F20
Narragansett ... F20
Nashville ... F20
Natchez ... F20
Natoma ... F20
Neenah ... F20
Neva ... E20
New England ... E20
Newcastle ... E20
Newland ... E20
Nordica ... E20
Normandy ... F20
Nottingham ... E20
Oak Park ... F20
Parkside ... F20,21
Rutherford ... F20
Sayre ... E20
State ... F21
71st Pl. ... E20
71st St. ... E20
72nd Pl. ... E20
72nd St. ... E20
73rd Pl. ... E20
73rd St. ... E20
74th Pl. ... E20
74th St. ... E20
75th St. ... E,G20
76th Pl. ... G20
76th St. ... G20
77th Pl. ... G20
77th St. ... E-G20
78th Pl. ... G20
78th St. ... E-G20
79th Pl. ... G20
79th St. ... E-G20
80th Pl. ... G20
80th St. ... E-G20
81st Pl. ... E-G21
81st St. ... E-G21
82nd Pl. ... E-G21
82nd St. ... E-G21
83rd Pl. ... F,G21
83rd St. ... E-G21
84th Pl. ... E-G21
84th St. ... E-G21
85th Pl. ... F,G21
85th St. ... E-G21
86th Pl. ... F,G21
86th St. ... E-G21
87th St. ... E-G21

SCHOOLS
Queen of Peace H.S. ... G20
Reavis H.S. ... F20
St. Laurence H.S. ... F,G20

BURNHAM

Page 14

STREETS
Bensley Ave. ... N26
Brainard Ave. ... P26
Burnham Ave. ... 026
Calhoun Ave. ... N26
Centre ... 026
Chippewa ... 026
Croissant ... N26
Exchange Ave. ... 026
Goodrich Ave. ... 026
Greenbay Ave. ... 026
Hammond Ave. ... 026
Hoxie Ave. ... N26
Kettleson St. ... N26
Mackinaw Ave. ... 026
Pierson St. ... N26
State St. ... N26
138th St. ... 026
139th St. ... 026
140th St. ... 026
141st St. ... 026
142nd St. ... 026
143rd St. ... 026

MISCELLANEOUS
Village Hall ... 026

CALUMET CITY

Page 14

STREETS
Allen Ln. ... N26
Arthur St. ... 026-28
Baker St. ... 027
Balmoral Ave. ... 028
Bensley Ave. ... N27
Buffalo Ave. ... 027,28
Burnham Ave. ... 026-28
Calhoun Ave. ... N27
Calumet Expwy. ... 027
Campbell Ave. ... 026,27
Cedar ... 026
Chappel Ave. ... N27
Chestnut Ct. ... N28
Cleveland Ave. ... N26
Clyde Ave. ... N27
Commercial Ave. ... 027
Cornell Ave. ... N26
Crandon Ave. ... N27
Dawn Ln. ... 026
Detroit St. ... P28
Dogwood Ct. ... N28
Dolton (State St.) ... N26
Douglas Ave. ... P27
Downs Dr. ... N26
East-West Rd. ... N28
Elizabeth St. ... P27
Elm Ct. ... N28
Escanaba ... 027
Euclid St. ... 027
Exchange Ave. ... 027
Forest Dale Ave. ... P28
Forest Hill ... 028
Forest Pl. ... 028
Forsythe Ave. ... P27
Freeland Ave. ... 026-28
Garfield Ave. ... 027
George, S. ... 026
Golf Ct. ... P27
Gordon Ave. ... 027,28
Greenbay Ave. ... 027,28
Greenwood Rd. ... N28
Harbor Ave. ... N26
Harding Ave. ... N27
Harness St. ... 027
Harrison St. ... 027
Henry St. ... 027
Hickory Ct. ... N28
Highland St. ... P28
Hirsch Ave. ... 027,28
Hirsch Blvd. ... 028
Houston Ave. ... 027
Hoxie Ave. ... N27
Imperial Ave. ... 028
Ingraham ... P27
Jeffery Ave. ... N27
Jennifer Ln. ... 026
Kenilworth Dr. ... P28
Lincoln Ave. ... 028,P27
Lincoln Pl. ... 028
Locust Ct. ... N28
Lucas St. ... 027
Luella ... N26,27
Mackinaw Ave. ... 026-28
Madison Ave. ... N27
Manistee ... 027
Marquette Ave. ... 027
Mason St. ... P27
Memorial Dr. ... 027
Merrill Ave. ... N27
Michigan City Rd. ... N-P27
Muskegon ... 027
Oglesby ... N26,27
Patricia Pl. ... N26
Patton Ln. ... N26
Paxton ... 026-28
Prairie Ave. ... N26
Price Ave. ... 027,28
Pulaski Rd. ... N27
Ridgeland Ave. ... N27
Ring Rd. ... N28
River Dr. ... 028
River Oaks Dr. ... 028
Rudolph ... 028
Ruth ... 0,P27
Saginaw Ave. ... 027
Schrum ... P28
Shirley Dr. ... P28
Sibley Blvd. ... N-P27
Stanley Blvd. ... 028
State Line Rd. ... P27
State St. ... N-P26
Stewart Ave. ... N26
Superior Ave. ... 027,28
Sycamore Ct. ... N28
Timothy Ln. ... 026
Torrence ... 026,27
Twilight Ln. ... 026
Virginia St. ... 027
Wabash Ave. ... 027
Waltham ... P27
Warren ... 027
Webb St. ... 027
Wentworth Ave. ... P27
West Dr. ... 028
William ... 028
Willow Ct. ... N28
Wilson Ave. ... 0,P27
Woodview ... 028
Yates Ave. ... N27
142nd St. ... N26
151st St. ... 027
152nd Pl. ... 027
152nd St. (Memorial Dr.) ... N27
153rd Pl. ... 027
153rd St. ... N27
154th Pl. ... 027
155th Pl. ... 027
155th St. ... 027
156th Pl. ... 027
156th St. ... 027
157th Pl. ... 027
157th St. ... 027
158th Pl. ... N28
159th St. ... 028
160th Pl. ... M29
160th St. ... 028
161st St. ... 028
162nd Pl. ... P28
162nd St. ... 028
163rd Pl. ... 028
163rd St. ... 0,P28
164th Pl. ... P28
164th St. ... 0,P28
165th Pl. ... P28
165th St. ... 0,P28
166th Pl. ... P28
166th St. ... 0,P28
167th Pl. ... P28
167th St. ... P21

PARKS
Calumet City Pk. ... P27
Forestdale Pk. ... P28

SCHOOLS
Thornton Frac. Twp. H.S. ... 027

SHOPPING CENTERS
River Oaks ... 028

MISCELLANEOUS
City Hall ... P27

CALUMET PARK

Page 13

STREETS
Aberdeen, S. ... K24,25
Ada, S. ... K25
Ashland ... K25
Bishop, S. ... K25
Carpenter, S. ... K24,25
Elizabeth, S. ... K25
Green ... L24,25
Halsted ... L24
High ... K24
Honore ... K25
Justine, S. ... K25
Laflin, S. ... K25
Lincoln ... K25
Loomis, S. ... K25
Marshfield ... K25
May, S. ... K24,25
Morgan ... K24,25
Page ... K24,25
Paulina ... K24,25
Peoria ... L24,25
Racine, S. ... K25
Sangamon ... K24,25
Throop, S. ... K25
Vermont ... L24
Winchester ... K25
Wood ... K24,25
York ... K24
119th St. ... K24
120th St., W. ... K24
121st St., W. ... K24
122nd St., W. ... K24
123rd St., W. ... K24
124th St., W. ... K24
125th St., W. ... K24
126th St., W. ... K25
127th St. ... K,L25
128th St., W. ... K25

MISCELLANEOUS
Raceway Park ... K25

CHICAGO

STREETS
Abbott ... Pg.10 ... L21
Aberdeen ... Pg.7,13 ... K13-24
Ada ... Pg.3 ... K12-24
Adams ... Pg.6 ... F-L14
Adams Blvd. ... Pg.6 ... F14
Addison ... Pg.1 ... D-L11
Agatite ... Pg.1 ... D-L10
Ainslie ... Pg.2 ... F-L10
Albany ... Pg.3 ... J7-24
Albion ... Pg.2 ... E-K8
Aldine ... Pg.3 ... K-L11
Alexander ... Pg.7 ... L15
Algonquin ... Pg.2 ... G8
Allen ... Pg.3 ... H11
Allport ... Pg.7 ... K15
Almond ... Pg.6 ... J14
Alta Vista Ter ... Pg.3 ... K10-11
Altgeld ... Pg.2 ... E-L12
Anacona ... Pg.7 ... K13
Anson Pl. ... Pg.6 ... J13
Anthony ... Pg.11 ... M19,021
Arbour Pl. ... Pg.7 ... K14
Arcade Pl. ... Pg.7 ... K14
Arch ... Pg.7 ... K16
Archer ... Pg.7 ... L15,H18
Ardmore ... Pg.2 ... E-K9
Argyle ... Pg.1 ... D10,E-L9
Arlington Pl. ... Pg.3 ... L12
Armitage ... Pg.2 ... E-K12
Armour ... Pg.7 ... K13
Armstrong ... Pg.2 ... G9
Artesian ... Pg.3 ... J7-24
Arthington ... Pg.6 ... F-L14
Arthur ... Pg.2 ... E-K8
Ashland ... Pg.3 ... K7-22
Astor ... Pg.7 ... L13
Attrill ... Pg.3 ... J12
Augusta Blvd. ... Pg.6 ... C-K13
Austin ... Pg.2 ... F9-19
Avalon ... Pg.10 ... M21-22
Avenue A ... Pg.11 ... P23
Avenue B ... Pg.11 ... P23
Avenue C ... Pg.11 ... P23
Avenue D ... Pg.11 ... P23
Avenue E ... Pg.11 ... P22-23
Avenue F ... Pg.11 ... P23-24
Avenue G ... Pg.11 ... P22-23
Avenue H ... Pg.11 ... P23
Avenue J ... Pg.11 ... P23
Avenue K ... Pg.14 ... 025
Avenue L ... Pg.11 ... 022-25
Avenue M ... Pg.11 ... 023-25
Avenue N ... Pg.11 ... 023-25
Avenue O ... Pg.11 ... 021-25
Avers ... Pgs.2,3,6,9 ... H9-23
Avondale ... Pg.2 ... E8,J-K12
Baker ... Pg.11 ... 021
Balbo Dr. ... Pg.7 ... M-L14
Baldwin ... Pg.11 ... N20
Balmoral ... Pg.2 ... E-K9
Baltimore ... Pg.11 ... 021-25
Banks ... Pg.7 ... L13
Barber ... Pg.7 ... L15
Barry ... Pg.2 ... E-L11
Bauwans ... Pg.7 ... K13
Beach ... Pg.6 ... H-K13
Beacon ... Pg.3 ... K10
Beaubien Ct. ... Pg.7 ... L14
Belden ... Pg.2 ... E-K12
Bell ... Pg.3 ... J7-24
Belle Plaine ... Pg.1 ... L-D10
Bellevue Pl. ... Pg.7 ... L13
Belmont ... Pg.2 ... E-L11
Belmont Harbor Dr ... Pg.3 ... L11
Bennett ... Pg.11 ... N19-22
Bensley ... Pg.11 ... N22-25
Benson ... Pg.7 ... K16
Berenice ... Pg.2 ... F-K10
Berkeley ... Pg.7 ... M17
Bernard ... Pg.3 ... H9-12
Berteau ... Pg.1 ... D-K10
Berwyn ... Pg.1 ... E-K9
Besly Ct. ... Pg.3 ... K12
Best Dr. ... Pg.11 ... M19
Beverly ... Pg.10 ... K21-23
Bingham ... Pg.3 ... J12
Birchwood Ave. ... Pg.2 ... E-K7
Birkoff ... Pg.10 ... L21
Bishop ... Pg.7 ... K13-24
Bissell ... Pg.3 ... K-L12
Bittersweet Pl. ... Pg.3 ... L10
Blackhawk ... Pg.7 ... K-L13
Blackstone ... Pg.7 ... N18-22
Blake ... Pg.6 ... J17
Blanchard Ct. ... Pg.7 ... L16
Bliss ... Pg.7 ... K13
Bloomingdale ... Pg.2 ... E-K12
Blue Island ... Pg.6 ... J-K15
Bonaparte ... Pg.7 ... K16
Bond ... Pg.11 ... 021
Bonfield ... Pg.7 ... K16
Bosak Ave. ... Pg.10 ... J22
Bosworth ... Pg.3 ... K7-13
Boulevard Way ... Pg.6 ... J16
Bowen ... Pg.7 ... M17
Bowler ... Pg.6 ... J14
Bowmanville ... Pg.3 ... J9
Bradley Pl. ... Pg.3 ... J-L11
Brainard ... Pg.14 ... 025
Brandon ... Pg.11 ... 020-25
Brayton ... Pg.13 ... L24
Brennan ... Pg.11 ... N22
Briar Pl. ... Pg.3 ... L11
Brighton Pl. ... Pg.6 ... J17
Broad ... Pg.7 ... K16
Broadway ... Pg.3 ... K9,L11
Brodman ... Pg.1 ... D10
Brompton ... Pg.3 ... L11
Bross ... Pg.6 ... J16
Browning ... Pg.7 ... M16
Bryn Mawr ... Pg.1 ... D-K9
Buckingham Pl. ... Pg.3 ... K-L11
Buena ... Pg.3 ... K-L10
Buffalo ... Pg.11 ... 021-25
Burley ... Pg.11 ... 021-25
Burling ... Pg.3 ... L11-12
Burnham ... Pg.11 ... 020-21
Burnside ... Pg.10 ... M21
Burton Pl. ... Pg.7 ... L13
Busse ... Pg.2 ... E9
Butler Dr. ... Pg.13 ... M-N25
Bypass ... Pg.2 ... F12
Byron ... Pg.1 ... K-D10
Cabrini ... Pg.7 ... K-L14
Caldwell ... Pg.2 ... F8,G9
Calhoun ... Pg.11 ... N22-25
California ... Pg.3 ... J8-23,L11
Calumet ... Pg.7 ... M15-25
Cambridge ... Pg.3 ... L11-13
Campbell ... Pg.3 ... J7-24
Canal ... Pg.7 ... L14-17
Canalport ... Pg.7 ... L-K15
Canfield ... Pg.2 ... E8-9
Carmen ... Pg.1 ... D-L9
Carondolet ... Pg.14 ... 025
Carpenter ... Pg.7 ... K13-24
Carpenter Rd. ... Pg.2 ... G8
Carroll ... Pg.6 ... G-L14
Castleisland Ave. ... Pg.1 ... D10
Castlewood Ter. ... Pg.3 ... K-L10
Catalpa ... Pg.1 ... E-K9
Caton ... Pg.3 ... J12
Cedar ... Pg.7 ... L13
Central ... Pg.2 ... G8-19
Central Park ... Pg.3 ... H8-24
Cermak Rd. ... Pg.6 ... G-M15
Champlain ... Pg.7 ... M17-23
Chanay ... Pg.3 ... J12
Chappel ... Pg.11 ... N19-25
Charles ... Pg.10 ... K22-23
Charleston ... Pg.3 ... J12
Chase Ave. ... Pg.2 ... E-K8
Chelsea Pl. ... Pg.10 ... K23
Cheltenham Pl. ... Pg.11 ... 020
Cherry ... Pg.7 ... K13
Chester ... Pg.1 ... D9-10
Chestnut ... Pg.7 ... K-L13
Chicago ... Pg.6 ... G-M13
Chicago Beach Dr. (Pvt) ... Pg.7 ... N18
Chicora ... Pg.2 ... F-G8
Chippewa ... Pg.14 ... N24
Christiana ... Pg.3 ... H9-20
Church ... Pg.10 ... K23
Churchill ... Pg.3 ... J12
Cicero ... Pg.2 ... G8-23
Claremont ... Pg.3 ... J8-23
Clarence ... Pg.2 ... E-F8
Clarendon ... Pg.3 ... L10
Clark St. ... Pg.3 ... K7-11,L11-15
Cleaver ... Pg.7 ... K13
Cleveland ... Pg.7 ... L13
Clifford ... Pg.2 ... G9
Clifton ... Pg.3 ... K10-12
Clifton Park ... Pg.10 ... H23
Clinton ... Pg.7 ... L14-15
Clover ... Pg.2 ... G10
Clybourn ... Pg.3 ... J11-K12
Clyde ... Pg.11 ... N19-25
Coast Guard Dr. ... Pg.11 ... N19
Coles ... Pg.11 ... 020-21
Colfax ... Pg.11 ... 020-21
Columbia ... Pg.3 ... K8
Columbia Dr. ... Pg.11 ... N18
Columbus Ave. ... Pg.10 ... J20
Columbus Dr. ... Pg.7 ... N18
Commercial ... Pg.11 ... 021-25
Commonwealth ... Pg.3 ... L11-12
Concord Pl. ... Pg.2,3,7 ... G-L12
Congress Pkwy. ... Pg.6 ... G-L14
Constance ... Pg.11 ... N19-22
Corbett ... Pg.7 ... K15-16
Corliss ... Pg.11 ... M23-25
Cornelia ... Pg.1 ... D-L11
Cornell ... Pg.7 ... N18-21
Cortez Dr. ... Pg.6 ... G-K13
Cortland ... Pg.2 ... E-K12
Cottage Grove ... Pg.7 ... M15-25
Couch Pl. ... Pg.7 ... L14
Court Pl. ... Pg.7 ... L14
Coyle Ave. ... Pg.2 ... E-J8
Crandon ... Pg.11 ... N19-25
Cregier ... Pg.11 ... N19-21
Crestline ... Pg.9 ... H21
Crilly ... Pg.3 ... L12
Crosby ... Pg.7 ... L13
Crowell ... Pg.7 ... K16
Crystal ... Pg.6 ... G-K13
Cullerton ... Pg.6 ... H-L15
Cullom ... Pg.2 ... F-K10
Cumberland ... Pg.1 ... D10
Cuyler ... Pg.2 ... F-L10
Cyril ... Pg.11 ... N20
Dakin ... Pg.2 ... F-L10

Street	Page	Grid
Damen	Pg.3	K7-22
Daniel Dr.	Pg.13	L-M25
Dante	Pg.11	N19-21
Dauphin	Pg.10	M21-23
Davlin Ct.	Pg.3	H11
Davol	Pg.10	K23
Dawson	Pg.3	H11
Dayton	Pg.3	K10-12
Dean	Pg.7	K13
Dearborn	Pg.7	L13-18
Dekoven	Pg.7	L14
Delaware Pl.	Pg.7	L13
Delphia Ave.	Pg.1	D10
Deming Pl.	Pg.2	G-L12
Denvir	Pg.6	J14
Depot Pl.	Pg.7	L15
Des Plaines	Pg.7	L13-15
Devon	Pg.2	E-K8
Dewitt Pl.	Pg.7	L13
Dickens	Pg.2	E-L12
Dickinson	Pg.2	G10
District	Pg.6	H17
Diversey	Pg.2	E-L11
Diversey Dr.	Pg.3	L11
Diversey Pkwy.	Pg.3	K11
Division	Pg.6	F-L13
Dobson	Pg.11	M20-25
Dominick	Pg.3	K12
Dorchester	Pg.7	M17-22
Douglas Blvd.	Pg.6	H15
Dover	Pg.3	K10
Dowagiac	Pg.2	G8
Drake	Pg.3	H9-17
Draper	Pg.2	K12
Drew	Pg.10	K23
Drexel	Pg.7	M17-25
Drexel Blvd.	Pg.7	M17
Drexel Sq. Dr.	Pg.7	M18
Drummond Pl.	Pg.2	G-L12
Dunbar, S.	Pg.10	M21-22
Early	Pg.3	K9
East End	Pg.11	N20
East River Rd.	Pg.1	D9-10
Eastlake Terr.	Pg.3	K7
Eastman	Pg.7	K-L13
Eastview Pk.	Pg.3	N18
Eastwood	Pg.2	D-L10
Eberhart	Pg.7,10,11,13	M16-25
Edbrooke	Pg.13	L25-27
Eddy	Pg.2	F-K11
Edgebrook Ter.	Pg.1	F8
Edgewater	Pg.3	K9
Edmaire	Pg.10	K23
Edmund	Pg.2	F-G10
Edward Ct.	Pg.3	L12
Eggleston	Pg.10	L19-25
Elaine Pl.	Pg.3	L11
Elbridge	Pg.3	H11
Eleanor	Pg.7	K16
Elias Ct.	Pg.7	K16
Elizabeth	Pg.7	K13-24
Elk Grove	Pg.3	K12-13
Ellen	Pg.7	K13
Elliot	Pg.11	N20
Ellis	Pg.7	M16-25
Ellsworth Dr.	Pg.7	M18
Elm	Pg.7	L13
Elmdale	Pg.3	K9
Elston	Pg.2,3,7	F9,H11,J12,K13
Emerald	Pg.7	L16-25
Emerald S.	Pg.10	L19
Emmett	Pg.3	H11
Englewood	Pg.10	L19
Erie	Pg.6	F-L13
Ernst Ct.	Pg.7	L13
Escanaba	Pg.11	O20-24
Esmond	Pg.10	K23
Essex	Pg.11	N21-22
Estes Ave.	Pg.2	E-K8
Euclid	Pg.11	N19-22
Eugenie	Pg.3	L12
Evans	Pg.7	M17-25
Evans Ct.	Pg.7	L13
Everett	Pg.7	N18
Evergreen	Pg.2,6,7	E8,H-L13
Ewing	Pg.11	O22-23
Exchange	Pg.11	O20-25
Fair Pl.	Pg.7	L13
Fairbanks Ct.	Pg.7	L13
Fairfield	Pg.3	J7-24
Fargo Ave.	Pg.2	E-K7
Farragut	Pg.2	E-K9
Farrell	Pg.7	K16
Farwell Ave.	Pg.2	E-K8
Federal	Pg.7	L14-19
Felton Ct.	Pg.7	L13
Ferdinand	Pg.6	G-J13
Fern Ct.	Pg.3	L12
Field Plaza Dr.	Pg.7	M15
Fielding	Pg.10	L20
Fifth	Pg.6	G-J14
Fillmore	Pg.6	G-K14
Financial	Pg.7	L14
Fitch Ave.	Pg.2	E-J8
Fletcher	Pg.2	E-L11
Flournoy	Pg.6	G-K14
Ford	Pg.7	L15
Ford City Dr.	Pg.9	G20
Forest	Pg.10	M21-24
Forest Glen	Pg.2	G9
Forest Preserve	Pg.1	D11,E10
Forrestville	Pg.7	M17-25
Foster	Pg.2	E-L9
Foster Pl.	Pg.2	E9
Francis Pl.	Pg.2	K13
Francisco	Pg.3,6,10,12,13	J7-21
Franklin	Pg.7	L14
Franklin Blvd.	Pg.6	J-H13
Fremont	Pg.3	K10-13
Front	Pg.10,11,13	M23
Frontier	Pg.3	L10
Fry	Pg.7	K13
Fuller	Pg.7	K13
Fullerton	Pg.2	E-L12
Fulton	Pg.6	E-L14
Fulton Blvd.	Pg.6	H14
Gale	Pg.2	G10
Garfield	Pg.2	F14
Garfield Blvd.	Pg.6,7,10	K-L18
Garland Ct.	Pg.7	L14
Geneva Ter.	Pg.3	L12
Genoa	Pg.10	L21-22
George	Pg.2	E-L11
Germania Pl.	Pg.7	L13
Gettysburg	Pg.2	G9
Giddings	Pg.1	E-K10
Gilbert Ct.	Pg.10	L21
Giles	Pg.7	M16
Givins Ct.	Pg.10	L21
Gladys	Pg.6	G-L14
Glenlake	Pg.2	E-K9
Glenwood	Pg.3	K8-9
Goethe	Pg.7	L13
Goodman	Pg.2	F9
Gordon Ter.	Pg.3	K-L10
Governor's Pkwy.	Pg.6	H14
Grace	Pg.3	D-L10
Grady Ct.	Pg.7	K13
Grand	Pg.2,6,7	E-G12,J-L13
Grant Pl.	Pg.3	L12
Granville	Pg.2	H-K8
Gratten	Pg.3	K16
Green	Pg.7	L14-25
Green Bay	Pg.11	O21-25
Greenleaf	Pg.2	E-K8
Greenview	Pg.3	K7-13
Greenwood	Pg.7	M17-25
Gregory	Pg.1	D-K9
Grenshaw	Pg.6	G-L15
Gresham	Pg.3	H11
Grove	Pg.7	L15
Grover	Pg.3	F10
Gunnison	Pg.1	F-L10
Haddon	Pg.6	G-K13
Haft	Pg.7	F8
Haines	Pg.7	L13
Hale	Pg.10	K23-24
Halsted	Pg.3	L11-25
Halsted Pkwy.	Pg.10	L19
Hamilton	Pg.3,6,7,10	J8-22
Hamlin	Pg.6	H8-23
Hamlin Blvd.	Pg.6	H14
Hampden Ct.	Pg.3	L11-12
Harbor	Pg.11	O22
Harding	Pg.2	H8-23
Harlem	Pg.2	E8-19
Harper	Pg.7	M17-25
Harrison	Pg.7	G-L14
Hart	Pg.2	F8
Hartland Ct.	Pg.7	K13
Hartwell	Pg.10	L19
Harvard	Pg.10	L19-25
Haskins	Pg.3	K7
Hastings	Pg.3	J-K15
Hawthorne Pl.	Pg.3	L11
Hayes	Pg.2	E-F8
Hayes Dr.	Pg.11	N19
Hayford Pl.	Pg.9	H20
Haynes Ct.	Pg.7	K16
Hazel	Pg.3	K10
Heath	Pg.6	J15
Helen Mikols Dr.	Pg.9	G19
Henderson	Pg.2	E-K11
Henry Ct.	Pg.3	J12
Hermione	Pg.2	F9
Hermitage	Pg.3	K8-21
Hermosa	Pg.10	K23
Hiawatha	Pg.2	F8-G9
Hickory	Pg.7	F8
Higgins	Pg.1	B8,F9
Higgins Rd.	Pg.1	B-C8,E9
Highland	Pg.2	E-K8
Hill	Pg.7	L13
Hillock	Pg.7	K16
Hirsch	Pg.6	F-J13
Hobart	Pg.3	E-F9
Hobbie	Pg.7	L13
Hobson	Pg.2	F9
Hoey	Pg.7	K16
Holbrook	Pg.2	F9
Holland Rd.	Pg.10	L21
Hollett Dr.	Pg.10	H19-20
Holly	Pg.3	K12
Hollywood	Pg.2	G-K9
Homan	Pg.6	H13-24
Homer	Pg.2	G-K12
Homewood	Pg.10	K23
Honore	Pg.3	K8-24
Hood	Pg.2	E-K9
Hooker	Pg.7	K13
Hopkins Pl.	Pg.10	K21
Horner	Pg.3	J12
Hortense	Pg.2	E8
Houston	Pg.11	O21-25
Howard St.	Pg.2	E-K7
Howe	Pg.3	L12-13
Howland	Pg.10	K21
Hoxie	Pg.11	O22-25
Hoyne Ave.	Pg.3,6,7,10	J8-23
Hoyt	Pg.6	J16
Hudson	Pg.3	L11-13
Huguelet Pl.	Pg.7	L13
Humboldt Blvd.	Pg.6	J12
Humboldt Dr.	Pg.3	J13
Hunt Pl.	Pg.10	K21
Huntington	Pg.2	F8
Hurlbut	Pg.2	F-F9
Huron	Pg.6	F-M13
Hutchinson	Pg.2	F-L10
Hyacinth	Pg.2	F9
Hyde Park Blvd.	Pg.7	M-N18
Ibsen	Pg.2	E8
Illinois	Pg.7	L13
Imlay	Pg.2	E-F8
Independence Blvd	Pg.6	H14
Indian Rd.	Pg.2	F8,G9
Indiana	Pg.7	L15-25
Indianapolis	Pg.11	P22-23
Ingleside	Pg.7	M17-25
Institute Pl.	Pg.7	L13
Ionia	Pg.2	G8-9
Iowa	Pg.6	G-K13
Irene	Pg.3	J11
Iron	Pg.7	K16
Irving Park Rd.	Pg.1	D-L10
Isham	Pg.2	E8
Jackson Blvd.	Pg.6	J-L14
Jackson Dr.	Pg.7	L-M14
James	Pg.2	K18
Jarlath Ave.	Pg.2	E-J8
Jarvis Ave.	Pg.2	E-K7
Jasper Pl.	Pg.7	K16,17
Jean	Pg.2	F8
Jefferson	Pg.7	L14-15
Jeffery	Pg.14	N24-25
Jeffery Blvd.	Pg.11	N19-22
Jenssen Blvd.	Pg.3	K11
Jerome	Pg.2	E-J7
Jersey	Pg.2	H9
Jessie Ct.	Pg.6	J13-14
Jones	Pg.3	J12
Jonquil Ter.	Pg.2	K7
Jourdan Ct.	Pg.7	L15
Joyce	Pg.2	F10
Julia Ct.	Pg.3	J12
Julian	Pg.7	K13
Juneway Ter.	Pg.2	K7
Junior Ter.	Pg.3	L10
Justine	Pg.3	K14-22
Kamerling	Pg.6	G-H13
Karlov	Pg.6	H8-21
Kasson	Pg.2	H10
Kearsage	Pg.2	H11
Keating	Pg.2	G8-21
Kedvale	Pg.6	H8-21
Kedzie Ave.	Pg.2,3,6,10	J7-23
Kedzie Blvd.	Pg.3	J12
Keefe	Pg.11	M19
Keeler	Pg.6	H8-21
Keeley	Pg.7	K16
Keene	Pg.2	G8
Keller Dr.	Pg.9	H8-21
Kemper Pl.	Pg.3	L12
Kenmore	Pg.3	K8-12
Kennedy	Pg.2	H10
Kennicott	Pg.2	H10
Kennison	Pg.2	G9-10
Kenosha	Pg.2	H11
Kensington	Pg.10	L-M24
Kent	Pg.2	G8-21
Kentucky	Pg.6	G10
Kenwood	Pg.7	M17-22
Keokuk	Pg.3	H10
Keota	Pg.2	F8
Kerbs	Pg.2	G9
Kercheval	Pg.6	G9
Kerfoot	Pg.10	K21-24
Kewanee	Pg.2	H10
Keystone	Pg.6	H8-14
Kilbourn	Pg.2	H8-23
Kildare	Pg.6	H9-21
Kilpatrick	Pg.2	H8-23
Kimball	Pg.2	H8-12
Kimbark	Pg.7	M17-22
Kimberly	Pg.2	G9
King, Dr. M.L. Dr.	Pg.7,10,11,13	M15-25
Kingsbury	Pg.3	K12-14
Kingsdale	Pg.2	G9
Kingston	Pg.11	O20-22
Kinzie	Pg.6	F-L14
Kinzua	Pg.2	G8
Kiona	Pg.2	H10
Kirby	Pg.2	G9
Kirkland	Pg.7	H20
Kirkwood	Pg.2	G8-9
Knox	Pg.6	H9-21
Kolin	Pg.6	H13-21
Kolmar	Pg.2	K21
Komensky	Pg.6	H15-21
Kostner	Pg.6	G9-21
Kruger	Pg.2	G10
LaCrosse	Pg.2	G9-19
LaSalle St.	Pg.7	L18
Lacey	Pg.2	G9
Lafayette	Pg.7	L17-24
Laflin	Pg.7	K13-24
Lake	Pg.6	F-L14
Lake Park	Pg.7	M16-18
Lake Shore Dr.	Pg.3	K9,L13,M17,N19
Lake Shore Dr. E.	Pg.3	L11
Lake View	Pg.3	L11-12
Lakeside Pl.	Pg.3	K10
Lakewood	Pg.3	K8-12
Lambert	Pg.2	G9
Lamed	Pg.2	G9
Lamon	Pg.2	G9-19
Landers	Pg.2	G8-9
Langley	Pg.7	M17
Lansing	Pg.2	G9-19
Laporte	Pg.2	F8,G9
Laramie	Pg.2	G9-18
Larchmont	Pg.2	K10
Larned	Pg.2	G9
Larrabee	Pg.3	L12-13
LasCasas	Pg.2	G9
Latham	Pg.7	K13
Latrobe	Pg.2	G9-19
Lavergne	Pg.2	G9-19
Lawler	Pg.2	G9-19
Lawndale	Pg.3,6,9,10,12	H8-23
Lawrence	Pg.2	F-L10
Lawrence Ct.	Pg.3	L10
Le Mai	Pg.2	G8
Le Moyne	Pg.6	F-K13
Leader	Pg.2	G8-9
Leamington	Pg.2	G9-18
Leavenworth	Pg.2	G9
Leavitt	Pg.3	J8-22
Leclaire	Pg.2	G9-19
Lee Pl.	Pg.2	J-K13
Legett	Pg.2	G8-9
Lehigh	Pg.2	G9
Lehmann Ct.	Pg.3	L11
Leland	Pg.1	D-L10
Lemont	Pg.2	G8-9
Lenox	Pg.2	G8-9
Leona	Pg.2	G8
Leonard	Pg.2	F-G9
Leoti	Pg.2	F8,G9
Leroy	Pg.2	G9
Lessing	Pg.7	K13
Lester	Pg.2	G9-10
Levee	Pg.7	K16
Lexington	Pg.6	G-L14
Leyden	Pg.13	M25
Liano	Pg.2	G9
Libbey	Pg.7	K13
Liberty	Pg.7	K-L15
Lieb	Pg.2	G9
Lightfoot	Pg.2	F8
Lill	Pg.3	K12
Lincoln	Pg.3	H8,J10,K11,L12
Lincoln Park W.	Pg.3	L12
Lind	Pg.2	G9
Linden Pl.	Pg.3	D9,J12
Linder	Pg.2	G9-19
Lipps	Pg.2	G10
Lister	Pg.3	K12
Lituanica	Pg.7	K16
Livermore	Pg.2	G8
Lloyd	Pg.7	K16
Lock	Pg.2	G9
Lockwood	Pg.2	G9-19
Locust	Pg.7	L13
Logan Blvd.	Pg.3	J12
Loleta	Pg.2	F8
London	Pg.3	G10
Long	Pg.2	G9-19
Longwood Dr.	Pg.10	K21-24
Loomis	Pg.7	K14-24
Loomis Blvd.	Pg.10	K19-22
Loomis Pl.	Pg.7	K16,17
Lorel	Pg.2	G9-19
Loring	Pg.2	G9
Loron	Pg.2	G8
Lothair	Pg.10	J23-24
Lotus	Pg.2	G9-18
Louis Munoz Marin Dr.	Pg.6	J13
Louise	Pg.2	F8,G9
Lovejoy	Pg.2	F9
Lowe	Pg.7	L15-18
Lowell	Pg.6	H8-12
Loyola	Pg.3	K8
Lucerne	Pg.2	G9
Ludlam	Pg.2	G9
Luella	Pg.11	N20-25
Lumber	Pg.7	K-L15
Luna	Pg.2	G9-18
Lundy	Pg.2	F8
Lunt Ave.	Pg.2	E-K8
Luther Pl.	Pg.6	J16
Lyman	Pg.7	K16
Lyndale	Pg.2	G-J12
Lyon	Pg.11	M22
Lytle	Pg.7	K14-15
Mackinaw	Pg.11	O21-25
Madison	Pg.6	F-L14
Madison Ave. Pk. E.	Pg.7	M18
Magnet	Pg.2	G9
Magnolia	Pg.3	K8-12
Major	Pg.2	G9-19
Malden	Pg.3	K10
Mandel	Pg.7	L11
Mango	Pg.2	G9-12
Manila	Pg.2	G9
Manistee	Pg.11	O20-25
Mankato	Pg.2	G9
Mann Dr.	Pg.10	H-J19
Manor	Pg.3	D9,J10
Mansfield	Pg.2	G9-19
Manton	Pg.2	G9
Maple	Pg.7	L13
Maplewood	Pg.3	J7-24
Marcey	Pg.3	K12
Margate Ter.	Pg.3	K-L9
Marine Dr.	Pg.3	L9-10
Marion	Pg.2	G9
Marion Ct.	Pg.7	K13
Market St.	Pg.13	L25
Markham	Pg.2	F9
Marmora	Pg.2	G9-12
Marquette	Pg.11	O20-25
Marquette Dr.	Pg.7	N18
Marquette Rd.	Pg.9	G-N19
Marshall Blvd.	Pg.6	J15
Marshfield	Pg.3	K7-22
Mary	Pg.7	K16
Maryland	Pg.11	M18-23
Mason	Pg.2	G9-19
Massasoit	Pg.6	F13-19
Matson	Pg.2	G9
Maud	Pg.3	K12
Mautene Ct.	Pg.7	K13
Maxwell	Pg.7	K-L15
May	Pg.7	K13-24
Mayfield	Pg.2	F12-19
Maypole	Pg.6	G-K14
McAlpin	Pg.2	F8
McClellan	Pg.2	F8
McClurg Ct.	Pg.7	M13
McCook	Pg.2	F9
McCormick Blvd.	Pg.3	H6-8
McDowell	Pg.7	K17
McFetrige Dr.	Pg.7	M15
McLean	Pg.3	F-K12
McLeod	Pg.2	F8
McVicker	Pg.2	F8-19
Meade	Pg.2	F8-19
Medford	Pg.2	F8
Medill	Pg.2	E-K12
Medina	Pg.2	F9
Meis Van Der Rohe	Pg.7	L13
Melrose	Pg.2	E-L11
Melvina	Pg.2,5,6,9	F8-12
Menard	Pg.2	F8,K12
Mendell	Pg.7	F8,K12
Mendota	Pg.2	F8
Menominee	Pg.3	L12
Meredith	Pg.2	F8
Merrill Ave.	Pg.11	N19-26
Merrimac	Pg.2,5,6,9	F8-19
Merrion	Pg.11	N22
Meyer	Pg.3	L12
Miami	Pg.2	F9
Michigan	Pg.7	L13-25
Midway	Pg.6	F13
Midway Plaisance	Pg.11	M-N19
Mildred	Pg.3	K11
Millard	Pg.6,8,10,12	
Miller	Pg.7	K14-15
Milltmore	Pg.2	F9
Milwaukee	Pg.2,3,7	E7,H11,K13
Moffat	Pg.3	J-K12
Mohawk	Pg.3	L12
Monon Ave.	Pg.2	F8
Monitor	Pg.2	F9-19
Monroe	Pg.6	G-L14
Monroe Dr.	Pg.7	L-M14
Montana	Pg.2	G-K12
Montclare	Pg.2	E11-12
Monterrey	Pg.10	K23
Montgomery	Pg.6	J17
Monticello	Pg.3	H8-13
Montrose	Pg.1	D-L10
Montrose Harbor Dr.		L10
Montvale	Pg.10	K23
Moody	Pg.2	F8-19
Moore	Pg.7	L13
Moorman	Pg.7	K13
Morgan	Pg.7	K14-25
Morse Ave.	Pg.2	G-K8
Moselle	Pg.2	E8
Mozart	Pg.3	J8-21
Mulligan	Pg.2,5,6,9	F8-19
Museum Dr.	Pg.11	N18
Muskegon	Pg.11	O20-25
Myrtle	Pg.2	E8
Nada	Pg.7	K13
Nagle	Pg.2	F8-19
Naper	Pg.2	F8-9
Naples	Pg.2	F8-9
Napoleon	Pg.2	F9
Narragansett	Pg.2,5,6,9	F10-19
Nashotah	Pg.2	F9
Nashville	Pg.2	F8-19
Nassau	Pg.2	F8-9
Natchez	Pg.2	F9-19
Natoma	Pg.2	F8-19
Navajo	Pg.3	J7-24
Navarre	Pg.2	E-F9
Neenah	Pg.2	F8-19
Nelson	Pg.3	E-L11
Neola	Pg.2	F8-10
Nettleton	Pg.2	E8-9
Neva	Pg.2	F8-19
New	Pg.7	M13-14
New England	Pg.2	E8-19
New Hampshire	Pg.2	E9
Newark	Pg.2	E8-9
Newberry	Pg.7	L15
Newburg	Pg.2	L15
Newcastle	Pg.2	E8-19
Newgard	Pg.3	K8
Newland	Pg.2	E8-19
Newport	Pg.2	E-L11
Newton	Pg.2	E9
Niagara	Pg.2	E9
Nickerson	Pg.2	E8-9
Nicolet	Pg.2	E9
Nina	Pg.2	E9
Nixon	Pg.2	E9
Nobel	Pg.2	F10
Noble	Pg.3	K12-13
Nokomis	Pg.2	F8
Nora	Pg.2	E10-11
Nordica	Pg.2	E8-18
Normal	Pg.7	L15-24
Normal Blvd.	Pg.10	L19-20
Normal Pkwy.	Pg.10	L19
Normandy	Pg.2	F8-19
North	Pg.2,3,5,7	E-L12
North Branch	Pg.3	K13
North Park	Pg.3	L12-13
North Shore	Pg.2	E-K8
North Water	Pg.7	M13
Northcott	Pg.2	E8,F9
Northeast Cir.	Pg.2	E9
Northwest Cir.	Pg.2	E9
Northwest Hwy.	Pg.2	E8,F9
Norton	Pg.7	K14
Norwood	Pg.2	E-K9
Nottingham	Pg.2	E9-19
Nursery	Pg.2	K12
O'Brien	Pg.7	L15
Oak Park	Pg.2	F8-19
Oak Pl.	Pg.7	L13
Oakdale	Pg.2	E-L11
Oakenwald	Pg.7	M17
Oakley Blvd.	Pg.6	J13
Oakview	Pg.1	D10
Oakwood Blvd.	Pg.7	M17
Oconto	Pg.2	E7-11
Octavia	Pg.2	E7-11
Odell	Pg.2	E7-11
Ogallah	Pg.2	F8
Ogden	Pg.7	
Ogden Blvd.	Pg.7	K14
Oglesby	Pg.11	N19-26
Ohio	Pg.6	F-M13
Oketo	Pg.2	E7-11
Olcott	Pg.2	E7-11
Oleander	Pg.2	E7-11
Olive	Pg.3	E-K9
Olmsted	Pg.2	E8
Olympia	Pg.2	E8-9
Onarga	Pg.2	E8
Oneida	Pg.2	E8

CHICAGO

Chicago-Lake Shore Hospital . . . Pg.3 . . . L10
Children's Memorial Hospital . . . Pg.3 . . . L12
Columbus Hosp. . . . Pg.3 . . . L12
Cook Co. Hosp. Pg.7 . . . K14
Cuneo Hosp. . Pg.3 . . . L10
Edgewater Hosp. . . . Pg.3 . . . K9
Franklin Blvd. Comm. Hospital . . . Pg.6 . . . H13
Grant Hospital Pg.3 . . . L12
Halco Hospital Pg.7 . . . L13
Holy Cross Hospital . . . Pg.10 . . . J19
Ill. Masonic Medical Center . . . Pg.3 . . . K11
Jackson Park Hospital . . . Pg.11 . . . N20
LaRabida Children's Hosp. & Research Center . . . Pg.11 . . . N19
Little Company of Mary Hospital . . . Pg.10 . . . J22
Loretto Hosp. . Pg.6 . . . G14
Louis Burg Hosp. . . . Pg.7 . . . L15
Martha Washington Hosp . . . Pg.3 . . . J10
Mary Thompson Hospital . . . Pg.7 . . . K14
Mercy Hosp. . Pg.7 . . . M16
Michael Reese Medical Center . . . Pg.7 . . . M16
Mt. Sinai Hospital Medical Center . . . Pg.6 . . . J15
Mun. Communicable Disease Hosp. . . . Pg.6 . . . J16
Mun. T.B. Sanitarium . . . Pg.3 . . . H9
Nicholas J. Pritzker Children's Hosp. . . . Pg.11 . . . M18
Northeast Comm. Hospital . . . Pg.3 . . . K8
Northwest Hosp. . . . Pg.2 . . . F11
Northwestern Memorial Hosp. . . . Pg.7 . . . L13
Norwegian Amer. Hosp. . . . Pg.6 . . . J13
Pinel Hosp. . . Pg.3 . . . L11
Provident Hosp. Pg.7 . . . M18
Ravenswood Hosp. . . . Pg.3 . . . K10
Rest Haven Hosp. . . . Pg.6 . . . J15
Resurrection Hospital . . . Pg.2 . . . E9
Ridgeway Hosp. Pg.6 . . . H13
Roosevelt Memorial Hospital . . . Pg.3 . . . L12
Roseland Comm. Hospital . . . Pg.10 . . . L23
Rush Presby. St. Luke's Med. Ctr . . . Pg.7 . . . K14
Scott Clinic . . Pg.7 . . . M18
Sheridan Rd. Hospital . . . Pg.3 . . . K9
South Chicago Comm. Hospital . . . Pg.11 . . . N22
South Shore Hospital . . . Pg.11 . . . N20
St. Anne's Hosp. Pg.6 . . . G13
St. Anthony's Hospital . . . Pg.6 . . . J15
St. Bernard's Hospital . . . Pg.10 . . . L19
St. Elizabeth Hospital . . . Pg.6 . . . J13
St. Georges Hospital . . . Pg.10 . . . L20
St. Joseph Hosp. . . . Pg.3 . . . L11
St. Mary of Nazareth Hospital . . . Pg.6 . . . J13
St. Vincent's Hospital . . . Pg.7 . . . L13
State T.B. Hosp. Pg.7 . . . K15
Swedish Covenant Hospital . . . Pg.3 . . . J9
Thorek Hosp. . Pg.3 . . . K10
U. of Chicago Clinics . . . Pg.11 . . . M18
U. of IL. Med. Ctr. . . . Pg.7 . . . K14
Veterans Admin. Hospital . . . Pg.7 . . . K14
Veterans Admin. Research Hosp. . . . Pg.7 . . . M13
Von Solbrig Hospital . . . Pg.9 . . . H19
Walther Mem. Hospital . . . Pg.6 . . . H13
Weiss Mem. Hospital . . . Pg.3 . . . L10
Woodlawn Hosp. . . . Pg.11 . . . M19

SCHOOLS

Academy of Our Lady . . . Pg.10 . . . K22
Alvernia H.S. . Pg.3 . . . H10
Amundson H.S. Pg.3 . . . J9
Austin H.S. . . Pg.6 . . . G14
Bogan H.S. . . Pg.9 . . . H20
Bowen H.S. . . Pg.11 . . . O21
Bradley Univ. . Pg.10 . . . J22
Calumet H.S. . Pg.10 . . . K21
Cardinal Stritch H.S. . . . Pg.2 . . . F10
Career Metro H.S. . . . Pg.7 . . . L13
Carver H.S. . . Pg.13 . . . M25
Catholic Theo. Union of Chicago . . . Pg.11 . . . N18
Chicago Bible College . . . Pg.3 . . . K11
Chicago H.S. for Agri. Sci. . . . Pg.9 . . . H23
Chicago Medical Sch. . . . Pg.6 . . . H15
Chicago State University . . . Pg.11 . . . M22
Chicago Tech. College . . . Pg.7 . . . L15
Chicago Voc. H.S. . . . Pg.11 . . . N21
Clemente H.S. Pg.6 . . . J13
Collins H.S. . . Pg.6 . . . J15
Cooley Voc. H.S. Pg.7 . . . L13
Corlis H.S. . . . Pg.11 . . . M22
Crane H.S. . . . Pg.6 . . . J14
Cregier Voc. H.S. . . . Pg.7 . . . K14
Curie H.S. . . . Pg.6 . . . H18
Daley College . Pg.9 . . . H20
De LaSalle H.S. Pg.7 . . . L16
DePaul Univ. . Pg.3 . . . K12
DeVry Inst. of Tech. . . . Pg.2 . . . H11
Decatur Sch. . Pg.3 . . . J8
Dominican Coll. Pg.5 . . . E13
Du Sable H.S. Pg.7 . . . L18
Dunbar Voc. H.S. . . . Pg.7 . . . M16
Englewood H.S. Pg.10 . . . L19
Farragut H.S. . Pg.6 . . . H16
Felician Coll. . Pg.3 . . . H9
Fenger H.S. . . Pg.10 . . . L23
Flower Voc. H.S. Pg.6 . . . H14
Foreman H.S. . Pg.2 . . . G11
Frederick Stock Sch. . . . Pg.2 . . . E8
Good Council H.S. . . . Pg.3 . . . H9
Gordon Tech. H.S. . . . Pg.3 . . . J11
Gunsaulus Sch. Acad. . . . Pg.6 . . . J17
Gurden Hubbard H.S. . . . Pg.9 . . . H19
Harlan H.S. . . Pg.10 . . . L22
Harold Washington College . . . Pg.7 . . . L14
Harper H.S. . . Pg.10 . . . K19
Hirsch H.S. . . Pg.11 . . . M20
Holy Family Acad. . . . Pg.7 . . . K13
Holy Trinity H.S. Pg.7 . . . K13
House of the Good Shepherd H.S. . . . Pg.3 . . . K10
Hyde Park H.S. Pg.11 . . . N19
Ida Crown H.S. Pg.3 . . . J8
Ill. Coll. of Optometry . . . Pg.7 . . . L16
Immaculata H.S. Pg.3 . . . L12
Jones Comm. H.S. . . . Pg.7 . . . L14
Juarez H.S. . . Pg.7 . . . K15
Kelly H.S. . . . Pg.6 . . . J17
Kelvyn Park H.S. Pg.2 . . . H12
Kennedy H.S. . Pg.9 . . . F18
Kennedy-King College . . . Pg.10 . . . L19
Kenwood H.S. Pg.7 . . . N18
King H.S. . . . Pg.7 . . . M17
La Casas Occup. H.S. . . . Pg.11 . . . O22
Lake View H.S. Pg.3 . . . K10
Lane Tech. H.S. Pg.3 . . . J11
Leo H.S. . . . Pg.10 . . . L20
Lindblom H.S. Pg.10 . . . K19
Loretto Academy . . . Pg.11 . . . N19
Lourdes H.S. . Pg.9 . . . H18
Loyola Univ. . Pg.3 . . . K8
Luther H.S. North . . . Pg.2 . . . F10
Luther H.S. South . . . Pg.10 . . . J21
Madonna H.S. Pg.2 . . . H11
Malcolm X College . . . Pg.7 . . . K14
Manley H.S. . . Pg.6 . . . J14
Marshall H.S. . Pg.6 . . . H14
Mather H.S. . . Pg.3 . . . J9
Meadville Lombard Theo. Sch. . . . Pg.11 . . . M18
Mendel H.S. . . Pg.11 . . . M23
Moody Bible Inst. . . . Pg.7 . . . L13
Mt. Carmel H.S. Pg.11 . . . M19
Mundelein Coll. Pg.3 . . . K8
North Park Coll. & Theo. Sem. . . . Pg.3 . . . H9
Northeastern Ill. University . . . Pg.3 . . . H9
Northwestern Bus. College . . . Pg.3 . . . J12
Northwestern Univ. (Chicago Campus) . . Pg.7 . . . M13
Notre Dame H.S. . . . Pg.2 . . . F11
Olive-Harvey Coll. . . . Pg.11 . . . M22
Orr H.S. . . . Pg.6 . . . H13
Phillips H.S. . . Pg.7 . . . M17
Prosser H.S. . Pg.2 . . . G12
Providence H.S. Pg.6 . . . H14
Richards Voc. H.S. . . . Pg.6 . . . J18
Roosevelt H.S. Pg.3 . . . H10
Roosevelt Univ. Pg.7 . . . L14
Sacred Heart H.S. . . . Pg.10 . . . K20
Savcedo H.S. . Pg.6 . . . J15
Schurz H.S. . . Pg.2 . . . H11
Senn H.S. . . . Pg.3 . . . K9
Shoop H.S. . . Pg.10 . . . K23
Siena H.S. . . . Pg.6 . . . F14
Simeon Voc. H.S. . . . Pg.10 . . . L21
South Shore H.S. . . . Pg.11 . . . N20
Spaulding H.S. Pg.7 . . . K14
St. Alphonsus Comm. H.S. . . . Pg.3 . . . K11
St. Ann H.S. . . Pg.6 . . . J15
St. Barbara H.S. Pg.7 . . . K16
St. Benedict H.S. . . . Pg.3 . . . J10
St. Columbus Comm. H.S. . . . Pg.7 . . . K13
St. Elizabeth H.S. . . . Pg.7 . . . L17
St. Ignatius H.S. Pg.7 . . . K15
St. Juliana Sch. Pg.2 . . . E8
St. Mary H.S. . Pg.7 . . . K15
St. Mary of Perpetual Help H.S. . . . Pg.7 . . . K16
St. Michaels Central H.S. . . . Pg.3 . . . L12
St. Patrick H.S. Pg.2 . . . F11
St. Paul H.S. . Pg.9 . . . F19
St. Phillip Basilica H.S. . . . Pg.6 . . . J14
St. Pias Comm. H.S. . . . Pg.7 . . . K15
St. Procopius H.S. . . . Pg.7 . . . K15
St. Sebastian H.S. . . . Pg.3 . . . L11
St. Stanislaus Kostka H.S. . . . Pg.7 . . . K13
Steinmetz H.S. Pg.2 . . . F11
Sullivan H.S. . Pg.3 . . . K8
Taft H.S. . . . Pg.2 . . . F9
Tilden Tech. H.S. Pg.7 . . . L17
Truman Coll. . Pg.3 . . . K10
Tuley H.S. . . Pg.6 . . . J13
Turner Sch. . .
Unity H.S. . . . Pg.11 . . . M21
Univ. of Chicago Pg.11 . . . M18
Univ. of Ill. (Chicago Campus) . . . Pg.7 . . . L14
Von Stueben H.S. . . . Pg.3 . . . H9
Washburne Trade H.S. . . . Pg.6 . . . H16
Washington H.S. . . . Pg.11 . . . O23
Weber H.S. . . Pg.2 . . . G12
Wells H.S. . . . Pg.7 . . . K13
Westinghouse Voc. H.S. . . . Pg.6 . . . H13
Wilson Occup. H.S. . . . Pg.2 . . . G9
Wright Coll. . . Pg.2 . . . F11

SHOPPING CENTERS

Brickyard Mall Pg.2 . . . F11
Century Mall . Pg.3 . . . L11
Evergreen Plaza . . . Pg.10 . . . J22
Ford City . . . Pg.9 . . . G20
Lake Meadows Pg.7 . . . M16
North Riverside Park Plaza . . . Pg.5 . . . E15
Scottsdale Shopping Ctr. . . . Pg.9 . . . G20

TRANSPORTATION

Chicago & Northwestern R.R. Sta. . . . Pg.7 . . . L14
Chicago Midway Airport . . . Pg.9 . . . G18,19
Dearborn St. R.R. Station . . . Pg.7 . . . L14
LaSalle St. R.R. Sta. . . . Pg.7 . . . L14
Meigs Field . . Pg.7 . . . M15
O'Hare Int'l Airport . . . Pg.1 . . . B9
Union R.R. Sta. Pg.7 . . . L14

MISCELLANEOUS

Adler Planetarium . . . Pg.7 . . . M15
Art Institute . . Pg.7 . . . L14
Belmont Harbor Yacht Club . . . Pg.3 . . . L11
Buckingham Fountain . . . Pg.7 . . . L14
Burnham Park Yacht Club . . . Pg.7 . . . M15
Calumet Boating Center . . . Pg.13 . . . K25
Calumet Yacht Club . . . Pg.11 . . . P22
Chicago Acad. of Sciences . . . Pg.3 . . . L12
Chicago Corinthian . . . Pg.3 . . . L10
Chicago Hist. Society . . . Pg.3 . . . L12
Chicago Lighthouse for the Blind . . . Pg.7 . . . K15
Chicago Nursery & Orphan Asylum . . . Pg.3 . . . J9
Chicago Parental Sch. . . . Pg.3 . . . H9
Chicago Public Library . . . Pg.7 . . . L14
Chicago Stadium . . . Pg.7 . . . K14
Chicago Yacht Club . . . Pg.7 . . . M14
Chinatown . . . Pg.7 . . . L15
City Hall . . . . Pg.7 . . . L14
Coast Guard Sta. . . . Pg.7 . . M14,P22
Coliseum . . . . Pg.7 . . . L15
Comiskey Park (White Sox) . . . Pg.7 . . . L16
Cook Co. Juvenile Home . . . Pg.6 . . . J15
County Building Pg.7 . . . L14
Courthouse . . Pg.6 . . . J16
Criminal Court Pg.6 . . . J16
Daley Center . Pg.7 . . . L14
Diversey Yacht Club . . . Pg.3 . . . L12
Douglas Tomb State Mem. . . . Pg.7 . . . M16
Eckersall Stadium . . . Pg.11 . . . N21
Federal Bldg. . Pg.7 . . . L14
Field Museum Pg.7 . . . L15
Fifth Army Hdqrs. . . . Pg.7 . . . N18
Filtration Plant Pg.11 . . . O20
Fullerton Pavilion . . . Pg.3 . . . L12
Grant Monument . . . Pg.3 . . . L12
Home for the Aged . . . Pg.1 . . . H9
Hull House Museum . . . Pg.7 . . . L14
Ill. Air Nat'l. Guard . . . Pg.9 . . . G19
Int'l Amphitheatre . . . Pg.7 . . . L17
Jackson Park Y.C. . . . P g.11 . . . N19
Knute Rockne Sta. . . . Pg.6 . . . G15
Lake Calumet Boat & Gun Club . . . Pg.13 . . . K25
Lawrence Hall Orphanage . . . Pg.3 . . . J10
Lincoln Monument Statues . . . Pg.3 . . . L12
Lincoln Park . Pg.3 . . . L12
Lincoln Park Archery Club . . . Pg.3 . . . L12
Lincoln Park Bath House . . . Pg.3 . . . L12
Lincoln Park Bird Sanctuary . . . Pg.3 . . . L11
Lincoln Park Conservatory . . . Pg.3 . . . L12
Lincoln Park Gun Club . . . Pg.3 . . . L11
Lincoln Park Totem Pole . . . Pg.3 . . . L11
Lincoln Park Zoo . . . Pg.3 . . . L12
McCormick Place Expo. Center . . . Pg.7 . . . M15
Merchandise Mart . . . Pg.7 . . . L14
Museum of Science & Industry . . . Pg.11 . . . N18
Naval Res. Armory . . . Pg.7 . . . M13
Navy Pier . . . . Pg.7 . . . M13
Newberry Library . . . Pg.7 . . . L13
Opera House . Pg.7 . . . L14
Port of Chicago Calumet Harbor . . . Pg.14 . . . N25
Post Office-Main Pg.7 . . . L14
Post Office-O'Hare Airport . . . Pg.11 . . . B10
Regenstein Lib. Pg.11 . . . M18
Rosemont Horizon . . . Pg.1 . . . B8
Shedd Aquarium . . . Pg.7 . . . M15
South District Filtration Plant . . . Pg.11 . . . O20
Southern Shore Y.C. . . . Pg.11 . . . N19
U.S. Army Admin. Ctr . . . Pg.7 . . . K17
U.S. Military Res . . . Pg.14 . . . P24
Water Tower . Pg.7 . . . L13
Wrigley Field (Cubs) . . . Pg.3 . . . K11

CICERO

Page 6

STREETS

Austin . . . F15
Central Ave. . . . G15-17
Cermak Rd. . . . F,G16
Cicero . . . G15-17
Edgewood . . . F16
Laramie . . . G15,16
Lombard . . . F15
Ogden Ave. . . . F16
Park . . . F16
Pershing Rd. . . . F17
Roosevelt Rd. . . . F,G15
12th Pl. . . . G15
13th Pl. . . . G15
13th St. . . . F,G15
14th St. . . . F,G15
15th Pl. . . . G15
15th St. . . . F,G15
16th St. . . . F,G15
18th St. . . . F,G15
19th Pl. . . . F17
19th St. . . . F,G15
20th St. . . . G15
21st Pl. . . . G15
21st St. . . . G15
22nd Pl. . . . F,G15
23rd Pl. . . . G15
23rd St. . . . G15
24th Pl. . . . G16
24th St. . . . F,G16
25th Pl. . . . G16
25th St. . . . F,G16
26th St. . . . F,G16
27th St. . . . F16
28th Pl. . . . G16
28th St. . . . G16
29th Pl. . . . G16
29th St. . . . G16
30th Pl. . . . G16
30th St. . . . G16
31st Pl. . . . G16
31st St. . . . F,G16
32nd Pl. . . . G16
32nd St. . . . G16
33rd St. . . . F,G16
34th St. . . . F,G16
35th St. . . . F,G16
36th St. . . . F,G17
37th St. . . . F,G17
38th St. . . . F,G17
46th Ct. . . . G15
46th St. . . . G15
47th Ct. . . . G15
47th St. . . . G15
48th Ct. . . . G15
49th Ct. . . . G15
49th St. . . . G15
50th Ct. . . . G15,16
50th St. . . . G15,16
51st Ct. . . . G15
51st St. . . . G15
52nd St. . . . G15-17
53rd Ct. . . . G17
53rd St. . . . G15-17
54th Ct. . . . G17-17
54th St. . . . G17-17
55th Ct. . . . G15-17
55th St. . . . G15-17
56th Ct. . . . F15-17
56th St. . . . G15
57th Ct. . . . F15-17
57th St. . . . F15-17
58th Ct. . . . F15-17
58th St. . . . F15-17
59th Ct. . . . F15-17
59th St. . . . F15-17
60th Ct. . . . F15-17
61st Ct. . . . F15-17
61st St. . . . F15-17

CRESTWOOD

PARKS

Clyde Park . . . F16
Columbus Playground . . . G16
Hawthorne Park . . . G16
Manor Park . . . F16
N. Warren Park . . . F15
Parkholm Park . . . G15
South Clyde Park . . . F17
Warren Park . . . F15

SCHOOLS

Morton East H.S. & Jr. Coll. . F16

MISCELLANEOUS

Hawthorne Race Track . . . G17
Sportsmans Park Race Track G16
Village Hall . . . G16

COUNTRYSIDE

Page 8

STREETS

Ashland . . . C18
Barton Rd. . . . C19
Bob-O-Link Dr. . . . C18
Brainard Ave. . . . C19
Cantigny . . . B19
Catherine . . . C18
Constance Ln. . . . C19
Crestview Rd. . . . B19
Dasher Rd. . . . C18
Dawn . . . B19
East Ave. . . . C18
Edgewood . . . B18
Forestview . . . B19
Francis . . . C19
Golf View Dr. . . . B19
Hillsdale . . . B20
Joliet Rd. . . . C19
Kensington Ave. . . . C18,19
La Grange Rd. . . . C19
Leitch . . . B18
Longview Dr. . . . C18,19
Lorraine Dr. . . . B20,C19
Madison . . . C18
Maplewood Rd. . . . B20
Merry Court . . . C19
Park Rd. . . . C18
Parkside . . . B19
Peck . . . B18
Plainfield Rd. . . . B,C18
Rose Ct. . . . C19
Rosemary Ct. . . . C19
S.E. Ct. . . . B18
Stafford Rd. . . . B19
Sunset . . . B20
Terry Ln. . . . C18
Vail Rd. . . . B,C18
Willow Springs Rd. . . . B19,20
5th St. . . . B20
6th Ave. . . . C18
7th Ave. . . . C18
8th Ave. . . . C18
9th Ave. . . . C18
10th Ave. . . . C18
51st St. . . . C18
53rd St. . . . C18
54th St. . . . C18
55th Pl. . . . B18
55th St. . . . B,C18
56th St. . . . C18
57th St. . . . C18
58th St. . . . C18
59th St. . . . C19
61st Pl. . . . C19
61st St. . . . C19
63rd St. . . . C19
67th St. . . . B19
71st Pl. . . . B20
74th St. . . . C20
75th St. . . . C20

MISCELLANEOUS

Village Hall . . . C18

CRESTWOOD

Page 12

STREETS

Arbor Ln. . . . G25
Calumet Sag Rd. . . . G25
Carriage Ln. . . . G25
Central Ave. . . . G25,26
Charles Ln. . . . G26
Cicero Ave. . . . G25
Circle Ave. . . . G25
Circle Ct. . . . G25
Crawford Ave. . . . H26
Crescent Ct. . . . G25
Crestview Ct. . . . G26
Crestwood Ct. . . . G25
Crestwood Dr. . . . G25
Di Roe Ct. . . . G25
Dori Ln. . . . G26
Fairway Dr. . . . G25
Forestview Ct. . . . G25
Forestview Ln. . . . G25
Harding . . . H26
Highland Ct. . . . G25
Hill St. . . . F25
Homestead Dr. . . . G25

James Ct. G26
James Dr. G26
Karlov Ave. H26
Keeler H25
Kenton Ave. G25
Kildare Ave. H26
Kolmar Ln. H26
Kostner H25
Lamon Ave. G26
Laramie Ave. G25
Lavergne Ave. G26
Lawler Ave. G25
Leclaire Ave. G25
Leonard Dr. G26
Linder St. G25
Long Ave. G25
Loomis Ct. G25
Loomis Ln. G25
Midlothian Tpke. H26
Model Ct. G25
Park Ct. G25
Park Ln. G25
Parkview Ct. G25
Playfield Dr., W. G25
Pleasant Ct. G25
Pleasant Ln. G25
Regal Rd. G25
Royal Ct. G25
S. End Ln. G26
Sandra Ln. G26
Short Dr. G25
Terrace Ln. G25
Village Ct. G25
Village Ln. G25
Walter Dr. G26
Waterbury Ct. G26
Waterbury Dr. G26
Waterbury Ln. G26
Waterbury Way G26
West End Ln. G25
Willow Ln. G26
128th Pl. G25
128th St. F25
129th St. G25
130th St. G25
131st St. G25
132nd St. G25
133rd St. G25
134th Pl. G25
135th Ct. G25
135th Pl. G25
135th St. G25
136th St. G25
137th Pl. G,H25
137th St. G25
138th Ct. G26
138th Pl. G26
138th St. G26
139th St. G26
140th Pl. H26
140th St. G,H26
141st St. G,H26
142nd St. G,H26
143rd St. G,H26

MISCELLANEOUS
Village Hall G26

DES PLAINES

Page 1

STREETS
Alden Ln. C8
Andy Ct. C8
Andy Ln. C8
Armstrong Ct. A8
Armstrong Rd. A8
Ash B7
Bennett Pl. C7
Birch St. C7,C8
Birchwood Ave. B7,C7
Bittersweet Ct. B7
Bradock Dr. A7
Briar Ct. B7
Cedar Ct. C7
Cedar St. C8
Central Ave. C8
Chase Ave. C8
Chestnut St. B7
Circle St. B7
Cora St. B7
Craig Dr. C8
Curtis St. C8
Dale St. C8
David Dr. C8
Des Plaines River Rd. C8
Devon Ave. C8
Dexter Ln. B7
Douglas Ave. B8
Eastview Dr. B8
Eisenhower Ct. C8
Eisenhower Dr. C8
Elm St. B7
Elmira Ave. B8
Esser Ct. C7
Estes Ave. C8
Everett Ave. B,C7
Everett Ln. B7
Fargo Ave. B8,C7
Farwell Ave. C8
Fox Ln. C8
Frontage Rd. B8
Greco Ave. C8
Greenleaf C8
Halsey Dr. C8
Hazel Ct. B7
Hickory St. C8
Higgins Rd. A,C8
Highland Dr. B7
Howard Ave. A,C7
Illinois St. B7
Iris Ln. C8
Irwin Ave. B7
Jariath B8
Jarvis Ave. A-C8
Joseph Ave. C8
Kennicott Ct. C7
Koehler Dr. B7
Laura Ln. C8
Linden St. C7
Locust St. C7
Lunt Ave. C8
Magnolia St. C8
Mannheim Rd. B7,8
Maple St. C7,8
Marshall Dr. A6,7
Morse Ave. C8
Mt. Prospect Rd. A8
Nebel Ln. B7
Nimitz Dr. C8
North Shore Ave. C8
Northwest Tollway C8
Nuclear Dr. A7
Oakton Pl. B7
Oakton St. A-C7
Orchard St. C7,8
Oxford Rd. B8
Park Ave. C8
Parkwood Ln. C8
Patton Dr. C8
Paula Ln. C8
Pearle Dr. C8
Peter Rd. C8
Pine St. B7
Plainfield Dr. B7
Pratt Ave. C8
Prospect Ave. B,C7
Prospect Ln. B7
Riverview Ave. C7
Rusty Dr. C8
Santa Rosa Dr. B8
Scott St. C8
Shepard Dr. B7
Sherwin Ave. C8
South Ct. C8
Spruce Ave. B8
Sprucewood Ave. B8
Stillwell Dr. C8
Stockton Ave. B,C7
Sunset Ave. C8
Sycamore St. C7,8
Times Dr. B7
Touhy Ave. A,C8
Tri-State Tollway C8
Tures Ln. B7
Webster Ave. C8
Webster Ln. B7
Welwyn Ave. C7
Westview Dr. B8
White St. C7
Willie Rd. A7
Winthrop Dr. A7

PARKS
Eton Field C8
Majewski Metro Park A7
Seminole Park C8
South Park B7

SCHOOLS
Maine Twp. H.S. West B7

MISCELLANEOUS
Opeka Lake B7

DIXMOOR

Page 13

STREETS
Ashland K26
Calumet K26
Circle Dr. K26
Cooper K26,27
Davis Ave. J26
Davis Ct. J26
Division St. K26
Dixie Hwy. J26
Elm K26
Honore K26
Hoyne K27
Joliet J27
Leavitt K26
Lincoln K26
Maple K26
Marshfield K26
Norris J,K26
Oak K26
Oakley J26
Page Ave. K26
Paulina Ave. K26
Prairie K26
Robey K27
Seeley K27
Sibley Blvd. K27
Spaulding Ave. K26
Vail K26
Walnut K26
Western J26
Winchester K27
Wood K26
139th St. J,K26
140th St. K26
141st St. K26
142nd St. K26
143rd St. K26
144th St. K26
145th St. J,K26
146th St. K26

MISCELLANEOUS
Village Hall K26

DOLTON

Pages 13,14

STREETS
Adams St. M26
Ann St. M26
Arthur Ct. M26
Atlantic Ave. L26
Avalon N26
Beachview M26,27
Blackstone N26,27
Blouin Dr. M27
California M26
Calumet Ave. N26
Calumet Expwy. N26,27
Catalpa Ln. M26
Center Ave. M26
Champlain M26,27
Chicago M26,27
Clark Ave. L27
Clausen Ct. M26
Cornell N27
Cottage Grove M26-28
Dante N26,27
Dearborn L27
Diekman Ct. N27
Dilner Pl. M26
Dobson M26,27
Dorchester N26,27
Drexel Ave. M26,27
East End N27
Edbrooke Ave. L27
Ellis M26,27
Empire M26
Evans M26,27
Evers M26,27
Forest M26
Grant St. M26,27
Greenwood Rd. M26,27
Harding M,N27
Harper N26,27
Harvard L26
Hastings Dr. M27
Indiana Ave. M26,27
Ingleside M26,27
Irving M26,27
Jackson Ave. M26
Jefferson St. M26
Kanawha M26
Kasten Dr. N26
Kenwood N26
Kimbark M26,27
La Salle Ave. L26
Lakeside M26
Langley M26,27
Lincoln Hwy. M26
Main St. L,M26
Manor Ct. M26
Margaret M26
Maryland Ave. M26,27
McArthur Ct. M26
Meadow Ln. M27
Memorial Dr. M26
Michigan Ave. L27
Michigan City Rd. M26
Minerva M26,27
Monroe St. M26
Murray M26
Oak St. M26,27
Ohio M26
Park Ave. M26
Parkside Dr. L26
Pennsylvania N26
Pohlers M26
Princeton Ave. L26
Riverside Dr., N. L26
Sanderson St. M26
Sheridan St. M26
Sibley Blvd. L-N27
State St. L27
Stein St. L26
Stewart M,N26
Sunset Dr. N27
University M26,27
Vanburen M26
Wabash Ave. L27
Washington St. M26
Wentworth L26
Woodlawn M26,27
139th Pl. M26
140th Pl. L26
141st Pl. L26
142nd Pl. L26
143rd St. M,N26
144th Pl. M26
144th St. M,N26
145th St. M,N26
146th St. M,N26
147th Pl. M26
147th St. L-N26
148th St. L,M26
149th St. M27
151st St. M,N27
152nd St. M,N27
153rd St. M,N27
154th Pl. N27
154th St. M,N27
155th Pl. N27
155th St. M27
157th St. M27
158th St. M,N27

PARKS
Dolton Park M26

SCHOOLS
Thornridge H.S. M27

MISCELLANEOUS
City Hall M26

EAST CHICAGO, IN

Page 14

STREETS
Beacon Q26
Columbus Dr. Q26
Exchange Q26
Homer Lee Q27
Kosciusko Q27
Northcote Q26
Reading Q26,27
Ruth Q26,27
Shell Q27
Walsh Q26,27
Wegg Q26,27
142nd Q26
143rd Q26
144th Q26
148th Q26
151st Q27

SCHOOLS
Indiana Univ. of East Chicago Q26

ELMWOOD PARK

Page 2

STREETS
Armitage E12
Atgeld E12
Barry St. E11
Belden E12
Belmont Ave. E11
Birchdale E11
Bloomingdale E12
Brook Rd. D12
Cortland E12
Country Club Ln. E12
Cresset E11
Dickens E12
Diversey E11
Elmgrove Dr. E11
Fletcher D11
George St. E11
Grand Ave. E12
Harlem Ave. E12
Marwood E12
Medill E12
Nelson D11
Oakleaf E11
Pacific D11
Palmer E12
Pleasant Pl. E12
Schubert E12
Sunset E11
Thatcher Rd. D12
Wabansia E12
Wellington E11
Westwood Dr. E12
Wrightwood E12
72nd Ct. E12,13
73rd Ave. E12,13
73rd Ct. E12,13
74th Ave. E12,13
74th Ct. E12,13
75th Ave. E12,13
75th Ct. E12,13
76th Ave. E11-13
76th Ct. E11-13
77th Ave. E11-13
77th Ct. E11-13
78th Ave. E11-13
78th Ct. E11-13
79th Ave. E11-13
79th Ct. D11-13
80th Ave. D12

MISCELLANEOUS
Village Hall E12

EVERGREEN PARK

Pages 9,10

STREETS
Albany J21,22
Avers H22
Balmoral J22
Beck Ct. H22
California J22
Campbell J22
Central Park H22
Clark H22
Clifton Park H22
Country Club J22
Crawford Ave. H21,22
Elm Pl. H22
Fairfield J21
Francisco J22
Grove Pl. H22
Hamlin H22
Harding H22
Homan H22
Lawndale H22
Maple H22
Maplewood J22
Millard H22
Mozart J22
Richmond J22
Ridgeway H22
Ross Pl. H22
Sacramento J22
Sawyer J22
Sheridan J21
Spaulding H22
Springfield H22
St. Louis H22
Talman J21
Troy J22
Trumbull H22
Turner H22
Utica J22
Washtenaw J21,22
Western Ave. J21,22
87th St. J21
88th St. J21
89th Pl. J21
89th St. J21
90th Pl. J21
90th St. J21
91st St. J21
92nd St. J21
93rd Pl. J22
93rd St. J22
94th Pl. J22
94th St. J22
95th Pl. J22
95th St. J22
96th Pl. J22
96th St. J22
97th Pl. J22
97th St. H,J22
98th Pl. H,J22
98th St. H,J22
99th Pl. J22
99th St. H,J22
100th Pl. J22
100th St. H,J22
101st Pl. J22
101st St. H22
102nd Pl. J22
102nd St. H,J22

GOLF COURSES
Beverly C.C. J21
Evergreen C.C. J22

PARKS
Evergreen Park H22

SCHOOLS
Brother Rice H.S. H22
Evergreen Pk. Comm. H.S. J22
Fox College J22
Luther H.S. South J21
Mother McAuley H.S. H22
St. Xavier Coll. H22

SHOPPING CENTERS
Evergreen Shopping Plaza J22

MISCELLANEOUS
Convalescent Home H22
Little Company of Mary Hosp. J22
Village Hall J22

FOREST PARK

Page 5

STREETS
Adams E14
Beloit E14,15
Belvidere E14
Bergman E14
Brown E14
Burkhardt Ct. E14
Central E14
Cermak Rd. E15
Circle E14,15
Des Plaines E14,15
Dixon E14
Dunlop E15
Elgin E14,15
Ferdinand E14,15
Fillmore E15
Franklin E14
Hannah E14,15
Harlem E15
Harrison E14
Harvard E14
Jackson Blvd. E14
Lathrop E14,15
Lehmer E14
Lincoln Ct. E14
Madison E14
Marengo E14,15
Monroe E14
Polk E14
Randolph E14
Rockford E14
Roosevelt Rd. E15
Taylor E15
Thomas E14,15
Troost E15
Van Buren E14
Warren E14
Washington E14
Wilcox E14
York E14
Yuba E15
13th St. E15
14th St. E15
15th St. E15
16th St. E15

PARKS
Forest Park E14

SHOPPING CENTERS
Forest Park Plaza D15

MISCELLANEOUS
City Hall E14
Riverside Hosp. D15

FOREST VIEW

Pages 5,6

STREETS
Austin F18
Central G18
Clinton E17
East E17
Grove E17
Harlem Ave. E17
Home E17
Kenilworth E17
Laramie F18
Latrobe G18
Lockwood G18
Long G18
Lorel G18
Major F18
Maple E17
Mason F18
Meade F18
Menard F18
Merrimac F18
Monitor F18
Oak Park E17
Ridgeland E17
Wenonah E17
Wisconsin E17
47th St. G17
51st St. G18

MISCELLANEOUS
Village Hall E17

FRANKLIN PARK

Page 1

STREETS
Acorn Ln. B11
Addison Ave., W. B,C11
Alta St. B11
Anderson Pl. B11
Ashland C11
Atlantic C11,12
Belmont Ave. A-C11
Birch C11
Bright B11
Britta C11
Byron C11
Calwagner C11,12
Carnation B11
Carol Ln. B11
Center Ave. B11
Centralia Blvd. B11
Cherry C11
Chestnut C11
Copenhagen Ct. A11
County Line Rd. B11
Crescent Dr. C11
Crown Rd. B11
Cullerton St. B11
Davis C11
DeSota Ct. C11
Des Plaines River Rd. D11
Dodge Ave. C11
Dora C11,12
Edgington C11,12
Elder Ln. C12
Elm D11
Emerson C11
Ernst C11

Exchange Pl. D11
Fairfield C12
Finley C12
Fleetwood Ln. B10
Fletcher B11
Franklin B,C11
Front C11
Fullerton C12
Gage C11
George C11,12
Grand C11
Greenfield Rd. C11
Gustav C11
Hackey Ln. C11
Hart Dr. B11
Hawthorne C11
Herrick C12
Herschberg C11
Houston Dr. B11
Iona Ave. C11
James B11
Jill B11
Johanna C12
Kimmey Ln. C11
King Ave., W. B11
Kirschoff C12
LaSalle Ct. C11
Latoria B11
Lee St. B10
Leona C12
Lesser C11
Leyden C11
Lincoln C11,12
Lombard C11
Lonquist Dr. C11
Louis C11
Lucy Ln. B11
Mannheim Rd. C12
Maple D11
Martens C11
McNerney Dr. C11
Medill D12
Melrose Ave. B11
Minneapolis C11
Montana C12
Nerbonne C11
Nevada C12
Nichols C11
Nona C12
Oak C12
Pacific C,D11
Panoramic Dr. C11
Park C12
Parker C12
Parklane Ave. C11
Pearl C11
Podlin Dr. A11
Powell St. B11
Prairie Rd. B11
Reeves Ct. C11
Reuter C12
Richard C12
Riverside Dr. C12
Robinson Rd. C11
Rose C11
Ruby C11
Runge St. B11
Ruth B11
Sandra St. B11
Sarah C11,12
Schierhorn Ct. D11
Schiller Blvd. C11
Scott C11
Seymour B10
Sheila C12
Silver Creek Dr. C12
Sonia C12
Sunset C11
Tugwell St. B10
United Pkwy. B10
Walnut C11
Washington C11
Waveland B11
Wehrman C11
Wellington B11
Westbrook C12
Williams Dr. B11
Willow C11
Wolf Rd. B11
Wrightwood C12
25th Ave. C11

SCHOOLS
Leyden East Twp. H.S. C11
Mannheim Sch. B11

MISCELLANEOUS
City Hall C11
Leyden Comm. Ext. Care Ctr. B11
Leyden Fire Sta. B11
Leyden Twp. Hall C11
O'Hare Stadium B10

HAMMOND, IN
Page 14

STREETS
Alice P27
Ames P29
Ann P27
Ash Q26
Atlas Q27
Baltimore P25,26
Baring Q29
Bauer P27
Beall P27
Becker P27
Beech Q27,29
Belmont Q29
Benjamin P24
Bertram Q28,29
Birch Q27-29
Brown P24
Brunswick P26
Burton Ct. P24
Calumet P24,26,29
Cameron P26
Caroline P24
Carroll P,Q27
Catalpa Q27,29
Cedar P26
Cherry P28
Chesapeake Q28
Chestnut Q27,29
Chicago P26
Clark P26
Claude P27
Cleveland P,Q28
Clinton P27
Columbia Q27,29
Columbus Dr. Q26
Condit P,Q27
Conkey P28
Coolidge P28
Crescent P28
Dearborn P26
Doty P27
Douglas P27
Drackert P27
Dyer P28
Eaton P27
Elm Q26
Erie P27
Euclid P28
Fernwood P28
Field Q28
Florence P28
Forest P28
Garfield P28
Glendale P28
Golf Way Q29
Gostlin P26
Grover P26
Hanover P26
Hanson Ct. Q28
Harrison P28,29
Havana P28
Henry P25,26
Hickory Q26
Highland P,Q28
Hoffman P26
Hohman P26,27
Howard Q27-29
Hudson P26
Huehn P26
Hump Rd. Q27
Hyslop P28
Indiana P,Q27
Indiana East-West Toll Road P25
Jackson P28,29
Jarnecke Q29
Jefferson P28,29
Jessie P27
Johnson P25,26
Kane P27
Kent Q27
Kenwood P28
Lawndale P28
Lewis P28
Linden Q27,29
Logan P,Q27
Lyman P29
Lyons P,Q27
Madison P27-29
Magnolia Q27-29
Malden P24
Maplewood P29
Marble P26
May P27
Maywood P27
Meadow Ln. P28,29
Merrill Q28
Michigan P27
Molsberger Q27
Monroe P28,29
Moraine P28
Morris Q28
Morton Ct. P27
Moss Q28
Muenich Ct. P27
Mulberry P28
Murray Q27
Nobel Q28
Northcote Q28
Oak Q26
Oakdale Q29
Oakley P27
Oakwood P28
Ogden P27
Park P29
Park Pl. P28
Parkview P24
Paxton P27
Pine P26
Plummer P27
Porter Rd. Q27
Price P27
Ray Q28
Rhode P28
Ridge P28
Ridgeland Q28
Rimbach P27
Roosevelt P24,Q27
Roselawn P28
Rosewood P28
Russell P27
Sheffield P25,26
Shell Q27
Sherman Q27
Sirley P28
Sohl P27
Southeastern Q28
Southmoor P29
Spruce P28
State P27
State Line Rd. P28
Stewart P24
Summer P27
Tapper P29,Q28
Tell Q27
Thornton P27
Tilly Dr. Q29
Torrence P25,26
Towle P26
Truman P,Q27
Van Buren P28,29
Victoria P26
Vine P28
Vine Ct. P28
Wabash P26
Wallace Q28
Walnut Q27-29
Walter P27
Warwick P24
Washington P28
Webb P27
Webster P27
White Oak Q27,29
White Oak Pl. Q29
Wilcox P,Q27
Wildwood Rd. P28
Willard Q28
Williams P27
Willis Q27
Willow Ct. P27
Wood P27
Woodlawn P29
114th P23
115th P24
116th P24
117th P24
117th Pl. P24
118th P24
119th P24
129th P25
133rd P25
134th P25
136th P25
137th P25
138th P26
139th P26
140th P26
141st P26
142nd P26
143rd P,Q26
145th Q26
149th P27
150th P27
164th Pl. Q28
165th Q28
167th P,Q28
169th P,Q28
169th Pl. P28
170th P,Q28
170th Pl. Q28
171st P,Q28,Q29
171st Pl. Q29
172nd P,Q29
172nd Pl. P29
173rd P,Q29
173rd Pl. P,Q29
174th P,Q29
174th Pl. P,Q29
175th P29
175th Pl. P29
176th P29
177th Q29
177th Pl. P29

CEMETERIES
Concordia Cem. P28
Elmwood Cem. Q28
Oak Hill Cem. P28

PARKS
Columbia Park Q27
Douglas Park P26
Edison Park P28
Forsyth Park P24
Harrison Park P27
Maywood Park P28
Turner Park P27

SCHOOLS
Don Gavitt H.S. Q29
Hammond H.S. P27
Kennedy Memorial Center P27
Technical H.S. P27

MISCELLANEOUS
City Hall P28
Columbia Center Housing Project Q29
St. Margaret Hospital P27

HARVEY
Page 13

STREETS
Artesian J27
Ashland K27,28
Belden L28
Broadway K27
California J27
Calumet Blvd. K,L26
Campbell J27,28
Carol L28
Carse L28
Center K27,28
Clairemont Ave. J27
Clairemont Ct. J27
Clinton L27,28
Commercial K27
Cooper K27
Des Plaines L27
Dixie Hwy. J27,K28
Emerald L28
Fairfield J27
Finch L28
Fisk K28
Gauger K28
Geneva L28
Green L28
Halsted L27,28
Harvey K27
Honore K27
Hoyne K27
Jefferson L27,28
Justine K28
Kentucky K27
Lathrop L28
Leavitt K27
Lexington K27,28
Lincoln K27
Loomis K27,28
Lowe L28
Madison L27
Main L27
Maplewood J27
Markham Dr. L27
Marshfield K28
Morgan L27
Myrtle K28
Oakdale L27
Oakley Ave. J27
Oakley Ct. J27
Page K28
Park K28
Parkside L27
Parnell L27
Paulina K28
Peoria K27
Rockwell J27
Sangamon K26
Seeley K27
Shore Dr. L26
Sibley Blvd. J-L27
Streamside Dr. L26
Talman J27
Thornton Rd. K27
Turlington K28
Union L27
Vincennes L27
Vine K28
Wallace L27,28
Washington L27
Washtenaw J27
Wells K26
West K28
Western J27
Willard L28
Winchester K27
Wood K27,28
Woodbridge L28
144th Ct. K26
145th St. J-L26
146th St. J-L26
147th Pl. L27
147th St. L27
148th Pl. J,L27
148th St. J,K27
149th Pl. J27
149th St. J,K27
150th Pl. J27
150th St. J,K27
151st Pl. J27
151st St. J27
151st Terr. J27
152nd Ct. J27
152nd Pl. J27
152nd St. J-L27
153rd St. J,K27
154th Pl. J,K27
154th St. J,K27
155th Pl. K27
155th St. K27
156th Pl. K27
156th St. K27
157th Pl. K27
157th St. K27
158th Pl. K28
158th St. K28
159th St. K28
160th Pl. L28
160th St. K,L28
161st St. K,L28
162nd St. L28
163rd St. L28
164th St. L28
165th St. L28
166th St. L28
167th St. L28
168th Pl. L28
168th St. L28

PARKS
Ashland Park K27
Holmes Park L28
Lexington Park K27

MISCELLANEOUS
City Hall K27
Ingalls Mem. Hosp. K27

HARWOOD HEIGHTS
Page 2

STREETS
Ainsley E10
Argyle E10
Carmen E10
Foster Pl. E10
Gunnison E,F10
Harlem Ave. E10
Lawrence E10
Leland E10
Montrose F10
Mulligan F10
Nagle F10
Narragansett F10
Nashville F10
Natchez F10
Neenah F10
New England E10
Newcastle E10
Newland E10
Norridge E10
Norwood F10
Oak Park E10
Oconto E10
Octavia E10
Odell E10
Oketo E9
Oriole E10
Ronald E10
Rutherford E10
Sayre E10
Senior Pl. E10
Strong E10
Sunnyside E,F10
Wilson E10
Winnemac E10
Winona E10

GOLF COURSES
Ridgemoor C.C. F10

MISCELLANEOUS
Village Hall E10

HILLSIDE
Page 4

STREETS
Adams B14
Ashbel B14
Bellwood B14
Berkeley B14
Bosworth Ave. B15
Broadview B14
Buckthorn Rd. B14
Butterfield Rd. C14
Canterbury C15
Center B15
Charles C15
Chicago B14
Clayton Rd. B14
Craig B14
Cypress Ct. B14
Cypress Dr. B14
Darmstadt B14
Dickens B14
Division B15
East B15
East End B14
Edgewater B15
Electric Ave. B14
Elm B14
Englewood B14
Fencl Ln. B15
Fenwood Ln. B14
Fielding B15
Forest B14,15
Frontage Rd. B14
Geneva B14
Golf Ln. B14
Granville Ave. B14
Harrison B14
Hawthorne B14
High Ridge Rd. B14
Hillside B14
Howard B14
Hyde Park B14
Idlewild B14
Iroquois Rd. B14
Irving B14
Jackson Blvd. B14
Laverne B14
Lee B14
Lind B14
Locust B14
Madison B14
Mannheim Rd. C14
Maple Ave. B14
Maple Ln. B14
May B15
Melrose B14
Morris B14
Mueller B14
Oak B14
Oak Ridge B15
Orchard B15
Railroad B,C14
Randolph B14
Raymond B14
Ridge Ave. A14
Rohde B14
Roosevelt Rd. B15
School St. A14
Spenchley B14
St. Paul Ct. B14
Sunnyside Dr. B14
Taft B14
Terrace Ln. B16
Van Buren B14
Vanna Ct. B14
Warren B14
Washington Blvd. C14
Washington St. B14
Westwood B16
Wolf Rd. B15
50th Ave. B15
51st Ave. B14
53rd Ave. B14

PARKS
Eisenhower Park B14

SCHOOLS
Hillside Sch. B14
Proviso West H.S. B14

SHOPPING CENTERS
Hillside Shopping Center B14

MISCELLANEOUS
Village Hall B14

HODGKINS
Page 8

STREETS
Belfast Ln. C19
Cantigny Rd. C19
Catherine Ann Dr. C19
Chester C19
Cobb C19
Conrad C19
East Ave. C19
Fransean Dr. C19
Kane Rd. C19
Kimball C19
Lagrange Rd. C19,20
Lenzi C19
Lyons C19
Mance Rd. C19
Normandy Ln. C19
Roger Ln. C19
Santa Fe C19,20
Sharon Ln. C19
Stratford Ct. C19
Weeping Willow Rd. C19
Wenz C19
Westgate C19
67th St. C19

MISCELLANEOUS
Village Hall C19

HOMETOWN
Page 9

STREETS
Beck H21
Corcoran H21
Duffy G21
Keeler H21
Kenton G21
Kilbourn G21
Kildare H21
Kilpatrick G21
Kolin H21
Kolmar G21

Komensky H21
Kostner G21
Main H21
Ryan H21
Southwest Hwy. G,H21
87th Pl. G,H21
87th St. G,H21
88th Pl. G,H21
88th St. G21
89th Pl. G,H21
89th St. G21
90th Pl. G,H21
90th St. H21
91st St. G,H21

MISCELLANEOUS
Village Hall H21

INDIAN HEAD PARK

Page 8

STREETS
Acacia Cir. B19
Acacia Dr. B19
Acacia Ln. B19
Algonquin Dr. B19
Apache Dr. B19
Arrowhead Tr. B20
Big Bear Ct. B19
Big Bear Dr. B19
Blackhawk Trail B19
Cascade Dr. B19
Cherokee Dr. B19
Cochise Dr. B19
Edgewood View Rd. B19
Golf View Rd. B20
Hiawatha Ln. B19
Howard Ave. B19
Indian Wood Ln. B19
Joliet Rd. B19
Keokuk B19
Laurel Ave. B19
Mohawk Ct. B19
Osceola Terr. B19
Plainfield Rd. B19
Pontiac Dr. B19
Sequoia Ln. B19
Shabbona Ln. B19
Sioux Tr. B19
Tecumseh Ln. B19
Thunderbird Dr. B19
Vine St. B19
Waubansee Ln. B19
Willow Springs Rd. B19
Wolf Rd. B19
63rd St. B19
65th Pl. B19
65th St. B19
70th Pl. B20
72nd St. B20

LA GRANGE

Page 4

STREETS
Arlington B17
Ashland C17
Bassford B17
Beach C17
Bell C17
Benton C17
Blacktone B17
Bluff C17
Brainard C17
Brewster C17
Brighton B18
Burlington C17
Calendar C17
Calle View Dr. C18
Carriage Ln. B18
Catherine C17
Cossitt C17
Country Club Dr. C18
Dover B17
Drexel B17
East Ave. C18
Eberly C17
Edgewood B17,18
Elder Ln. B17
Elm B17
Fairway B18
Gilbert B17
Goodman B17
Harris C17
Hayes C17
Hazel C17
Hillgrove Ave. B17
Kensington C17
La Grange Rd. C17,18
Leitch B17
Lincoln C17
Linden C17
Locust C17
Madison C17
Malden B17
Maple B17
Mason Dr. B18
Newberry C17
Ogden Ave. B17
Park Ave. C17
Peck B17
Poplar Pl. B17
Sawyer C17
Shawmut C17
Southview C17
Spring C17
Stone C17
Sunset B17
Tilden C17
Waiola C17
Washington C17
6th Ave. C17,18
7th Ave. C17,18
8th Ave. C17,18
9th Ave. C17,18
10th Ave. C17,18
11th Ave. C18
12th Ave. C18
47th St. B,C18
48th St. C18
49th St. C18
50th Pl. B18
50th St. C18
51st St. C18
52nd Pl. B18
52nd St. C18
53rd Pl. B18
53rd St. C18
54th Pl. B18
54th St. C18
55th St. C18

GOLF COURSES
La Grange C.C. B,C18

PARKS
Gilbert Park B17

SCHOOLS
Lyons Twp. H.S. North C17

MISCELLANEOUS
Community Mem. Hosp. B18
Village Hall B17

LA GRANGE PARK

Page 4

STREETS
Alma C16
Ashland C17
Barnesdale Rd. C16
Beach C16
Blanchan C16
Brainard C17
Brewster C17
Catherine C17
Cleveland C16
Community Dr. C16
Deerpath C16
Dover B17
Edgewood B17
Elmwood C17
Fairview C17
Finsbury Ln. C16
Forest Rd. C16,17
Garfield C16
Grant C17
Harding C16
Harrison C16
Homestead Rd. C16,17
Huntington Ct. C16
Jackson C16
Kemman C16
Kensington C17
Kings Ct. C16
La Grange Rd. C16
Lincoln C17
Logan Blvd. C16
Malden B17
Meadowcrest C16
Monroe C16
Morgan C16
Newberry C16
Oak C17
Ogden Ave. B17
Ostrander C16
Park Rd. C17
Pine C17
Pine Tree C16
Plymouth Pl. C17
Raymond C16
Richmond C17
Robinhood Ln. C16,17
Scotdale C16
Sherwood Rd. C16
Southview C17
Spring C17
Stone C17
Stonegate Rd. C16
Thorpe Ct. C16
Timber Ln. C16
Waiola C17
Woodlawn B17
Woodside Rd. C16
26th St. C16
28th St. C16
29th St. C16
30th St. C16
31st St. (Logan Blvd.) C16

PARKS
Memorial Park C17
North-East Park C16
Robin Hood Park C16
Stone Monroe Park C16

SCHOOLS
Nazareth H.S. B17

MISCELLANEOUS
Village Hall C17

LEYDEN TOWNSHIP

Page 1

STREETS
Alcoa B12
Alta B11
Altgeld B12
Armitage C12
Atlantic C12
Balmoral D9
Barry B11
Behrns B11
Belden C12
Belmont B11
Belwood B12
Bryn Mawr D9
Calwagner C12
Catalpa D9
Charles B11
Cornell C12
Courtland D9
Crescent D9
Crown B11
Derrough B11
Dickens C12
Diversey B11
Dora C12
Drummond Pl. B12
Emerson C12
Fairview D9
Fleetwood Ln. B10
Fletcher B11
Franklin B11
Fullerton B12
Gary Dr. B11
Geneva B12
Geneva B12
Grand B11
Granville B11
Gregory D9
Gustav C12
Haber B11
Harold B11
Hawthorne C12
Hyde Park B12
Inland Dr. A11
Landan Dr. B11
Laporte B11
Lee B11
Louis C12
Lyndale C12
Mannheim Rd. B12
Manor D9
Manor Dr. C12
Marian B11
Martin B11
McDonough St. A10
McKay B11
McLean C12
Medill B12
Melrose B12
Montana B12
Nevada B12
Palmer C12
Park C12
Parker B,C12
Pearl B11
Prater B11
Prospect D9
Rascher D9
Redwood D9
Rhodes B11
Roberta Ave. B11
Rowlet B11
Roy B11
Ruby C12
Sandra B11
Sarah C12
Schubert B12
Scott C12
Summerdale D9
Taft Ave. B10
Valor Rd. A10
Vine D9
Washington D9
Wellington B11
Winters Dr. B12
Wolf Rd. B11
Wrightwood B12

CEMETERIES
All Saints Parish Cem. D9
St. Nickolas Ukranian Cem. D9

PARKS
West Dale Pk. B11

SCHOOLS
Apostle Sch. B11

MISCELLANEOUS
Camp Fort Dearborn D9

LINCOLNWOOD

Pages 2,3

STREETS
Albion G,H8
Arthur G,H8
Avers H8
Carpenter Rd. G8
Central Park H8
Chase Ave. H8
Christiana Ave. H8
Cicero G8
Cicero Ave., N. G8
Columbia G8
Crawford Ave. H8
Devon H8
Drake H8
East Prairie Rd. H8
Estes Ave. H8
Farwell G,H8
Fitch Ave. G,H8
Greenleaf G,H8
Hamlin Ave. H8
Harding H8
Jarlath St. H8
Karlov Ave. H7,8
Keating G8
Keating, N. G8
Kedvale Ave. H7,8
Keeler Ave. H7,8
Kenneth Ave. G8
Kenton Ave. G8
Keystone Ave. H7,8
Kilbourn G8
Kildare H7,8
Kilpatrick G8
Kimball Ave. H8
Knox G8
Kolmar G8
Kostner G8
La Porte G8
Lawndale H8
Lemay G8
Leroy G8
Lincoln St. G7,H8
Longmeadow G8
Lowell H7,8
Loyola H8
Lunt Ave. G,H8
Minehaha G8
Morse Ave. G,H8
Nakomis G8
Navajo G8
North Shore G,H8
Pratt G8
Proesel H8
Ramona G8
Range Terr. H8
Ridgeway H8
Sauganash G8
Schreiber G,H8
Sherwin Ave. H8
Spaulding H8
Spokane G8
Springfield H8
St. Louis H8
Tower Circle Dr. G8
Tower Ct. G8
Tripp Ave. H7,8
Trumbull H8
Wallen H8

GOLF COURSES
Bryn Mawr C.C. H8

SCHOOLS
Todd Sch. H8

MISCELLANEOUS
Police Dept. H8

LYONS

Page 5

STREETS
Abbot Terr. D17
Amelia E17
Anna D17
Barrypoint Rd. E17
Center E17
Clyde D17
Collins E17
Cracow D17
Custer D17
Elm E17
Fern D17
First D17
Fishermans Terr. E17
Gage E17
Haas E17
Hawthorne D17
Joliet Ave. E17
Joliet Rd. E17
Kenwood D17
Konrad D17
Lawndale D17
Leland D17
Lincoln Dr. D17
Maple E17
Oak Ave. E17
Ogden Ave. E17
Patricia D17
Plainfield Rd. D17
Powell E17
Prescott E17
Pulaski D17
Riverside D17
Rose D17
Salisbury E17
Warsaw D17
White E17
Winchester D17
38th Pl. E17
39th St. E17
40th St. D,E17
41st Ct. E17
41st Pl. E17
42nd Ct. E17
42nd Pl. E17
42nd St. E17
43rd Pl. D17
43rd St. D17
44th Pl. D17
44th St. D,E17
45th Pl. D,E17
45th St. D,E17
46th St. E17
47th St. D18

MISCELLANEOUS
Village Hall E17

LYONS TOWNSHIP

Page 8

STREETS
Acacia Ln. B19
Arbor B20
Barton Rd. C18
Bielby Ave. B19
Bielby Ave. B20
Blackstone C19
Both Pl. B19
Brainard C19
Burr Oak Ln. C20
Central B20
Circle Dr. B20
Commonwealth B20
Cook-DuPage Rd. C17
Coronet Ln. C19
County Line Rd. B20,21
Dana Way B20
Edgewood B19,20
Fairelms B20
Franklin B18,19
German Church B21
German Church Rd. B18
Golf View B19
Harvey Ave. B18
Hess Ave. B19
Howard B19
Howard B18-20
Jann Ct. B19
Joliet Rd. C19
Laurel B18,19
Lincoln C19
Linden B19
Linn Ct. B19
Locust B19
Lorraine B20
Maple Ave. B21
Maridon C20
N.E. Ct. B18
N.W. Ct. B18
Oak Grove B21
Orchard St. B21
Parkside Ln. B19
Peck C19
Plainfield Rd. B19
Pleasant View B21
Pleasantview B18
Public St. B21
Railroad Ave. (91st St.) B21
S.W. Ct. B18
Sunset B18,19
Terry Ln. C18
Timber View Ln. B19
Valley Rd. B20
Vial Pkwy. B18
Vine B19
Willow Springs B20
Wolf Rd. B21
52nd Pl. B18
53rd Pl. B18
54th Pl. B18
54th St. B18
55th Pl. B18
55th St. B18
56th St. B18
57th St. B18
58th Pl. B18
58th St. B19
59th Pl. B19
59th St. B19
60th St. B19
61st Pl. B19
61st St. B19
62nd Pl. B19
62nd St. B19
63rd Pl. B19
63rd St. B19
64th St. B19
70th St. B20
71st Pl. B20
72nd St. B20
73rd Pl. B20
74th St. B20
75th St. B20
77th St. B20
79th St. A20
79th St. B18
80th Pl. B21
87th St. C18
87th St. B21
114th Ave. B21

GOLF COURSES
Edgewood Valley C.C. B20
Maple Crest G.C. B19
Par Three G.C. B19
Timber Trails G.C. B19

SCHOOLS
Pleasantdale Sch. B19

MISCELLANEOUS
Santa Fe Speedway B22

MARKHAM

Pages 12,13

STREETS
Afton Dr. J27
Albany Ave. J28
Alta Rd. H27
Arthur Terr. H28
Ashland Ave. K28
Belleplaine Dr. H28
Berkshire Dr. J28
Birch Rd. H27
Blackstone Ave. H28
California Ave. J28
Central Park Ave. H27,28
Cherry Ln. H27
Circle Dr. J28
Clifton Park Ave. H27,28
Country Aire Dr. J27
Crawford Ave. H27,28
Crocket Ln. J27
Cypress Rd. J27
Damen Ave. K28
Dixie Hwy. K28
Frontage Rd. H27
Hamlin Ave. H27,28
Heather Dr. H27
Hermitage Ave. K28
Hillcrest Dr. H28
Homan Ave. J27,28
Honore Ave. K28
Hoyne K28
Justine St. K28
Kedzie Ave. J27,28
Laflin St. K28
Lancaster Dr., E. J28
Lathrop Ave. K28
Lawndale Ave. H27,28
Lincoln Dr. J27
Magnolia Dr. H27
Maple Ln. H27
Marshfield Ave. K28
Millard Ave. H27
Mozart St. J28
Nottingham Ave. J28
Oakley J28
Oxford Dr. J28
Parkside Dr. J27
Paulina St. K28
Plainview Dr. H28
Plymouth Dr. J28
Richmond Ave. J28
Ridgeway Ave. H27
Rockwell St. J27
Roesner Dr. H27
Rose Manor Terr. H28
Sacramento Ave. J28
Sawyer Ave. J27,28
Sherwood Ave. J28
Spaulding Ave. J27,28
Springfield Ave. H28
St. Louis Ave. H27,28
Stafford Ave. N21
Sunset Ave. H28
Sussex Ave. J28
Sussex Ct. J28
Troy Ave. J27,28
Trumbull Ave. H27,28
Turner Ave. J27,28
Wedgewood Dr. H28
Western Ave. J28
Whipple St. J28
Willow Ln. H27
Wilshire Ave. J28
Wilshire Ct. J28
Winchester K28
Wolcott Ave. K28
Wood Ave. K28
149th St. H,J27
151st St. H27

MARKHAM
152nd St. J27
154th Pl. H27
154th St. H27
155th St. H,J27
156th St. H,J27
157th St. H,J27
158th Pl. J28
158th St. J28
159th Pl. H28
159th St. J28
160th St. H28
161st St. H28
162nd Pl. H28
162nd St. H-K28
163rd Pl. J,K28
163rd St. H-K28
164th St. H-K28
165th St. J28
166th St. H,J28
167th St. H,J28
168th St. H,J28

MISCELLANEOUS
City Hall J28

MAYWOOD
Pages 4,5

STREETS
Adams D14
Augusta D13
Chicago D13
Congress D14
Erie D13
Eugene C14
Gage C14
Green D14
Greenwood D14
Harrison D14
Harvard D14
Huron D13
Iowa D13
Lake St. D13
Lexington D14
Madison D14
Main D13
Maple D14
Maywood Dr. D14
Monroe D14
Oak C14
Ohio D13
Orchard D14
Pine D14
Quincy D14
Randolph C14
Russel C14
School St. D14
Sherman C14
Stanley C14
Superior C14
Van Buren C14
Walnut D14
Walton D13
Warren C14
Washington C14
West End C14
Wilcox D14
William C14
1st Ave. D13,14
2nd Ave. D13,14
3rd Ave. D13,14
4th Ave. D13,14
5th Ave. D13,14
6th Ave. D13,14
7th Ave. D13,14
8th Ave. D13,14
9th Ave. D13,14
10th Ave. D13,14
11th Ave. D13,14
12th Ave. D13,14
13th Ave. D13,14
14th Ave. D13
15th Ave. D13
16th Ave. D13
17th Ave. D13
18th Ave. C13
19th Ave. C13
20th Ave. C13
21st Ave. C13
22nd Ave. C14
23rd Ave. C14

PARKS
Maywood Grove D13
Maywood Park D14
Memorial Park D14
Playground C,D14

SCHOOLS
Proviso East H.S. D14

MISCELLANEOUS
Loyola University Med. Ctr. D15
Veterans Administration Hosp. (Hines) D15
Village Hall D14

MC COOK
Page 8

STREETS
Clyde Terr. D18
East Ave. C18
Egandale D18
Glencoe D18
Grand D18
Hinsdale D18
Joliet Rd. C18
Lawndale D18
Plainfield Rd. D18
Riverside D18
47th St. D18
50th D18
53rd D18
55th C18
71st D20

MISCELLANEOUS
Village Hall D18

MELROSE PARK
Pages 1,4,5

STREETS
Alvin Pg.1 B12
Andy Dr. Pg.5 D13
Armitage Pg.1 C12
Augusta Pg.4,5 C13
Bank Rd. Pg.4 B13
Belden Pg.1 C,D12
Bloomingdale Pg.1 C,D12
Braddock Dr. Pg.5 D13
Broadway Pg.4 C13
Caryl Pg.4 B13
Channing Ct. Pg.4,5 D13
Charleston Ct. Pg.4,5 D13
Chicago Pg.4,5 D13
Clay Ct. Pg.5 D13
Clinton Ct. Pg.4,5 D13
Concord Dr. Pg.5 D13
Cornell Pg.1 C12
Cortez Pg.4,5 C13
Davis Pg.4,5 D13
Division Pg.4,5 C,D13
Doris Pg.5 D13
Elsie Pg.4,5 D13
Geneva Pg.1 B12
George Pg.1 B12
Grant Pg.4,5 D13
Haddon Pg.4 C13
Harold Pg.4 B13
Hawthorne Pg.1 C12
Helen Dr. Pg.4,5 D13
Hirsch Pg.4 C13
Iowa Pg.4 C13
James Pl. Pg.1 B12
Janice Pg.1 B12
Lake Pg.4 C13
Lee Pg.4,5 D13
Lemoyne Pg.4 C13
Main Pg.4,5 C,D13
Mannheim Pg.1 B12
North Pg.4 B13
Norwood Pg.4 C13
Park Pg.4,5 D13
Rice Pg.4 C13
Roberta Pg.1 B12
Rose Pg.5 D13
Roy Pg.4 B13
Ruby Pg.1 C12
Sherman Pg.4,5 D13
Soffel Pg.4,5 C13
Superior Pg.4,5 D13
Thomas Pg.4 C13
Walton Pg.4 C13
Winston Dr. Pg.4,5 D13
1st Ave. Pg.5 D13
9th Ave. Pg.4,5 D13
10th Ave. Pg.4,5 D13
11th Ave. Pg.4,5 D13
12th Ave. Pg.4,5 D13
13th Ave. Pg.4,5 D13
14th Ave. Pg.4,5 D13
15th Ave. Pg.1,4 D12,13
16th Ave. Pg.4,5 C13
17th Ave. Pg.1,4 C12,13
18th Ave. Pg.1,4 C12,13
19th Ave. Pg.1,4 C12,13
20th Ave. Pg.4,5 C13
21st Ave. Pg.4,5 C13
22nd Ave. Pg.4,5 C13
23rd Ave. Pg.4,5 C13
24th Ave. Pg.4,5 C13
25th Ave. Pg.1 C12
30th Ave. Pg.4,5 C13
31st Ave. Pg.4,5 C13
32nd Ave. Pg.4,5 C13
33rd Ave. Pg.4,5 C13
34th Ave. Pg.4,5 C13
35th Ave. Pg.4,5 C13
36th Ave. Pg.4,5 C13
37th Ave. Pg.4,5 C13
38th Ave. Pg.4,5 C13
43rd Ave. Pg.4 B13
44th Ave. Pg.4 B13
45th Ave. Pg.4 B13
46th Ave. Pg.4 B13
47th Ave. Pg.4 B13

PARKS
Bulger Park Pg.4,5 D13

SHOPPING CENTERS
Winston Park Shopping Center Pg.4,5 D13

MISCELLANEOUS
Gottlieb Hosp. Pg.1 D12
Maywood Park Racetrack Pg.4,5 D13
Village Hall Pg.4 D13
Walther Lutheran Hospital Pg.4 D13
Westlake Comm. Hospital Pg.4 D13

MERRIONETTE PARK
Pages 10,12

STREETS
Albany Dr. Pg.10 J24
Central Park Pg.10 H24
Mahoney Pg.10 J24
Meadow Pg.10 J24
Morgan Park Pg.12 H24
Palisade Dr. Pg.10 J24
Park Lane Dr., S. Pg.10 J24
Sacramento Dr. Pg.10 J24
St. Louis Pg.12 H24
Troy Pg.10 J24
Whipple Dr. Pg.12,13 J24
113th Pl. Pg.10 J23
113th St. Pg.10 J23
114th Pl. Pg.10 J23
114th St. Pg.10 J23
115th St. Pg.10 J24
118th St. Pg.10 J24
119th St. Pg.10 J24

CEMETERIES
Beverly Cem. Pg.12 H24
Mt. Hope Cem. Pg.10 J24
Mt. Olivet Cem. Pg.10 J23
Oak Hill Cem. Pg.12 H24

MIDLOTHIAN
Page 12

STREETS
Avers Ave. H26,27
Central Park Ave. H26
Clifton Park Ave. H26
Crawford Ave. H26
Hamlin Ave. H26,27
Harding Ave. H27
Homan Ave. H26
Karlov Ave. H26
Keating Ave. G26
Kedvale Ave. H26,27
Kedzie Ave. J26
Keeler Ave. H26
Kenneth Ave. H26,27
Kenton G26
Keystone Ave. H26
Kilbourn Ave. G26
Kildare Ave. H26
Kilpatrick Ave. G26
Knox Ave. G26
Kolin Ave. H26
Kolmar Ave. G26,27
Kostner H26
Lawndale Ave. H26,27
Maple Ln. G26
Maxey Ct. H26
Millard H26,27
Raday Dr. H27
Ridgeway Ave. H26,27
Sawyer Ave. J26
Spaulding Ave. H26
Springfield Ave. H26
St. Louis Ave. H26
Terrace Ln. H27
Tripp Ave. H26
Trumbull Ave. H26
Turner H26
Waverly H26
143rd Pl. G,H26
143rd St. G,H26
144th Pl. G26
144th St. G,H26
145th St. G,H26
146th St. G,H26
147th Pl. H,J26
147th St. G,H26
148th Pl. H27
148th St. G,H26
149th St. G,H27
150th St. G,H27
151st St. H27
152nd St. H27
153rd Pl. H27
153rd St. H27
154th St. H27

GOLF COURSES
Midlothian C.C. G26

SCHOOLS
Bremen Twp. Community H.S. H27

MISCELLANEOUS
Village Hall H27

NILES
Page 2

STREETS
Albion E8
Austin Ave. F8
Birchwood Ave. E7
Brummel F7
Caldwell F8
Central Ave. G8
Cherry E8
Concord Ln. F8
Croname Rd. F7
Days Terr. F8
Dobson St. E7
Ebinger Ave. E8
Evergreen E8
Fargo Ave. E7
Forest View Ave. E8
Franks Ave. E8
Greenleaf Ave. F8
Gross Point Rd. F8
Harlem Ave. E7
Harts Rd. F8
Harvard St. E7
Howard St. F7
Jarvis Ave. E,F7
Jarvis St. E7
Jonquil Terr. E7
Kirk Dr. E7
Kirk Ln. E7
Kirk St. E7
Lawler Ave. E7
Lehigh F8
Lexington Ln. F8
Mason F7
Melvina Ave. F8
Menard Ave. F7
Merrimac Ave. F7
Mulford St. E,F7
Natchez Ave. F7
Neva Ave. E7
Nieman Ave. E8
Niles Ter. E7
Nora Ave. E7
Nordica E7
Nottingham E7
Oak Park Ave. F7
Oakton Ct. E7
Oakton St. E7
Oconto Ave. E7,8
Octavia Ave. E7,8
Odell Ave. E7,8
Oketo Ave. E7,8
Olcott Ave. E7,8
Oleander Ave. E7
Oriole Ave. E7
Osceola Ave. E7,8
Riverside Dr. E8
Riverview Ave. E8
Rosemary Ave. E8
School St. E8
Touhy Ave. F8
Vapor Ln. F7
Waukegan Rd. E7

CEMETERIES
St. Adalberts Cem. E8

GOLF COURSES
Tam Golf Course F7

FOREST PRESERVES
Smith Woods F8

PARKS
Jazwiak Park E8
Jonquil Terrace Park E7
Kirk Lane Park E7

SCHOOLS
Niles College E8
Niles Twp. H.S. West F7
Oakton Comm. College F7

SHOPPING CENTERS
Lawrencewood Shopping Ctr. E7

MISCELLANEOUS
Village Hall E8

NORRIDGE
Pages 1,2

STREETS
Agatite D,E10
Ainslie D10
Argyle D,E10
Belle Plaine E10
Berteau E10
Canfield D10
Carmen D,E9
Charmaine Rd. D9
Chester D9
Coral Dr. D10
Courtland D10
Crescent D10
Cullom E10
Delphia D10
Denal D10
Eastwood D10
Elm Dr. D10
Forest Preserve Dr. E10
Frank D10
Giddings D,E10
Greenwood D10
Gunnison D,E10
Irving Park F10
Knight D10
Leland D10
Leonard Dr. D10
Lincoln D10
Maple D10
Memory Ln. D9
Mission Dr. E9
Monterey D10
Montrose E10
Moreland D9
Neva E10
Newland E10
Nordica E10
Nottingham E10
Oak D10
Octavia E10
Odell E10
Oketo E10
Olcott E10
Oleander E10
Oneida E10
Opal E10
Orange Dr. E10
Oriole E10
Osage D10
Osceola E10
Ottawa E10
Overhill E10
Ozaman E10
Ozark E10
Paris D10
Pensacola E10
Pittsburgh D10
Plainfield D10
Pontiac D10
Prospect D10
Redwood Dr. D10
Ridgewood D10
Sayre E10
Strong D,E10
Sunnyside D,E10
Sunrise Ln. D10
Thatcher Rd. D10
Vine D10
Wilson D,E10
Windsor E10
Winnemac D10
Winona D9

CEMETERIES
Acacia Park Cem. D10
Irving Park Cem. E10
Westlawn Cem. D10

PARKS
Norridge Park E10

SCHOOLS
Ridgewood H.S. E10

SHOPPING CENTERS
Harlem Irving Shopping Ctr. E10

MISCELLANEOUS
Chicago State Hosp. F10
Norridge Home for the Aged D10
State Police Headquarters E10
Village Hall E10

NORTH RIVERSIDE
Page 5

STREETS
Burr Oak E15
Cermak Rd. E15
Country Club Ln. E16
Des Plaines E15,16
Edgewater Rd. D16
Elm D15
Forest E15
Forest View Dr. D16
Groveland D16
Hainsworth E15
Harlem Ave. E15
Keystone E15
Lathrop E15
Lewe Ct. D16
Lincoln D16
Madison D15
Northgate E15
Park E15
Prairie D15
Traube E15
Westover E15
1st Ave. E15
2nd Ave. D15
3rd Ave. D15
4th Ave. D15
5th Ave. D15
6th Ave. D15
7th Ave. D15
8th Ave. D15
9th Ave. D15
10th Ave. D15
11th Ave. D15
12th Ave. D15
13th Ave. D15
17th Ave. D15
22nd Pl. D15
23rd Pl. D16
23rd St. D15
24th St. D16
25th St. D,E16
26th St. D16
27th St. D16
28th St. D16
30th St. D16
31st St. D16

GOLF COURSES
Riverside G.C. D16

SHOPPING CENTERS
Shopping Ctr. E15

MISCELLANEOUS
Village Hall D16

NORTHLAKE
Pages 1,4

STREETS
Alvin Pg.1 B12
Armitage Pg.1 B12
Ashbel Pg.4 B13
Belle Dr. Pg.1 B12
Bernice Pg.1 B12
Caryl Pg.1,4 B12,13
Charles Dr. Pg.1 B12
Country Club Dr. Pg.1 B12
Dewey Pg.1 B12
Dickens Pg.1 B12
Diversey Pg.1 B11
Dodd Pg.4 B13
East Dr. Pg.1 B12
Edward Pg.1 B12
Elm Pg.4 B13
Franklin Dr. Pg.1 B12
Fullerton Pg.1 B12
Gail Pg.4 B13
Geneva Pg.1 B12
Golf View Pg.1 B12
Grand Ave. Pg.1 B11
Haber Ct. Pg.1 B12
Harold Pg.1 B12
Harvard Pg.4 B13
Hayes Pg.1 B12
Hillside Pg.1,4 B12,13
Hirsch Pg.4 B13
Irving Pg.4 B13
Jerome Pg.1 B12
Lake Pg.4 A13
Lakewood Pg.4 B13
Landen Dr. Pg.1 B12
Laporte Pg.1 B12
Lavergne Pg.1 B12
Lemoyne Pg.4 B13
Lind Pg.4 B13
Longfield Pg.1 B12
Lyndale Pg.1 B12
MacArthur Dr. Pg.1 B12
Major Dr. Pg.1 B13
Maplewood Pg.4 B13
Marilyn Pg.1,4 B12,13
McLean Pg.1 B12
Medill Pg.1 B12
Morse Pg.1,4 B13
North Ave. Pg.1,4 B13
Northwest Ave. Pg.1 A12
Palmer Pg.1 B12
Parkview Dr. Pg.1 B12
Prater Pg.1,4 B12,13
Railroad Ave. Pg.1 B12
Rhodes Pg.1 B11
Roberta Pg.1 B12
Roy Pg.1 B12
Sandra Pg.1 B12
Soffel Pg.4 B13
Tri-State Tollway Pg.1 A12
Victoria Dr. Pg.4 B13
Village Dr. Pg.1 B12
Wagner Dr. Pg.1 B12
West Dr. Pg.1 B12
Westward Ho Dr. Pg.1 B12
Whitehall Pg.1 B12
William Pg.1 B12
Winters Dr. Pg.1 B12
Wolf Rd. Pg.1 B12
43rd Ave. Pg.4 B13
44th Ave. Pg.4 B13
45th Ave. Pg.4 B13

CEMETERIES
Memorial Estates Cem. Pg.1 B12

PARKS
Grant Park Pg.1 B12
Park Pg.1 B12

SCHOOLS
Ben Franklin Sch. Pg.1 B12
Mark Twain Sch. Pg.4 B13
Riley Sch. Pg.4 B13
Roy Sch. Pg.1 B12
St. John Sch. Pg.1 B12

NORTHLAKE

- West Leyden H.S. Pg.1 B12
- Westdale Sch. Pg.1 B11
- Whittier Sch. Pg.1 B12

MISCELLANEOUS

- City Hall Pg.4 B13
- Fire Dept. Pg.1 B12
- Home for the Aged Pg.1 B12
- Library Pg.4 B13
- Northlake Community Hosp. Pg.1 B13
- Public Works Pg.4 B13

OAK LAWN

Page 9

STREETS

- Adeline H23
- Alexander G21
- Alice Ct. G22
- Arnold H23
- Austin F22
- Avery G21
- Brandt G22
- Buell G22
- Campbell G22
- Cass G22
- Center Dr. G22
- Cicero G21-23
- Circle G22
- Columbus Dr. G22
- Cook G22
- Cranbrook E21
- Crescent Ct. F21
- David Ct. F22
- Dean Dr. H23
- Drury Ln. G22
- Dumke G22
- Eastshore Dr. G22
- Edgelake F23
- Edison F22
- Elm G22
- Fairfax H23
- Franklin G22
- Georgia G23
- Grant H23
- Harlem Ave. E22
- Harnew Rd. G22
- Hartford E21
- High G23
- Hilton Dr. G22
- James F22
- Karlov H21-23
- Kathleen H23
- Keating G21,23
- Kedvale H21-23
- Keeler H21-23
- Kenneth Ave. G22
- Kenneth Pl. G23
- Kenton G21-23
- Kilbourn G22,23
- Kildare H22,23
- Kilpatrick G21-23
- Kimball Pl. G21
- Knox G21-23
- Kolin H22,23
- Kolmar G21-23
- Komensky H21-23
- Kostner H22,23
- Lacrosse G23
- Lamb Dr. G22
- Lamon G23
- Laporte G23
- Laramie G22,23
- Lavergne G23
- Lawler G23
- Lawrence Ct. G22
- Lawton G22
- Leclaire G23
- Linder G22
- Lockwood G23
- Long G23
- Lorel G23
- Luna G21
- Lynwood Dr. F21
- Major F21-23
- Mansfield F22
- Maple G22
- Marion F22
- Marmora F23
- Mason F22,23
- Massasoit F22
- Mayfield F21,22
- McVicker F21,22
- Meade F21,22
- Melvina F22
- Menard F22
- Merrimac F21,22
- Merton F22
- Minnick G22
- Mobile F21
- Monitor F22
- Moody F21,22
- Moore G23
- Mulberry G22
- Mulligan Dr. F21
- Nashville F22
- Natchez F22
- Natoma F21,22
- Neva E22
- New England E21,22
- Newland E21
- Nora E22
- Nordica E22
- Normandy F22
- North St. G21
- Oak G22
- Oak Center Dr. G22
- Oak Park E22
- Oakdale Dr. G22
- Olympic E21
- Otto Pl. G21
- Pacific F22
- Park G22
- Parkside F22
- Paxton Rd. G22
- Raymond Ave. G22
- Ridgeland F22
- Ruby G22
- Rumsey G22
- Rutherford F22
- Sayre E21
- Scott Ln. G22
- Southwest Hwy. G22
- Spring Rd. G22
- Stevens Dr. G21
- Stilwell Pl. H23
- Stony Circle G22
- Stony Creek Dr. G23
- Tripp H21-23
- Tulley G21,22
- Wainwright H23
- Warren G22
- Washington G22,23
- Westshore Dr. G22
- Wick Dr. G22
- William Pl. G22
- Wolfe Dr. G23
- Yourell G22
- 48th St. G22
- 49th Ct. G22
- 49th St. G22
- 50th Ct. G22
- 50th St. G22
- 51st Ct. G23
- 51st St. G22
- 52nd St. G22
- 53rd Ct. G21,22
- 53rd St. G21,22
- 54th Ct. G21,22
- 54th St. G21,22
- 55th Ct. G21,22
- 55th St. G21,22
- 68th Ct. E22
- 69th Ct. E22
- 87th Pl. E,F21
- 87th St. E-G21
- 88th Pl. E,F21
- 88th St. E,F21
- 89th Pl. E,F21
- 90th Pl. E,F21
- 90th St. E,F21
- 91st Pl. E-G21
- 91st St. E-G21
- 92nd Pl. E-G22
- 92nd St. E-G22
- 93rd Pl. E-G22
- 93rd St. E-G22
- 94th Pl. E-G22
- 94th St. E-G22
- 95th St. E-G22
- 96th Pl. E-G22
- 96th St. E-G22
- 97th Pl. E-G22
- 97th St. E-G22
- 98th Pl. F-H22
- 98th St. F-H22
- 99th Pl. F-H22
- 99th St. F-H22
- 100th Pl. F-H22
- 100th St. F-H22
- 101st Pl. F-H22
- 101st St. F-H22
- 102nd Pl. F-H22
- 102nd St. F-H22
- 103rd St. F-H22
- 104th St. F-H23
- 105th Pl. F-H23
- 105th St. F-H23
- 106th Pl. F-H23
- 106th St. F-H23
- 107th Pl. G,H23
- 107th St. G,H23
- 108th Pl. F,G23
- 108th St. F,G23
- 109th St. F,G23
- 110th Pl. F,G23
- 110th St. F,G23
- 111th St. F,G23

PARKS

- Beverly Lawn Park H22
- Oak Meadows Park G22

SCHOOLS

- Oak Lawn Comm. H.S. F22
- Richards H.S. Campus Bldg. F23
- Richards H.S. N.E. Bldg. H23

SHOPPING CENTERS

- Shopping Center G21

MISCELLANEOUS

- Christ Comm. Hospital H22
- Village Hall G22

OAK PARK

Pages 5,6

STREETS

- Adams E,F14
- Augusta Blvd. E13
- Austin Blvd. F13-15
- Belleforte E13
- Berkshire E13
- Carpenter E14
- Chicago E13
- Clarence E14,15
- Clinton E15
- Columbian F13
- Common F14
- Cuyler F13,14
- Division E13
- East F13-15
- Edmer F13
- Elizabeth Ct. E13
- Elmwood F13-15
- Erie E13
- Euclid F13-15
- Fair Oaks F13
- Fillmore E15
- Flournoy F14
- Forest E13
- Garfield E14
- Greenfield E,F13
- Grove E13,14
- Gunderson F15
- Harlem E13,14
- Harrison F14
- Harvard E14
- Harvey F13-15
- Hayes F13
- Highland F15
- Home E15
- Humphrey F13
- Iowa E13
- Jackson Blvd. E,F14
- Kenilworth E13,14
- Lake E13
- Le Moyne Pkwy. E,F13
- Lenox F13
- Lexington E,F14
- Linden F13,14
- Lombard F13-15
- Lyman F15
- Madison E,F14
- Maple E15
- Mapleton F13
- Marion E13,14
- Miller E13
- Monroe E14
- North Ave. E13
- Oak Park E12-15
- Ontario E,F13
- Paulina E13
- Pleasant E,F14
- Pleasant Pl. E14
- Randolph E14
- Ridgeland F13-15
- Roosevelt Rd. E15
- Rossell F13
- Schneider E13
- Scoville F14,15
- South Blvd. E14
- Superior E,F13
- Taylor F13-15
- Thomas E13
- Van Buren E,F14
- Washington Blvd. E14
- Wenonah E15
- Wesley F14,15
- Westgate E14
- Wisconsin E15
- Woodbine E13

PARKS

- Anderson Playground F13
- Austin Gardens E13
- Barrie Plg. Park F14
- Carroll Plg. Park E14
- Field Park E13
- Fox Park F14
- Lindberg Park E13
- Longfellow Park F14
- Maple Park E14
- Mills Park E14
- Rehm Park F14
- Scoville Park E13
- Stevenson Plg. Park F14
- Taylor Park F13

SCHOOLS

- Fenwick H.S. F14
- Oak Park River Forest H.S. F13

MISCELLANEOUS

- City Hall F14
- Euclid Sq. F15
- Frank Lloyd Wright Home E13
- Oak Park Hospital E14
- Unity Temple E13
- West Suburban Hosp. F13
- Wright Hist. Dist. F13

PARK RIDGE

Pages 1,2

STREETS

- Albion D8
- Aldine D7,8
- Archbury Ln. C8
- Arthur D8
- Ascot Dr. C8
- Ashland D7-9
- Austin D7
- Avondale D7
- Babetta D7
- Belle Plaine D8
- Berry Pkwy. E8
- Bonita Dr. D8
- Bonnie D8
- Bouterse D7
- Broadway D7,8
- Brophy D9
- Busse Hwy. D7
- Canfield Rd. E8
- Carolyn D7
- Castle Dr. D8
- Cedar C,D8
- Cherry C,D7
- Chester D7,8
- Cleveland E8
- Clifton D7-9
- Clinton D8
- Columbia D8
- Courtland D8,9
- Crescent D8,9
- Cumberland D7,8
- Curtiss D7
- Cynthia D7
- Dee Rd. C7,D9
- Delphia D7,8
- Des Plaines D8
- Devon D8
- East E7
- Edgemont Ln. C-E7
- Ellison D7
- Elm C,D7
- Elmore E7
- Engel Blvd. D8
- Euclid D8
- Fairview D8,9
- Florence C7
- Forestview C7
- Frances Pkwy. D9
- Garden D8
- Gillick D8
- Glenlake D9
- Goodwin C7
- Grace D7-9
- Grand Blvd. D7
- Grant Pl. D7
- Granville D9
- Greenwood D7,8
- Grove E8
- Hamlin D7,8
- Hansen Pl. D7
- Harrison E8
- Hastings D7
- Higgins Rd. D9
- Home D7,8
- Imperial D8
- Irwin D7
- James Pl. D8
- Jonquil Terr. E7
- Joyce Pl. E7
- Kathleen E7
- Kent D8
- Knight D7,8
- Lahon C-E7
- Lake D8
- Laverne D7
- Leonard D7
- Lincoln D7-9
- Linden D8,9
- Lois D9
- Marvin Pl. D7
- Mary Jane D7
- Meacham D7
- Merrill E7
- Michael John Dr. D7
- Milton D7
- Morris D8
- Newton D9
- Norman D8
- Northwest Hwy. C7,E8
- Ozanam E8
- Park Pl. D8
- Park Ridge Blvd. D8
- Parkplaine C7
- Parkwood C7
- Peale D8
- Peterson D9
- Prairie D8
- Prospect D7-9
- Rabe D7
- Redfield Ct. D7,8
- Ridge Terr. D8
- Root D7
- Rose Ct. D7,8
- Rosemont D8
- Rowe D7
- Scottylynne Dr. C7
- Seeley D7
- Seminary D7,8
- Sibley D7
- Spring D8
- Stanley D8
- Stewart D8
- Summit E8
- Sylviawood C7
- Talcott Pl. D8
- Talcott Rd. C7
- Thames Pkwy. C8
- Thorndale D9
- Touhy D8
- Vine D8,9
- Virginia C7
- Warren D8
- Washington D7-9
- Wesley C7
- Western D7-9
- Wilkinson Pkwy. D7
- Wilma Pl. E7
- Yost E9

GOLF COURSES

- Park Ridge C.C. D7

PARKS

- Centennial Park D8
- Hinkley Park D8
- Jaycee Park D9
- Maine Park C7
- Northeast Park E7
- South Park D8
- Southwest Park D9

SCHOOLS

- Maine Twp. H.S. South D8

MISCELLANEOUS

- Camp Ft. Dearborn D9
- Lutheran Boys Home E9
- Village Hall D8

PHOENIX

Page 13

STREETS

- Frances St. L27
- Halsted St. L27
- Vandrunen Rd. L27
- Vincennes L27
- Wallace L27
- Welton L27
- 1st Ave. L27
- 2nd Ave. L27
- 3rd Ave. L27
- 4th Ave. L27
- 5th Ave. L27
- 6th Ave. L27
- 7th Ave. L27
- 8th Ave. L27
- 9th Ave. L27
- 149th L27
- 151st Pl. L27
- 151st St. L27
- 153rd St. L27
- 154th Pl. L27
- 154th St. L27
- 155th Pl. L27
- 155th St. L27
- 156th St. L27

MISCELLANEOUS

- Village Hall L27

POSEN

Pages 12,13

STREETS

- Albany J26
- Albert J26
- Ash J26
- Blaine J26
- California J26
- Campbell J26
- Cleveland J26
- Division J26
- Elm J26
- Francisco J26
- Grove J26
- Harrison J26
- Kedzie J26
- Maple J26
- McKinley J26
- Mozart J26
- Palmer J26
- Richmond J26
- Sacramento J26
- Sherman J26
- Short J26
- Troy J26
- Utica J26
- Western Ave. J26
- Whipple J26
- 139th Pl. J26
- 139th St. J26
- 140th St. J26
- 141st St. J26
- 142nd St. J26
- 143rd St. J26
- 144th St. J26
- 145th St. J26
- 146th St. J26
- 148th St. J26
- 149th St. J26
- 150th St. J26

MISCELLANEOUS

- Village Hall J26

PROVISO TOWNSHIP

Page 4

STREETS

- Alexandria B16
- Buck Rd. A14
- Burton Ct. A16
- Concord St. A15
- Degener A15
- Dickens A15
- Duncan St. A15
- Hamilton A15
- Harvard A15
- Hawthorne A15
- Marion A15
- Monticello Pl. B16
- Turner A15

GOLF COURSES

- Fresh Meadow G.C. B15
- Meadowlark G.C. B16

RIVER FOREST

Page 5

STREETS

- Ashland E14
- Auvergne Pl. F13
- Berkshire E13
- Bonnie Brae E13
- Central E14
- Chicago E13
- Clinton E14
- Clinton Pl. E13
- Edgewood Pl. F13
- Forest E13,14
- Franklin E14
- Gale D14
- Garden D14
- Harlem Ave. E13
- Hawthorne E14
- Holly Ct. E13
- Iowa E13
- Jackson E14
- Keystone E13,14
- Lathrop E14
- Linden E14
- Monroe E14
- North Ave. E13
- Oak E13
- Park Ave. E14
- Park Dr. E14
- Quick E13
- River Oaks F13
- Thatcher D13
- Thomas E13
- Vine E14
- Vinson D13
- Washington Blvd. E14
- William E13,14

PARKS

- Keystone Field E14
- North Park E13

SCHOOLS

- Concordia Teachers College E13
- Rosary College E13
- Trinity H.S. E13

MISCELLANEOUS

- Village Hall E14

RIVER GROVE

Pages 1,2

STREETS

- Arnold D11
- Ashland Ave. D11
- Aux Plaines D11
- Belden D12
- Belmont Ave. D11
- Beulah D11
- Boyle D11
- Budd D12
- Carey D12
- Center D11
- Cherry D11
- Chestnut D11
- Clarke D12
- Clinton D12
- Davisson D12
- Des Plaines River Rd. D12
- Elm D12
- Enger D11
- Erie D12
- Finley D12
- Forest D11
- Forestview D12
- Franklin St. D11
- Fullerton D12
- Grand Ave. D12

RIVER GROVE

Greenwood Terr. D12
Grove D12
Haymond D12
Herrick D12
Hessing D12
Indian Bdry. Rd. D11
Julian Terr. D11
Kennedy St. D11
Leyden D12
Lyndale D12
Maple D12
Marwood D11
O'Connor Dr. D11
Oak D11
Pacific D11
Palmer D11
Paris D11
Park D11
Rhodes D11
Richard D11
Ridge D11
River Grove D12
Roosevelt Ln. D12
Smith Ln. D11
Spruce D11
Struckmann D12
Thatcher Ave. D12
Trumbull D11
Walnut D11
Walsh D11
West D12
Wood D12
Wrightwood D12
5th Ave. D12

SCHOOLS

Holy Cross H.S. D11
St. Paul Guerin H.S. D11
Triton Jr. College D11

MISCELLANEOUS

Village Hall D12

RIVERDALE

Page 13

STREETS

Acme L25
Ashland K26
Atlantic St. L25,26
Blue Island-Riverdale Rd. . L25
Clark L26
Eggleston L26
Emerald L26
Forestview L26
Halsted St. L25,26
Illinois St. L26
Indiana Ave. L25,26
Jackson K25
La Salle L26
Lowe Ave. L25,26
Normal Ave. L25,26
Pacesetter Pkwy K,L26
Parnell Ave. L25,26
Perry Ave. L25
Roll K25
School L25,26
State St. L25
Stewart Ave. L26
Tracy L26
Union L26
Wabash L25
Wallace St. L25,26
Wentworth L25,26
135th Pl. L25
136th Pl. L25
136th St. L26
137th Pl. L25
137th St. L25
138th St. K,L26
139th St. L26
140th Ct. L26
140th St. L26
141st St. K,L26
142nd St. L26
143rd St. L26
144th St. L26
145th St. L26
146th St. L26

GOLF COURSES

Pipe O'Peace G.C. K25

PARKS

Ivanhoe Park L26
Riverdale Park L25

MISCELLANEOUS

Calumet Boating Center . . K25
Village Hall & Fire Dept. . . L26

RIVERSIDE

Page 5

STREETS

Addison Rd. E16
Akenside Rd. E16
Arlington E16
Audubon Pkwy. E16
Barrypoint D17
Bartram Rd. E16
Berkley Rd. E16
Black Hawk Rd. E17

Bloomingbank D17
Blythe Rd. E16
Burling Rd. E17
Burlington D17,E16
Byrd Rd. E16
Columbus Blvd. E17
Cowley Rd. E16
Delaplaine Rd. E16,17
Des Plaines D16
Downing Rd. E16
East Grove Rd. E16
Evelyn E16
Fairbank Rd. D17
Forest D16
Gage Rd. E17
Gatesby Rd. E16
Gladstone E17
Groveland D16
Haas Ave. E17
Harlem Ave. E17
Harris Rd. E17
Herbert Rd. E16,17
Herrick Rd. E16
Kent E16
Kimbark E16
La Fayette Rd. E17
Lawton Rd. E16
Leesley E16
Lincoln D16
Lindberg Rd. E16
Lionel Rd. E17
Long Common Rd. E16
Loudoun Rd. E16
Maplewood Dr. D16
Michaux Rd. E16
Miller Rd. E17
Northgate Rd. E16
Northwood Rd. E16
Nuttall Rd. E17
Ogden Ave. E17
Olmsted Rd. E17
Park Pl. D,E16
Parkway Rd. E16
Pine D17,E16
Quincy D17,E16
Quincy E16
Repton Rd. E16
Ridgewood D16
Riverside Dr. E17
Robinson Rd. E17
Scottswood D17
Selbourne Rd. E16
Shakespeare E17
Shenstone Rd. E16
Southcote Rd. E16
Stanley E17
Uvedale Rd. E16
Washington E17
Waubansee D17
West D16
Woodside Rd. E16
York Rd. E16
39th St. E17

PARKS

Long Common Park E16

MISCELLANEOUS

Village Hall E17

ROBBINS

Page 12

STREETS

A St. H26
Albany J26
Aldia H26
Avers H25
Broadway J25
Central Park J26
Clifton Park H25,26
Emery Ln. H26
Finley H26
Francisco Ave. J25
Glenn H26
Grace H26
Hamlin H25
Harding H25
Hendricks H26
Homan H25
Karlov H25
Kedvale H25
Kedzie J25
Keystone H26
Kildare H25
Kinne Rd. H26
Kolin H25
Lawndale H25
Lincoln Ln., E. H25
Lydia H26
Lydia Ct. H26
Maxey Ct. H26
McBreen H26
Midlothian Tpk. H25,26
Monticello H25
Nelson Ave. H26
Reeves Rd. H26
Rexford Rd. H26
Richardson J26
Richmond J25

Ridgeway H25
Sacramento J25
Sawyer J25
Spaulding H25,H,J26
Springfield H25
St. Louis H25,26
Tripp H25
Troy J26
Trumbull H25,26
Turner J26
Utica J26
Woodlawn J25
134th Pl. H25
134th St. H25
135th Pl. H25
135th St. H25
136th Pl. H25
136th St. H,J25
137th St. H,J25
138th St. H,J26
139th Pl. H,J26
139th St. H26
140th Pl. H26
140th St. H26

MISCELLANEOUS

Village Hall H26

ROSEMONT

Page 1

STREETS

Allen C9
Ardmore C9
Barry B8
Berwyn C9
Bryn Mawr C9
Byron C9
Chestnut B8
Des Plaines River Rd. . . . C8
Devon C8
Emerson C9
Estelle Dr. C8
Evenhouse C9
Farragutt C9
Gage C9
Glenlake C9
Graff Dr. C9
Granville C9
Hawthorne C9
Higgins Rd. B8
Hope Dr. C8
Kirschoff B8
Lee St. B8
Lunt B8
Lyndon B8
Mannheim Rd. B8
Maple Dr. C9
Milton Pkwy. C9
Morse B8
Norwood C9
Otto C9
Pearl C9
Rose C9
Rosemont C8
Ruby C9
Schaffer Ct. C9
Scott C9
Thorndale C9
Touhy B8
Wesley Ter. C9
William C9
Willow Creek Dr. C9

MISCELLANEOUS

Village Hall C9

SCHILLER PARK

Page 1

STREETS

Agitite Ave. C10
Agitite Ct. C10
Ainslie C10
Atlantic C10
Belle Plaine C10
Berteau C10
Bobby Ln. C10
Byron St. C10
Cary C11
Cora (Foster) Ave. C10
Cullom C10
Delta Pkwy. B10
Des Plaines River Rd. . . . C10
Eastwood Ave. C10
Eastwood Ct. C10
Eden C10
Emerson Ave. C10
Emerson Dr. C10
Fifth C10
Forest C9
Foster C10
Garden Ct. C10
Goss C10
Grace C10
Gremley C10
Harold C10
Hartford Ct. C10
Hirschberg Ct. C10
Indian Rd. C10

Irving Park Rd. C10
Ivanhoe Ave. C11
Ivanhoe Cir. C11
Ivanhoe Ct. C11
Ivanhoe St. C11
Jill Ln. C10
Judd C10
Kelvin Ln. C10
Kolze C10
Lawrence C10
Lawrence Ct. C10
Leland C10
Linn C10
Marie Ct. C10
Michigan C10
Montrose Blvd. C10
Moore Ln. C10
Pan American Dr. B10
Panoramic Dr. C11
Prairie C10
River C10
Rose C10
Ruby (9th) C10
Sally C10
Scott (5th) Ave. C10
Scott St. C10
Seymour C10
South C10
Sterling Ln. C10
Sunnyside C10
Susy Ln. C10
Transworld Rd. B10
United Pkwy. B10
Wagner C10
Waveland Ave. C11
Wehrman Pl. C11
Wesley Terr. C10
Willow C11
Wilson C10
Winona C9
25th Ave. C11

MISCELLANEOUS

Village Hall C10

SKOKIE

Pages 2,3

STREETS

Austin Ave. F7
Babb Ave. G7
Birchwood G,H7
Birchwood Ave. G,H7
Brummel St. G,H7
Carpenter Rd. G8
Central Ave. G8
Central Park Ave. H8
Chase Ave. G8
Coyle Ave. G8
Crawford Ave. H7
Dobson G,H7
East Prairie Rd. H7
Edens Expy. G7,8
Estes Ave. G8
Fairview Ln. G,H7
Fargo Ave. G,H7
Farwell Ave. G8
Fitch Ave. G8
Galitz St. G7
George St. G7
Harvard St. G,H7
Howard St. F–H7
Hull St. G,H7
Jarlath Ave. G,H8
Jarvis Ave. G,H7
Jerome Ave. G,H7
Joneway Terr. G7
Jonquil Terr. G7
Karlov Ave. H7
Kedvale Ave. H7
Keeler Ave. H7
Kenneth Ave. H7
Kenton Ave. G7
Keystone Ave. H7
Kilbourn Ave. H7
Kildare Ave. H7
Kilpatrick Ave. H7
Kirk St. G,H7
Knox Ave. G7
Kolmar Ave. H7
Kostner Ave. H7
LaCrosse Ave. G7
Lamon Ave. G8
Laramie Ave. G8
Latrobe Ave. G8
Lavergne Ave. G7,8
Lawndale Ave. H8
LeClaire Ave. G7,8
Linder Ave. G8
Lockwood Ave. G7
Long Ave. G7
Lorel Ave. G8
Louise St. G,H7
Lunt Ave. G8
Major Ave. F7
Mango Ave. F7
Marmora Ave. F7
Mason F7
McCormick Blvd. H7
Menard Ave. F7

Monticello Ave. H8
Morse Ave. G8
Mulford St. G,H7
New Gross Point Rd. F7
Niles Ave. G7
Niles Center Rd. G8
Oakton St. G,H7
Park Ave. G7
Parkside Ave. F7
Pratt G8
Ridgeway Ave. H8
Sherwin Ave. G8
Skokie Blvd. G7
St. Louis Ave. H8
Touhy Ave. G8

PARKS

Birch Park G7
Coyle Park G8
Emily Park G7
Frontage Park F7
George Park G7
Hamlin Park H7
Kostner Park H7
Laramie Park G8
Little League Park H7
Oakton Park G7

SCHOOLS

Hebrew Theological College . G8
Niles Twp. H.S. East G8
Niles Twp. H.S. West F7

MISCELLANEOUS

Village Hall G7

SOUTH HOLLAND

Pages 13,14

STREETS

Avalon Ave. M27,28
Bennet Ave. N29
Betty Ln. M28
Calumet Ave. L27
Calumet Expwy. M27,28
Canal St. L28
Caryn Cir. M28
Champlain St. M27
Church Dr. M27
Claire Ln. M28
Clark L27
Clyde N28,29
Constance Ave. N29
Cornell Ave. N28
Cottage Grove Ave. . . . M27,28
Cregier Ave. N29
Dante Dr. N27
Dearborn L27
Debbie Ln. M27,28
Dobson Ave. M27–29
Dorchester N27
Drexel Ave. M27,28
Ellis Ave. M27,28
Ellis Ct. M28,29
Elm Ct. M28
Elm St. M28
Evans Ave. M28,29
Evans Ct. M28
Everett Ave. N29
Godwens Ln. M27
Greenwood Ave. M28,29
Halsted St. M28
Ingleside Ave. M27,28
Ingleside Ct. M28
Joyce Cir. M28
Joyce Ct. M28
Kenwood Ave. M27–29
Kenwood Ct. M28
Kimbark M27,28
La Salle L27
Langley Ave. M28,29
Louis Ave. M28,29
Louis Ct. M29
Lowell Ave. M28
Luella Ave. N28
Maple Ct. M28
Maple St. M27,28
Marian Dr. M27,28
Maryland Ave. M28,29
Merrill N28
Michigan Ave. M28
Minerva M27
Mutual Terr. M27
Naughton Ave. M28
Orchid Dr. M27
Park Ln. M27
Parkside Ave. M27–29
Parkside Ct. M27
Paxton Ave. N28
Perry L27
Prairie Ave. L28
Prince Dr. N27
Riverside Dr. L,M27
Riverside Dr., E. L28
Riverside Dr., W. L28
Riverview St. M27
Robin Ln. M27
Rose Dr. M27
School St. M27–29
Shirley Ct. M27
South Park Ave. M27–29

State St. L27,28
Suntone Rd. L27,28
Taft Dr. L28
Thornton Ave. M28
Thornton-Blue Island Rd. . . L28
Thornwood Dr. M28,29
Union St. L29
University Ct. M28
Vandrunen L27,28
Vincennes Rd. L27,28
Volbrecht Ave. N29
Volbrecht Rd. N29
Wabash Ave. L27,28
Wabash Ct. L27
Wallace Ave. L28
Waterman Dr. M27
Wausau Ave. M28,29
Wausau St. M28
Wentworth Ave. L27
Westview Ave. L29
Woodlawn Ave., E. M27
Yates Ave. N29
147th St. (Sibley Blvd.) . . . L27
150th Pl. L27
152nd St. L28
153rd Pl. M27
153rd St. M27
154th Pl. L–N27
154th St. L27
155th Pl. L,M27
155th St. L,M27
156th Pl. M27
156th St. M,N27
157th Pl. M28
157th St. M27,28
158th Pl. L27,28
158th St. M,N27
159th Ct. M27
159th Pl. M27
159th St. M27
160th Ct. M27
160th Pl. M27
160th St. L,M27
161st Pl. M28
161st St. M28
162nd Pl. M28
162nd St. L,M28
163rd Ct. M28
163rd Pl. M28
163rd St. M28
164th Ct. M28
164th Pl. M28
164th St. L–N28
165th Pl. M28
165th St. M28
166th Pl. M,N28
166th St. L,M28
167th Pl. M28
167th St. L–N28
168th Ct. M28
168th Pl. M,N28
168th St. L–N28
169th Pl. M,N28
169th St. L–N28
170th Pl. M,N28
170th St. L–N28
171st Pl. M,N28,29
171st St. L–N28
172nd St. L29
173rd Pl. M28
173rd St. M,N29

PARKS

Van Oostenbrugge Park . . . M27
Veterans Mem. Park M27

SCHOOLS

South Suburban Coll. L28
Thornwood H.S. M28

MISCELLANEOUS

Village Hall M28

STICKNEY

Pages 5,6

STREETS

Central G17
Cicero G17
Clarence F17
Clinton E17
East F17
Elmwood F17
Grove F17
Gunderson F17
Harlem Ave. E17
Home F17
Kenilworth E17
Laramie G17
Lorraine Terr. F17
Maple F17
Oak Park F17
Pershing Rd. E17
Ridgeland F17
Scoville F17
Wenonah F17
Westley F17
Wisconsin E17
39th St. E17
40th Pl. E17

STICKNEY

40th St. ... E17
41st St. ... E17
42nd St. ... E17
43rd St. ... E17
44th St. ... E17
45th St. ... F17

MISCELLANEOUS
Village Hall ... F17

STONE PARK

Pages 4,5

STREETS
Division ... C13
Lake ... C13
Lemoyne ... C13
Mannheim Rd. ... B13
North ... C13
Soffel ... C13
32nd Ave. ... C13
33rd Ave. ... C13
34th Ave. ... C13
35th Ave. ... C13
36th Ave. ... C13
37th Ave. ... C13
38th Ave. ... C13
39th Ave. ... C13
40th Ave. ... C13
43rd Ave. ... B13
44th Ave. ... B13
45th Ave. ... B13

SCHOOLS
Sacred Heart Seminary ... C13

MISCELLANEOUS
Village Hall ... B13

SUMMIT

Pages 5,8,9

STREETS
Archer ... Pg.5,9 . E18,19
Center ... Pg.5,9 . E18,19
Douglas ... Pg.5 ... E18
Harlem ... Pg.5,9 . E18,19
Hunt ... Pg.9 ... E18,19
Lawndale ... Pg.5,8 . D18,18
Park Ave. ... Pg.9 ... E18
53rd St. ... Pg.9 ... E18
55th Pl. ... Pg.9 ... E18

56th Pl. ... Pg.9 ... E18
57th Pl. ... Pg.9 ... E18
57th St. ... Pg.9 ... E18
58th Pl. ... Pg.9 ... E19
58th St. ... Pg.9 ... E19
59th Pl. ... Pg.9 ... E19
59th St. ... Pg.5,8,9 ... E19
60th Pl. ... Pg.9 ... E19
60th St. ... Pg.9 ... E19
61st Pl. ... Pg.9 ... E19
61st St. ... Pg.9 ... E19
62nd Pl. ... Pg.9 ... E19
62nd St. ... Pg.9 ... E19
63rd Pl. ... Pg.9 ... E19
63rd St. ... Pg.9 ... E19
64th Pl. ... Pg.9 ... E19
64th St. ... Pg.9 ... E19
72nd Ct. ... Pg.5 ... E18
73rd Ave. ... Pg.5,9 . E18,19
73rd Ct. ... Pg.5 ... E18
74th Ave. ... Pg.5,9 . E18,19
75th Ave. ... Pg.5,9 . E18,19
76th Ave. ... Pg.9 ... E19

PARKS
Summit Park . Pg.9 ... E18

SCHOOLS
Argo H.S. ..... Pg.9 ... E19

WESTCHESTER

Pages 4,5

STREETS
Alexandria Ln. ... B16
Ashley Woods ... B16
Balmoral Blvd. ... C15
Bassford ... B16
Beckett ... B16
Bedford ... B16
Belleview ... B15
Berkshire ... B16
Boeger Ave. ... B15,16
Boeger Ct. ... B15
Bond ... C15
Brighton ... B16
Bristol ... C15
Broadway ... C15
Buckingham ... B15,16
Burns ... B15
Burton Dr. ... B16
Cambridge ... C15
Camelot ... B15

Canterbury ... B,C15
Carlisle ... B16
Cermak Rd. ... B15
Charles ... B15
Chaucer ... C15
Claridge ... B15
Concord ... B16
Constitution Dr. ... B16
Crestwood ... C15
Cromwell ... C15
Denton ... B16
Derby Ln. ... C15
Devonshire Ln. ... C15
Devonshire St. ... C15
Dickens ... B,C15
Dorchester ... B15
Dover ... C15
Downing ... B15,16
Drake ... B16
Drury Ln. ... C15
Eaton ... B16
Edgewood Ave. ... B16
Elizabeth ... B16
Enterprise Dr. ... B16
Essex ... B16
Evers ... B15
Fairfield ... B16
Fielding ... B15
Fleet ... B16
Forest ... B16
Gardner Rd. ... C15
Gladstone ... C15
Haas ... B15
Halifax ... B16
Hastings ... B16
Hawthorne ... B15
Heidorn ... B15
High Ridge Pkwy. ... B15,16
Hull ... C15
Kensington ... B15,16
Kent ... C15
Kings ... C15
Kingston ... B16
Kipling ... C15
Kitchener ... C15
La Grange Rd. ... C16
Lancaster ... B16
Manchester ... C15
Mandel ... B15
Mandel Ct. ... B15
Mannheim Rd. ... C15

Martindale Dr. ... B16
Mayfair ... B15,16
Millford ... C15
Monticello ... B16
Nelson Sq. ... B16
Nelson St. ... B16
Newbury ... B16
Newcastle ... C15
Norfolk ... C15
Oxford ... B,C15
Park ... B16
Pelham ... C15
Pell ... B16
Plymouth ... B16
Portsmouth ... C15
Prescott ... B16
Preston ... B16
Princess ... B16
Queens ... B16
Raleigh ... B16
Regency ... B16
Robinhood ... B15
Roosevelt Rd. ... B,C15
Shakespeare ... B15
Shaw ... B15
Shelly ... B15
Sherwood ... B16
Somerset Dr. ... B16
Stratford ... B15,16
Suffolk ... C15
Sunnyside ... B15,16
Terrace Ln. ... B16
The Strand ... C15
Wakefield ... B15
Waterford ... B15
Waverly ... B15
Wellington ... B16
Westminster ... B16
Westwood ... B16
Wight ... C15
Winchester ... C15
Windsor ... B16
Wolf Rd. ... B15
Woodlawn ... B16
Worcester ... C15
24th St. ... B16
26th St. ... B16
28th St. ... B16
29th St. ... B16
30th St. ... B16
31st St. ... B16

CEMETERIES
Glenn Oak Cem. ... B15
Oak Ridge Cem. ... B15

PARKS
Gladstone Park ... C15

SCHOOLS
High Ridge Sch. ... B15
Immaculate Heart of Mary H.S. ... B15
St. Joseph H.S. ... B15

MISCELLANEOUS
Village Hall ... C15

WESTERN SPRINGS

Page 8

STREETS
Birch Ln. ... B17,18
Burlington ... B17
Caroline ... B18
Central ... B17,18
Chestnut ... B17
Clausen ... B17,18
Commonwealth ... B18
Courtland Cir. ... B18
Crest Ln. ... B18
Crestview ... B18
Dierks Dr. ... B18
Ellington ... B17,18
Elm Ave. ... B17
Ernst Ct. ... B18
Fairelms ... B18
Forest ... B17
Franklin ... B17,18
Garden ... B18
Gilbert ... B17
Grand ... B17,18
Grove ... B17
Hampton ... B17
Harvey Ave. ... B17,18
Hillgrove ... B17
Howard ... B17,18
Johnson ... B17,18
Kirkland Ave. ... B18
Lawn Ave. ... B17,18
Lawn Cir. ... B18
Lawn Ct. ... B18
Lawn Dr. ... B18
Linden Ave. ... B17,18
Linden Cir. ... B19

Linden Ct. ... B19
Linden Ln. ... B19
Longmeadow Ln. ... B18
Maple Ln. ... B18
Maple St. ... B17
Oak Ln. ... B19
Oak St. ... B17
Ogden ... B17
Park Ln. ... B18
Park Pl. ... B17
Prospect ... B17
Race St. ... B17
Ridge Ln. ... B19
Ridgewood Dr. ... B18
Ried St. ... B17
Rose ... B18
Rugeley Rd. ... B17
Sunset Terr. ... B17
Walker ... B17
Walnut ... B17
Western ... A17
Willow St. ... B17
Wolf Rd. ... B17,18
Woodland ... B17-19
39th St. ... B17
40th St. ... B17
41st St. ... B17
42nd St. ... B17
43rd St. ... B17
45th St. ... B17
46th St. ... B17
47th St. ... B18
48th St. ... B18
49th St. ... B18
50th Pl. ... B18
50th St. ... B18
51st Pl. ... B18
51st St. ... B18
52nd St. ... B18
53rd St. ... B18
54th Pl. ... B18
54th St. ... B18
55th St. ... B18

PARKS
Laidlaw Park ... B17
Ridge Acres Park ... B17
Spring Rock Pk. ... B17

SCHOOLS
Lyons Twp. H.S. South ... B18

MISCELLANEOUS
Village Hall ... B17

COOK CO. SUBURBS
SECTION 2

LEGEND

▬▬▬ EXPRESSWAY FREE & TOLL	🛡 INTERSTATE
▬▬▬ MULTI-LANE DIVIDED	🛡 U.S.
▬▬▬ PRIMARY THROUGH ROUTE	🛡 STATE
▬▬▬ OTHER THRU ROADS	▱ PARK
▬▬▬ OTHER STREETS	▱ FOREST PRESERVE
┼┼┼┼┼ RAILROAD	▱ GOLF COURSE
⬭ RIVER OR LAKE	▨ CEMETERY
	▱ AIRPORT

TURN PAGE FOR ORIENTATION MAP

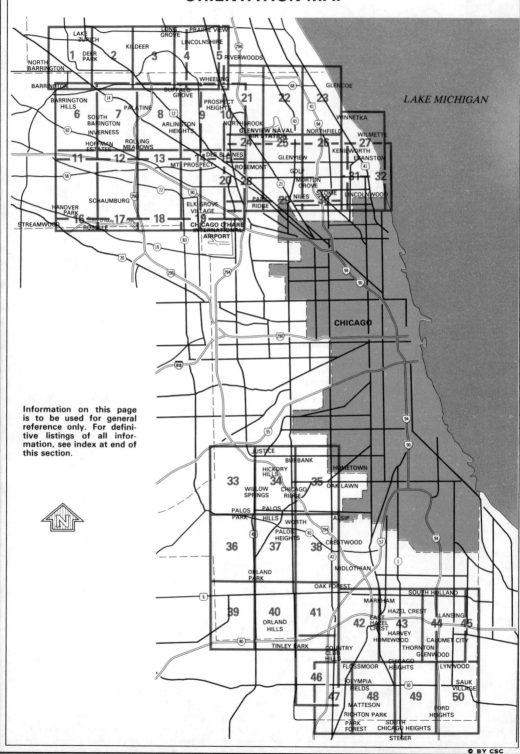

SECTION 2
ORIENTATION MAP

LAKE MICHIGAN

Information on this page is to be used for general reference only. For definitive listings of all information, see index at end of this section.

© BY CSC

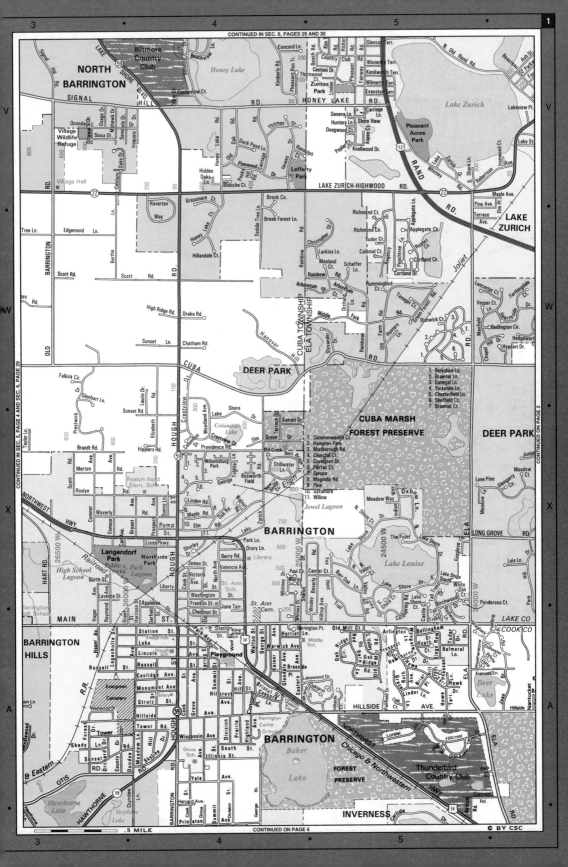

CONTINUED IN SEC. 6, PAGES 30 AND 31

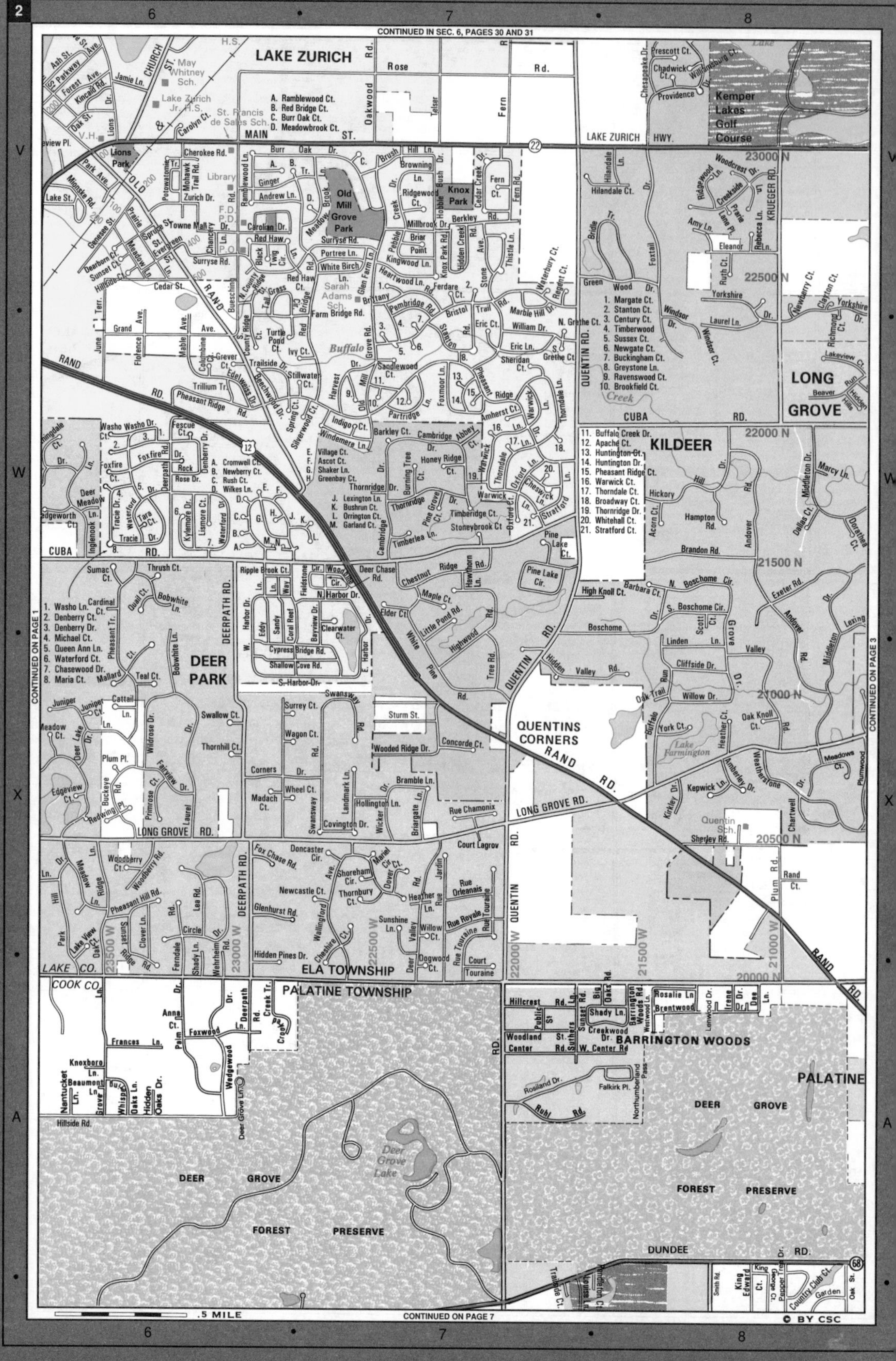

6
7
8
V
W
X
A
LAKE ZURICH
KEMPER LAKES GOLF COURSE
LONG GROVE
KILDEER
DEER PARK
QUENTINS CORNERS
ELA TOWNSHIP
PALATINE TOWNSHIP
BARRINGTON WOODS
PALATINE
LAKE CO.
COOK CO.
DEER GROVE FOREST PRESERVE
Deer Grove Lake
Old Mill Grove Park
Knox Park
Lions Park
Buffalo Creek
Lake Farmington
May Whitney Sch.
Lake Zurich Jr. H.S.
St. Francis de Sales Sch.
Sarah Adams Sch.
Quentin Sch.
Library
MAIN ST.
LAKE ZURICH HWY.
RAND RD.
OLD RAND
QUENTIN RD.
CUBA RD.
LONG GROVE RD.
DEERPATH RD.
DUNDEE RD.
Rose
Fern Rd.
Telser
Oakwood Rd.
23000 N
22500 N
22000 N
21500 N
21000 N
20500 N
20000 N
23500 W
23000 W
22500 W
22000 W
21500 W
21000 W
A. Ramblewood Ct.
B. Red Bridge Ct.
C. Burr Oak Ct.
D. Meadowbrook Ct.
1. Margate Ct.
2. Stanton Ct.
3. Century Ct.
4. Timberwood
5. Sussex Ct.
6. Newgate Ct.
7. Buckingham Ct.
8. Greystone Ln.
9. Ravenswood Ct.
10. Brookfield Ct.
11. Buffalo Creek Dr.
12. Apache Ct.
13. Huntington Ct.
14. Huntington Dr.
15. Pheasant Ridge Ct.
16. Warwick Ct.
17. Thorndale Ct.
18. Broadway Ct.
19. Thornridge Dr.
20. Whitehall Ct.
21. Stratford Ct.
A. Cromwell Ct.
B. Newberry Ct.
C. Rush Ct.
D. Wilkes Ln.
E. Village Ct.
F. Ascot Ct.
G. Shaker Ln.
H. Greenbay Ct.
J. Lexington Ln.
K. Bushrun Ct.
L. Orrington Ct.
M. Garland Ct.
1. Washo Ln.
2. Denberry Ct.
3. Denberry Dr.
4. Michael Ct.
5. Queen Ann Ln.
6. Waterford Ct.
7. Chasewood Dr.
8. Maria Ct.
.5 MILE
© BY CSC

CONTINUED ON PAGE 1

CONTINUED ON PAGE 3

CONTINUED ON PAGE 7

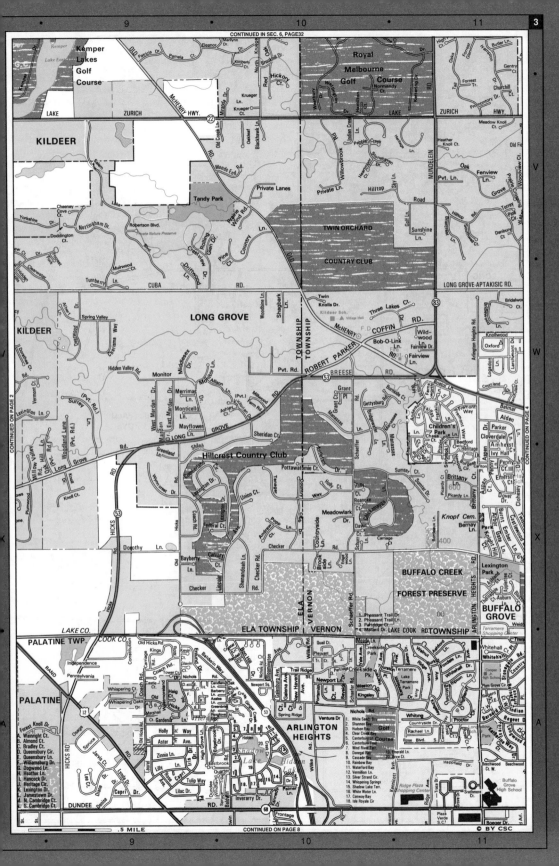

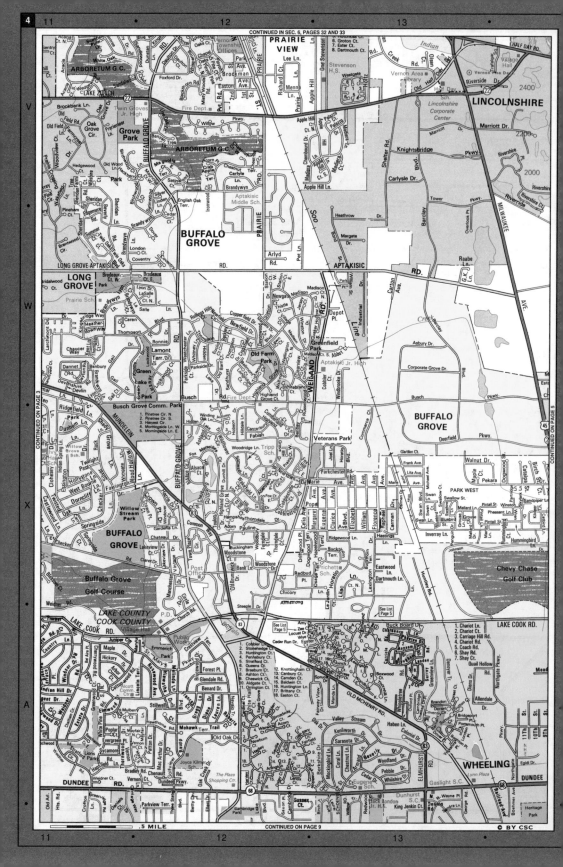

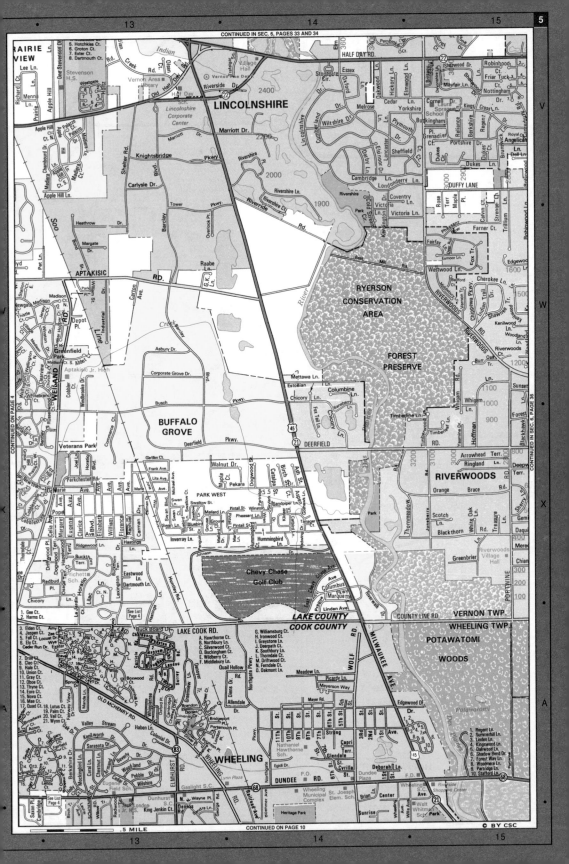

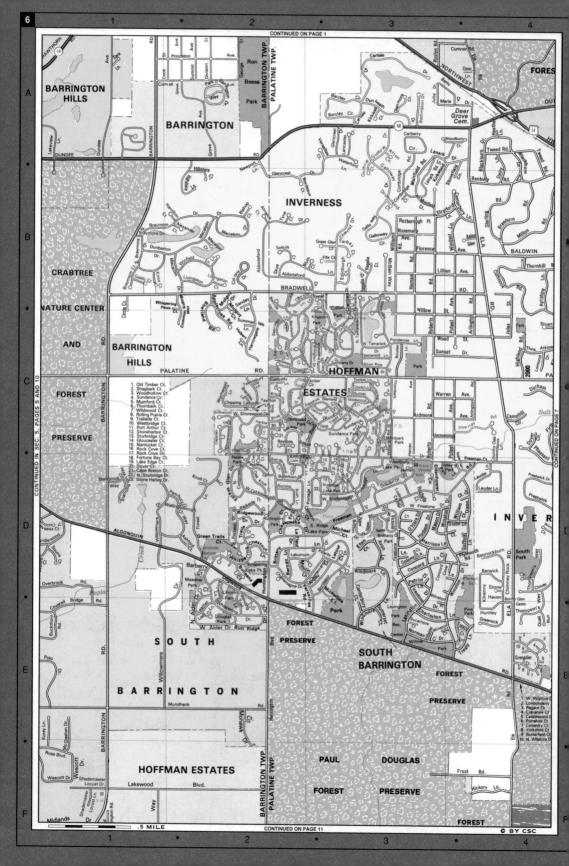

CONTINUED ON PAGE 2

CONTINUED ON PAGE 6

CONTINUED ON PAGE 8

CONTINUED ON PAGE 12

CONTINUED ON PAGE 3

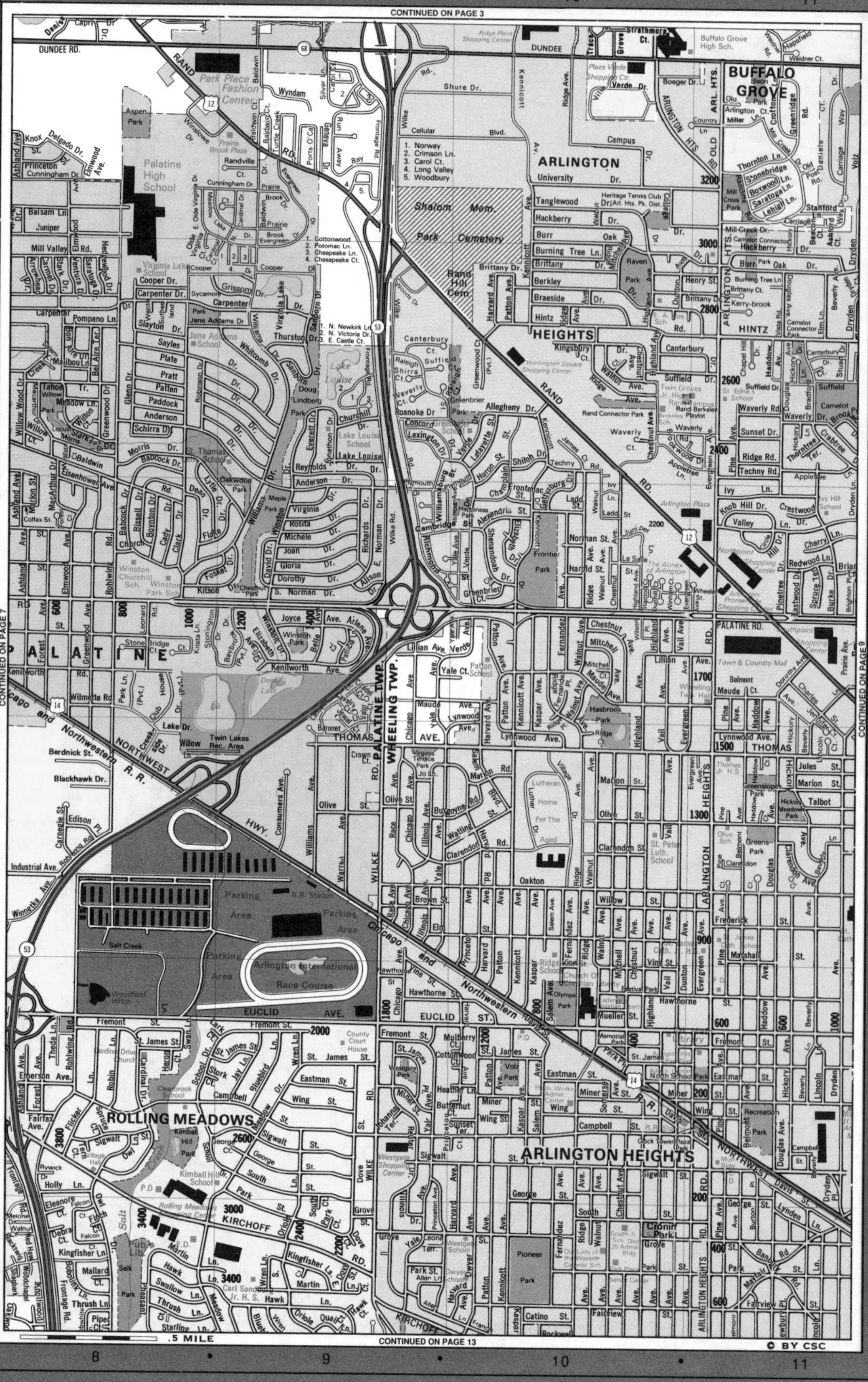

CONTINUED ON PAGE 7

CONTINUED ON PAGE 9

CONTINUED ON PAGE 13

BUFFALO GROVE

ARLINGTON HEIGHTS

PALATINE

ROLLING MEADOWS

WHEELING TWP.

PALATINE TWP.

THOMAS

HINTZ

Palatine High School

Virginia Lake School

Park Place Fashion Center

Aspen Park

Shalom Mem. Park

Rand Hill Cem.

Lake Louise

Arlington International Race Course

Woodfield Hilton

Twin Lakes Rec. Area

Arlington Plaza

Town & Country Mall

1. Norway
2. Crimson Ln.
3. Carol Ct.
4. Long Valley
5. Woodbury

1. Cottonwood
2. Potomac Ln.
3. Chesapeake Ln.
4. Chesapeake Ct.

1. N. Newkirk Ln.
2. N. Victoria Dr.
3. E. Castle Ct.

DUNDEE RD.

RAND RD.

PALATINE RD.

EUCLID AVE.

KIRCHOFF RD.

NORTHWEST HWY.

Chicago and Northwestern R.R.

.5 MILE

© BY CSC

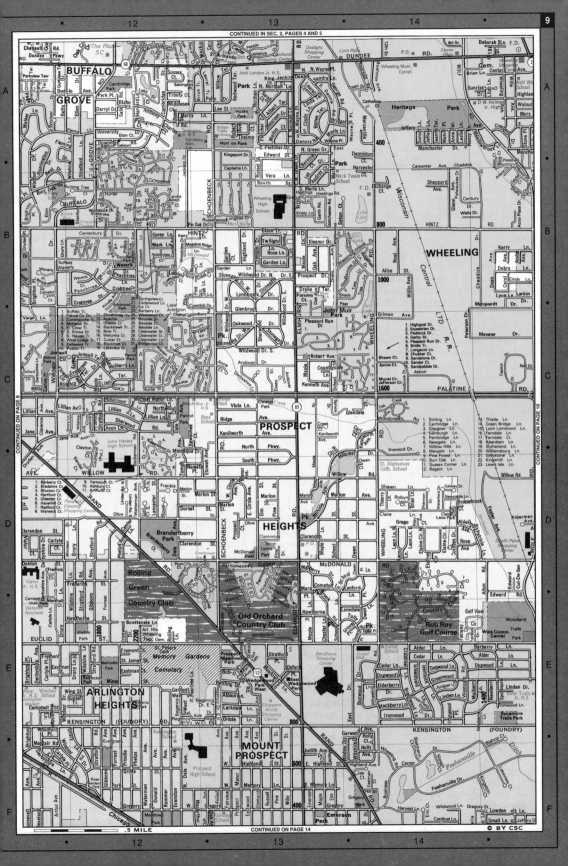

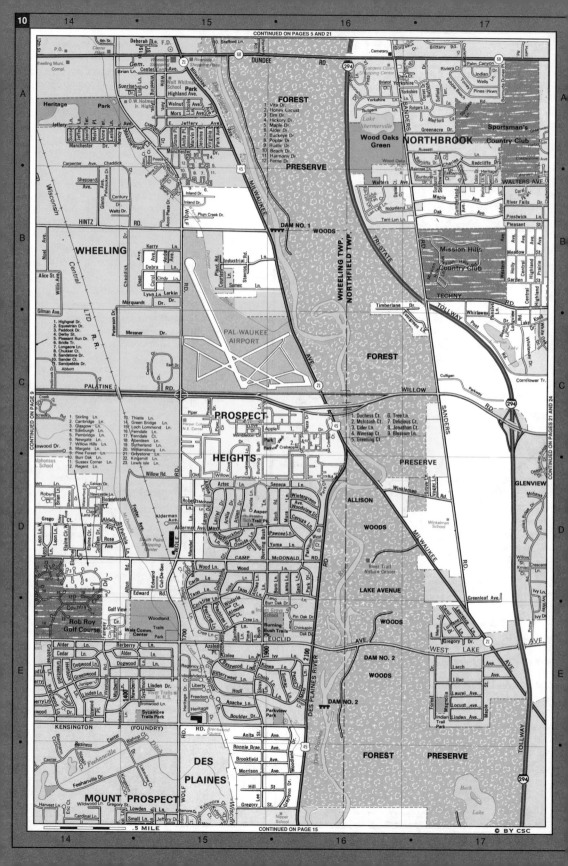

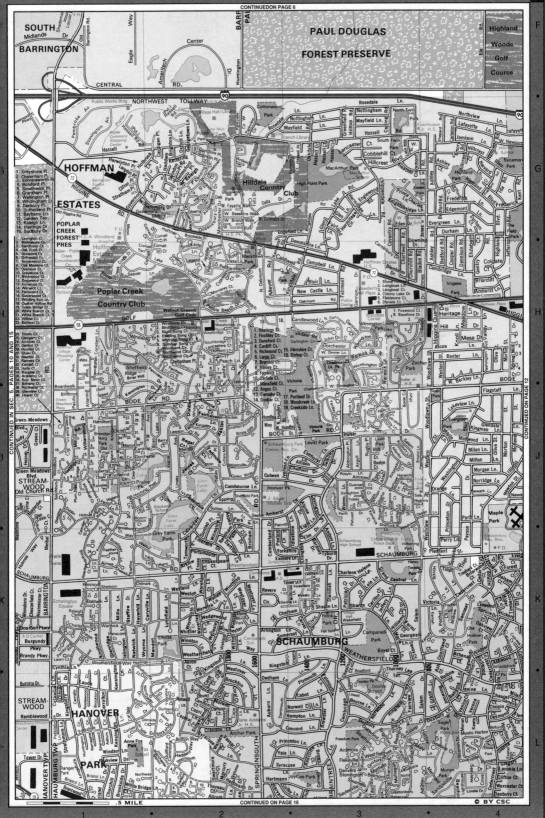

CONTINUED ON PAGE 6

CONTINUED ON PAGE 16

CONTINUED ON PAGE 12

CONTINUED IN SEC. 5 PAGES 10 AND 15

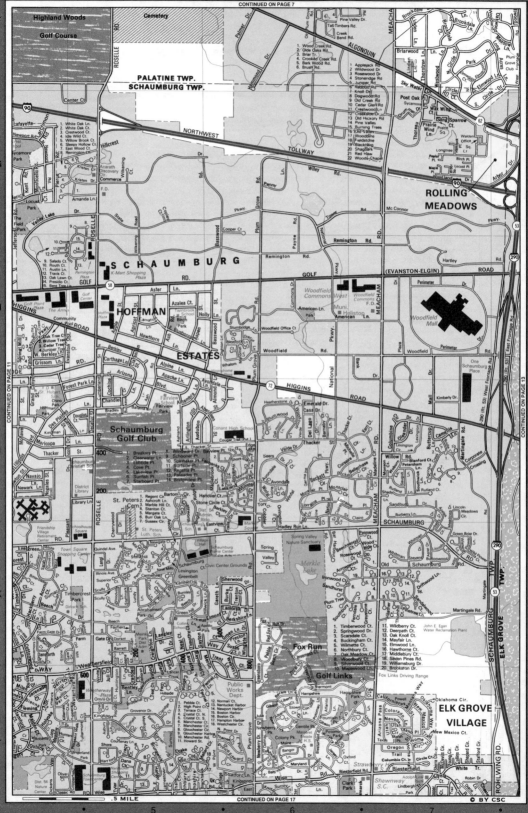

CONTINUED ON PAGE 7

CONTINUED ON PAGE 11

CONTINUED ON PAGE 13

.5 MILE

© BY CSC

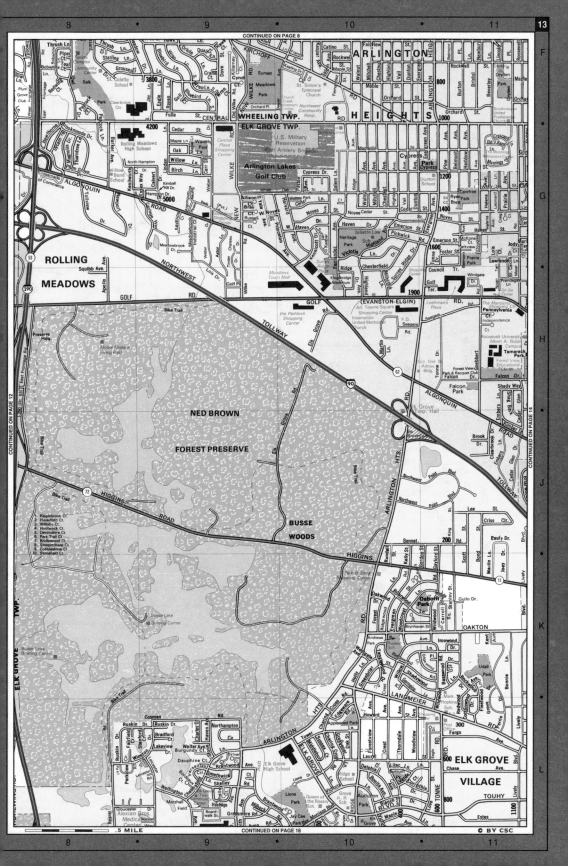

CONTINUED ON PAGE 8

13

CONTINUED ON PAGE 12

CONTINUED ON PAGE 14

CONTINUED ON PAGE 18

ARLINGTON

HEIGHTS

WHEELING TWP.

ELK GROVE TWP.

U.S. Military
Reservation
145th Artillery Brigade

Arlington Lakes
Golf Club

ROLLING

MEADOWS

NED BROWN

FOREST PRESERVE

BUSSE
WOODS

ELK GROVE TWP.

ELK GROVE

VILLAGE

TOUHY

© BY CSC

.5 MILE

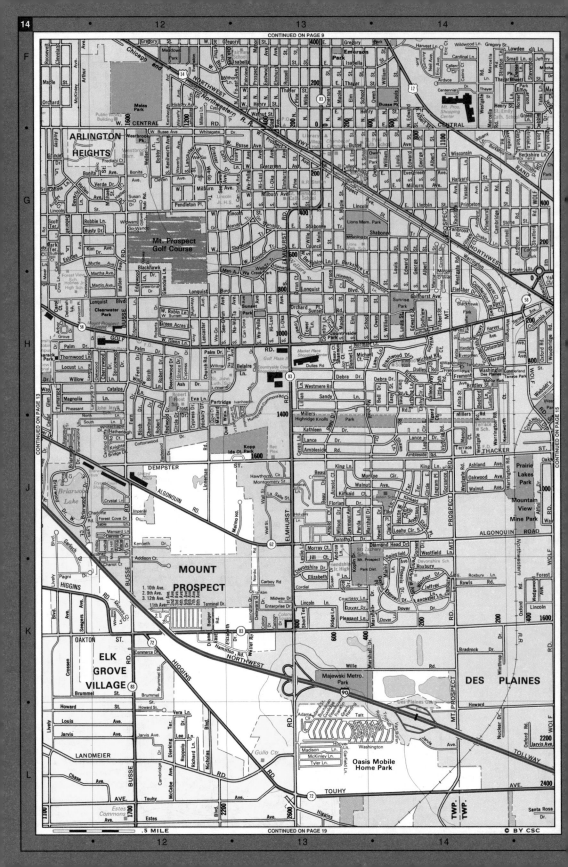

CONTINUED ON PAGE 9

CONTINUED ON PAGE 13

CONTINUED ON PAGE 15

ARLINGTON HEIGHTS

Mt. Prospect Golf Course

MOUNT PROSPECT

ELK GROVE VILLAGE

DES PLAINES

Oasis Mobile Home Park

CONTINUED ON PAGE 19

.5 MILE

© BY CSC

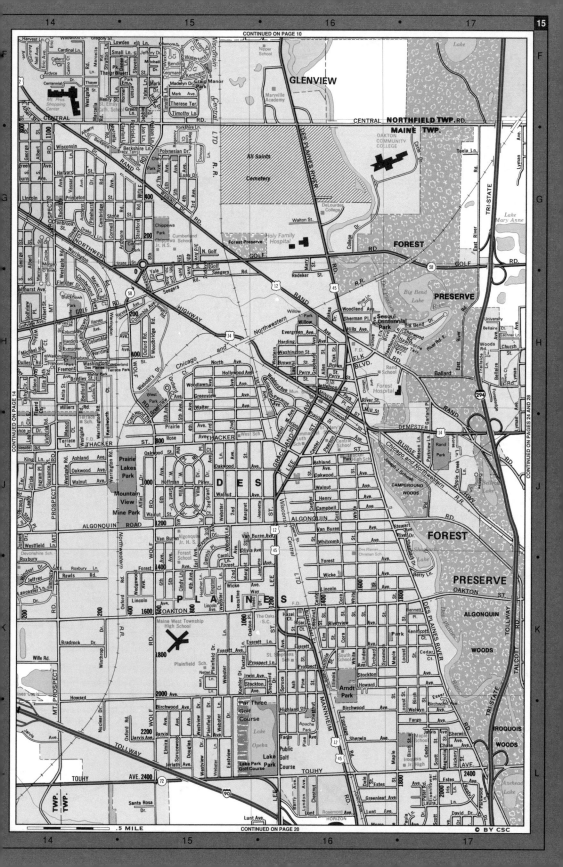

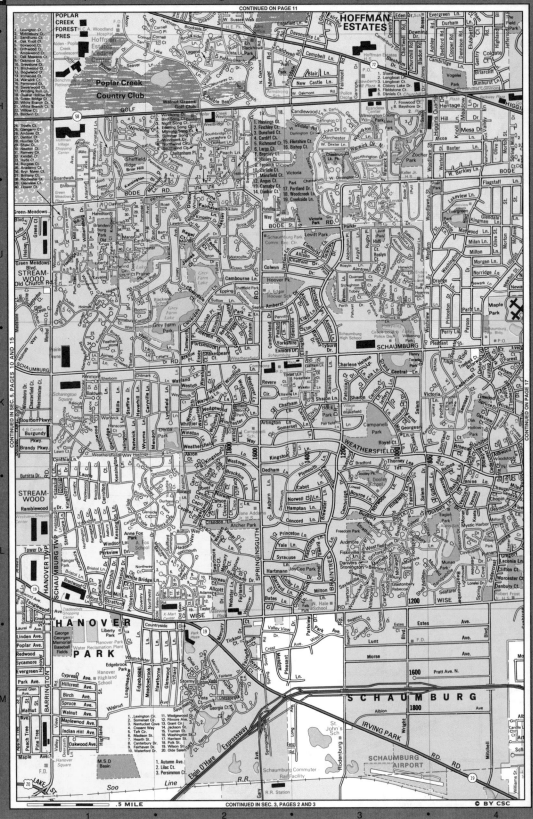

CONTINUED ON PAGE 11
CONTINUED ON PAGE 17
CONTINUED IN SEC. 5, PAGES 10 AND 15
CONTINUED IN SEC. 3, PAGES 2 AND 3

.5 MILE

© BY CSC

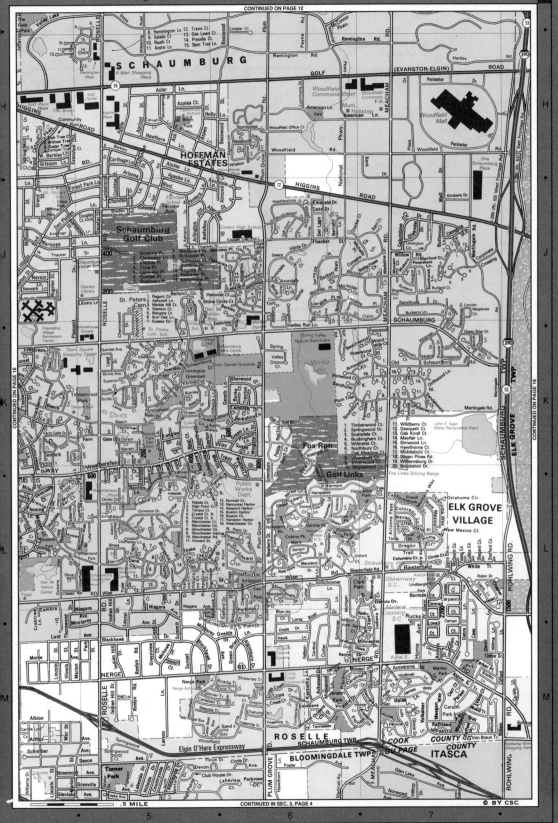

CONTINUED ON PAGE 16

CONTINUED ON PAGE 18

SCHAUMBURG

HOFFMAN ESTATES

ELK GROVE VILLAGE

NERGE

ROSELLE

SCHAUMBURG TWP.

BLOOMINGDALE TWP.

COOK DU PAGE

COUNTY ITASCA

CONTINUED ON PAGE 13

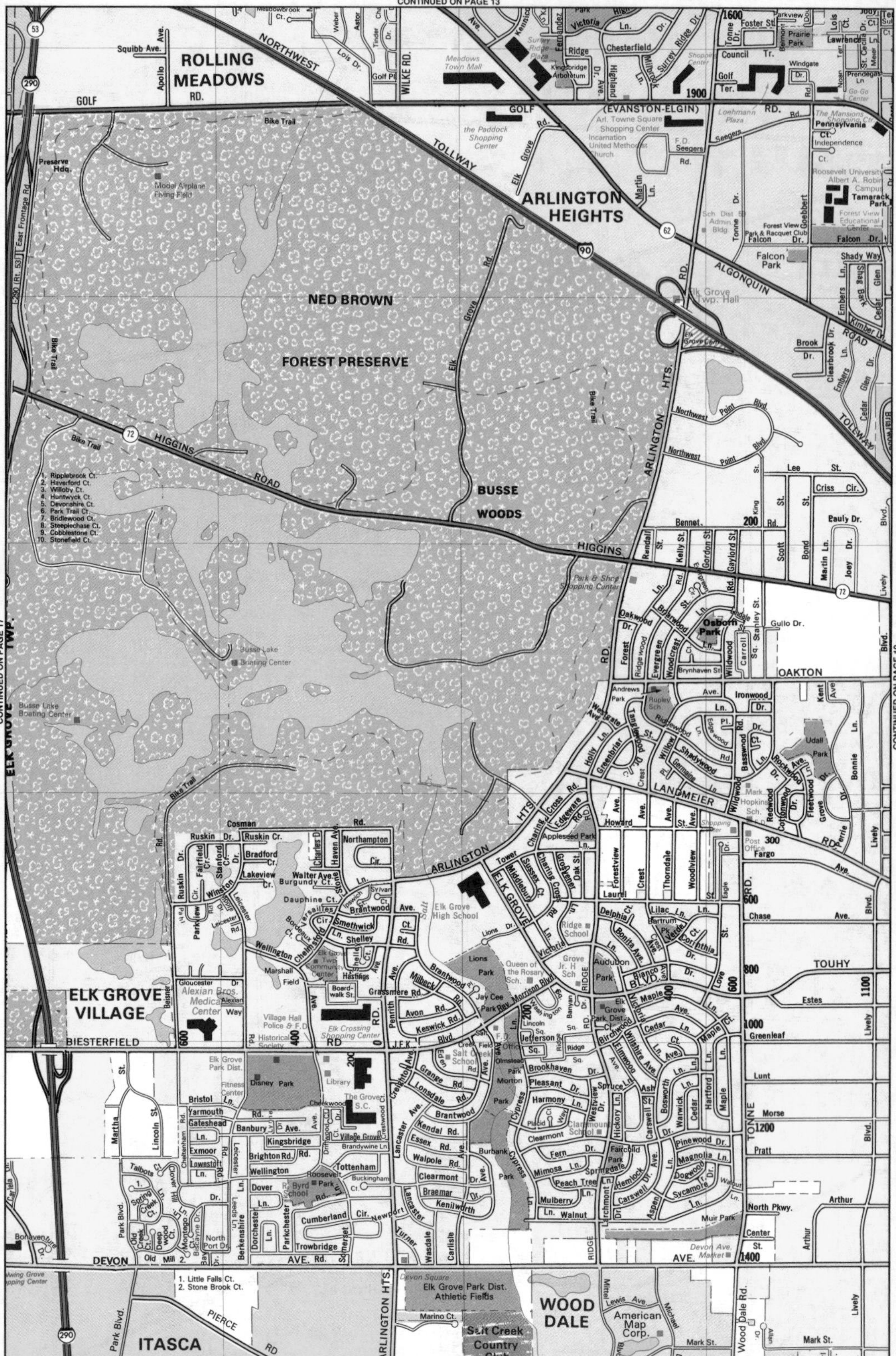
8
9
10
11
H
J
K
L
M
ROLLING MEADOWS
ARLINGTON HEIGHTS
NED BROWN
FOREST PRESERVE
BUSSE WOODS
ELK GROVE VILLAGE
ELK GROVE TWP.
WOOD DALE
ITASCA
NORTHWEST
TOLLWAY
GOLF RD.
(EVANSTON-ELGIN)
HIGGINS ROAD
ALGONQUIN ROAD
ARLINGTON HTS. RD.
LANDMEIER RD.
OAKTON
TOUHY
BIESTERFIELD RD
DEVON AVE.
PIERCE RD
TONNE
ELK GROVE BLVD.
1. Ripplebrook Ct.
2. Haverford Ct.
3. Willoby Ct.
4. Huntwyck Ct.
5. Devonshire Ct.
6. Park Trail Ct.
7. Bridlewood Ct.
8. Steeplechase Ct.
9. Cobblestone Ct.
10. Stonefield Ct.
1. Little Falls Ct.
2. Stone Brook Ct.
Preserve Hdq.
Model Airplane Flying Field
Busse Lake Boating Center
Elk Grove High School
Alexian Bros. Medical Center
Elk Grove Twp. Hall
Salt Creek Country Club
Elk Grove Park Dist. Athletic Fields
American Map Corp.
Meadows Town Mall
the Paddock Shopping Center
Arl. Towne Square Shopping Center
Park & Shop Shopping Center
Elk Crossing Shopping Center
Devon Square
.5 MILE

CONTINUED ON PAGE 17
CONTINUED ON PAGE 19
CONTINUED IN SEC. 3, PAGE 5

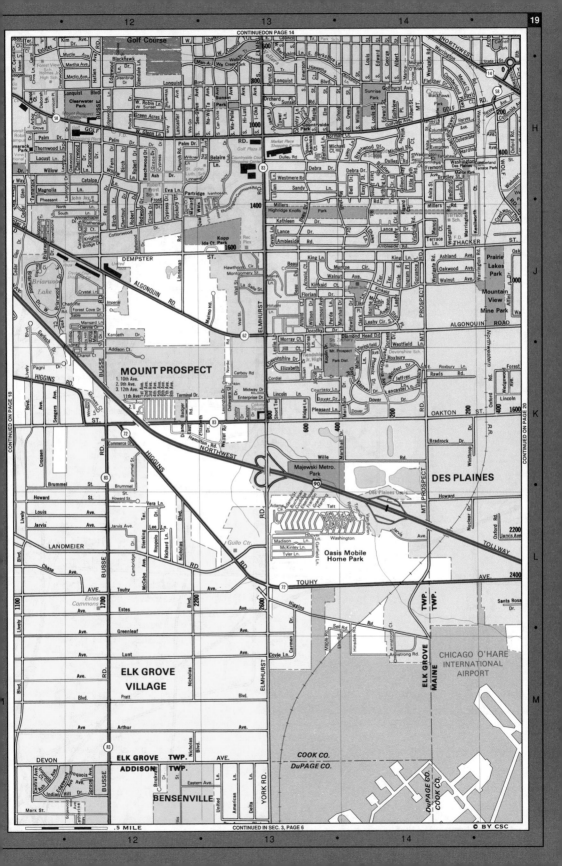

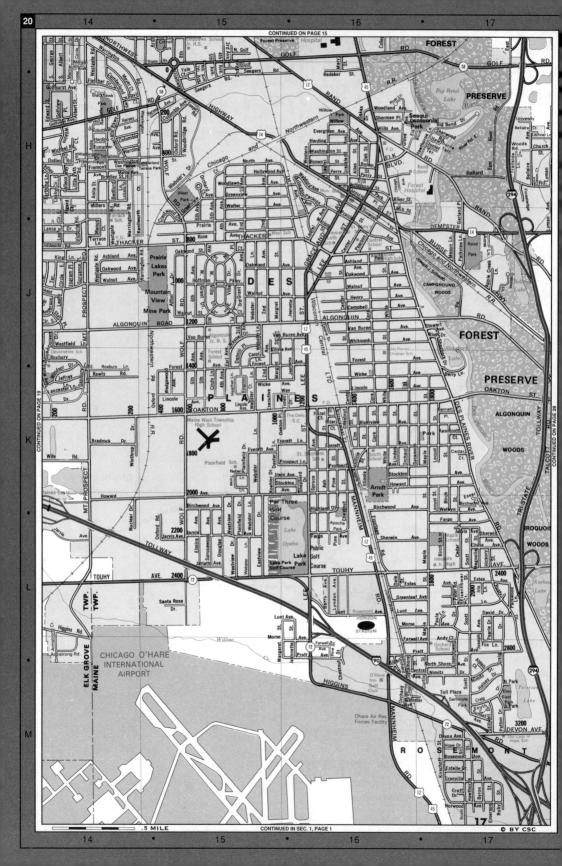

CONTINUED ON PAGE 15
CONTINUED ON PAGE 19
CONTINUED ON PAGE 28
© BY CSC

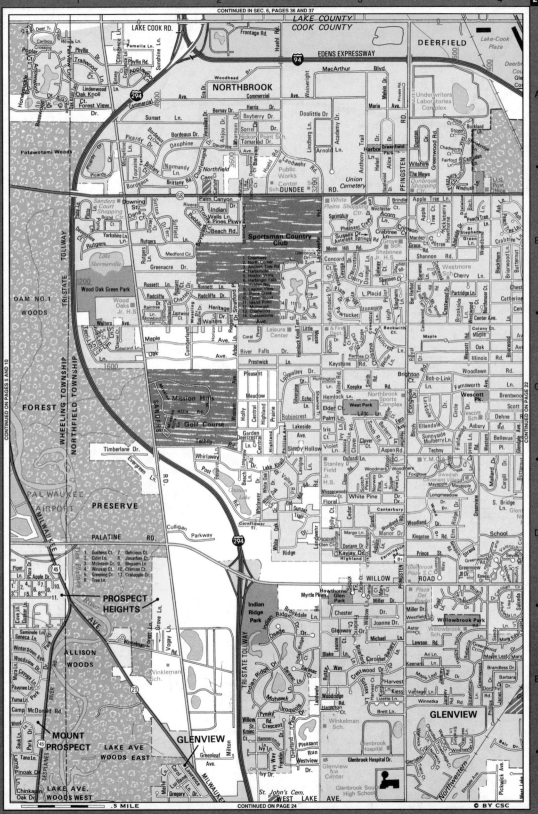

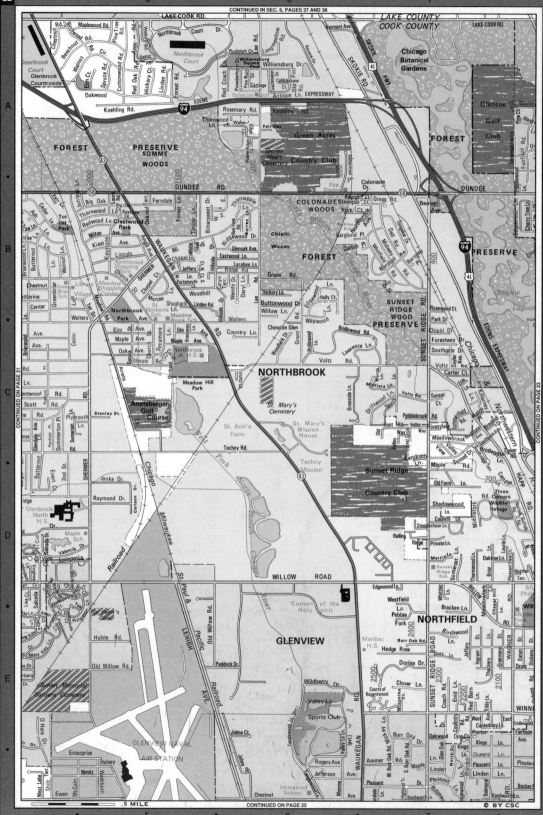

CONTINUED IN SEC. 6, PAGES 37 AND 38

LAKE-COOK RD.

LAKE COUNTY
COOK COUNTY

LAKE-COOK RD.

Chicago
Botanical
Gardens

FOREST

Glencoe
Golf
Club

FOREST

PRESERVE
SOMME
WOODS

PRESERVE

DUNDEE RD.

DUNDEE

COLONADE
WOODS

FOREST

SUNSET
RIDGE
WOOD
PRESERVE

NORTHBROOK

St. Mary's
Cemetery

St. Ann's
Farm

St. Mary's
Mission
House

Techny
Mission

Anetsberger
Golf
Course

Meadow Hill
Park

Sunset Ridge
Country Club

Glenbrook
North
H.S.

WILLOW ROAD

Three
Corners
Wildlife
Refuge

NORTHFIELD

GLENVIEW

Convent of
Holy Spirit

Marillac
H.S.

Sunset Memorial
Gardens Cemetery

GLENVIEW NAVAL
AIR STATION

Immanuel
School

CONTINUED ON PAGE 21

CONTINUED ON PAGE 23

.5 MILE

© BY CSC

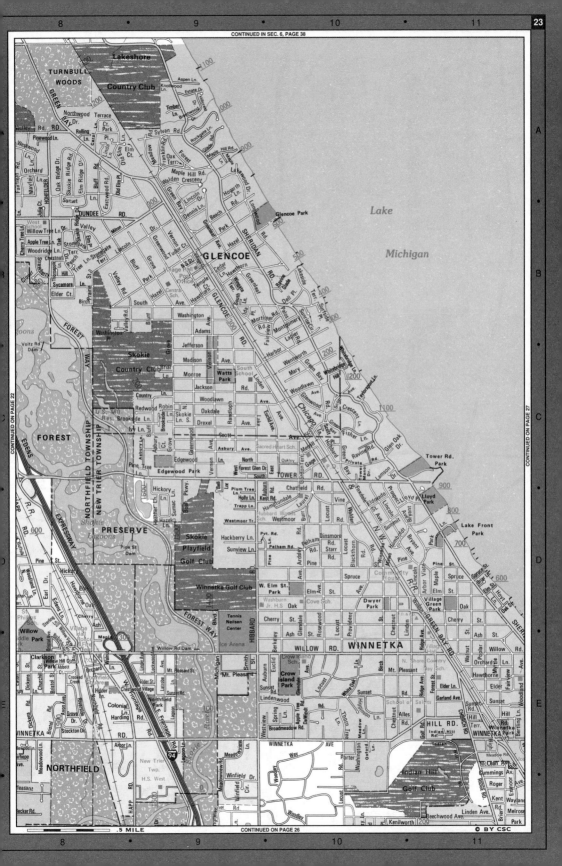

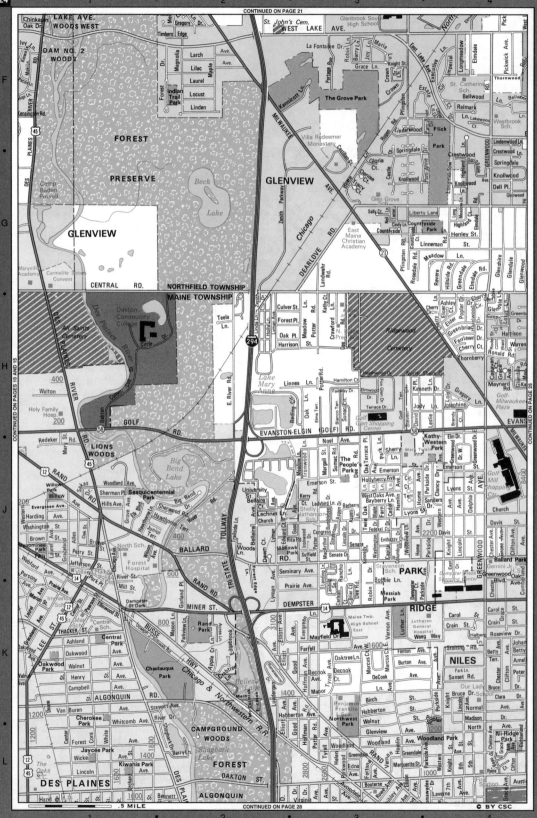

CONTINUED ON PAGE 21

CONTINUED ON PAGES 10 AND 15

CONTINUED ON PAGE 25

CONTINUED ON PAGE 28

.5 MILE

© BY CSC

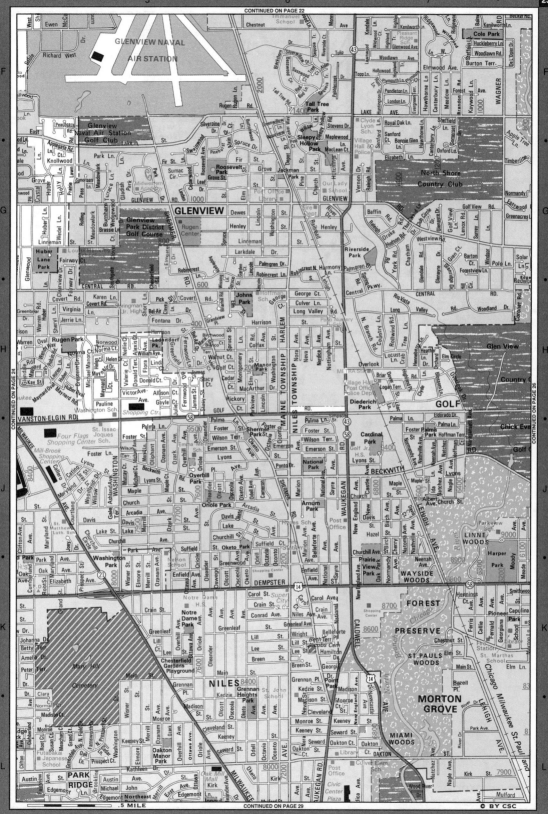

CONTINUED ON PAGE 22

CONTINUED ON PAGE 24

CONTINUED ON PAGE 26

CONTINUED ON PAGE 29

.5 MILE

© BY CSC

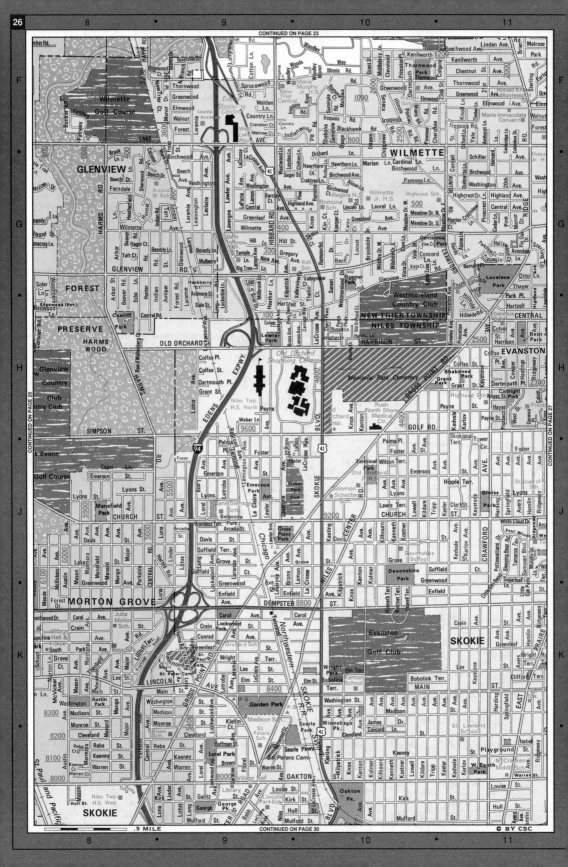

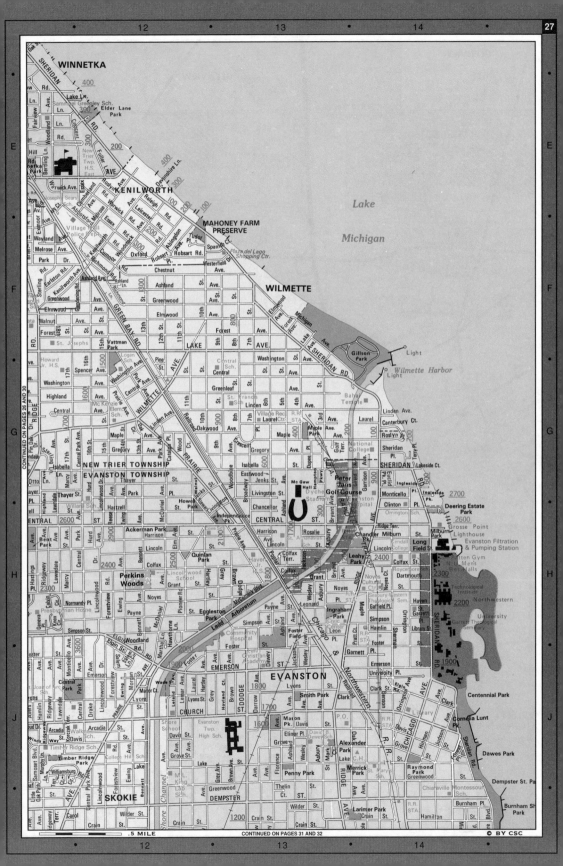

CONTINUED ON PAGE 24

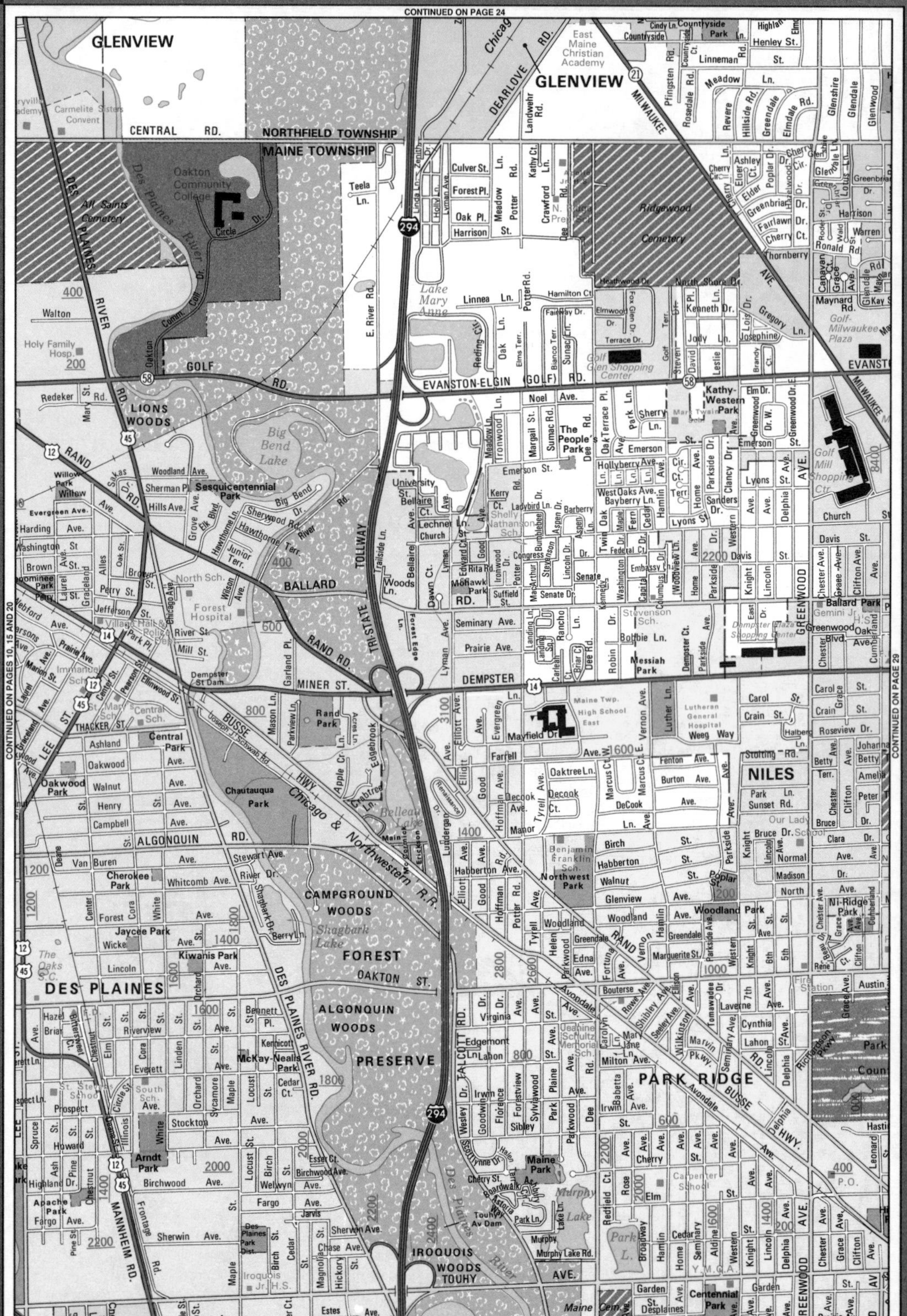

GLENVIEW

GLENVIEW

CENTRAL RD.

NORTHFIELD TOWNSHIP

MAINE TOWNSHIP

Oakton Community College

Ridgewood Cemetery

EVANSTON-ELGIN

GOLF RD.

Golf Mill Shopping Ctr.

DES PLAINES

NILES

PARK RIDGE

FOREST

ALGONQUIN WOODS PRESERVE

CAMPGROUND WOODS

IROQUOIS WOODS TOUHY

ROSEMONT

.5 MILE

© BY CSC

CONTINUED ON PAGES 10, 15 AND 20

CONTINUED ON PAGE 29

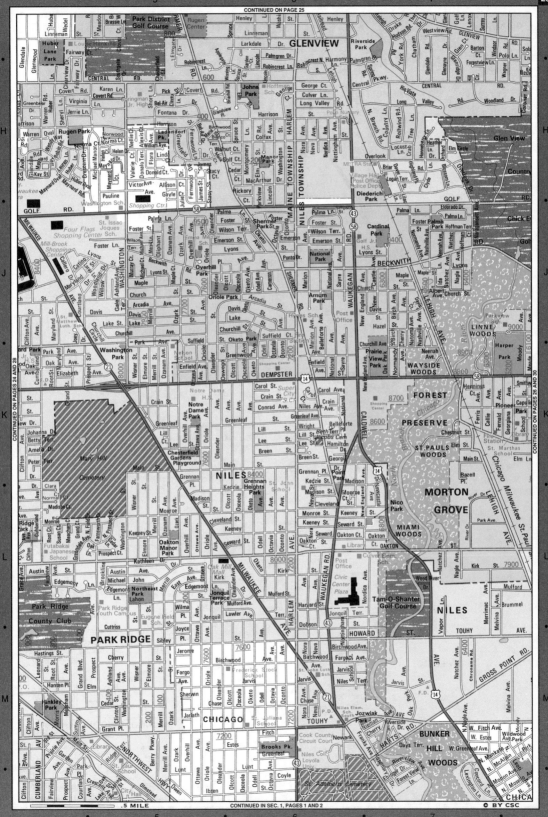

CONTINUED ON PAGE 25

CONTINUED ON PAGES 24 AND 28

CONTINUED ON PAGES 26 AND 30

CONTINUED IN SEC. 1, PAGES 1 AND 2

GLENVIEW

NILES TOWNSHIP

MAINE TOWNSHIP

BECKWITH

DEMPSTER

NILES

FOREST PRESERVE

MORTON GROVE

PARK RIDGE

CHICAGO

NILES

BUNKER HILL WOODS

.5 MILE

© BY CSC

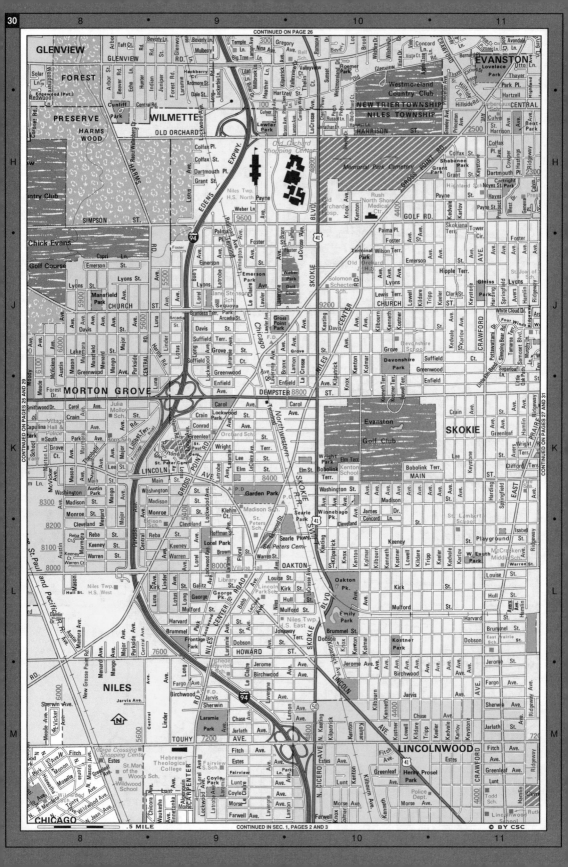

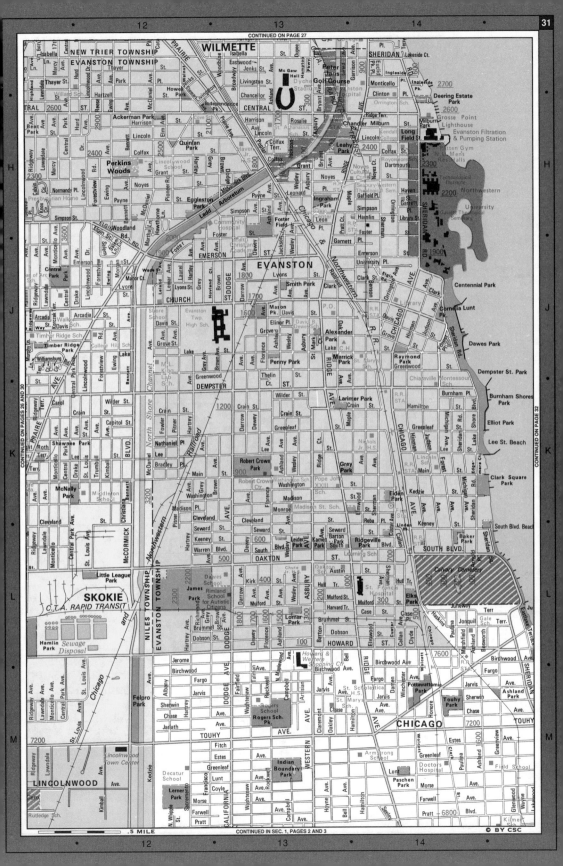

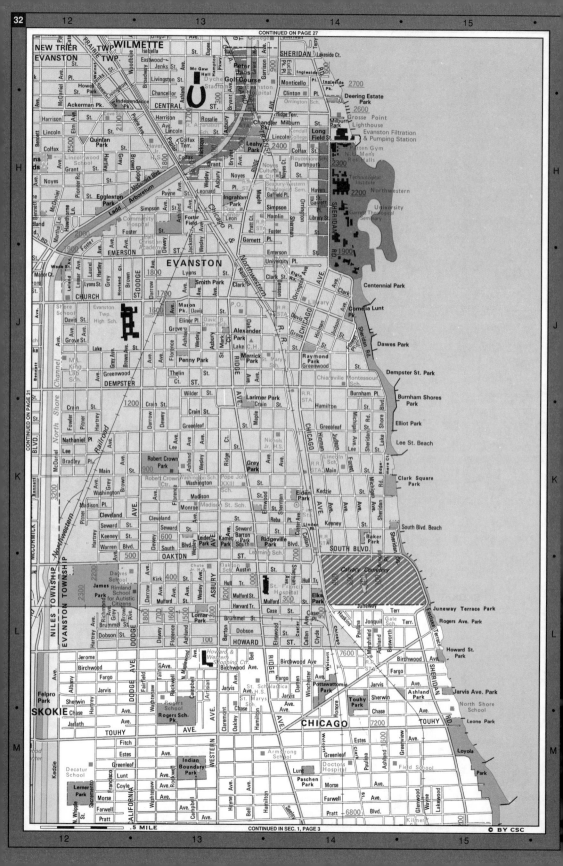

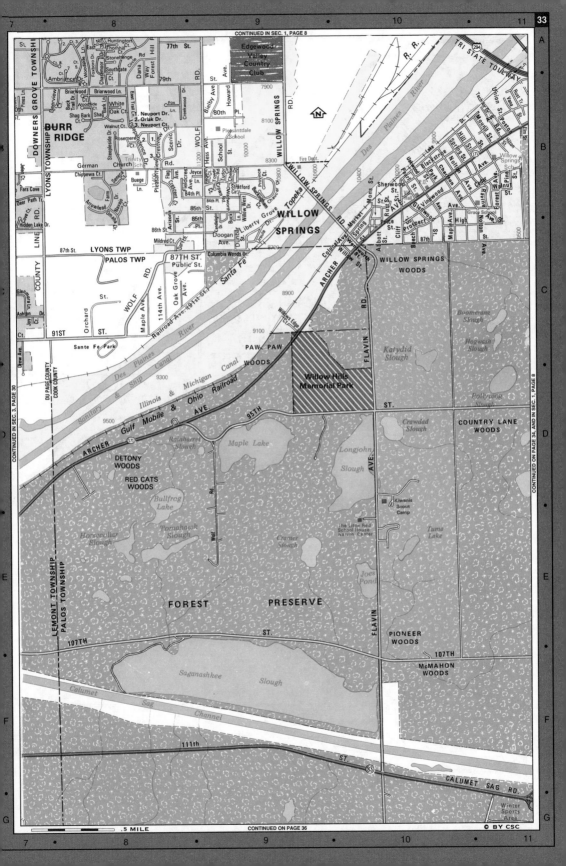

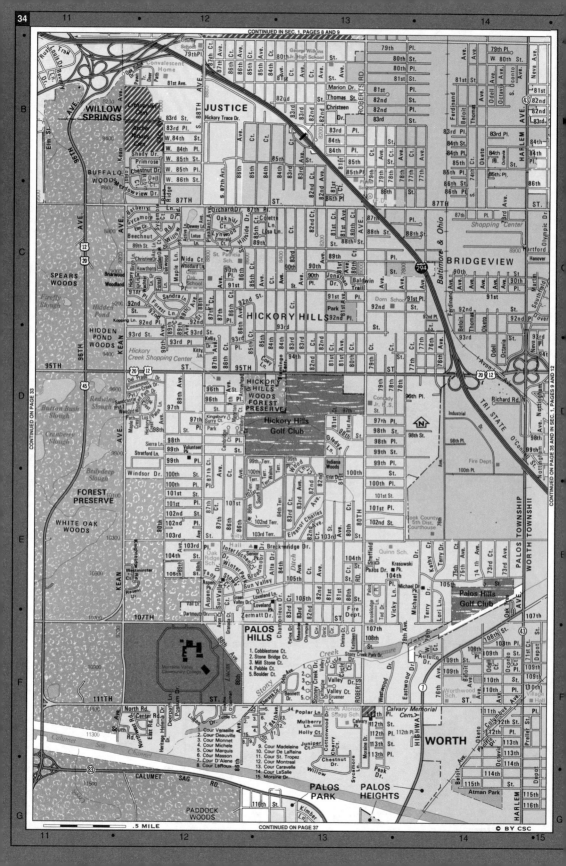

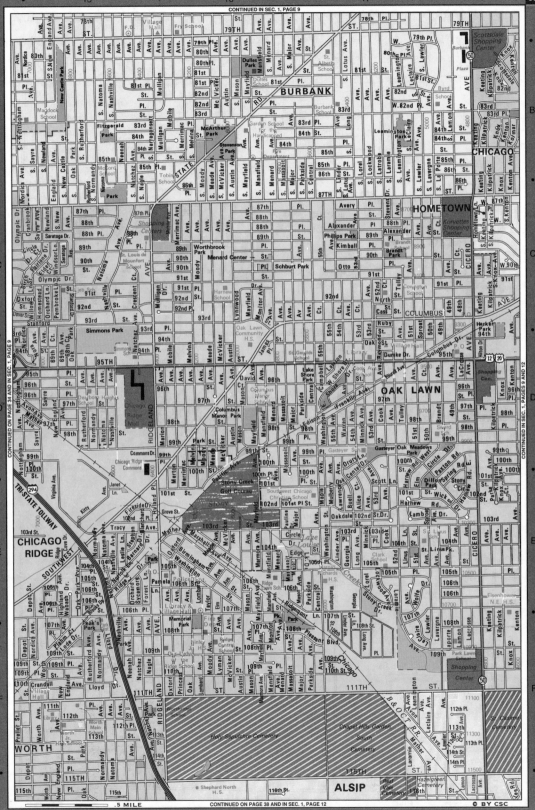

BURBANK

CHICAGO

HOMETOWN

COLUMBUS

OAK LAWN

CHICAGO RIDGE

WORTH

ALSIP

CONTINUED ON PAGE 34 AND IN SEC. 1, PAGE 9

CONTINUED IN SEC. 1, PAGES 9 AND 12

.5 MILE

© BY CSC

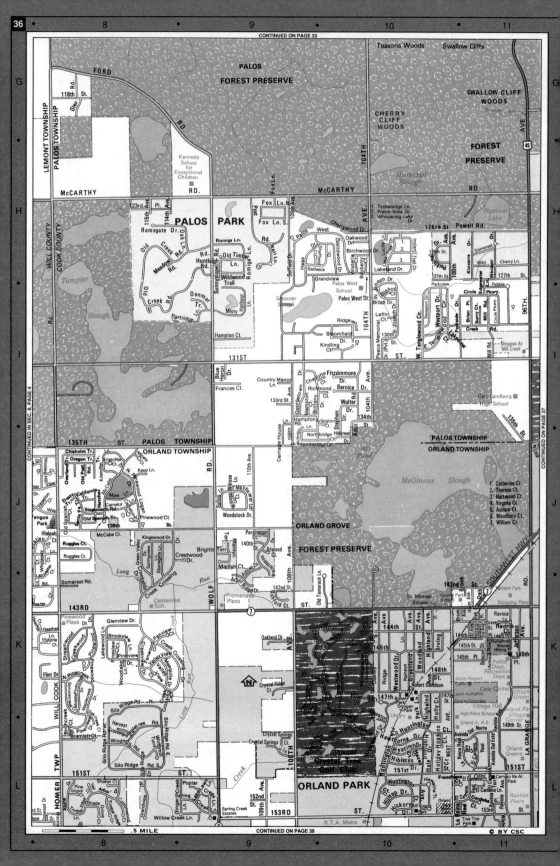

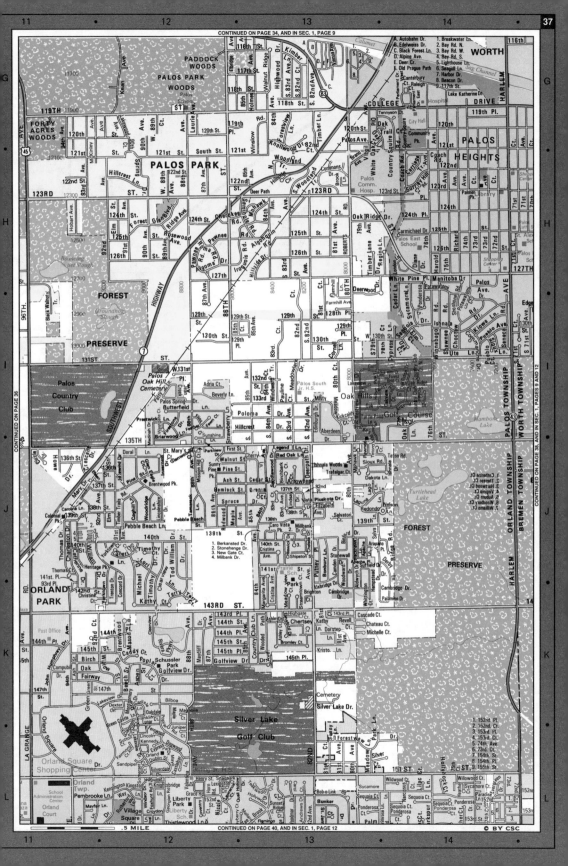

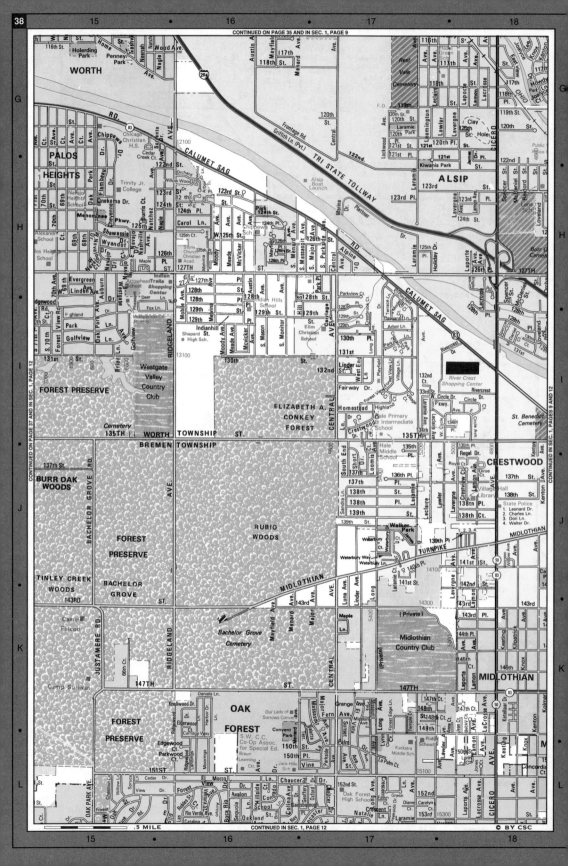

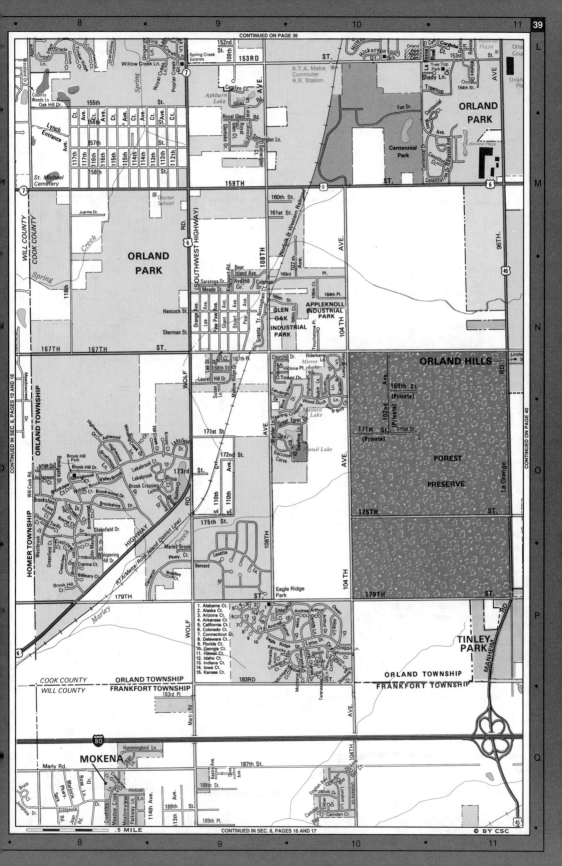

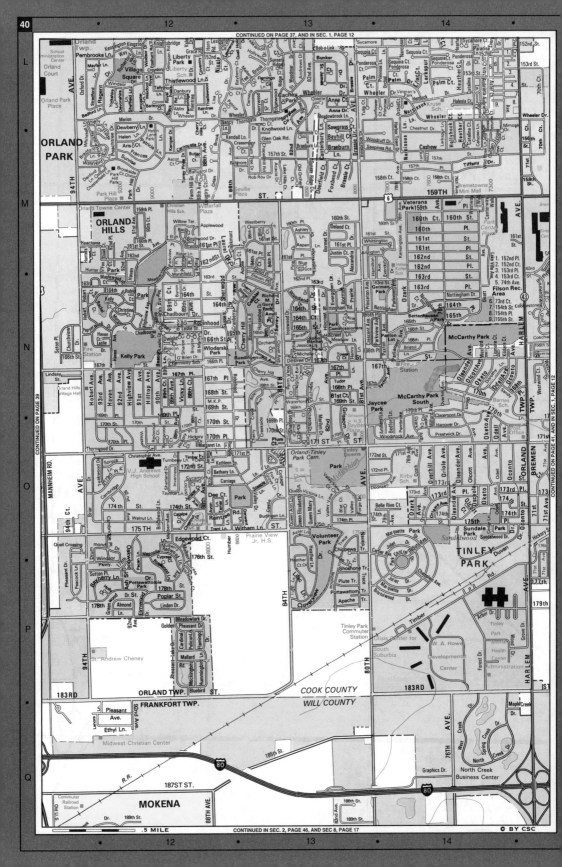

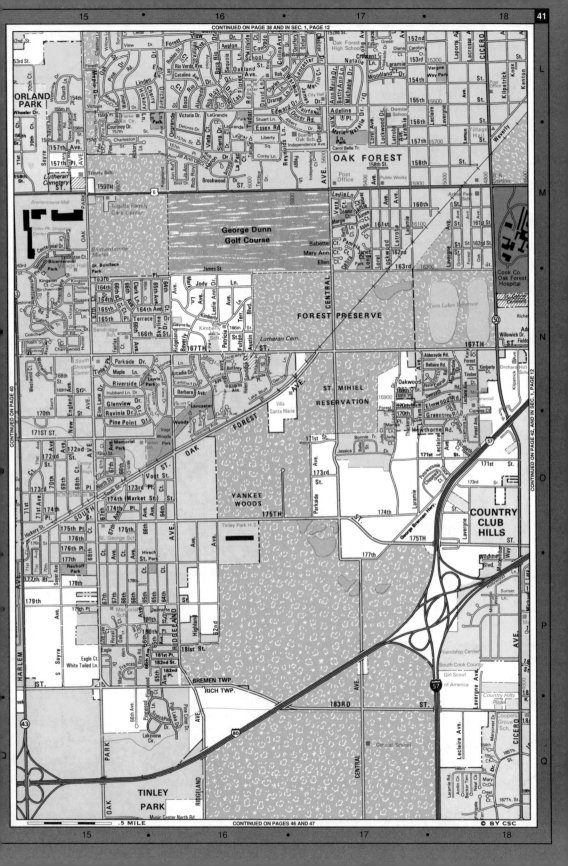

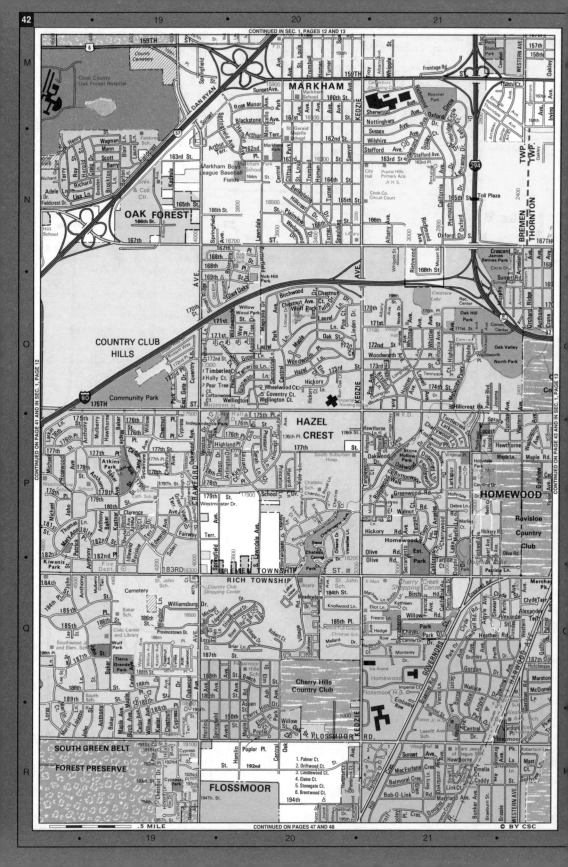

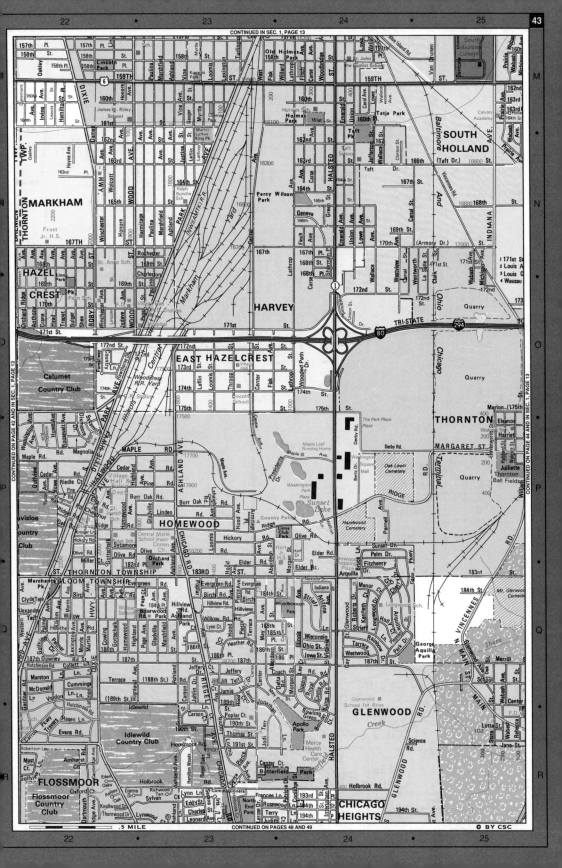

MARKHAM

SOUTH HOLLAND

HAZEL CREST

HARVEY

EAST HAZELCREST

THORNTON

HOMEWOOD

Calumet Country Club

THORNTON TOWNSHIP

BLOOM TOWNSHIP

GLENWOOD

FLOSSMOOR

Flossmoor Country Club

CHICAGO HEIGHTS

Idlewild Country Club

CONTINUED ON PAGE 42 AND IN SEC. 1, PAGE 13

CONTINUED ON PAGE 44 AND IN SEC. 1, PAGE 13

.5 MILE

© BY CSC

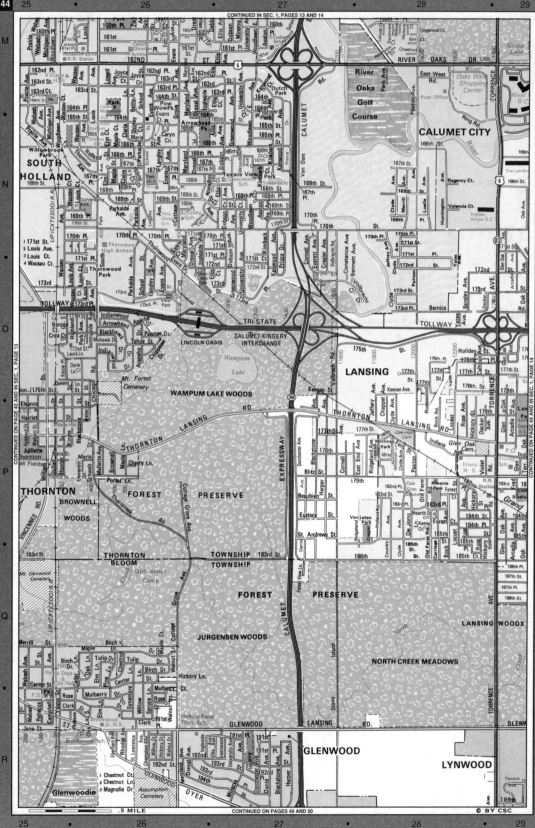

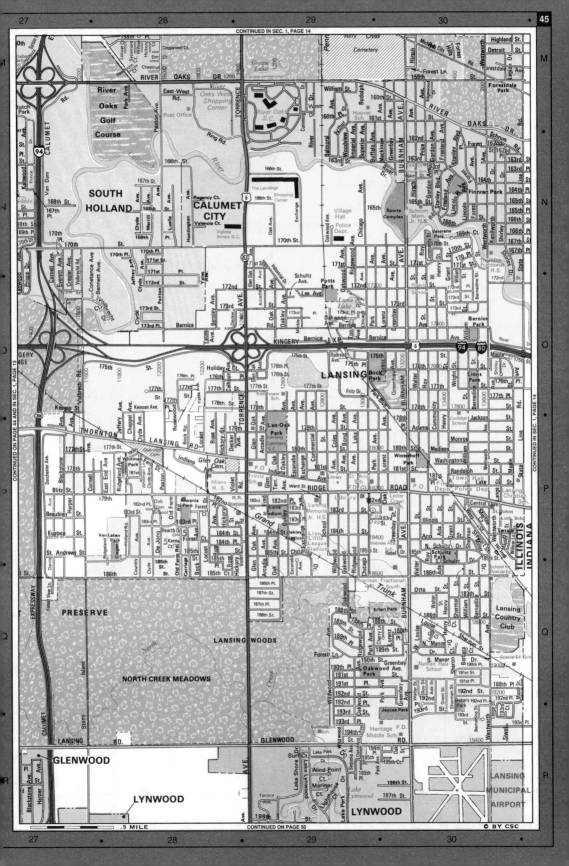

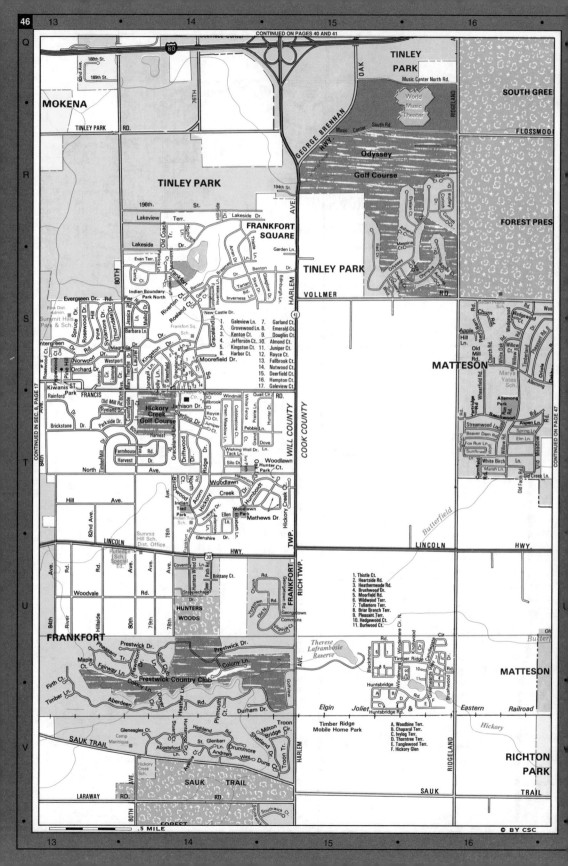

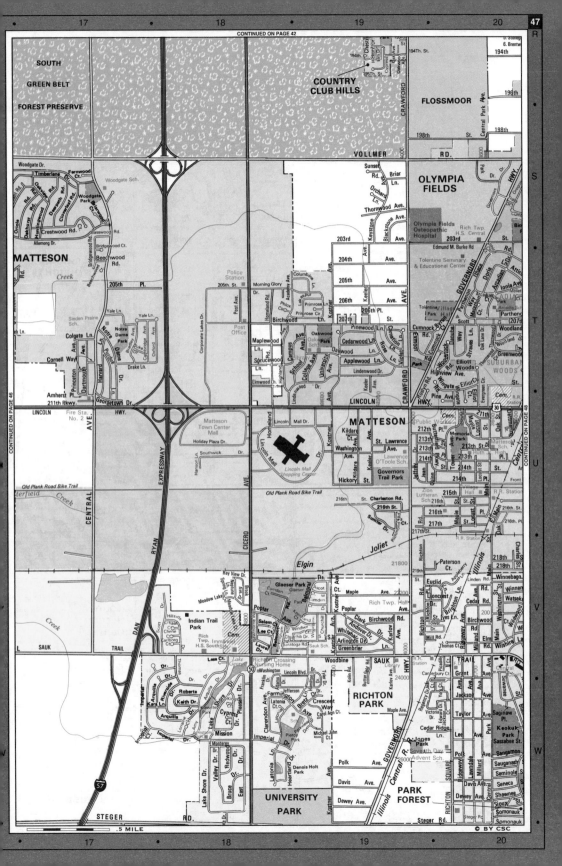

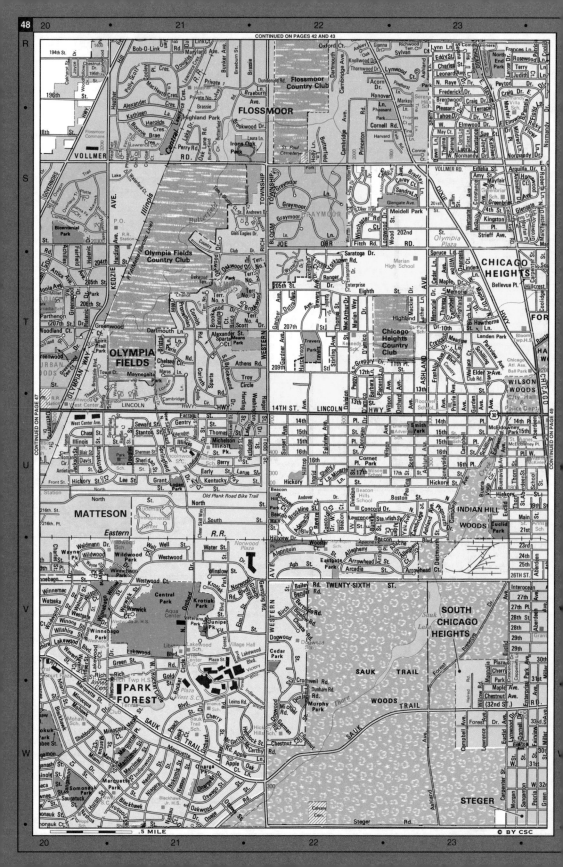

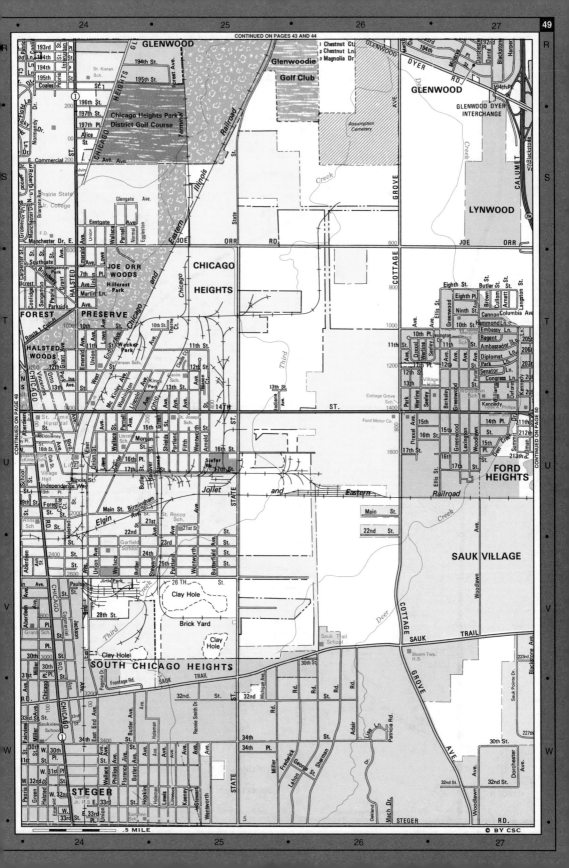

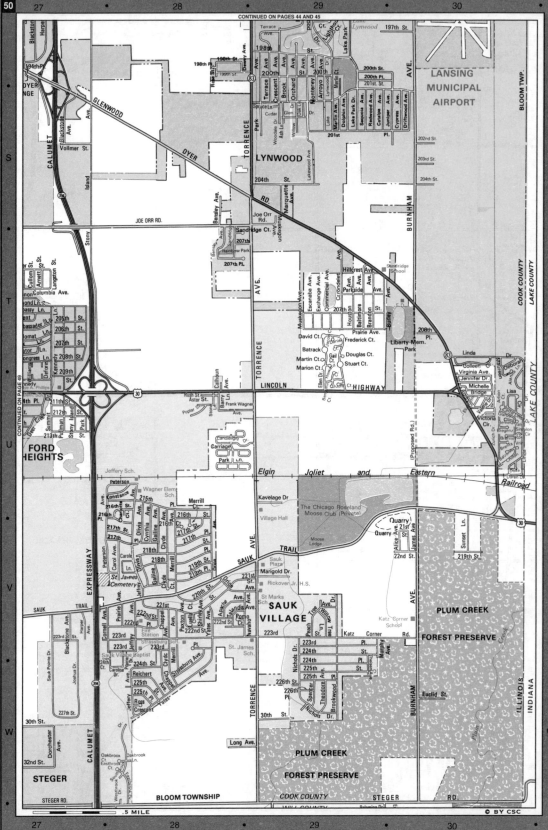

CONTINUED ON PAGES 44 AND 45

LANSING
MUNICIPAL
AIRPORT

LYNWOOD

FORD
HEIGHTS

STEGER

SAUK
VILLAGE

PLUM CREEK
FOREST PRESERVE

PLUM CREEK
FOREST PRESERVE

CONTINUED ON PAGE 49

.5 MILE

© BY CSC

INDEX TO SUBURBAN COOK COUNTY

ARLINGTON HEIGHTS

Pages 3,8,9,13,14

STREETS

Alexandria St. . Pg.8 . . . . . C10
Algonquin Rd. . Pg.13 . . . . H11
Allegheny Dr. . . Pg.8 . . . . . B10
Allen Ln. . . . . . Pg.8 . . . . . F9
Allison Ct. . . . Pg.13 . . . . G9
Amhurst Ct. . . . Pg.9 . . . . D12
Appletree Ln. . . Pg.8 . . . . B11
Arlington Heights Rd.
. . . . Pg.8,13 . . A-H11
Arthur Ave. . . . Pg.14 . . . . F11
Ashbury Dr. . . . Pg.9 . . . . . D12
Ashford Ln. . . . Pg.3 . . . . . A11
Avon Ct. . . . . . Pg.9 . . . . . C12
Avon Ln. . . . . . Pg.9 . . . . . C12
Banbury Rd. . . . Pg.8 . . . . . F11
Barberry Ct. . . Pg.9 . . . . . E12
Bayside Dr. . . . Pg.3 . . . . . A10
Bel Aire Dr. . . . Pg.9 . . . . . E12
Belmont Ave. . Pg.8,13 . . D-G11
Belmont Ct. . . . Pg.8 . . . . . G11
Berkley Dr. . . . Pg.8 . . . . . B10
Best Dr. . . . . . Pg.9 . . . . . B12
Betty Dr. . . . . . Pg.9 . . . . . A12
Beverly Ave. . . Pg.8 . . . . C-F11
Beverly Ln. . . Pg.8,13 . . C-F11
Birchwood Ln. . Pg.9 . . . . . C12
Bloomington Ave.
. . . . Pg.3 . . . . . A10
Boeger Dr. . . . Pg.8 . . . . . A10
Bradford Dr. . . Pg.8 . . . . . B11
Bradshire Ct. . . Pg.9 . . . . . D12
Braeside Dr. . . Pg.8 . . . . . B11
Brampton Ln. . . Pg.3 . . . . . A11
Brandenberry Ct. .
. . . . Pg.3 . . . . . A10
Bray Ct. . . . . . Pg.13 . . . . G9
Briar Ln. . . . . . Pg.8 . . . . . C11
Brighton Pl. . . . Pg.9 . . . . B-E11
Bristol Ln. . . . . Pg.13 . . . . F11
Brittany Ct. . . . Pg.8 . . . . . B10
Brittany Dr. . . . Pg.8 . . . . . B10
Brocton Ct. . . . Pg.9 . . . . . D12
Brook Dr. . . . . Pg.13 . . . . J11
Brookwood Dr. Pg.8 . . . . B10-11
Brown St. . . . . Pg.8 . . . . . D9
Buffalo Grove Rd.
. . . . Pg.9 . . . . A-C12
Burgoyne Rd. . . Pg.8 . . . . . D10
Burke Dr. . . . . Pg.8 . . . . . A11
Burkitt Pl. . . . . Pg.3 . . . . . A11
Burning Tree Ct. Pg.9 . . . . . B12
Burning Tree Ln. Pg.8 . . . . B10,11
Burr Oak Dr. . . Pg.8 . . . . A10-12
Burton Pl. . . . . Pg.13 . . . . F11
Butternut Ct. . . Pg.9 . . . . . E10
Cambridge St. . Pg.8 . . . . C9,E10
Camelot Ct. . . . Pg.8 . . . . . B11
Campbell St. . Pg.8,9 . . E10-12
Campus Dr. . . . Pg.8 . . . . . A10
Canterbury Ct. . Pg.8 . . . . . B9
Canterbury Dr. . Pg.8 . . . . . B9
Carlyle Ct. . . . . Pg.9 . . . . . D12
Carlyle Ln. . . . . Pg.9 . . . . . E11
Carlyle Pl. . . . . Pg.9 . . . . . F12
Carriage Way Dr. . .
. . . . Pg.8 . . . . . A11
Catino St. . . . . Pg.8 . . . . . C10
Cedar Glenn Dr. Pg.13 . . . . J11
Cedar Ln. . . . . Pg.13 . . . . G10
Cedar St. . . . . Pg.13 . . . . G10
Cellular Blvd. . . Pg.8 . . . . . A9
Central St. . . . Pg.13 . . . . F9-11
Champlain St. . Pg.8 . . . . . B10
Chapel Hill Dr. . Pg.8 . . . . . B11
Charles St. . . . Pg.8 . . . . . C11
Charter Point Dr. (Pvt.) . .
. . . . Pg.9 . . . . . C12
Chatham Pl. . . . Pg.8 . . . . . F11
Cherry Hill Dr. . . Pg.9 . . . . . C12
Cherry Ln. . . . . Pg.8 . . . . . C11
Chesterfield Dr. Pg.13 . . . . G10
Chestnut Ave. . Pg.8,13 . . B-G10
Chicago Ave. . . Pg.8 . . . . . D9
Circle Hill Dr. . . Pg.8 . . . . . C11
Clarence Ave. . Pg.8 . . . . . D11
Clarendon Ave. Pg.8 . . . . . D11
Clarendon Ct. . Pg.8 . . . . . D11
Clarendon Rd. . Pg.8 . . . . . D10
Clarendon St. . Pg.8 . . . . . D10
Clayton Ct. . . . Pg.9 . . . . . C12
Clearbrook Dr. . Pg.13 . . . . J11
Cleveland Ave. Pg.9,14 . . . F11
Coldspring Rd. (Pvt.) . .
. . . . Pg.9 . . . . . C13
College Dr. . . . Pg.8 . . . . . A10
Concord Dr. . . . Pg.8 . . . . . B9
Cottonwood Ct. Pg.8 . . . . . E10
Council Tr. . . . Pg.13 . . . . H11
Country Lake Rd.
. . . . Pg.9 . . . . . C13
Country Ln. . . . Pg.8 . . . . . A11
Courtland Dr. (Pvt.) . .
. . . . Pg.9 . . . . . C12
Crabtree Dr. . Pg.8,9 . . B11-12
Crescent Ln. . Pg.13 . . . . G11
Crestwood Dr. . Pg.8 . . . . . C11
Cypress Dr. . . Pg.13 . . . . G10
Cypress St. . . Pg.13 . . . . G10
Dale Ave. . . . . Pg.9 . . . . C-D12
Daniels Ct. . . . Pg.8 . . . . . B11
Davis St. . . . . . Pg.8 . . . . E10-11

Derbyshire Ave. Pg.9 . . . . . E11
Derbyshire Dr. . Pg.9 . . . . . F11
Derbyshire Ln. . Pg.9 . . . C,F11
Donald Ave. . . . Pg.9 . . . . . F12
Dorothy Ave. . . Pg.8 . . . . . C11
Douglas Ave. . Pg.13 . . B,D,E,G11
Dover Ct. . . . . . Pg.9 . . . . . C12
Dover Ln. . . . . . Pg.9 . . . . . C12
Drury Ln. . . . . . Pg.9 . . . . B-E12
Dryden Ave. . . . Pg.8 . . C11,E11
Dryden Ct. . . . . Pg.9 . . . . . B11
Dryden Ln. . . . . Pg.11 . . . . C11
Dryden Pl. . . . Pg.8,13 . . A-F11
Dundee Rd. . . . Pg.8 . . . . . A11
Dunhill Ct. . . . . Pg.8 . . . . . C10
Dunton Ave. . . Pg.8,13 . . B,D,G10
Dwyer Ave. . . . Pg.8 . . . . . F10
Eastman Ct. . . . Pg.9 . . . . . E11
Eastman St. . . . Pg.8 . . . . . E11
Eastwood Dr. . . Pg.8 . . . . . C11
Elizabeth Dr. . . Pg.8 . . . . . C11
Elizabeth Ln. . . Pg.9 . . . . . B12
Elk Grove Rd. . Pg.13 . . . . H10
Ellen Dr. . . . . . Pg.9 . . . . . A12
Elm Ln. . . . . . . Pg.8 . . . . . B11
Elm St. . . . . . . Pg.8 . . . . . D9
Elmwood Cir. . . Pg.9 . . . . . C12
Embers Ln. . . . Pg.13 . . . . H11
Emerson St. . . . Pg.13 . . . . G10
Eton Dr. . . . . . Pg.9 . . . . . B12
Euclid St. . . . . . Pg.8 . . . . . E11
Evanston Ave. . Pg.9 . . . . . F12
Evergreen Ave. Pg.8,13 . . B-G11
Evergreen Terr. Pg.9 . . . . . C12
Fairview St. . . . Pg.8 . . . . . F10
Falcon Dr. . . . . Pg.13 . . . . H11
Fernandez Ave. Pg.8,13 . . C-G10
Fernandez Pl. . . Pg.8 . . . . . C10
Fernandez St. . Pg.13 . . . . F10
Fleming Dr. . . . Pg.9 . . . . . A12
Flentie Ln. . . . . Pg.9 . . . . . A12
Flower Circle . . Pg.9 . . . . . C12
Forrest Ave. . . . Pg.9 . . . D-F12
Forrest Dr. . . . Pg.8 . . . . . B12
Forrest Ln. . . . . Pg.9 . . . . . B12
Foster St. . . . . Pg.13 . . . . G11
Foxdale Ln. . . . Pg.8 . . . . . A11
Francis Dr. . . . . Pg.8 . . . . . F10
Frederick Ct. . . Pg.9 . . . . . D11
Frederick St. . . Pg.9 . . . . . D11
Fremont Ct. . . . Pg.9 . . . . . E12
Fremont St. . . . Pg.8 . . . . E9-11
Frontenac St. . . Pg.9 . . . . . B11
Garden Walk . . Pg.9 . . . . E10-11
George St. . . . . Pg.9 . . . . E10-11
Gettysburg Dr. . Pg.8 . . . . . C10
Gibbons Ave. . . Pg.9 . . . . D-F12
Goebbert Rd. . . Pg.13 . . . . H11
Golf (Evanston-Elgin Rd.) . .
. . . . Pg.13 . . . . H10
Golf Terr. . . . . . Pg.13 . . . . H11
Greenbrier Ct. . Pg.8 . . . . . C10
Greenwood Ct. (Pvt.) . .
. . . . Pg.8 . . . . . B9
Gregory St. . . . Pg.9 . . . . . F12
Greshan Ct. . . Pg.13 . . . . G11
Grove St. . . . . . Pg.8 . . . . F9-12
Hackberry Dr. . Pg.8 . . . . . A10
Haddow Ave. . Pg.8,13 . . B-G11
Haddow Ct. . . . Pg.8 . . . . . D11
Happifield Dr. . . Pg.3 . . . . . A11
Harold St. . . . . Pg.8 . . . . . C10
Hartford Ct. . . . Pg.9 . . . . . D12
Harvard Ave. . Pg.8,13 . . . .
. . . . F9,B-G10
Harvard Rd. . . . Pg.8 . . . . . D10
Haven Dr. . . . . Pg.13 . . . . G10
Haven Dr. W. . . Pg.13 . . . . G10
Haverhill Ct. . . . Pg.9 . . . . . D12
Hawthorne St. . Pg.8 . . . . . E9
Heather Ln. . . . Pg.8 . . . . . E10
Henry St. . . . . . Pg.8 . . . . . B10
Hickory Ave. . . Pg.8 . . . D-E11
Hickory Ln. . . . Pg.8 . . . . . B11
Highland Ave. . Pg.3,8 . . . . .
. . . . A11,B-H10
Hintz Rd. . . . . . Pg.8 . . . . B10-12
Hunter Dr. . . . . Pg.9 . . . . . C12
Huntington Dr. . Pg.9 . . . . . A11
Huron St. . . . . . Pg.8 . . . . . B10
Illinois Ave. . . . Pg.8 . . . . . C11
Illinois St. . . . . Pg.9 . . . . . E9
Independence Ct. . .
. . . . Pg.13 . . . . H11
Ironwood Dr. . . Pg.9 . . . . . E12
Ivy Ln. . . . . . . Pg.13 . . . . H11
James Ct. . . . . Pg.8 . . . . . B10
Jane Ave. . . . . Pg.8 . . . . . E10
Jennifer Ct. . . . Pg.8 . . . . . B11
Jo Ln. . . . . . . Pg.8 . . . . . D9
Johanna Terr. . . Pg.9 . . . . . C12
Jonquil Cir. . . . Pg.9 . . . . . C12
Jonquil Terr. . . Pg.9 . . . . . C12
Jules St. . . . . . Pg.8 . . . . . C11
Juniper Ln. . . . Pg.8 . . . . . C11
Kaspar Ave. . Pg.8,13 . . C-G10
Keating Ct. . . . Pg.9 . . . . . C12
Kendal Ct. . . . . Pg.8 . . . . . B11
Kennicott Ave. Pg.3,8,13 . .
. . . . A10,B-G10
Kennicott Ct. . . Pg.13 . . . . G10
Kensington (Foundry Rd.) . .
. . . . Pg.9 . . . . E12
Kerry-Brook Ct. Pg.8 . . . . . B11
Kimber Ln. . . . Pg.13 . . . . J11
Kingsbury Dr. . . Pg.8 . . . . . B10

Kingsbury Dr. . Pg.8 . . . . . B10
Kingsley Ln. . . . Pg.3 . . . . . A11
Kirchoff Rd. . . Pg.13 . . . . F10
Knob Hill Dr. . . Pg.8 . . . . . C11
La Salle St. . . . Pg.8 . . . . . C10
Ladd St. . . . . . Pg.8 . . . . . C10
Lafayette St. . . Pg.8 . . . . . B10
Lake Arlington Dr. . .
. . . . Pg.9 . . . . C12
Lake Shore Cir. Pg.9 . . . . . C12
Lake-Cook Rd. . Pg.3 . . . . . A10
Lancaster . . . . Pg.9 . . . . . C12
Lawrence Ln. . Pg.13 . . . . G11
Leona St. . . . . Pg.8 . . . . . F9
Lexington Dr. . . Pg.9 . . . . . B9
Lilac Terr. . . . . Pg.9 . . . . . C12
Lillian Ave. . . . Pg.8 . . . . . C10
Lillian Ln. . . . . Pg.8 . . . . . C10
Lincoln Ln. . . . Pg.8 . . . . . D11
Lincoln Ln. . . . Pg.8 . . . . . E11
Luther Dr. . . . . Pg.8 . . . . . F11
Lynden Ln. . . . Pg.8 . . . . . F11
Lynnwood Ave. Pg.8 . . . . . D10
Magnolia St. . . Pg.13 . . . . G10
Mallard Dr. . . . Pg.3 . . . . . A10
Maple Ln. . . . . Pg.9 . . . . . C12
Maple St. . . . . Pg.13 . . . . F10
Marion Rd. . . . Pg.8 . . . . . B10
Marion St. . . . . Pg.8 . . . D10-11
Marshall Ct. . . . Pg.9 . . . . . E12
Marshall St. . . Pg.8 . . . . . E12
Martin Ln. . . . . Pg.13 . . . . H10
Maude Ave. . . . Pg.8 . . . . . D11
Mayfair Rd. . . Pg.8,9 . . . F11-12
McKinley Ave. . Pg.9,14 . . . F11
McKone Ct. . . . Pg.13 . . . . G11
Meade Ln. . . . . Pg.3 . . . . . A10
Meier Rd. . . . . Pg.13 . . . . H11
Michael Manor Ln. . .
. . . . Pg.9 . . . . C12
Milida . . . . . . Pg.13 . . . . G10
Millbrook Ln. . Pg.13 . . . . H10
Miner St. . . . . . Pg.8 . . . . . B10
Mitchell Ave. . Pg.8,13 . . . .
. . . . B10,D-G10
Mitchell Ct. . . . Pg.8 . . . . . C10
Mitchell Dr. . . . Pg.3 . . . . . A11
Moorings Dr. . . Pg.9 . . . . . C12
Mueller St. . . . Pg.8 . . . . . E10
Mulberry Ct. . . Pg.8 . . . . . E10
Mulberry Ln. . . Pg.9 . . . . . C12
New Wilke Rd. . Pg.13 . . . F,G9
Newbury Pl. . . Pg.13 . . . . H11
Newport Ct. . . Pg.3 . . . . . A10
Newport Ln. . . . Pg.3 . . . . . A10
Nichols Rd. . . . Pg.3 . . . . . A10
Norman St. . . . Pg.8 . . . . . C10
Normandy Ct. . Pg.9 . . . . . C12
Northwest Hwy. Pg.8 . . . . . E11
Northwest Tollway . .
. . . . Pg.13 . . . . J11
Northwood Ct. . Pg.13 . . . . G10
Noyes St. . . . Pg.13 . . . . G10
Noyes St. W. . Pg.13 . . . . G9
Oakton St. . . . . Pg.9 . . . . . D11
Oakwood Dr. . . Pg.9 . . . . . C12
Old Arlington Hts. Rd. . .
. . . . Pg.8 . . . . A10
Old Barn Ln. . . Pg.13 . . . . G11
Olive St. . . . . . Pg.8 . . . . . D10
Orchard Pl. . . . Pg.13 . . . . F9
Orchid Ln. . . . . Pg.9 . . . . . F11
Oxford Ln. . . . . Pg.8 . . . . . D11
Page Rd. . . . . . Pg.9 . . . . . A12
Palatine Rd. . . . Pg.8 . . . . . B10
Park Pl. . . . . . . Pg.8 . . . . . E10
Park St. . . . . . . Pg.8 . . . . F9-12
Parkview . . . . . Pg.13 . . . . G11
Partridge Ct. . . Pg.3 . . . . . A10
Partridge Ln. . . Pg.3 . . . . . A10
Patton Ave. . . . Pg.8 . . . C-F10
Patton Cir. . . . . Pg.8 . . . . . C10
Peachtree Dr. . Pg.9 . . . . . B12
Peachtree Ln. . Pg.9 . . . . . B12
Peartree Ln. . . Pg.9 . . . . . E12
Pennsylvania Pl. Pg.13 . . . . H11
Pheasant Trail Ct. . .
. . . . Pg.3 . . . . A10
Pheasant Trail Dr. . .
. . . . Pg.3 . . . . A10
Pheasant Trail Ln. . .
. . . . Pg.3 . . . . A10
Phelps Ave. . . . Pg.8 . . . . . A12
Pickwick Rd. . . Pg.13 . . . . G10
Pin Oak Dr. . . . Pg.8 . . . . . B13
Pine Ave. . . . Pg.8,13 . . B-G11
Pine Ct. . . . . . Pg.13 . . . . G11
Pinetree Dr. . . . Pg.9 . . . . . B12
Plymouth Dr. . . Pg.8 . . . . . A12
Plymouth St. . . Pg.8 . . . . . C9
Portsmith Ln. . . Pg.3 . . . . . A10
Prairie Ave. . . . Pg.8 . . . . . C11
Princeton Ave. Pg.8 . . . . . D11
. . . . D-F9,G10
Princeton Ct. . . Pg.8 . . . . . D11
Prindle Ave. . . . Pg.9 . . . . B-F12
Proctor Cir. . . . Pg.3 . . . . . A11
Quail Ct. . . . . . Pg.8 . . . . . C11
Race Ave. . . . . Pg.9 . . . . . D9
Radford Ct. . . . Pg.9 . . . . . D12
Raleigh Ct. . . . Pg.8 . . . . . B9
Raleigh St. . . . Pg.8 . . . . . B9
Rammer Ave. . . Pg.9 . . . . . E12
Rand Rd. . . . . Pg.8,9 . . B10,D12
Redwood Ln. . . Pg.8 . . . . . C11

Regency Ct. . . . Pg.9 . . . . . E13
Regency Dr. . . . Pg.9 . . . . . E13
Reuter Dr. . . . . Pg.8 . . . . . E9
Richmond St. . . Pg.8 . . . . . C9
Ridge Ave. . . . Pg.3,8 . . . . .
. . . . A11,A-G10
Ridge Ct. . . . . Pg.8 . . . . . D10
Ridge Dr. . . . . Pg.13 . . . . H10
Ridge Pl. . . . . . Pg.8 . . . . . C10
Ridge Rd. . . . . Pg.8 . . . . . B11
Roanoke Dr. . . Pg.8 . . . . . B9
Robinhood Ln. . Pg.9 . . . . . C12
Rockwell St. . . Pg.13 . . . . F11
Rolling Ln. . . . Pg.9 . . . . . C12
Roosevelt Ave. Pg.9,14 . . . F11
Rosehill Dr. . . . Pg.9 . . . . . C12
Russell Ct. . . . Pg.13 . . . . G9
Russetwood Dr. Pg.9 . . . . . C12
Salem Ave. . . Pg.8,13 . . E-F10
Salem Blvd. . . . Pg.8 . . . . . D10
Salem Ct. . . . . Pg.3 . . . . . A10
Salem Ln. . . . Pg.13 . . . . G10
Schaefer Rd. . . Pg.3 . . . . . A10
Scottsvale Ln. . Pg.9 . . . . . E12
Seegers Rd. . . Pg.13 . . . . H11
Shady Way . . Pg.13 . . . . H11
Shag Bark . . . Pg.13 . . . . H11
Shenandoah Cir. Pg.13 . . . . H10
Shenandoah Dr. Pg.8 . . . . . C10
Sherwood Rd. . Pg.9 . . . . . C12
Shiloh Dr. . . . . Pg.8 . . . . . B12
Shirra Ct. . . . . Pg.8 . . . . . B9
Shure Dr. . . . . Pg.8 . . . . . A12
Sigwalt St. . . . Pg.8 . . . . . E9
Silver Lake Rd. Pg.9 . . . . . C13
Somerset Ave. . Pg.8 . . . . . E10
South St. . . . . . Pg.8 . . . . . F10
Spring Ridge Dr. Pg.3 . . . . . A10
Spruce Terr. . . Pg.8 . . . . . C11
St. James Pl. . . Pg.8 . . . . . C11
St. James St. . . Pg.8 . . . E10-12
Stanford . . . . . Pg.9 . . . . . B12
Stanton Ct. . . . Pg.8 . . . . . C11
Stillwater Rd. (Pvt.) . .
. . . . Pg.9 . . . . C12
Stratford Dr. . . Pg.9 . . . . . C12
Stratford Ln. . . Pg.3 . . . . . A12
Stratford Rd. . . Pg.9 . . . . . C12
Stuart Dr. . . . . Pg.8 . . . . . B11
Suffield Ct. . . . Pg.8 . . . . . B9
Suffield Dr. . . Pg.8,9 . . B10-12
Sunset Dr. . . . Pg.8 . . . . . B11
Sunset Terr. . . Pg.8,9 . . E10-12
Surrey Ln. . . . Pg.13 . . . . G10
Surrey Park Ln. Pg.13 . . . . G9
Surrey Ridge Dr. Pg.13 . . . . G10
Talbot St. . . . . Pg.8 . . . . . C11
Tanglewood Dr. Pg.8 . . . . . A10
Techny Rd. . . Pg.8 . . . . B10-11
Terramere Ave. Pg.3 . . . . . A11
Thomas Ave. . . Pg.8 . . . . . B11
Thorntree Terr. Pg.8 . . . . . B11
Thurston Pl. . . . Pg.3 . . . . . A10
Tonne Dr. . . . Pg.13 . . . . G11
Towne Blvd. . . Pg.9 . . . . . C12
University Dr. . . Pg.8 . . . . . A11
Vail Ave. . . . . Pg.8,13 . . C-G10
Valley Ln. . . . . Pg.8 . . . . . B11
Vargo Ln. . . . Pg.9 . . . . C11-12
Ventura Dr. . . . Pg.3 . . . . . A10
Verde Ave. . . . Pg.8 . . . . . C10
Verde Dr. . . . . Pg.8 . . . . . C10
Viator Ct. . . . . Pg.8 . . . . . D11
Victoria Ln. . . Pg.13 . . . . G10
Village Dr. . . . . Pg.9 . . . . . D10
Vine St. . . . . . Pg.8 . . . . D9-10
Vista Rd. . . . . Pg.8 . . . . . B11
Volz Dr., E. . . . Pg.9 . . . . . A11
Volz Dr., W. . . . Pg.9 . . . . . A11
Walden Ln. . . . Pg.9 . . . . . C12
Walker Ln., E. . Pg.9 . . . . . A11
Walker Ln., W. . Pg.9 . . . . . A11
Walnut Ave. . Pg.3,8,13 . . . .
. . . . A11,B-G10
Walnut Dr. . . . Pg.8 . . . . . B10
Warwick Ct. . . Pg.9 . . . . . D12
Waterman Ave. Pg.9 . . . . B,D-F12
Watling St. . . . Pg.8 . . . . . D10
Waverly Ct. . . . Pg.8 . . . . . B9
Waverly Dr. . . Pg.8,9 . . D11-12
Waverly Pl. . . . Pg.9 . . . . . B12
Waverly Rd. . . . Pg.8 . . . . . B12
West Haven Dr. Pg.13 . . . . G10
Weston Dr. . . . Pg.9 . . . . . C12
Wheeler St. . . . Pg.8 . . . . . C11
White Oak St. . Pg.13 . . . . G10
Whitehall Dr. . . Pg.3 . . . . . A11
Whiting Ln. . . . Pg.8 . . . . . B11
Wilke Rd. . . . . Pg.9 . . . . . A-D9
Williamsburg St. . .
. . . . Pg.8 . . . . C10
Willow Rd. . . . Pg.9 . . . . . D12
Willow Dr. . . . . Pg.8 . . . . . B11
Wilshire Ave. . . Pg.9 . . . . . C12
Wilshire Ln. . . Pg.13 . . . . G10
Wilshire Rd. . . Pg.9 . . . . A-E12
Wilson Pl. . . . . Pg.8 . . . . . C11
Windgate Dr. . Pg.13 . . . . H11
Windsor Dr. . . Pg.9 . . . . A-F12
Windy St. . . . Pg.8,9 . . E11-12
Winham Ct. . . . Pg.8 . . . . . B10
Woodbury Dr. . Pg.9 . . . . . C13
Woodford Dr. . . Pg.13 . . . . G10
Woodford Pl. . . Pg.9 . . . . . B12
Woodland Ln. . Pg.13 . . . . G10
Woodridge Ln. . Pg.9 . . . . . E11
Woods Dr. . . . . Pg.8 . . . . . B9

Yale Ave. . . . . Pg.8 . . . . C-F9
Yale Ave. S. . . Pg.13 . . . . G9
Yarmouth Ct. . Pg.9 . . . . . D12

CEMETERIES

Arl. Hts. Wheeling Twp. Cem. . . .
. . . . Pg.9 . . . . E12
Memory Gardens Cem. . . .
. . . . Pg.9 . . . . E12
Rand Hill Cem. . Pg.8 . . . . . B10
Shalom Mem. Pk. Cem. . . .
. . . . Pg.8 . . . . A9
St. Peters Cem. . Pg.9 . . . . E12

GOLF COURSES

Arlington Lakes Golf Club . . .
. . . . Pg.13 . . . . G9
Rolling Green C.C. . . .
. . . . Pg.9 . . . . D12

PARKS

Arlington Hts. Pk. Dist. Admin. Ctr.
. . . . Pg.8 . . . . E11
Banta Park . . . Pg.9 . . . . . E11
Berbecker Park Pg.9 . . . . . E12
Brandenberry Park . . .
. . . . Pg.9 . . . . D12
Camelot Park . . Pg.8 . . . . . B11
Carousel Park . Pg.9 . . . . . B12
Carriage Walk Pk. . .
. . . . Pg.8 . . . . D11
Centennial Pk. . Pg.8 . . . . . B11
Clock Tower Plaza Pk. . .
. . . . Pg.8 . . . . E11
Creekside Park Pg.3 . . . . . A10
Cronin Park . . . Pg.8 . . . . . F10
Cypress Park . Pg.13 . . . . G11
Dryden Park . . Pg.13 . . . . F11
Evergreen Park Pg.9 . . . . . C12
Falcon Park . . Pg.13 . . . . H11
Festival Park . . Pg.9 . . . . . E11
Forest View Pk. & Racquet Club .
. . . . Pg.9 . . . . H11
Frontier Park . . Pg.8 . . . . . C10
Greenbrier Park Pg.8 . . . . . D11
Greens Park . . Pg.8 . . . . . A12
Greenslopes Pk. Pg.8 . . . . . C11
Happiness Park Pg.8 . . . . . C10
Hasbrook Park Pg.13 . . . . G10
Heritage Park . Pg.13 . . . . G10
Heritage Tennis Club . . .
. . . . Pg.8 . . . . A10
Hickory Meadows Pk. . .
. . . . Pg.8 . . . . D11
Kingsbridge Arboretum . . .
. . . . Pg.3 . . . . A10
Klehm Park . . . Pg.9 . . . . . E12
Lake Arlington . Pg.9 . . . . . C12
Lake Terramere Park . . .
. . . . Pg.3 . . . . A10
Memorial Pk. . . Pg.8 . . . . . E10
Methodist Pk. . Pg.9 . . . . . D10
North School Park . . .
. . . . Pg.8 . . . . E11
Olympic Park . . Pg.8 . . . . . E10
Patriot Park . . . Pg.8 . . . . . E10
Pioneer Park . . Pg.8 . . . . . F10
Rand Connector Park . . .
. . . . Pg.8 . . . . B10
Rand-Berkley Playlot . . .
. . . . Pg.8 . . . . B10
Raven Park . . . Pg.8 . . . . . B10
Recreation Pk. . Pg.8 . . . . . E11
Rose Garden Park . . .
. . . . Pg.9 . . . . F12
Sunset Meadows Park . . .
. . . . Pg.13 . . . . F9
T.N. Cronan Pk. Pg.8 . . . . . F10
Victory Park . . Pg.13 . . . . G10
Virginia Terr. Pk. Pg.8 . . . . . D9
Volz Park . . . . Pg.8 . . . . . E11
Westgate Pk. . . Pg.8 . . . . . E9
Wildwood Park Pg.8 . . . . . B11
Willow Park . . . Pg.8 . . . . . C11

SCHOOLS

Academy of Christian Liberty . . .
. . . . Pg.9 . . . . C12
Berkeley Sch. . Pg.8 . . . . . B10
Dryden Sch. . . Pg.13 . . . . F11
Dunton Sch. . . Pg.13 . . . . G11
Dwyer Sch. . . . Pg.8 . . . . . F10
Greenbrier Sch. Pg.8 . . . . . B10
Ivy Hill Sch. . . Pg.8 . . . . . C11
John Hersey H.S.
. . . . Pg.9 . . . . C12
Juliette Low Sch. . .
. . . . Pg.13
. . . . G10
Kensington Sch. Pg.9 . . . . . E12
Miner Jr. H.S. . Pg.13 . . . . G9
Olive Sch. . . . Pg.9 . . . . . B12
Our Lady of Wayside Cath. Sch. .
. . . . Pg.8 . . . . F10
Patton Sch. . . Pg.13 . . . . G11
Poe Sch. . . . . Pg.9 . . . . . B12
Rand Campus . Pg.8 . . . . . B10
Ridge Sch. . . . Pg.8 . . . . . B11
Riley Sch. . . . . Pg.8 . . . . . C11
School Dist. 59 Admin. Bldg. . .
. . . . Pg.8 . . . . B11
South Jr. H.S. . Pg.13 . . . . G11
St. Edna's Cath. Sch. . . .
. . . . Pg.8 . . . . B11
St. James Cath. Jr. H.S.
. . . . Pg.8 . . . . D11

St. James Cath. Sch.
. . . . Pg.8 . . . . D11
St. Peter's Luth. Sch.
. . . . Pg.8 . . . . D10
St. Viator Cath. H.S.
. . . . Pg.9 . . . . D11
Thomas Jr. H.S. Pg.8 . . . . . D11
Twin Groves Jr. H.S.
. . . . Pg.8 . . . . B10
Westgate Sch. . Pg.8 . . . . . F10
Windsor Sch. . Pg.9 . . . . . E11

SHOPPING CENTERS

Arlington Market . . .
. . . . Pg.8 . . . . E11
Arlington Plaza Pg.8 . . . . . C10
Arlington Promenade . . .
. . . . Pg.8 . . . . C11
Brook Run Shopping Ctr. . . .
. . . . Pg.8 . . . . B11
Central Plaza . Pg.13 . . . . G9
Huntington Sq. Pg.8 . . . . . B10
Lohmann's Plaza . . .
. . . . Pg.13 . . . . H11
Mansions Shopping Ctr. . . .
. . . . Pg.13 . . . . H11
Northpoint Shopping Ctr. . . .
. . . . Pg.8 . . . . C11
Ridge Plaza . . . Pg.8 . . . . . A10
Southpoint Shopping Ctr. . . .
. . . . Pg.8 . . . . C11
Surrey Ridge Shopping Ctr. . . .
. . . . Pg.13 . . . . H10
Terramere Shopping Ctr. . . .
. . . . Pg.3 . . . . A11
The Annex of Arlington . . .
. . . . Pg.8 . . . . C10
Town & Country Mall . . .
. . . . Pg.8 . . . . C11
Westgate Shopping Ctr. . . .
. . . . Pg.8 . . . . E-9

MISCELLANEOUS

Americana Nursing Home . . .
. . . . Pg.13 . . . . G10
Arl. Mem. Library . . .
. . . . Pg.8 . . . . E11
Church Creek Retirement Ctr. . . .
. . . . Pg.8 . . . . E11
Fire Dept. . . . . Pg.8 . . . . . E11
Lutheran Home for the Aged . . .
. . . . Pg.8 . . . . D10
Moorings Retirement Ctr. . . .
. . . . Pg.13 . . . . G11
Municipal Bldg. Pg.8 . . . . . E10
Northwest Comm. Hosp. . . .
. . . . Pg.8 . . . . F10
Park Place Senior Ctr. . . .
. . . . Pg.13 . . . . F10
Post Office . . . Pg.8 . . . . . E10
Public Works . . Pg.8 . . . . . E10
Railroad Sta. . . Pg.8 . . . . . E10
U.S. Military Reservation . . .
. . . . Pg.13 . . . . G10
Viatorian Novitiate . . .
. . . . Pg.9 . . . . D11
Wheeling Township Hall . . .
. . . . Pg.8 . . . . C11

BARRINGTON

Page 1

STREETS

Applebee St. X4
Balmoral St. A5
Barrington Pt. A4
Bellingham Dr. A5
Bent Bridge Ln. X4
Berry Rd. X4
Beverly Rd. X5
Birch X4
Birchwood Dr. X5
Braeside Dr. A4
Bristol Dr. A4
Bryant Ave. X4
Burr Oak Ln. X5
Carl Ave. X4
Castle Ct. X5
Center Ct. X5
Chestnut St. X4
Church Hill Ct. X4
Coldspring Rd. X5
Commonwealth Ct. X4
Concord Ct. A4
Concord Ln. A4
Concord Pl. A4
Cook St. A,X4
Coolidge Ave. A4
Cornell Ave. X4
County Dr. A4
Covington X4
Cumnor Ave. X3
Division St. X4
Drury Ln. X4
Dundee Ave. X4
Dundee Rd. B4
Eastern Ave. X4
Ela St. X4
Elm Ave. X4
Elm Park Ave. X4
Exmoor Ave. X4
Fairfax St. X4
Forest Dr. A3
Fox Hunt Trail X5
Foxglove Ln. X4
Franklin St. X4

BARRINGTON

Garfield St. ... X4
George St. ... A,B4
George Towne Ln. ... X4
Glendale Ave. ... A,X4
Grant St. ... X4
Grove Ave. ... A,B4
Hager Ave. ... A3
Harriet Ln. ... X4
Harrison St. ... X4
Hart Rd. ... X3
Hawthorne Rd. ... X4
Heath Ct. ... A,C5
Highland Ave. ... A4
Highland Ct. ... A4
Hill St. ... A4
Hillcrest Ave. ... A4
Hillside Ave. ... A4
Hillside Ave. Ext. ... A3
Hilltop Ave. ... X5
Home Ave. ... A4
Hough St. ... A4
Illinois St. ... A4
Indian Way ... X5
James St. ... X4
June Terr. ... A5
Kainer Ave. ... A4
Kings Row ... A5
Lageshulte St. ... A3
Lake Shore Ct. ... X5
Lake Shore Dr. ... X5
Lake Shore Dr. S. ... X5
Lake St. ... X4
Lake Zurich Rd. ... X4
Lakeview Ln. ... A1
Laverne St. ... A4
Liberty St. ... A4
Lincoln Ave. ... A4
Linden Ave. ... A4
Lions Pkwy. ... X4
Magnolia Rd. ... X4
Main St. ... A,A4
Maple ... X4
Marlbourough Rd. ... X4
Martin Ct. ... A4
Meadow Ln. ... A4
Meadow Way ... X5
Monument Ave. ... A4
New Bridge Ct. ... X4
New Hart Rd. ... X4
North Ave. ... A4
North St. ... X3
Northwest Hwy. ... X3
Oak Rd. ... X4
Oak Ridge Cir. ... A5
Oak Ridge Rd. ... A5
Old Creek Ct. ... A5
Old Mill Ct. ... A5
Old Mill Rd. ... A5
Orchard Dr. ... A3
Oxbow Ln. ... X5
Park Ave. ... A4
Park Barrington Dr. ... A2
Park Barrington Way ... A2
Park Ln. ... X4
Park N. ... X4
Paul Cir. ... X4
Pine ... A4
Ponderosa Ct. ... X5
Prairie Ave. ... A4
Prospect Rd. ... X4
Providence Rd. ... X4
Pump St. ... X4
Queens Cove ... X4
Railroad St. ... X4
Raymond Ave. ... A4
Red Barn Ln. ... A5
Redwood Ln. ... X4
Roslyn Rd. ... X3
Roslyn Rd., W. ... X3
Russell St. ... A3-4
Scott Ave. ... X3
Shady Ln. ... A3
Sharon St. ... X5
Shore Ct. N. ... X5
Shore Ct. S. ... X5
Shorley Dr. ... A4
Skyline Dr. ... A4
South St. ... A5
Spring St. ... A5
Spruce ... X5
Station St. ... X4
Stillwater Ln. ... X4
Strutz St. ... X4
Summit St. ... X4
Sunny Ln. ... X4
Sunny Rd. ... X4
Sunset Rd. ... X3
Surrey Ln. ... X5
Sycamore ... X4
Tall Trees Dr. ... X5
Tall Trees Rd. ... X5
The Point ... X5
Tower Ln. ... X4
Tower Rd. ... A4
Tudor Dr. ... X4
Valencia Ave. ... X4
Valley Ct. N. ... X5
Valley Rd. ... X5
Valley Rd. N. ... X5
Vernon ... X4
Victoria Ave. ... X4
Walnut ... X4
Walton St. ... A4
Warwick Ave. ... A4
Washington St. ... X4
Waverly Rd. ... X4

Werten Rd. W. ... X3
Wesley ... X3
Western Ave. ... X3
Westwood Dr. ... A3
White Oak Ct. ... X5
Whitney Dr. ... X4
Willow ... X4
Wisconsin Ave. ... A4
Woodside Ln. ... A5
Wool St. ... A4
Wool St. ... A4
Wyngate Ave. ... A5
13th St. ... X3

CEMETERIES
Evergreen Cem. ... A3
St. Anne Cemetery ... A4

PARKS
Bosworth Field ... X4
Hampton Park ... X4
Langendorf Park (Northside Park) ... X4
Northside Park ... X4
Playground ... A4
Ron Breese Park ... A2
Williamsburg Park ... X4

SCHOOLS
Barrington H.S. ... X3
Grove Sch. ... X4
Hough Sch. ... X4
Middle Sch. ... X5
Roslyn Sch. ... X4
St. Ann Sch. ... X4

MISCELLANEOUS
Barrington Camp Ground ... A4
Library ... A4
Village Hall ... A4

BARRINGTON HILLS
Page 1
STREETS
Sara Ln. ... A1
Barrington Rd. ... C1
Dundee Ln. ... A1
Dundee Rd. ... A1
Hart Rd. ... X3
Hawthorne Ln. ... B3
Hawthorne Rd. ... B3
Lakeview Ln. ... A1
Otis Rd. ... A3
Palatine Rd. ... C1
Sara Ln. ... A1

BARRINGTON TOWNSHIP
Pages 1,6
STREETS
Circle St. ... B1
Cook St. ... A4
Division St. ... A4
George St. ... A4
Grove Ave. ... A4
Harvard Ave. ... A4
Princeton Ave. ... A4
Summit Ave. ... A4
Yale Ave. ... A4

SCHOOLS
Willow Creek Comm. Sch. ... D2

BLOOM TOWNSHIP
Pages 43,44,45,48,49,50
STREETS
Alice Ave. ... Pg.50 ... V30
Arnett St. ... Pg.49 ... T27
Ashland Ave. ... Pg.48 ... W22
Audry ... Pg.50 ... U30
Baltimore Ave. ... Pg.50 ... T29
Batrack ... Pg.50 ... T29
Benjamin St. ... Pg.50 ... T29
Bensley Ave. ... Pg.50 ... S28
Blackstone Ave. ... Pg.50 ... S27
Brandon Ave. ... Pg.50 ... T29
Bridge ... Pg.50 ... U30
Brown St. ... Pg.49 ... T27
Burley Ave. ... Pg.50 ... T29
Burnham Ave. ... Pg.45,50 ... W30
Butler St. ... Pg.49 ... T27
Calhoun Ave. ... Pg.50 ... T29
Calumet Expy. ... Pg.50 ... W27
Candlelight ... Pg.50 ... U28
Carondellet Ave. ... Pg.50 ... T29
Carriage ... Pg.50 ... U28
Coales St. ... Pg.49 ... R24
Collom St. ... Pg.49 ... T27
Columbia Ave. ... Pg.49 ... T27
Commercial Ave. ... Pg.50 ... T29
Coolidge St. ... Pg.43 ... R24
Cottage Grove Ave. ... Pg.44,49 ... V26
Daniel Ct. ... Pg.50 ... T29
Daren St. ... Pg.50 ... U30
David Ct. ... Pg.50 ... T29
Division St. ... Pg.42 ... T22
Douglas Ct. ... Pg.50 ... T29
Dutra Ave. ... Pg.49 ... V24
East End ... Pg.49 ... V24
Eighth St. ... Pg.50 ... T27
Elizabeth St. ... Pg.50 ... U30

Ellen Dr. ... Pg.50 ... U29
Ellis St. ... Pg.49 ... T27
Escanaba Ave. ... Pg.50 ... T29
Euclid St. ... Pg.50 ... W30
Exchange Ave. ... Pg.50 ... T29
Forest Ln. ... Pg.44 ... Q27
Frederick Ct. ... Pg.50 ... T29
Gail Ct. ... Pg.50 ... T29
Gardner Ave. ... Pg.48 ... T22
Glenwood Dyer Rd. ... Pg.50 ... R26
Glenwood-Lansing Rd. ... Pg.44,45 ... R27
Halsted ... Pg.43 ... R24
Hammond Ln. ... Pg.49 ... T27
Hillcrest Ave. ... Pg.50 ... T29
Holbrook Rd. ... Pg.43 ... R24
Houston Ave. ... Pg.50 ... T29
Howard Ct. ... Pg.50 ... U29
Hutchinson Ave. ... Pg.48 ... T22
Indiana Ave. ... Pg.49 ... U25
Interurban Ave. ... Pg.43 ... R24
Jacob Ct. ... Pg.50 ... T29
James Ave. ... Pg.50 ... V30
Jennifer Dr. ... Pg.50 ... U30
Joe Orr Rd. ... Pg.49 ... S27
Judith Ct. ... Pg.50 ... U29
Katz Corner Rd. ... Pg.50 ... V29
Langston St. ... Pg.49 ... T27
Lincoln Hwy. ... Pg.50 ... U29
Long Ave. ... Pg.49 ... W29
Main St., N. ... Pg.49 ... Q25
Marion Ct. ... Pg.49 ... T29
Martin Ct. ... Pg.50 ... T29
Michelle ... Pg.50 ... U30
Michigan Ave. ... Pg.49 ... W25
Muskegon Ave. ... Pg.50 ... T29
Park ... Pg.50 ... U27
Park Ln. ... Pg.50 ... U28
Parkside Ave. ... Pg.50 ... T29
Prairie Ave. ... Pg.50 ... V29
Pullman St. ... Pg.49 ... U27
Rhodes ... Pg.44 ... R26
Sauk Trail Rd. ... Pg.49 ... W22
St. Lawrence ... Pg.44 ... R26
State St. ... Pg.50 ... W25
Steger Rd. ... Pg.49 ... W22
Stirling Ave. ... Pg.48 ... T22
Stony Island Ave. ... Pg.50 ... S,U27
Stuart Ct. ... Pg.50 ... T29
Summit Dr. ... Pg.49 ... U27
Sunset Ln. ... Pg.50 ... V30
Torrence Ave. ... Pg.49 ... W29
Travers Ave. ... Pg.48 ... T22
Valerie Dr. ... Pg.50 ... U30
Vincinnes Rd. ... Pg.43 ... Q25
Vollmer Rd. ... Pg.48 ... S20
Vollmer St. ... Pg.50 ... S27
Wentworth Ave. ... Pg.45,49 ... R30,W25
Western Ave. ... Pg.48 ... T22
Woodlawn Ave. ... Pg.49 ... W27
10th St. ... Pg.50 ... T27
13th St. ... Pg.49 ... T25
14th St. ... Pg.49 ... U25
16th St. ... Pg.49 ... U25
21st St. ... Pg.50 ... V30
22nd St. ... Pg.49,50 ... V30
26th St. ... Pg.49 ... V22
28th St. ... Pg.49 ... V24
30th St. ... Pg.50 ... W27
32nd St. ... Pg.49 ... W25
34th St. ... Pg.49 ... W25
184th St. ... Pg.43,45 ... Q25
186th St. ... Pg.44 ... Q28
193rd Pl. ... Pg.43 ... R24
194th St. ... Pg.49,50 ... R24
194th St. ... Pg.44 ... Q28
195th St. ... Pg.49 ... R24
196th St. ... Pg.44 ... R24
205th St. ... Pg.48 ... T22
207th St. ... Pg.48,50 ... T22
209th St. ... Pg.48 ... T22
211th St. ... Pg.50 ... U27
212th St. ... Pg.49 ... U27
213th St. ... Pg.49 ... U27
219th St. ... Pg.50 ... V30
223rd St. ... Pg.50 ... V29

CEMETERIES
Assumption Cem. ... Pg.49 ... S26
Calvery Cem. ... Pg.48 ... W22
Mt. Glenwood Cem. ... Pg.44 ... Q25

FOREST PRESERVES
Jurgensen Woods ... Pg.44 ... Q26
Lansing Woods Pg.44 ... Q29
North Creek Meadows ... Pg.44 ... Q28
Plum Creek F.P. ... Pg.50 ... W29
Sauk Trail Woods ... Pg.48 ... V22

GOLF COURSES
Glenwood Country Club ... Pg.49 ... R26
Idlewild Country Club ... Pg.43 ... R23

SCHOOLS
Katz Corner Sch. Pg.50 ... V30
Sandridge Sch. Pg.50 ... T30

MISCELLANEOUS
Girl Scout Camp Pg.44 ... Q26

BREMEN TOWNSHIP
Pages 38,41,42
STREETS
Anne Ct. ... Pg.38 ... K18
Artesian Ave. ... Pg.41 ... M21
Austin Blvd. ... Pg.41 ... N16
Bachelor Grove Rd. ... Pg.38 ... J15
Beverly Ave. ... Pg.41 ... N16
Central Ave. ... Pgs.38,41 ... K17
Elmdale ... Pg.42 ... M21
Fairway Terr. ... Pg.42 ... P19
Forest Ave. ... Pg.41 ... O18
Fulton Terr. ... Pg.41 ... N16
Gaynelle Rd. ... Pg.41 ... N16
George Brennan Hwy. ... Pg.41 ... O17
Harlem Ave. ... Pg.40 ... P15
Highland Ave. ... Pg.41 ... P16
Jean Ct. ... Pg.38 ... K18
Jody Ln. ... Pg.41 ... N16
Justamere Rd. ... Pg.38 ... K15
Kedvale ... Pg.41 ... N19
Kenneth Ave. ... Pg.38 ... L18
Kilbourne Ave. ... Pg.38 ... L18
Kilpatrick ... Pg.41 ... N18
Kimberly Ln. ... Pg.41 ... N16
LaCrosse ... Pg.38 ... K18
Lamon Ave. ... Pg.38 ... J18
Laramie Ave. ... Pg.41 ... J,O17
Lavergne Ave. ... Pg.38,41 ... J,O,P18
Lawndale Ave., S. ... Pg.42 ... P20
Leclaire Ave. ... Pg.38,41 ... J17
Leslie Ann Dr. ... Pg.41 ... N16
Linder Ave. ... Pg.38,41 ... K17
Lockwood ... Pg.41 ... O17
Long Ave. ... Pg.38 ... J17
Luna Ave. ... Pg.38 ... K18
Major Ave. ... Pg.38 ... K17
Mark Ln. ... Pg.41 ... N16
Mayfield Ave. ... Pg.38 ... K16
Menard Ave. ... Pg.38 ... K16
Midlothian Turnpike ... Pg.38 ... J16
New England Ave. ... Pg.41 ... M15
Oak Forest Ave. ... Pg.41 ... N16
Oak Park Ave. ... Pg.41 ... P15
Parkside Ave. ... Pg.41 ... N16
Patricia Ave. ... Pg.41 ... N16
Poplar ... Pg.42 ... M21
Ridgeland Ave. ... Pg.38,41 ... K16
Sayre Ave. S. ... Pg.41 ... M,P15
Springfield Ave. ... Pg.42 ... P19
Thorndale ... Pg.42 ... M21
Waverly Ave. ... Pg.41 ... L18
62nd Ave. ... Pg.41 ... P16
135th ... Pg.38 ... I17
136th Pl. ... Pg.38 ... J17
137th St. ... Pg.38 ... J15
139th St. ... Pg.38 ... J17
141st St. ... Pg.38 ... J18
142nd St. ... Pg.38 ... J18
143rd ... Pg.38 ... K20
143rd St. ... Pg.38 ... J18
147th St. ... Pg.38 ... K15
148th St. ... Pg.38 ... J,K18
149th St. ... Pg.38 ... J18
151st St. ... Pg.38 ... L21
152nd St. ... Pg.38 ... L18
153rd St. ... Pg.40 ... L15
157th Ave. ... Pg.41 ... M15
157th Pl. ... Pg.41 ... P,M15
159th Ct. ... Pg.42 ... M21
162nd St. ... Pg.42 ... N21
163rd St. ... Pg.42 ... N19
166th St. ... Pg.41 ... N16
167th St. ... Pg.41 ... N16,18
171st St. ... Pg.41 ... O17,18
173rd St. ... Pg.41 ... O17,18
174th St. ... Pg.41 ... O17
175th St. ... Pg.41 ... O17
177th St. ... Pg.41 ... O17,P16,20
178th St. ... Pg.41 ... P15
179th St. ... Pg.41,42 ... P15,16,19
180th St. ... Pg.41 ... P15
181st St. ... Pg.41 ... P15
182nd St. ... Pg.41 ... P15
183rd St. ... Pg.41 ... P15,16

CEMETERIES
Bachelor Grove Cem. ... Pg.38 ... K15
County Cem. ... Pg.42 ... M19
Lutheran Cem. ... Pg.41 ... M15
St. Gabriel Cem. ... Pg.41 ... N18

FOREST PRESERVES
Bachelor Grove Pg.38 ... J15
Burr Oak Woods Pg.38 ... J15
Rubio Woods Pg.38 ... J16
Tinley Creek Woods ... Pg.38 ... J15
Yankee Woods Pg.41 ... O16

GOLF COURSES
Midlothian C.C. Pg.38 ... K17

SCHOOLS
Kimberly Heights Sch. ... Pg.41 ... N16
Orchard Hill Sch.Pg.41 ... M15
Trinity Sch. ... Pg.41 ... M15

MISCELLANEOUS
Camp Falcon ... Pg.38 ... K15
Camp Sullivan ... Pg.38 ... K15
Oak Forest Infirmary ... Pg.41 ... M18
South Cook Girl Scouts of America ... Pg.41 ... P18
Villa Santa Maria ... Pg.41 ... O16
Walter Fierke Educ. Center ... Pg.41 ... L15

BUFFALO GROVE
Pages 3,4,8,9
STREETS
Aber ... Pg.4 ... X12
Aberdeen Ln. ... Pg.4 ... X13
Acacia Ct. N. ... Pg.4 ... V11
Acacia Ct. S. ... Pg.4 ... V11
Acacia Terr. ... Pg.4 ... V11
Acorn Ct. ... Pg.4 ... X12
Acorn Pl. ... Pg.4 ... X11
Alden Ln. ... Pg.3 ... X11
Amherst Ct. ... Pg.3 ... X11
Anderson Ln. ... Pg.4 ... X11
Anthony Ct. ... Pg.9 ... A12
Anthony Rd. ... Pg.9 ... B12
Arbor Ct. ... Pg.4 ... A12
Arbor Gate Ln. ... Pg.3 ... X11
Arlington Heights Rd. ... Pg.3 ... A-X11
Armstrong Dr. ... Pg.4 ... X12
Asbury Dr. ... Pg.4 ... W13
Ashford Ct. ... Pg.8 ... X11
Aspen Ct. ... Pg.3 ... X11
Aspen Dr. ... Pg.3 ... X11
Auburn Ln. ... Pg.4 ... X11
Autumn Ct. ... Pg.4 ... X12
Banberry ... Pg.4 ... W11
Banyon Tree Ln. ... Pg.4 ... V12
Barclay Blvd. ... Pg.4 ... W13
Beacon Ct. ... Pg.3 ... B11
Bedford Ct. ... Pg.3 ... X10
Beechwood Ct. E. ... Pg.4 ... A11
Beechwood Ct. W. ... Pg.3 ... A11
Beechwood Rd. ... Pg.4 ... A11
Bel Aire Ct. ... Pg.4 ... A11
Bel Aire Dr. ... Pg.4 ... A11
Bellmont Ct. ... Pg.4 ... W12
Belmar Ct. ... Pg.3 ... X11
Belmar Ln. ... Pg.3 ... X11
Bentley Pl. ... Pg.3 ... X12
Berkley Ct. ... Pg.4 ... X11
Bernard Ct. W. ... Pg.3 ... A11
Bernard Dr. ... Pg.4 ... A11-12
Betty Dr. ... Pg.9 ... A11
Birchwood Ct. ... Pg.3 ... V12
Birchwood Ln. ... Pg.4 ... X12
Blackthorn Dr. ... Pg.4 ... X11
Blaho Ct. ... Pg.9 ... A12
Blue Ash Ct. ... Pg.3 ... V12
Bordeaux Ct. W. ... Pg.4 ... W11
Bourdeaux Ct. E. ... Pg.4 ... W11
Boxwood Ln. ... Pg.3 ... B11
Brandywn Ct. ... Pg.4 ... W11
Brandywn Ln. ... Pg.4 ... W11
Brentwood Terr. ... Pg.4 ... A11
Bristol Ln. ... Pg.3 ... W11
Brucewood Dr. ... Pg.4 ... A12
Buckingham Ln. ... Pg.4 ... X12
Buckthorn Ct. ... Pg.4 ... X13
Buckthorn Terr. ... Pg.4 ... X12
Buffalo Grove Rd. ... Pg.3 ... A-X12
Bunescu Ln. ... Pg.3 ... X11
Burgess Cir. ... Pg.3 ... X11
Burnt Ember Ct. ... Pg.4 ... X11
Burnt Ember Ln. ... Pg.3 ... X11
Busch Pkwy. ... Pg.4 ... X13
Busch Rd. ... Pg.4 ... X12
Cambridge Dr. ... Pg.9 ... B12
Camden Ct. ... Pg.3 ... X11
Cameron Way ... Pg.4 ... A11
Canterbury Ln. ... Pg.4 ... X12
Caren Ct. ... Pg.4 ... W12
Caren Ln. ... Pg.4 ... W12
Carlton Pl. ... Pg.3 ... X11
Carman Dr. ... Pg.4 ... X13
Carriage Way Dr. ... Pg.8 ... A11
Cary Ln. ... Pg.4 ... X11
Castlewood Ln. ... Pg.4 ... X11
Chapel Oaks Dr. ... Pg.3 ... V12
Charles Ct. ... Pg.3 ... B12
Chase Ct. ... Pg.4 ... X11
Chatham Ct. ... Pg.4 ... A11
Chaucer Way ... Pg.4 ... W11
Checker Dr. ... Pg.4 ... X11
Chenault Rd. ... Pg.4 ... A12
Cherrywood Rd. ... Pg.4 ... A11
Chestnut Ct. E. ... Pg.4 ... V12
Chestnut Ct. W. ... Pg.4 ... V12
Chestnut Terr. ... Pg.4 ... V12
Chevy Chase Ave. E. ... Pg.5 ... X14

Chicory Ct. ... Pg.4 ... X12
Chicory Ln. ... Pg.4 ... X12
Churchill Ct. ... Pg.3 ... W13
Circle Dr. ... Pg.4 ... X12
Clearwater Ct. ... Pg.3 ... W13
Clohesey Dr. ... Pg.3 ... X11
Cloverdale ... Pg.3 ... X11
Cobblestone Ln. ... Pg.4 ... X12
Cocoawood Cir. ... Pg.3 ... X13
Commerce Ct. ... Pg.4 ... X13
Cooper Ct. ... Pg.3 ... X11
Copperwood Dr. ... Pg.4 ... W12
Corporate Grove Dr. ... Pg.4 ... W13
Cottonwood Rd. ... Pg.4 ... A11-12
Country Ln. ... Pg.3 ... A11
Court 'N.' ... Pg.3 ... X11
Courtland Dr. ... Pg.3 ... W11
Coventry Ct. ... Pg.3 ... W12
Coventry Ln. ... Pg.3 ... W12
Covington Terr. ... Pg.4 ... A11
Crab Apple Terr. ... Pg.4 ... V12
Crestview Terr. ... Pg.4 ... A12
Crofton Ln. ... Pg.8 ... B11
Crossfield Ct. ... Pg.4 ... W12
Crown Point Dr. ... Pg.4 ... X12
Cumberland Ln. ... Pg.3 ... X13
Dannet Ct. ... Pg.4 ... W11
Dannet Rd. ... Pg.4 ... W11
Darryl Dr. ... Pg.9 ... A12
Dartmouth Ln. ... Pg.4 ... X13
Daulton Ct. ... Pg.3 ... V12
Daulton Dr. ... Pg.3 ... V12
Dayton Rd. ... Pg.4 ... X13
Deerfield Pkwy. ... Pg.4 ... X13
Depot Pl. ... Pg.4 ... A12
Devonshire Rd. ... Pg.4 ... W11
Devonwood Ct. ... Pg.4 ... W12
Diane Dr. ... Pg.4 ... A12
Dogwood Terr. ... Pg.3 ... X13
Dorncliff Ln. ... Pg.3 ... X11
Dover Ct. ... Pg.3 ... W12
Dover Dr. ... Pg.3 ... W12
Downing Rd. ... Pg.4 ... X12
Driftwood Pl. ... Pg.4 ... X12
Dun-lo Ave. ... Pg.9 ... A12
Dundee Pkwy. ... Pg.4 ... A12
Dundee Rd. ... Pg.4 ... A12
Dunham Ln. ... Pg.4 ... X11
Dunhill Dr. ... Pg.4 ... X11
Dunston Ln. ... Pg.3 ... V12
Eastwood Ln. ... Pg.4 ... X13
Ellen Dr. ... Pg.9 ... A12
Elmwood Dr. ... Pg.9 ... A11
English Oak Terr. Pg.4 ... W12
Essington Ln. ... Pg.4 ... X12
Estate Dr. ... Pg.4 ... A11
Eton Ct. ... Pg.3 ... A12
Euclid Ct. ... Pg.3 ... A12
Evergreen Pl. ... Pg.3 ... A11
Fabish Dr. ... Pg.4 ... X12
Fairfax Ln. ... Pg.3 ... X11
Farnsworth Ln. ... Pg.3 ... W11
Farrington Dr. ... Pg.4 ... X11
Ferndale Ct. ... Pg.4 ... A12
Forest Pl. ... Pg.4 ... A12
Forest Way Dr. ... Pg.3 ... X11
Fox Ct. E. ... Pg.4 ... X12
Fox Ct. W. ... Pg.4 ... X12
Fox Hill Dr. ... Pg.4 ... X12
Fox Tail Ct. ... Pg.5 ... X14
Foxford Dr. ... Pg.3 ... V12
Frances Ct. ... Pg.4 ... A12
Franklin Ln. ... Pg.3 ... W11
Fremont Way ... Pg.4 ... W-X11
Gail Dr. ... Pg.9 ... A11
Garden Ct. ... Pg.4 ... A12
Gardenia Ln. ... Pg.4 ... X13
Glendale Rd. ... Pg.4 ... X12
Golfview Terr. ... Pg.4 ... A12
Green Knolls Dr. ... Pg.4 ... W-X12
Greenbridge Rd. ... Pg.8 ... B11
Greenwood Ct. N. ... Pg.4 ... A11
Greenwood Ct. S. ... Pg.4 ... A11
Gregg Ln. ... Pg.4 ... X11
Grove Cir. ... Pg.3 ... A11
Grove Dr. ... Pg.3 ... A11
Hackberry Ct. ... Pg.3 ... V12
Hampshire Ct. ... Pg.4 ... X12
Happsfield Ln. ... Pg.8 ... A11
Harris Dr. ... Pg.4 ... X12
Harvard Ln. ... Pg.9 ... A12
Harvest Cir. ... Pg.4 ... X12
Hastings Ln. ... Pg.4 ... X12
Hawthorne Rd. ... Pg.4 ... A11-12
Hazelwood Terr. ... Pg.4 ... X13
Heatherdown Way ... Pg.4 ... W11
Hiawatha Dr. ... Pg.4 ... X11
Hickory Dr. ... Pg.4 ... A11
Hidden Lake Dr. ... Pg.4 ... X11
Highland Grove Ct. N. ... Pg.4 ...
Highland Grove Dr. ... Pg.4 ... X12
Hill Ct. E. ... Pg.4 ... X13
Hill Ct. W. ... Pg.4 ... X13
Hilldale Ln. ... Pg.4 ... X12
Hobson Dr. ... Pg.4 ... X12
Hollystone Ln. ... Pg.4 ... X13
Horatio Blvd. ... Pg.4 ... X13
Indian Hill Dr. ... Pg.4 ... A11
Indian Spring Ln. ... Pg.4 ... X11

Ivy Hall Ln. ... Pg.3 ... X11
Jersey Ct. ... Pg.4 ... W12
Juniper Ct. ... Pg.4 ... A12
Katherine Ct. ... Pg.3 ... A11
Ken Ln. ... Pg.4 ... W11
Kingsbridge Way ... Pg.4 ... W11
Kingston Dr. ... Pg.3 ... V12
Kirkwood Dr. ... Pg.4 ... X12
Knight Hill Ct. ... Pg.3 ... X11
Knollwood Dr. ... Pg.3 ... W11
La Salle Ct. N. ... Pg.4 ... W12
La Salle Ln. ... Pg.4 ... W12
Lake Cook Rd. ... Pg.3,4 ... A11,12
Lake St. ... Pg.9 ... A12
Lamont Ter. ... Pg.4 ... W12
Landcaster Ct. ... Pg.4 ... X12
Larchmont Dr. ... Pg.4 ... W11
Larraway Dr. ... Pg.4 ... X12
Lauren Ln. ... Pg.4 ... A12
Le Parc Cir. ... Pg.4 ... X13
Lee Ct. ... Pg.3 ... X11
Lehigh Ln. ... Pg.8 ... A11
Lexington Dr. ... Pg.4 ... X13
Lilac Ln. ... Pg.4 ... X13
Lincoln Terr. ... Pg.4 ... A12
Linden Ave. ... Pg.5 ... X14
Live Oak Ln. ... Pg.4 ... V12
Lockwood Ct. ... Pg.4 ... W12
Lockwood Dr. ... Pg.4 ... W12
Logsdon Ln. ... Pg.3 ... W11
London Ct. ... Pg.3 ... W12
Long Grove Aptakisic Rd. ... Pg.4 ... W11-14
Long Ridge Ct. ... Pg.4 ... W12
Longwood Ct. ... Pg.3 ... A11
Longwood Dr. ... Pg.3 ... A11
Lyon Ct. ... Pg.4 ... W11
Lyon Dr. ... Pg.4 ... W12
MacArthur Ct. ... Pg.4 ... A12
MacArthur Dr. ... Pg.4 ... A12
Madison Ct. N. ... Pg.4 ... W13
Madison Ct. S. ... Pg.4 ... W13
Madison Dr. ... Pg.4 ... W12
Magnolia Ct. E. ... Pg.4 ... V12
Magnolia Ct. W. ... Pg.3 ... V12
Maple Dr. ... Pg.4 ... A11
Margate Dr. ... Pg.4 ... W12
Marie Ave. ... Pg.4 ... X13
Marylu Ln. ... Pg.4 ... A12
Mayfair Ct., N. ... Pg.4 ... A11
Mayfair Ct., S. ... Pg.4 ... A11
Mayfair Ln. ... Pg.4 ... A11
Melinda Ln. ... Pg.4 ... A12
Middlesex Ct. ... Pg.9 ... A12
Millcreek Dr. ... Pg.8 ... A12
Miller Ln. ... Pg.8 ... B11
Milwaukee Ave. ... Pg.5 ... A14
Misty Woods ... Pg.3 ... V12
Mohawk Ct. ... Pg.3 ... A12
Mohawk Trail ... Pg.4 ... A12
Morningside Ln. E. ... Pg.4 ... X12
Morningside Ln. W. ... Pg.4 ... X12
Mulberry Ct. ... Pg.4 ... A11
Mundelein Rd. ... Pg.4 ... X11
Navajo Trail ... Pg.4 ... A12
New Dover ... Pg.3 ... V12
Newfield Dr. ... Pg.4 ... W12
Newport Ct. ... Pg.3 ... X11
Newtown Ct. ... Pg.4 ... X13
Newtown Dr. ... Pg.4 ... X12
Oak Creek Dr. ... Pg.4 ... A12
Old Arlington Ct. ... Pg.4 ... A11
Old Arlington Heights Rd. ... Pg.8 ... A11
Old Oak Ct., E. ... Pg.4 ... A12
Old Oak Ct., W. ... Pg.4 ... A12
Old Oak Dr. ... Pg.4 ... A12
Old Post Rd. ... Pg.8 ... A11
Osage Terr. ... Pg.4 ... X13
Oxford Dr. ... Pg.3 ... W11
Palmgren Ct. ... Pg.9 ... A12
Park Ln. ... Pg.3 ... X11
Park Pl. ... Pg.9 ... A12
Parker Ln. ... Pg.3 ... X11
Parkside Dr. ... Pg.4 ... W12
Parkview Terr. ... Pg.9 ... A11
Patton Dr. ... Pg.4 ... A12
Pauline Ave. ... Pg.4 ... X13
Penny Ln. ... Pg.3 ... X11
Pinehurst Ln. ... Pg.4 ... X12
Pinetree Cir. N. ... Pg.4 ... X12
Pinetree Cir. S. ... Pg.4 ... X12
Pinyon Ct. ... Pg.3 ... V12
Plum Grove Cir. ... Pg.3 ... A11
Poplar Ct. ... Pg.4 ... A11
Prairie ... Pg.4 ... X12
Prairie Ln. ... Pg.4 ... X12
Providence Ln. ... Pg.3 ... X11
Quaker Hollow Ct. N. ... Pg.4 ... W13
Quaker Hollow Ct. S. ... Pg.4 ... W13
Rachel Ln. ... Pg.3 ... A10
Radcliffe Rd. ... Pg.3 ... A11
Ranchview Ct. ... Pg.3 ... W11
Raphael Ave. ... Pg.4 ... X13
Raupp Blvd. ... Pg.4 ... A12
Red Oak Ct. ... Pg.4 ... A12
Redbud Pl. ... Pg.4 ... X12
Regent Ct. E. ... Pg.3 ... A11
Regent Ct. W. ... Pg.3 ... A11
Regent Dr. ... Pg.3 ... A11
Ridgefield Ln. ... Pg.4 ... X11
Ridgewood Ln. ... Pg.4 ... X13
Rivershire Ln. ... Pg.5 ... V14
Roberta Ct. ... Pg.4 ... A12
Ronnie Dr. ... Pg.4 ... W12
Rose Blvd. ... Pg.3 ... A10
Rose Ct. W. ... Pg.3 ... A11
Rosewood Ave. ... Pg.4 ... A12
Russellwood Ct. ... Pg.4 ... W13
Salk Rd. ... Pg.9 ... A12
Sandalwood Ct. ... Pg.4 ... V12
Sandalwood Rd. ... Pg.4 ... V12
Sandhurst Dr. ... Pg.4 ... W12
Saratoga Ln. ... Pg.8 ... A11
Satinwood Ct. ... Pg.4 ... V12
Satinwood Terr. ... Pg.4 ... W12
Saxon Ct. ... Pg.9 ... A12
Saybrook Ln. ... Pg.3 ... X11
Scottish Pine Ln. ... Pg.4 ... V11
Selwyn Ln. ... Pg.9 ... A12
Shady Grove Ln. ... Pg.4 ... X11
Shambliss Ct. ... Pg.3 ... X11
Shambliss Ln. ... Pg.3 ... X11
Silver Linden Ln. ... Pg.4 ... W12
Silver Rock Ln. ... Pg.4 ... X11
Somerset Ln. ... Pg.4 ... X12
Somerset Ln. ... Pg.4 ... X12
Springside Ct. ... Pg.4 ... X11
Springside Ln. ... Pg.4 ... X11
St. Mary's Pkwy. ... Pg.4 ... A12
Stanford Ln. ... Pg.8 ... A11
Station Ct. E. ... Pg.4 ... W12
Station Ct. W. ... Pg.4 ... W12
Station Dr. ... Pg.4 ... W12
Steeple Dr. ... Pg.4 ... X12
Stillwell Dr. ... Pg.4 ... A12
Stonebridge ... Pg.8 ... A11
Stonegate Ct. ... Pg.3 ... A11
Stonegate Rd. ... Pg.3 ... A11
Strathmore Ct. ... Pg.3 ... A11
Sunridge Ln. ... Pg.4 ... X12
Sussex Ct. ... Pg.9 ... A12
Sycamore Rd. ... Pg.4 ... A11
Teakwood Cir. ... Pg.4 ... X13
Terrace Pl. ... Pg.3 ... A11
Thistle Ct. ... Pg.4 ... W12
Thompson Blvd. ... Pg.4 ... W11
Thompson Ct. ... Pg.4 ... W12
Thorndale Ct. ... Pg.4 ... X12
Thorndale Dr. ... Pg.3 ... X12
Thornton Ln. ... Pg.8 ... A11
Thornwood Rd. ... Pg.4 ... A12
Three States Blvd. ... Pg.9 ... A11
Timber Hill Rd. ... Pg.4 ... A11
Trace Dr. ... Pg.3 ... A11
Trinity Ct. ... Pg.9 ... A12
Trotwood Ct. ... Pg.4 ... W12
Twilight Pass ... Pg.4 ... X11
Twisted Oak Ln. ... Pg.3,4 ... A11
University Dr. ... Pg.9 ... A12
Vernon Ct., N. ... Pg.4 ... A11
Vernon Ct., S. ... Pg.4 ... A11
Vernon Ln. ... Pg.4 ... A11
Villa Verde Dr. ... Pg.8 ... A11
Village Ct. ... Pg.4 ... W12
Wakefield Ln. ... Pg.4 ... X13
Wedgewood Ct. ... Pg.4 ... V11
Weidner Ct. ... Pg.4 ... A11
Weidner Rd. ... Pg.4 ... A11
Weiland Rd. ... Pg.4 ... A-X12
Wellington Ct. N. ... Pg.4 ... W12
Wellington Ct. S. ... Pg.4 ... W12
Westbourne Ln. ... Pg.4 ... X11
Westchester Ln. ... Pg.4 ... W12
Wheeling Ave. ... Pg.4 ... X13
Whispering Oaks Ct. ... Pg.3 ... V12
Whispering Oaks Dr. ... Pg.3 ... V12
White Oak ... Pg.4 ... V11
White Pine Rd. ... Pg.4 ... A11
Whitebranch Ct. ... Pg.4 ... X12
Whitehall Ct. ... Pg.3 ... A11
Whitehall Pl. ... Pg.3 ... A11
Whitney Ln. ... Pg.4 ... W12
Wildflower Ct. ... Pg.4 ... X12
Willow Pkwy. ... Pg.4 ... V12
Windbrooke Dr. ... Pg.4 ... X13
Winding Oak Ln. ... Pg.4 ... X12
Windover Ct. ... Pg.4 ... X12
Windsor Dr. ... Pg.4 ... A11
Windwood Ct. ... Pg.4 ... X12
Wood Hollow Ln. ... Pg.4 ... X12
Woodbury Ln. ... Pg.4 ... X12
Woodridge Ln. ... Pg.4 ... X12
Wyngate Ln. ... Pg.4 ... X12

CEMETERIES

Knopf Cem. ... Pg.3 ... X11

GOLF COURSES

Buffalo Grove G.C. ... Pg.4 ... X11
Chevy Chase C.C. ... Pg.5 ... X14

PARKS

Bicentennial Park ... Pg.3 ... W11
Bison Park ... Pg.3 ... A11
Cambridge Park ... Pg.9 ... A12
Emmerich Park ... Pg.4 ... A12
Kingsbridge Park ... Pg.3 ... W11
Lions Park ... Pg.4 ... A11
Longfellow Park ... Pg.3 ... A11
Mill Creek Park ... Pg.4 ... A11
Willow Stream Park ... Pg.4 ... X12

SCHOOLS

Buffalo Grove H.S. ... Pg.3 ... A11
Cooper Jr. H.S. ... Pg.3 ... A11
Ivy Hall Sch. ... Pg.4 ... X11
Joyce Kilmer Sch. ... Pg.4 ... A12
Longfellow Sch. ... Pg.3 ... A11
Willow Grove Sch. ... Pg.4 ... X11

SHOPPING CENTERS

Plaza Verde S.C. ... Pg.4 ... A10
The Plaza ... Pg.4 ... A12

MISCELLANEOUS

Alcott Community Ctr. ... Pg.4 ... A12

CHICAGO HEIGHTS

Pages 48,49

STREETS

Abbott Ave. ... S23
Aberdeen St. ... U24
Adams St. ... U22
Alden Ct. ... U23
Alice St. ... R24
Alvin Pl. ... S24
Amy St. ... S23
Andover Ct. ... U22
Andover Dr. ... U22
Arnold St. ... U25
Arquilla Ave., N. ... S23
Arquilla Dr., E. ... S23
Ash St. ... V24
Ashland Ave. ... R23
Ashland Ln. ... R23
Avonelle Dr. ... S23
Barbara Ln. ... T22
Beacon Blvd. ... U22
Beacon Ct. ... U22
Bellevue Pl. ... T24
Birch Ln. ... T23
Birmingham Ave. ... U24
Boston St. N. ... U23
Bradley Ln. ... S23
Bradoc St. ... T22
Brentwood Dr. ... R23
Briargate Ave. ... S24
Broadway ... T24
Brookline St. ... U22
Buena Vista Ave. ... U23
Buena Vista Cir. ... U23
Bunker St. ... U22
Butler St. ... U24
Butterfield Ave. ... V25
Caldwell Ave. ... S23
Cambridge St. ... U23
Campbell Ave. ... T23
Carey Ct. ... S23
Carpenter St. ... T24
Cedar Ln. ... T23
Center Ave. ... U24
Charing Cross Rd. ... S23
Charles St. ... R23
Chicago Heights-Glenwood Rd. ... R24
Chicago Rd. ... R23
Circle Ct. ... U24
Claude Ct. ... T24
Coales St. ... R24
Commercial Ave. ... S24
Concord Ct. ... U22
Concord Dr. ... U22
Concord Dr.,S. ... U22
Concord Dr.,W. ... U22
Constance ... S23
Coolidge St. ... R,T24
Cottage Grove Ave. ... T26
Country Club Rd. ... T23
Cove Dr. ... S22
Craig Dr., E. ... R23
Craig Dr., W. ... R23
Crescent Dr. ... T23
D'Amico Dr. ... T22
Dartmouth Dr. ... U23
Dawn Ln. ... S23
Deangels Ct. ... T23
Deer Trail Rd. ... S22
Diane Ln. ... R23
Division St. ... T22
Dixie Hwy. ... S23
Donovan Dr. ... U22
Doris Ln. ... S23
Dutra Ave. ... T22
East End Ave. ... U24
Eastgate Ave. ... S24
Eddy St. ... R23
Edgewood Ave. ... U23
Eggleston Ave. ... S24
Eighth St. ... T23
Elder Ave. ... T23
Elmwood Dr.,E. ... S23
Elmwood Dr.,W. ... S23
Emelia St. ... S23
Emerald Ave. ... S24
Enterprise Ct. ... T22
Enterprise Dr. ... T22
Euclid Ave. ... U23
Fairview Ave. ... U22
Fifth Ave. ... U25
Fitch Rd. ... S22
Flossmoor Rd. ... R23
Floyd Ln. ... S24
Forest Ave. ... U24
Frances Ln. ... R23
Franklin Ave. ... T23
Frederick Dr. ... R23
Gail Ln. ... S23
Garden Ave. ... U23
Glengate Ave. ... S23,24
Glengate,W. ... S23
Grace Ln. ... S23
Grant Ave. ... T24
Green St. ... U25
Greenbrier Ave. ... S23
Gregory Dr. ... T22
Grosvenor Pl. ... S24
Halsted St. ... R24
Hamilton Woods ... R23
Hanover St. ... U24
Hawthorne Ln. ... T23
Hickory St. ... U22
Highland Dr. ... T23
Hillcrest Ave. ... T24
Hilltop Ave. ... U22
Hillview Dr. ... U22
Holbrook Cir. ... R23
Holbrook Rd. ... R23
Homewood Ct. ... S24
Hutchinson Ave. ... T22
Illinois St. ... U24
Independence Way ... U24
Ingrid Ln. ... U22
Iris Ln. ... T23
Irving Blvd. ... T23
Isa Ave. ... T24
Joe Orr Rd. ... S23
Joyce Ln. ... S23
Judith Ln. ... R24
Kathleen Ln. ... S23
Kingston Pl. ... S23
Laflin St. ... S23
Laura ... S23
Lawrence St. ... U22
Leonard Ave. ... R23
Lerose Dr. ... R23
Lexington Dr. ... T22
Lincoln Ave. ... T24
Lincoln Hwy. ... U22
Linden Ln. ... T23
Longwood Ct. ... S22
Longwood Dr. ... S22
Lowe Ave. ... S24
Luther Ln. ... T23
Lynn Ln. ... R23
MacArthur Dr. ... T22
Mackler Dr. ... T23
Main St. ... U22
Manchester Dr., E. ... S24
Manchester Dr., N. ... S24
Maple Dr., N. ... T23
Maple Dr., W. ... T23
Marian Way ... T22
Martin Ln. ... T24
Mason Ct. ... T23
May Ct. ... S23
Mayfair Pl. ... S23
McEldowney Pl. ... U24
McKinley Ave. ... T24
Meadow Ln. ... T23
Memorial Dr. ... T23
Mildred Ln. ... S23
Minette Ln. ... U22
Morgan St. ... U24
Normal Ave. ... S24
Normandy Dr. ... S23
Normandy Dr., E. ... S23
Normandy Dr., W. ... S23
Oak St. ... U24
Orchard Ave. ... U23
Otto Blvd. ... T24
Pamela Dr. ... R24
Park Ave. ... T24
Parkside Ave. ... T24
Parkview Ave. ... T23
Parnell Ave. ... S24
Patricia Dr. ... R24
Paulina St. ... U23
Peggy Ln. ... T22
Peoria St. ... R,T24
Peyton Dr. ... R23
Piacenti Ln. ... T22
Pleasant Dr. ... S23
Plymouth Dr. ... U23
Plymouth St. ... U23
Portland Ave. ... U25
Prairie Ave. ... U23
Ranger Dr. ... T22
Raye Dr. ... R23
Revere Ct. ... U22
Ricky Dr. ... S24
Roberta Ln. ... S24
Roberts ... S22
Rosewood Ln. ... R23
Route 1 Cutoff ... T24
Sandra Ln. ... S23
Sangamon St. ... T24
Saratoga Dr. ... T22
Sauk Tr. ... W24
Schilling Ave. ... T23
School St. ... U24
Scott Ave. ... U23
Serena Dr. ... R23
Shea Dr. ... S22
Shelly Ln. ... U22
Sherry Ln. ... S23
Shields Ave. ... U25
Southgate Ave. ... T24
Spruce Ln. ... T23
Standish St. ... U23
State St. ... S25
Stewart Ave. ... U25
Stirling Ave. ... T22
Strieff Ave. ... S23
Sue Ct. ... S23
Sunnyside Ave. ... U23
Sunset Ave. ... U22
Tahoe Dr. ... S23
Terrace Dr. ... S23
Terry Ct. ... R23
Terry Ln. ... R23
Thelma Ln. ... S23
Theresa Ln. ... T23
Thomas St. ... T22
Thorn St. ... U23
Thorne Ct. ... T25
Travers Ave. ... T22
Travers Ct. ... T22
Union Ave. ... S24
Union St. ... U24
Vincennes Ave. ... T24
Vollmer Rd. ... S23
Wallace Ct. ... T23
Wallace St. ... U24
Washington Ave. ... T24
Wentworth Ave. ... U25
West End Ave. ... T24
Western Ave. ... T22
Westgate Ave. ... S23
Willow Dr. ... T23
Wilson Ave. ... U23
Winchester Rd. ... S22
Winston Ln. ... S22
Wood St. ... S23
Wooster Ct. ... U22
Yale Ave. ... U23
Yorktown Rd. ... T22
4th St. ... S23
7th Pl. ... T24
8th St. ... T22
10th St. ... T25
11th Pl. ... T23
11th St. ... T25
12th St. ... T25
13th St. ... U22,T25
14th Pl. ... U22
14th St. ... U22
15th Pl. ... U22
15th St. ... U22
16th Pl. ... U22
16th St. ... U22
17th St. ... U24
19th Pl. ... U24
19th St. ... U24
21st St. ... U24
22nd St. ... U24
23rd St. ... V25
24th St. ... V25
25th St. ... V25
26th St. ... V24
28th St. ... V24
193rd Pl. ... R24
195th St. ... R24
196th St. ... R24
197th Pl. ... R24
197th St. ... R24
201st St. ... S23
202nd St. ... S23
205th St. ... T22
209th St. ... T22

FOREST PRESERVES

Halsted Woods ... T24
Indian Hill Woods ... U23
Joe Orr Woods ... T24
Wilson Woods ... T24

GOLF COURSES

Chicago Heights C.C. ... T23
Chicago Heights Pk. Dist. G.C. ... S24

PARKS

Beacon Hill Park ... U22
Chicago Hts. Athletic Ball Pk. ... T24
Commissioners Park ... R23
Cornet Park ... U22
Euclid Park ... U23
Hillcrest Park ... T24
Jirtle Park ... V24
King Park ... U24
Landen Park ... T23
McEldowney Park ... U23
Meidell Park ... S23
North End Park ... R23
Sangamon Park ... T24
Siefer Park ... U25
Smith Park ... U23
Traverse Park ... T22
Wacker Park ... T24

SCHOOLS

Beacon Hills Sch. ... U22
Bloom Twp. H.S. ... T23
Emanuel Adventis Sch. ... U23
Garfield Sch. ... V24
Gavin Sch. ... T25
Greenbriar Sch. ... S23
Highland Sch. ... T23
Jefferson Sch. ... T24
Kennedy Sch. ... T22
Lincoln Sch. ... U24
Marian H.S. ... T23
Normandy Villa Sch. ... S23
Prairie St. Jr. College ... S24
Roosevelt Sch. ... U23
Serena Hills Sch. ... R23
St. Agnes Sch. ... U24
St. Anns Sch. ... U24
St. Josephs Sch. ... U23,25
St. Kieran Sch. ... R24
St. Pauls Sch. ... T23
St. Rocco Sch. ... U25
Washington McKinley Sch. ... U24
Wilson Sch. ... U22

SHOPPING CENTERS

Olympia Plaza ... S23

MISCELLANEOUS

City Hall & Police Department ... U24
Fire Department ... S24
Library ... U24
Post Office ... U24
St. James Hospital ... U24

CHICAGO RIDGE

Page 34,35

STREETS

Anderson Ave. ... E15
Austin Ave. ... F16
Barnard Dr. ... E15
Birmingham St. ... E16
Blanchard ... E15
Central Ave. ... F16
Donna Ave. ... D15
Fireside Dr. ... E15
Forest Ln. ... E15
Grove St. ... E15
Hyland Pl. ... E15
Janet Ln. ... E15
Kitty Ave. ... E15
Klein Ave. ... E15
Leslie Ln. ... E15
Lombard Ave. ... E16
Lyman Ave. ... E,F16
Major Ave. ... F16
Mansfield Ave. ... F16
Marshall Ave. ... E16
Mason Ave. ... E,F16
Massasoit Ave. ... F16
Mather Ave. ... D15,E16
Mayfield Ave. ... E16
McVicker Ave. ... E,F16
Meade Ave. ... E16
Melvina ... F16
Menard Ave. ... E,F16
Monitor Ave. ... E16
Moody Ave. ... E,F16
Mormora ... F16
Nashville Ave. ... D,E15
Natoma Ave. ... D,E15
New England Ave. ... D15
Norfolk Ln. ... E15
Normandy Ave. ... D,E15
Nottingham Ave. ... D14
O'Connell St. ... D14
Oak Ave. ... F16
Oak Park Ave. ... D,E15
Orchard Ln. ... E15
Oxford Ave. ... E,F16
Pacific Ave. ... D16
Pamela Ln. ... E15
Parkside Ave. ... E17,F16
Pleasant Blvd. ... F17
Princess Ave. ... F16
Ridge Dr. ... E15
Ridgeland Ave. ... F16
Ridgemont Ln. ... E16
Sayre ... D15
Southwest Hwy. ... E15
Stephen Dr. ... E15
Sycamore ... E15
Tracy Ave. ... E15
Tri-State Tollway ... D14
Washington St. ... E16
97th Pl. ... D15
98th St. ... D14,15
99th Pl. ... D14
99th St. ... D14-16
100th St. ... D15
101st St. ... E16
103rd St. ... E16
104th Pl. ... E15
104th St. ... E15
105th St. ... E15,16
106th Pl. ... E15
106th St. ... E15,16
107th Pl. ... E16
107th St. ... E16
108th Pl. ... F16
108th St. ... F16
109th Pl. ... F16
110th St. ... F16
111th St. ... F16

PARKS

Memorial Park ... E16

CHICAGO RIDGE

SCHOOLS
- Finley Jr. H.S. F16
- Our Lady of the Ridge Sch. F16
- Ridge Central Sch. F16
- Ridge Lawn Sch. E16
- Ridge Sch. E15
- Youth / Senior Ctr. E16

SHOPPING CENTERS
- Chicago Ridge Commons D15
- Chicago Ridge Mall D15

MISCELLANEOUS
- Fire Department E16
- Police Department E16
- Village Hall & Library E16

COUNTRY CLUB HILLS

Page 41,42

STREETS
- Amherst Ct. P19
- Amlin Cir. Q18
- Anthony P18,19,Q18,R19
- Apple Tree Dr. O20
- Arlington Dr. P20
- Baker Ave. P,Q,R19
- Baker St. P19
- Becker Terr. Q18
- Birch Ave. P,R19
- Briargate N20
- Butterfield N20
- Cedar Ave. P,Q,R19
- Cedar Ct. R19
- Central Park Ave. P20
- Chestnut Ave. P,Q,R19
- Chestnut Dr. R19
- Cicero Ave. Q18
- Clarence Ave. P19
- Cottonwood Ct. O19
- Country Club Dr. P20
- Coventry Ln. O19
- Crawford Ave. P19
- Crest Ct. Q18
- Cypress Ave. P,Q19
- Cypress Ct. R19
- Cypress Dr. R19
- Devon Dr. P19
- East Gate Dr. O19
- Edwards Ave. P19
- Elm Dr. R19
- Fairway Terr. P19
- Farmcrest Terr. R19
- Glen Oaks O20
- Green View Terr. P19
- Harvard Ln. P20
- Hawthorne P19
- Hickory Ave. R19
- Hickory Dr. R19
- Highland Pl. P20
- Hillcrest Dr. P20
- Holly Ct. O19
- Hollywood Ln. P18
- Huntleigh Ct. P19
- Idlewild Dr. P19
- Indian Hill Dr. O19
- John Ave. P18
- John St. Q18,R19
- Junew Ct. P19
- Keeler Ave. Q19
- Keeler Dr. R19
- Kirk Ct. P20
- Kostner Ave. P19
- Laramie Rd. Q18
- Larkin Ln. P18
- Laurel Ln. O20
- Lavergne Ave. O,P18
- Lee St. Q18
- Loras Ln. R19
- Loretto Ln. R19
- Maple Ave. P,Q,R19
- Martin Ct. R18
- Martin Ln. R18
- Mary Ann Ln. P18
- Mary Ct. Q18
- Marycrest Dr. Q18
- Mayfair Ct. P19
- Michael Ave. P18
- Mocombo Way P18
- Mulberry P19
- Mulberry Terr. Q19
- Neal Cir. Q18
- Nightingale Ter. Q18
- Oak Ave. R19
- Oakwood Ave. P,Q,R19
- Oakwood Ct. R19
- Old Elm O19
- Olympic Dr. P19
- Orchard Ln. O19
- Park Ln. O19
- Patrick P18
- Pear Tree Ct. O19
- Pheasant Ln. P20
- Pine Dr. R19
- Princeton Ln. P20
- Provincetown Dr. Q19
- Ravisloe Terr. P19
- Rosewood P18
- Russett Way O19
- Sarah Ct. P20
- Sarah Ln. P20
- School Dr. P20
- Soleri Dr. P19
- Springfield Ave. P19
- Sunset Ln. P18
- Sunset Ridge O19
- Sycamore Ave. P19
- Thomas Ln. P18
- Timberlea Ct. O19
- Walnut Ave. Q19
- Wildwoode Way O20
- Williamsburg Dr. Q19
- Willow Ave. P,Q,R19
- Willow Ct. Q19
- Wilshire Blvd. P18
- Windsor Ln. Q19
- Winston Ct. O19
- Winston Dr. P19
- Yale Ln. R20
- 40th Ct. Q19
- 167th Pl. N19
- 167th St. N19
- 168th Pl. N19
- 168th St. N19
- 169th St. O19
- 171st Pl. O19
- 171st St. O19
- 172nd Pl. O19
- 172nd St. O19
- 173rd St. O18
- 175th Pl. O20,P18
- 175th St. O19
- 176th Pl. P18,19,20
- 176th St. P18,19,20
- 177th Pl. P19
- 177th St. P18,19,20
- 178th Pl. P19
- 178th St. P18,19
- 179th Pl. P18
- 179th St. P19
- 180th St. P19
- 181st Pl. P18
- 181st St. P18,19
- 182nd Pl. P19
- 182nd St. P19
- 184th Ct. Q18
- 184th Pl. Q18
- 184th St. Q18
- 185th Ct. Q18
- 185th Pl. Q18
- 185th St. Q18
- 186th Pl. Q18,19
- 186th St. Q19
- 187th Pl. Q19
- 187th St. Q18,19
- 188th Pl. Q19
- 188th St. Q18,19
- 189th Pl. R19
- 189th St. Q18,19
- 190th Pl. R19
- 190th St. R19
- 191st Ct. R19
- 191st St. R19
- 192nd Pl. R19
- 192nd St. R19
- 193rd St. R19
- 194th Ct. R19
- 194th St. R19
- 195th St. R19

PARKS
- Atkins Park P19
- Community Park O19
- Cypress Park R19
- Independence Park P19
- Kiwanis Park Q18
- Nob Hill Park O20
- Tierra Grande Park Q19
- Willow Wood Park O20
- Wulf Park Q19

SCHOOLS
- Baker Sch. Q19
- Cooper Grove Sch. Q18
- Hillcrest H.S. O19
- Knob Hill Sch. N20
- Meadowview Sch. P18
- South Sch. Q19
- Southwood Jr. H.S. Q18
- St. Emeric Cath. Sch. P19
- St. John Sch. Q19

SHOPPING CENTERS
- Country Club Hills Shopping Plaza P18
- Country Club Shopping Center Q19

MISCELLANEOUS
- City Hall & Police Department O20
- Civic Center & Library Q19
- Fire Department Q19
- Friendship Center P18

DEER PARK

Page 1-2

STREETS
- Bobwhite Ln. X6
- Bramble Ln. X7
- Briargate Ln. X7
- Cardinal Ct. X6
- Cheshire Ct. X7
- Circle Dr. X6
- Clover Ln. X6
- Court Lagrov X7
- Court Touraine X7
- Corners Dr. X6
- Covington Dr. X7
- Deer Lake Dr. X6
- Deer Valley Rd. X7
- Dogwood Ct. X7
- Doncaster Cir. X7
- Dover Ct. X7
- Edgeview Ct. X6
- Fairview Dr. X6
- Ferndale Rd. X6
- Fox Chase Rd. X6
- Glengarry Cir. X6
- Glenhurst Rd. X6
- Heather Ln. X7
- Hollington Ln. X7
- Juniper Ct. X6
- Juniper Ln. X6
- Lake View Ct. X6
- Lake-Cook Rd. X7
- Landmark Ln. X7
- Laurel Dr. X6
- Lea Rd. X6
- Lois Ln. X6
- Lone Pine X6
- Long Grove Rd. X5
- Madach Ct. X7
- Mallard Ct. X6
- Mariel Ct. X7
- Meadow Ct. X6
- Newcastle Ct. X7
- Oak Ridge Ln. X6
- Park Hill Dr. X6
- Pheasant Hill Rd. X6
- Pheasant Tr. X6
- Primrose Ct. X6
- Quail Ct. X6
- Rand Rd. X7
- Rue Chamonix X7
- Rue Orleanais X7
- Rue Touraine X7
- Shady Ln. X6
- Shoreham Ct. X7
- Sunset Ridge Rd. X6
- Sunshine Ln. X7
- Surrey Ct. X7
- Swallow Ct. X6
- Swansway Rd. X7
- Teal Ct. X6
- Thornbury Ct. X7
- Thronhill Ct X6
- Wagon Ct. X7
- Wallingford Ave. X7
- Wehrheim Rd. X6
- Wheel Ct. X7
- Wicker Dr. X7
- Wildrose Dr. X6
- Willow Ct. X7
- Woodberry Ct. X6
- Woodberry Rd. X6

DEERFIELD

Page 21,22

STREETS
- Huehl Rd. A2
- Lake-Cook Rd. A2
- Pfingsten Rd. A3
- Waukegan Rd. A4

DES PLAINES

Pages 14,15,19,20,28,29

STREETS
- Acres Ln. Pg.15 J17
- Albany Ln. Pg.15 G14
- Alden Ct. Pg.20 M17
- Alfini Dr. Pg.15 J15
- Alger Pg.20 M16
- Algonquin Rd. Pg.15 J16
- Alles St. Pg.15 H16
- Ambleside Rd. Pg.14 J13,14
- Amherst Ave. Pg.14 G14
- Anderson Ter. Pg.19 J14
- Andrea Ln. Pg.14 J13
- Andy Ct. Pg.15 L17
- Anita St. Pg.15 H14
- Apple Creek Ln. Pg.15 J17
- Ardmore Rd. Pg.15 G15
- Arlington Ave. Pg.15 H16
- Armstrong Ct. Pg.19 M14
- Armstrong Rd. Pg.19 M14
- Arnold Ct. Pg.19 J13
- Ash St. Pg.15 K16
- Ashbury Cir. Pg.28 M3
- Ashland Ave. Pg.14,15 J14-16
- Ballard Rd. Pg.15 H17
- Beau Ct. Pg.14 J13
- Beau Dr. Pg.14 J13
- Bedford Ln. Pg.14 H14
- Bell Dr. Pg.14 H14
- Bellaire Ave. Pg.15 H17
- Bellaire Ct. Pg.28 J2
- Bellaire Ct. Pg.15 H17
- Bender Rd. Pg.15,20 H17
- Bending Ct. Pg.15 F15
- Bennett Ln. Pg.14 H13
- Bennett Pl. Pg.15 K17
- Berkshire Ct. Pg.15 G15
- Berkshire Ln. Pg.15 G15
- Berry Ln. Pg.15 K17
- Big Bend Dr. Pg.15 H17
- Birch St. Pg.15 L17
- Birchwood Ave. Pg.15 L17
- Bittersweet Ct. Pg.24 L1
- Boardwalk Pg.28 M3
- Bradley St. Pg.14 H14
- Bradrock Dr. Pg.14 K14
- Brentwood Dr. Pg.14 H14
- Briar Ct. Pg.15 K16
- Broadway Pg.15 H15
- Brown St. Pg.15 H16
- Busse Hwy. Pg.15 J17
- Cambridge Rd. Pg.14 G14
- Campbell Ave. Pg.15 J16
- Carlow Dr. Pg.15 F15
- Carol Ln. Pg.15 K15
- Cavan Ln. Pg.14 J13
- Cedar Ct. Pg.15 K17
- Cedar St. Pg.15 L17
- Center St. Pg.15 J16
- Central Ave. Pg.20 M16
- Central Rd. Pg.14 G14
- Chase Ave. Pg.15 L17
- Chestnut St. Pg.15 K-L16
- Chicago Ave. Pg.24 J1
- Church St. Pg.15 H17
- Cindy Ln. Pg.15 K15
- Circle Dr. Pg.15 G17
- Circle St. Pg.15 K16
- Clark Ln. Pg.19 J14
- Clayton Ln. Pg.15 G15
- College Dr. Pg.15 G16
- Columbia Ave. Pg.15 H14-15
- Concord Ln. Pg.15 G15
- Cora St. Pg.15 K16
- Cordial Dr. Pg.14 K13
- Cornell Ave. Pg.14 G14
- Courtesy Ln. Pg.14 K13
- Crabtree Ln. Pg.15 J17
- Craig Dr. Pg.20 M17
- Cranbrook St. Pg.14 G14
- Crestwood Dr. Pg.15 J15
- Cumberland Pkwy. Pg.14 H14
- Curtis St. Pg.20 M17
- Dale St. Pg.15 L16
- Danbury Ln. Pg.14 K14
- Dara James Rd. Pg.14 H14
- David Dr. Pg.20 L17
- Davis Ct. Pg.14 H14
- Dawn Ct. Pg.15 H17
- Dayton Pl. Pg.14 K13
- Deane St. Pg.15 J-K16
- Debra Dr. Pg.14 H13
- Dempster St. Pg.15 J17
- Dennis Pl. Pg.15 K15
- Denver Dr. Pg.14 K14
- Des Plaines River Rd. Pg.15 K17
- Devon Ave. Pg.20 M17
- Devonshire Dr. Pg.14 K13
- Dexter Ln. Pg.15 K15
- Diamond Head Dr. Pg.14 J13-14
- Doreen Dr. Pg.14 J14
- Dorothy Dr. Pg.14 J13
- Douglas Ave. Pg.15 L15
- Dover Dr. Pg.14 K13-14
- Dover Ln. Pg.14 K14
- Drake Ln. Pg.14 G14
- Dulles Rd. Pg.14 H14
- Eaker Pl. Pg.19 J14
- Earl Ave. Pg.15 K15
- East Grant Dr. Pg.15 J15
- East River Rd. Pg.15 H17
- East Villa Dr. Pg.15 J15
- Eastview Dr. Pg.15 L15
- Easy St. Pg.14 H14
- Edgebrook Pg.28 K2
- Edward Ct. Pg.28 J2
- Eisenhower Ct. Pg.15 L17
- Eisenhower Dr. Pg.20 M17
- Elizabeth Ln. Pg.14 K13
- Elk Blvd. Pg.15 H16
- Ellinwood St. Pg.15 J16
- Elm St. Pg.15 K16
- Elmhurst Rd. Pg.14 K13
- Elmira Ave. Pg.15 L15
- Emerson St. Pg.28 J3
- Esser Ct. Pg.15 K17
- Estes Ave. Pg.15 L17
- Estes St. Pg.28 M2
- Everett Ave. Pg.15 K16
- Everett Ln. Pg.15 K16
- Evergreen Ave. Pg.15 H14,16
- Executive Way Pg.15 K15
- Farewell Ave. Pg.20 L16
- Fargo Ave. Pg.15 L16-17
- Farthing Ln. Pg.14 H14
- Figard Ct. Pg.14 H14
- Fletcher Dr. Pg.14 H14
- Florian Dr. Pg.14 J13
- Forest Ave. Pg.15 K15
- Forest Edge Ln. Pg.15 H17
- Fox Ln. Pg.20 M17
- Fremont Ave. Pg.14 H14
- Fremont Ct. Pg.15 H14
- Frontage Rd. Pg.15 L16
- Galleon Way Pg.14 H14
- Garland Pl. Pg.15 J17
- Golf Rd. Pg.15 G16
- Good Ave. Pg.24 J2
- Graceland Ave. Pg.15 H16
- Grant Dr. E. Pg.15 J15
- Grant Dr. W. Pg.15 J15
- Greco Ave. Pg.15 L16
- Greenleaf Ave. Pg.15 L16
- Greenview Ave. Pg.15 H15
- Gregory St. Pg.10 F15
- Grove Ave. Pg.15 H16
- Halsey Dr. Pg.20 M17
- Harding Ave. Pg.14,15 H14,16
- Harvard St. Pg.14 G14
- Harvey Ave. Pg.14,15 H14,15
- Hawthorne Ln. Pg.15 H17
- Hawthorne Terr. Pg.15 H17
- Hazel Ct. Pg.15 K16
- Heather Ln. Pg.15 J15
- Henry Ave. Pg.15 J16
- Hewitt Dr. Pg.14 J14
- Hickory St. Pg.15 L17
- Higgins Rd. Pg.20 M16
- Highland Dr. Pg.15 L16
- Hills Ave. Pg.15 H16
- Hoffman Pkwy. Pg.15 J15
- Holiday Ln. Pg.19 J13
- Hollywood Ave. Pg.15 H15
- Horne Terr. Pg.19 J14
- Howard Ave. Pg.15 K16,L14
- Ida St. Pg.15 H16
- Illinois St. Pg.15 K16
- Ingram Pl. Pg.19 J14
- Inner Circle Dr. Pg.15 H14
- Iris Ln. Pg.15 L17
- Ironwood Dr. Pg.24 J2
- Irwin Ave. Pg.15 K15
- Jarlath Ave. Pg.15 L15
- Jarvis Ave. Pg.15 L15-17
- Jeanette St. Pg.15 J16
- Jefferson St. Pg.15 H16
- Jeffrey Ln. Pg.14 K14
- Jill Ct. Pg.14 J13
- Jon Ct. Pg.14 H13
- Jon Ln. Pg.15 G15
- Joseph Ave. Pg.20 L17
- Joseph J. Schwab Rd. Pg.15,20 J17
- Joyce Dr. Pg.14 K13
- Junior Terr. Pg.15 H17
- Kathleen Dr. Pg.14 J13
- Kenilworth Ct. Pg.14 J14
- Kenmare Ct. Pg.15 F15
- Kenmare Dr. Pg.15 F15
- Kennicott Ct. Pg.15 K17
- Kerry Ct. Pg.24 J3
- Kincaid Ct. Pg.14 J13,14
- King Ln. Pg.19 J13,14
- Kingston Ct. Pg.15 K15
- Koehler Dr. Pg.15 K15
- Koplin Dr. Pg.14 K13
- Kylemore Ct. Pg.15 F15
- Kylemore Dr. Pg.15 F15
- LaSalle St. Pg.19 H14
- Lancaster Ln. Pg.14 K14
- Lance Dr. Pg.14 J14
- Laura Ln. Pg.15 L17
- Laurel Ave. Pg.15 J-H16
- Lawn Ln. Pg.14 H14
- Leahy Circle E. Pg.19 J14
- Leahy Circle S. Pg.19 J14
- Lechner Ln. Pg.15 H17
- Lee St. Pg.15 K16
- Leslie Ln. Pg.14 J13
- Lillian Ln. Pg.14 H13
- Lincoln Ave. Pg.15 K15,16
- Lincoln Ln. Pg.14 K13
- Linden St. Pg.15 K16
- Lismore Dr. Pg.15 F15
- Little Path Rd. Pg.14 H14
- Locust St. Pg.15 K17
- Luau Dr. Pg.15 G15
- Lunt Ave. Pg.15 L16
- Lyman Ave. Pg.15 H-J17
- Lynn Ct. Pg.14 H14
- Madelyn Dr. Pg.15 F15
- Magnolia St. Pg.15 L17
- Mannheim Rd. Pg.15 L16
- Manor Ct. Pg.14 J14
- Maple St. Pg.15,20 K-L17
- Marcella Rd. Pg.14 G14
- Margaret St. Pg.15,20 J,K15
- Marina St. Pg.15 H14
- Marion St. Pg.15 J16
- Mark Ave. Pg.15 F15
- Marshall Dr. Pg.14 H-K14
- Mary St. Pg.15 H16
- Mason Ln. Pg.15 J17
- McCain Ct. Pg.14,19 J14
- Meyer Ct. Pg.14 H14
- Miami Ln. Pg.14 K14
- Michael Ct. Pg.14 H13
- Michael Rd. Pg.14 H14
- Mill St. Pg.15 H16
- Millers Rd. Pg.14 H14
- Miner St. Pg.15 H16
- Mitchell Ln. Pg.15 F15
- Moody Pg.29 M8
- Morgan-O'Brien Pg.15 H14
- Morray Ct. Pg.14 J13
- Morse Ave. Pg.20 L16
- Mt. Prospect Rd. Pg.14 J14
- Munroe Cir. Pg.14,19 J13,14
- Murray Ln. Pg.14 J13
- Nebel N. Pg.15 K15
- Nelson Ln. Pg.15 G15
- Nimitz Dr. Pg.20 M17
- Norman Ct. Pg.14 H13
- North Ave. Pg.15 H15
- North Golf Pg.15 G15
- North Shore Ave. Pg.20 M17
- Northeast Ct. Pg.15 J15
- Northeast Pl. Pg.15 J15
- Northwest Hwy. Pg.15 H15
- Northwest Pl. Pg.15 J15
- Northwest Tollway Pg.15 L15
- Nuclear Dr. Pg.14 L14
- Oak St. Pg.15 H16
- Oakton St. Pg.15 K15
- Oakwood Ave. Pg.14,15 J14-16
- Oakwood St. Pg.15 J15
- Olivia Ave. Pg.15 K15
- Orchard Ct. Pg.15 H15
- Orchard Pl. Pg.20 M16
- Orchard St. Pg.15 K16
- Oxford Rd. Pg.15 H,K-L15
- Park Ln. Pg.28 M3
- Park Pl. Pg.15 H16
- Park, N. Pg.20 M17
- Park, S. Pg.20 M17
- Parkview Ln. Pg.15 J17
- Parkwood Ln. Pg.15 L17
- Parsons Ave. Pg.15 H16
- Patricia Ln. Pg.15 G15
- Patton Dr. Pg.20 M17
- Paula Ln. Pg.20 L17
- Pearle Dr. Pg.20 L17
- Pearson St. Pg.15 J16
- Pennsylvania Ave. Pg.14 K14
- Perda Ln. Pg.14 J13
- Perry St. Pg.15 H16
- Peter Rd. Pg.15 L17
- Phoenix Dr. Pg.14 K14
- Pine St. Pg.15 K16
- Pinehurst Dr. Pg.14 G14
- Plainfield Dr. Pg.15 K15
- Pleasant Ln. Pg.14 K13
- Polynesian Dr. Pg.15 G15
- Potter Rd. Pg.28 J13
- Prairie Ave. Pg.15 J15-16
- Pratt Ave. Pg.20 M17
- Princeton St. Pg.14 G14
- Prospect Ave. Pg.15 K16
- Prospect Ln. Pg.15 K16
- Radcliffe Ave. Pg.14,15 G,H14
- Railroad Ave. Pg.15 L16
- Rand Rd. Pg.15 G15
- Rawls Rd. Pg.14 K14
- Redeker Rd. Pg.15 H16
- Regency Pg.15 G15
- Ridge Ln. Pg.14 K13
- Rita Rd. Pg.28 J2
- River Dr. Pg.15 J17
- River Ln. Pg.15 H16
- River St. Pg.15 H16
- Riverview Ave. Pg.15 K16
- Rose Ave. Pg.15 J15
- Roxbury Ln. Pg.14 K14
- Roxbury Ln. E. Pg.15 K14
- Rusty Dr. Pg.15 L17
- Sakas Dr. Pg.15 H16
- Sandy Ln. Pg.14 H13
- Santa Rosa Dr. Pg.15 L15
- Scott St. Pg.20 L-M17
- Seegers Rd. Pg.15 H15
- Seminary Ave. Pg.24 J2
- Seymour Ave. Pg.14 J13
- Shagbark Dr. Pg.15 J17
- Shannon Ct. Pg.14 H13
- Shawn Ln. Pg.14 J14
- Shepherd Dr. Pg.15 K16
- Sherman Pl. Pg.15 H16
- Sherwin Ave. Pg.15 K16-17
- Sherwood Rd. Pg.15 H17
- Short Terr. Pg.14 K13
- Simone Dr. Pg.15 G15
- Small Ln. Pg.15 F15
- South Golf Pg.15 H15
- Southeast Ct. Pg.15 J15
- Southeast Pl. Pg.15 J15
- Southwest Pl. Pg.15 J15
- Springfield Ave. Pg.14 J14
- Spruance Pl. Pg.14,19 J14
- Spruce Ave. Pg.15 K16
- Sprucewood Ave. Pg.15 L15
- Stark Pl. Pg.14,19 J14
- State St. Pg.15 G15
- Stewart Ave. Pg.15 J17
- Stillwell Dr. Pg.20 M17
- Stockton Ave. Pg.15 K16
- Stone St. Pg.15 G15
- Stratford Rd. Pg.15 G15
- Suffield St. Pg.24 J2
- Sunset Ave. Pg.20 M17
- Susan Dr. Pg.14 K13
- Sycamore St. Pg.15,20 K-M16
- Teela Ln. Pg.15 G17
- Terrace Ln. Pg.14 J14
- Thacker St. Pg.15 J15
- Therese Terr. Pg.15 F15
- Times Dr. Pg.15 K16
- Timothy Ln. Pg.15 F15
- Touhy Ave. Pg.15 L16
- Tracy Terr. Pg.15 G15
- Trailside Ln. Pg.15 H17
- Tri-State Tollway Pg.15 K17
- Tures Ln. Pg.15 K15
- University Ln. Pg.15 H17
- University St. Pg.15 H17
- Van Buren Ave. Pg.15 J15-16
- Vassar Ln. Pg.14 G14
- Victoria Rd. Pg.14 J14
- Villa Dr. E. Pg.15 J15
- Villa Dr. W. Pg.15 J15
- Village Ct. Pg.14 G14
- Waikiki Dr. Pg.15 G15
- Walnut Ave. Pg.15,19 J14,15
- Walnut St. Pg.15 J15
- Walter Ave. Pg.15 H15
- Walton Pg.24 H1
- Walton St. Pg.15 G16

Warrington Rd. Pg.14 ... G-J14
Washington Ave. Pg.14 ... H14
Washington Ct. Pg.15 ... H14
Washington St. Pg.15 ... H16
Waterford Ct. ... Pg.15 ... F15
Waterford Dr. ... Pg.15 ... F15
Wayne Dr. ... Pg.15 ... J15
Webford Ave. ... Pg.15 ... H16
Webster Ave. ... Pg.20 ... M16
Webster Ln. ... Pg.15 ... J-L15
Wedgewood Ave. ... Pg.15 ... K15
Welwyn Ave. ... Pg.15 ... L17
West Grant Dr. ... Pg.15 ... J15
West Villa Dr. ... Pg.15 ... J15
Western ... Pg.15 ... H16
Westfield Ln. ... Pg.14 ... J14
Westgate Rd. ... Pg.15 ... G-J14
Westmere Rd. ... Pg.14 ... H13,14
Westview Dr. ... Pg.15 ... L15
Wexford Ct. ... Pg.15 ... F15
Whitcomb Ave. Pg.15 ... J16
White St. ... Pg.15 ... K16
Wicke Ave. ... Pg.15 ... K16
Wieboldt's Dr. ... Pg.15 ... H15
Wilkins Dr. ... Pg.14 ... H14
Wille Rd. ... Pg.14 ... K13
Willow Ave. ... Pg.15 ... H16
Wilson Ave. ... Pg.24 ... J1
Wilson Dr. ... Pg.14 ... J13
Windsor Dr. ... Pg.14 ... K14
Winthrop Dr. ... Pg.14 ... K14
Wisconsin Dr. ... Pg.14 ... G14
Wolf Rd. ... Pg.15 ... K15
Woodbridge Rd. Pg.15 ... H15
Woodland Ave. Pg.15 ... H16
Woodlawn Ave. Pg.15 ... H15
Woods Ln. ... Pg.15 ... H17
Yale Ct. ... Pg.15 ... H15
Yorkshire Ln. ... Pg.15 ... G15
1st ... Pg.15 ... H16
2nd Ave. ... Pg.15 ... H-K15
3rd Ave. ... Pg.15 ... G-J15
4th Ave. ... Pg.15 ... G-K15
5th Ave. ... Pg.15 ... G-K15
5th Ct. ... Pg.15 ... H15
6th Ave. ... Pg.15 ... G-J15
7th Ave. ... Pg.15 ... G15
8th Ave. ... Pg.15 ... G15

CEMETERIES

All Saints Cem. Pg.15 ... G16

FOREST PRESERVES

Lions Woods ... Pg.24 ... J1

PARKS

Apache Park ... Pg.15 ... L16
Arndt Park ... Pg.15 ... K16
Blackhawk Park Pg.14 ... H14
Central Park ... Pg.24 ... K1
Chautauqua Pk. Pg.28 ... K2
Cherokee Park ... Pg.24 ... L1
Cheyenne Park Pg.15 ... G15
Chino Park ... Pg.14 ... J14
Chippewa Park Pg.15 ... G15
Cornell Park ... Pg.15 ... G15
Craig Manor Park ... Pg.15 ... F15
Cumberland Terr. Park ... Pg.15 ... H15
Des Plaines Park Dist. ... Pg.15 ... L17
Eton Field ... Pg.20 ... M17
Highridge Knolls Park ... Pg.14 ... J13
Jaycee Park ... Pg.24 ... L1
Kiwanis Park ... Pg.24 ... L1
Lake Park ... Pg.28 ... M1
Majewski Metro Park ... Pg.14 ... K13
McKay-Nealis Park ... Pg.24 ... L2
Menominee Park ... Pg.24 ... J1
Mountain View Mine ... Pg.20 ... J15
Oakwood Park ... Pg.24 ... K1
Prairie Lakes Park ... Pg.15 ... J15
Rand Park ... Pg.15 ... J17
Seminole Park ... Pg.20 ... M17
Sesquicentennial Pk. ... Pg.15 ... H16
Tomahawk Park Pg.14 ... H14
West Park ... Pg.15 ... H15
Willow Park ... Pg.15 ... H16

SCHOOLS

Algonquin Jr. H.S. ... Pg.15 ... J15
Brentwood Sch. Pg.14 ... H14
Central Sch. ... Pg.15 ... J16
Chippewa Jr. H.S. ... Pg.15 ... G15
Cumberland Sch. ... Pg.15 ... G15
Des Plaines Christian Sch. ... Pg.15 ... K16
Devonshire Sch. Pg.14 ... K14
Einstein Sch. ... Pg.14 ... J14
Forest Sch. ... Pg.15 ... K15
Friendship Jr. H.S. ... Pg.14 ... K13
High Ridge Knoll Sch. ... Pg.14 ... H14
Immanuel Lutheran Sch. ... Pg.15 ... J16
Iroquois Jr. High ... Pg.15 ... L17
Main West Township H.S. ... Pg.15 ... K15
Maple Sch. ... Pg.15 ... L17
Maryville Academy ... Pg.15 ... F16
Nipper Sch. ... Pg.15 ... F16
North Sch. ... Pg.15 ... H16
Oakton Comm. Coll. ... Pg.15 ... G16
Orchard Sch. ... Pg.20 ... M17
Plainfield Sch. ... Pg.15 ... K15
South Sch. ... Pg.15 ... K16
St. Mary's Sch. Pg.15 ... J16
St. Stephens Sch. ... Pg.15 ... K16
St. Zachary Catholic Sch. ... Pg.14 ... J13
Terrace Sch. ... Pg.14 ... J14
Thacker Jr. H.S. Pg.15 ... J16
West Sch. ... Pg.15 ... J15

SHOPPING CENTERS

Market Place Shopping Ctr. ... Pg.14 ... H13
The Oaks ... Pg.15 ... K16

MISCELLANEOUS

Carmelite Sisters Convent ... Pg.28 ... H1
Fire Dept. ... Pg.24 ... L1
Forest Hospital Pg.15 ... H17
Holy Family Hospital ... Pg.15 ... G16
Police Dept. ... Pg.24 ... K1
Village Hall ... Pg.24 ... K1

EAST HAZEL CREST

Page 43

STREETS

Ashland Ave. ... P23
Center St. ... O23
Country Ln. ... O22
Dixie Hwy. ... P22
Fisk Ave. ... O23
Forestway Dr. ... O22
Halsted St. ... N24
Hawthorne Dr. ... O22
Laflin St. ... O23
Lathrop St. ... O24
Loomis St. ... O23
Park Ave. ... O22
Throop St. ... O23
Wooded Path Dr. ... O24
171st St. ... O23
172nd Pl. ... O23
172nd St. ... O22,23
173rd St. ... O23
174th St. ... O22,23
175th St. ... O19,23

SCHOOLS

Lincoln Sch. ... O23

MISCELLANEOUS

R.R. Station ... O22
Village Hall ... O23

ELA TOWNSHIP

Pages 1,2,3
(Lake County)

STREETS

Buckeye Rd. ... X6
Dorothy Ln. ... X9
Hazel Crest Rd. ... X8
Lake-Cook Rd. ... A10
Old Hicks Rd. ... X9
Plum Pl. ... X6
Plum Rd. ... X8
Rand Ct. ... X8
Rand Rd. ... X8
Redwing Pl. ... X6
Sherley Rd. ... X8

ELK GROVE TOWNSHIP

Pages 13,14,18,19

STREETS

Aker Pl. ... Pg.19 ... J14
Anderson Terr. ... Pg.19 ... J14
Arnold Ct. ... Pg.19 ... J13
Blackhawk Dr. ... Pg.19 ... H12
Brian Ln. ... Pg.18 ... K11
Briarwood Dr. E. ... Pg.19 ... J11
Briarwood Dr. W. ... Pg.19 ... J11
Busse Rd. ... Pg.19 ... J12
Central Ave. ... Pg.13 ... G11
Clark Ln. ... Pg.19 ... J14
Council Tr. ... Pg.13 ... G11
Crest Ave. ... Pg.18 ... K13
David St. ... Pg.18 ... K11
Dempster St. ... Pg.19 ... J12
Denise St. ... Pg.18 ... K11
Diane East ... Pg.19 ... K12
Edgewood Ln. ... Pg.19 ... H12
Elane Ct. ... Pg.19 ... J11
Elizabeth Dr. ... Pg.19 ... K13
Elm Rd. ... Pg.19 ... L13
Emerson St. ... Pg.13 ... G11
Forest View Ave. Pg.18 ... L10
Foster St. ... Pg.13 ... G11
Glendale Ln. ... Pg.19 ... H12
Greenbriar Dr. ... Pg.19 ... H12
Hamilton Rd. ... Pg.19 ... K13
Hayen St. ... Pg.13 ... G11
Hickory Ave. ... Pg.13 ... G11
Higgins Rd. ... Pg.19 ... K12
Hinsdale Rd. ... Pg.19 ... L13
Horne Terr. ... Pg.19 ... J14
Howard St. ... Pg.18 ... L10
Imperial Ct. ... Pg.19 ... J12
Ingram Pl. ... Pg.19 ... J14
Kenneth Dr. ... Pg.19 ... J12
King Ln. ... Pg.19 ... J13-14
King St. ... Pg.18 ... K11
Kinkaid Ct. ... Pg.19 ... J13
Laurel St. ... Pg.18 ... L10
Leahy Cir. E. ... Pg.19 ... J14
Leahy Cir. S. ... Pg.19 ... J14
Lee Ln. ... Pg.19 ... L12
Lela St. ... Pg.19 ... L13
Lincoln St. ... Pg.18 ... M8
Linneman Rd. ... Pg.19 ... J12
Lund Rd. ... Pg.19 ... L13
Malmo Rd. ... Pg.19 ... J13
Maple Rd. ... Pg.19 ... L13
Martha St. ... Pg.18 ... M8
McCain Ct. ... Pg.19 ... J14
Meyer Ave. ... Pg.19 ... H12
Munroe Cir. ... Pg.19 ... J14
Northwest Point Rd. ... Pg.13 ... J10,11
Northwest Tollway ... Pg.19 ... K13
Oakton St. ... Pg.19 ... K13
Prairie Ave. ... Pg.13 ... G11
Prospect Rd. ... Pg.19 ... J14
Richard Ln. ... Pg.19 ... L12
Roppolo Dr. ... Pg.19 ... L12
Sell Rd. ... Pg.19 ... L13
Spruance Pl. ... Pg.19 ... J14
Stark Pl. ... Pg.19 ... J14
Sunset Rd. W. ... Pg.19 ... H12
Susan Lane ... Pg.14 ... G12
Thorndale ... Pg.18 ... L10
Tina Ln. ... Pg.18 ... K11
Tonne Dr. ... Pg.13 ... G11
Touhy Ave. ... Pg.19 ... L13
Vera Ln. ... Pg.19 ... L12
Walnut Ave. ... Pg.19 ... J14
Weiler Rd. ... Pg.19 ... K13
Woodview Ave. Pg.18 ... L10
1st Ave. ... Pg.14 ... K12
2nd Ave. ... Pg.14 ... K12
3rd Ave. ... Pg.14 ... K12
4th Ave. ... Pg.14 ... K12
5th Ave. ... Pg.14 ... K12
6th Ave. ... Pg.14 ... K12
7th Ave. ... Pg.14 ... K12
8th Ave. ... Pg.14 ... K12
9th Ave. ... Pg.14 ... K12
10th Ave. ... Pg.14 ... K12
11th Ave. ... Pg.14 ... K12
12th Ave. ... Pg.14 ... K12

FOREST PRESERVES

Busse Lake Boating Center ... Pg.13 ... K9
Busse Woods ... Pg.18 ... J10
Model Airplane Flying Field ... Pg.13 ... H8
Ned Brown Forest Preserve ... Pg.18 ... J9

PARKS

Carefree Park ... Pg.13 ... G11
Prairie Park ... Pg.13 ... G11

SCHOOLS

Einstein Sch. ... Pg.19 ... J14

ELK GROVE VILLAGE

Pages 17,18,19

STREETS

Addison Ct. ... Pg.19 ... K12
Alabama ... Pg.17 ... M6
Albany Ct. ... Pg.17 ... L6
Aldrin Tr. ... Pg.17 ... M7
Alexian Way ... Pg.18 ... L9
Allen Dr. ... Pg.18 ... N11
American Ln. ... Pg.19 ... M13
Anders Dr. ... Pg.17 ... M7
Arizona Pass ... Pg.17 ... L7
Arkansas Dr. ... Pg.17 ... M6
Arlington Heights Rd. ... Pg.18 ... L9
Armstrong Ct. ... Pg.17 ... M7
Armstrong Ln. ... Pg.17 ... M7
Arthur Ave. ... Pg.19 ... M12
Ash St. ... Pg.18 ... M10
Aspen Ln. ... Pg.18 ... M10
Atlantic Ln. ... Pg.17 ... L6
Augusta Ct. ... Pg.17 ... L6
Avon Rd. ... Pg.18 ... L9
Badger Rd. ... Pg.19 ... K12
Baltimore Dr. ... Pg.17 ... L6
Banbury Ave. ... Pg.18 ... M9
Bangor Ln. ... Pg.17 ... L6
Banyan Dr. ... Pg.18 ... L10
Basswood Ct. ... Pg.18 ... K11
Basswood Dr. ... Pg.18 ... K11
Bay Dr. ... Pg.17 ... M7
Beisner Rd. ... Pg.18 ... L8
Bennett Rd. ... Pg.18 ... J10
Berkenshire Ln. Pg.18 ... M9
Bianco Dr. ... Pg.18 ... L10
Biesterfield Rd. Pg.17,18 ... L7,M8
Birchwood Ave. Pg.18 ... L10
Biscayne Dr. ... Pg.18 ... M8
Bismark Ct. ... Pg.17 ... M7
Blue Jay Cir. ... Pg.17 ... M6
Boardwalk St. ... Pg.13 ... L9
Bonaventure Dr. Pg.18 ... M8
Bond St. ... Pg.18 ... J11
Bonita Ave. ... Pg.18 ... L10
Bonnie Ln. ... Pg.18 ... K11
Boosa Ln. ... Pg.17 ... M7
Bordeaux Ct. ... Pg.13 ... L9
Borman Ct. ... Pg.17 ... L7
Bosworth Ln. ... Pg.18 ... M10
Bradford Cr. ... Pg.18 ... L9
Bradley Ln. ... Pg.17 ... M7
Braemer Dr. ... Pg.18 ... M9
Brandywine Ln. Pg.18 ... M9
Brantwood Ave. Pg.18 ... L9
Brantwood Ct. ... Pg.18 ... L9
Briarwood Ln. ... Pg.18 ... K10
Brickvale Ln. ... Pg.19 ... M12
Brighton Rd. ... Pg.18 ... M9
Bristol Ln. ... Pg.18 ... M8
Brookhaven Dr. Pg.18 ... M10
Brown Cir. ... Pg.17 ... L6
Brummel St. ... Pg.19 ... K11
Brynhaven Ct. ... Pg.18 ... K10
Brynhaven St. ... Pg.18 ... K10
Buckingham Ct. Pg.18 ... M9
Burgundy Ct. ... Pg.13 ... L9
Busse Rd. ... Pg.19 ... L12
California St. ... Pg.17 ... L7
Cambridge Dr. ... Pg.19 ... L12
Carboy Ln. ... Pg.19 ... K13
Cardinal Ln. ... Pg.17 ... M6
Carl St. ... Pg.18 ... M11
Carlela Ln. ... Pg.17 ... M8
Carlisle Ave. ... Pg.18 ... M9
Carmen Dr. ... Pg.19 ... M13
Carolina ... Pg.17 ... M7
Carpenter Ct. ... Pg.17 ... L7
Carr Ct. ... Pg.17 ... M7
Carroll Sq. ... Pg.18 ... K11
Carswell Ave. ... Pg.18 ... M10
Cass Ln. ... Pg.17 ... M7
Cedar Ln. ... Pg.18 ... L10
Center St. ... Pg.18 ... M11
Cernan Ct. ... Pg.17 ... M7
Chaffee Ct. ... Pg.17 ... M7
Charing Cross Rd. ... Pg.18 ... L10
Charlela Dr. ... Pg.17 ... M8
Charles Dr. ... Pg.18 ... L9
Chase Ave. ... Pg.18 ... L11
Cheekwood Dr. Pg.18 ... M9
Chelmsford Ln. Pg.18 ... L9
Cheltenham Rd. Pg.18 ... M8
Chester Ln. ... Pg.17 ... L7
Christa Ct. ... Pg.17 ... L7
Cindy Ln. ... Pg.17 ... M7
Circle Ct. ... Pg.17 ... L7
Clearmont Dr. ... Pg.18 ... M10
Clearmont Rd. ... Pg.18 ... M9
Clifford Ln. ... Pg.17 ... M7
Clover Hill Ct. ... Pg.18 ... M8
Clover Hill Ln. ... Pg.18 ... M8
Collins Cir. ... Pg.17 ... L7
Colorado Ln. ... Pg.17 ... L7
Columbia Ct. ... Pg.17 ... L7
Commerce Dr. ... Pg.19 ... K12
Concord Ln. ... Pg.17 ... L6
Conrad Ct. ... Pg.17 ... L7
Cooper Ct. ... Pg.17 ... L7
Corinthia Ct. ... Pg.18 ... L10
Corinthia Dr. ... Pg.18 ... L10
Cosman Rd. ... Pg.18 ... L9
Cottonwood Dr. Pg.18 ... L11
Coyle Ln. ... Pg.19 ... M13
Creighton Ave. ... Pg.18 ... M9
Crest Ave. ... Pg.18 ... K10
Crestwood Ct. ... Pg.18 ... M9
Criss Cir. ... Pg.18 ... J11
Crossen Ave. ... Pg.19 ... K11
Cumberland Cir. Pg.18 ... M9
Cunningham Cir. Pg.17 ... M7
Cutter Ln. ... Pg.17 ... M6
Cypress Ln. ... Pg.18 ... M10
Dakota Dr. ... Pg.17 ... M7
Dauphine Ct. ... Pg.18 ... L9
David Ln. ... Pg.17 ... M7
Debra Ln. ... Pg.17 ... M7
Deep Wood Ct. Pg.18 ... M8
Delaware Ln. ... Pg.17 ... L6
Delmar Ct. ... Pg.12 ... L6
Delphia Ave. ... Pg.18 ... L10
Delphia Ct. ... Pg.18 ... L10
Delta Ln. ... Pg.19 ... M13
Denise St. ... Pg.18 ... K11
Devon Ave. ... Pg.19 ... M11
Diane East ... Pg.19 ... K12
Diane Ln. ... Pg.17 ... L7
Dierking Terr. ... Pg.19 ... L12
Dogwood Tr. ... Pg.18 ... M10
Doral Ct. ... Pg.12 ... L6
Dorchester Ln. Pg.18 ... M9
Dover Ln. ... Pg.18 ... M9
Driftwood Ct. ... Pg.18 ... M9
Dupont Ct. ... Pg.12 ... L6
Eagle Dr. ... Pg.18 ... L11
Eastern Ave. ... Pg.19 ... M13
Eden Rd. ... Pg.18 ... M9
Edgeware Rd. ... Pg.18 ... L10
Edgewood Ln. ... Pg.18 ... K10
Elizabeth Dr. ... Pg.19 ... K13
Elk Grove Blvd. Pg.18 ... L10
Elmwood Ln. ... Pg.18 ... M10
Erie Ct. ... Pg.17 ... L6
Essex Rd. ... Pg.18 ... M9
Estes Ave. ... Pg.18 ... L11
Evans Ct. ... Pg.17 ... M7
Evergreen Cir. ... Pg.13 ... K10
Evergreen St. ... Pg.18 ... K10
Exmoor Rd. ... Pg.18 ... M8
Fairfield Cir. ... Pg.18 ... L8
Fargo Ave. ... Pg.18 ... L11
Fern Dr. ... Pg.18 ... M10
Fleetwood Ln. ... Pg.18 ... L11
Florida Ln. ... Pg.17 ... M6
Forest Ln. ... Pg.18 ... K10
Forestview Ave. Pg.18 ... L10
Fox Run Dr. ... Pg.17 ... K6
Franklin Ln. ... Pg.17 ... L7
Galleon Ln. ... Pg.17 ... M6
Garlisch Dr. ... Pg.18 ... J11
Gateshead Ln. ... Pg.18 ... M8
Gaylord St. ... Pg.18 ... K11
Geneva ... Pg.17 ... M6
Georgia Dr. ... Pg.17 ... M6
Germaine Ln. ... Pg.18 ... K10
Germaine Pl. ... Pg.18 ... K10
Gibson Dr. ... Pg.17 ... L6
Glen Tr. S. ... Pg.17 ... M7
Glen Tr. W. ... Pg.17 ... M7
Gloria Dr. ... Pg.17 ... M7
Gloucester Dr. ... Pg.18 ... L8
Gordon St. ... Pg.18 ... K11
Grange Rd. ... Pg.18 ... M9
Grassmere Rd. Pg.18 ... L9
Greenbriar St. ... Pg.18 ... K10
Greenleaf Ave. ... Pg.19 ... L12
Greensboro Ct. Pg.12 ... L6
Gregory Ct. ... Pg.17 ... M7
Grissom Tr. ... Pg.17 ... M7
Grosvener Ln. ... Pg.18 ... L10
Grove Dr. ... Pg.18 ... L11
Gullo Dr. ... Pg.18 ... K11
Haar Ln. ... Pg.17 ... M7
Haise Ct. ... Pg.17 ... M7
Haise Ln. ... Pg.17 ... M7
Hamilton Rd. ... Pg.19 ... K13
Hampshire Dr. ... Pg.17 ... L6
Harmony Ln. ... Pg.18 ... M10
Hartford Ln. ... Pg.18 ... M11
Hastings Ave. ... Pg.18 ... L9
Hawk Ln. ... Pg.17 ... M6
Helen Ln. ... Pg.17 ... L7
Hemlock Dr. ... Pg.18 ... M10
Hickory Ln. ... Pg.18 ... M10
Higgins Rd. ... Pg.18 ... K10
Hodlmair Ct. ... Pg.17 ... M7
Hodlmair Ln. ... Pg.17 ... M7
Holly Ln. ... Pg.18 ... K10
Home Ave. ... Pg.17 ... L-M7
Home Cir. ... Pg.17 ... L7
Howard St. ... Pg.18,19 ... L10-12
Hudson Ct. ... Pg.17 ... L6
Idaho Pl. ... Pg.17 ... L7
Indiana Ln. ... Pg.17 ... M7
Inverness Ct. ... Pg.17 ... K6
Iowa Dr. ... Pg.17 ... M6
Ipswich Ct. ... Pg.18 ... L9
Ironwood Dr. ... Pg.18 ... K11
Jackson Cir. ... Pg.17 ... M6
James Way ... Pg.17 ... M7
Jarvis Ave. ... Pg.19 ... L11
Jefferson Sq. ... Pg.18 ... L10
Jersey Ln. ... Pg.17 ... L6
Joey Ln. ... Pg.18 ... K11
Joplin ... Pg.17 ... M7
Judy Dr. ... Pg.17 ... M7
Julie Dr. ... Pg.17 ... L6
Katherine ... Pg.19 ... M12
Kathleen Way ... Pg.17 ... M7
Kelly St. ... Pg.18 ... K10
Kendal Rd. ... Pg.18 ... M9
Kenilworth Ave. Pg.18 ... M9
Kennedy, J.F. Blvd. ... Pg.18 ... L9
Kent ... Pg.18 ... K11
Kentucky Ln. ... Pg.17 ... M6
Keswick Rd. ... Pg.18 ... L9
King St. ... Pg.18 ... K11
Kingsbridge Rd. Pg.18 ... M9
Lakeview Cr. ... Pg.18 ... L9
Lancaster Ave. ... Pg.18 ... M9
Landmeier Rd. ... Pg.18 ... L10
Larchmont Dr. ... Pg.18 ... M10
Laurel St. ... Pg.18 ... L10
Lee Ln. ... Pg.18,19 ... L12
Lee St. ... Pg.18 ... J11
Leeds Ln. ... Pg.18 ... M8
Leicester Rd. ... Pg.18 ... L-M9
Lela St. ... Pg.19 ... L13
Liberty Ct. ... Pg.17 ... L6
Lilac Ln. ... Pg.18 ... L10
Lincoln Sq. ... Pg.18 ... L10
Lincoln St. ... Pg.18 ... M8
Lindale St. ... Pg.18 ... K11
Lions Dr. ... Pg.13 ... L10
Little Falls Ct. ... Pg.18 ... M8
Lively Blvd. ... Pg.19 ... J-L11
Long Boat Dr. ... Pg.17 ... M6
Lonsdale Rd. ... Pg.18 ... M9
Louis Ave. ... Pg.19 ... L11
Louisiana Dr. ... Pg.17 ... M6
Love St. ... Pg.18 ... L11
Lovell Ct. ... Pg.17 ... M7
Lowestoft Rd. ... Pg.18 ... M8
Lund Rd. ... Pg.19 ... L13
Lunt Ave. ... Pg.19 ... M12
Lynn Ct. ... Pg.19 ... J12
Lynne Dr. ... Pg.18 ... M9
Madison ... Pg.17 ... M6
Magnolia Ln. ... Pg.18 ... M10
Maine Dr. ... Pg.17 ... L6
Maple Ct. ... Pg.18 ... L11
Maple Ln. ... Pg.18 ... L10
Mark St. ... Pg.18 ... M11
Martha St. ... Pg.18 ... M8
Martin Ln. ... Pg.18 ... K11
Maryland Dr. ... Pg.17 ... L6
McCabe Ave. ... Pg.19 ... L12
McDevitt Cir. ... Pg.17 ... L7
Meacham Rd. ... Pg.17 ... M7
Meegan Way ... Pg.17 ... M7
Memphis Cir. ... Pg.17 ... M6
Michigan Ln. ... Pg.17 ... M6
Middlebury Ln. Pg.18 ... L10
Midway Ct. ... Pg.14 ... K12
Milbeck Rd. ... Pg.18 ... L9
Mimosa Ln. ... Pg.18 ... M10
Minnesota Dr. ... Pg.17 ... M7
Minot Ct. ... Pg.17 ... L7
Mississippi Ln. Pg.17 ... M6
Missouri Dr. ... Pg.17 ... M6
Mitchell Tr. ... Pg.17 ... M7
Mobile ... Pg.17 ... M7
Montana Way ... Pg.17 ... L7
Montego Ct. ... Pg.18 ... M8
Montego Dr. ... Pg.18 ... M8
Moore Ln. ... Pg.18 ... L9
Morgan Dr. ... Pg.17 ... M7
Morse Ave. ... Pg.18 ... M11
Mulberry Ln. ... Pg.18 ... M10
Nebraska Dr. ... Pg.17 ... M7
Nerge Rd. ... Pg.17 ... M7
Nevada ... Pg.17 ... L7
New Mexico Ct. Pg.12 ... L7
New Mexico Trail ... Pg.17 ... L7
New York Ln. ... Pg.17 ... L6
Newberry Ln. ... Pg.17 ... L6
Newport ... Pg.18 ... M9
Nicholas Blvd. ... Pg.19 ... M12
North Pkwy. ... Pg.18 ... M11
North Port Dr. ... Pg.18 ... M8
Northampton Cir. ... Pg.18 ... L9
Northwest Tollway ... Pg.18 ... J11
Northwest Point Blvd. ... Pg.18 ... J10
Oak St. ... Pg.18 ... L10
Oakton St. ... Pg.18 ... K11
Oakwood Dr. ... Pg.18 ... K10
Oklahoma Cir. ... Pg.17 ... L7
Oklahoma Way Pg.17 ... L7
Old Creek Ct. ... Pg.18 ... M8
Old Mill Ln. ... Pg.18 ... M8
Omaha ... Pg.17 ... M6
Oregon Trail ... Pg.17 ... L7
Oriole Dr. ... Pg.17 ... M6
Orleans Ct. ... Pg.17 ... M6
Oxford Ct. ... Pg.17 ... L7
Pagni Dr. ... Pg.19 ... K11
Pahl Rd. ... Pg.18 ... L8
Pan Am Blvd. ... Pg.19 ... M13
Park Blvd. ... Pg.18 ... M8
Parkchester Rd. Pg.18 ... M9
Parker Pl. ... Pg.17 ... M7
Parkview Cr. ... Pg.18 ... L8
Patricia Ct. ... Pg.17 ... M7
Pauly Dr. ... Pg.18 ... J11
Peach Tree Ln. ... Pg.18 ... M10
Pebble Beach Cir. ... Pg.12 ... L6
Penrith Ave. ... Pg.18 ... L9
Perrie Dr. ... Pg.18 ... L11
Pierce Rd. ... Pg.18 ... M8
Pinewood Dr. ... Pg.18 ... M10
Placid Way ... Pg.18 ... M10
Pleasant Dr. ... Pg.18 ... M10
Potomac Ln. ... Pg.17 ... L6
Pratt Blvd. ... Pg.19 ... M12
Racine Dr. ... Pg.17 ... M7
Randell St. ... Pg.18 ... K10
Red Fox Ln. ... Pg.17 ... K6
Redwood Ave. ... Pg.18 ... K11
Rev. Morrison Blvd. ... Pg.18 ... L10
Revere Ln. ... Pg.17 ... L6
Richard Ln. ... Pg.19 ... L12
Richmond Cir. ... Pg.17 ... M7
Ridge Ave. ... Pg.18 ... L10
Ridge Ct. ... Pg.18 ... L10
Ridge Rd. ... Pg.18 ... L-M10
Ridge Sq. ... Pg.18 ... L10
Ridgewood Rd. Pg.18 ... K10
Robin Dr. ... Pg.17 ... L7
Rockwood Dr. ... Pg.18 ... K11
Rohlwing Rd. ... Pg.17 ... M7
Roosa Ln. ... Pg.17 ... M7
Roppolo Dr. ... Pg.19 ... L12
Ruskin Cr. ... Pg.18 ... L9
Ruskin Dr. ... Pg.18 ... L8
Rutgers Ln. ... Pg.17 ... L6
Salem Ct. ... Pg.17 ... L7
Schirra Cir. ... Pg.17 ... L7
Schooner Ln. ... Pg.17 ... M6
Scott St. ... Pg.18 ... J11
Seegers Ave. ... Pg.19 ... K11
Shadywood Ln. Pg.18 ... K10
Shelley Ct. ... Pg.18 ... L9
Shelley Rd. ... Pg.18 ... L9

ELK GROVE VILLAGE

Shepard Cir. . . . Pg.17 . . . . L7
Smethwick Ln. . . Pg.18 . . . . L9
Somerset Ln. . . . Pg.18 . . . . M9
South Glen Tr. . . Pg.17 . . . . M7
Spring Creek Ct. . Pg.18 . . . . M8
Springdale Ln. . . Pg.18 . . . M10
Spruce Ln. . . . . Pg.18 . . . M10
Stafford Cir. . . . Pg.17 . . . . L8
Stanford Cir. . . . Pg.18 . . . . L8
Stanley St. . . . . Pg.13 . . . K11
Stone Brook Ct. . Pg.18 . . . . M8
Stone Haven Ave.
. . . . Pg.17 . . . . L9
Stowe Cir. . . . . Pg.17 . . . . L9
Susan Ct. . . . . . Pg.17 . . . . L7
Sussex Ct. . . . . Pg.18 . . . L10
Sycamore Dr. . . Pg.18 . . . M10
Sylvan Ct. . . . . Pg.13 . . . . L9
Talbots Ln. . . . . Pg.18 . . . . M8
Tanglewood Ct. . Pg.13 . . . K10
Tanglewood Dr. . Pg.18 . . . K10
Tennessee Ln. . . Pg.17 . . . . M8
Terminal Dr. . . . Pg.19 . . . K12
Texas St. . . . . . Pg.17 . . . . L7
Thorndale Ave. . Pg.18 . . . L10
Timber Dr. . . . . Pg.17 . . . . L8
Tonne Rd. . . . . Pg.18 . . . M11
Tottenham Ln. . . Pg.18 . . . . L9
Touhy Ave. . . . . Pg.18 . . . L11
Tower Ln. . . . . . Pg.18 . . . L10
Trowbridge Rd. . Pg.18 . . . . M9
Turner . . . . Pg.17 . . . . M7
Union Cir. . . . . . Pg.17 . . . . L7
United Ln. . . . . . Pg.19 . . . M13
University Ln. . . Pg.17 . . . . L6
Utah Cir. . . . . . Pg.19 . . . L12
Vera Ln. . . . . . . Pg.18 . . . L10
Verde Ln. . . . . . Pg.18 . . . L10
Vermont Dr. . . . Pg.17 . . . . L6
Vernon Cir. . . . . Pg.17 . . . . L6
Versailles Cir. . . Pg.18 . . . . L9
Victoria Ln. . . . . Pg.18 . . . K11
Village Grove Dr.
. . . . Pg.18 . . . . M9
Vine Ln. . . . . . . Pg.17 . . . . L6
Virginia Dr. . . . . Pg.17 . . . . M6
Volkamer Tr. . . . Pg.17 . . . . M7
Von Braun Tr. . . Pg.17 . . . . M7
Walnut Ln. . . . . Pg.18 . . . M10
Walpole Rd. . . . Pg.18 . . . . M9
Walter Ave. . . . . Pg.17 . . . . L7
Warwick Ln. . . . Pg.18 . . . M10
Wasdale . . . . . . Pg.18 . . . . M9
Washington Sq. . Pg.18 . . . L10
Wellington Ave. . Pg.18 . . . L10
Wellington Ct. . . Pg.18 . . . . M8
West Glen Tr. . . Pg.17 . . . . M7
Westgate Ave. . . Pg.17 . . . K10
Westview Dr. . . . Pg.18 . . . M10
White Tr. . . . . . Pg.17 . . . . L7
Wildwood Pl. . . . Pg.18 . . . K11
Wildwood Rd. . . Pg.18 . . . K11
William Clifford Ln.
. . . . Pg.17 . . . . M7
Willow Ln. . . . . . Pg.18 . . . K10
Wilma Ln. . . . . . Pg.17 . . . . M7
Wilshire Ave. . . . Pg.18 . . . M10
Windsor Ln. . . . Pg.19 . . . K12
Winston Dr. . . . . Pg.18 . . . . L8
Wisconsin . . . . . Pg.17 . . . . M6
Wood Tr. . . . . . Pg.17 . . . . M7
Woodcrest Ln. . . Pg.18 . . . K10
Woodview Ave. . Pg.18 . . . L10
Worden Way . . . Pg.17 . . . . M7
Yale Ct. . . . . . . Pg.17 . . . . L7
Yarmouth Rd. . . Pg.18 . . . . M8
York Rd. . . . . . . Pg.19 . . . M13
Young Cir. . . . . Pg.17 . . . . L7

CEMETERIES
Elk Grove Cem. . Pg.18 . . . H11
Rohlwing Grove Cem.
. . . . Pg.17 . . . . M8

PARKS
Appleseed Park Pg.18 . . . L10
Audubon Park . . Pg.18 . . . L10
Batram Park . . . Pg.18 . . . L10
Burbank Park . . Pg.18 . . . M10
Colony Park . . . Pg.17 . . . . L6
Fairchild Park . . Pg.18 . . . M10
Fountain Square Park
. . . . Pg.17 . . . . L6
Gentile Park . . . Pg.17 . . . . L6
Jaycee Park . . . Pg.18 . . . L10
Lions Park . . . . Pg.18 . . . L10
Mather Park . . . Pg.17 . . . . M7
Morton Park . . . Pg.18 . . . M10
Muir Park . . . . . Pg.18 . . . M11
Newberry Park . . Pg.17 . . . . L6
Olmstead Park . . Pg.18 . . . M10
Osborn Park . . . Pg.18 . . . K10
Udall Park . . . . Pg.18 . . . K11

SCHOOLS
Adlai E. Stevenson Sch.
. . . . Pg.17 . . . . M7
Adolph Link Sch.
. . . . Pg.17 . . . . L7
Byrd Sch. . . . . . Pg.18 . . . . M9
Claremount Sch.
. . . . Pg.18 . . . M10
Elk Grove H.S. . . Pg.18 . . . . L9
Grantwood Sch. . Pg.18 . . . L10
Grove Jr. H.S. . . Pg.18 . . . L10
Lively Jr. H.S. . . Pg.18 . . . . M9

Mark Hopkins Sch.
. . . . Pg.18 . . . K11
Patricia Marshall Sch.
. . . . Pg.18 . . . . L9
Queen of Rosary Sch.
. . . . Pg.18 . . . L10
Ridge Sch. . . . . Pg.18 . . . L10
Rupley Sch. . . . Pg.18 . . . L10
Salt Creek Sch. . Pg.18 . . . . M9
Westbrook Sch. . Pg.19 . . . K12

SHOPPING CENTERS
Devon Ave. Market
. . . . Pg.18 . . . M11
Devon Square . . Pg.18 . . . . M9
Elk Crossing S.C.
. . . . Pg.18 . . . . L9
Estes Commons Pg.19 . . . L12
Gullo Center . . . Pg.19 . . . L13
Mallard Crossing
. . . . Pg.17 . . . . M7
Park and Shop . Pg.18 . . . K10
Shawnmy S.C. . . Pg.17 . . . . L7
Strawberry Hill S.C.
. . . . Pg.17 . . . . L7
The Grove S.C. . Pg.18 . . . . M9

MISCELLANEOUS
Alexian Bros. Hosp.
. . . . Pg.18 . . . . L8
Elk Grove Park Dist.
. . . . Pg.18 . . . . M9
Fire Department Pg.17 . . . . L7
Fire Department Pg.18 . . . . M9
Fire Dept. Office Pg.18 . . . M10
Fitness Center . . Pg.18 . . . . M9
Historical Society
. . . . Pg.18 . . . . M9
Library . . . . Pg.18 . . . . M9
Post Office . . . . Pg.18 . . . L11

EVANSTON
Pages 27,30,31

STREETS
Arnold Pl. . . . . . Pg.31 . . . . L14
Asbury Ave. . . . Pg.27,31 . H-L13
Ashland Ave. . . Pg.27,31 . H-L13
Austin St. . . . . . Pg.31 . . . . L13
Barton Ave. . . . Pg.27 . . . . H12
Bennett Ave. . . . Pg.27 . . . . H12
Benson . . . . Pg.27 . . . . J14
Bernard Pl. . . . . Pg.30 . . . G11
Bradley Pl. . . . . Pg.27 . . . . H12
Broadway . . . . . Pg.31 . . L12-13
Brown Ave. . . . . Pg.27,31 . H-L13
Brummel St. . . . Pg.31 . . L12-13
Bryant Ave. . . . Pg.27 . . . . H13
Burnham Pl. . . . Pg.27 . . . K14
Callan Ave. . . . . Pg.31 . . . . L14
Calvin Cir. . . . Pg.27,30,31 H11
Case Pl. . . . . . . Pg.31 . . . . L14
Case St. . . . . . . Pg.31 . . . . L14
Central Park Ave.
. . . . Pg.27 . . . . H11
Central St. . . . Pg.27,30 H11,13
Chancellor . . . . Pg.31 . . . . L14
Chicago Ave. . . Pg.27,31 . K14
Church St. . . . . Pg.31 . . . . J12
Clark St. . . . . . . Pg.27 . . J13-14
Cleveland St. . . Pg.31 . . K12-13
Clifford St. . . . . Pg.30 . . . G11
Clinton Pl. . . . . Pg.27 . . . H14
Clyde . . . . Pg.31 . . . . L14
Colfax . . . . Pg.27 . . . . H13
Colfax Pl. . . . . . Pg.30 . . . H11
Colfax St. . . . . . Pg.31 . . H12-14
Colfax Terr. . . . Pg.27 . . . . H13
Cowper Ave. . . . Pg.30 . . . H11
Crain St. . . . . . . Pg.27 . . K12-14
Crawford Ave. . Pg.30 . . . G11
Culver St. . . . . . Pg.31 . . . . L14
Custer Ave. . . . Pg.31 . . . . L14
Darrow Ave. . . . Pg.27,31 . J-L13
Dartmouth . . . . Pg.27 . . . . J14
Dartmouth Pl. . . Pg.30 . . . H11
Davis St. . . . . . . Pg.27 . . J12-14
Dempster St. . . Pg.27 . . . K12
Dewey Ave. . . . Pg.27,31 . J-L13
Dobson St. . . . . Pg.31 . . L12-13
Dodge . . . . Pg.27 . . . . J14
Dodge Ave. . . . Pg.27,31 . J-L13
Eastwood . . . . . Pg.27 . . . G13
Edgemere Ct. . . Pg.31 . . . K14
Elgin Rd. Pg.27 H-J12,J14
Elinor Pl. . . . . . . Pg.27 . . . . J13
Elm Ave. . . . . . . Pg.27 . . . . H12
Elmwood . . . . . Pg.27 . . . . L14
Elmwood Ave. . Pg.27,31 . K14
Emerson St. . . . Pg.27 . . J13-14
Euclid Pk. Pl. . . Pg.27 . . . . J13
Ewing Ave. . . . . Pg.27 . . . . H12
Florence Ave. . . Pg.27,31 J,K-L13
Forest Ave. . . . . Pg.27 . . . K14
Forest Pl. . . . . . Pg.27,31 . J14
Forestview Rd. . Pg.27 . . . H12
Foster . . . . Pg.27 . . . . J12
Foster St. . . . . . Pg.27 . . H13-14
Fowler . . . . Pg.31 . . . K12
Gaffield Pl. . . . . Pg.27 . . . H14
Garnett Pl. . . . . Pg.31 . . J13-14
Garrett Pl. . . . . Pg.27 . . . H14
Garrison Ave. . . Pg.31 . . . G14
Geneva Pl. . . . . Pg.31 . . . H11
Girard Ave. . . . . Pg.31 . . . G13
Grant . . . . Pg.27 . . . H13

Grant St. . . . . . Pg.27 . . . H12
Greeley Ave. . . Pg.30 . . . H11
Greenleaf St. . . Pg.31 . . K13-14
Greenwood St. . Pg.27 . . J12-14
Grey Ave. Pg.27,31
. . . . J12-13,K12
Grove St. . . . . . Pg.27 . . J12-14
Hamilton St. . . . Pg.31 . . . K14
Hamlin . . . . Pg.27 . . . H14
Hampton Pkwy. Pg.27 . . . G13
Harrison Ave. . . Pg.27 . . . H13
Harrison St. . . Pg.27,30 H11-12
Hartley Ave. . . . Pg.31 . . H-L12
Hartrey Ave. . . . Pg.31 . . H-L12
Hartzell St. . . Pg.27,30 H11-12
Harvard Tr. . . . . Pg.31 . . . . L13
Hastings Ave. . . Pg.30 . . . H11
Haven St. . . . . . Pg.27 . . . H12
Hawthorne Ln. . Pg.27 . . . H12
Hayes . . . . Pg.30 . . . H11
Highland Ave. . . Pg.30 . . . H11
Hillside Ln. . . . . Pg.31 . . . H11
Hillside Rd. . . . . Pg.31 . . . H11
Hinman Ave. . . Pg.27,30 . J-K14
Hovland Ct. . . . Pg.27 . . . . J13
Howard St. . . . . Pg.31 . . . . L14
Hull Tr. . . . . Pg.31 . . L13-14
Hurd Ave. . . . . Pg.27 . . . H12
Ingleside Pk. Pl. Pg.27 . . . G14
Jackson . . . . . . Pg.27 . . . H-J13
Jenks St. . . . . . Pg.27 . . G12-13
Judson Ave. . . Pg.27,31 . J-K14
Kedzie St. . . . . Pg.31 . . . . L13
Keeney St. . . . . Pg.31 . . L12-14
Kirk St. . . . . Pg.31 . . . . L13
Knox Cir. . . Pg.27,30,31 H11
Lake Shore Blvd. Pg.31 . . K14
Lake St. . . . . . . Pg.27 . . J12-13
Lakeside Ct. . . . Pg.27 . . . . J12
Laurel . . . . Pg.27 . . . . J12
Lawndale Ave. . Pg.27 . . . H11
Lee St. . . . . Pg.31 . . K12-14
Leland Ave. . . . Pg.27 . . . . J12
Lemar Ave. . . . . Pg.27 . . . . J12
Leon Pl. . . . . . . Pg.27 . . . . H13
Leonard Pl. . . . Pg.27 . . . . H13
Library St. . . . . Pg.27 . . . H14
Lincoln St. . . . . Pg.27 . . H12-14
Lincolnwood Dr. Pg.27 . . . H12
Linden Pl. . . . . . Pg.31 . . . H11
Livingston St. . . Pg.27 . . . G13
Lyons St. . . . . . Pg.27 . . J12-13
Madison Pl. . . . Pg.31 . . . K12
Madison St. . . . Pg.31 . . . K12
Main St. . . . . . . Pg.31 . . K12-14
Maple . . . . Pg.27 . . . . J13
Maple Ave. . . . . Pg.31 . . . H13
Marcy Ave. . . . . Pg.27 . . G-H11
Martha Ln. . . . . Pg.27 . . . H12
McCormick Blvd.
. . . . Pg.27 . . . H11
McDaniel Ave. . Pg.27 . . G-K12
Michigan Ave. . Pg.31 . . . K14
Milburn Park . . Pg.27,31 . H14
Milburn St. . . . Pg.27,31 . H14
Monroe St. . . . . Pg.31 . . . K13
Monticello . . . . Pg.27 . . . G14
Mulford St. . . . . Pg.31 . . L13-14
Nathaniel Pl. . . Pg.31 . . . K12
Normandy Pl. . . Pg.27 . . . H11
Noyes Ct. . . . . . Pg.27 . . . H14
Noyes St. . . . Pg.27,30 H11-13
Oak Ave. . . . . . Pg.27 . . . . J14
Oakton St. . . . . Pg.31 . . . . L13
Orrington Ave. . Pg.31 . . . H11
Otto Ln. . . . . . . Pg.30 . . . G11
Park Pl. . . . . . Pg.27,30 . G12
Payne St. . . . . . Pg.27 . . . H12
Pioneer Rd. . . . Pg.27 . . . H12
Pitner . . . . Pg.27 . . . H12
Pitner Ave. . . . Pg.27,31 . K12
Poplar . . . . Pg.27 . . . H14
Prairie Ave. . . . Pg.27 . . G,H12
Pratt Ct. . . . . . . Pg.31 . . . . L14
Princeton Ave. . Pg.30 . . . G11
Prospect Ave. . . Pg.27 . . . H14
Railroad . . . . . . Pg.31 . . . . L13
Reba Pl. . . . . . . Pg.31 . . . K14
Reese Ave. . . . . Pg.27 . . . H12
Richmond Ave. . Pg.31 . . . . L12
Ridge Ave. . . . . Pg.27 . . H-J14
Ridge Ct. . . . . . Pg.31 . . . K13
Ridge Terr. . . . . Pg.31 . . . H13
Ridgeway Ave. . Pg.27,30 . H11
Rosalie . . . . Pg.27 . . . H13
Roslyn Pl. . . . . . Pg.27 . . . G14
Seward St. . . . . Pg.27 . . L12-13
Sheridan Pl. . . . Pg.27 . . . G14
Sheridan Rd. . Pg.27,31 . G-K14
Sheridan Sq. . . Pg.31 . . . L15
Sherman Ave. . Pg.31 . . . K14
Simpson St. . . . Pg.27 . . . H12
South Blvd. . . . Pg.31 . . L13-14
St. Mark St. . . Pg.27,31 . J14
Stewart Ave. . . Pg.27 . . . G12
Terry Pl. . . . . . . Pg.27 . . . H12
Thayer St. . . . Pg.27,30
. . . . G11-12
Thelin Ct. . . . . . Pg.27 . . . . J13
University Pl. . . Pg.27 . . . J14
Wade St. . . . . . Pg.27 . . . G12
Walnut . . . . Pg.27 . . . G12
Warren Blvd. . . Pg.31 . . . L12
Washington . . . Pg.27 . . . H14
Washington St. . Pg.31 . . . K13

Wesley Ave. . . Pg.27,31 . H-L13
West Dr. . . . . . . Pg.30 . . . H11
Wilder St. . . . . . Pg.27 . . . K13
Woodbine . . . . Pg.27 . . . G13
Woodland Rd. . Pg.27 . . . H12

CEMETERIES
Calvary Cem. . . Pg.31 . . . L14

FOREST PRESERVES
Perkins Woods . Pg.31 . . . H12

GOLF COURSES
Peter Jan's G.C. Pg.31 . . . H13

HOSPITALS
Community Hosp.
. . . . Pg.27 . . . H12
Evanston Hosp. Pg.27 . . . G14
St. Francis Hosp.
. . . . Pg.31 . . . . L14

PARKS
Ackerman Park Pg.31 . . . H12
Alexander Park Pg.27 . . . . J13
Baker Park . . . . Pg.31 . . . . L14
Barton Park . . . Pg.27 . . . . J13
Bent Park . . . . Pg.30 . . . H11
Burnham Shores Park
. . . . Pg.31 . . . K15
Cartright Park . Pg.30 . . . H11
Centennial Park Pg.31 . . . . J14
Chandler Park . Pg.31 . . . H14
Clark Square Park
. . . . Pg.31 . . . K14
Cornelia Lunt Park
. . . . Pg.27 . . . . J14
Dawes Park . . . Pg.31 . . . . J14
Deering Estate Park
. . . . Pg.31 . . . K14
Dempster St. Park
. . . . Pg.31 . . . K14
Eggleston Park Pg.31 . . . H12
Eiden Park . . . . Pg.31 . . . K14
Elks Park . . . . . Pg.31 . . . . L14
Elliott Park . . . . Pg.31 . . . K15
Foster Field . . . Pg.27 . . . H13
Grey Park . . . . Pg.31 . . . K13
Howell Park . . . Pg.17 . . . G12
Independence Park
. . . . Pg.31 . . . H12
Ingraham Park . Pg.31 . . . H12
James Park . . . Pg.31 . . . . L12
Kamen Park . . . Pg.31 . . . . L14
Larimer Park . . Pg.31 . . . . L14
Leahy Park . . . Pg.31 . . . . L13
Leider Park . . . Pg.31 . . . . L13
Lomar Park . . . Pg.31 . . . . L13
Lovelace Park . Pg.30 . . . H11
Mason Park . . . Pg.27 . . . . J13
Merrick Park . . Pg.31 . . . . J13
Penny Park . . . Pg.31 . . . H12
Quinlan Park . . Pg.31 . . . H12
Raymond Park . Pg.27 . . . . J14
Ridgeville Park . Pg.31 . . . . L14
Robert Crown Park . . .
. . . . Pg.31 . . . K14
Smith Park . . . . Pg.31 . . . . J13

SCHOOLS
Barbereaux Sch. Pg.26 . . . H11
Chiaravalle Montessori Sch.
. . . . Pg.27 . . . H14
Chute Jr. H.S. . Pg.27 . . . . L13
Cove Sch. . . . . Pg.27 . . . H13
David B. Dewey Sch.
. . . . Pg.27 . . . . J13
Dawes Sch. . . . Pg.31 . . . . L13
Evanston Twp. H.S.
. . . . Pg.27 . . . . J12
Faith Christian Academy
. . . . Pg.31 . . . . J13
Haven Jr. H.S. . Pg.27 . . . H14
Kendall College Pg.31 . . . H14
King Lab Sch. . Pg.27 . . . H12
Learning Sch. . Pg.31 . . . . L13
Lincoln Sch. . . Pg.27 . . . H12
Lincolnwood Sch.
. . . . Pg.27 . . . H12
Madison Street Sch.
. . . . Pg.31 . . . K13
Nichols Sch. . . Pg.31 . . . . L12
Northwestern University
. . . . Pg.31 . . . H14
Oakton Sch. . . Pg.31 . . . . L13
Orrington Sch. Pg.27 . . . H14
Pope John XXIII Sch.
. . . . Pg.31 . . . K14
Rimland Sch. for Autistic Citizens
. . . . Pg.27 . . . H14
Roycemore Sch.
. . . . Pg.31 . . . H14
Shore Sch. . . . Pg.31 . . . . J12
Skiles Jr. H.S. . Pg.27 . . . . J12
St. Athanasius Sch.
. . . . Pg.31 . . . H13
St. Mary's Sch. Pg.31 . . . H13
Washington Sch.
. . . . Pg.31 . . . . L13
Willard Sch. . . Pg.31 . . . H12

MISCELLANEOUS
Dyche Stadium Pg.27 . . . H13
Fire Station . . . Pg.31 . . . K14
Ladd Arboretum Pg.31 . . . H13
Lee St. Beach . Pg.31 . . . K15

FLOSSMOOR
Pages 42,43,48

STREETS
Acorn Dr. . . . . . Pg.48 . . . . R22
Alexander Cres. Pg.48 . . . . R21
Amherst Ct. . . . Pg.43 . . . . R22
Argyle Ave. . . . Pg.42 . . . . Q21
Arquilla . . . . . . Pg.42 . . . . R21
Ash St. . . . . Pg.42 . . . . Q21
Ashland Ave. . . Pg.43 . . . . R23
Ashland Ln. . . . Pg.42 . . . . R20
Ashley Oak . . . Pg.43 . . . . R22
Aspen St. . . . . . Pg.42 . . . . Q20
Avers Ave. . . . . Pg.42 . . . . R20
Balmoral Cres. Pg.42 . . . . R21
Balmoral Glen Pg.42 . . . . R21
Baythorne Dr. . Pg.42 . . . . R21
Beech St. . . . . . Pg.42 . . . . Q20
Berry Rd. . . . . . Pg.42 . . . . R21
Bob-O-Link Rd. Pg.48 . . . . R21
Bonnie Brae Cresent
. . . . Pg.48 . . . . S21
Braeburn Ave. . Pg.42,48 R21,22
Braeburn St. . . Pg.48 . . . . S21
Braemer Rd. . . Pg.42 . . . . Q21
Brassie Ave. . . . Pg.42,48
. . . . R22,S21
Brentwood Ct. . Pg.48 . . . . R20
Brookwood Dr. Pg.48 . . . . S21
Bruce Ave. . . . . Pg.42 . . . . Q21
Brumley Dr. . . . Pg.42 . . . . R21
Bunker Ave. . . Pg.42,48 . R21
Burns Ave. . . . . Pg.42 . . . . Q21
Butterfield Cir. . Pg.48 . . . . S21
Butterfield Rd. . Pg.42 . . . . S21
Caddy St. . . . . Pg.42 . . . . Q21
Cambridge Ave. Pg.43,48 . R,S22
Candlewood Ct. Pg.42 . . . . R20
Cardinal Ct. . . . Pg.48 . . . . S21
Carmel Dr. . . . Pg.42 . . . . Q21
Caroll Pkwy. . . Pg.43 . . . . R22
Central Dr. . . . . Pg.42 . . . . R21
Central Park Ave.
. . . . Pg.42 . . . R,S20
Cherry Hills Dr. Pg.42 . . . . R20
Chestnut Dr. . . Pg.42 . . . . Q20
Collett Ln. . . . . Pg.43 . . . . Q22
Connie Ct. . . . . Pg.48 . . . . S23
Cooley Pl. . . . . Pg.42 . . . . R21
Cornell Rd. . . . Pg.48 . . . . S22
Crawford Ave. . Pg.42 . . . . R19
Cummings Ln. . Pg.43 . . . . Q22
Dartmouth Rd. Pg.48 . . . . S22
Dixie Hwy. . . . Pg.42 Q22,S23
Douglas Ave. . . Pg.42 . . . . Q21
Driftwood Ct. . Pg.48 . . . . R20
Dundonald Ln. Pg.48 . . . . R21
Eden Oaks . . . Pg.42 . . . . R22
Elaine Ct. . . . . Pg.48 . . . . R21
Elm Ct. . . . . . . Pg.42 . . . . R20
Elm St. . . . . . . Pg.42 . . . . Q20
Embassy Row . Pg.42 . . . . Q21
Emelia Ct. . . . . Pg.48 . . . . R21
Evans Rd. . . . . Pg.42 . . . . R20
Flossmoor Rd. . Pg.42,43 . R20
Gardner Rd. . . Pg.43 . . . . Q22
Gianna Dr. . . . Pg.43 . . . . Q22
Golfview Ln. . . Pg.42 . . . . R21
Gordon Dr. . . . Pg.42 . . . . Q21
Governors Hwy. Pg.42 . . . . Q21
Hagen Ln. . . . . Pg.42 . . . . R20
Hamlin Ave. . . Pg.42 . . . . R20
Hampton Ct. . . Pg.42 . . . . R21
Hanover Ln. . . Pg.43 . . . . R22
Harding Ave. . . Pg.42 . . . . R19
Harold's Cres. . Pg.48 . . . . S21
Harvard . . . . . . Pg.48 . . . . R21
Harwood Ave. . Pg.42 . . . . Q22
Hawthorne Ln. Pg.42 . . . . R21
Heather Hill Cresent
. . . . Pg.42 . . . . R21
Heather Hill Ct. Pg.48 . . . . R21
Heather Rd. . . . Pg.42 . . . . R21
Holbrook Rd. . . Pg.43 . . . . Q22
Holly Ln. . . . . . Pg.48 . . . . S22
Hutchinson Rd. Pg.43 . . . . Q22
Imperial Ct. . . . Pg.42 . . . . Q21
Joyce Dr. . . . . . Pg.48 . . . . S21
Kathleen Ln. . . Pg.48 . . . . S21
Kedzie Ave. . . . Pg.42 . . . . R20
Knollwood Dr. . Pg.42 . . . . Q20
Lake Dr. . . . . . Pg.42 . . . . Q22
Latimer Ln. . . . Pg.48 . . . . S21
Laura Ln. . . . . Pg.48 . . . . R21
Laurel Ave. . . . Pg.42 . . . . R22
Lawrence Crescent
. . . . Pg.42 . . . R,S21
Leavitt Ave. . . . Pg.42 . . . . R21
Link Ct. . . . . . . Pg.48 . . . . R21
Lynwood Ct. . . Pg.48 . . . . R23

Library . . . . Pg.31 . . . . J14
McGaw Hall . . . Pg.27 . . . G13
Noyes Cultural Center
. . . . Pg.31 . . . H14
Post Office . . . . Pg.27 . . . H11
Presbyterian Home for the Aged .
. . . . Pg.27 . . . H11
Robert Crown Center
. . . . Pg.31 . . . K14
Seabury Western Theological Sem.
. . . . Pg.31 . . . H14
South Blvd. Beach
. . . . Pg.31 . . . . L15

MacFarlane Cresent . . . .
. . . . R21
MacHeath Cresent . . . .
. . . . Pg.48 . . . . R21
Maple Rd. . . . . Pg.42 . . . . R20
Markey Ln. . . . Pg.48 . . . . R23
Marston Ln. . . . Pg.43 . . . . Q22
Maryland Ave. . Pg.42 . . . . R21
Mast Ct. . . . . . Pg.42 . . . . R21
McDonald Ln. . Pg.42 . . . . Q22
Monterey Dr. . . Pg.42 . . . . R22
Oak Ct. . . . . . . Pg.42 . . . . R20
Oak Lane Rd. . . Pg.48 . . . . S21
Oak St. . . . . . . Pg.42 . . . . R20
Oakherst St. . . Pg.42 . . . . R20
Oakmont Ave. . Pg.42 . . . . R21
Oxford Ct. . . . . Pg.42 . . . . R22
Palmer Ct. . . . . Pg.42 . . . . R20
Park Dr. . . . . . . Pg.42 . . . Q,R21
Patricia Ln. . . . Pg.48 . . . . S21
Perry Rd. . . . . . Pg.42 . . . . R21
Perth . . . . Pg.42 . . . . Q21
Pheasant Ct. . . Pg.48 . . . . S21
Pinehurst . . . . . Pg.48 . . . . R23
Polly Ln. . . . . . Pg.48 . . . . R21
Poplar . . . . Pg.42 . . . . R20
Poplar Pl. . . . . Pg.42 . . . . R20
Princeton Rd. . Pg.48 . . . . S21
Quail Ct. . . . . . Pg.48 . . . . S21
Redwood . . . . . Pg.48 . . . . Q21
Redwood Ct. . . Pg.48 . . . . R21
Richwood Terr. Pg.48 . . . . R23
Robertson Ln. . Pg.42 . . . . R22
School St. . . . . Pg.42 . . . . Q21
Scott Ave. . . . . Pg.42 . . . . Q21
Scott Cres. . . . Pg.48 . . . . Q21
Sequoia . . . . . . Pg.48 . . . . S21
Springfield Ave. Pg.42 . . . . R19
Sterling Ave. . . Pg.42 . . . Q,R21
Stonegate . . . . Pg.42 . . . . R20
Stonegate Ct. . Pg.48 . . . . R21
Strieff Ln. . . . . Pg.42 . . . . R21
Sunset Ave. . . . Pg.42 . . . . R21
Sylvan Ct. . . . . Pg.42 . . . . R23
Tanglewood Dr. Pg.42 . . . . R20
Thomas Ct. . . . Pg.48 . . . . S23
Thornwood Ct. Pg.42 . . . . R22
Tina Ln. . . . . . . Pg.48 . . . . S23
Travers Ln. . . . Pg.42 . . . . R21
Vardon Ct. . . . Pg.43 . . . . Q22
Vardon Pl. . . . . Pg.42 . . . . Q22
Verne Ln. . . . . Pg.42 . . . . Q21
Vollmar Rd. . . . Pg.42 . . . . S20
Wallace Dr. . . . Pg.42 . . . . Q21
Western Ave. . . Pg.42 . . . . T22
Willow St. . . . . Pg.42 . . . . R20
Woodhollow Dr. Pg.42 . . . . R20
Yale Rd. . . . . . . Pg.42 . . . . S23
187th St. . . . . Pg.43 . . Q19,22
188th St. . . . . Pg.42 . . . . Q19
189th St. . . . . Pg.42 . . . . Q19
190th St. . . . . Pg.42 . . . . R20
192nd St. . . . . Pg.42 . . . . R20
194th St. . . . . Pg.42 . . . . R20
195th St. . . . . Pg.48 . . . . R20
196th St. . . . . Pg.42 . . . . R20
198th St. . . . . Pg.48 . . . . S20

CEMETERIES
St. Paul Cem. . Pg.48 . . . . S22

GOLF COURSES
Cherry Hill Country Club
. . . . Pg.42 . . . . Q20
Flossmoor Country Club
. . . . Pg.48 . . . . R22

PARKS
Flossmoor Pk. . Pg.42 . . . . R22
Highland Park . Pg.48 . . . . S21
Iron Oak Pk. . . Pg.42 . . . . S21
Pheasant Pk. . . Pg.48 . . . . S22

SCHOOLS
Flossmoor Hills Sch.
. . . . Pg.42 . . . . Q20
Flossmoor Montessori Sch.
. . . . Pg.42 . . . . Q22
Heather Hill Sch. Pg.48 . . . . R21
Homewood Flossmoor H.S.
. . . . Pg.42 . . . . Q21
Infant Jesus of Prague Sch.
. . . . Pg.42 . . . . R21
Leavitt Ave. Sch. Pg.48 . . . . S21
Parker Jr. H.S. . Pg.42 . . . . R21
Western Avenue Sch.
. . . . Pg.42 . . . . R22

SHOPPING CENTERS
Flossmoor Commons
. . . . Pg.48 . . . . S20

MISCELLANEOUS
Fire Dept. . . . . Pg.42 . . . . Q21
Ice Arena . . . . Pg.48 . Q21,R22
Police Dept. . . Pg.42 . . . . R21
R.R. Station . . . Pg.42 . . . . R21
Village Hall . . . Pg.48 . . . . R21

FORD HEIGHTS
Pages 49,50

STREETS
Ambassador Ln. T27
Berkeley Ave. T27
Calumet Expwy. R,T27

FORD HEIGHTS

Cannon Ln. T27
Columbia Ave. T27
Congress Ln. T27
Cottage Grove Ave. T26
Deer Creek Ln. U27
Defores T27
Diplomat Ln. T27
Drexel Ave. T26
Eighth Pl. T27
Eighth St. T27
Ellis St. T27
Embassy Ln. T27
Greenwood Ave. T27
Hammond Ln. T27
Hickory St. R26
Kennedy Ln. T27
Lexington Ave. T27
Lexington Cir. T27
Lincoln Hwy. U27
Ninth St. T27
Park Ave. T26
Park Ln. T27
Park St. T27
Porter Ave. T27
Pullman T27
Regent T27
Seeley Ave. T27
Senator Ln. T27
Stoney Island T27
Summit Dr. U27
Vincennes Rd. Q25
Werline T26
Williams T27
Willow St. R26
Woodlawn Ave. T27
10th Pl. T26
10th St. T26
11th Pl. T26
11th St. T27
12th St. T27
13th St. T26
14th Pl. U27
14th St. U27
15th Pl. U27
15th St. U26
16th St. U26
15th St. U26
17th St. U26
205th St. T27
206th St. T27
207th St. T27
208th St. T27
209th St. T27

CEMETERIES

Mt. Glenwood Cem. Q25

FOREST PRESERVES

Jurgensen Wood Q26

GOLF COURSES

Glenwoodie G.C. R25

SCHOOLS

Cottage Grove Sch. U26
Medgar Evers Sch. T27
Tideye A. Phillips Elem. Sch. U27
Woodlawn Sch. U27
Ann Rutledge Sch. for Special
Education U14

MISCELLANEOUS

Fire Department R25
Police Department R25
Village Hall U27
Summit Hill Sch. Dist. Office U14

GLENCOE

Pages 22,23

STREETS

Adams B9
Apple Tree Ln. B8
Aspen Ln. A9
Beach Rd. B8
Birch B8
Bluff B,C9
Bluff Rd. A8
Brentwood Dr. A9
Briar Ln. C9
Brookside C9
Brookside Ln. C9
Carol Ln. A8
Cedar Ln. B9
Cherry Tree Ln. B8
Chestnut Ln. B8
Clover Ln. B8
Country Ln. C9
County Line Rd. A7
Dell Pl. B10
Dennis Ln. B9
Drexel Ave. C9
Dundee Rd. B7
Eastwood Rd. B8
Edgebrook Ln. B8
Elder Ct. A9
Elm Ct. A8
Elm Pl. A8
Elm Ridge Dr. A8
Estate Dr. A9
Euclid Ave. C9
Fairfield Rd. A8
Fairview Rd. B10
Forest A9
Forest Way B8
Franklin Rd. A9
Glade Rd. A9

Glencoe Rd. B9
Glenwood Ave. C10
Green Bay A9,C10
Green Bay Rd. A8,E11
Greenleaf Ave. B9
Greenwood B-C9
Grove B,C9
Harbor C9
Hawthorne B9
Hazel B9
Hillcrest Dr. A9
Hogarth Ln. A9
Hohfelder Rd. A8
Ida Pl. B9
Ivy Ln. C9
Jackson Rd. C9
Jefferson B9
Julia Ct. B8
Knollwood Ln. A9
Lake C9
Lakeside Terr. B10
Lakewood Dr. A9
Lapier B10
Lincoln Dr. A9-B8
Linda Ln. A9
Linden Ave. C9
Longmeadow Ln. A8
Longwood Rd. B9
Madison Ave. A9
Maple Hill Rd. A9
Maple Ln. A9
Mary C10
Mayfair Ln. A8
Meadow Rd. A9
Milton B8
Monroe B10
Montgomery Ln. B9
Mortimer Rd. B8
N-S St. B9
Northwood Dr. A8
Oak Dr. B8
Oak Ridge Dr. A9
Oak Terr. A9
Oakdale C9
Old Elm Ln. A8
Old Elm Pl. A8
Orchard Ln. A8
Palos Rd. B10
Park B9
Park Pl. A8
Peach Tree Ln. B8
Pebblewood Ln. A8
Pine Ct. A8
Pinewood Ln. A8
Prairie St. B8
Ravine Glade B10
Redwood Ln. A9
Ronlin Ln. C9
Rockgate Ln. A9
Rolling Ln. A8
Scott Ave. C10
Scott Ln. C10
Sheridan Rd. B9
Skokie Ln., N. C9
Skokie Ln., S. C9
Skokie Ridge Dr. A8
Skokie Ridge Rd. A8
South Ave. B9
South Ln. B8
Stonegate Terr. B8
Strawberry Hill B8
Sunrise Cir. B10
Sunset Ln. A8
Surfside Pl. B10
Sycamore Ln. A9
Sylvan Rd. A9
Temple Ct. A8
Terrace Ct. A8
Thornapple Ln. B8
Timber Ln. A9
Tudor Ct. B8
Valley Rd. B9
Vernon Ave. B-C9
Village Ct. B9
Walden Crescent A9
Washington B9
Washington Pl. B8
Wentworth C10
Westley Rd. A8
Westwood Ln. A8
Whitebridge Hill C10
Willow Tree Ln. B8
Wingate Terr. B8
Woodlawn Ave. C9-10
Woodridge Ln. B8

GOLF COURSES

Glencoe G.C. A7
Lake Shore C.C. A8-9
Skokie C.C. C8

PARKS

Glencoe Park B10
Watts Park C9

SCHOOLS

Central Sch. B9
North Sch. C9
South Sch. C9
West Sch. B8

MISCELLANEOUS

Post Office B9
Village Hall C9

GLENVIEW

Pages 21,22,24,25,26

STREETS

Alder Pl. . . . . Pg.25 . . . . . F6
Alvin Ct. . . . . Pg.25 . . . . . G6
Ammer Rd. . . Pg.22 . . . . . F7
Apple Gate . . Pg.25 . . . . . H5
Apple Tree Ln. Pg.25 . . . . . G8
Arbor Ln. . . . Pg.26 . . . . . G8
Arbor St. . . . . Pg.26 . . . . . G9
Ardmore St. . . Pg.26 . . . . . G9
Ari Ln. . . . . . Pg.21 . . . . . E4
Astor Ct. . . . . Pg.21 . . . . . E4
Baffin Rd. . . . Pg.25 . . . . . G7
Balmoral . . . . Pg.22 . . . . . E7
Barbara Dr. . . Pg.21 . . . . . E4
Barbary Ln. . . Pg.21 . . . . . E3
Barry Ln. . . . . Pg.24 . . . . . F3
Barton Ct. . . . Pg.25 . . . . . F7
Basswood Cir. . Pg.25 . . . . . F6
Basswood Ct. . Pg.25 . . . . . F6
Beaver Rd. . . Pg.26 . . . . . G8
Becker Rd. . . . Pg.22 . . . . . F8
Beech Dr. . . . Pg.26 . . . G8,9
Beir Dr. . . . . Pg.21 . . . . . E4
Bel Air Dr. . . . Pg.25 . . . . . H5
Bellwood Ln. . Pg.24 . . . . . F4
Bette Ln. . . . . Pg.24 . . . . . G3
Beverly Ln. . . Pg.26 . . . . . G9
Bianco Terr. . . Pg.25 . . . . . H5
Birchwood Ct. . Pg.25 . . . . . H5
Blackthorn Dr. . Pg.25 . . . . . F6
Blake Ln. . . . . Pg.21 . . . . . E3
Bonnie Glen Ln. Pg.25 . . . . . G7
Branch Rd. N. . Pg.25 . . . . . H7
Brandless Dr. . Pg.21 . . . . . E4
Brandon Rd. . . Pg.22,25 . . . F7
Brassie Ln. . . . Pg.21 . . . . . E3
Briarford . . . . Pg.21 . . . . . E3
Briar hill Rd. . . Pg.25 . . . . . H6
Brook Ln. . . . . Pg.25 . . . . . G8
Brookdale Ln. . Pg.21 . . . . . D3
Bucknell Ln. . . Pg.25 . . . . . D5
Burnham Ct. . . Pg.25 . . . . . G5
Burr Oak Ct. . . Pg.25 . . . . . E7
Burr Oak Dr. E. . Pg.22 . . . . . F7
Burr Oak Dr. W. Pg.22 . . . . . F7
Burton Terr. . . Pg.25 . . . . . F7
Buttonwood Ln. Pg.25 . . . . . G6
Canterbury Ln. . Pg.25 . . . . . G7
Cariann Ln. . . Pg.26 . . . . . G8
Carol Ln. . . . . Pg.24 . . . . . F2
Carousel Dr. . . Pg.21 . . . . . E3
Carpington . . . Pg.21 . . . . . E3
Castilian Ct. . . Pg.24 . . . . . F3
Castle Dr. . . . Pg.24 . . . . . G3
Cedar Ct. . . . Pg.25 . . . . . H6
Cedarwood Ln. Pg.25 . . . . . G5
Central . . . . . Pg.26 . . . . . H6
Central Pkwy. . Pg.25 . . . . H6-7
Central Rd. . . . Pg.25 . . . . H5-8
Chandler Ln. . . Pg.21 . . . . . F4
Chatham Dr. . . Pg.25 . . . . . G7
Chester Dr. . . Pg.21 . . . . . D3
Chesterfield St. . Pg.25 . . . . . H5
Chestnut Ave. . Pg.25 . . . . . F6
Church St. . . . Pg.25 . . . . . G6
Cindy Ln. . . . Pg.21 . . . . . G3
Clavey Ln. . . . Pg.25 . . . . . H4
Clearview Dr. . Pg.25 . . . . . H4
Clover Ct. . . . Pg.25 . . . . . G5
Club Circle Dr. . Pg.25 . . . . . G7
Colfax St. . . . Pg.25 . . . . . H6
Cornell Ct. . . . Pg.25 . . . . . D5
Coronet Rd. . . Pg.25 . . . . . H8
Country Ln. . . Pg.25 . . . . . H7
Countryside Dr. . Pg.24 . . . . . G3
Countryside Ln. . Pg.24 . . . . . G3
Covert Rd. . . . Pg.25 . . . . . H7
Crab Tree Ln. . Pg.25 . . . . . H7
Crain Ln. . . . . Pg.26 . . . . . G9
Crescent . . . . Pg.21 . . . . . E2
Crestwood Dr. . Pg.21 . . . . . E3
Crestwood Ln. . Pg.24 . . . . . G4
Crown Ln. . . . Pg.24 . . . . . F3
Crystal . . . . . Pg.25 . . . . . G4
Culver Ln. . . . Pg.25 . . . . . H6
Dale St. . . . . Pg.26 . . . . . H9
Dartmouth Ct. . Pg.25 . . . . . D5
De L'Ogier Dr. . Pg.25 . . . . . F8
Dearlove Rd. . Pg.24 . . . . G3-4
Dell Pl. . . . . . Pg.24 . . . . . G4
Denise Ct. . . . Pg.24 . . . . . G3
Depot St. . . . Pg.25 . . . . . G6
Dewes St. . . . Pg.25 . . . . . G6
Dorothy Rd. . . Pg.21 . . . . . E4
Drake Rd. . . . Pg.25 . . . . . G7
East Lake St. . Pg.24 . . . . F3-4
Eastwood Ln. . Pg.25 . . . . . G8
Echo Ln. . . . . Pg.25 . . . . . G8
Edgewood (Pvt) Pg.26 . . . . . H8
Elizabeth Ln. . Pg.25 . . . . . G7
Elm St. . . . . . Pg.25 . . . . G-H6
Elmdale Ave. . Pg.21 . . . . . D4
Elmgate Dr. . . Pg.25 . . . . . G5
Elmwood Ave. . Pg.25 . . . . . F7
Estate Ln. . . . Pg.24 . . . . . F4
Evanston/Elgin Rd. . . . .
. . . . H5
Evergreen Terr. . Pg.25 . . . . . F7
Executive Ln. . Pg.24 . . . . . F4
Fairhope Ave. . Pg.22 . . . . . E8
Fairway Ct. . . Pg.25 . . . . . G4
Fairway Dr. . . Pg.25 . . . . . H4
Ferndale Rd. . Pg.26 . . . . . G8

Fernwood Ln. . Pg.25 . . . . . H5
Fir St. . . . . . . Pg.25 . . . . G5-6
Fontana Dr. . . Pg.25 . . . . . H5
Forest Ave. . . Pg.25 . . . . . F7
Forest Dr. . . . Pg.24 . . . . . F2
Forest Rd. . . . Pg.26 . . . . . G9
Forestview Ln. . Pg.25 . . . . . H7
Franklin Ln. . . Pg.21 . . . . . E2
Frederick St. . . Pg.25 . . . . . F7
Garden Ct. . . Pg.25 . . . . . G6
George Ct. . . . Pg.25 . . . . . H6
Gladish Ln. . . Pg.25 . . . . . G5
Glen Ct. . . . . Pg.25 . . . . . G7
Glen Oak Dr. . Pg.22 . . . . . E7
Glenayre Dr. . Pg.25 . . . . G,H7
Glenbrook Hosp. Dr. . . . . . .
. . . . Pg.21 . . . . . E3
Glendale Rd. . Pg.25 . . . . . H7
Glenlake Dr. . . Pg.21 . . . . . F4
Glenridge Dr. . Pg.25 . . . . . H7
Glenview Rd. . Pg.25,26 . . G5-7
Glenway Dr. . . Pg.21 . . . . . E3
Glenwood . . . Pg.25,26 . F7,G9
Glenwood Rd. . Pg.25 . . . . . G4
Gloria Ln. . . . Pg.24 . . . . . G3
Golf Ct. . . . . . Pg.25 . . . . . H6
Golf Rd. . . . . Pg.25 . . . . . I5
Golf View Ln. . Pg.25 . . . . . H5
Golf View Rd. . Pg.25 . . . . . G7
Grace Ln. . . . Pg.24 . . . . . F3
Grandview Pl. . Pg.25 . . . . H5-6
Green Willow Ln. . . . .
. . . . Pg.25 . . . . . F6
Greenacres Ln. . Pg.25 . . . . . G8
Greenbrier Dr. . Pg.24 . . . . . H4
Greenfield Dr. . Pg.25 . . . . . H5
Greenwood Ct. Pg.21 . . . . . E4
Greenwood Rd. Pg.21 . . . . . E4
Gregory Dr. . . Pg.24 . . . . . F2
Grove St. . . . Pg.25 . . . . . G6
Hackberry Ct. . Pg.26 . . . . . G9
Hager Ct. . . . Pg.26 . . . . . G8
Hammersmith Dr. . . . .
. . . . Pg.21 . . . . . E2
Hampton Ct. . Pg.21 . . . . . E3
Happy Hollow Rd. . . . .
. . . . Pg.21 . . . . . E4
Harlem Ave. . . Pg.25 . . . . . H6
Harmony Ln. . Pg.25 . . . . . H6
Harrison St. . . Pg.25 . . . . H5-6
Harvard Ct. . . Pg.25 . . . . . D5
Harvest Ct. . . Pg.21 . . . . . E3
Harvest Ln. . . Pg.21 . . . . . E3
Hawthorne Ln. . Pg.25 . . . . . G7
Heather (Pvt) . Pg.25 . . . . . H7
Heatherfield Ln. Pg.26 . . . . . G8
Henley St. . . . Pg.25 . . . . . H6
Henneberry Ln. Pg.25 . . . . . H7
Hickory Ct. . . Pg.25 . . . . . H6
Highland Ln. . Pg.24 . . . . . G4
Highland Tr. . . Pg.25 . . . . . F7
Hill Cir. . . . . . Pg.25 . . . . . H7
Hollywood . . . Pg.25 . . . . . F7
Holste Rd. . . . Pg.22 . . . . . E5
Huber Ln. . . . Pg.25 . . . . . H4
Huckelberry Ln. Pg.25 . . . . . G7
Hudson Rd. . . Pg.25 . . . . . G7
Hunt Ln. . . . . Pg.25 . . . . . G6
Hunter Rd. . . . Pg.26 . . . . . G8
Huntington Dr. . Pg.25 . . . . . F7
Hutchings Ave. Pg.25 . . . . . G6
Imperial . . . . Pg.24 . . . . . F4
Indian Rd. . . . Pg.26 . . . . . G9
Indian Ridge Ct. . . . .
. . . . Pg.21 . . . . . E2
Indian Ridge Dr. . Pg.21 . . . . . E2
Inverness Ln. . Pg.21 . . . . . F4
Iroquois Dr. . . Pg.21 . . . . . E2
Ivy Dr. . . . . . Pg.21 . . . . . F2
Ivy Ln. . . . . . Pg.21 . . . . . E2
Ivy Way . . . . Pg.21 . . . . . E2
Janet Dr. . . . . Pg.21 . . . . . E4
Janny Rd. . . . Pg.21 . . . . . E4
Jefferson Ave. . Pg.22 . . . . . F6
Jerrie Ln. . . . Pg.25 . . . . . H4
Joanne Dr. . . Pg.21 . . . . . D3
Johns Ct. . . . Pg.22 . . . . . E6
Johns Dr. . . . Pg.22 . . . . . F6
Joy Ln. . . . . . Pg.24 . . . . . F3
Juniper St. . . . Pg.26 . . . . . G9
Juniper Terr. . . Pg.26 . . . . . G9
Karen Ln. . . . Pg.25 . . . . . H5
Kaywood Ln. . Pg.25 . . . . . F7
Keenan Ln. . . Pg.21 . . . . . E4
Kendale Ln. . . Pg.25 . . . . . F7
Kenilworth Ln. Pg.25 . . . . . F7
Kennicott Ln. . Pg.24 . . . . . F3
Kiess . . . . . . Pg.25 . . . . . E3
Kings Ln. . . . Pg.25 . . . . . F6
Kinker Way . . Pg.25 . . . . . F6
Kmiec Ct. . . . Pg.21 . . . . . D5
Knight . . . . . . Pg.24 . . . . . F3
Knollwood . . . Pg.24 . . . . . G3
LaFontaine Dr. Pg.25 . . . . . F6
Lake Ave. . . . Pg.25 . . . . . H5
Lake St. E. . . Pg.25 . . . . . F3
Lakewood Ct. . Pg.24 . . . . . F4
Landreth Ln. . Pg.22 . . . . . C7
Laramie Ln. . . Pg.26 . . . . . G9
Larch Ave. . . Pg.25 . . . . . F2
Larkdale Dr. . . Pg.25 . . . . . G6
Laurel Ave. . . Pg.24 . . . . . F2
Lawnwood Terr. Pg.25 . . . . . F7
Lawrence . . . Pg.25 . . . . . F2
Lawson Rd. . . Pg.21 . . . . . E4
Leaf Dr. . . . . Pg.25 . . . . . G5

Leanne Ct. . . Pg.21 . . . . . E3
Lehigh . . . . . Pg.25 . . . . . H6
Lenox Rd. . . . Pg.25 . . . . . G7
Lexington Ln. . Pg.25 . . . . . D4
Liberty Ln. . . . Pg.24 . . . . . G4
Lilac Ave. . . . Pg.24 . . . . . F2
Limar Ln. . . . Pg.25 . . . . . H6
Lincoln . . . . . Pg.25 . . . . . H6
Lincoln Ave. . . Pg.25 . . . . F-H6
Linden . . . . . Pg.25 . . . . . G5
Linden Ave. . . Pg.24 . . . . . F2
Linden Ln. . . . Pg.22 . . . . . F7
Lindenwood . . Pg.24 . . . . . G3
Linneman St. . Pg.25 . . . . . G6
Lizette Ln. . . . Pg.21 . . . . . E3
Locust Ave. . . Pg.24 . . . . . F2
Locust Ln. . . . Pg.25 . . . . . H7
London Ln. . . Pg.25 . . . . . F7
Long Rd. . . . . Pg.26 . . . . . G9
Long Valley Rd. Pg.25 . . . . H6-7
Longmeadow . Pg.24 . . . . . F4
Lori Dr. . . . . . Pg.22 . . . . . E4
Lotus Ln. . . . . Pg.24 . . . . . H4
Lurilane . . . . Pg.24 . . . . . F2
MacArthur Dr. . Pg.25 . . . . . H6
MacLean Ct. . Pg.25 . . . . . G6
Magnolia . . . . Pg.24 . . . . . F2
Malik Ct. . . . . Pg.25 . . . . . H5
Maple Leaf Dr. Pg.21 . . . . . E4
Maple Ln. . . . Pg.22 . . . . . F7
Maple St. . . . Pg.21 . . . . . E2
Maplewood Ln. Pg.25 . . . . . G6
Maria Ct. . . . Pg.25 . . . . . H5
Marie Ln. . . . Pg.24 . . . . . F3
Mark Dr. . . . . Pg.26 . . . . . G9
Mark Ln. . . . . Pg.21 . . . . . D3
Mary Ct. . . . . Pg.25 . . . . . H5
Mary Kay Ln. . Pg.21 . . . . . E4
Meadow Ln. . . Pg.25 . . . . . F7
Meadowlark . . Pg.25 . . . . . G5
Merle Ln. . . . Pg.24 . . . . . F2
Michael Ln. . . Pg.21 . . . . . E3
Mickey Ln. . . Pg.24 . . . . . F2
Miller Dr. . . . Pg.21 . . . . . D3
Milwaukee Ave. Pg.24 . . . . . F3
Mohawk Ln. . . Pg.21 . . . . . E2
Monroe . . . . . Pg.22 . . . . . F6
Montgomery Ln. . . . .
. . . . Pg.25 . . . . . H6
Mulberry Ln. . Pg.26 . . . . . G9
Myrtle Pkwy. . Pg.21 . . . . . D3
Neil Ln. . . . . Pg.24 . . . . . G3
Neva Ave. . . . Pg.25 . . . . . H6
Nora Ave. . . . Pg.25 . . . . . H6
Nordica Ave. . Pg.25 . . . . . H6
Norma Ct. . . . Pg.25 . . . . . H5
Normandy Ln.(Pvt) . . . .
. . . . Pg.25 . . . . . G8
North Dr.(Pvt) . Pg.22 . . . . E-F7
Norwich Ct. . . Pg.21 . . . . . F4
Norwood Terr. . Pg.25 . . . . . H5
Nottingham Ave. Pg.25 . . . . . H6
O'Hare Ln. . . Pg.22 . . . . . E4
Oakwood . . . Pg.22 . . . . . E7
Old Willow Rd. Pg.22 . . . . . D5
Overlook Dr. . . Pg.25 . . . . . H7
Oxford Ln. . . . Pg.25 . . . . . G7
Paddock Dr. . . Pg.22 . . . . . D5
Palmgren Dr. . Pg.25 . . . . G6-7
Pam-Anne Dr. Pg.24 . . . . . G3
Park Dr. . . . . Pg.25 . . . . . G5
Park Ln. . . . . Pg.25 . . . . . G5
Parkview Rd. . Pg.25 . . . . . H6
Pebble Creek Dr. . . . .
. . . . Pg.25 . . . . . F6
Pebble Dr. . . Pg.25 . . . . . G5
Pebblewood Ln. Pg.22 . . . . . D5
Pendleton Ln. . Pg.25 . . . . . F7
Penn Ct. . . . . Pg.25 . . . . . D5
Pfingsten . . . Pg.24 . . . . . F3
Pfingsten Rd. . Pg.21 . . . . . E3
Phillips Dr. . . Pg.21 . . . . . E4
Pick Dr. . . . . Pg.25 . . . . . H5
Pine Ct. . . . . Pg.25 . . . . . G6
Pine St. . . . . Pg.25 . . . . . G6
Pinehurst Dr. . Pg.25 . . . . G5-6
Pleasant Dr. . . Pg.22 . . . . . F7
Pleasant Ln. . . Pg.22 . . . . . F7
Plymouth Ct. . Pg.25 . . . . . F7
Plymouth Ln. . Pg.25 . . . . . F7
Polo Ln. . . . . Pg.25 . . . . . G8
Portage Run . Pg.24 . . . . . F3
Porter Ct. . . . Pg.21 . . . . . D3
Potter Rd. . . . Pg.25 . . . . . F7
Prairie St. . . . Pg.25 . . . . . G6
Princeton Ln. . Pg.25 . . . . . D5
Pynsky Rd. . . Pg.21 . . . . . F2
Queens Ln. . . Pg.22 . . . . . F7
Rackliff Ct. . . Pg.25 . . . . . D5
Railroad . . . . Pg.25 . . . . . G6
Raleigh Dr. . . Pg.25 . . . . . G7
Raleigh Rd. . . Pg.25 . . . . . G7
Ralmark Ln. . . Pg.24 . . . . . F4
Rebecca Ln. . Pg.21 . . . . . E4
Red Bud Ln. . Pg.25 . . . . . F6
Redwood Ln. . Pg.26 . . . . . H8
Ridgewood Ln. (E&W) . . . . . .
. . . . Pg.25 . . . . . F7
Rio Vista (Pvt) . Pg.25 . . . . . H7
River Dr. . . . . Pg.25 . . . . . G6
Riverside Ct. . Pg.25 . . . . . F6
Robin Ln. . . . Pg.24 . . . . . F3
Robincrest Ln. N. . . . .
. . . . Pg.25 . . . . . H6
Robincrest Ln., S. . . . .

Rogers Ave. . . Pg.25 . . . . . H6
Rolfe Rd. . . . Pg.22 . . . . . F6
Rolling Pass . Pg.25 . . . . . G5
Rollwind Rd. . Pg.25 . . . . . H7
Roosevelt Ave. Pg.25 . . . . . G5
Royal Oak Ln. . Pg.25 . . . . . G7
Rugen Ctr. . . Pg.25 . . . . . F6
Rugen Ln. . . . Pg.25 . . . . . F6
Rugen Rd. . . . Pg.25 . . . . . F6
Russet Way . . Pg.21 . . . . . E3
Rutgers Ct. . . Pg.22 . . . . . D5
Sally Ct. . . . . Pg.24 . . . . . G3
Sandy Ln. . . . Pg.21 . . . . . E4
Sanford Ct. . . Pg.25 . . . . . G7
Sanford Ln. . . Pg.25 . . . . F-G7
Saranac Ct. . . Pg.21 . . . . . E3
Saranac Ln. . . Pg.21 . . . . . E3
Sequoia Trail . Pg.25 . . . . . F6
Sheffield Ln. . . Pg.25 . . . . . G7
Shermer Rd. . Pg.25 . . . . . G5
Sherwood Rd. . Pg.26 . . . . . G8
Sheryl Ln. . . . Pg.25 . . . . . H4
Short Ln. . . . Pg.25 . . . . . H5
Silver Willow Dr. . . . .
. . . . Pg.25 . . . . . F6
Silverpine Dr. . Pg.25 . . . . . G5
Simonson . . . Pg.25 . . . . . G5
Sioux Tr. . . . . Pg.21 . . . . . D3
Sleepy Hollow Rd. . . . .
. . . . Pg.25 . . . . . G6
Solar Ln. . . . Pg.25 . . . . . G7
Somerset Dr. . Pg.25 . . . . . G7
Southgate Dr. . Pg.25 . . . . . H5
Spring Rd. . . . Pg.25 . . . . . F6
Springdale Ave. Pg.24 . . . . . G4
Spruce Dr. . . . Pg.25 . . . . . G6
Spruce St. . . . Pg.25 . . . . G-H6
Steffens Ln. . . Pg.25 . . . . . F7
Stevens Dr. . . Pg.25 . . . . . F6
Stratford Ln. . . Pg.21 . . . . . E4
Strawberry . . Pg.21 . . . . . E4
Sumac Cir. . . Pg.25 . . . . . F6
Sunset Ridge Rd. . . . .
. . . . Pg.22 . . . . . E7
Surrey Ln. . . . Pg.25 . . . . . H7
Sussex Ln. . . Pg.21 . . . . . E3
Swainwood Dr. Pg.25 . . . . . G5
Taft Ct. . . . . . Pg.26 . . . . . G8
Tall Tree Rd. . Pg.25 . . . . . F6
Tamer Ln. . . . Pg.24 . . . . . G3
Tanglewood Ln. Pg.22 . . . . . F6
Terrace Ln. . . Pg.25 . . . . . G5
Thornwood Ln. Pg.25 . . . . . G7
Timberline Dr. . Pg.25 . . . . . G8
Timbers Edge . Pg.24 . . . . . F2
Tinker Way . . Pg.25 . . . . . G6
Topp Ln. . . . . Pg.25 . . . . . F7
Tracy Ct. . . . Pg.24 . . . . . G3
Tri-State Tollway Pg.21 . . . . . E2
Trowbridge Ct. Pg.21 . . . . . E4
Tulip Tree Ln. . Pg.25 . . . . . F6
Valley Lo Ln.(Pvt) . . . .
. . . . Pg.25 . . . . . E6
Vantage Ln. . . Pg.21 . . . . . E3
Vernon Dr. . . Pg.22 . . . . . E4
Virginia Ln. . . Pg.25 . . . . . H4
Wagner Rd. . . Pg.25 . . . . . F8
Walnut Ct. . . . Pg.25 . . . . H5-6
Warren Rd. . . Pg.25 . . . . . F4
Warrington Ct. Pg.21 . . . . . F4
Warwick . . . . Pg.21 . . . . . F4
Washington St. Pg.25 . . . . G-H6
Waukegan Rd. Pg.22,25 . . F-K6
Wedgewood Ct. Pg.25 . . . . . G5
Wedgewood Dr. Pg.25 . . . . . G5
Wellesley Ct. . Pg.25 . . . . . G5
West Lake Ave. Pg.24 . . . . F2-4
Westfield Ln. . Pg.24 . . . . . F2
Westview Rd. . Pg.25 . . . . . G5
Wildberry Dr. . Pg.22 . . . . . E6
Wildwood . . . Pg.25 . . . . . F7
Willow . . . . . Pg.25 . . . . . G6
Willow Ln. . . . Pg.25 . . . . . G6
Wilmette Ave. . Pg.25 . . . . . G8
Winchester Ln. Pg.21 . . . . . F4
Windsor Rd. . . Pg.25 . . . . . G7
Winnetka Rd. . Pg.21 . . . . . F4
Wissing Ln. . . Pg.25 . . . . . H6
Woodland Dr. . Pg.25 . . . . . H7
Woodlawn Ave. Pg.25 . . . . . F7
Woodlawn Rd. Pg.25 . . . . . G5
Woodmere Ln. Pg.26 . . . . . G8
Woodridge Rd. Pg.21 . . . . . E3
Woodview Ln. . Pg.25 . . . . . G6
Yale Ct. . . . . Pg.25 . . . . . D5
York Rd. . . . . Pg.25 . . . . . H6
Zenith Pkwy. . Pg.24 . . . . . G2

CEMETERIES

Sunset Mem. Gdns. Cem. . . . .
. . . . Pg.22 . . . . . E4

GOLF COURSES

Glenview N.A.S. G.C. . . . .
. . . . Pg.25 . . . . . G5
Glenview Pk. G.C. . . . .
. . . . Pg.25 . . . . . G5
North Shore C.C. Pg.25 . . . . . G7
Northwestern/
. . . . Pg.26 . . . . . J8
Valley-Lo Sports Club . . . . . .
. . . . Pg.22 . . . . . E6

PARKS

Cole Park . . . Pg.25 . . . . . F7

Country Lane Pk. Pg.24 G3
Countryside Pk. Pg.24 G3
Cunliff Park Pg.26 H8
Flick Park Pg.24 F3
Hawthorn Glen Park Pg.21 D3
Huber Lane Pk. Pg.25 G4
Indian Trail Pk. Pg.24 F2
Jackman Park Pg.25 G6
John's Park Pg.25 H6
Manor Park Pg.25 H6
Riverside Park Pg.25 H6
Roosevelt Park Pg.25 G5
Rugen Park Pg.25 H4
Sleepy Hollow Pk. Pg.25 G6
Tall Tree Park Pg.25 F6
The Grove Park Pg.24 F3
Willowbrook Park Pg.21 E4

SCHOOLS
Avoca W. Sch. Pg.26 G9
Clyde Lyons Sch. Pg.25 G7
Glen Grove Sch. Pg.24 G3
Glenbrook South H.S. Pg.21 F3
Hoffman Sch. Pg.25 H6
Immanuel Sch. Pg.22 F6
Louise Henking Sch. Pg.25 G4
Midwestern Academy Pg.25 G5
Our Lady Sch. Pg.25 G6
Pleasant Ridge Sch. Pg.25 F7
Poko Nursery Sch. Pg.25 H6
Rugen Sch. Pg.25 G5
Springman Jr. H.S. Pg.25 H5
Westbrook Sch. Pg.24 F4
Willowbrook Elem. Sch. Pg.24 E4
Winkleman Sch. Pg.21 E3

SHOPPING CENTERS
Golfview S.C. Pg.25 H6
Plaza del Prado Pg.21 D3

MISCELLANEOUS
Convent of the Holy Spirit Pg.22 D6
Fire Department Pg.25 G6
Glenbrook Hospital Pg.21 E3
Glenview Ice Center Pg.21 F3
Library Pg.25 G6
Post Office Pg.25 G6
Village Hall / Police Pg.25 G7

GLENWOOD
Pages 43,44,49

STREETS
Arizona Ave. Pg.43 Q24
Arquilla Dr. Pg.43 Q24
Avalon Pg.44 R27
Birch Dr. Pg.44 Q26
Blackstone Ave. Pg.44 R27
Bruce Ln. Pg.43 P24
Campbell Ave. Pg.44 R25
Carol Pkwy. Pg.43 Q24
Cedar Ln. Pg.44 Q26
Center St. Pg.44 Q25
Champlain Pg.44 R26
Cherry Dr. Pg.43 Q24
Chestnut Ct. Pg.44 R26
Chestnut Ln. Pg.44 Q26
Chicago Heights- Glenwood Rd. Pg.43,49 R24
Clark St. Pg.44 R26
Cottage Grove Ave. Pg.44 Q26
Dante Ave. Pg.44,49 R27
Dorchester Ave. Pg.44 R27
Drexel Ave. Pg.44 R26
Eberhart Pg.44 R26
Ellis Pg.44 R27
Elm Ln. Pg.44 Q26
Fitzhenry Dr. Pg.43 Q24
Forest Ave. Pg.49 R25
Gay Ct. Pg.43 Q24
Glenwood Ave. Pg.43 Q25
Glenwood Dyer Rd. Pg.44 R25
Glenwood Lansing Rd. Pg.44 R27
Greenwood Pg.43 R27
Halsted St. Pg.43 R24
Harper Ave. Pg.44 R27
Hickory Ln. Pg.44 Q26
Holbrook Rd. Pg.43 R24
Holly Ct. Pg.43 Q24
Illinois Ave. Pg.43 Q24
Indiana Pg.43 Q24
Ingleside Ave. Pg.44 R26
Iowa St. Pg.43 Q24
Jane St. Pg.44 R25
Kenneth Ct. Pg.43 Q24
Lee Ct. Pg.43 Q24
Longwood Ct. Pg.43 Q24
Longwood Dr. Pg.43 Q24
Lotta St. Pg.43 R25
Magnolia Dr. Pg.44 Q26
Main St. Pg.43 R25
Main, N. Pg.43 R25
Manor Ct. Pg.43 Q24
Maple Ct. Pg.44 Q26
Maple Dr. Pg.44 Q26
Maryland Ave. Pg.44 R26
Merrill St. Pg.44 Q25
Minerva Ave. Pg.44 R27
Mulberry Ct. Pg.44 R26
Mulberry Dr. Pg.44 R26
Nevada St. Pg.43 Q24
Oak Lane S. Pg.44 R26
Oak Ln. Pg.43 Q26
Oak St. Pg.43 Q25
Ohio St. Pg.43 Q24
Palm Dr. Pg.43 P24
Park Dr. Pg.43 Q24
Pickens Pg.44 R25
Pine Ln. Pg.44 Q26
Pleasant Dr. Pg.43 Q24
Rainbow Dr. Pg.43 Q24
Rebecca St. Pg.44 R25
Rhodes Pg.44 R26
Roberts Dr. Pg.43 Q24
Rose Ct. Pg.44 R26
Rose St. Pg.44 R26
School St. Pg.43 Q25
Science Rd. Pg.43 R24
Spruce Ln. Pg.44 R26
St. Lawrence Pg.44 R26
State St. Pg.43 R25
Strieff Ln. Pg.43 Q24
Sunset Dr. Pg.43 P24
Sycamore Ln. Pg.44 R26
Terrace Pg.43 Q24
Tulip Dr. Pg.44 Q26
University Pg.44 R27
Virginia Ave. Pg.43 Q24
Wabash Ave. Pg.43 R25
Walnut Ln. Pg.44 Q26
Westwood Pg.43 Q24
Willow Ln. Pg.44 R26
Wisconsin Pg.43 Q24
Young St. Pg.44 R25
187th St. Pg.43 Q24
191st Pl. Pg.44 R26
192nd Pl. Pg.44 R27
192nd St. Pg.44 R26
193rd Pl. Pg.44 R27
193rd St. Pg.44 R27
194th Pl. Pg.49 R27
194th St. Pg.43,44 R24,27
195th St. Pg.49 R24

PARKS
George Aquilla Park Pg.43 Q24

SCHOOLS
Brookwood Jr. H.S. Pg.44 R26
Brookwood Sch. Pg.44 R26
Glenwood Sch. for Boys Pg.43 Q24
Hickory Bend Elem. Sch. Pg.44 R26
Longwood Sch. Pg.43 Q24

SHOPPING CENTERS
Glenwood Plaza Pg.43 Q24

MISCELLANEOUS
City Hall R25

GOLF
Page 25

STREETS
Blossom Ln. H7
Briar Rd. H7
Clyde Ln. H7
Dover St. H7
Elm Cir. H7
Highland Pl. H7
Lilac Ln. H7
Logan Terr. H7
Orchard Ln. H7
Overlook Dr. H7

GOLF COURSES
Glen View C.C. H8

PARKS
Diederich Park H7

MISCELLANEOUS
Metra Station H7
Police Department H7
Post Office H7
Village Hall H7

HANOVER PARK
Page 16

STREETS
Adams St. M2
Apple Tree St. M1
Applewood Ct. L1
Asbury Cir. L1
Barrington Rd. M1
Berkshire Dr. L1-2
Birch Ave. M1
Bolton Way M1
Brentwood Ct. L1
Briar Ln. L1
Briarwood Ave. L1
Briarwood St. M1
Bristol Ct. L1
Bristol Dr. L1
Bristol Ln. L1
Brockton Ct. L1
Brookside Dr. L1
Canterbury Dr. M1
Carlisle Ct. L1
Carlisle Dr. L1
Carnaby Ct. L1
Carrolton Ct. L1
Catawba Ln. L1
Churchill Dr. L1
Countryside Dr. M1-2
Coventy Dr. L1
Crescent Way M1
Cumberland Dr. L1
Cynthia Ln. L1
Cypress Ave. M1
Dartmouth Ct. L2
Dartmouth Ln. L1-2
Deerpath Ln. M1
Durham Ct. L2
Edgebrook Ln. M1
Essex Ct. L2
Evergreen M1
Fairhaven Dr. M2
Filmore Ave. M2
Forest Glen Ave. M1
Glenside Ct. L1
Glenwood Ln. M2
Grant Cir. M2
Greenwood Ave. M1
Guilford Commons L2
Haddam Way M1
Hanover St. M1
Harrison St. M2
Hartman Dr. L1
Hasting Ln. L1-2
Hawthorn Ln. M2
Hearth St. M1
Highland St. M1
Hillcrest Ave. M1
Huntington Cir. L1
Indian Hill Ave. M1
Irving Park Rd. L1
Jackson St. M2
Jenson Blvd. L1
Kensington Ln. L1
Kent Ct. L2
Kingsbury Dr. L1
Kingsbury Ln. L1
Laurel Ave. M1
Laurie Dr. L1
Lexington Cir. M1
Lexington Pk. L2
Linden Ave. M1
Long Meadow Ln. M1
Longmeadow Ct. M1
Madison St. M1
Manchester Manor L2
Maple Ave. M1
Maplewood Ave. M1
Meadowbrook Ln. M1
Nantucket Cove L2
Northway Ct. L1
Northway Dr. L-M1
Oakwood Ave. M1
Old Mill Ln. L1
Olde Salem Cir. M2
Olde Salem Dr. L2
Olivia Ln. L1
Orchard Ln. M2
Oxford L1
Park Ave. M1
Parkview Dr. L1
Peach Tree M1
Pebblebrook Ln. L1
Pine Tree M1
Polk St. M2
Poplar Ave. M1
Princeton Cir. L1
Ramblewood Dr. L1
Ramsgate Cir. L1
Redwood M1
Rocton Way L2
Rosewood St. M1
Roxbury Ct. L1
Sarson Way M1
Shelbourne Ct. L1-2
Sherwood Cir. L1
Somerset Cir. M1
Spruce Ave. M1
Stratford Ln. L1
Strathmore Ln. L1
Sycamore M1
Taft Cir. M1
Tanglewood Ave. M1
Taylor St. M2
Tower Dr. L1
Truman St. M2
Valley View Rd. M1
Walnut Ave. M1
Washington St. M2
Waterford Dr. M2
Wedgewood Dr. M2
Westchester Dr. M1-2
Weymouth Cir. L2
White Bridge Ct. L1
White Bridge Ln. L1
Wilson St. M2
Windsor Ln. L1
Wise M2
Yorkshire Ct. L2
Yorkshire Dr. L1-2

SCHOOLS
A. Fox Sch. L1
Hanover Highland Sch. M1

SHOPPING CENTERS
Hanover Square M1
Tradewinds Shopping Center L1

HAZEL CREST
Pages 42,43

STREETS
Adrian Ln. Q19
Albany Ave. O21
Annetta N22
Anthony Ave. O22
Arlington Ln. P21
Artesian N,O22
Balmoral Ln. P21
Birchwood O20
Bordeaux Ct. P20
Briar Ln. Q20
Bryant Ln. O21
Bulger Ave. O22
Burgundy Ln. P20
Burr Oak Ln. O20
Butternut O21
Buttonwood Walk P21
California Ave. O21
Cannes Ct. P20
Carriage Way P21
Central Park Ave. O20
Chambord P20
Chantilly Ln. P20
Charlemagne Ave. P20
Charleston N23
Charters Ct. P20
Cherry Creek Dr. O21
Cherrywood Ln. P21
Chestnut Ave. O20
Chestnut Ct. O20
Circle Dr. N21
Coach Ln. P21
Concord Pl. O21
Cottonwood Ct. O20
Coventry Ct. O20
Crane Ave. O22
Crawford Ave. P19
Crescent Dr. N21
Crystal Ct. Q20
Dogwood Ln. P21
Edgewater Dr. Q19
Elm Dr. O20
Emerson Ave. O21
Eylsees Ct. P20
Fontainbleau Dr. P20
Glynwood Ln. O20
Golfview Dr. Q20
Grandview Dr. P21
Grenoble Dr. Q20
Harseile Ln. Q20
Hawthorne Ln. P21
Hazel Ln. O20
Head Ave. O22
Hickory Ct. O20
Hickory Ln. O20
Highland Ave. O21
Highland Ct. O21
Hillside O21
Holmes Ave. O21
Indi Ct. Q20
Jodave Ave. O22
Jovanna O21
Kedzie Ave. O20
Knollwood Pl. P21
Lakeview Dr. Q20
Larkspur Ln. P21
Laurel Ln. O20
Lawndale Ave., S. P20
Lexington Dr. O21
Lexy Ct. Q19
Lincoln Ave. O22
Linden Dr. O20
Locust Dr. O20
Longfellow Ave. O21
Lowell Ave. O21
Magnolia Dr. O20
Mahoney Pkwy.,W. O21
Maple Ln. O20
Meadow Dr. Q20
Michael Ct. Q19
Michael Dr. Q19
Millstone Rd. P21
Montmarte Ave. P20
Murphy O21
Normandy Ln. P20
Novak Dr. O21
Oak St. O20
Oakwood Dr. P21
Old Trail Rd. P21
Orchard Ridge Ave. O22
Orleans Dr. P20
Page St. O23
Palmer Blvd. O21
Park Ave. N23
Paulina O23
Peach Grove Ln. O20
Pebblewood P21
Pine Ct. O20
Poe Ave. O21
Recreation Ct. O21
Ridgewood Dr. P21
River Rd. Q20
Robert Ct. Q20
Roby St. O22
Rochester Ave. N23
Rockwell Ave. O21
Royale Ln. P20
Seine Ct. P20
Shagbark Ln. P21
Shea Ave. O22
Smoketree P21
Springfield Ave. P20
Springtide Ln. O20
Spruce O21
Stonebridge Dr. P21
Streamwood Dr. Q20
Summit Ave. O21
Sunset Rd. O22
Surrey Ln. P21
Tamarino Ln. O20
Tanglewood Ct. P21
Tennyson Pl. O21
Trapet Ave. O22
Tulip Dr. O20
Turtlecreek Dr. P21
Versailles Ln. P20
Village Dr. Q20
Village Rd. Q20
Wellington O20
Wellington Ct. O20
Western O22
Wheelwood Ct. O20
Whipple St. N21
Whitman Ave. O21
Whittier Ave. O21
Winchester Ave. O22
Wood St. O22
Woodworth Pl. O20,21
167th St. N22
168th St. N22,23
169th St. O21,22
170th Pl. O21
170th St. O21,22
171st St. O21,22
172nd Ct. O19
172nd St. O21
173rd St. O19,21
174th St. O21
175th St. O19
176th St. P20
177th St. P20
183rd St. Q23
187th St. Q19

GOLF COURSES
Calumet C.C. O22

PARKS
Chateau Park P20
Hillcrest Park O21
James Setnes Park N21
Lions Park O22
Oak Hill Park O21
Oak Valley North Park O21
Stone Hollow Park P21
Wolf Park O20

SCHOOLS
Chataux Sch. P20
Highland Sch. O20
Palm Sch. O22
St. Anne Sch. N22
St. John Sch. Q20

MISCELLANEOUS
Community Center O21
Fire Department O21,22
Hazel Crest Hospital O23
Imperial Nursing Home O20
Library Q20
R.R. Station O23
South Suburban Hospital P20
Village Hall O21,23

HICKORY HILLS
Page 34

STREETS
Active Ln. C12
Active Ln. N. C12
Active Ln. S. C12
Ash Ln. C12
Baldwin Trail C13
Barberry Ln. C12
Beechnut Rd. C12
Birch Ln. C12
Blue Ridge C12
Briarwood C12
Chestnut Dr. B12
Christina Dr. C12
Coey Ln. D13
Colette Ln. C12
Dell Ct. B12
Elm Dr. C12
Emerald Ave. C12
Flamingo Terr. D13
Forest B11
Forest Ln. C12
Forest Ln. East C12
Golden Oak Ct. C12
Hawthorn Dr. C12
Hickory Ln. C12
Hillside Dr. C12
Jonathan Dr. C13
Kean Ave. C11
Kells Dr. D12
Kitty Ln. D12
Kopping Ln. C12
Lisa Ln. C12
Lynwood C12
Maple Ln. C12
Meadowview Dr. C11
Nida Ct. C12
Oak Hill Ct. C12
Oakwood C12
Orchard Dr. C12
Pleasant Ave. C12
Primrose Ln. B12
Robin Ct. B12
Sandra Ln. C12
Shady Dr. B12
Sycamore Ct. C12
Sycamore Dr. C12
Wachter Ln. C12
Willow Rd. C12
Woodard Ln. C12
Woodland C12
76th Ave. D14
76th Ct. D14
77th Ave. D14
77th Ct. D14
78th Ave. D13
78th Ct. D13
79th Ave. D13
79th Ct. D13
80th Ave. (Roberts Rd.) D13
80th Ct. D13
81st Ave. D13
81st Ct. D13
82nd Ave. D13
82nd Ct. D13
83rd Ave. D13
83rd Ct. D13
84th Ave. D13
84th Ct. D13
85th Ave. D12
85th Ct. D12
85th St. B13
86th Ave. D12
86th Ct. D12
86th Pl. C13
87th Ave. D12
87th Ct. C12
87th Pl. C12,13
87th St. C12
88th Ave. D12
88th Ct. C12
88th St. C13
89th Ave. D12
89th Ct. D12
89th Pl. C13
89th St. C12
90th Ave. D12
90th Pl. C13
90th St. D12,13
91st Pl. C12,14
91st St. C12
92nd Pl. C12,13
92nd St. C12,13
93rd Pl. D12
93rd St. D12,C13
94th St. D13
95th St. D12
96th Pl. D14
97th Pl. D13
97th St. D13
98th Pl. D13
98th St. D13,14
99th St. D13

FOREST PRESERVES
Hickory Hills Woods D12

GOLF COURSES
Hickory Hills G.C. D13

SCHOOLS
Conrady Jr. H.S. D13
Dorn Sch. C13
Glen Oak Sch. C12
St. Patricia Sch. C12

SHOPPING CENTERS
Hickory Creek Shopping Ctr. D12

HOFFMAN ESTATES
Pages 6,11,12

STREETS
Abbey Wood Dr. Pg.11 G2
Aberdeen St. Pg.12 J6
Alcoa Ln. Pg.11 H4
Alder Ct. Pg.6 E2
Alder Dr. N. Pg.6 E2
Alder Dr. W. Pg.6 E2
Algonquin Rd. Pg.7 F5
Alhambra Ln. Pg.12 J5
Almond Ln. Pg.12 J6
Alpine Ln. Pg.12 H5
Amber Cir. Pg.6 C3
Ameritech Center Dr. (Pvt.) Pg.11 F2
Amherst Ln. Pg.11 H4
Anjou Ln. Pg.6 D3
Apache Ln. Pg.12 H5
Apple St. Pg.12 H5
Apricot St. Pg.12 H5
Arizona Blvd. Pg.12 H5
Arlington St. Pg.12 J5
Arrowwood Ln. Pg.6 D2
Ascot Ct. Pg.11 J3
Ash Rd. Pg.12 J5
Ashland St. Pg.12 J5

HOFFMAN ESTATES

Street	Page	Grid
Ashley Ct.	Pg.11	G4
Ashley Rd.	Pg.11	G4
Aspen St.	Pg.12	H5
Aster Ln.	Pg.12	H5
Atlantic Ave.	Pg.11	J1
Audubon St.	Pg.12	J5
Avondale Ln.	Pg.6	H2
Azalea Ln.	Pg.12	H5
Barberry Ct.	Pg.6	D2
Barcroft Dr.	Pg.6	B2
Barcroft St.	Pg.6	B2
Bardwick Ct.	Pg.6	C3
Barrington Rd.	Pg.11	H1
Basswood St.	Pg.12	H6
Batavia Ln.	Pg.12	J5
Baxter Ln.	Pg.11	H4
Bayberry Ln.	Pg.11	F1
Bayside Cir.	Pg.11	D1
Bayside St. E.	Pg.6	D2
Beacon Ct.	Pg.6	C2
Bedford Rd.	Pg.11	G4
Berkley Ln., E.	Pg.11	H5
Berkley Ln., W.	Pg.11	H4
Bernay Ln.	Pg.6	D2
Bicek Ct.	Pg.6	C2
Bicek Dr.	Pg.6	C2
Blair Ln.	Pg.11	H3
Bluebonnet Ln., E.	Pg.12	H5
Bluebonnet Ln.	Pg.11	H5
Boardwalk Blvd.	Pg.11	H1
Bode Cir.(Pvt)	Pg.11	J3
Bode Rd.	Pg.11	H4
Bolleana Ct.	Pg.6	D2
Bonnie Ln.	Pg.6	H2
Bordeaux Dr.	Pg.6	D3
Botsford Pl.	Pg.11	F1
Boulder Ln.	Pg.6	C3
Bradley Ln.	Pg.12	J5
Bradwell Rd.	Pg.6	B2
Briarcliff Ln.	Pg.11	H4
Brigantine Ct.	Pg.6	C2
Brigantine Ln.	Pg.6	C2
Brighton Pl.	Pg.11	G2
Bristol Walk	Pg.11	G2
Brittany Ln.	Pg.6	D2
Brookside Dr.	Pg.11	H2
Brookside Ln.	Pg.6	D2
Buckeye Dr.	Pg.12	J5
Buckingham Ct.	Pg.11	J3
Buckthorn Dr.	Pg.6	D2
Bulrush Dr.	Pg.6	H2
Burnham Rd.	Pg.6	C3
Burning Bush Ln.	Pg.6	D2
Burr Ridge Dr.	Pg.6	D2
Buttercreek Ct.	Pg.12	H4
Butterfield Ct.	Pg.6	E4
Caldwell Ln.	Pg.11	H2
Cambridge Ln.	Pg.11	H4
Camelot Ln.	Pg.6	B2
Cameron Ct.	Pg.6	C3
Candlewood Ln.	Pg.11	H3
Cape Breton Ct.	Pg.6	D2
Capstan Dr.	Pg.6	C2
Cardigan Pl.	Pg.11	G2
Carleton Rd.	Pg.11	G4
Carling Rd.	Pg.11	G3
Carmel Ct.	Pg.11	H2
Carnation Ln.	Pg.11	H4
Carthage Ln.	Pg.12	H5
Castaway Ct.	Pg.6	C2
Castaway Ln.	Pg.6	C2
Castlewood Ct.	Pg.6	E4
Cedar Tree Ct.	Pg.12	H4
Central Rd.	Pg.11	F1
Chambers Dr.	Pg.6	B3
Chandler Ln.	Pg.12	J5
Charlemagne Dr., N.	Pg.6	D3
Charlemagne Dr., W.	Pg.6	D2
Charleston Ln.	Pg.11	H2
Chatsworth Ln.	Pg.11	J3
Chelmsford Pl.	Pg.6	E3
Cheltenham Pl.	Pg.11	G1
Cherry Ct.	Pg.6	D2
Chesapeake Ct.	Pg.6	D2
Chesapeake Dr.	Pg.6	D2
Chestnut Ln.	Pg.6	D2
Chippendale Rd.	Pg.11	G3
Claremont Rd.	Pg.11	G3
Clarendon St.	Pg.12	H5
Claridge Cir.	Pg.11	J3
Clifton Pl.	Pg.11	J4
Clover Ln.	Pg.6	C3
Cobblehill Ct.	Pg.11	H2
Cochise Ct.	Pg.12	J5
Colgate Ct.	Pg.11	G1
Colony Ln.	Pg.6	D3
Concord Cove	Pg.6	D3
Concord Ln.	Pg.6	D3
Cooper Rd.	Pg.11	H4
Cornell Ct.	Pg.11	H1
Cornell Ln.	Pg.11	H2
Cornell Dr.	Pg.11	H2
Cornell Terr.	Pg.11	H1
Cottonwood Tr. N.	Pg.6	D2
Cottonwood Tr. W.	Pg.6	D2
Cougar Trail (Pvt.)	Pg.12	J6
Cove Ln.	Pg.6	C2
Coventry Ct.	Pg.6	E4
Crab Orchard Dr.	Pg.6	C3
Cranshire Ct.	Pg.6	E4
Creekside Dr.	Pg.11	H2
Crescent Ln.	Pg.11	H2
Crimson Ct.	Pg.6	D2
Crimson Dr.	Pg.6	D2
Crowfoot Cir. N.	Pg.11	H2
Cumberland St.	Pg.12	J5
Cypress Ct.	Pg.11	H2
Danbury Pl.	Pg.11	F1
Darien Ct.	Pg.11	J3
Darlington Cir. N.	Pg.11	H3
Darlington Ct.	Pg.11	H3
Decatur St.	Pg.12	J5
Deerpath Cir.	Pg.11	H3
Deerpath Ln.	Pg.11	H3
Della Dr.	Pg.11	G2
Dennison Rd.	Pg.11	G4
Des Plaines Ln.	Pg.12	J4
Devonshire Ln.	Pg.11	H3
Dexter Ln. N.	Pg.11	H3
Dexter Ln. W.	Pg.11	H3
Diamond Dr.	Pg.6	C3
Dixon Ct.	Pg.6	D4
Dixon Dr.	Pg.6	G4
Dogwood Ct.	Pg.6	D2
Dorchester Ln.	Pg.11	H3
Douglas Ln.	Pg.12	J5
Dover Ct.	Pg.6	D2
Dovington Ct.	Pg.11	H3
Dovington Dr. N.	Pg.11	H3
Dovington Dr. W.	Pg.11	J3
Downey St.	Pg.11	J3
Downing Dr.	Pg.6	C3
Dresden Ct.	Pg.6	D3
Dresden Dr.	Pg.6	D3
Driftwood Ct.	Pg.6	C3
Dukesberry Ln.	Pg.6	C3
Dunmore Pl.	Pg.11	G2
Durham Ct.	Pg.11	G4
Durham Ln.	Pg.11	G4
Eagle Way	Pg.11	F1
Edgefield Ln.	Pg.11	G4
Edgemont Ln.	Pg.11	G4
Eisenhower Cir.	Pg.6	D3
Elizabeth Ct.	Pg.11	H4
Emory Rd.	Pg.11	G4
Englewood Rd.	Pg.11	G3
Erie Ln.	Pg.11	G2
Essington Ct.	Pg.6	C2
Essington Ln.	Pg.6	C2
Evanston St.	Pg.12	H4
Evergreen Ln.	Pg.11	H4
Exeter Ct.	Pg.11	B3
Fairfield Ln.	Pg.11	H4
Fairmont Rd.	Pg.11	G4
Fairway Ct.	Pg.11	G2-3
Fayette Walk	Pg.11	G2
Fir Ct.	Pg.6	D2
Firestone Dr. N.	Pg.6	D3
Firestone Dr. W.	Pg.6	D3
Firestone Ln.	Pg.6	D3
Flagstaff Ln.	Pg.11	J4
Foltz Dr.	Pg.11	J3
Forest Glen Dr.	Pg.6	D2
Forest Park Ln.	Pg.12	H5
Fortune Bay Ct.	Pg.6	D2
Franklin Pl.	Pg.11	G2
Frederick Ln.	Pg.6	D3
Freeman Rd.	Pg.6	D3
Fremont Rd.	Pg.6	D3
Gannon Ct.	Pg.11	H3
Gannon Dr.	Pg.11	H3
Garden Terr.	Pg.11	F1
Garnet Ct.	Pg.6	D3
Gentry Rd.	Pg.11	H4
Georgetown Ln.	Pg.11	G2
Geronimo St.	Pg.12	G4
Glen Lake Rd.	Pg.11	H3
Glen Ln.	Pg.11	G3
Glendale Ln.	Pg.11	J4
Glenwood Ln.	Pg.6	C3
Gloucester Ct.	Pg.11	H4
Goldenrod Ln.	Pg.6	C3
Golf Rd. (Rte. 58)	Pg.11	H1
Governors Ln.	Pg.11	G1
Grand Canyon Pkwy.	Pg.12	H4
Grand Canyon St.	Pg.12	J4
Grantham Rd.	Pg.11	F1
Greenfield Rd.	Pg.6	D3
Greens Ct.	Pg.11	H2
Greenspoint Pkwy.	Pg.11	G1
Greystone Pl.	Pg.11	F1
Grissom Ln.	Pg.12	H4
Haddam Pl.	Pg.11	G2
Haman Ave.	Pg.6	D3
Haman Ct.	Pg.6	D3
Hampton Rd.	Pg.11	H4
Hancock Dr.	Pg.11	G2
Harbor Cir.	Pg.6	D2
Harrison Ln.	Pg.6	D3
Hartford Ln.	Pg.11	G4
Harvard Ln.	Pg.11	G4
Harwinton Pl.	Pg.11	G1
Hassell Cir.	Pg.11	G3
Hassell Ct.	Pg.11	G3
Hassell Dr.	Pg.11	G3
Hassell Pl.	Pg.11	G3
Hassell Rd.	Pg.11	G1-3
Hastings Dr.	Pg.11	F1
Hawthorn Ln.	Pg.12	H5
Heather Ln.	Pg.11	G3
Heritage Dr.	Pg.11	H4
Hermitage Ct.	Pg.11	G3
Hermit age Ln.	Pg.11	G3
Higgins Quarter Dr.	Pg.11	H4
Higgins Rd. (Rte. 72)	Pg.11	G2
Highland Blvd.	Pg.11	H4
Hill Dr.	Pg.11	H4
Hillcrest Blvd.	Pg.11	G3
Hillcrest Ct.	Pg.11	G4
Hillside Ln.	Pg.6	E3
Hilltop Rd.	Pg.11	G3
Holbrook Ln.	Pg.11	G1
Holly Ln.	Pg.12	H5
Hudson Dr.	Pg.6	D3
Hundley St. N.	Pg.11	J2
Hundley St. W.	Pg.11	J2
Hundley Way	Pg.11	J2
Huntington Blvd.	Pg.11	G2
Huttner Ct.	Pg.11	G2
Ida Rd.	Pg.11	G4
Illinois Blvd.	Pg.11	J4
Islandview Ln.	Pg.11	G2
Jamestown Cir.	Pg.11	G2
Jamison Ln.	Pg.11	G4
Jefferson Rd.	Pg.11	G3
Jennifer Ln.	Pg.11	H2
Jody Ln.	Pg.11	H2
John Dr.	Pg.11	H3
Jones Rd.	Pg.11	G4
Juniper Tree Ct.	Pg.12	H4
Kenilworth Ct.	Pg.11	G2
Kensington Ln.	Pg.11	G4
Kent Rd.	Pg.11	G4
Kenwood Rd.	Pg.11	G2
Kettering Rd.	Pg.11	G2
Kingston Dr.	Pg.11	C3
Knoll Ln.	Pg.11	H2
Laburnum Rd.	Pg.6	C2
Lafayette Ln.	Pg.11	G4
Lafleur Ln.	Pg.6	D2
Lake Edge Ct.	Pg.6	D2
Lakeside Plaza N.	Pg.11	G3
Lakeside Plaza W.	Pg.11	G3
Lakeview Ln.	Pg.11	J4
Lakewood Blvd.	Pg.11	F1-2
Lancaster Ct.	Pg.12	G3
Langdon Pl.	Pg.11	G1
Larchmont Rd.	Pg.12	G4
Latour Ct.	Pg.6	D3
Leatherleaf Ct.	Pg.6	E2
Leatherleaf Ln.	Pg.6	E1
Legend Ln.	Pg.11	H2
Lexington Dr.	Pg.6	E3
Liberty Pl.	Pg.11	G2
Lichfield Dr.	Pg.6	C3
Lincoln St.	Pg.12	J4
Lincolnshire Ln.	Pg.11	J3
Lombardy Ln.	Pg.11	D3
London Sq.	Pg.11	J3
Londonderry Ct.	Pg.11	E4
Ludington Ct.	Pg.11	G2
Manchester Dr.	Pg.6	G3
Maple Ln.	Pg.11	J4
Maricopa Ln.	Pg.12	J4
Marquette Ln.	Pg.6	D3
Mason Dr.	Pg.6	D3
Mayfield Ln.	Pg.11	J4
Maywood Ln.	Pg.11	J4
McCormack Dr.	Pg.11	G4
Meadow Ln.	Pg.11	H4
Mesa Dr.	Pg.11	H4
Meyer Rd.	Pg.11	H2
Michael Ct.	Pg.6	D3
Michelline Ct.	Pg.6	D3
Milan Ct.	Pg.11	J4
Milton Ln.	Pg.11	J4
Mohave St.	Pg.11	J4
Monarch Ln.	Pg.6	C3
Monterey Ct.	Pg.11	H2
Monticello Rd.	Pg.12	G4
Moon Lake Blvd.	Pg.11	H1-2
Morgan Ln.	Pg.11	J4
Morton St.	Pg.11	J-H4
Moulin Ln.	Pg.6	D3
Mumford Ct.	Pg.6	D2
Mumford Rd.	Pg.6	D2
Nantucket Ln.	Pg.6	D2
Navajo Ln.	Pg.12	J4
New Britton Dr. N.	Pg.6	D3
New Britton Dr. W.	Pg.6	D3
Newark Ln.	Pg.6	J4
Newcastle Ln.	Pg.11	H3
Newman St.	Pg.6	D3
Newport Rd. N.	Pg.12	G4
Newport Rd. W.	Pg.12	G4
Newton St.	Pg.11	J4
Nogales St.	Pg.12	J4
Norman Dr.	Pg.6	E3
Norridge Ln.	Pg.11	G4
Northview Ln.	Pg.11	G4
Nottingham Ln.	Pg.11	G3
O'Hare Ln.	Pg.6	D3
Oak Knoll Ln.	Pg.6	D2
Oak Tree Ct.	Pg.12	H4
Oakdale Rd.	Pg.11	G3
Oakmont Rd. N.	Pg.11	H2
Oakmont Rd. W.	Pg.11	H3
Old Barrington Rd.	Pg.11	H3
Old Higgins Rd.	Pg.11	G1
Old Timber Ct.	Pg.6	C3
Old Timber Ln.	Pg.6	C3
Olive St.	Pg.11	J-H4
Olmstead Dr.	Pg.6	C3
Opal Dr.	Pg.6	C3
Orange Ln.	Pg.11	J4
Osage Ln.	Pg.11	J4
Oxford Ln.	Pg.11	J4
Pacific Ave.	Pg.11	J1
Paisley Ct.	Pg.6	B2
Paris Ln.	Pg.11	J4
Park Ln.	Pg.6	D3
Parkside Dr. N.	Pg.11	D2
Parkside Dr. W.	Pg.6	D2
Parkview Cir. E.	Pg.11	G2
Parkview Cir. W.	Pg.11	G2
Partridge Hill Dr.	Pg.11	J3
Patriot Ln.	Pg.11	F1
Payson Dr.	Pg.11	G2
Pebble Beach Ct.	Pg.11	H2
Pebble Beach Dr.	Pg.11	H2
Pebblewood Ln.	Pg.6	D2
Pembroke Ln.	Pg.11	G1
Perry Ln.	Pg.11	K4
Picardy Ln.	Pg.6	D2
Pierce Rd.	Pg.12	J4
Pleasant St.	Pg.11	K4
Plum Grove Rd.	Pg.12	J6
Plymouth Rd.	Pg.6	B2
Ponderosa Ln.	Pg.12	J4
Poplar Creek Dr.	Pg.11	H1
Port Arthur Ct.	Pg.6	D2
Portage Ln.	Pg.6	D2
Portshire Ct.	Pg.6	E4
Prestwick Rd.	Pg.6	C3
Princeton St.	Pg.11	J4
Queensbury Cir.	Pg.11	G2
Raleigh Ln.	Pg.11	F1
Raleigh Pl.	Pg.11	F1
Randi Ln.	Pg.11	H3
Rebecca Dr.	Pg.11	H2
Regan Ct.	Pg.6	E4
Regent Dr.	Pg.6	E4
Ridgewood Ln.	Pg.6	D2
Robin Cir.	Pg.11	H2
Robin Ln.	Pg.11	H2
Rochester Dr.	Pg.11	C3
Rock Cove Ct.	Pg.6	D2
Rock Cove Dr.	Pg.6	D2
Rolling Prairie Ct.	Pg.6	D2
Rosedale Ln.	Pg.11	H2
Sandlewood Ln.	Pg.6	C3
Sapphire Dr. N.	Pg.6	C2-3
Sessions Walk	Pg.11	G2
Shagbark Ct.	Pg.11	G2
Shepard Rd.	Pg.11	G4
Shoe Factory Rd.	Pg.11	G1
Shorewood Ct.	Pg.6	C2
Shorewood Dr., N.	Pg.6	C2
Shorewood Dr., W.	Pg.6	C2
Silver Pine Dr.	Pg.6	C3
Smethwick Ln.	Pg.11	F1
Somersworth Pl.	Pg.11	F1
Somerton Dr.	Pg.11	C3
Spring Mill Dr.	Pg.11	H4
Stockton Dr.	Pg.6	D2
Stoneharbor Ct.	Pg.6	D2
Stoneharbor Dr. N.	Pg.6	D1
Stonington Ave.	Pg.11	G1
Stratham Pl.	Pg.11	G1
Sturbridge Ct.	Pg.6	C3
Sturbridge Dr. N.	Pg.6	D3
Sturbridge Dr. W.	Pg.6	D3
Sudbury Dr.	Pg.11	F1
Suffolk Ln.	Pg.6	D4
Sumac Tr.	Pg.6	C3
Sundance Ct.	Pg.6	C3
Sunflower Ln.	Pg.6	C3
Sussex Walk	Pg.11	G2
Sutherland Pl.	Pg.11	F1
Sweetflower Dr.	Pg.11	H2
Swindon Pl.	Pg.11	F1
Sycamore Ct.	Pg.6	E3
Tamarack Ct.	Pg.6	B3
Tamarack Dr. W.	Pg.6	C3
Tarrington Dr.	Pg.11	C2
Thacker St. E.	Pg.12	J4
Thacker St. W.	Pg.12	J4
Thornbark Ct.	Pg.6	C3
Thornbark Dr.	Pg.6	C3
Topaz Dr.	Pg.11	C3
Trailside Ct.	Pg.6	E3
Treaty Ln.	Pg.11	E3
Turnberry Dr.	Pg.6	C3
Valley Ln.	Pg.12	H4
Versailles Ln.	Pg.6	D3
Victoria Dr.	Pg.6	D3
Victoria Dr. N.	Pg.6	D3
Vista Ln.	Pg.11	H2
Volid Dr.	Pg.11	J3
Wainsford Dr.	Pg.11	J3
Warington Ln.	Pg.11	H2
Warwick Cir. N.	Pg.11	H3
Warwick Cir. S.	Pg.11	H3
Washington Blvd.	Pg.11	J3-4
Wellington Pl.	Pg.11	H4
Westbridge Ct.	Pg.6	C3
Westbury Dr.	Pg.6	C3
Western St.	Pg.11	J3
Westhaven Ct.	Pg.11	J3
Westview St.	Pg.11	J4
Whispering Trails Ct.	Pg.6	D2
Whispering Trails Dr.	Pg.6	E2
Whitingham Ln.	Pg.11	H2
Wildwood Ct.	Pg.6	C3
William Ct.	Pg.11	H2
Williams Rd.	Pg.6	C3
Williamsburg Ct.	Pg.11	H4
Willow Tree Ct.	Pg.12	H4
Wilmington Ln.	Pg.11	H2
Wilshire Dr. N.	Pg.6	E4
Wilshire Dr. W.	Pg.6	E4
Winding Trail Ln.	Pg.6	E2
Winston Cir.	Pg.6	D3
Winston Ct.	Pg.6	D3
Winston Ln.	Pg.6	D3
Winston Pl.	Pg.6	E3
Woodcreek Ln.	Pg.11	H2
Woodhollow Ct.	Pg.6	C3
Woodlawn St.	Pg.11	H,J4
Worthington Dr.	Pg.11	H2
Yardley Ln.	Pg.11	J3
Yorkshire Ct.	Pg.6	E4

GOLF COURSES

Name	Page	Grid
Highland Woods G.C.	Pg.11,12	F4
Hilldale C.C.	Pg.11	G3
Poplar Creek C.C.	Pg.11	H1

PARKS

Name	Page	Grid
Chestnut Park	Pg.3	H3
Chino Park	Pg.12	J4
Cottonwood Park	Pg.6	F2
Douglas Park	Pg.6	C3
Evergreen Park	Pg.11	J4
Field Park, The	Pg.11	H3
High Point Park	Pg.11	G3
Lincoln Park	Pg.6	C3
Locust Park	Pg.12	G4
Meadow Park	Pg.6	C3
Pebble Park	Pg.6	D2
Pine Park	Pg.6	E4
Seminole Nature Area	Pg.6	D2
Valley Park	Pg.6	D4
Victoria Park	Pg.11	H3
Vogelei Park	Pg.11	H4
Whispering Lake Park	Pg.6	D2
Willow Park	Pg.6	E3

SCHOOLS

Name	Page	Grid
Armstrong Sch.	Pg.11	H2
Conant H.S.	Pg.12	J6
Eisenhower Jr. H.S.	Pg.11	G3
Enders Salk Sch.	Pg.11	J3
Fairview Sch.	Pg.12	H3
Hillcrest Sch.	Pg.11	G4
Hoffman Estates H.S.	Pg.11	H3
Lakeview Sch.	Pg.11	J4
MacArthur Sch.	Pg.11	G3
Twinbrook Sch.	Pg.12	H5

SHOPPING CENTERS

Name	Page	Grid
Barrington Square Mall	Pg.11	G1
Crossroads Commons	Pg.12	H4
Forest View S.C.	Pg.6	D2
Hoffman Plaza	Pg.12	H5
Huntington Plaza	Pg.6	D2
Poplar Commons S.C.	Pg.11	G1

MISCELLANEOUS

Name	Page	Grid
Fire Station	Pg.6	C3
Hoffman Estates Medical Center	Pg.11	H2
Hoffman Estates Park Dist. Admin. Office	Pg.11	H2
Library, Schaumburg Twp.	Pg.11	H2
Woodland Hosp.	Pg.11	G1

HOMEWOOD

Pages 42,43

STREETS

Street	Grid
Aberdeen St.	P,Q23
Alexander St.	Q22
Alexander Terr.	Q22
Argyle Ave.	Q21
Armitage Pl.	P23
Ashland Ave.	P,Q23
Bertz Dr.	P24
Beth Ct.	P21
Birch Rd.	Q21-23
Boulder Ct.	R24
Bowling Green	R24
Briar Ave.	P22
Burr Oak Rd.	P23
California Ave.	P,Q21
Caroline Dr.	P21
Carpenter Ave.	Q24
Carson Ct.	R23
Carson Dr.	Q,R23
Castle Rd.	Q24
Cedar Rd.	P22
Center Ave.	P22
Center Ct.	R23
Center St.	Q23
Chayes Park Dr.	Q21
Chayes Park Dr.	Q21
Cherrycreek Dr.	P21
Cherrywood Ln.	P21
Chestnut Rd.	P22
Chicago Rd.	P23
Clyde Rd.	Q21
Clyde St.	Q21
Clyde Terr.	Q22
Coach Rd.	Q24
Cowing Ave.	Q22
Crescent Rd.	Q21
Debra Ln.	P21
Delta Rd.	Q24
Dixie Hwy.	P,Q22
Dixmoor Dr.	P22
Dolphin Lake Dr.	P21
Downey Rd.	Q22
Dundee Ave.	P,Q22
Elder Rd.	P23,P,Q24
Eliot Ln.	Q21
Elm Rd.	P22
Evergreen Rd.	Q23
Francisco Ave.	Q21
Fresno Ln.	Q21
Gladville Ave.	P,Q23
Golfview Ave.	P,Q22
Gottshalk Ave.	P,Q22
Governors Hwy.	Q21
Greenwood Rd.	P21
Halsted St.	R24
Hart Dr.	P24
Harwood Ave.	P22
Hawthorne Rd.	P22
Heather Ct.	Q23
Heather Rd.	Q21-23
Hedgerow Ln.	Q21
Hickory Rd.	P21-23
Highland Ave.	P,Q22
Hillside Ave.	P22
Hillview Rd.	Q23
Holbrook Rd.	R23
Hollydale Ct.	P21
Homewood Ave.	P,Q22
Hood Ave.	P,Q23
Howe Ave.	P22
Idlewild Ln.	Q22
Jamie Ct.	Q23
Jamie Ln.	Q23
Jeffery Ct.	Q23
Jeffery Dr.	Q23
Jill Ct.	Q23
Jill Terr.	Q23
Jodi Terr.	Q23
Jonathan Ln.	Q23
Juhlin Dr.	Q23
Kathleen Ct.	Q21
Kedzie Ave.	R20
Kimball Ave.	Q20
Kings Rd.	Q24
Klimm Ave.	Q22
Knollwood Ln.	Q20
Kroner Ln.	P22
Lahaigh Rd.	P23
Larkspur Ln.	P21
Lexington Ave.	Q22
Lincoln	P21
Linden Rd.	P23
Locust	Q23
Loomis Ave.	P,R23
Los Angeles Ave.	P21
Los Angeles Rd.	P21
Lynn Ct.	Q23
Magnolia Rd.	P22
Mallard Dr.	Q20
Maple Ave.	P24
Maple Ln.	Q21
Maple Rd.	P22
Marlin Ct.	P21
Marlin Ln.	P21
Marshfield Ave.	Q23
Martin Ave.	Q22
Mathew Ln.	Q21
May Ave.	Q23
May St.	Q23
Miller Ct.	P22
Morgan St.	P,Q24
Morris Ave.	Q22
Oak Rd.	P22
Olive Rd.	P21-24
Page Ave.	Q23
Page Ct.	Q23
Palmer Ave.	Q22
Palmer Ct.	Q22
Patricia Ln.	Q21
Perth Ave.	P21
Pierce Ave.	Q,R23

HOMEWOOD

Pierce Ct. ... R23
Pierce Terr. ... Q23
Pine Ct. ... P22,23
Poplar Ave. ... C4
Poplar Ct. ... R23
Presidents Dr. ... P24
Queens ... Q24
Ridge Rd. ... P22,23
Riedle Ct. ... P22
Riegel Oaks Ln. ... R23
Riegle Ct. ... Q23
Robin Ln. ... Q21
Rockwell Ave. ... P21
Roosevelt Ave. ... P22
Royal Rd. ... Q24
Sacramento ... Q21
Sacramento Ave. ... P21
San Diego Ave. ... P21
Spruce ... Q21
Stedhall Rd. ... Q21
Stewart Ave. ... P,Q21
Stockton Ave. ... Q21
Sycamore ... P22
Sycamore Dr. ... P22
Tarpon Ct. ... P21
Terrace Rd. ... Q22
Thomas St. ... P22
Tipton Ave. ... P22
Turtlecreek Dr. ... Q24
Virginia Pl. ... P21
Walnut Ave. ... P21
Walton Ln. ... P24
Washington Ave. ... P22
Western Ave. ... P,Q22
Willow Rd. ... Q21-23
174th St. ... Q25
175th St. ... Q24
182nd Pl. ... Q22
183rd St. ... Q23
184th Pl. ... Q23
184th St. ... Q20,23
185th Pl. ... Q20,23
185th St. ... Q23
186th Pl. ... Q23,24
186th St. ... Q22,23
187th St. ... Q22,23
188th St. ... Q23
189th St. ... Q22,23
190th St. ... R23
191st St. ... R23

CEMETERIES
Hazelwood Cem. ... P24

GOLF COURSES
Idlewild Country Club ... R23
Ravisloe Country Club ... P22

PARKS
Apollo Park ... R24
Ashland Park ... Q23
Briarwood Park ... Q23
Butterfield Park ... R24
Hollydale Park ... P21
Homewood Estates Park ... P21
Lions Club Park ... P21
Merchants Park ... Q22
Orchard Park ... P23
Woodborough Park ... Q24

SCHOOLS
Central Sch. ... P23
Churchill Sch. ... R23
Full Gospel Christian Sch. ... Q20
Hart Jr. H.S. ... P24
Ridge Sch. ... P22
St. Joseph Sch. ... P22
Willow Sch. ... Q22

SHOPPING CENTERS
Cherry Creek Shopping Center ... Q21
Park Place Plaza ... Q24
Washington Park Plaza ... P24
Washington Square Mall ... P24

MISCELLANEOUS
County Police ... P23
Governors Medical Center. ... P21
Maple Leaf Nursing Home ... P24
Marie Irwin Community Center ... P23
Mercy Health Care Center ... R24
R.R. Station ... P22
Village Hall & Police Dept. ... P22

INVERNESS
Pages 6,7
STREETS
Abbotsford Dr. ... B2
Aberdeen Ln. ... B5
Aberdeen Rd. ... B5
Afton Cir. ... A3
Alexander Ct. ... B2
Alnwick ... B2
Appleby Rd. ... C4
Applecross Rd. ... C2
Ardmore Ave. ... C3
Arlington Rd. ... B,C4
Atkinson Rd. ... C2
Ayrshire Ln. ... B4
Balmoral Cir. ... D5
Balmoral Dr. ... D5
Balmoral St. ... D5
Banbury Rd. ... B4

Bannockburn ... D4
Barclay Cir. ... A3
Barra Ln. ... B5
Beaver Pond Rd. ... C4
Bedlington Dr. ... A3
Berwick ... A3
Betty Dr. ... A3
Bishop Ct. ... B2
Blackburn Dr. ... A4
Blair Ln. ... B2
Blyth Ct. ... B2
Bonnie Ln. ... B5
Bonny Glen Gates ... D4
Bordeaux Ct. ... B2
Borthwick Ln. ... C4
Bradwell Ave. ... B2-3
Braeburn Rd. ... B4
Braymore Ln. ... B1
Braymore Dr, N. ... B1
Braymore Dr, S. ... B1
Brodick Ln. ... B5
Burleigh Ln. ... B5
Camphill Cir. ... A3
Canterbury Ln. ... B3
Carberry Cir. ... A3
Carlisle Dr. ... A3
Cawdor Ln. ... B4
Cheviot Dr. ... B3
Chimmey Rock ... D4
Clover Dr. ... D4
Colonial Pkwy. ... E5
Colony Dr. ... B2
Common Ridings Way ... B2
Cornell Ave. ... B5
Country Oak Ln. ... C4
Courtbridge Ln. ... B3
Courtbridge Rd. ... B3
Craigie Ln. ... B5
Crichton Ln. ... C4
Cumnock Rd. ... B4
Day Ct. ... C5
Dewey Rd. ... C4
Diary Ln. ... B4
Direlton Ln. ... B5
Dover Cir. ... A4
Drummond Ct. ... B3
Dublin Ct. ... D5
Dumfries Ct. ... D5
Dunbar Rd. ... B5
Dunbarton Dr. ... B1
Dundee Rd. ... A4
Dunheath Ave. ... A3
Dunheath Dr. ... A3
Durham Dr. ... A3
Edinburgh Ct. ... B3
Ela Rd. ... B-D4
Fife Ct. ... B3
Fincharn Ln. ... C4
Firth Rd. ... D4
Florence Ave. ... D5
Fox Tr. ... D5
Gaelic Ln. ... B1
Galloway Cir. ... B3
Galloway Dr. ... B3
Glamis Ln. ... B5
Glen Eagles Ct. ... B5
Glencrest Dr. ... B2,A3
Glenmore Ct. ... A3
Grayfriars Ln. ... C5
Great Glen Ct. ... B3
Greenrock ... D4
Guthrie Ct. ... A3
Guthrie Dr. ... A3
Halbert Ln. ... C2
Halkirk Dr. ... C5
Haman Ave. ... B3
Hamilton Dr. ... B2
Harmening ... C3
Harrow Gate Dr. ... C2
Heather Ln. ... A4
Highland Rd. ... B2
Hillshire Ct. ... B2
Hillshire Dr. ... B2
Huntly ... D4
Inverray Rd. ... B3
Inverway Rd. ... B4-5
Jules St. ... C4
Julie Dr. ... A3
Kelso Glen ... D4
Kilrenny ... C4
Kirkwall Ct. ... A3
Kirkwood Dr. ... B3
Kitson Ct. ... C4
Knockderry Ln. ... B5
Knox Ct. ... B2
Lamond Dr. ... A3
Lanark ... A3
Lancaster Ct. ... A3
Lauder Ln. ... D4
Lillian Ave. ... B4
Livingston Ct. ... B2
Livingston Dr. ... B2
Loch Lomond Dr. ... C5
Lochleven Ln. ... B5
Macalpin Cir. ... B2
Macalpin Dr. ... B2
Macalpin Ln. ... B2
Marie Dr. ... A3
McBain Way ... B3
Midmar Ln. ... C4
Milton Rd. ... B4
Muirfield Cir. ... B3
Muirfield Rd. ... B3
Mulgay Ct. ... C2
Mulgay Dr. ... C2
Newport Ln. ... B2

Northwest Hwy. ... A4
Oldwick Ln. ... B5
Palatine Rd. ... C4
Pheasant Tr. ... C4
Plymouth Ct. ... A4
Plymouth Rd. ... C-D5
Poteet Ave. ... C3
Prestwick Dr. ... D4
Quail Run ... D4
Ravenscraig Ln. ... B,C5
Regalia Ct. ... B3
Regalia Dr. ... B3
Rob Roy Ct. ... B5
Roberts Rd. ... C3
Roselle Rd. ... C-E5
Rosemary Ave. ... B3
Rosslyn Ln. ... B5
Rozborough Pl. ... B4
Sanday Ln. ... B2
Scotts Ct. ... B5
Selkirk ... B2
Shetland Rd. ... C2
Shire Cir. ... E5
Skye Ln. ... B2
St. Andrews Ln. ... B2
Sterling Rd. ... B4
Stonefield Cir. ... B3
Stonehaven ... D4
Stratford Ln. ... B3
Stuart Ln. ... B4
Summer Isle Ln. ... C2
Sunset Dr. ... C4
Tarbat Ct. ... B3
Thompson's Way ... D4
Thor Dr. ... E5
Thornhill Rd. ... B4
Thyra Ct. ... E4
Turkey Ct. ... E4
Turkey Tr. ... E5
Tweed Rd. ... A4
Tyne Ct. ... B2
Valley Lake Dr. ... E5
Warren Ave. ... C4
Waterford Ln. ... A3
Whispering Pines Ct. ... B5
Whithorn Ln. ... B5
Williams Rd. ... B5
Willow St. ... B3
Windsor Cir. ... D4
Windsor Dr. ... D4
Windsor Rd. ... B3
Windsor Rd. ... D4
Winfield Ln. ... B2
Wood St. ... B3
Woodburn Ct. ... A4

CEMETERIES
Cady Cem. ... A4
Deer Grove Cem. ... A4

GOLF COURSES
Inverness Golf Club ... B5
South Park ... D4

MISCELLANEOUS
Village Hall ... B5

JUSTICE
Page 34
STREETS
Christeen Dr. ... B13
Deer Path ... B12
Hickory Trace Dr. ... B12
Kean Ave. ... B11
Marion St. ... B13
Oak Ridge Dr. ... B12
Pawn Tr. ... B12
Thomas St. ... B13
78th St. ... B13
79th Ave. ... B13
79th St. ... B13
79th Pl. ... B12
80th Ave. ... B13
80th St. ... B13
81st Ave. ... B12,13
81st St. ... B13
82nd Ave. ... B13
82nd Ct. ... B13
82nd St. ... B13
83rd Ave. ... B13
83rd Pl. ... B12,13
83rd St. ... B13
84th Ave. ... B13
84th Ct. ... B13
84th Pl. ... B13
84th Pl. W. ... B13
84th St. ... B13
85th Ave. ... B12
85th Ct. ... B13
85th Pl. ... B13
85th Pl. W. ... B13
85th St. ... B13
85th St. W. ... B13
86th Ave. ... B12
86th Ct. ... B13
86th St. ... C13
86th St. W. ... B12
87th Ave. ... B12
87th Ave. S. ... B12
87th Ct. ... B13
87th Pl. ... B12
88th Ave. S. ... B12
90th Ave. ... B12

CEMETERIES
Archer Woods Cem. ... B12
Lithuanian Cem. ... B12

SCHOOLS
Dosher Sch. ... B12
George Wilkins Jr. H.S. ... B13
Player Sch. ... B13

MISCELLANEOUS
Convalescent Home ... B12
Fire Department ... C13

KENILWORTH
Pages 23,27
STREETS
Abbotsford Rd. Pg.27 ... F12
Abingdon Ave. Pg.27 ... F12
Brier ... Pg.23 ... F11
Cumberland Ave. ... Pg.27 ... E12
Cummings Ave. Pg.23 ... E11
Cumnor Rd. ... Pg.27 ... E11,F12
Devonshire Ln. Pg.27 ... F11
Earlston Rd. ... Pg.27 ... F11
Essex Rd. ... Pg.27 ... F12
Exmoor Rd. ... Pg.27 ... F11
Greenwood Ave. Pg.27 ... F11
Ivy Ct. ... Pg.27 ... F12
Kenilworth Ave. Pg.27 ... E-F12
Kent Rd. ... Pg.23 ... F11
Leicester Rd. ... Pg.27 ... E12
McLean Ave. ... Pg.23 ... E11
Melrose Ave. ... Pg.27 ... E12,F11
Oxford Rd. ... Pg.27 ... F12
Park Dr. ... Pg.27 ... F11
Raleigh Rd. ... Pg.27 ... E12
Richmond Rd. ... Pg.27 ... F12
Robsart Pl. ... Pg.27 ... F12
Robsart Rd. ... Pg.27 ... F12
Roger Ave. ... Pg.23 ... F11
Roslyn Rd. ... Pg.27 ... E12
Sheridan Rd. ... Pg.27 ... E11-12
Sterling Rd. ... Pg.27 ... F11
Tudor Pl. ... Pg.27 ... F12
Warwick Rd. ... Pg.27 ... F11
Wayland Ave. ... Pg.27 ... F11
Woodstock Ave. Pg.27 ... F12

MISCELLANEOUS
Village Hall ... Pg.27 ... F12

KILDEER
Pages 2,3
STREETS
Abbey Ct. ... W7
Acorn Ct. ... W8
Amberley Dr. ... X8
Amy Ln. ... V8
Andover Rd. ... W8
Barbara Ct. ... W8
Barkley Ct. ... W7
Boschome Cir. N. ... W8
Boschome Cir. S. ... X8
Boschome Dr. ... X8
Boschome, N. ... W8
Boschome, S. ... X8
Brandon Rd. ... W8
Bridal Tr. ... W8
Buffalo Run ... X8
Burning Tree Ct. ... W7
Cambridge Dr. ... W7
Chadwick Ct. ... V8
Chartwell Dr. ... X8
Chestnut Ridge Rd. ... W7
Circle Bay Rd. ... X7
Clayton Ct. ... V8
Cliffside Dr. ... X8
Concorde Ct. ... X7
Cuba Rd. ... W8
Dallas Ct. ... W8
Dorothea Ct. ... W9
Elder Ct. ... W7
Eleanor Ln. ... V8
Exeter Rd. ... W9
Foxtail Dr. ... W8
Green Wood Dr. ... W8
Grove Dr. ... X8
Hampton Rd. ... W8
Hanaford Ct. ... X7
Hawthorn Ln. ... W7
Heather Ct. ... X8
Hickory Hill Dr. ... W8
Hidden Valley Rd. ... X7
Highwood Rd. ... X7
Hilandale Ct. ... V8
Hilandale Rd. ... V8
Honey Ridge Ct. ... W8
Hopewell Ct. ... W8
Kerwick Ln. ... X8
Kirkley Dr. ... X8
Krueger Rd. ... V8
Lake Zurich Rd. ... V8
Laurel Ln. ... W8
Lexington Ln. ... X8
Linden Ln. ... X8
Little Pond Rd. ... X7
Long Meadow Dr. ... X8
Maple Ct. ... W7
Marcy Ln. ... X8
Meadows Ct. ... X8
Middleton Dr. ... W9
Newberry Dr. ... V9
Oak Knoll Ct. ... X8

Oak Trail ... X8
Pine Grove Ct. ... W8
Pine Lake Cir. ... X7
Pine Lake Dr. ... X7
Plumwood Dr. ... X8
Providence Dr. ... V8
Quentin Rd. ... V7
Rand Rd. ... X8
Rebecca Ln. ... V8
Richmond Ct. ... W8
Ruth Ct. ... V8
Salem Lake Dr. ... V9
Scott Ct. ... X8
Sherley Rd. ... X8
South Rd. ... V8
Stoneybrook Ct. ... W7
Thornridge Dr. ... W7
Timberidge Ct. ... W8
Timberleaf Ln. ... W7
Tree Ave. ... X7
Valley Rd. ... X8
Vermont Ct. ... W8
Weatherstone Ct. ... X8
Weatherstone Rd. ... X8
White Pine Rd. ... X7
Willow Dr. ... X8
Wooded Ridge Dr. ... X7
York Ct. ... X8
Yorkshire Dr. ... V9

LANSING
Page 45
STREETS
Ada St. ... P,Q30
Adams St. ... P30
Ann St. ... P30
Arcadia Ave. ... O,P29
Barbara Ct. ... Q30
Bensley Ave. ... P30
Bernadine St. ... O,O,R30
Bernice Ave. ... O29,30
Bernice Rd. ... O28,29
Blackstone Ave. ... P27
Bock Ave. ... P28
Bond Ave. ... P29
Burnham Ave. ... O,Q30
Calhoun Ave. ... O28
Carriage Ln. ... P28
Central ... P30
Cherry ... O29
Chicago Ave. ... N-P29
Christina Dr. ... P28
Clyde Ave. ... P28
Coles Ave. ... P29
Commercial Ave. ... P29
Community St. ... N,O30
Country Ave. ... P28
Cregier ... P28
DeJong Ln. ... P28
Decker Ave. ... O,P28
Decker St. ... O28
Dorchester Ave. ... P27
Escanaba Ave. ... O29
Exchange Ave. ... N,P29
Flannigan Dr. ... O29
Forest Ct. ... P28
Forest View Ln. ... P28
Fred St. ... P29
Fritz Dr. ... P28
Glen Oak Ave. ... O,P29
Glen Terr. ... P28
Grant St. ... N,P,Q30
Greenbay Ave. ... O,Q30
Greenbay St. ... P30
Harper Ave. ... P27
Hearth Ct. ... P28
Henry Ct. ... O30
Henry St. ... N,O,Q30
Hickory St. ... O29,30
Holiday Ct. ... O28
Holland Rd. ... P28
Illi-Indi Dr. ... P30
Illinois St. ... P30
Indiana Ave. ... P28,29
Industrial Dr. ... N29
Jackson St. ... O30
Jason Ln. ... P28
Jeffery Ave. ... O28
Keegan Ave. ... O28
Keegan St. ... O27
Kettle Ct. ... P28
Kingery Expressway ... N29
Lake Ave. ... P29
Lake St. ... P30
Lange St. ... R,P30
Lee Ave. ... O29
Locust St. ... P28
Lorenz Ave. ... O-Q30
Louise Ct. ... Q30
Louise Dr. ... Q30
Louise Dr.,W. ... Q30
Madison St. ... P30
Manor Dr.,N. ... Q30
Manor Dr.,S. ... Q30
Maple Ave. ... O30
Maple St. ... P,Q30
Marble Ave. ... O29
Mertile Ct. ... P30
Miller Dr. ... P30
Monroe St. ... Q30
Oak Ave. ... N-P29,P30
Oak St. ... R30
Oakley Ave. ... O,P29
Oakwood Ave. ... N-Q29
Old Farm Rd. ... P28

Otto St. ... Q30
Park Ave. ... O-R29,Q30
Park Blvd. ... O29
Railroad Ave. ... O29
Randolph St. ... P30
Rebel Dr. ... P30
Ridge Rd. ... P29
Ridgeland ... P28
Ridgewood Ave. ... N,P,Q29
River Dr. ... O30
Rose Ave. ... P29
Rosewood Dr. ... O28
Roy St. ... N-Q30
School St. ... P29
Schultz Ave. ... O29
Schultz Dr.,N. ... P30
Schultz Dr.,S. ... P30
Sharon Ct. ... Q30
Sherman St. ... P,Q30
Shirley Dr. ... O30
Siwel ... R30
State Line Rd. ... P30
Stewart St. ... P30
Terrace Dr. ... P30
Thornton Lansing Rd. ... P28
Ton Ave. ... O29
Torrence Ave. ... O29
Violet Rd. ... P28
Volbrech Rd. ... O27
Walter St. ... O,Q30
Ward St. ... P29
Washington St. ... P30
Wentworth St. ... P30
West St. ... P30
Whitman Ln. ... P28
Wildwood Ave. ... P-R29
William St. ... N-Q30
Willow Ln. ... Q30
Wright St. ... O30
Yates Ave. ... O28
166th St. ... N29
168th St. ... N30
170th Pl. ... N30
170th St. ... N29,30
171st St. ... N29,30
172nd Pl. ... O30
172nd St. (Elizabeth Ave.) ... O28,30
173rd Ct. ... O30
173rd St. ... O28,30
174th St. ... O30
175th St. ... O30
176th Pl. ... O28,29
176th St. ... O29,30
177th Pl. ... O28,30
177th St. ... O28-30,P27,28
178th Pl. ... O30
178th St. ... O28-30,P27
179th St. ... P28,29
180th St. ... P28,29
181st Pl. ... P30
181st St. ... P28,29
182nd Pl. ... P28,29
182nd St. ... P29
183rd Pl. ... P28,29
183rd St. ... P28,29
184th Pl. ... P28
184th St. ... P28,29
185th Pl. ... Q28
185th St. ... P28
185th St. ... P28-30
186th Pl. ... Q28
186th St. ... Q28
187th Pl. ... O28
187th St. ... Q29,30
188th Pl. ... O28
188th St. ... Q29,30
189th Pl. ... Q29,30
189th St. ... Q29,30
190th Pl. ... Q29,30
190th St. ... Q29
191st Pl. ... Q29,30
191st St. ... Q29
192nd Pl. ... Q29,30
192nd St. ... Q29,30
193rd Ct. ... R30
193rd Pl. ... R29,30
193rd St. ... R29,30
194th Pl. ... R29
194th St. ... R30
195th St. ... R30

CEMETERIES
Glen Oak Cem. ... P28

GOLF COURSES
Lansing C.C. ... Q30

PARKS
Bernice Park ... O30
Bock Park ... O29
Erfert Park ... Q30
Jaycee Park ... R30
Kiwanis Park ... P28
Lan-Oak Park ... P29
Lions Park ... O30
Oakley Playlot ... P29
Oakwood Park ... O29
Potts Park ... P29
Rotary Park ... P29
Schultz Park ... P30
Van Laten Park ... N30
Veterans Park ... P28
Whitman Park ... P28

Winterhoff Park P30

SCHOOLS
Coolidge Sch. O30
Eisenhower Sch. O29
Hebrew Acad. Sch. P30
Heritage Middle Sch. R29
Illiana H.S. P28
Lansing Christian Sch. P30
Lansing Memorial Jr. H.S. P29
Lester Crawl Sch. P30
Nathan Hale Sch. Q30
Oak Glen Sch. P28
Reavis Sch. O30
Special Ed. Sch. Q30
St. Anns Sch. P29
St. John's Luth Sch. P30
Sunnybrook Sch. R29
Thornton Fractional South H.S. Q30
Trinity Sch. P29

SHOPPING CENTERS
Landings Shopping Center N20
Lansing Commons P29

MISCELLANEOUS
Fire Dept. P29,30,R30
Lansing Muni. Airport R30
Library P29
Lions Little League Stadium P29
Post Office P29,30
R.R. Station P28
Sports Complex N30
Village Hall & Police Dept. N29

LONG GROVE
Page 3

STREETS
Andrew Ct. X10
Antietam Dr. X10
Arlington Heights Rd. X11
Bayberry Ln. X9
Bernay Ln. X11
Bordeaux Ln. X11
Bridgewater Ct. X10
Brittany Ct. X11
Brittany Ln. X11
Brookside Ln. X10
Calvary Ct. X9
Carriage Ct. X10
Checker Rd. X9-10
Chickamauga Ln. X10
Coach Rd. X9
Country Club X10
Countryside Ln. X10
Cumberland Cir. X9
Dawn Ct. X10
Dorothy Ln. X9
Edgewood Ln. X10
Federal Ct. X9
Holly Ct. X10
Holly Ct. X10
Juniper Ln. X9
Knoll Ct. X9
Knoll Dr. X9
Lake Cook Rd. X9
Lexington Dr. X9
Lincoln Ave. X10
Long Grove Rd. X9
Manasas Ct. X10
Manasas Ln. X10
Meadowlark Dr. X10
Oak Hill Ln. X9
Old Hicks Rd. X9
Picardy Ct. X11
Picardy Ln. X11
Popp Ln. X10
Pottawatomie Ct. X10
Roanoke Ct. X10
Shaeffer Rd. X10
Shenandoah Ln. X10
Sheridan Ct. X10
Sumter Dr. X10
Tanager Way X10
Union Ct. X10
Walnut Ln. X9
Willow Valley Rd. X9
Woodland Ln. X9

LYNWOOD
Pages 45,50

STREETS
Alanna Ln. Pg.50 T30
Arbon Ct. Pg.50 U30
Arroyo Ave. Pg.50 S29
Ash Ln. Pg.50 S29
Balzano Pg.50 U30
Bensely Ave. Pg.50 T28
Bergenz Pg.50 U30
Bernina Pg.50 U30
Brenner Pg.50 U30
Brenta Pg.50 U30
Brook Ave. Pg.50 S29
Burnham Ave. Pg.50 S30
Carondelet Ave. Pg.50 T29
Catalpa Ave. Pg.50 S29
Cedar Glen Dr. Pg.50 S29
Chillon Pg.50 U30
Colleen Dr. Pg.50 T30
Crescent Ave. Pg.50 S29
Cypress Ave. Pg.50 S30
Deborah Pg.50 T30
Dewey Ave. Pg.50 R28
Dolphin Ave. Pg.50 S29
Driftwood Ave. Pg.50 S30
Duke Pg.50 U30
Glarus Pg.50 U30
Glenwood Dyer Rd. Pg.50 S28
Glenwood Rd. Pg.45 R29
Joe Orr Rd. Pg.50 S27
Juniper Ave. Pg.50 S30
Lake Lynwood Dr. Pg.45 S29
Lake Park Ct. Pg.45 R29
Lake Park Dr. Pg.45,50 S29
Lake Shore Dr. Pg.45 R29
Lakewood Ave. Pg.50 S29
Lighthouse Ct. Pg.50 R29
Linda Dr. Pg.50 T30
Lisa Cir. Pg.50 U30
Mariner Ct. Pg.45 R29
Marlin Ave. Pg.50 S29
Marquette Ave. Pg.50 S29
Maureen Ct. Pg.50 T30
Merlin Ct. Pg.50 S29
Monterey Ave. Pg.50 S29
Muskegan Ave. Pg.50 S29
Oak Ln. Pg.50 S29
Oakwood Ave. Pg.50 R29
Orchard Ave. Pg.50 S29
Park Ave. Pg.50 S29
Pattie Pg.50 U30
Redwood Ave. Pg.50 S29
Rose St. Pg.50 R28
Sandridge Ct. Pg.50 T28
Sandridge Rd. Pg.50 T28
Sequoia Ave. Pg.50 S29
Simplon Cir. Pg.50 U30
Spruce Ln. Pg.50 S29
Stony Island Ave. Pg.45 S27
Surf Ct. Pg.45 R29
Terrace Ave. Pg.45 S29
Torrence Ave. Pg.50 S29
Vals Pg.50 U30
Victoria Cir. Pg.50 U30
Vollmer St. Pg.45 S27
Vrin Pg.50 U30
Willow Dr. Pg.50 S29
Wind Point Ct. Pg.45 R29
Woodale Dr. Pg.50 S29
Zurich Dr. Pg.50 U30
195th Pl. Pg.45 R29
196th St. Pg.45 R30
197th St. Pg.50 R30
198th Pl. Pg.50 R28
198th St. Pg.50 R28
199th St. Pg.50 R28
200th Pl. Pg.50 R29
200th St. Pg.50 R29
201st Pl. Pg.50 S29
201st St. Pg.50 S29
202nd St. Pg.50 S30
203rd St. Pg.50 S30
204th St. Pg.50 S29,30
207th Pl. Pg.50 T28
207th St. Pg.50 T28
208th Pl. Pg.50 T30

PARKS
Liberty Memorial Park Pg.50 T30
Rainbow Park Pg.50 T28

SCHOOLS
Sandridge Sch. Pg.50 T30

MISCELLANEOUS
Fire Department Pg.50 T30

LYONS TOWNSHIP
Page 33,34

STREETS
Bielby Ave. B9
Both Pl. B9
Cook-DuPage Rd. C7
German Church Rd. B8
Hess Ave. B9
Howard B9
Pleasantview B8
79th St. B8
87th St. C8

FOREST PRESERVES
Buffalo Woods B11

GOLF COURSES
Edgewood Valley C.C. A9

SCHOOLS
Pleasantdale Sch. B9

MAINE TOWNSHIP
Pages 24,25

STREETS
Alexis Ct. H5
Allison Ct. H5
Ashley Dr. H4
Aspen Dr. J3
Aspen Ln. J3
Ballard Rd. J2
Barberry Ln. J3
Bayberry Ln. J3
Bianco Terr. H3
Bobbie Ln. K3
Brandy Ct. H4
Briar Ct. K3
Bumblebee Dr. J3
Burton Ave. K3
Capital Dr. J3
Carleah Ct. K3
Cedar Ln. J3
Central Rd. H4
Cherry Cir. H4
Cherry Ct. H4
Cherry Ln. J3
Chester Ave. J4
Clancy Dr. J4
Columbus Dr. J3
Congress Dr. J3
Crawford Ln. H3
Crescent Dr. H5
Culver St. H2
David Pl. J3
Davis St. J4
Decook Ave. K3
Decook Ct. K3
Dee Rd. J-K3
Dee Rd. J-K3
Delphia Ave. J4
Delphia Ave. J4
Dempster St. K3
Dempster St. K3
Des Plaines River Rd. H1
Donald Ct. H5
Donald Terr. H5
East Dr. J4
East River Rd. H2
Elder H4
Elder Ct. H4
Elm Dr. J4
Elms Terr. H3
Elmwood Dr. H3
Embassy Ln. J3
Emerson St. J3-4
Evanston-Elgin (Golf) Rd. J3
Fairlawn Dr. H4
Fairway Dr. H3
Farwell Ave. M16
Fernwood Dr. H5
Flora Ave. H5
Forest Pl. H2
Foster St. J5
Fox Glen Dr. H3
Gayle Ct. H5
Glendale Ln. H4
Glendale Rd. H4
Glenshire H4
Golf Rd. J3
Golf Terr. H3
Greenbriar Dr. H4
Greenwood Ave. H-K4
Greenwood Dr. (E & W) J4
Gregory Ln. H4
Hamilton Ct. H3
Hamlin Ave. J3
Harrison St. H2-4
Hazelwood Dr. H4
Heathwood Dr. H3
Helen Ct. H5
Helen Dr. H5
Holly Ln. H2
Hollyberry Ave. J3
Home Ave. J3
Home Cir. J3
Home Ct. J3
Home Terr. J3
Ironwood Ln. J3
James Ct. H5
James St. H5
Jody Ln. H3
Josephine Ln. H4
Julie Dr. H5
Kathy Ct. H3
Kennedy J3
Kenneth Dr. H3
Knight Ave. J4
Ladybird Ln. J3
Landing Ln. J3
Landing Sq. J3
Leslie Ln. J4
Lincoln Ave. J4
Lincoln Dr. J3
Linda Ct. H5
Linda Ln. H2
Linnea Ln. H3
Lois Dr. H4
Lyman Ave. H2
Lyons St. J3-4
MacArthur J3
Manor Ln. K3
Maple Ln. J3
Marcus Ct. E. K3
Marcus Ct. W. K3
Margail St. J3
Maynard Ct. H4
Maynard Dr. H4
Meadow Ln. H3
Michael Manor H5
Milwaukee Ave. H4
Nellie Ct. H5
Noel Ave. H5
Norma Ct. H5
North Shore Dr. H3
Oak Ave. J3
Oak Ln. H3
Oak Pl. H2
Oaktree Ln. K3
Park Ln. J3
Parkside Ave. J-K3
Parkside Dr. J3
Pauline Ave. H5
Poplar Dr. H4
Potter Rd. H-J3
Rancho Ln. J-K3
Reding Cir. H3
River Rd. E. H2
Robin Dr. K3
Roder St. H4
Ronald Rd. H4
Sanders Dr. J4
Senate Dr. J3
Sherry Ln. J3
Stacy Ct. H5
Stacy St. H5
Steven Dr. J3
Stevenson Dr. J3
Sumac Ln. H3
Sumac Rd. J3
Teela Ln. H2
Terrace Dr. H3
Terrace Pl. J3
Thornberry H4
Tri-State Tollway J2
Twin Oak Ln. J3
Tyrell Ave. K3
Valerie Ct. H5
Victor Ave. H5
Wald St. H4
Washington Dr. J3
West Oaks Ave. J3
Western Ave. H-J4
William Ave. H5
Zenith Dr. H2

CEMETERIES
Ridgewood Cem. H3-4

PARKS
Ladendorf Park H5
The People's Park J3

SCHOOLS
Apollo Jr. H.S. H3
N. Ridge Prep. Sch. H3
Shelley Nathanson Sch. J3
Stevenson Sch. J3
Washington Sch. H5

SHOPPING CENTERS
Dempster Plaza K4
Golf Glen S.C. J3

MATTESON
Pages 46,47

STREETS
Allemong Dr. S16
Amherst Pl. U17
Apple Hill Ln. S16
Applewood Ln. T19
Aspen Ln. T16
Basswood Rd. S17
Beachwood Ct. T17
Beachwood Rd. T16,17
Beaver Dam Rd. T16
Birchwood Ln. T18
Bradley Ave. T17
Briarwood Ct. S17
Bridgewood Ct. S17
Bridgewood Rd. T17
Butterfield Pkwy. U20
Cambridge Ave. T17
Campus Ave. T18
Carnation Ln. T19
Cedarwood Ln. T19
Central Ave. U17
Charles St. V20
Charleston Rd. U19
Church Rd. S16
Churn Rd. S16
Cicero Ave. V18
Cloverleaf Rd. S17
Colgate Ln. T17
College Ave. T19
Columbine Ln. T19
Cornell Way T17
Cornfield Rd. T16
Corporate Lakes Dr. T18
Crawford Ave. T19
Crestwood Ct. S17
Crestwood Rd. S17
Dan Ryan Expwy. U18
Dartmouth Ave. T17
Deerpath Rd. S17
Dettmering Dr. U20
Drake Ln. T17
Duke Dr. T17
Elm Ln. T16
Elmwood Ln. T18
Fernwood Ct. S17
Fox Run Ln. T16
Front St. U20
Georgetown Dr. U17
Goldenrod Cir. T18
Hanson Ln. U18
Harvard Ln. T17
Hickory St. U19
Highland Ave. T18
Highland Rd. T16
Holiday Plaza Dr. U18
Homan Ave. U20
Homeland Rd. T18
Huntingwood Rd. S17
Jean U19
Jeffrey Dr. U19
Keeler Ave. T,U19
Kildare Ave. U19
Kildare Ct. U19
Kostner Ave. T,U19
Lakespur T19
Lincoln Hwy. U19
Lincoln Mall Dr. U18
Lindenwood Dr. T19
Locust St. U20
Main St. U,V20
Main St.,E. U20
Maple St. U20
Marsh Ln. T16
Morning Glory Dr. T18
North St. U20
Notre Dame Dr. T17
Oak St. U20
Oakhurst Rd. S17
Oakview Rd. S17
Oakwood Ln. T19
Old Creek Ln. T16
Old Farm Rd. T16
Old Meadow Rd. T16
Old Mill Rd. S16
Oriole Rd. S17
Oxford Ave. T17
Partridge Rd. T16
Paterson Ct. V20
Pheasant Rd. S16
Phlox Cir. T18
Pinewood Ln. T19
Post Ave. T18
Primrose Cir. T19
Primrose Ln. T19
Princeton Ave. T17
Purdue Ln. T17
Quail Run Rd. T16
Quinn U20
Red Barn Rd. S16
Richmond Ct. U19
Richmond Rd. U19
Richton Rd. V19
Ridgeland R16
Rose Ln. T19
School Ave. T19
Southwick Dr. U18
Spring Ln. T16
Sprucewood Ln. T18
St. Lawrence Ave. U19
Streamwood Rd. T16
Sumter Dr. U19
Sunflower Dr. T16
Timberlane Dr. S16,17
Tower Ave. U20
University Ave. T19
Violet Ln. T19
Vollmer Rd. S15
Washington Ave. U19
Wedgewood Ct. S16
Wedgewood Rd. S16
Wheatfield Rd. S16
White Birch Ln. T16
White Oaks Rd. S16
Willow Ct. S16
Willow Rd. S16
Wolf Rd. T16
Woodgate Dr. S17
Yale Ln. T17
205th Pl. T17
205th St. T18
206th Pl. T19
207th St. T19
211th Pkwy. U17
211th St. U20
212th Pl. U19
213th Pl. U19,20
213th St. U19,20
214th Pl. U20
214th St. U19,20
215th St. U20
216th Pl. U20
216th St. U19,20
217th St. U19,20
218th Pl. V20
218th St. V20
219th St. V19

PARKS
Allemong Park T16
Memorial Park U20
Notre Dame Park T17
Oakwood Park T19
Woodgate Park S17

SCHOOLS
Hurth Jr. H.S. U20
Marya Yates Sch. S16
Matteson Sch. U20
Oakwood Sch. T19
Sieden Prairie Sch. T17
St. Lawrence O'Toole Sch. U19
Woodgate Sch. S17
Zion Lutheran Sch. U19

SHOPPING CENTERS
Lincoln Mall U18
Matteson Town Ctr. Mall U18

MISCELLANEOUS
Fire Station No. 2 U17
Old Plank Road Bike Trail U18
Police Station T18
Post Office T18
Public Works U20
R.R. Station U,V20
Village Hall U20

MORTON GROVE
Pages 29,30

STREETS
Albert Ave. J7
Arcadia St. J5-6
Austin Ave. J-L8
Bazell Pl. K7
Beckwith Rd. J5-7
Belleforte Ave. J6
Birch Ave. J7
Callie Ave. K7
Cameron Ave. J6
Capri Ln. J8
Capulina Ave. K7-8
Carol Ave. K8
Central Ave. K-L8
Central Rd. J8
Cherry Ave. J7
Chestnut St. K7
Church St. J5-8
Churchill Ave. J5
Churchill St. J6-7
Cleveland L8
Crain St. K8
Davis St. J5-8
Dempster St. K6
Eldorado Dr. J7
Elm Ln. K8
Elm St. K7
Emerson St. J6-8
Enfield Ave. K5-6
Fernald Ave. K7
Ferris Ave. K7
Forest Dr. K8
Foster St. J5-7
Frontage Rd. K8
Georgiana Ave. K8
Greenwood Ave. K6,J8
Gross Point Rd. K9
Grove Ct. K8
Harms Rd. H8,J9
Hazel St. J7
Hennings Ct. K7
Hoffman Ct. J7
Hoffman Terr. J7
Keeney Ct. L8
Keeney St. L8-9
Kirk St. L9
Lake St. J5-8
Lee St. K8
Lehigh Ave. J-L7
Lillibet Terr. K8
Lincoln Ave. K9
Linder Ave. J-L9
Long Ave. L9
Lotus Ave. L9
Luna Ave. J-L9
Lyons St. J5-8
Madison St. K8-9
Main St. K8-9
Major Ave. J-K8
Mango Ave. J-K8
Mansfield Ave. J8
Maple Ave. J7
Maple Ct. J5
Maple St. J5-7
Marion Ave. J6
Marmora Ave. J-L8
Mason Ave. J-K8
McVickers Ave. J-K8
Meade Ave. J-K8
Menard Ave. J-L8
Merril Ln. J5
Merrill St. J5
Michael Ave. J5
Michael Ct. J5
Monroe St. K8-9
Moody Ave. K8
Morton Ln. K8
Murray Ct. J5
Nagle Ave. J-L7
Narragansett Ave. J7
Nashville Ave. J7
Natchez Ave. J-L7
National Ave. J-K6
Natoma Ave. J7
Neenah Ave. J,K7
New Castle Ave. J7
New England Ave. J-K7
Normandy Ave. K7
Oak Park K7
Oakton St. L7
Oconto Ave. J-K6
Octavia J-K6
Odell Ave. J-K6
Oketo Ave. J6
Olcott J-K6
Oleander St. K5
Oliphant Ave. J5
Oriole Ave. J5
Osceola Ave. J6
Oswego St. K6
Ottawa Ave. K5
Overhill Ave. J5
Ozanam Ave. J5
Ozark Ave. J5
Ozark St. J5
Palma Ln. J5-7
Park Ave. L7
Park Ave. S. K8
Parkside Ave. H-L8
Ponto Dr. J6
Prospect J-K6
Reba Ct. L8
Reba St. L8-9

MORTON GROVE

STREETS

River Dr. L7
Sayre Ave. J-K6
School St. K8
Shermer Rd. J6
Simpson St. J6
Smithwood Dr. K7
Suffield J5
Suffield Ct. J6
Theobald Rd. J6
Warren L8
Warren St. L8-9
Washington K8
Waukegan Rd. J6
Wilson Terr. J5-6
104 Ln. J7

PARKS

Arnum Park J6
Austin Park K8
Cardinal Park J7
Harper Park K7-8
Mansfield Park J8
National Park J6
Oketo Park J6
Oriole Park J5
Overhill Park J5
Palma Ln. Park J7
Pioneer Park K8
Prairie View Park K7
Shermer Park J6

SCHOOLS

Blanche Borg Sch. K8
Edison Sch. L9
Emma Meltzer Sch. J5
Golf Jr. H.S. J6
Hynes Sch. J6
Julia Molloy Sch. J6
Parkview Sch. J7
St. Marthas Sch. K8

MISCELLANEOUS

Fire Station K7
Fire Station J6
Library K8
Police Department K8
Post Office J6
Village Hall K8

MOUNT PROSPECT

Pages 9,10,13,14,15

STREETS

Addison Ct. . . Pg.14 . . . . J12
Albert St. . . . . Pg.14 . F,G14
Albion Ln. . . . Pg.9 . . . . E13
Alder Ln. . . . . Pg.14 . E14,15
Algonquin Ln. . Pg.14 . . . . J11
Almond Ct. . . . Pg.10 . . . E15
Andoa Ln. . . . Pg.14 . . . D15
Ann-Marie . . . Pg.14 . . . E15
Apache Ln. . . . Pg.9 . . . . E15
Apple Ct. . . . . Pg.9 . . . . D13
Apricot Ct. . . . Pg.9 . . . . D13
Aralia Dr. . . . . Pg.10 . . . D15
Ardyce Ln. . . Pg.14,15 . . F14
Arthur Ave. . . . Pg.14 . . . F11
Ash Dr. . . . . . Pg.14 . . . H12
Aspen Dr. . . . Pg.10 . . . G11
Audrey Ln. . . . Pg.14 . . . G11
Autumn Ave. . Pg.14 . . . E15
Azalea Ln. . . . Pg.10 . . . G11
Azalea Pl. . . . Pg.10 . . . G11
Aztec Ln. . . . Pg.10 . . . D15
Barberry Ln. . . Pg.9 . . . . E14
Basswood Ln. . Pg.10 . . . E15
Beechwood Dr. Pg.14 . . . H12
Belaire Ln. . . . Pg.14 . . . E14
Berkshire Ln. . Pg.14 . . . G13
Beverly Ln. . . . Pg.14 . . . F14
Biermann Ct. . . Pg.9 . . . . F14
Birch Dr. . . . . Pg.14 . . . H12
Birch Rd. . . . . Pg.10 . . . D15
Bishop Ct. . . . Pg.14 . . . E15
Bittersweet Ln. Pg.14 . . . E15
Blackhawk Dr. . Pg.14 . . . E15
Blue Jay Ct. . . Pg.9 . . . . F14
Bob-O-Link Rd. Pg.9 . . . . E13
Bobby Ln. . . . Pg.14 . . . G12
Bonita Ave. . . Pg.14 . . . F14
Boro Ln. . . . . Pg.10 . . . D16
Boulder Dr. . . . Pg.10 . . . E14
Boxwood Dr. . . Pg.14 . . . E14
Brentwood Ln. Pg.14 . . . E14
Bridgeport Dr. . Pg.9 . . . . D13
Brighton Pl. . . Pg.9 . . . . D13
Brownstone Ln. Pg.14 . . . J11
Buckthorn Rd. . Pg.10 . . . D15
Bunting Ln. . . . Pg.9 . . . . E13
Burning Bush Ln. . . . .
. . . . Pg.10 . . . E15
Burr Oak Dr. . . Pg.10 . . . E16
Business Center Dr. . . . . . .
. . . . Pg.14 . . . F14
Busse Ave. . . . Pg.14 . . . G13
Busse Rd. . . . . Pg.14 . . . F14
Butternut Dr. . . Pg.9 . . D12,13
Byron Ct. . . . . Pg.14 . . . F14
Callero Cir. . . . Pg.14 . . . E14
Camp McDonald Rd. . . . . . .
. . . . Pg.10 . D15,16
Can-Dota Ave. S. . . . .
. . . . Pg.14 . . H,G13
Canford Cliffs Dr. . . . .
. . . . Pg.14 . . . J12

Cannon Dr. . . . Pg.14 . . . K13
Carboy Rd. . . . Pg.14 . . . K13
Cardinal Ln. . . Pg.14 . . . F14
Carib Ln. . . . . Pg.10 . . . D15
Carol Ct. . . . . Pg.14 . . . H11
Carol Ln. . . . . Pg.14 . . . G11
Carriage Hill . . Pg.14 . . . H13
Catalpa Ln. . . . Pg.14 . . . H12
Cathy Ln. . . . . Pg.14 . . . G12
Catino Ct. . . . . Pg.14 . . . F14
Cayuga Ln. . . . Pg.10 . . . D16
Cedar Ln. . . . . Pg.9 . . . . E14
Centennial Dr. . Pg.14 . . . F14
Central Rd. . . . Pg.14 . . . E14
Chariot Ct. . . . Pg.14 . . . J12
Charlotte Rd. . . Pg.14 . . . J11
Cherrywood Dr. Pg.14 . . . H12
Chestnut Dr. . . Pg.14 . . . H12
Chinkapin Oak . Pg.14 . . . E16
Cholo Ln. . . . . Pg.10 . . . E15
Chris Ln. . . . . Pg.14 . . . H11
Church Rd. . . . Pg.14 . . . E14
Circle Dr. . . . . Pg.14 . . . J12
Clevin Ave. . . . Pg.14 . . . H13
Clove Ct. . . . . Pg.9 . . . . D12
Colony Dr. . . . Pg.14 . . . K13
Columbine Dr. . Pg.10 . . . D15
Connie Ln. . . . Pg.14 . . . G11
Corktree Ln. . . Pg.10 . . . E15
Cottonwood Dr. Pg.14 . . . J12
Council Tr. . . . Pg.14 . . . G13
Country Ln. . . . Pg.14 . . . H13
Coventry Pl. . . Pg.9 . . . . D13
Crabtree Ln. . . Pg.9 . . . . E14
Craig Ct. . . . . Pg.13 . . . H11
Cree Ln. . . . . Pg.10 . . . E15
Crestwood Ave. Pg.14 . . . G11
Crystal Ln. . . . Pg.14 . . . J12
Cypress Dr. . . . Pg.14 . . . H12
Dale Ave. . . . . Pg.9 . . . . F12
Debbie Dr. . . . Pg.14 . . . F15
Deborah Ln. . . Pg.14 . . G,H11
Dempster Ln. . . Pg.14 . . . J12
Deneen Ln. . . . Pg.14 . . . F15
Dennis Dr. . . . Pg.14 . . . J12
Des Plaines River Rd. . . . .
. . . . Pg.10 . . . E16
Dogwood Ln. . . Pg.9 . . . . E14
Dover Pl. . . . . Pg.9 . . . . D13
Dover Dr. . . . . Pg.14 . . . H12
Dresser Dr. . . . Pg.14 . . . F14
East Dr. . . . . . Pg.9 . . . . F14
Eastman Ct. . . Pg.9 . . . . F14
Eastwood Ave. Pg.14 . . . F13
Edgewood Ln. . Pg.14 . . . H12
Edward St. . . . Pg.14 . . . F14
Elayne Ct. . . . Pg.14 . . . J11
Elderberry Dr. . Pg.9 . . . . E14
Elm St. . . . . . Pg.14 . F-H13
Elmhurst Ave. . Pg.14 . . . F13
Elmhurst Rd. . . Pg.9 . . E-J13
Elmhurst Rd. . . Pg.14 . . . J13
Emerson St. . . Pg.14 . . . F13
Emmerson St. . Pg.14 . . . F15
Enterprise Dr. . Pg.14 . . . K13
Eric Ave. . . . . Pg.14 . . . F14
Eric Ct. . . . . . Pg.14 . . . F14
Estates Dr. . . . Pg.14 . . . G11
Euclid Ave. . . . Pg.14 . . . F14
Eva Ln. . . . . . Pg.14 . . . H12
Evanston Ave. . Pg.14 . . . F12
Evergreen Ave. Pg.14 . . . G13
Fairmont . . . . . Pg.9 . . . . D13
Fairview St. . . . Pg.14 . . . F13
Feehanville Dr. . Pg.9 . . . . E14
Fern Dr. . . . . . Pg.14 . . . H12
Forest Ave. . . . Pg.9 . . . . F13
Forest Cove Dr. Pg.14 . . . J12
Franklin Dr. . . . Pg.14 . . . K13
Freedom Ct. . . Pg.10 . . . E15
Frost Dr. . . . . Pg.14 . . . H12
Garwood Ave. . Pg.9 . . . . G14
George St. . . . Pg.14 . . . F14
Glendale Ln. . . Pg.14 . . . H11
Glenn Ln. . . . . Pg.14 . . . G12
Go-Wan-Do Tr. . Pg.9 . . G12,13
Golf (Evanston-Elgin) . . . . .
. . . . Pg.14 . H13-14
Golfhurst Ave. . Pg.14 . . . H12
Golfview Ave. . . Pg.14 . . . H12
Golfview Pl. . . . Pg.14 . . . H12
Grace Dr. . . . . Pg.14 . . . H12
Green Acres Ln. Pg.14 . . . H12
Green Ln. . . . . Pg.14 . . . F15
Greenbriar Dr. . Pg.14 . . . G14
Greenfield Ct. . Pg.9 . . . . E14
Greenfield Ln. . Pg.9 . . . . E14
Greenwood Ln. Pg.9 . . . . E14
Gregory Ln. . . . Pg.14 . . . F14
Gregory St. . . . Pg.9 . . . . F13
Grindel Dr. . . . Pg.14 . . . G11
Grove Dr. . . . . Pg.14 . . . H11
Hackberry Ln. . Pg.14 . . . F14
Hanover Pl. . . . Pg.9 . . . . D13
Harvest Ln. . . . Pg.14 . . . F14
Hatlen Ave. . . . Pg.14 . . . G13
Hawthorn St. . . Pg.14 . . . J13
Hayden St. . . . Pg.13 . . . G11
Hazelhill . . . . . Pg.14 . . . J12
Heatherleigh Ct. Pg.14 . . . D15
Helena Ave. . . Pg.13,14 . . J11
Hemlock Ln. . . Pg.9 . . . . E14
Henry St. . . . . Pg.14 . . . F14
Heritage Dr. . . Pg.14 . . . G13
Hi-Lusi Ave. . . Pg.14 . . . G13
Hiawatha Ct. . . Pg.14 . . . G13

Hickory Ave. . . Pg.13 . . . G11
Hickory Ct. . . . Pg.14 . . . H12
Highland Dr. . . Pg.9 . . . . F14
Highland St. . . Pg.9 . . . . F13
Hill St. . . . . . . Pg.9 . . . . F14
Holly Ave. . . . . Pg.14 . . . E14
Holly Ct. . . . . . Pg.14 . . . E14
Hopi Ln. . . . . . Pg.10 . . . E16
Horner Ln. . . . Pg.14 . . . F15
Hunt Club Dr. . Pg.14 . . . H13
Huntington Commons Dr. . . .
. . . . Pg.14 . . . H13
I-Oka Ave. . . . Pg.14 . . . G13
Ida Ct. . . . . . . Pg.14 . . . J13
Imperial Ct. . . . Pg.14 . . . J12
Independence Ct. . . . .
. . . . Pg.10 . . . E15
Indigo Ct. . . . . Pg.14 . . . E15
Indigo Ln. . . . . Pg.10 . D,E15
Ironwood Ct. . . Pg.10 . . . E15
Ironwood Ln. . . Pg.9 . . . . E14
Ironwood Pl. . . Pg.14 . . . E14
Isabella St. . . . Pg.14 . . . F13
Ivanhoe Ln. . . Pg.14 . . . H13
Ivy Ln. . . . . . . Pg.14 . . . E16
Jeffery Dr. . . . . Pg.15 . . . F15
Jerry Dr. . . . . . Pg.14 . . . F15
Jody Ct. . . . . . Pg.13 . . . G11
Judith Ann Dr. . Pg.9 . . . . F13
Juniper Dr. . . . Pg.14 . . . E15
Kenilworth Ave. Pg.14 . . . F12
Kenneth Dr. . . Pg.14 . . . F14
Kensington Rd. Pg.9 . E12-15
Kim Ave. . . . . Pg.14 . . . G13
Kingston Ct. . . Pg.9 . . F14,15
Kiowa Ln. . . . . Pg.10 . . . E16
Knights Bridge Dr. . . . .
. . . . Pg.14 . . . J12
La Vergne Dr. . Pg.14 . . . H12
Lakeview . . . . Pg.14 . . . H13
Lakeview Ct. . . Pg.14 . . . F15
Lama Ln. . . . . Pg.10 . . . E16
Lams Ct. . . . . Pg.14 . . . G13
Lancaster Ave. Pg.14 . F-H12
Larch Dr. . . . . Pg.14 . . . D15
Larkdale Ln. . . Pg.9 . . . . E13
Lasalle Dr. . . . Pg.14 . . . J13
Laurel Dr. . . . . Pg.14 . . . D15
Lexington Dr. . . Pg.14 . . . K13
Liberty Ct. . . . Pg.14 . . . E15
Lincoln Rd. . . . Pg.9 . . . . G11
Lincoln St. . . . Pg.14 . . . G13
Linden Dr. . . . Pg.9 . . . . F15
Linden Dr. . . . Pg.9 . . . . E15
Linden Ln. . . . Pg.9 . . . . E14
Linneman Rd. . Pg.14 . . . H13
Locust Ln. . . . Pg.14 . . . H11
Lois Ct. . . . . . Pg.13 . . . G11
Lonquist Blvd. . Pg.14 . . . H12
Louis St. . . . . Pg.14 . . . F14
Lowden Ln. . . . Pg.14 . . . F15
Lynn Ct. . . . . . Pg.14 . . . J11
MacArthur Blvd. . . . .
. . . . Pg.14 . . . F12
Magnolia Ln. . . Pg.14 . . . H11
Main St. . . . . . Pg.14 . . . G13
Mallard Ln. . . . Pg.14 . . . J13
Mamio Rd. . . . Pg.14 . . . G13
Man-A-Wa Tr. . Pg.14 . . . G13
Mandel Ln. . . . Pg.10 . . . D15
Mansard Ln. . . Pg.14 . . . J12
Manshire Pl. . . Pg.9 . . . . D13
Maple Ct. . . . . Pg.9 . . . . F13
Maple St. . . . . Pg.14 . . . F13
Marcella Rd. . . Pg.14 . . . F14
Mark Dr. . . . . Pg.15 . . . F15
Mark Terr. . . . . Pg.14 . . . G11
Martha Ave. . . Pg.14 . . . G12
Martin Ave. . . . Pg.14 . . . G12
Maya Ln. . . . . Pg.10 . . . D15
Meadow Ln. . . Pg.9 . E13,14
Meier Rd. . . . . Pg.13 . . . G11
Memory Ln. . . . Pg.14 . . . F13
Michael St. . . . Pg.14 . . . G12
Midway Dr. . . . Pg.14 . . . K13
Milburn Ave. . . Pg.14 . . . G12
Millers Ln. . . . Pg.14 . . . F12
Mitchell Dr. . . . Pg.15 . . . F15
Moehling Dr. . . Pg.14 . . . H13
Mohawk Ln. . . Pg.10 . . . F15
Moki Ln. . . . . . Pg.10 . . . E16
Montgomery St. . . . .
. . . . Pg.14 . . . J13
Morrisohill . . . Pg.14 . . . J12
Mt. Prospect Rd. . . . .
. . . . Pg.14 . . . G14
Mulberry Ln. . . Pg.9 . . . . E14
Mura Ln. . . . . Pg.10 . . . D16
Myrtle Ave. . . . Pg.14 . . . G12
Na-Wa-Ta Ave. Pg.14 . . . H13
Neil Ave. . . . . Pg.15 . . . F14
Newberry Ln. . . Pg.14 . . . E15
Noan Terr. . . . Pg.13 . . . H11
Nordic Rd. . . . Pg.14 . . . K13
Northwest Hwy. Pg.14 . . . F13
Nutmeg Ct. . . . Pg.9 . . D,E13
Oak Ave. . . . . Pg.14 . . . F13
Oakwood Dr. . . Pg.14 . . . H12
Ojibwa Tr. . . . . Pg.10 . . . G12
Oneida Ct. . . . Pg.10 . . . D15
Oneida Ln. . . . Pg.14 . . . D15
Orange Ct. . . . Pg.9 . . . . D13
Orchard Pl. . . . Pg.14 . . . H13
Oriole Ln. . . . . Pg.9 . . . . E13
Owen St. . . . . Pg.14 . . . F14
Oxford Pl. . . . . Pg.9 . . . . E13
Palm Dr. . . . . Pg.14 . . . H12

Park Dr. . . . . . Pg.10 . . . D16
Parliament Pl. . Pg.9 . . . . D13
Partridge . . . . Pg.14 . . . H13
Pawnee Ln. . . Pg.10 . . . D16
Peachtree Ln. . Pg.10 . . . E15
Peartree Ln. . . Pg.10 . . . E15
Pecos Ln. . . . Pg.10 . . . E16
Pendleton Pl. . . Pg.14 . . . G12
Persimmon Ln. Pg.9 . . D12,13
Pheasant Ln. . . Pg.14 . . . J11
Phillip . . . . Pg.14 . . . J12
Picadilly Cir. . . Pg.9 . . . . D13
Pin Oak Ct. . . . Pg.10 . . . E15
Pin Oak Dr. . . . Pg.10 . . . E16
Pine County . . Pg.14 . . . H13
Pine St. . . . . . Pg.14 . . . F,G13
Plum Ct. . . . . . Pg.9 . . . . D12
Prendegast Ln. Pg.13 . . . H11
Prospect Ave. . Pg.14 . F12,G13
Prospect Manor Ave. . . . . . .
. . . . Pg.9,14 . . E,F13
Quail Walk . . . Pg.14 . . . J13
Quince Ct. . . . Pg.10 . . . E15
Quince Ln. . . . Pg.10 . . . E15
Raleigh Pl. . . . Pg.9 . . . . D13
Rand Rd. . . . . Pg.14 . . . E13
Redwood Dr. . . Pg.14 . . . J12
Regency Ct. . . Pg.10 . . . E15
Ridge Ave. . . . Pg.14 . . . F13
River West Ct. . Pg.10 . . . D16
Rob Rd. . . . . . Pg.14 . . . F12
Robbie Ln. . . . Pg.14 . . . G12
Roberts Dr. . . . Pg.14 . . . H12
Robin Ln. . . . . Pg.14 . . . H12
Rosetree Ln. . . Pg.10 . . . D15
Russell St. . . . Pg.14 . . . F13
Rusty Dr. . . . . Pg.14 . . . G12
Sable Ln. . . . . Pg.9 . . . . J11
Santee Ln. . . . Pg.10 . . . E15
Sauk Ln. . . . . Pg.10 . . . D16
School St. . . . Pg.14 . . . F14
Scott Terr. . . . . Pg.14 . . . F14
See-Gwun Ave. Pg.14 . . . H13
Seminole Ln. . . Pg.10 . . . D15
Seneca Ln. . . . Pg.10 . . . D16
Shabonee Tr. . . Pg.14 . G13-14
Sioux Ln. . . . . Pg.10 . . . E15
Sir Galahad Ln. Pg.14 . . . J13
Sir Lancelot . . Pg.14 . . . J13
Sitka Ln. . . . . Pg.10 . . . D15
Sivio St. . . . . . Pg.14 . . . G12
Slawin Ct. . . . Pg.14 . . . F14
Small Ln. . . . Pg.9,10 . . F15
Sprucewood Dr. Pg.14 . . . H12
St. Celicia Dr. . Pg.13 . . . H11
Stevenson Ln. . Pg.14 . . . H11
Stratford Pl. . . Pg.14 . . . E13
Stratton Ln. . . Pg.14 . . . F14
Sullivan Ct. . . . Pg.14 . . . G13
Sumac Ln. . . . Pg.10 . . . E16
Sunset Rd. . . . Pg.14 . . . G13
Susan Dr. . . . . Pg.14 . . . G12
Sycamore Ln. . Pg.9 . . . . E14
Tamarack Dr. . . Pg.14 . . . H11
Tano Ln. . . . . Pg.10 . . . D15
Thackery Pl. . . Pg.14 . . . D13
Thayer St. . . . Pg.14 . . . G13
Thomas Moore Terr. . . . . . .
. . . . Pg.9 . . . . E13
Thornwood Ln. Pg.14 . . . H11
Tower Dr. . . . . Pg.14 . . . H13
Tower Ln. . . . . Pg.14 . . . H13
University Dr. . . Pg.9 . . . . D13
Verde Ct. . . . . Pg.14 . . . G12
Verde Dr. . . . . Pg.14 . . . G12
Victoria Dr. . . . Pg.14 . . . J12
Village Dr. . . . . Pg.14 . . . F14
Vista St. . . . . . Pg.14 . . . G13
Wall St. . . . . . Pg.14 . . . J13
Walnut St. . . . . Pg.14 . . . F13
Wapella Ave. . . Pg.14 . . . G13
Waverly Ave. . . Pg.14 . F-H12
We-Go Tr. . . . . Pg.14 . G,H12
Wedgewood Ln. . . . .
. . . . Pg.9 . . . . E13
Weller Ln. . . . . Pg.14 . . . G12
Westgate Rd. . . Pg.14 . . . F14
Wheeling Rd. . . Pg.9 . . . . F14
White Chapel Dr. . . . .
. . . . Pg.14 . . . H12
Whitegate Dr. . Pg.14 . . . G12
Whithorn Ln. . . Pg.14 . . . F12
Wigwam . . . . . Pg.14 . . . G12
Wildwood Ln. . Pg.9 . . . . F13
Wille St. . . . . . Pg.14 . . . F13
William St. . . . Pg.14 . . . F12
Willow Ln. . . . . Pg.14 . . . H12
Wilshire Dr. . . . Pg.9 . . . . E14
Wimbolton Dr. . Pg.9 . . . . E13
Windsor Tr. . . . Pg.9 . . . . E13
Wintergreen Ave. . . . .
. . . . Pg.10 . . . D16
Wistoria Ct. . . . Pg.10 . . . F15
Wolf Rd. . . . . . Pg.14 . . . F15
Wood Ln. . . . . Pg.10 . . . D15
Woodview Dr. . Pg.10 . . . D16
Yarmouth Pl. . . Pg.14 . . . E13
Yates Ln. . . . . Pg.14 . . . F15
Yuma Ln. . . . . Pg.10 . . . D16

Rob Roy C.C. . . Pg.9 . . . . D14

PARKS

Aspen Trail Park Pg.9 . . . D15
Bluett Park . . . . Pg.14 . . . F15
Burning Busk Trails Park . . .
. . . . Pg.14 . . . E16
Busse Park . . . Pg.14 . . . F14
Clearwater Park Pg.14 . . . H12
Countryside Park . . . .
. . . . Pg.14 . . . H13
East Wedgewood Park . . . . .
. . . . Pg.9 . . . . E13
Emerson Park . Pg.14 . . . F13
Gregory Park . . Pg.9 . . . . F14
Kopp Park . . . . Pg.14 . . . J13
Lions Memorial Park . . . . . .
. . . . Pg.14 . . . G13
Meadows Park . Pg.9 . . . . F12
Melas Park . . . Pg.14 . . . F12
Owen Park . . . Pg.14 . . . G14
Parkview Park . Pg.9 . . . . E15
Prospect Meadows Park . . . .
. . . . Pg.9 . . . . E13
Sunrise Park . . Pg.9 . . . . H14
Sunset Park . . . Pg.14 . . . H13
Sycamore Trails Park . . . . . .
. . . . Pg.9 . . . . E15
Tamarack Park . Pg.14 . . . H11
We-Go Park . . Pg.14 . . . G12
Weller Creek . . Pg.14 . . . H12
West Wedgewood Park . . . . .
. . . . Pg.14 . . . E13
Westbrook Park . . . .
. . . . Pg.14 . . . G12
Woodland Trails Park . . . . . .
. . . . Pg.9 . . . . E15

SCHOOLS

Busse Sch. . . . Pg.14 . . . F14
Dempster Jr. H.S. . . . .
. . . . Pg.14 . . . J13
Euclid Sch. . . . Pg.14 . . . E14
Fairview Sch. . . Pg.9 . . . . F13
Forest View Sch. . . . .
. . . . Pg.14 . . . H11
Frost Sch. . . . . Pg.14 . . . D15
Gregory Sch. . . Pg.14 . . . F14
Holmes Jr. H.S. Pg.14 . . . H11
Indian Grove Sch. . . . .
. . . . Pg.14 . . . G11
John Jay Sch. . Pg.9 . . . . H12
Lincoln Jr. H.S. Pg.14 . . . G13
Lions Park Sch. Pg.14 . . . G13
Parkview Sch. . Pg.14 . . . G11
Prospect H.S. . Pg.9 . . . . F12
River Trails Jr. H.S. . . . .
. . . . Pg.14 . . . E15
Robert Frost Sch. . . . .
. . . . Pg.14 . . . H12
Shadrach Bond Sch. . . . . . .
. . . . Pg.14 . . . F15
St. Emily Cath. Sch. . . . .
. . . . Pg.14 . . . F15
St. John Luth. Sch. . . . .
. . . . Pg.14 . . . H13
St. Paul Luth. Sch. . . . .
. . . . Pg.14 . . . G13
St. Raymond Cath. Sch. . . . .
. . . . Pg.14 . . . G13
Sunset Park Sch. . . . .
. . . . Pg.14 . . . H13
Westbrook Sch. Pg.14 . . . G12

SHOPPING CENTERS

Countryside Court S.C. . . . .
. . . . Pg.14 . . . H13
Golf Shopping Plaza . . . . . .
. . . . Pg.14 . . . H12
Mt. Prospect S.C. . . . .
. . . . Pg.14 . . . F14
Randhurst S.C. Pg.9 . . . . E13
Shoppers World S.C. . . . . . .
. . . . Pg.9 . . . . E13

MISCELLANEOUS

Fire Department . . . .
. . . . Pg.10 . . . E16
Police & Fire Station . . . . . .
. . . . Pg.14 . . . G13
Post Office . . . Pg.14 . . . F13
RR Station . . . Pg.14 . . . F13
Rec Plex . . . . Pg.14 . . . J13
Village Hall . . . Pg.14 . . . G13

NEW TRIER TOWNSHIP

Pages 23,26

STREETS

Cotton Ln. . . . Pg.26 . . . . F9
Illinois Rd. . . . Pg.23 . . F9,10
Indian Hill Rd. . Pg.23 . . . E11
Locust Rd. . . . Pg.23 . . . E10
Longmeadow Rd. . . . .
. . . . Pg.26 . . . . F9
Oxford Ln. . . . Pg.26 . . . E10
Porter . . . . . . Pg.23 . . . E10
Washington . . Pg.23 . . . E10
Woodley Manor Pg.26 . . . F10
Woodley Way . Pg.26 . . . F10
Woodley Woods Pg.26 . . . . F9

GOLF COURSES

Old Orchard C.C. . . . .
. . . . Pg.9 . . . . D13

FOREST PRESERVES

Turnbull Woods Pg.23 . . . . A8

NILES

Pages 28,29,30

STREETS

Amelia St. . . . Pg.29 . . . . K4
Ashland Ave. . . Pg.29 . . . . J5
Belleforte Pl. . . Pg.29 . . . . K6
Betty Terr. . . . . Pg.29 . . . . K4
Birchwood Ave. Pg.29 . . . . M6
Breen St. . . . . Pg.29 . . . . K6
Bruce Dr. . . . . Pg.28 . . . . L4
Brummel . . . . Pg.29 . . . . L8
Callero Dr. . . . Pg.29 . . . . J4
Canavan Ct. . . Pg.28 . . . . H4
Carol Ave. . . . Pg.29 . . . . K6
Carol Ct. . . . . Pg.29 . . . . K6
Carol St. . . . Pg.28,29 . K4,6
Catino . . . . . . Pg.29 . . . . J4
Cedar Ln. . . . . Pg.25 . . . . L5
Chase . . . . . . Pg.29 . . . . M6
Cherry . . . . . . Pg.29 . . . . M7
Chester Ave. . . Pg.28 . . . . K4
Chroname Rd. . Pg.29 . . . . M7
Church St. . . . Pg.29 . . . J4-5
Churchill Ave. . Pg.25 . . . . J5
Churchill Cir. . . Pg.29 . . . . J5
Clara Ct. . . . . Pg.28 . . . . L4
Clara Dr. . . . . Pg.28 . . . . L4
Cleveland St. . Pg.29 . . . L5-6
Clifton Ave. . . . Pg.29 . . . J-K4
Concord Ln. . . Pg.29 . . M-N7
Conrad Ave. . . Pg.29 . . . . K6
Courtland Dr. . . Pg.29 . . . . J4
Crain Ave. . . . Pg.29 . . . K4-6
Crain St. . . . . Pg.28 . . . K4-6
Cumberland Ave. . . . .
. . . . Pg.29 . . . . K4
Davis St. . . . . Pg.28 . . . J4-5
Days Terr. . . . . Pg.29 . . . . M7
Dempster St. . . Pg.29 . . . . K6
Dobson St. . . . Pg.29 . . . . L6
Ebinger Dr. . . . Pg.29 . . M-N7
Elizabeth Ave. . Pg.29 . . . K-L5
Elmore St. . . . Pg.29 . . . . K6
Fargo Ave. . . . Pg.29 . . . . M6
Farnsworth Dr. Pg.29 . . . . L5
Field Dr. N. . . . Pg.25 . . . . L5
Forest View Ln. Pg.29 . . M-N7
Foster Ln. . . . . Pg.29 . . . . J5
Franks Ave. . . Pg.29 . . . . M6
Gale Ter. . . . . Pg.29 . . . . J5
Georgia Dr. . . . Pg.29 . . . . K6
Glendale Rd. . . Pg.29 . . . . H4
Golf(Evanston-Elgin Rd.) . . . .
. . . . Pg.29 . . . . J4
Grace Ave. . . . Pg.29 . . . . K4
Grand Ct. . . . . Pg.29 . . . . K4
Grand St. . . . . Pg.29 . . . . K4
Greendale Ave. Pg.29 . . . L4-5
Greenleaf . . . . Pg.29 . . . . K5
Greenleaf St. . . Pg.29 . . . . K6
Greenwood Ave. Pg.28 . . J-K4
Greenwood Blvd. . . . .
. . . . Pg.28 . . . . K4
Grennan Pl. . . Pg.29 . . . K5-6
Gross Point Rd. Pg.29 . . . . M7
Hamilton Dr. . . Pg.29 . . . . K6
Harlem Ave. . . Pg.29 . . . . L6
Harts Rd. . . . . Pg.29 . . . . M7
Harvard St. . . . Pg.29 . . . . L6
Howard St. . . . Pg.29 . . . M6-8
Huber Ln. . . . . Pg.29 . . . . H4
Huber Oval . . . Pg.29 . . . . H4
Jarvis Ave. . . . Pg.30 . . . . M8
Jarvis St. . . . . Pg.29 . . . M6-7
Joey Dr. . . . . . Pg.29 . . . . K6
Johanna Dr. . . Pg.29 . . . . K6
Jonquil Ter. . . . Pg.29 . . . L5-6
Kay St. . . . . . Pg.29 . . . . H4
Kedzie St. . . . Pg.29 . . . . K6
Keeney St. . . . Pg.29 . . . L5-7
Kirk Dr. . . . . . Pg.29 . . . . J4
Kirk Ln. . . . . . Pg.29 . . . . J4
Kirk St. . . . . . Pg.29 . . . . L5
Knight . . . . . . Pg.28 . . . . L4
Lake St. . . . . . Pg.29 . . . . H4
Lauren Ln. . . . Pg.29 . . . . H4
Lawler Ave. . . Pg.29 . . . . J4
Lee St. . . . . . Pg.29 . . . K5-6
Lexington Ln. . Pg.29 . . . M-N7
Lill Ct. . . . . . . Pg.29 . . . . K5
Lill St. . . . . . . Pg.29 . . . . K6
Lincoln Ave. . . Pg.29 . . . . K4
Loras Ln. . . . . Pg.29 . . . . J5
Lyons St. . . . . Pg.29 . . . . J5
Madison St. . . Pg.29 . . . . L4
Madison Dr. . . Pg.29 . . . . L4
Main St. . . . . Pg.29 . . . K5-6
Maryland St. . . Pg.29 . . . J-K4
Maynard Oval . Pg.25 . . . . J4
Maynard Rd. . . Pg.29 . . . . J4
Maynard Ter. . . Pg.29 . . . . J4
Meacham Ct. . Pg.29 . . . . J4
Melvina Ave. . . Pg.29 . . L7,M8
Menard Ave. . . Pg.30 . . . . M8
Merrill St. . . . . Pg.29 . . . K,L6
Merrimac Ave. . Pg.29 . . . . L7
Milwaukee Ave. Pg.29 . . J4,L6
Monroe Ct. . . . Pg.29 . . . . K4
Monroe St. . . . Pg.29 . . . L4-6
Mulford Ave. . . Pg.29 . . . . L6
Mulford St. . . . Pg.29 . . . L6-8
Natchez Ave. . Pg.29 . . . . M7
National . . . . . Pg.29 . . . . K6

NILES

Neva St. . . . . . Pg.29 . . . . . . L6
New England Ave. . . . .
. . . . Pg.29 . . . . K-L6
Newark . . . . . . Pg.29 . . . . . . M6
Newcastle Ave. . Pg.29 . . . . . . L7
Nieman Ave. . . . Pg.29 . . . . . . M7
Niles Ave. . . . . . Pg.29 . . . . . . K6
Niles Terr. . . . . . Pg.29 . . . . . . M6
Nora Ave. . . . . . Pg.29 . . . . . . M6
Nordica Ave. . . . Pg.29 . . . . . . L7
Norma Ct. . . . . . Pg.29 . . . . . . H5
Normal Ave. . . . Pg.28 . . . . . . L4
Normal Ct. . . . . Pg.29 . . . . . . L4
North Ave. . . . . Pg.28 . . . . . . L4
Nottingham . . . . Pg.29 . . . L-M6
Oak Ave. . . . . . Pg.28 . . . . . . K4
Oak Ln. . . . . . . Pg.29 . . . . . . L5
Oak Park Ave. . . Pg.29 . . . . . . M7
Oakton Ct. . . . . Pg.29 . . . . L6-7
Oakton St. . . . . Pg.29 . . . . . . L6
Oconto Ave. . . . Pg.29 . . . . . . L6
Octavia Ave. . . . Pg.29 . . . . . . L6
Odell Ave. . . . . . Pg.29 . . . . . . L6
Oketo Ave. . . . . Pg.29 . . . . K-L6
Olcott Ave. . . . . Pg.29 . . . . . . L6
Oleander Ave. . . Pg.29 . . . K5,L6
Oriole Ave. . . . . Pg.29 . . . . K-L5
Osceola Ave. . . . Pg.29 . . . . K-L5
Ottawa Ave. . . . Pg.29 . . . . K-L5
Oval . . . . Pg.29 . . . . . . H4
Overhill Ave. . . . Pg.29 . . . . K-L5
Ozanam Ave. . . . Pg.29 . . . . K-L5
Ozark Ave. . . . . Pg.29 . . . . . . L5
Park Ave. . . . . . Pg.28 . . . . . . K4
Park Ln. . . . . . . Pg.24 . . . . . . K4
Peter Ter. . . . . . Pg.29 . . . . . . K4
Prospect Ave. . . Pg.29 . . . . . . L5
Prospect Ct. . . . Pg.29 . . . . . . L5
Prospect St. . . . Pg.29 . . . . . . K5
Riverside Dr. . . . Pg.29 . . . . . . M7
Riverview Ave. . . Pg.29 . . . . . . M7
Robin Rd. . . . . . Pg.29 . . . . . . H4
Root Ct. . . . . . . Pg.29 . . . . . . L4
Root St. . . . . . . Pg.29 . . . . . . K4
Rosemary Dr. . . Pg.29 . . . . . . M7
Roseview Ct. . . . Pg.29 . . . . . . K4
School St. . . . . . Pg.29 . . . . . . M6
Seward St. . . . . Pg.29 . . . . . . L6
Shermer Rd. . . . Pg.29 . . . . J-L6
Sibley St. . . . . . Pg.29 . . . M5-6
Stolting Rd. . . . . Pg.29 . . . . . . K4
Sunset Rd. . . . . Pg.28 . . . . . . L4
Waukegan Rd. . . Pg.29 . . . . . . L6
Wendy Way . . . . Pg.29 . . . . . . H4
Willow . . . . Pg.29 . . . . . . J5
Wisner St. . . . . . Pg.29 . . . . K-L5
Woodland Dr. . . . Pg.29 . . . . . . J5
Wright Ter. . . . . Pg.29 . . . . . . K6

CEMETERIES
Beth Jacobs Cem. . . . .
. . . . Pg.29 . . . . . . K6
Mary Hill Cem. . . Pg.29 . . . . . . K5
St. Adalberts Cem. . . . .
. . . . Pg.29 . . . . . . N6

GOLF COURSES
Chick Evans G.C. . . . .
. . . . Pg.30 . . . . . . J8
Tam-O-Shanter G.C. . . . .
. . . . Pg.29 . . . . . . L7

PARKS
Ballard Park . . . Pg.25 . . . . . . J4
Chesterfield Gardens Playground
. . . . K5
Greenleaf Park . Pg.25 . . . . . . K6
Grennan Hts. Park . . . .
. . . . Pg.29 . . . . . . L6
Jonquil Terr. Pk. Pg.25 . . . . . . L5
Jozwiak Park . . . Pg.29 . . . . . . M6
Kathy-Western Park . . . .
. . . . Pg.24 . . . . . . J4
Notre Dame Pk. Pg.25 . . . . . . K5
Oakton Manor Park . . . .
. . . . Pg.25 . . . . . . L5
Point Park . . . . Pg.25 . . . . . . K6

SCHOOLS
Culver Elem. Sch. . . . .
. . . . Pg.29 . . . . . . L7
Futabakai Japanese Sch. . . . . .
. . . . Pg.25 . . . . . . L4
Gemini Jr. H.S. . Pg.28 . . . . . . K4
Mark Twain Sch. Pg.28 . . . . . . J3
Nelson Sch. . . . Pg.29 . . . . . . K5
Niles Coll. / Loyola Univ. . . . . .
. . . . Pg.29 . . . . . . M6
Niles Elem. Sch. S. . . . .
. . . . Pg.29 . . . . . . M6
Notre Dame H.S. Pg.29 . . . . . . K5
Our Lady Sch. . . Pg.28 . . . . . . L4
St. Issac Joques Sch. . . . .
. . . . Pg.25 . . . . . . J5
St. John Luth. Sch. . . . .
. . . . Pg.29 . . . . . . M6
St. John Sch. . . Pg.29 . . . . . . K6
St. Mary of the Woods Sch. . . .
. . . . Pg.30 . . . . . . M8
St. Matthew Luth. Sch. . . . . . .
. . . . Pg.29 . . . . . . J4
Wildwood Sch. . Pg.30 . . . . . . M8

SHOPPING CENTERS
Dempster Plaza S.C. . . . .
. . . . Pg.28 . . . . . . K4

Four Flags S.C. Pg.29 . . . . . . J4
Golf Mill S.C. . . Pg.29 . . . . . . J4
Golf-Milwaukee Plaza . . . .
. . . . Pg.24 . . . . . . H4
Mill-Brook S.C. . Pg.29 . . . . . . H5
Oak Mill Mall . . Pg.29 . . . . . . L5
Village Crossing S.C. . . . .
. . . . Pg.30 . . . . . . M8

MISCELLANEOUS
Civic Center Plaza . . . .
. . . . Pg.25 . . . . . . L6
Fire Departments . . . .
. . . . Pg.24,29 . . K4,M7
Library . . . . Pg.25 . . . . . . L6
Police Dept. . . . Pg.29 . . . . . . M6
Post Office . . . . Pg.25 . . . . . . L6

NILES TOWNSHIP
Pages 25,26

FOREST PRESERVES
Harms Woods H8
Linne Woods J7-8
Miami Woods L7
St. Pauls Woods K7
Wayside Woods K7

NORTHBROOK
Pages 21,22

STREETS
Academy Dr. A3
Acorn Ln. B3
Adelaide Dr. B4
Adirondack Dr. B3
Alice Rd. A3
Alleghany B3
Allen Dr. E4
Ancient Tree B2-3
Angle Ave. B5
Anjou Dr. A2
Antelope Sprs. Rd. B3
Anthony Trail A3
Antique Ln. A6
Apple Tree Ct. B4
Apple Tree Ln. B3-4
Applewood Ln. A1
Arbeleda Ln. E4
Arbor Ln. C2
Arnold Ln. A3
Arrowwood Dr. A1
Asbury Rd. C4
Ash Ln. B4
Aspen Rd. C3
Astor Pl. C7
Auburn Ln. D3
Bach B4
Banyan Dr. A2
Bar Harbor Terr. B3
Barberry C3
Barnsley Pl. B7
Basswood Dr. A1
Bayberry Dr. A2
Beaver Ave. B7
Beckwith Ct. C3
Bellevue Pl. C4
Berglund Pl. B6
Bernay Dr. A2
Big Oak B5
Birch Rd. C3
Bittersweet Dr. E. B5
Bittersweet Dr. S. B5
Bittersweet Dr. W. B5
Blackthorn B4
Blue Hill B3
Bob-O-Link Ln. C4
Bordeaux Dr. A2
Braeside Ln. C6
Breesway Ln. D4
Brentwood Rd. C4
Brian Dr. A3
Briarwood Ln. B4
Bridge Ln. S. D4
Bridlewood Ln. C6
Bridlewood Rd. C6
Brighton Ct. C3
Brindle Ct. B3
Bristol Ct. B1
Brittany Ct. A2
Brittany Rd. A2
Brookside Ln. A4
Buckland Ln. A4
Buckthorne Cir. A1
Burgundy Ln. D4
Burmuda Dunes Pl. B2
Butternut Ln. B-D4
Buttonwood Dr. B6
Cambridge Dr. D3
Campden Ln. C3
Candlewood Hill Rd. B3
Canterbury Dr. D3
Cargill Dr. A3
Caribou Crossing A1
Carlson Dr. D5
Carlyle Ct. A2
Carol Ct. C5
Carriage Ln. A6
Carter Ct. C7
Caryn Ter. B6
Castilian Cir. D-E4
Catherine B4
Cayuga Dr. B3
Cedar Ln. B4
Center Ave. B4

Chadworth Ct. A4
Chapel Ct. B5
Chapel Dr. B5
Charlemagne Dr. A2
Charles Dr. B2
Charlwood B2
Chartries C3
Chesapeake Ln. B4
Chestnut B4
Chipiti Dr. C7
Christiana Ln. C3
Church St. B,C5
Clover Ct. C3
Clover Rd. C3
Coachmaker Dr. A6
Cobblestone B2
Cobblestone Ct. A6
Cobblewood Dr. D4
Colonade Dr. B6
Colony Ct. C4
Commercial Ave. A2
Concord Ct. B3
Cornflower Tr. D2
Cotswolds Ln. A4
Cotswolds Way A4
Country Ln. C6
Coventry Ln. B3
Crabtree Ln. B3
Crestwood Dr. B4
Crimson Ct. B3
Cuyler Ave. C7
Cypress Ln. C3
Dalton Pl. B7
Dana Ct. B1
Daniel Ct. C1
Daryl Ln. B5
Dauphine A2
Debra Ln. E4
Deer Trail A1
Deer Trail Ct. A1
Dehne Rd. C4
Dell Rd. B7
Dennis Dr. A7
Devonshire Dr. B1
Division St. B4
Donegal Ln. C3
Donovan Glen Ct. D3
Doolittle Dr. A3
Doriann Dr. B5
Dorset Dr. B2
Downing St. B7
Driftwood Ln. C7
Dundee Rd. B2-5
Dunsten Cir. A3
Eastwind Ct. B2
Eastwood Ln. B6
Echo Ln. B3
Edgewood Ln. B6
El Cid Ln. C3
Elder Ct. D4
Ellendale Dr. A3
Elm Ave. C5
Elm Ridge Dr. C4
Era Dr. A2
Eric Ln. C7
Eskin Dr. A17
Eskine Dr. B2
Essex Dr. A1
Estate Ct. A1
Euclid Ave. A6,B7
Evert Ct. D4
Fair Ln. A4
Fairford Ln. A4
Fairview Ln. A6
Fairway A6
Farmington Rd. D3
Farnsworth Ln. C4
Fern Ave. B5
Ferndale B5
Fieldwood Dr. A1
Floral Dr. D3
Forest Ln. B5
Forest View Dr. A1
Forestway Dr. C7
Four Winds Ln. A1
Fox Run Dr. A6
Foxglove Rd. D4
Galway Ct. B3
Glenbrook Dr. B3
Glendale Ave. D4
Glenoak Ave. B6
Grace Rd. B5
Grand D5
Grant Rd. B,C6
Greenacre Dr. B4
Greenbriar Ln. B4
Greenview Rd. D4
Greenway B2
Greenwood Rd. A4,E4
Gregg Rd. B7
Hampton Ln. B3
Harbinger Falls B2
Harbor Ln. B2
Harborside A2
Harris Dr. B7
Hawthorne Lane A4,B4
Hazelwood Dr. B4
Heather Ct. C3
Heather Ln. C3
Helen Dr. A3
Hemlock Knoll Terr. C3
Hemlock Ln. C3
Henrici Dr. A7
Heritage Dr. B2
Hickory Ln. B6
Hidden Bay B2

Hidden Wells B2
High Point B3
Highland Dr. D3
Hill B4
Hill Rd. A7
Hillcrest Ln. B4
Hillside Dr. B5,6
Holly B6
Holste Rd. E5
Honeysuckle Dr. A1
Horizon Ln. B4
Huckleberry B4
Huehl Rd. C3
Huntington Ln. C3
Illinois Rd. C4-5
Indian Wells Ln. B2
Iris Ct. C3
Island Point B2
Ivy Ln. C3
Janke Dr. D5
Jeffrey Ct. B5
Jeffrey Ct., N. B5
Jeffrey Ct., S. B5
Jeffrey Ct., W. B5
Jeffrey Ln. B5
Juli-Lyn Cir. C1
Juli-Lyn Ln. C1
Juniper Ln. A4
Kayjay Dr. D3
Keyston Rd. B5
Keystone B5
Keystone Cir. B5
Kiest Ave. B5
Killarney Ln. A3
Kingsport Ct. B3
Kingston Rd. D3
Koehling Rd. A6
Koepke Rd. A4
L. Placid B3
Laburnum Dr. A2
Lagoon View Dr. B2
Lake Knoll Dr. C2
Lake Knoll Rd. D2
Lake-Cook Rd. B2
Lakeside C3
Landwehr Rd. A-D3
Lane Winchester A3
Larabee Ln. B6
Larkdale Rd. C4
Laurel Rd. B5
Lavigne Ln. C6
Lawrence Ln. B6
Lee Rd. A-B6
Lilac Ln. D3
Lincoln B5
Lincoln Dr. A7
Lindberg Ln. A4
Linden Ave. A7
Linden Rd. B5
Lindenwood Ln. A1
Lisa Ct. D4
Little Moose Ln. C3
Longaker Rd. B7
Longmeadow Dr. D3-4
Longmeadow Rd. A6
Longvalley Dr. B2
Longview Rd. C2
Lorette Ln. C3
Lori-Lyn Ln. C1
MacArthur Blvd. A3
Mallard Dr. D4
Manor Dr. A7
Maple Ave. C4-5
Maple Hill Rd. A7
Marcee Ln. B5
Marden Ct. B3
Margo Ln. C4
Maria Ave. A3
Marshall Rd. B7
Mayapple A4
Mayapple Ct. A4
Meadow Rd. B5
Medford Cir. B2
Melvin Dr. A3
Micheline A1
Midfield Ln. C7
Midway Rd. B7
Mill Rd. B2
Miller Rd. C3
Milton Ave. A7
Milton Dr. A7
Mission Hills Ln. C2
Mission Hills Rd. W. C2
Moon Hill Rd. B3
Mountain Dr. B3
Mt. Vernon Ter. B4
Muirwood B4
Mulberry Ln. C4
Newport Rd. D4
Normandy Ln. A2
North Corner B2
North Ln. C7
Northbrook Ave. B7
Northmoor Ct. B4
Northwood A7
Norway Pine Ln. D3
Oak Ave. C4-5
Oak Knoll Ct. A1
Oak Knoll Ter. A1
Oak Leaf Ter. B5
Old Mill Cir. D3
Old Mill Rd. D3
Old Post Rd. B5
Old Willow Rd. E5
Orchard C5
Otis Pl. B7
Oxford Ln. C3

Palm Canyon Dr. B2
Palm Ln. C3
Park Way B7
Partridge Ln. B4
Pawtucket B3
Peach Tree Ln. B4
Pebble Beach Rd. B2
Pebblebrook Rd. C5
Penfold Pl. C4
Pfingsten Rd. A3
Pheasant Creek Dr. B3
Phillips Ave. B7
Phyllis Dr. A1
Phyllis Rd. C3
Picardy Dr. A1
Pinto Ln. A1
Pleasant St. C2
Plum Is. Dr. B2
Plymouth Ln. C4
Pondside Dr. C3
Pony Ln. B1
Poplar Ct. A5
Portsmouth Ct. B5
Post Rd. D2
Powderhorn Dr. C4
Prairie C2
Prestbury Ct. A4
Prestwick Ln. C2
Prince St. C4
Private Rd. A3
Quail Ln. C4
Queens Way D4
Radcliffe Dr. B3
Raintree Ln. D4
Raleigh Ct. B6-7
Raymond Dr. D5
Red Coach Ln. A6
Red Haw Rd. B6
Redwood Ln. A4
Regent Dr. B2
Rennes Ct. A2
Revere Dr. A6
Ridge Dr. A4
Ridge Rd. B6
Ridgeland Ln. B4
Ridgewood Dr. B2
Ring Rd. A5
River Falls Dr. C2-3
Riviera Dr. B2
Robincrest Dr. C3
Rosemary Rd. A6
Rosewood Ct. B7
Royal Dr. C3
Rudolph Dr. A6
Russett Ct. B2
Russett Ln. B2
Rutgers Ln. B1
Salceda Dr. A2
Sanders Rd. C2
Saranac Ln. A3
School Dr. D4
Scotch Pine Ln. D3
Scott Rd. C5
Seton Rd. A5
Seville Circle C5
Shagbark Ln. B5
Shannon Ct. B3
Shannon Rd. B3-4
Shawnee Trail C4
Shermer Rd. D5
Silverpine Dr. C3
Skokie Rd. A6
Sleepy Hollow C3
Smith Rd. C3
Snowbird Ln. C3
Somerset Ln. C4
Sorrel Dr. C1
South Ln. C7
Southgate Dr. C4
Southwind Dr. B2
Springhill Dr. B4
Spruce St. C5
Spyglass Ln. A7
St. Stephens Green B4
Stanley St. C7
Stone Creek B2
Stonebridge Ln. A4
Stonegate B3
Stowe Ct. A4
Stratford Pl. B2
Suffield Terr. B2
Sugar Pine Ln. C7
Summer Field Rd. C7
Summerton Pl. C4
Sunburst Ln. B2
Sunnyside Circle C4
Sunset Ct. C3
Sunset Ridge Rd. B,C7
Sunset Tr. D2
Surrey Ln. B6
Sussex Dr. B3
Sutton Dr. B3
Sycamore Ln. C5
Tamarind Ln. A2
Techny Rd. C2-5
Terri-Lyn Ct. C1
Terri-Lyn Rd. C1
The Mews A3
The Strand A4
Thornapple Ln. B6
Thornwood Ln. A6,B5
Timber Ln. B5
Torrey Pines Pkwy. B2
Toulon Dr. A2
Touraine Ter. A1
Trail B2

Trailwood Ct. A1
Trailwood Ln. A1
Tri-State Tollway B1
Tyron Woods B2
Valencia Dr. D4
Valley Rd. D3
Vermont Ave. A6
Versailles Dr. A2
Vicki Ln. D3
Violet Ln. C3
Virginia Ln. D4
Vista Ct. D4
Voltz Ct. C3
Voltz Rd. C6-7
Wainwright A3
Walnut Ln. B4
Walters Ave. B2-6
Wateredge Ct. A6
Wateredge Ln. A6
Waukegan Rd. B5
Weller Ln. C3
Wellington Rd. A5
Wendy Dr. B6
Wessling Dr. B2
Westcott Rd. C4
Western Ave. C2-4
Westwood Ct. B4
Whirlaway Dr. D2
Whisperwoods Dr. D3
White Dr. B3
White Hall Dr. B5
White Oak Dr. D2
White Pine Dr. D3
Whitefield Rd. B7
Wildwood Ln. B6
Williamsburg Dr. A6
Willow Ln. B6
Willow Rd. D3
Wilshire Ln. A3
Windrush Ln. B4
Windsor Lane D4
Wintercress Cir. D4
Wood Dr. D4
Woodbine Ln. B4
Woodhead Dr. A2
Woodhill Dr. B5
Woodland Dr. D3-4
Woodlark Dr. C6
Woodlawn Rd. C4
Woodmere Ct. D3
Woodmere Dr. D3
York Ct. B6-7
Yorkshire Ln. B1
1st St. B5
2nd St. D4

CEMETERIES
Northfield Cem. A2
Sacred Heart Cem. A6
St. Mary's Cem. C6
St. Peter's Cem. E5
Union Cem. B3

GOLF COURSES
Anetsberger G.C. C5
Green Acres C.C. A6
Mission Hills G.C. C2
Sportsman C.C. B2
Sunset Ridge C.C. C7

PARKS
Colonades Woods B6
Crestwood Park B5
Greenfield Park A3
Meadow Hill Park C5
Northbrook Park B5
Wescott Park C4
West Park C3
Williamsburg Park A6
Wood Oak Green Park. B1

SCHOOLS
Glenbrook North H.S. D5
Green Briar Sch. B4
Grove Sch. B3
Hickory Point Sch. A2
Maple Sch. C3
Meadow Brook Sch. B5
Northbrook Jr. H.S. C5
Oaklane Sch. B6
Shabonee Jr. H.S. B3
Solomon Schecter Sch. A6
St. Norberts Sch. B5
Stanley Field Jr. H.S. D3
Westcott Sch. C4
Westmoor Sch. B4
Wood Oaks Jr. H.S. B1

SHOPPING CENTERS
Dunnbrook S.C. A3
Meadow Shopping Plaza B5
Northbrook Court A5
Northbrook Shopping Plaza B5
Sanders Court S.C. B1
Village S.C. B5
White Plains S.C. B3

MISCELLANEOUS
Fire Station B6
Leisure Center C2
Library B4
Police / Fire Department C3
Post Office B4
Sports Complex C3
St. Mary's Mission House. C6
Swedish Covenant Village. . . . D4

Village Hall B5
YMCA C3

NORTHFIELD

Pages 22,23

STREETS

Abbott Ct. E8
Alice Pl. E8
Arbor Ln. E8
Ash D8
Avon Ave. E8
Birchwood Ln.(Pvt.) E7
Bosworth Ln. E8
Bracken Ln. D7
Briar Ln. D7
Bridlegate Ln. C7
Bridlewood Ln. E8
Bristol Ave. E8
Bristol Rd. E8
Bristol St. E8
Brookhill Dr. C7
Burr Oak Rd. E7
Camden Ln. D8
Canterbury Ln. (E&W) E7
Central Rd. E8
Chapel Hill Ln. D7
Cherry D8
Churchill St. E8
Clover Ln. E7
Coach Rd. E7
Country Ln. D7
Coventry Rd. E7
Crooked Creek E8
Dickens Rd. E8
Dickens St. E8
Dorina Dr. E7
Drury Ln.(Pvt.) E7-8
Earl Dr. D8
Eaton St. E8
Eddy Ln. E7
Edens Expwy. C8
Edens Ln. D8
Edgewood Ln. D7
Elder St. E9
Elm D8
Enid Ln. E7
Graemere St. E7
Grove Dr. E8
Happ Rd. D-E8
Harding Rd. E8
Hawthorne D8
Heather Terr. D8
Hedge Row E7
Hickory D8
Hickory Ln. E7
Holder Ln. E8
Ingram St. E7
Jeffery St. E7
Lagoon Dr. E9
Lagoon Ln. E9
Latrobe Ave. E9
Laurie Ln. D8
Linder Ave. E9
Lockwood Ave. E9
Maple St. E8
Martin Ln. D7
Meadowview Ln. E9
Meadowview Rd. F9
Meadowwood Ln. E8
Middlefork Rd. D7
Mt. Pleasant St. E9
Norfolk Rd. D8
Northfield Rd. E8
Northgate Ave. C7
Oak D8
Oak Tree Ln. D7
Old Farm Ln. D7
Old Willow Rd. D7
Orchard Ln. E8
Pebble Fork E7
Pine St. D8
Pleasant View Ln. D8
Red Barn Ln. E7
Riverside Dr. E8
Robinhood Ln. E8
Somerset Ln. D7
South Ridge Ter. C7
Southgate Ave. C7
Southgate Terr. C7
Steeplechase Ln. D7
Steifel Ln. E8
Sterling Ln. D8
Stockton Dr. E8
Suffolk Rd. D8
Sunset Rd. E9
Sunset Ridge Rd. E7
Thackery Ln. E7
Thornwood Ln. D7
Tower Rd. C8
Wagner Rd. E8
Walnut E8
Westfield Ln. D7
Whittier Ln. D7
Willow Rd. E8
Willow Rd.(Old) D7
Willow Ter. E8
Willow View Terr. E8
Winfield Cir. F9
Winfield Dr. E9
Winnetka Ct. E7
Winnetka Rd. E8
Woodland Ln. (N&S) D8

PARKS

Clarkson Park E8
Northfield Park E8
Three Corners Wildlife Refuge D8
Willow Park E8

SCHOOLS

Marillac H.S. D7
Middle Fork Sch. D8
New Trier H.S. West E9
St. Phillips Sch. D8
Sunset Ridge D7

SHOPPING CENTERS

Northfield Square E8

NORTHFIELD TOWNSHIP

Pages 21-25

STREETS

Anets Dr. Pg.22 C5
Applegate Ct. Pg.25 G4
Beach Ln. Pg.21 D2
Beechnut Rd. Pg.22 A4
Birchwood Pg.22 A4
Castillian Ct. Pg.24 G3
Central Pg.21 C2
Central Rd. Pg.24 H1-2
Charlie Ct. Pg.21 D3
Chestnut Ave. Pg.25 F6
Chestnut Rd. Pg.22 A4
Constance Ln. Pg.21 A1
Cottonwood Rd. Pg.22 A5
Countryside Ln. Pg.24 G3
Culligan Pkwy. Pg.21 D2
Cumberland Ave. Pg.21 C2
Dearlove Rd. Pg.24 G3
Dundee Rd. Pg.21 B1
East Pg.21 C2
East Lake St. Pg.24 G4-5
East Valley Cir. Way Pg.22 C7
Elm Ct. Pg.22 A5
Elmdale Rd. Pg.24 F-H4
Enterprise Pg.22 F4
Evergreen Ln. Pg.21 C1
Ewen Pg.25 F4
Forest Ln. Pg.21 E2
Forest Rd. Pg.22 A5
Forestview Rd. Pg.21 A1
Garden Pg.21 C2
Glendale Pg.24 G4
Glenshire Pg.21 G4
Glenview Rd. Pg.24 G4
Glenwood Ln. Pg.25 G4
Greenleaf Pg.21 E2
Greenwood Rd. Pg.24 G4
Grove Ln. Pg.21 E2,G3-4
Halsey Pg.22 F5
Henley St. Pg.24 G4
Hickory Ct. Pg.22 A5
Highland Pg.21 C2
Highland Ct. Pg.24 G4
Hillside Rd. Pg.24 G4
Holly Pg.21 C2
Holly Ct. Pg.21 D3
Holly Ln. Pg.25 G4
Huber Ln. Pg.25 G4
Huehl Rd. Pg.21 A2
Johns Dr. Pg.22 F6
Kennicott Ln. Pg.24 F2
Knollwood Pg.24 G3-5
Koehling Rd. Pg.22 A5
Landwehr Pg.21 D-G3
Lee Rd. Pg.22 A6
Lehigh Ave. Pg.22 E5
Linden Rd. Pg.22 A5
Linneman St. Pg.24 G3-4
Long Meadow Ln. Pg.24 G3
Longmeadow Dr. Pg.24 F-G4
Longview Rd. Pg.21 C2
Maple Ave. Pg.21 C,F2
Maple Rd. Pg.22 D7
Maplewood Rd. Pg.22 A5
McCain Pg.24 F4
Meadow Pg.21 C2
Meadow Ln. Pg.24 G4
Meadowbrook Pg.22 C7
Milwaukee Ave. Pg.21 D1,F2
Nimitz Pg.22 F5
Oak Ave. Pg.21 C2
Oakwood Pg.22 A5
Old Farm Ln. Pg.22 D7
Old Hunt Rd. Pg.22 C7
Overland Pass Pg.21 E3
Palatine Rd. Pg.21 D1-2
Pamela Ln. Pg.21 A1
Peachgate Rd. Pg.25 G4
Pensive Ln. Pg.21 D2
Pfingsten Rd. Pg.24 F-G3
Phyllis Rd. Pg.21 A1
Pickwick Ave. Pg.21 F4
Pine Tree Rd. Pg.22 A5
Pleasant Pg.21 C2
Pleasant Run Pg.22 E3
Post Rd. Pg.21 D2
Prairie Pg.21 C2
Prairie Lawn Rd. Pg.25 G4
Red Oak Rd. Pg.22 A5
Revere Rd. Pg.24 G4
Richard West Dr. Pg.25 F4
Riverdale Pg.22 C7
Rolling Ridge Pg.22 D7
Rollings Ridge Pg.22 D7
Rosedale Rd. Pg.24 G3
Sable Pg.25 F4
Sanders Rd. Pg.21 C2
Shadowwood Ln. Pg.22 D7
Shermer Rd. Pg.22 D5
Shilt Pg.22 F4
Southridge Terr. Pg.22 C7
Spruce Rd. Pg.22 A5
Steeplechase Ln. Pg.22 D7
Sunset Dr. Pg.22 C7
Sunset Ln. Pg.21 A1-2
Sunset Ridge Rd. Pg.22 C7
Sunset Trail Pg.21 D2
Sunshine Ln. Pg.21 A2
Techny Rd. Pg.21 C2-5
Thornwood Pg.24 F4
Timberlane Dr. Pg.21 C1
Tri-State Tollway Pg.21 B1,E2
Valley View Pg.22 C7
Valley Way Pg.22 C7
Vogay Ln. Pg.21 E2
Walnut Cir. Pg.22 A5
Washburn Pg.24 F5
Waukegan Rd. Pg.22 A4
Wedel Ln. Pg.25 G4
West Lake Terr. Pg.24 F4
Western Pg.21 C2
Westview Dr. Pg.21 F3
Whirlaway Dr. Pg.21 D2
White Oak Dr. Pg.21 D2
Willow Rd. Pg.21 D3,6
Wilton Pg.21 E2
Winkelman Rd. Pg.21 E1
Woodridge Pg.21 E3

CEMETERIES

St. John's Cem. Pg.21 F2

FOREST PRESERVES

Allison Woods Pg.21 E1
Camp Pine Woods Pg.24 F1
Colonades Woods Pg.22 B6
Lake Avenue Woods East Pg.21 E1
Lake Avenue Woods West Pg.21 F1
Potowatomie Woods Pg.21 A1
Somme Woods Pg.22 A5
Sunset Ridge Woods Pg.22 B7

GOLF COURSES

Green Acres C.C. Pg.22 A6
Mission Hills G.C. Pg.21 C2
Sunset Ridge C.C. Pg.22 D7

PARKS

Country Lane Park Pg.24 G3-4
Countryside Park Pg.24 G3-4
Flick Park Pg.24 F-G4
Garden Park Pg.24 G4
Huber Lane Park Pg.25 G4

SCHOOLS

East Main Christian Acad. Pg.24 G3
St. Catherine Sch. Pg.24 F4
Villa Redeemer Monastery Pg.24 G3

MISCELLANEOUS

Camp Pine Pg.24 F1
Glenview N.A.S. Pg.22 F5

OAK FOREST

Pages 38,41,42

STREETS

Abbe Ct. Pg.41 M17
Adele Pg.42 N18
Adeline Pl. Pg.41 L17
Aimee Ln. Pg.41 M17
Alameda Ave. Pg.41 L16
Albert Dr. Pg.41 L17
Aldersyde Dr. Pg.41 N19
Ann Marie Dr. Pg.41 L17
Ann Marie Ln. Pg.41 M17
Arroyo Dr. Pg.41 L,M16
Avalon Pg.38 L16
Babette Ct. Pg.41 M17
Barry Ln. Pg.42 N19
Barton Ln. Pg.42 N19
Bellaire Rd. Pg.41 N19
Belle St. Pg.41 O17
Beth Ct. Pg.41 M17
Betty Ann Ln. Pg.41 L17
Blair Ln. Pg.42 N19
Boca Rio Dr. Pg.41 L16
Bonnie Tr. Pg.41 O17
Bramblewood Rd. Pg.41 M15
Brendon Ln. Pg.42 N19
Bret Dr. Pg.41 M16
Brianne Ln. Pg.41 L15
Briar Ln. Pg.41 L16
Brockton Ln. Pg.42 N19
Brookwood Dr. Pg.41 M16
Carol Belle Tr. Pg.41 M17
Carolyn Ct. Pg.38 L17
Carriage Way Pg.38 L16
Catalina Ave. Pg.41 L16
Cedar Pg.38 L15
Central Ave. Pg.38 N19
Charles Pg.41 L16
Charleston St. Pg.41 M15
Chaucer Dr. Pg.38 L16
Cherry Ln. Pg.41 L16
Chestnut Ln. Pg.38 L15
Church Pg.41 L15
Cicero Ave. Pg.41 L18
Colina Ave. Pg.41 L16
Concha Ct. Pg.41 L16
Condado Pg.38 L16
Corey Ln. Pg.41 M16
Coulter Rd. Pg.41 N18
Courtney Ln. Pg.41 M15
Craig Dr. Pg.42 N19
Creekside Dr. Pg.41 L17
Crescent Ln. Pg.38 L17
Cypress Ct. Pg.41 O18
Daniels Ln. Pg.38 K16
David Ln. Pg.41 L16
Debra Dr. Pg.41 M17
Deerpath Rd. Pg.41 N18
Dennis Ct. Pg.41 M17
Diane Ct. Pg.38 L17
Dolores St. Pg.41 M16
Dover Rd. Pg.41 L17
Duncan Rd. Pg.41 M17
Edgewood Ct. Pg.38 L16
Edward Dr. Pg.41 L16
El Morro Ln. Pg.38 L16
El Vista Ave. Pg.38 K17
Elderwood Ct. Pg.38 K16
Elizabeth Ct. Pg.41 O18
Ellen Ct. Pg.41 M17
Elm Ln. Pg.41 L16
Elmwood Rd. Pg.41 N18
Essex Rd. Pg.41 M16
Fairfax Rd. Pg.41 L17
Farmsley Ct. Pg.41 N18
Fawn Ct. Pg.41 L17
Fern Pg.38 K17
Fieldcrest Ln. Pg.42 N18
Forest Ave. Pg.41 M18
Forest Ct. Pg.41 N,O18
Forest Edge Ln. Pg.38 K17
Forest Tr. Pg.41 N17
Forest View Dr. Pg.38 L16
Gainsborough Pl. Pg.41 L17
Galetta Terr. Pg.38 K17
Geoffrey Rd. Pg.38 L17
George Dr. Pg.42 N18
Grange Ave. Pg.38 K17
Green Ln. Pg.38 L17
Greentree Rd. Pg.41 O18
Grove Ave. Pg.41 M18
Harbor Dr. Pg.38 K16
Harold St. Pg.42 N18
Hawthorne Pg.41 O17
Henry Pg.42 N18
Heron Dr. Pg.41 M16
Hickory Ln. Pg.41 L,M15
Hillside Ave. Pg.38 L16
Hillside Ct. Pg.41 L16
Independence Ave Pg.41 M17
Independence Ct. Pg.41 M17
James Dr. Pg.41 L17
Jamie Ct. Pg.41 M17
Janet Ct. Pg.41 M17
Jessica Dr. Pg.41 O17
Jill Ann Ln. Pg.41 M16
Joann Pg.41 M16
Jon Rd. Pg.41 M16
Jones Ct. Pg.38 L18
Judy Ct. Pg.41 O17
Kara Ct. Pg.41 N18
Kenton Ave. Pg.41 L18
Kilbourne Pg.42 L18,N19
Kilpatrick Ave. Pg.41 L,N18
Kimberly Ct. Pg.41 N18
Knollwood Dr. Pg.38 K16
Knox Pg.41 L18
La Grande Ave. Pg.41 M16
La Grande Ct. Pg.41 L16
La Grange Ave. Pg.41 M16
La Palm Ct. Pg.38 L17
La Palm Dr. Pg.38 L17
La Paz Ct. Pg.41 M16
La Paz Dr. Pg.41 M16
La Porte Ave. Pg.38 L18
Lacrosse Ave. Pg.38 L18
Lamon Pg.41 L,M18
Lancaster Dr. Pg.41 L17
Landings Ln. Pg.38 L16
Langley Ct. Pg.41 O18
Laramie Ave. Pg.41 M,O17
Laramie Ct. Pg.41 L17
Las Flores Ave. Pg.41 L16
Las Robles Pg.38 L16
Latrobe Ave. Pg.41 M17
Laura Ln. Pg.42 N19
Lavergne Ave. Pg.41 L,M18
Leclaire Ave. Pg.41 L,N18
Leslie Ln. Pg.41 M17
Liberty Sq. Pg.41 M16
Linden Dr. Pg.41 L16,M15
Lisa Ln. Pg.42 N18
Lockwood Ave. Pg.41 M17
Lockwood Dr. Pg.41 O17
Long Ave. Pg.41 K,M17
Lorel Ave. Pg.41 M17
Lorin Ct. Pg.38 L18
Lynne Ct Pg.38 L17
Major Ave. Pg.38 K17
Mann Pg.42 N19
Maple Ct. Pg.41 L15
Maple Dr. Pg.41 L15
Margie Ln. Pg.41 M17
Martha Ln. Pg.41 O17
Mary Ann Ct. Pg.41 M17
Massasoit Ave. Pg.38 K17
Meadowdale Dr. Pg.41 N18
Menard Ave. Pg.38 L17
Merlin Ct. Pg.38 L17
Michaele Dr. Pg.41 L17
Mission Ave. Pg.38 K17
Moorings Ln. Pg.38 L16
Natalie Dr. Pg.41 L17
New England Ave. Pg.41 M15
Newport Dr. Pg.41 N18
Oak Pg.38 M18
Oak St. Pg.41 L15
Oakland Ave. Pg.38 L16
Oakwood Pg.41 N17
Orange Ln. Pg.41 L16
Orchard Ln. Pg.41 L16
Orogrande Ct. Pg.41 L16
Orogrande St. Pg.41 L16
Oxford Dr. Pg.38 L17
Pamela Ct. Pg.41 M17
Park Ave. Pg.38 K17
Parkside Ave. Pg.38 L17
Parkwood Ct. Pg.38 L16
Peggy Ln. Pg.41 M17
Pine Ct. Pg.41 M15
Pine Dr. Pg.41 L15
Pine Rd. Pg.41 M15
Reynolds Dr. Pg.41 M16
Richard Ave. Pg.42 N18
Ridgeland Ave. Pg.38 M16
Ridgewood Dr. Pg.38 K,L16
Rio Verde Ave. Pg.38 L16
Rob Roy Ct. Pg.41 M16
Rob Roy Dr. Pg.41 L,M16
Roy St. Pg.42 N18
Sara Ann Ln. Pg.41 M16
Sayre Ave. Pg.41 M15
School Ln. Pg.38 L16
Scott Pg.42 N19
Sequoia St. Pg.38 L16
Sierra Dr. Pg.41 M16
Spruce Ln. Pg.38 L15
Stuart Ln. Pg.41 L16
Sunset Ave. Pg.38 K17
Sycamore Ln. Pg.41 O18
Temple Dr. Pg.38 K17
Terrace Dr. Pg.41 M16
Terry Ln. Pg.42 N18
Thackery St. Pg.41 O17
Timber Ct. Pg.41 N18
Tudor Rd. Pg.41 L16
Ventura Pg.38 L16
Vera Ct. Pg.41 M17
Victoria Ct. Pg.41 L16
Victoria Dr. Pg.41 L15,16
Vine St. Pg.38 L17
Vista Ct. Pg.41 M16
Wagman Pg.42 N19
Walnut Rd. Pg.41 L15
Warwick Pg.41 L17
Waverly Ave. Pg.41 M18
Westview Dr. Pg.41 L15
Willow Ln. Pg.38 L15
Willowwick Pg.42 N18
Woodland Dr. Pg.41 L17
66th Ct. Pg.38 K15
70th Ct. Pg.40 L15
148th St. Pg.38 K17
150th Pl. Pg.38 L16
150th St. Pg.38 L16,18
151st St. Pg.38 L16
152nd St. Pg.38 L17,18
153rd St. Pg.38 L15,17
154th Pl. Pg.41 L15
154th St. Pg.41 L17
155th Pl. Pg.41 L15
155th St. Pg.41 L17
156th Pl. Pg.41 M15
156th St. Pg.41 L17,M15
157th Ave. Pg.41 M15
157th Pl. Pg.41 M16
157th St. Pg.41 M15-17
158th St. Pg.41 M17
159th St. Pg.41 M15
160th St. Pg.41 M17,18
161st St. Pg.41 M17,18
162nd St. Pg.41 M18
163rd St. Pg.41 M17
165th St. Pg.42 N19
166th St. Pg.42 N19
167th St. Pg.41 N18,19
169th Pl. Pg.41 N17
169th St. Pg.41 N17
170th Pl. Pg.41 O17
170th St. Pg.41 N17

CEMETERIES

St. Gabriel Cem. Pg.41 N18

FOREST PRESERVES

Midlothian Meadows Pg.41 M19

GOLF COURSES

George Dunn G.C. Pg.41 M16

PARKS

Convent Park Pg.38 K16
Vergne Way Park Pg.41 L18

SCHOOLS

Arbor Park Sch. Pg.41 M18
Fieldcrest Sch. Pg.42 N19
Forest Ridge Sch. Pg.38 L17
Foster Sch. Pg.41 L16
Gingerwood Sch. Pg.41 N18
Jack Hills Sch. Pg.38 L16
Kerkstra Middle Sch. Pg.38 L17
Oak Forest H.S. Pg.38 L17
Orchard Hill Sch. Pg.41 N18
S.W. Case Sch. Pg.38 L16
Scarlet Oak Sch. Pg.41 M17
St. Damon Sch. Pg.41 L17
Walter Fierke Education Center Pg.41 L15

MISCELLANEOUS

City Hall Pg.41 L17
Commuter R.R. Station Pg.41 M18
Oak Forest Hosp. Pg.42 M18
Our Lady of Sorrows Convent Pg.38 K16
Post Office Pg.41 L18,M17
Public Works Pg.41 M17
Southwest Co Op Pg.38 L16
St. Mihiel Reservation Pg.41 N17

OLYMPIA FIELDS

Pages 47,48

STREETS

Achilles Ave. T20
Alexander St. T21
Apollo Cir. U21
Arcadian Ct. T20
Arcadian Dr. T20
Athens Rd. T21
Attica Rd. T20
Augusta Dr. S22
Birch Ln. T21
Bristol Ln. T21
Brookside Blvd. T20
Brookwood Dr T21
Brookwood Dr., S. T21
Byron Ct. T20
Cambridge Ln. U21
Chariot Ln. T21
Chelsea Cir. T21
Corinth Rd. T21
Country Club Dr. S21
Crawford Ave. T19
Cumberland Tr. S20
Cumnock Rd. T19
Danube Way T20
Dartmouth Ln. T21
Doria Ln. T20
Edmund M. Burke Rd. T20
Elliot Ct. T20
Evergreen Cir. U20
Exmoor Rd. T19
Fairfield Ave. T20
Glen Eagles Dr. S21
Governors Dr. S20
Governors Hwy. T20
Graymoor Ln. S22
Greenwood Center Ct. T20
Greenwood Ct. T20
Greenwood Dr. T20
Harding Ave. T21
Harding St. U21
Helenic Dr. T20
Highview Ave. T20
Hudson Tr. S20
Indiana Cir. T20
Inverness Ct. S21
Ionia Ave. T20
Ithaca Ct. T20
Ithaca Rd. T20
Joe Orr Rd. S22
Kedzie Ave. T21
Lake Dr. S21
Leland U22
Lincoln Hwy. U21
London Dr. U21
Marathon Ct. T20
Maros Ln. T21
Mellet Ct. T20
Mohawk Tr. S20
Oak Lane Dr. T20
Oakwood Dr. T21
Oakwood Terr. T21
Olympian Way T20
Orchard Dr. U21
Oregon Tr. S20
Overland Tr. S20

Paris Rd. T21
Park Dr. S20
Parthenon Ct. T20
Parthenon Way T20
Pine Ave. U20
Platte Tr. S20
Promethian Way T21
Rieger St. U22
Rockwell U21
Roslyn Rd. T19
Sante Fe Tr. S20
Scott Dr. T20,22
Sheffield Cir. T21
Sparta Ct. T21
Sparta Ln. T21
Spartan Way T20
St. Andrews Ct. S21
St. Andrews Dr. S21
Strauss Ln. T20
Tam-O-Shanter Ct. S21
Tenuta Ct. T21
Terr. No. 1 T22
Terr. No. 2 T22
Terr. No. 3 T22
Terr. No. 4 T22
Terr. No. 5 T21
Terr. No. 6 T21
Thaxed Cir. U20
Thomas St. U21
Thornwood Cir. T20
Thornwood Dr. T20
Tower Ct. T20
Trails Dr. S20
Troy Cir. T21
Vollmer Rd. S20
Warren Cir. T21
Washington Dr. U22
Waterford Ct. S21
Western Ave. T22
Wilderness Tr. S20
Wingate Rd. T,U20
Woodland Ct. T20
Woodland Dr. T20
Woodstock Rd. T20
Wysteria Dr. T22
203rd St. S20
204th St. T20
205th St. T20
206th St. T20
207th T20

FOREST PRESERVES
Elliott Woods T20

GOLF COURSES
Olympia Fields Country Club T21

PARKS
Bicentennial Park S20
Maynegaite Park U21
Means Park T21
Spirit Trail Park T21
Tolentine Park T20

SCHOOLS
Arcadia Sch. T20
Rich Twp. H.S. Central S20

MISCELLANEOUS
Olympia Fields Osteopathic Hosp. S20
Post Office S21
R.R. Station S21,U20
Tolentine Seminary & Educational Center T20
Village Hall T20

ORLAND HILLS

Page 40

STREETS
Beacon Ct. N12
Beacon Ln. N12
Birch Ct. M12
Birchwood Dr. M12
Brigitte Ct. N12
Cedarwood M12
Chadbourne Dr. N12
Christine Ct. N12
Christopher Ave. O12
Dwight Ct. N12
Elm Pl. M12
Fox Ct. M12
Haven Ave. M.N12
Haven Ct. N12
Hawthorn M11
Herbert Ct. N12
Hickory Ct. O12
Hickory Dr. O12
Highview Ave. N12
Hilltop Ave. N12
Hobart Ave. N11
Hobart Ct. N12
Hunter Ct. M11
Hunter Dr. M11
Kelly Ct. N12
Leslie Dr. N12
Lindsey St. N11
Maplewood Ct. N12
Marilyn Ct. N12
Marshfield N12
Meadowview N12
Morgan Ln. N12
O'Brien Dr. N12
Parkview Pl. M12
Pepperwood Dr. N12
Prairie Pl. M12
Pristine Pl. M12
Quail Ct. M12
Rachel Ct. N12
Redwood Ct. O12
Ridge Ln. M12
Robin Ct. N12
Sharon Ct. N12
Vicky Ln. N12
Westwood Ct. O12
Westwood Dr. O12
Willow Terr. M12
88th Ave. O12
88th Ct. N,O12
89th Ave. N,O12
89th Ct. N12
90th Ave. N12
90th Ct. M12
91st Ave. M,N12
92nd Ave. M,N12
92nd Pl. M12
93rd Ave. N12
94th Ave. P11
159th Pl. M12
159th St. M14
160th Pl. M12
161st St. M12
162nd St. M12
163rd St. N12
164th St. N12
167th Pl. N12
167th St. N12
169th Pl. N12
169th St. N12
170th Pl. O12
170th St. O12
171st St. O13

PARKS
Kelly Park N12

SCHOOLS
Christian Hills Sch. M12

SHOPPING CENTERS
Orland Towne Center M11

MISCELLANEOUS
Fire Station N11
Village Hall N11

ORLAND PARK

Pages 36,37,39-41

STREETS
Abby Ln. Pg.40 L12
Acacia Dr. Pg.40 M13
Adria Ct. Pg.37 I12
Alabama Ct. Pg.39 P9
Alaska Ct. Pg.39 P9
Aldwych Dr. Pg.37 J13
Alice Ln. Pg.39 P10
Alpine Dr. Pg.36 L8
Alveston St. Pg.36 K10
Andrea Ct. Pg.39 P10
Andrea Dr. Pg.39 P9
Anne Ct. Pg.40 L13
Anne Dr. Pg.40 L13
Apache Ln. Pg.37 J13
Apache Pl. Pg.37 J13
Arapaho Pl. Pg.37 J13
Arbor Dr. Pg.36 L8
Arbor Ridge Dr. Pg.36 K9
Aris Ct. Pg.40 M12
Arizona Ct. Pg.39 P9
Arkansas Ct. Pg.39 P9
Arrowhead Ct. Pg.37 J13
Arrowhead Ln. Pg.37 J13
Arthur Ct. Pg.39 P10
Arthur Dr. Pg.39 P10
Ascot Ct. Pg.40 M12
Ash St. Pg.37 J12,K11
Ashford Ct. Pg.36 K9
Ashley Ct. Pg.37 K13
Ashley Dr. Pg.37 K13
Ashton Ln. Pg.36 J9
Ashwood Ln. Pg.39 O8
Aspen St. Pg.37 K12
Aster Ln. Pg.40 L14
Atwood Ct. Pg.36 J9
Aubrieta Ct. Pg.40 L14
Aubrieta Ln. Pg.40 L14
Auburn Ct. Pg.37 J11
Avalon Ct. Pg.37 J13
Avenida Del Este Pg.36 L11
Avenida Del Notre Pg.36 L11
Baltusrol Dr. Pg.40 M12
Barleycorn Ct. Pg.40 L12
Bayberry Ct. Pg.40 L13
Bayhill Ct. Pg.40 M13
Beacon Ave. Pg.36 K11
Bear Island Ave. Pg.39 N9
Bedford Ln. Pg.40 L11
Beech St. Pg.37 K12
Begonia Ct. Pg.40 L14
Berkhansted Ct. Pg.37 J13
Beverly Ln. Pg.37 I12
Bilboa Pg.37 K12
Billinary Ct. Pg.39 P8
Biltmore Dr. Pg.40 M13
Binford Dr. Pg.37 J13
Birch St. Pg.37 K11
Birchbark Ct. Pg.37 J13
Black Friars Rd. Pg.40 L12
Blackhawk Ln. Pg.37 J13
Blarney Ct. Pg.39 N9
Blue Heron Dr. Pg.39 O9
Bob-O-Link Ct. Pg.37 K11
Bob-O-Link Rd. Pg.37 L13
Bonbury Ln. Pg.37 J13
Boyne Ct. Pg.39 O8
Bradford Ln. Pg.40 M12
Bradley Ct. Pg.39 P9
Braeburn Ln. Pg.40 M13
Bramlett Ct. Pg.36 L8
Brassie Ct. Pg.40 M13
Brassie Dr. Pg.40 L,M13
Brentwood Ave. Pg.37 K12
Briarwood Ln. Pg.37 I12
Brighton Ct. Pg.37 K13
Brigitte Terr. Pg.36 J9
Bromley St. Pg.37 K13
Brook Ave. Pg.36 K11
Brook Crossing Ct. Pg.39 O9
Brook Crossing Dr. Pg.39 O9
Brook Crossing Ln. Pg.39 O9
Brook Hill Ct. Pg.39 P8
Brook Hill Dr. Pg.39 O8
Brookdale Ct. Pg.39 O8
Brookgate Dr. Pg.39 O8
Brookshire Dr. Pg.39 O8
Brookside Ct. Pg.40 M12
Brookwood Ct. Pg.39 O8
Brookwood Dr. Pg.39 O8
Brushwood Ln. Pg.39 O8
Bunker Dr. Pg.40 L13
Butler Ct. Pg.40 M12
Butterfield Ln. Pg.37 I12
Byron Dr. Pg.40 N12
Caddy Ct. Pg.37 K12
California Ct. Pg.39 P9
Calypso Ln. Pg.40 M14
Cambridge Dr. Pg.37 K14
Camden Dr. Pg.37 J13
Camelia Ln. Pg.40 L13
Cameron Pkwy. Pg.39 P9
Canterbury Ln. Pg.40 M13
Cardinal Dr. Pg.39 N10
Carlisle Ln. Pg.37 K12
Carnousite Dr. Pg.40 M12
Carol Ct. Pg.37 L13
Carolina Ln. Pg.37 J11
Carolyn Ct. Pg.39 L9
Cascade Ln. Pg.37 K13
Cashew Dr. Pg.40 M14
Castlebar Ln. Pg.37 L12
Catalina Ct. Pg.40 M14
Catalina Dr. Pg.40 L14
Catherine Ct. Pg.36 J11
Catherine Dr. Pg.37 J11
Cedar St. Pg.37 J13
Centennial Ct. Pg.39 M11
Centennial Dr. Pg.39 M11
Chadbourn Dr. Pg.40 N12
Chapel Hill Rd. Pg.40 M13
Charleston Dr. Pg.37 J11
Chateau Ct. Pg.37 K13
Chaucer Dr. Pg.39 N9
Chelsea Dr. Pg.37 J13
Cherry Hills Ct. Pg.40 L12
Cherry Ln. Pg.40 J13
Cherrywood Ct. Pg.40 L13
Chertsey Ct. Pg.37 K13
Chesterfield Ln. Pg.40 M12
Chestnut Dr. Pg.40 M14
Cheswick Dr. Pg.37 J13
Christine Ct. Pg.37 K11
Churchill Dr. Pg.39 N9
Churchview Dr. Pg.40 N11
Clairmont Ct. Pg.37 L12
Clearview Ct. Pg.37 J12
Clearview Dr. Pg.37 J12
Cliffside Ln. Pg.40 M12
Coghill Ln. Pg.37 J12
Coleman Dr. Pg.39 N9
Colette Ct. Pg.40 L13
Colorado Ct. Pg.39 P9
Compubill Dr. Pg.37 K11
Concord Dr. Pg.37 J12
Connecticut Ct. Pg.39 P9
Constitution Ct. Pg.39 M11
Constitution Dr. Pg.39 M11
Cordoba Ct. Pg.36 L11
Cottonwood Ct. Pg.36 L8
Country Club Ln. Pg.37 K13
Country Ct. Pg.40 M12
Coventry Ct. Pg.37 L12
Cranna Ct. Pg.39 P8
Creek Crossing Dr. Pg.36 J,K8
Creekside Dr. Pg.36 J8
Cressmoor Ct. Pg.40 M13
Crestview Ct. Pg.39 P8
Crestview Dr. Pg.39 P8
Crestwood Dr. Pg.36 J8
Cristina Ave. Pg.37 J,K13
Croydon Ln. Pg.40 L12
Crystal Ridge Ct. Pg.36 K9
Crystal Springs Ct. Pg.36 L9
Crystal Springs Ln. Pg.36 L9
Crystal Tree Dr. Pg.36 K10
Cypress Ct. Pg.37 L12
Dakota Ln. Pg.37 J13
Danbury Ln. Pg.40 L12
Danford Ln. Pg.40 M12
Davids Ln. Pg.39 P10
Deer Run Dr. Pg.39 O9
Deerfield Ct. Pg.40 M13
Deerpath Dr. Pg.37 J13
Delaware Ct. Pg.39 P9
Devonshire Ln. Pg.40 L12
Dewberry Ln. Pg.40 L12
Dexter Ct. Pg.37 K12
Dogwood Ave. Pg.37 L12
Doorstep Ln. Pg.37 K13
Doral Ln. Pg.37 J12
Dublin St. Pg.37 L12
Eagle Ridge Dr. Pg.39 P9
Edgewood Dr. Pg.40 L13
Eileen Ct. Pg.37 J11
El Cameno Ct. Pg.36 L11
El Cameno Ln. Pg.36 L11
El Cameno Terr. Pg.36 L11
El Camino Re'Al Pg.36 L11
Elderberry Ln. Pg.39 N10
Elizabeth Ave. Pg.37 J13
Elm St. Pg.37 J12
Erin Ln. Pg.40 M12
Esther Dr. Pg.39 P9
Evergreen Dr. Pg.37 L14
Eynsford Dr. Pg.37 K13
Fairmont Ct. Pg.37 L12
Fairway Dr. Pg.37 K11
Fane Ct. Pg.39 O8
Farm Hill Dr. Pg.40 M12
Fawn Ct. Pg.37 I12
Feather Ct. Pg.37 I12
Fernwood Ct. Pg.37 L12
Fir St. Pg.37 J12
Firestone Dr. Pg.37 I12
First Ave. Pg.36 K11
Flamingo Cir. Pg.40 L13
Flint Ln. Pg.37 I12
Florida Ct. Pg.39 P9
Forestview Dr. Pg.37 L13
Foxbend Ct. Pg.40 M13
Frances Ln. Pg.40 M12
Franchesca Ct. Pg.36 L10
Franklin Ct. Pg.37 K12
Fun Dr. Pg.39 M10
Gardenview Ct. Pg.40 M14
Georgia Ct. Pg.39 P9
Ginger Creek Ln. Pg.36 L8
Glen Eagle Ct. Pg.37 J12
Glen Lake Dr. Pg.39 M9
Glen Oak Rd. Pg.40 M13
Glenlake Dr. Pg.39 M9
Glenwoody Ct. Pg.37 J12
Golf Rd. Pg.36 K10
Golfview Dr. Pg.37 K12
Grace Rd. Pg.37 L12
Grandview Dr. Pg.36 L8
Grange Dr. Pg.39 O8
Grants Tr. Pg.39 N9
Great Egret Dr. Pg.39 O9
Green St. Pg.37 K11
Green View Rd. Pg.36 K9
Greencastle Ln. Pg.37 K12
Greenfield Ct. Pg.39 O8
Greenfield Dr. Pg.39 O8
Greenland Ave. Pg.36 K10
Greenvalley Dr. Pg.36 J8
Hale Dr. Pg.36 L10
Halesia Ct. Pg.40 L14
Harbor Town Dr. Pg.40 M14
Harlem Ave. Pg.40 M15
Hartwood Ct. Pg.37 J11
Harvest Crossing Pg.36 L8
Harvest Hill Ct. Pg.39 O8
Harvest Hill Dr. Pg.39 O8
Hawaii Ct. Pg.39 P9
Hawthorne Dr. Pg.36 L10
Hazel Ct. Pg.36 L10
Heather Ct. Pg.40 L14
Helen Ln. Pg.40 M12
Hemlock Dr. Pg.40 J12,L14
Hempstead Dr. Pg.37 K13
Henry St. Pg.37 L12
Hiawatha Tr. Pg.36 L10
Hibiscus Dr. Pg.36 L10
Hickory Dr. Pg.36 L10
Hidden Brook Ct. Pg.39 O8
Highbush Rd. Pg.39 N10
Highgate Ct. Pg.37 K13
Highland Ave. Pg.36 K10
Highwood Ct. Pg.39 O8
Highwood Dr. Pg.39 O8
Hill Creek Ct. Pg.39 O9
Hilltop Ct. Pg.36 L10
Hilltop Dr. Pg.36 L10
Holiday Ct. Pg.36 L10
Hollow Tree Ct. Pg.36 K9
Hollow Tree Rd. Pg.36 K9
Holly Ct. Pg.36 K10
Hollyhock Ct. Pg.37 L,M14
Hollywood Dr. Pg.40 L13
Hopkins Ct. Pg.36 L10
Hughuelet Pl. Pg.37 L12
Huntington Ct. Pg.36 L10
Huntington Pl. Pg.36 L10
Hyacinth Dr. Pg.36 L10
Idaho Ct. Pg.39 P9
Idlewild Dr. Pg.37 J12
Illinois Ct. Pg.39 P10
Indiana Ct. Pg.39 P9
Innishmor Ct. Pg.39 P8
Innsbrook Dr. Pg.40 M13
Inverness Dr. Pg.37 J12
Iowa Ct. Pg.39 P9
Irving Ave. Pg.36 K10
Ishnala Dr. Pg.37 J14
Jean Creek Dr. Pg.37 I12
Jefferson Ave. Pg.36 K11
Jillian Rd. Pg.39 L9
John Charles Dr. Pg.39 P10
John Humphrey Dr. Pg.37 K11
John Mayher Sr. Dr. Pg.39 P8
Juniper Ct. Pg.37 L12
Kansas Ct. Pg.39 P9
Kathy Ct. Pg.37 K12,13
Katy Ln. Pg.37 K13
Kemper Dr. Pg.40 M12
Kendall Ln. Pg.40 M12
Kennedy Ct. Pg.37 L12
Kensington Way Pg.37 L12
Kentucky Ct. Pg.39 P9
Kingsport Rd. Pg.39 N9
Kingston Ln. Pg.37 L12
Kingswood Dr. Pg.36 J8
Knightsbridge Ln. Pg.37 L12
Knollwood Ln. Pg.40 M13
Kristen Ln. Pg.37 K13
Kristo Ln. Pg.37 K13
Kropp Ct. Pg.39 O9
La Grange Rd. (96th Ave.) Pg.36 L11
La Reina Ct. Pg.36 L11
La Reina Re'Al Pg.36 L11
Lago Ln. Pg.37 J13
Laguna Ln. Pg.37 J13
Lake Brook Dr. Pg.39 O9
Lake Hills Ct. Pg.40 M13
Lake Lawn Ln. Pg.36 L9
Lake Ridge Rd. Pg.36 K10
Lakebrook Ct. Pg.39 O9
Lakebrook Dr. Pg.39 O9
Lakefield Dr. Pg.39 O9
Lakeside Dr. Pg.39 M9
Lakeview Dr. Pg.37 K,L12
Lancaster Ln. Pg.40 L12
Landings Dr. Pg.40 N9
Larkspur Ln. Pg.40 L,M14
Laurel Dr. Pg.40 M12
Laurel Hill Dr. Pg.39 N9
Lawrence Ct. Pg.37 L12
Lee St. Pg.39 N9
Legend Ln. Pg.37 J13
Lexington Cir. Pg.37 L12
Lilac Ct. Pg.37 L14
Lincoln Ct. Pg.37 L12
Lincolnshire Dr. Pg.37 J12
Lindsay Dr. Pg.37 J13
Lisa Ct. Pg.40 L12
Lismore Ct. Pg.36 K10
Lissfannon Ct. Pg.39 O8
Lori Ln. Pg.37 J12
Louisiana Ct. Pg.39 P9
Lunar Pg.37 K12
Lynn Dr. Pg.39 P9
Magnolia Ct. Pg.37 K12
Mallard Cir. Pg.40 L13
Mallow Ridge Dr. Pg.39 N9
Maple Pg.37 K12
Maple Ave. Pg.37 J12
Margarita Ave. Pg.37 K13
Marilyn Ct. Pg.36 J9
Marilyn Terr. Pg.36 J9
Marley Brook Ct. Pg.39 P9
Mary Dr. Pg.37 J11
Mason Ln. Pg.37 K12
Maue Dr. Pg.39 P9
Maycliff Dr. Pg.37 K12
Mayfair Ln. Pg.37 L11
Mayo Dr. Pg.37 L12
Meade St. Pg.39 N9
Meadow Ln. Pg.37 L13
Meadowbrook Ln. Pg.40 L13
Meadowview Ct. Pg.37 K13
Medinah Dr. Pg.37 I12
Mellisa Dr. Pg.39 P10
Merion Dr. Pg.40 L12
Michael Dr. Pg.37 K12
Michelle Ct. Pg.37 K13
Michigan Ct. Pg.39 P9
Millbank Dr. Pg.37 J12
Mimosa Dr. Pg.40 L14
Mission Hill Ct. Pg.37 J12
Misty Hill Rd. Pg.36 M10
Mohawk Ln. Pg.37 J13
Montana Ct. Pg.39 P10
Montgomery Dr. Pg.37 K12
Morningside Ct. Pg.36 K10
Morningside Rd. Pg.36 K10
Nancy Ln. Pg.40 L12
Narcissus Ct. Pg.40 L14
Narcissus Ln. Pg.40 L,M14
Nebraska Ct. Pg.39 P10
Nelson Ln. Pg.37 J14
Nevada Ct. Pg.39 P9
Newgate Ct. Pg.37 J12
Nicole Ct. Pg.37 L12
Nottingham Ct. Pg.39 N9
O'Brien Dr. Pg.40 N12
Oak Pl. Pg.36 K11
Oak St. Pg.36 K11
Oakdale Ct. Pg.37 K12
Oakland Dr. Pg.36 K9
Oakley Ave. Pg.36 K10
Ohio Ct. Pg.39 P10
Oklahoma Ct. Pg.39 P10
Old Orchard Ct. Pg.40 M13
Old Tamarack Ln. Pg.36 K10
Orange Ave. Pg.39 N9
Orange Blossom Dr. Pg.40 M14
Orchid Ct. Pg.40 L14
Orchid Ln. Pg.40 L14
Oregon Ln. Pg.39 P10
Orenia Ct. Pg.37 J13
Oriole Ct. Pg.40 L12
Orland Brook Dr. Pg.40 M12
Orland Ct. Pg.37 L12
Orland Square Dr. Pg.37 L11
Owen Dr. Pg.39 P10
Oxford Dr. Pg.40 L11
Palm Ct. Pg.40 L13,14
Palm Dr. Pg.40 L14
Palos Spring Dr. Pg.37 I12
Paradise Ln. Pg.37 L14
Park Hill Dr. Pg.40 M12
Park Ln. Pg.36 K10
Parkview Dr. Pg.37 J12
Patricia Ln. Pg.40 M12
Patrick Ct. Pg.40 L12
Patty Ln. Pg.37 I12
Pawnee Rd. Pg.37 J13
Peachtree Dr. Pg.40 M12
Pebble Beach Ln. Pg.37 J12
Pebble Beach St. Pg.37 J12
Pembridge Rd. Pg.40 L12
Pembrooke Ln. Pg.37 L11
Persimmon Ct. Pg.36 J9
Persimmon Dr. Pg.36 J9
Petunia Ct. Pg.40 L14
Pine Grove Ct. Pg.36 L8
Pine St. Pg.37 J12
Pine Tree Rd. Pg.36 K9
Plum Tree Dr. Pg.40 M13
Pluskota Dr. Pg.37 J13
Ponderosa Ct. Pg.37 L13,14
Poplar Creek Ct. Pg.36 L9
Poplar Creek Ln. Pg.36 L9
Poplar Ct. Pg.37 K12
Poplar Rd. Pg.37 K12
Prestwick Ln. Pg.37 I12
Primrose Ct. Pg.40 L14
Primrose Ln. Pg.40 L14
Putney Pl. Pg.37 J13
Quail Hollow Dr. Pg.37 L13
Raccoon Curve Pg.39 O9
Raintree Dr. Pg.40 L12
Raintree Ln. Pg.40 L12
Raneys Ln. Pg.36 K10
Ravinia Ave. Pg.36 L,M11
Ravinia Ct. Pg.36 K11
Ravinia Ln. Pg.36 K11
Ravinia Pl. Pg.39 L11
Red Oak Ln. Pg.37 J13
Redondo Ln. Pg.37 J13
Redwood Dr. Pg.37 J12
Regent Dr. Pg.40 L12
Revell Ct. Pg.37 K13
Ridge Ave. Pg.36 K10
Riviera Pkwy. Pg.37 K12
Rob Roy Dr. Pg.40 M13
Robin Ln. Pg.39 N10,12
Robinhood Dr. Pg.40 N12
Royal Creek Ln. Pg.39 L9
Royal Foxhunt Rd. Pg.40 L12
Royal Georgian Rd. Pg.40 L12
Royal Glen Ct. Pg.39 M9
Royal Glen Rd. Pg.39 M9
Rutherford Ln. Pg.37 L12
Ryehill Ct. Pg.39 N9
Salvatori Ct. Pg.37 J13
Sandlewood Dr. Pg.37 J13
Sandpiper Ct. Pg.37 L12
Saratoga Dr. Pg.39 N9
Sawgrass Ct. Pg.40 L13
Seapines Rd. Pg.40 M13
Second Ave. Pg.36 K11
Selva Ln. Pg.37 J13
Seminole Ct. Pg.40 M13
Sequoia Ct. Pg.37 L13,14
Seton Pl. Pg.40 N11
Shade Cove Ct. Pg.36 L8
Shady Ln. Pg.39 L11
Shagbark Ct. Pg.37 L12
Shaker Ct. Pg.36 L8
Shannon Ct. Pg.39 O8
Sheffield Ln. Pg.40 L12
Sheri Ct. Pg.37 J12
Sheri Ln. Pg.37 J12
Sherwood Dr. Pg.40 N12
Shipston St. Pg.37 J13
Silo Ridge Dr. Pg.36 L8
Silo Ridge Rd., E. Pg.36 L8
Silo Ridge Rd., N. Pg.36 K8
Silo Ridge Rd., S. Pg.36 L8
Silo Ridge Rd., W. Pg.36 L8
Silverdale Dr. Pg.37 L12
Singletree Rd. Pg.36 L8

ORLAND PARK

Sioux Rd. . . Pg.37 . . . . . J13
Somerglen Ct. . Pg.39 . . . . M9
Somerset Ct. . Pg.37 . . . . L12
Song Bird Cir. . Pg.39 . . . . O10
Southwest Hwy. . Pg.36 . . . . P7
Spicebush Ln. . Pg.39 . . . . N10
Spring Creek Ln. . . . .
. . . . Pg.36 . . . . . L9
Springbrook Ct. . Pg.39 . . . . O8
Springview Ln. . Pg.36 . . . . J8
Spruce Dr. . . . Pg.37 . . . . J12
Spyglass Cir. . Pg.40 . . . . L13
St. Andrews Ct. . Pg.40 . . . . L13
St. Andrews Dr. . Pg.40 . . . . L13
St. James Ct. . Pg.40 . . . . L13
St. James Dr. . Pg.40 . . . . L13
St. James Dr. . Pg.40 . . . . L13
St. Mary's Cir. . Pg.37 . . . . J12
Stonegate Ln. . Pg.36 . . . . J8
Stonehenge Dr. . Pg.37 . . . . J13
Stonewall Ct. . Pg.37 . . . . J13
Stradford Ln. . Pg.40 . . . . L11
Strawberry Ln. . Pg.37 . . . . I12
Streamstown Ct. . . . .
. . . . Pg.37 . . . . K13
Suffield Ct. . . Pg.37 . . . . J13
Sunflower Ct. . Pg.40 . . . . L14
Sunny Ln. . . . Pg.37 . . . . J12
Sunrise Ln. . . Pg.40 . . . . M12
Sunset Ridge Ct. . . . .
. . . . Pg.40 . . . . L13
Sunset Ridge Dr. . . . .
. . . . Pg.40 . . . . L13
Sunshine Ct. . Pg.37 . . . . J12
Sunshine Ln. . Pg.37 . . . . I12
Susan Ln. . . . Pg.39 . . . . N9
Sussex Dr. . . Pg.40 . . . . N12
Sutton Ct. . . . Pg.37 . . . . J12
Swallow Ln. . . Pg.39 . . . . O10
Swilly Ct. . . . Pg.39 . . . . O8
Sycamore Ct. . Pg.37 . . . . L14
Sycamore Dr. . Pg.37 . . . . L14
Tally Ho Ln. . . Pg.40 . . . . L12
Tamarack Ln. . Pg.37 . . . . J12
Tea Brook Dr. . Pg.40 . . . . L13
Teakwood Ct. . Pg.37 . . . . L13
Tennessee Ln. . Pg.39 . . . . P10
Terry Ct. . . . . Pg.37 . . . . J12
Terry Dr. . . . . Pg.37 . . . . J12
Teton Ct. . . . . Pg.37 . . . . J13
Teton Rd. . . . Pg.39 . . . . J13
Texas Ct. . . . Pg.39 . . . . P10
Therese Ct. . . Pg.37 . . . . J11
Third Ave. . . . Pg.36 . . . . K11
Thistlewood Dr. . Pg.40 . . . . L12
Thistlewood Ln. . Pg.40 . . . . L12
Thomas Ct. . . Pg.37 . . . . J11
Thomas Dr. . . Pg.37 . . . . J11
Thorngate Ct. . Pg.40 . . . . L13
Thorngate Dr. . Pg.40 . . . . L13
Tiffany Dr. . . . Pg.40 . . . . M14
Timber Edge Ln. . . . .
. . . . Pg.36 . . . . . L8
Timber Ridge Ct. . . . .
. . . . Pg.36 . . . . . L8
Timber Trails Rd. . . . .
. . . . Pg.37 . . . . J12
Timberline Ct. . Pg.36 . . . . L10
Timothy Ct. . . Pg.37 . . . . K12
Timothy Dr. . . Pg.37 . . . . K12
Tod William Dr. . Pg.37 . . . . J12
Torrey Pines Dr. . Pg.37 . . . . M12
Tower Dr. . . . . Pg.39 . . . . N10
Trafalgar Ct. . . Pg.37 . . . . J13
Treetop Dr. . . Pg.39 . . . . L11
Trenton Dr. . . Pg.37 . . . . K12
Tulip Ct. . . . . Pg.40 . . L13,14
Union Ave. . . Pg.36 . . . . K11
Utah Ct. . . . . Pg.39 . . . . P10
Uxbridge Dr. . Pg.37 . . . . K13
Vail Ct. . . . . . Pg.36 . . . . . L8
Valentina Dr. . Pg.37 . . . . L12
Valley Brook Dr. . Pg.39 . . . . O8
Valley Ct. . . . Pg.36 . . . . . L9
Vermont Ct. . . Pg.39 . . . . P10
Victoria Pl. . . . Pg.39 . . . . N10
Villa Ct. . . . . Pg.37 . . . . J13
Violet Ct. . . . Pg.40 . . . . M14
Virginia Ct. . . Pg.37 . . . . J11
Vista Dr. . . . . Pg.37 . . . . J13
Vivian Ct. . . . Pg.39 . . . . . P9
Voss Dr. . . . . Pg.37 . . . . J12
Walnut St. . . . Pg.37 . . . . J12
Warbler Ln. . . Pg.39 . . . . O9
Waterford Ln. . Pg.40 . . . . M11
Wedgewood Glen Dr. . . . . . .
. . . . Pg.37 . . . . K13
West Ave. . . . Pg.36 . . L10,M11
Westbrook Dr. . Pg.39 . . . . O8
Westbrook Ct. . Pg.37 . . . . J12
Westgate Ct. . Pg.37 . . . . I12
Westminster Dr. Pg.40 . . . . M12
Westwood Dr. . Pg.36 . . K,L10
Wexford Ln. . . Pg.37 . . . . L12
Wheeler Dr. . . Pg.40 . . . . L14
Wherry Ln. . . Pg.40 . . . . L11
Whispering Hill Dr. . . . .
. . . . Pg.39 . . . . . P8
Whitehall Ct. . . Pg.37 . . . . J12
Wild Rose Ln. . Pg.40 . . . . M14
Wildflower Rd. . Pg.36 . . . . K10
Will-Cook Rd. . Pg.36 . . . . . L8
William Ct. . . . Pg.36 . . . . J11
William Dr. . . . Pg.37 . . . . J11
Willow Creek Ln. . . . .
. . . . Pg.36 . . . . . L8
Willow St. . . . Pg.37 . . . . K12

Willowood Ct. . Pg.40 . . . . L14
Wilshire Dr. . . Pg.39 . . . . L11
Winding Creek Ct. . . . .
. . . . Pg.39 . . . . . O8
Winding Creek Dr. . . . .
. . . . Pg.39 . . . . . O8
Windmill Rd. . . Pg.36 . . . . . L8
Windmill Turn . Pg.36 . . . . . L8
Windsor Dr. . . Pg.37 . . . . L12
Winterberry Ln. Pg.39 . . . . N10
Wittington Ct. . Pg.37 . . . . K13
Woburn Ct. . . Pg.36 . . . . K10
Wolf Rd. . . . . Pg.39 . . . . N9
Wood Duck Ln. Pg.39 . . . . O10
Woodbury Ct. . Pg.37 . . . . J11
Wooded Path Ln. . . . .
. . . . Pg.37 . . . . K13
Woodland Ave. Pg.36 . . . . K10
Woodmar Dr. . Pg.40 . . . . L13
Woodridge Ln. Pg.37 . . . . J12
Woodruff Dr. . . Pg.40 . . . . M13
Woodward Ct. . Pg.37 . . . . J13
Wyoming Ct. . Pg.39 . . . . P10
Yearling Crossing . . . .
. . . . Pg.39 . . . . . O9
Yorkshire Ln. . Pg.40 . . . . L14
Yorktown Ct. . . Pg.37 . . . . J12
Yorktown Dr. . Pg.37 . . . . K12
70th Ct. . . . . Pg.41 . . M14,15
71st Ct. . . . . Pg.41 . . M14,15
72nd Ct. . . . . Pg.40 . . . . L14
73rd Ave. . . . Pg.40 . . . . L14
73rd Ct. . . . . Pg.40 . . . . L14
74th Ave. . . . Pg.40 . . . . L14
74th Ct. . . . . Pg.40 . . . . L14
75th Ct. . . . . Pg.40 . . . . L14
76th Ave. . . . Pg.40 . . . . M14
77th Ave. . . . Pg.40 . . . . M14
78th Ave. . . . Pg.40 . . . . M14
80th Ave. . . . Pg.37 . J12,K,L13
81st Ave. . . . Pg.37 . . K,L13
81st Ct. . . . . Pg.37 . . K,L13
82nd Ave. . . . Pg.37 . . L,M13
82nd Pl. . . . . Pg.37 . . . . J13
83rd Ave. . . . Pg.37 . . . . J13
83rd Ct. . . . . Pg.37 . . . . J13
84th Ave. . . . Pg.37 . . J,K13
85th Ave. . . . Pg.37 . . J,K13
86th Ave. . . . Pg.37 . . J,M12
87th Ave. . . . Pg.37 . . . K12
88th Ave. . . . Pg.37,40 . . . . .
. . . . I,K,M12
89th Ave. . . . Pg.40 . . K,N12
89th Ct. . . . . Pg.40 . . . . N12
90th Ave. . . . Pg.40 . . . . N12
91st Ave. . . . Pg.37 . . . . J12
92nd Ave. . . . Pg.37 . . . . J11
92nd Ct. . . . . Pg.37 . . . . K11
93rd Pl. . . . . Pg.37 . . . . K11
94th Ave. . . . Pg.37,40 . K,M11
96th Ave. . . . Pg.39 . . . . M11
104th Ave. . . Pg.39 . . . . P10
105th Ct. . . . Pg.39 . . . . N10
106th Ct. . . . Pg.39 . . . . N10
107th Ave. . . Pg.39 . . . . N10
108th Ave. . . Pg.36 . . . . L,P9
110th Ave., S. . Pg.39 . . . . O9
118th Ave. . . Pg.39 . . . . N8
135th St. . . . Pg.37 . . . . J11
136th St. . . . Pg.37 . . . . J12
137th St. . . . Pg.37 . . J12,13
138th St. . . . Pg.37 . . . . J13
138th St. . . . Pg.37 . . J11,13
139th St. . . . Pg.37 . . J11-13
140th St. . . . Pg.37 . . J11-13
141st Pl. . . . Pg.37 . . . . J11
141st St. . . . Pg.37 . . . . J13
142nd St. . . . Pg.36 . . . . K11
143rd Pl. . . . Pg.37 . . K12,13
143rd St. . . . Pg.37 . . . . K8
144th St. . . . Pg.37 . . K11,12
144th St. . . . Pg.36 . . K10,12
145th Pl. . . . Pg.36 . . K11-13
145th St. . . . Pg.36 . . K10-12
145th St. . . . Pg.36 . . . . K10
146th St. . . . Pg.36 . . . . K10
147th St. . . . Pg.36 . . K10,12
148th St. . . . Pg.36 . . . . K11
149th St. . . . Pg.36 . . . . K11
151st St. . . . Pg.36 . . . L8,11
152nd Pl. . . . Pg.37 . . . . L14
152nd St. . . . Pg.37 . L12,14,15
153rd Ct. . . . Pg.37 . . . . L14
153rd Pl. . . . Pg.37,40 . . . L14
154th St. . . . Pg.40 . L9,11,14
154th St. . . . Pg.40 . . . . L14
154th St. . . . Pg.39,40 . . . . .

155th St. . . . Pg.40 . . . . L14
156th St. . . . Pg.40 . . . . M15
157th Pl. . . . Pg.40 . . . . M14
157th St. . . . Pg.40 . . . . M13
158th St. . . . Pg.40 . . . . M14
158th St. . . . Pg.40 . . . . M15
159th St. . . . Pg.39,40 . . . M9
160th St. . . . Pg.39 . . . . M9
161st Pl. . . . Pg.39 . . . . M12
161st St. . . . Pg.39 . . . . M9
162nd St. . . . Pg.40 . . . . M12
163rd Pl. . . . Pg.39 . . . . N9
163rd St. . . . Pg.39 . . N10,12
164th Pl. . . . Pg.39 . . . . N12
164th St. . . . Pg.39 . . . . N12
165th Pl. . . . Pg.40 . . . . N12
165th St. . . . Pg.39 . . . . N9
166th Pl. . . . Pg.39 . . . . N12
166th St. . . . Pg.40 . . N11,12

167th Pl. . . . Pg.40 . . . . N12
167th Pl. . . . Pg.39 . . . . . N9
167th St. . . . Pg.39,40 . . . N10
168th St. . . . Pg.40 . . . . N12
168th St. . . . Pg.39 . . . . . N9
169th St. . . . Pg.40 . . . . N12
170th Pl. . . . Pg.40 . . . . O12
170th St. . . . Pg.40 . . . . O12
171st St. . . . Pg.40 . . . . O12
175th St. . . . Pg.39 . . . . O9
179th St. . . . Pg.39 . . . . P8
183rd St. . . . Pg.39 . . . . P9

CEMETERIES
Orland Park Memorial Cem . . .
. . . . Pg.36 . . . . L10
Palos Oak Hill Cem. . . . .
. . . . Pg.37 . . . . I12
St. Michael Cem.Pg.37 . . . . K13

GOLF COURSES
Crystal Tree G.C. (Private) . . .
. . . . Pg.36 . . . . L10
Silver Lake G.C. Pg.37 . . . . K13

PARKS
Bill Young Park Pg.36 . . . . L10
Brentwood Pk. . Pg.37 . . . . J12
Brookhill Park . Pg.39 . . . . O8
Brown Park . . Pg.36 . . . . K10
Cachey Park . . Pg.40 . . . . L13
Cameno Re Al Park . . . .
. . . . Pg.36 . . . . L11
Carlo Vista Park Pg.37 . . . . J13
Colonial Park . Pg.37 . . . . J11
Community Park . . . .
. . . . Pg.39 . . . . M10
Country Club Estates Park . . .
. . . . Pg.37 . . . . K13
Dogwood Park Pg.37 . . . . L12
Doogan Park . Pg.36 . . . . K10
Eagle Ridge Park . . . .
. . . . Pg.39 . . . . . P9
Helen Lane Park Pg.40 . . . . M12
Heritage Pk. . . Pg.37 . . . . J12
Ishnala Woods Pg.37 . . . . J13
Ishnala Woods Park . . . .
. . . . Pg.37 . . . . J13
Liberty Park . . Pg.37 . . . . L12
Park Hill . . . . Pg.40 . . . . M12
Schussler Park Pg.37 . . . . K12
Spring Creek Estates Park . . .
. . . . Pg.39 . . . . . L9
Sunny Pine Park Pg.37 . . . . J12
Tree Top Park . Pg.39 . . . . L11
Veteran's Park . Pg.40 . . . . L14

SCHOOLS
Centennial Sch. Pg.38 . . . . K8
Fernway Elem. Sch. . . . .
. . . . Pg.40 . . . . N12
High Point Sch. Pg.36 . . . . K11
Jerling Jr. H.S. . Pg.37 . . . . L12
Kruse School . Pg.40 . . . . L14
Liberty Sch. . . Pg.37 . . . . L12
Orland Center Sch. . . . .
. . . . Pg.37 . . . . L11
Orland Park Jr. H.S. . . . .
. . . . Pg.36 . . . . L11
Orland Park Sch. . . . .
. . . . Pg.36 . . . . K10
Prairie Sch. . . Pg.37 . . . . J13
School Admin. Center . . . . . .
. . . . Pg.36 . . . . K10
St. Michael Sch. Pg.36 . . . . K10

SHOPPING CENTERS
Lakeview Plaza Pg.39 . . . . M11
Orland Greens . Pg.36 . . . . L11
Orland Park Place Mall . . . . .
. . . . Pg.36 . . . . L11
Orland Park Shopping Plaza . .
. . . . Pg.36 . . . . K11
Orland Square Shopping Center
. . . . Pg.37 . . . . L11
Park Hill Plaza . Pg.40 . . . . M12
Seville Plaza . . Pg.40 . . . . M13
Waterfall Plaza . Pg.40 . . . . M12

MISCELLANEOUS
Antique Row . . Pg.36 . . . . K11
Appleknoll Industrial Park . . . .
. . . . Pg.39 . . . . N10
Civic Center . . Pg.36 . . . . K11
Glen Oak Industrial Park . . . .
. . . . Pg.39 . . . . . N9
Humphrey Woods Hiking Trail . .
. . . . Pg.36 . . . . K11
Jacob Hastert Cabin . . . .
. . . . Pg.36 . . . . K11
John Humphrey Complex . . . .
. . . . Pg.36 . . . . K11
Orland Township Office . . . . .
. . . . Pg.37 . . . . L11
Palos Primary Care Medical Center
. . . . Pg.39 . . . . L10
Police Dept. . . Pg.36 . . . . K11
Post Office . . . Pg.37 . . . . K11
R.T.A. Metra Commuter Station. .
. . . . Pg.37 . . . . L10
Recreation Dept. . . . .
. . . . Pg.36 . . . . K11
Robert Davidson Center . . . .
. . . . Pg.36 . . . . K11
Village Center . Pg.39 . . . . N9
Village Hall . . . Pg.37 . . . . K11

ORLAND TOWNSHIP

Pages 36,37,39,40
STREETS
Arapaho Pl. . . Pg.37 . . . . J13
Aster Ln. . . . . Pg.40 . . . . L14
Bernard Dr. . . Pg.39 . . . . Q2
Birchcreek Ct. . Pg.36 . . . . . L8
Brighton Ct. . . Pg.37 . . . . L13
Brookview Ln. . Pg.36 . . . . K8
California Tr. . . Pg.36 . . . . J8
Camelot Ct. . . Pg.36 . . . . J8
Camelot Ln. . . Pg.36 . . . . J8
Chisholm Tr. . . Pg.36 . . . . J8
Circle Dr. . . . . Pg.37 . . . . J11
Creek Crossing Ct. . . . .
. . . . Pg.36 . . . . K8
Creekview Ln. . Pg.36 . . . . K8
Creekwood Dr. Pg.36 . . . . K8
Crescent Dr. . . Pg.37 . . . . J11
Dusty Tr. . . . . Pg.36 . . . . J8
Fenview Ct. . . Pg.36 . . . . K8
Fernwood Ct. . Pg.36 . . . . K8
Forestview Dr. . Pg.37 . . . . L13
Fun Dr. . . . . . Pg.39 . . . M10
Glenview Dr. . Pg.36 . . . . K8
Grant Ave. . . . Pg.39 . . . . N9
Hancock St. . . Pg.39 . . . . N9
Harlem Ave. . . Pg.40 . . . . J13
Howe Dr. . . . . Pg.37 . . . . J11
Juanita Dr. . . Pg.39 . . . . M8
Kaup Ln. . . . . Pg.36 . . . . J8
Kingwood Dr. . Pg.36 . . . . K11
Kristoffer Ct. . . Pg.36 . . . . J8
Kristoffer Ln. . . Pg.36 . . . . J8
Lakewood Ln. . Pg.36 . . . . K8
Lee Ave. . . . . Pg.39 . . . . N9
Logan Dr. . . . Pg.36 . . . . J8
Louetta Ln. . . Pg.40 . . . . Q13
Lynch Entrance Pg.39 . . . . M8
Maplecreek Dr. Pg.36 . . . . K8
Mark Ln. . . . . Pg.36 . . . . J8
McCabe Ct. . . Pg.36 . . . . J8
McCabe Dr. . . Pg.36 . . . . J8
Meade St. . . . Pg.39 . . . . N9
Meadow Ln. . . Pg.37 . . . . L13
Mesquite Dr. . Pg.36 . . . . K8
Middle Pinecreek Dr. . . . . . .
. . . . Pg.36 . . . . K8
Minetz Ct. . . . Pg.36 . . . . J8
N. Pinewood Ct. Pg.36 . . . . J8
N. Pinewood Dr. Pg.36 . . . . J8
Natchez Tr. . . Pg.36 . . . . J8
Oak Creek Dr. . Pg.36 . . . . . L8
Oak Hill Dr. . . Pg.39 . . . . L8
Old Post Rd. . . Pg.36 . . . . J8
Old Spanish Ct. Pg.36 . . . . N8
Old Spanish Tr. Pg.36 . . . . N8
Orange Ave. . . Pg.39 . . . . N9
Oregon Tr. . . . Pg.36 . . . . J8
Overland Tr. . . Pg.36 . . . . J8
Park Ln. . . . . Pg.37 . . . . L13
Paw Paw Ave. . Pg.39 . . . . N9
Pear Ave. . . . Pg.39 . . . . N9
Pinecreek Dr., N. Pg.36 . . . . K8
Pinecreek Dr., S. Pg.36 . . . . L8
Pineview Ct. . . Pg.36 . . . . J8
Pineview Dr. . . Pg.36 . . . . J8
Pinewood Ct. . Pg.36 . . J,K8
Pinewood Dr., N. . . . .
. . . . Pg.36 . . J,K8
Ruggles Ct. . . Pg.36 . . . . J8
Santa Fe Tr. . . Pg.36 . . . . J8
Selva Ln. . . . . Pg.37 . . . . J13
Sherman St. . . Pg.39 . . . . N9
Silver Ct. . . . . Pg.37 . . . . L13
Silver Lake Dr. . Pg.37 . . . . K13
Southwest Hwy. Pg.36 . . J11,P8
Sprucecreek Ln. Pg.36 . . . . K8
Stagecoach Rd. Pg.36 . . . . J8
Streamwood Dr. Pg.36 . . . . K8
Stuart Ave. . . Pg.39 . . . . N9
Touchstone Pl. Pg.39 . . . . N10
Valley View Ct. . Pg.36 . . . . K8
Woodale Ln. . . Pg.36 . . . . K8
Wolf Rd. . . . . Pg.36 . . . . K9
74th Ct. . . . . Pg.40 . . . . L14
80th Ave. . . . Pg.37 . J,O13
81st Ave. . . . Pg.37 . . . . L13
82nd Ave. . . . Pg.37 . . . . K13
84th Ave. . . . Pg.37 . . . . K13
92nd Ct. . . . . Pg.37 . . . . K11
94th Ave. . . . Pg.40 . . K,M11
94th Ct. . . . . Pg.40 . . . . O11
96th Ave. . . . Pg.40 . . . . O11
102nd Ave. . . Pg.39 . . . . O10
104th St. . . . Pg.39 . . . . N9
108th Ave. . . Pg.36 . . . J,N9
109th Ave. . . Pg.36 . . . . L9
110th Ave. . . Pg.39 . . . . O9
110th Ave. S. . Pg.39 . . . . O9
112th Ct. . . . Pg.36 . . . . M9
113th Ave. . . Pg.39 . . . . M9
113th Ct. . . . Pg.39 . . . . M9
114th Ct. . . . Pg.39 . . . . M8
114th St. . . . Pg.36 . . . . M8
115th Ave. . . Pg.39 . . . . M8
115th Ct. . . . Pg.39 . . . . M8
116th Ave. . . Pg.39 . . . . M8
116th St. . . . Pg.39 . . . . M8
117th Ave. . . Pg.36 . . . . M8
117th Ct. . . . Pg.39 . . . . M8
118th Ave. . . Pg.36,37,39 . N8
135th St. . . . Pg.36 . . . J8,11

136th St. . . . Pg.37 . . . . J11
139th St. . . . Pg.37 . . J8,12
143rd St. . . . Pg.36,37 . K8,12
145th Pl. . . . Pg.37 . . . . K13
145th St. . . . Pg.37 . . . . K11
151st St. . . . Pg.36,37 . L8,13
152nd St. . . . Pg.36 . . . . L9
153rd St. . . . Pg.40 . . . . L9
155th St. . . . Pg.39 . . . . L8
156th St. . . . Pg.39 . . . . M8
157th St. . . . Pg.39 . M8,13
158th St. . . . Pg.39 . . . . M8
159th St. . . . Pg.39,40 . . . M9
167th Pl. . . . Pg.39 . . . . N8
167th St. . . . Pg.39,40 . . . N8
169th St. . . . Pg.39 . . . . N10
171st St. . . . Pg.39 . . O9,10
172nd St. . . . Pg.39 . . . . O9
173rd St. . . . Pg.39 . . . . O9
175th St. . . . Pg.39,40 . O9,10
179th St. . . . Pg.39,40 . . . P8
183rd St. . . . Pg.39,40 . . . P11

FOREST PRESERVES
Orland Grove Forest Preserve . . .
. . . . Pg.36 . . . . J9

GOLF COURSES
Silver Lake Golf Club . . . .
. . . . Pg.37 . . . . K13

SCHOOLS
Doctor Sch. . . Pg.39 . . . . M9

SHOPPING CENTERS
Pinewood Plaza Pg.36 . . . . K8
Promenade Plaza . . . .
. . . . Pg.36 . . . . K9

PALATINE

Pages 7,8
STREETS
Abbey Hill Ln. D6
Aldridge Ave. C6
Alex A5
Allison Dr. C9
Almond Ct. B8-9
Anderson St. D6
Apple Tree Dr. A7
Arbor Ct. A4
Arbor Ln. A4
Arlene Ave. C9
Arrowhead Dr. B8
Ash St. C6
Ashland Ave. D5
Auburn Woods Ct. B6
Auburn Woods Dr. B6
Aurelia Ct. B6
Austin Ln. D5
Avondale Dr., W. A7
Babcock Dr. C8
Baldwin Ln. A9
Baldwin Rd. B6-9
Balsam Ln. A8
Bank Ct. B7
Barrington Woods Rd. A8
Baronet Ln. D9
Baybrook Dr. D6
Bedford Dr. W. D5
Bel Aire Terr. B8
Belle Ave. C9
Bennett Ave. D6
Benton St. D7
Big Oaks Rd. B6
Birchwood Ave. D6
Bishop Ct. D5
Bissell Dr. D6
Boardwalk Ct. D6
Boardwalk Dr. D6
Bombay Way C6
Bon Aire Dr. B8
Borders Dr. D5
Bothwell St. C7
Boynton Dr. C8
Bradley Ct. D6
Brandon Ct.(Pvt.) B7
Brighton D5
Bristol Ct. D5
Broadmoor Ave. A6
Brockway St. C7
Bryant Ave. C8
Burno Dr. D6
Cady Dr. C8
California St. D7
Cambridge Dr. N. B9
Cardinal Ct. A9
Cardinal Dr. N. A9
Carlton Ave. B6
Carmel Dr. C8
Carnageway Ln. A9
Carol Ct. A9
Carolyn Dr. C6
Carpenter Dr. B7-9
Carriage Way Ct. D6
Carriageway Ln. D6
Carter St. B9
Castle Ct. E. B9
Cavalry Ct. D7
Cedar Ave. D6
Cedar St. D6
Cedarwood Ct. A7
Center Rd. A7
Center Rd. W. A8
Charlotte St. C7
Charter Hall Dr. B6

Chatham Dr. D5
Cherrywood Dr. A6
Cheryl Ln. D6
Chesapeake Ct. B9
Chesapeake Ln. B9
Chestnut St. B6
Chewink St. B7
Church C8
Churchill Dr. B9
Citadel Ct. D9
Clark Dr. C8
Clearwater Ln. A5
Clinton Ct. D5
Club House Dr. C8
Coach Rd. A9
Cobblestone Ct. B6
Colfax St. C8
Comfort St. B7
Concord Way E6
Consumers Ave. D9
Cooper Dr. B8
Cornell Ave. B6
Cottonwood B9
Countryside Dr. B5
Cove Dr., N. B5
Creekside Dr. D8
Creekwood Dr. A8
Crescent Ct. C6
Crestview Dr. B7
Crimson Ln. A9
Crooked Willow Ln. D5
Cunningham Dr. A7,8
Daniels Rd. C6,D7
Dartmoor Ave. A6
David Dr. C9
Dean Dr. C8
Deer Run Dr. A6
Denton Ave. A6
Doral Ct. C9
Dorothy Dr. C9
Dorset Ave. D5
Dresden Ave. A6
Driftwood Ave. A6
Drovers Ln. C5
Eagle St. B7
Earls Ct. A5
Easy St. B7
Eaton Ct. D5
Echo Ln. D6
Edgewater Ct. A5
Edgeware Ln. A5
Eisenhower Ave. B8
Eliabeth Ct. C9
Elizabeth Ave. C9
Elm Ct. D6
Elm St. C6
Elmwood Ave. A,C8
Eric Dr. B6
Ethans Glen Dr. A5
Euclid Ave. E5
Everett Dr. B9
Evergreen Dr. D6
Exner Ct. D6
Fairfield Ct. A6
Fairway Ct. B7
Fairway Dr. B7
Falkirk Pl. E8
Falmore Dr. E5
Farm Gate Ln. A7
First Bank Dr. C7
Flake Dr. C8
Forest Ave. C8
Forest Ct. C8
Forest Knoll Dr. A9
Forest View Ct. A5
Fosket Dr. C8
Fremont St. C7
Frontage Rd. B9
Garden Ave. A7
Gatewood Ave. A6
Geri Ave. B6
Geri Ct. B6
Gilbert Ave. B7,D6
Gilbert Rd. D6
Glade Ave. D7
Glencoe Rd. C6
Glencoe St. C8
Glenn Dr. B8
Glenwood St. C7
Gloria Dr. C9
Golf Course Dr. B6
Golfview Terr. B7
Greeley St. C7
Greenwood Ave. C8
Greenwood Dr. B8
Grissom Dr. B8
Gull Ct. D5
Haddington Ln. D6
Hale St. C7
Hamilton Dr. B6
Hamilton Ln. B6
Hampton Ct. P5
Hampton Ln. C5
Harmstead Ct. C5
Harrison Ave. C5
Hart St. C6
Harvard Ct. D5
Harvard Dr. D5
Hawk St. B7
Heatherlea Dr. A,B7
Hedgewood Dr. B8
Helen Rd. C6-7
Heron Dr. B7
Hickory Ln. C6
Hicks Pl. C8
Hicks Rd. B7

PALATINE (continued)

Hidden Brook Tr. E5
Hill Ave. B5
Hillcrest Rd. A7
Home Ave. A7
Hunting Ct. D5
Hunting Dr. D5
Illinois Ave. D6
Imperial Ct. D7
Jane Addams Dr. B8
Jennifer Ln. B6
Jewel Ct. D9
Joan Dr. C9
Johnson St. C6-7
Jonathan D. B9
Joyce Ave. C9
Juniper Dr. A8
Karen Ln. B6
Kathleen Dr. D6
Kelly Ann Dr. D6
Kenilworth Ave. C5-9
Kenilworth Rd. C8
Kensington Ct. D5
Kerry Ct. D6
Kerwood St. C7
Kimball Ave. D6
King Arthur A7
King Charles Ct. A7
King Edward Ct. A7
King George Ct. A7
King Henry Ct. A7
Kitson Dr. C8
Knollwood Dr. A5
Krista Ct. C8
Krista Ln. C8
LaLonda Ave. E6
Laguna Ct. A5
Lake Dr. D8
Lake Louis Dr. B9
Lakeshore Dr. N. B6
Lakeview Ct. A5
Lakeview Dr. A5
Lanark Ln. D5
Lancelot Ln. D9
Leonard Rd. C8
Lincoln St. C7
Linden Ave. C8
Linden St. C8
Long Valley A9
Longview Dr. D6
Lynn Dr. B6
Lytle Dr. B8
MacArthur Dr. B8
Malibou Ln. B8
Mallard Ct. D5
Mallard Dr. D5
Maple St. C6
Marion St. C8
Marsha Dr. B7
Marshall Ct. A9
Mart Ct. B6
Meadow Lake Dr E. . . . A8,9
Meadow Ln. B8
Medford Dr. D6
Merrill Ave. C6
Michelle Dr. C9
Michigan Ave. D6
Middleton Ave. D5
Middleton Ct. D5
Mill Valley Rd. B8
Minafred Dr. C8
Minnesota Ave. B6
Monterey Rd. B8
Morris Dr. B8
Mozart St. C7
Mulligan Ct. B6
Newkirk Ln. N. B9
Nightingale Ct. E5
Norman Dr. C9
North Ct. B7
Northumberland Pass . . . A8
Northwest Hwy. C7
Norway A9
Oak Ridge Ct. A5
Oak St. C7
Old Bridge Rd. A7
Old Hicks Rd. A9
Olde Virginia Ct. A8
Olde Virginia Dr. E. . . . A8
Olive Ln. D9
Oxford Ct. D5
Paddock Dr. B8
Palatine Rd. C6-7
Panorama Dr. A6
Parallel St. C7
Park Ln. C8
Parkplace Dr. D6
Parkwood Dr. A6
Partridge Ct. D5
Partridge Dr. D5
Patricia Ct. C9
Patricia Ln. C9
Patten Dr. B8
Pebble Creek Rd. B8
Pebbles Dr. D5
Peder Ln. B6
Pendleton Ct. A6
Peregrine Ct. E5
Peregrine Dr. E5
Pine St. C6
Pinehill Ct. C6
Pineview Dr. D5
Pintail Ct. D5
Plate Dr. B8
Pleasant Hill Blvd. D6
Plum Grove Rd. C-D7
Plum Tree Ct. E6

Pompano Ln. B8
Ports O' Call A9
Potomac Ln. B9
Prairie Brook Dr. A9
Pratt Dr. B8
Providence Rd. B8
Public St. A7
Quail Hollow Ln. E5
Quinten St. C6
Randville Dr. A9
Raven Ct. D5
Ravine Hills Ct. E5
Reading Ct. D6
Reseda Pkwy. B7
Revere Ln. D6
Reynolds Dr. B9
Richards Dr. D5
Richmond St. C7
Ridge Tr. B7
Rimini Ct. B7
Roanoke Ct. C6
Robertson St. B7
Robinson Dr. B8
Rohlwing Rd. C8
Rose St. C6
Roselle Rd. E5
Rosewood Ct. A5
Rosiland Dr. A7
Rosita Dr. C9
Royal Ct. D7
Ruhl Rd. A7
Run Away Bay A9
Russet Way B7
Saddle Ridge Ct. E5
Salem Ct. B8
Sanborn Dr. D5
Sandpiper Ct. E5
Saratoga Dr. B8
Sayles Dr. B8
Schiller St. C7
Schirra Dr. B8
Schubert St. C7
Shady Ln. A8
Shadypine Ct. A7
Sherman St. B7
Sherwood Ct. A5
Sherwood Dr. A5
Shoreside Dr. B6
Silver Ln. A9
Skylark Ct. E5
Skylark Dr. E5
Slade St. C6-7
Slayton Dr. B8
Smith Rd. B7
Smith St. C7
Sparrow Ct. D5
Springwillow Bay C5
St. James Ct. B6
St. John's Pl. B6
Stark Dr. B8
Steeplechase Ln. B6
Stephen Dr. B6
Sterling Ave. A5
Stonebridge Ct. C8
Stonegate Ln. D6
Stuart Ln. D6
Sunset Rd. A7
Sutherland B8
Suthers Ln. A7
Tahoe Tr. B8
Tanglewood Ave. A6
Teal Ct. D5
Tern Dr. D5
Terrace Ct. D6
Thomas Ave. D9
Three Willows Ct. B8
Thurston Dr. B9
Timber Ln. A7
Timberlea A7
Topango Dr. A-B8
Tower Ct. A9
Tower Pl. B7
Trailside Ct. A6
Turtle Creek E6
Tymore E6
Valley Ln. D9
Valor Ct. D9
Ventura Dr. D6
Vermont Ave. D6
Vermont St. D6
Victoria Dr. N. B9
Virginia Dr. C9
Virginia Lake Dr. B9
Wainright Ct. A9
Walden Dr. B6
Walnut St. C6
Wanda Ln.(Pvt.) B6
Warren Ave. D9
Warwick Rd. A7
Washington Ct.(Pvt.) . . . E6
Washington St. C7
Wellington Dr. A7
Wellington Dr., N. A7
Wente B8
West Ct. B7
Westminster Dr. C6
Westmoreland Dr. A5
Whippoorwill Ln. E5
Whispering Dr. A8
Whispering Oaks Dr. . . . A9
Whitcomb Dr. B9
White Willow Bay D5
Whitehall Dr. B8
Whytecliff Rd. D5
Wilke Rd. D9
Williams Ave. D9

Williams Dr. B,C9
Willow Ct. B8
Willow Ln. D8
Willow Walk Dr. B8
Willow Wood Dr. B8
Wilmette Ave. D7
Wilmette Rd. C8
Wilshire Ct. B8
Wilson Ct. C6
Wilson St. C7
Wilton Ct. B8
Windmill Dr. C6
Winslowe Dr. A8
Winston Dr. C9
Wood St. C6
Woodbury A9
Woodland St. A7
Woodwork Ln. C6
Wren Ct. B7
Yale Ct. D5

CEMETERIES
Hillside Cem. C6
Immanuel Lutheran Cem. . . C6

GOLF COURSES
Palatine Hills G.C. & Rec. Area A6

PARKS
Ashwood Park B7
Aspen Park A8
Birchwood Park D6
Cedar Park C6
Cherrywood Park B7
Doug Lindberg Park B9
Locust Park D6
Mallard Park D5
Maple Park C9
Margreth Riemer Park . . . C6
Oakwood Park C6
Partridge Park D5
Peregrine Park E6
Sparrow Park C6
Sycamore Park B8
Tom T. Hamilton Park C6
Whippoorwill Park D6
Willow Park B8
Winston Park C9

SCHOOLS
Christ the King Sch. D7
Gray Sanborn Sch. C6
Hunting Ridge Sch. D5
Immanuel Lutheran Sch. . . . C7
Jane Addams Sch. B8
Lake Louise Sch. B9
Marion Jorden Sch. C6
Paddock Sch. C6
Palatine H.S. C8
Palatine Hills Jr. H.S. B6
Pleasant Hills Sch. D5
Samuel Kirk Sch. D7
School Dist. 211 . . . . E5
St. Therese Cath. Sch. E5
St. Thomas Cath. Sch. B8
Virginia Lake Sch. B8
William Fremd Sen. H.S. . . . C8
William Rainey Harper College E5
Winston Churchill Sch. . . . C8
Winston Park Sch. C8

SHOPPING CENTERS
Countryside Plaza B5
Eagle Plaza B7
Northwest Shopping Center . . A7
Palatine Mall Shopping Center B7
Palatine Plaza B7
Park Place Fashion Center . . A8
Prairie Brook Plaza A9
Regency Plaza A9
Village Oasis Shopping Center B6

MISCELLANEOUS
Community Center . . . C7,D6
Library B7
Police Department C7
St. Joseph's Cath. Home for the
  Elderly A7
Township Road Dist. B6

PALATINE TOWNSHIP
Pages 1-3,6-8,11,12

STREETS
Abbeywood Ct. Pg.3 . . . . A9
Abbotsford Ave. Pg.6 . . . . B2
Aldridge Ave. Pg.7 . . . . D6
Almond Ct. Pg.3 . . . . A9
Almwick Pg.6 . . . . B2
Alva St. Pg.7 . . . . A9
Amherst St. Pg.7 . . . . A7
Anna Ct. Pg.7 . . . . A6
Apple Tree Ct. Pg.7 . . . . A9
Arbor Cove Pg.7 . . . . B5
Ardmore Ave. Pg.6 . . . . C3
Arlington Heights Rd.
  Pg.3 . . . . A11
Arlington Ln. Pg.3 . . . . A9
Ashbury Ln. Pg.7 . . . . E4
Ashland Ave. Pg.7 . . . . D7
Aster Ave. Pg.7 . . . . A7
Azalea Ln. Pg.3 . . . . A9
Baldwin Ct. Pg.3 . . . . A9
Baldwin Dr. Pg.8 . . . . A9
Baldwin Rd. Pg.3 . . . . A-B9
Baldwin Way Pg.3 . . . . A9

Barberry Ln. Pg.3 . . . . A9
Bayer Dr. Pg.7 . . . . A5
Bayer Rd. Pg.7 . . . . A5
Bayside Dr. Pg.3 . . . . A10
Beaumont Ln. Pg.7 . . . . A9
Bedford Ln. Pg.3 . . . . A10
Benton St. Pg.7 . . . . E7
Bloomington Ave. . . . . . .
  Pg.3 . . . . A10
Bombay Way Pg.7 . . . . B5
Bon Hill Dr. Pg.3 . . . . A9
Bradley Ct. Pg.3 . . . . A9
Bradwell Ave. Pg.6 . . . . B3
Brentwood Dr. Pg.2 . . . . A8
Briar Cove Pg.7 . . . . A9
Briar Pl. Pg.1 . . . . A5
Briar Wood Ct. Pg.1 . . . . F7
Brookdale Ct. Pg.1 . . . . F7
Brookdale Ln. Pg.1 . . . . F7
Brookside St. Pg.7 . . . . C5
Bryant Ave. Pg.7 . . . . E7
California St. Pg.7 . . . . E7
Cambridge Ct. N. . . . . . .
  Pg.3 . . . . A9
Cambridge Ct. S. . . . . . .
  Pg.3 . . . . A9
Candlenut Ln. Pg.3 . . . . A9
Canterbury Ct. Pg.3 . . A10,B3
Canterbury Tr. Pg.3 . . . . A10
Capri Dr. Pg.3 . . . . A9
Carriage Ln. Pg.3 . . . . A9
Carriage Ln. Pg.3 . . . . A9
Carriage Ln.(Pvt.) . . . . . .
  Pg.3 . . . . A9
Cascade Bay Pg.3 . . . . A10
Castle Ct. Pg.3 . . . . A9
Chesapeake Ln. Pg.8 . . . . B9
Circle Dr. Pg.1 . . . . F7
Circle Ln. Pg.7 . . . . F7
Clear Creek Bay Pg.3 . . . . A10
Clyde Ave. Pg.7 . . . . C5
Coach Rd. Pg.7 . . . . A9
Coleen Ct. Pg.7 . . . . F7
Colonial Pkwy. Pg.7 . . . . E5
Conway Bay Pg.3 . . . . A10
Coolidge Ave. Pg.7 . . . . B5
Cottonwood Way . . . . . .
  Pg.8 . . . . B8
Country Club Ct. . . . . . .
  Pg.2 . . . . A-B8
Cove Dr., N. Pg.7 . . . . A9
Crescent Ave. Pg.7 . . . . C6
Crestwood Ln. Pg.7 . . . . F7
Crooked Creek Tr. . . . . . .
  Pg.3 . . . . A10
Crystal Ln. Pg.3 . . . . A10
Cumnor Rd. Pg.6 . . . . A4
Cumnor Rd. Pg.1 . . . . A4
Cunningham Dr. Pg.8 . . . . A9
Cypress Ct. Pg.7 . . . . A7
Daniels Rd. Pg.7 . . . . D7
Dee Ln. Pg.2 . . . . A8
Deer Ave. Pg.7 . . . . A9
Deer Ln. Pg.6 . . . . A4
Deerpath Rd. Pg.7 . . . . A9
Del Mar Dr. Pg.7 . . . . A7
Delgado Dr. Pg.7 . . . . A9
Denise Dr. Pg.7 . . . . A9
Diane Dr. Pg.7 . . . . A9
Doe Rd. Pg.7 . . . . A4
Dogwood Ln. Pg.7 . . . . A9
Donegal Bay Pg.3 . . . . A10
Dorchester St. Pg.7 . . . . D6
Dorset Ave. Pg.7 . . . . D6
Dundee Quarter Pg.3 . . . . A9
Dundee Rd. Pg.2 . . . . A8-11
Dupont Ave. Pg.7 . . . . E6
Echo Ln. Pg.2 . . . . A8
Edgar St. Pg.7 . . . . F7
Edgebrook Dr. Pg.3 . . . . A9
Ella Rd. Pg.1 . . . . A-F4
Ellis St. Pg.7 . . . . C6
Elm St. Pg.7 . . . A7,B5
Elmwood Ln. Pg.7 . . . . F7
Emerson Ave. Pg.7 . . . . E6
Enlund Dr. Pg.7 . . . . A9
Euclid Ave. Pg.7 . . . . E6
Evergreen Dr. Pg.8 . . . . A9
Fairfax Ave. Pg.7 . . . E7-8
Farm Gate Ln. Pg.7 . . . . A7
Fern Ct. Pg.7 . . . . D7
Florence Ave. Pg.6 . . . B3-4
Forest Ln. Pg.7 . . . . E7
Foxglove Ln. Pg.7 . . . . A9
Foxwood Ln. Pg.7 . . . . A9
Frances Ln. Pg.1 . . . A5-6
Franklin Ave. Pg.7 . . . . B6
Frost Rd. Pg.6 . . . . A3
Galena Ave. Pg.3 . . . . A9
Galesburg Ave. Pg.3 . . . . A10
Garden Ct. Pg.7 . . . . E7
Garden St. Pg.7 . . . . E7
Gardenia Ln. Pg.7 . . . . E7
Garfield Ave. Pg.7 . . . . E7
Geneva Dr. Pg.8 . . . . A9
Geri Ave. Pg.7 . . . . B6
Geri Ct. Pg.7 . . . . B6
Ginger Cr. Cir. Pg.3 . . . . A9
Ginger Cr. Dr. Pg.3 . . . . A9
Glavin Ct. Pg.3 . . . . A9
Glencoe Rd. Pg.7 . . A5-6,C5
Goodwin Dr. Pg.3 . . . . A9
Grace Ln. Pg.7 . . . . A5
Greenbriar Ln. Pg.3 . . . . A9
Greenwich Ct. Pg.7 . . . . F7
Grove Ln. Pg.7 . . . . A6
Guthrie Ct. Pg.6 . . . . A3

Haig Ct. Pg.3 . . . . A9
Haman Rd. Pg.6 . . . . C3
Hancock Dr. Pg.7 . . . . A9
Harrison Ave. Pg.7 . . . . C5
Hawk Dr. Pg.1 . . . . A5
Hawthorne Dr. Pg.1 . . . . A5
Heather Ln. Pg.3 . . . . A9
Heatherlea Dr. Pg.7 . . . . A7
Helen Rd. Pg.7 . . . . A6
Heritage Cir. Pg.3 . . . . A9
Heritage Dr. Pg.3 . . . . A9
Hickory Ln. Pg.6 . . . . F4
Hicks Rd. Pg.3 . . . . A10
Hidden Creek Dr. . . . . . .
  Pg.3 . . . . A10
Hidden Hill Ln. Pg.2 . . . . A9
Hidden Oaks Dr. Pg.2 . . . . A6
Hill Rd. Pg.7 . . . . A6
Hill St. Pg.7 . . . . A5
Hillcrest Ct. Pg.1 . . . . A5
Hillcrest Dr. Pg.1 . . . . A5
Hillcrest Terr. Pg.1 . . . . A5
Hillside Ave. Pg.7 . . . . C5
Hillside Dr. Pg.7 . . . . C5
Holly Way Pg.7 . . . . A9
Howe Terr. Pg.1 . . . . A5
Hudson Bay Pg.3 . . . . A10
Illinois Ave. Pg.7 . . . D6-7
Inverarry Dr. Pg.3 . . . . A9
Irene Dr. Pg.2 . . . . A8
Iris Dr. Pg.3 . . . . A9
Isle Royal Cir. Pg.3 . . . . A10
Ivy Pl. Pg.3 . . . . A9
Jamestown Dr. Pg.3 . . . . A9
Jarvis Ct. Pg.3 . . . . A9
Jennifer Ln. Pg.3 . . . . A9
Joan Dr. Pg.1 . . . . A6
Jody Ct. Pg.7 . . . . F7
Karen Ln. Pg.7 . . . . B6
Kelly Ann Dr. Pg.7 . . . . D6
Kenilworth Ave. Pg.7 . . . . C5
Kennedy Dr. Pg.3 . . . . A9
Kevin Ct. Pg.3 . . . . A10
Kimberly Ave. Pg.7 . . . . F7
Kings Row (Pvt.) . . . . . .
  Pg.3 . . . . A9
Knollwood Pg.8 . . . . F8
Knox St. Pg.7 . . . . A8
Knoxboro Ln. Pg.2 . . . . A6
LaLonde Dr. Pg.7 . . . . E6
Lake Cook Rd. Pg.3 . . . . X9
Lakeside Dr. Pg.7 . . . . A6
Laurel Ln. Pg.3 . . . . A9
Lee Ct. Pg.3 . . . . A9
Lenwood Dr. Pg.2 . . . . A9
Leonard St. Pg.7 . . . . C5
Lexington Dr. Pg.3 . . . . A9
Lilac Dr. Pg.3 . . . . A8
Lilac Pl. Pg.3 . . . . A9
Lily Ln. Pg.3 . . . . A9
Linden Ave. Pg.7 . . . . A7
Linden Ln. Pg.1 . . . . F7
Linder Ln. Pg.1 . . . . F7
Little City Dr. Pg.7 . . . . E4
Long Acres Ln. Pg.1 . . . . F8
Long Grove Rd. Pg.3 . . . . A10
Lorelei Ln. Pg.1 . . . . F7
Louise Ln. Pg.2 . . . A-B7
Lynda Dr. Pg.7 . . . . A9
Mallard Ln. Pg.3 . . . . A10
Maple Ave. Pg.7 . . . . B5
Marshall Ct. Pg.3 . . . . A9
Martin Dr. Pg.7 . . . . B6
Meadow Ln. Pg.1 . . . . C6
Merrill Ave. Pg.7 . . . . C6
Middleton Ave. Pg.7 . . . . C5
Morrison Ave. Pg.7 . . . . B5
Mudhank Rd. Pg.6 . . . . E1
Myrtle St. Pg.7 . . . . B5
Nantucket Ln. Pg.2 . . . . A6
New Haven Ave. Pg.3 . . . . A10
Newport Sq. Pg.3 . . . . A9
Nichols Rd. Pg.3 . . . A9,10
North St. Pg.7 . . . . A5
Oak Brook Dr. Pg.3 . . . . A10
Oak Ct. Pg.1 . . . . A5
Oak St. Pg.2 . . . . A8
Oaksbury Ln. Pg.7 . . . . E7
Oakwood Dr. Pg.3 . . . . A9
Old Mill Dr. Pg.7 . . . . A7
Old Northwest Hwy. . . . . . .
  Pg.7 . . . . B5
Olde Virginia Dr. Pg.8 . . . . A9
Palm Dr. Pg.2 . . . . A6
Palmer Ln. Pg.3 . . . . A9
Palos Ave. Pg.7 . . . . A5
Park Ave. Pg.7 . . . . A5
Park Dr. Pg.1 . . . . F7
Pepper Tree Dr. Pg.3 . . . . A9
Perry Dr. Pg.7 . . . . A6
Pheasant Ln. Pg.1 . . . . A5
Pheasant Tr. Pg.3 . . . . A10
Pinehill Ct. Pg.7 . . . . C5
Plum Grove Rd. Pg.7 . . . . C5
Pondview Dr. Pg.7 . . . . B6
Poplar St. Pg.7 . . . . A5
Portage Ave. Pg.7 . . . . A5
Portsmith Ln. Pg.3 . . . . A10
Poteet Ave. Pg.6 . . . . C3
Potomac Ln. Pg.3 . . . . A10
Princeton St. Pg.3 . . . . A8
Prospect Ct. Pg.1 . . . . A5
Quail Ct. Pg.3 . . . . A10
Queensbury Cir. Pg.3 . . . . A9
Queensbury Ln. Pg.3 . . . . A9
Quentin Rd. Pg.2 . . . . A7

PALOS HEIGHTS (continued)

Rainbow Bay . Pg.3 . . . . A10
Rand Rd. Pg.3 . . . . A8-9
Randall Ln. Pg.3 . . . . A10
Randville Dr. Pg.8 . . . . A8
Ridgewood Ln. Pg.7 . . . . A7
Roberts Rd. Pg.5 . . . . C3
Rosalie Ln. Pg.2 . . . . A8
Rose Ave. Pg.3 . . . . A9
Roslyn Rd. Pg.1 . . . . A5
Roth Ave. Pg.7 . . . . A5
Run Away Bay Pg.8 . . . . A9
Schaefer Rd. Pg.3 . . . . A10
Shadow Lake Terr. . . . . . .
  Pg.3 . . . . A10
Shady Dr. Pg.7 . . . . E7
Shagbark Ct. Pg.3 . . . . A5
Shannon Bay Pg.3 . . . . A10
Silver Ln. Pg.8 . . . . A9
Silver Strand Cir. . . . . . .
  Pg.3 . . . . A10
Smith St. Pg.7 . . . . E7
Spring Ridge Dr. Pg.3 . . . . A10
Stephen Dr. Pg.7 . . . . B6
Sterling Ave. Pg.7 . . . . B5
Stillwater Ct. Pg.3 . . . . A6
Tall Trees Ln. Pg.7 . . . . E7
Thackeray Dr. Pg.7 . . . . A7
Thorntree Ln. Pg.1 . . . . F7
Timberlea Dr. Pg.3 . . . . A9
Tower Ct. Pg.3 . . . . A9
Trail Ridge St. Pg.3 . . . . A10
Tulip Way Pg.3 . . . . A9
Tyne Ct. Pg.6 . . . . B2
Vermillion Ln. Pg.3 . . . . A10
Vermont St. Pg.7 . . . . D7
Wainwright Ct. Pg.3 . . . . A9
Warren Ave. Pg.6 . . . . C3
Waterford Bay Pg.3 . . . . A10
Weatherstone Rd. . . . . . .
  Pg.1 . . . . A6
Wedgewood Dr. Pg.2 . . . . A6
Westminster Dr. Pg.7 . . . . B6
Westmoreland Ct. . . . . . .
  Pg.3 . . . . A9
Westwood Ln. Pg.2 . . . . A8
Whispering Ct. Pg.3 . . . . A9
Whispering Oak Ln. . . . . . .
  Pg.2 . . . . A6
Whispering Oaks Dr. . . . . . .
  Pg.3 . . . . A10
White Gate Ct. Pg.1 . . . . A6
White Sand Bay Pg.3 . . . . A10
White Water Ln. Pg.3 . . . . A10
Wildwood Ct. Pg.7 . . . . F7
Wilke Rd. Pg.3 . . . . A10
Williamsburg Ct. . . . . . .
  Pg.7 . . . . E7
Williamsburg Dr. . . . . . .
  Pg.3 . . . . A9
Willow Ln. Pg.6 . . . . C3-5
Wilmette Rd. Pg.7 . . . . C5
Wilson St. Pg.7 . . . . C5
Wind River Terr. Pg.3 . . . . A10
Winnetka Ave. Pg.7 . . . . D7
Winnetka Dr. Pg.7 . . . . A5
Winter Haven Ct. . . . . . .
  Pg.7 . . . . D6
Wood St. Pg.7 . . . . C5
Woodcliff Ln. Pg.7 . . . . F7
Wyndam Pg.8 . . . . A9
Zinnia Ln. Pg.7 . . . . A9

CEMETERIES
St. John's Cem. Pg.7 . . . E-F5
St. Michael the Archangel Cem.
  . . . . . F5

FOREST PRESERVES
Barrington Woods . . . . . .
  Pg.2 . . . . A8
Deer Grove Forest Preserve . . .
  Pg.2 . . . A6-9
Paul Douglas Forest Preserve . .
  Pg.6 . . . E2-4

GOLF COURSES
Highland Woods Golf Course . . .
  Pg.1 . . . . F4

PARKS
Lake Park Pg.7 . . . . B6

SCHOOLS
Lincoln Sch. Pg.7 . . . . A7
Little City Sch. Pg.7 . . . . E4

MISCELLANEOUS
Camp Reinberg Pg.2 . . . . A7

PALOS HEIGHTS
Pages 37,38

STREETS
Aberdeen Ct. I13
Aberdeen Dr. I13
Arquilla Dr. I14
Auburn H15
Bachelor Grove Rd. J15
Bay Rd. G13
Bay Rd. N. G13
Beacon Dr. G13
Breakwater Way G13
Briar Ln. I15
Burris Ct. H15

PALOS HEIGHTS

Canterbury Ct. G14
Carmichael H14
Carol Ln. H16
Carriage Tr. H14
Cedar Creek Ct. G15
Cedar Ln. I14
Cheyenne Dr. H15
Chippewa Dr. G15
Choctaw Rd. I14
Coach Rd. H14
College Dr. Rd. G14
Comanche Dr. I14
Country Club Ct. I14
Country Club Ct., S. I14
Country Squire Ct., N. G14
Country Squire Rd. G14
Cypress Ln. I14
Deer Ln. I15
Diane Dr. H14
Dogwood Ln. H16
Edgewood Dr. I15
Edinburgh Dr. I13
Elm Ct. I14
Evergreen Ave. H15
Flambeau Dr. H15
Forest Hill Ct. I14
Forest Hill Ln. I14
Forest View Rd. I15
Fox Ln. I15
Golf Oak Dr. I14
Golfview Ln. I15
Harbor Ln. G13
Harlem Ave. G14
Harold Ave. H14
Highland Dr. I15
Hills Ct. I14
Ishnala Dr. I14
Justamere Rd. K15
Kiowa Ln. I14
Kirkaldy Ct. I13
Lake Katherine Dr. G14
Lakeview Ct. I13
Lighthouse Ln. G13
Linden Ave., W. H15
London Ln. H14
MacIntosh Dr. I14
Manitoba Dr. H14
Maple Ln. H15
Melvina Ave. H16
Menominee Pkwy. H15
Misty Meadow Dr. I13
Nagle Ave. H15
Nashville Ave. H15
Natchez Ave. H15
Natoma H15
Navajo Ct., E. H15
Navajo Ct., W. H15
Navajo Dr. H15
Navajo Dr., E. H15
Navajo Dr., W. H15
Oak Ct. I14
Oak Hills Pkwy. I13
Oak Ln. I14
Oak Park Ave. H,I15
Oak Ridge Ct. I14
Oak Trail Ct. G13
Old Georges Ct. I13
Old Oak Tr. G13
Onekema Dr. H15
Orchard Dr. H16
Palos Ave. H14
Park Ln. I15
Parliament Dr., E. G14
Parliament Dr., W. G14
Pheasant I15
Pine Arbor Pl. H16
Pine Arbor Tr. H16
Pine Pl. H16
Ponderosa Dr. I14
Ponderosa Ln. H14
Potawatomi Ct. H14
Potawatomi Dr. H14
Pueblo Ave. I14
Pueblo Ct. I14
Quail I15
Raleigh Ct. G14
Richard Ave. H14
Ridgeland Ave. K16
Seagull Ln. G13
Seneca Rd. I14
Sequoia Dr. I14
Shawassie Dr. H15
Shawnee Rd. I14
Shoshone Rd. I14
Sioux Ln. I14
Sorrento Dr. G15
Spruce Pl. H16
Surrey Hill H14
Surrey Hill Ct. H14
Sycamore Ln. I14
Tennyson Ct. G14
Turtle Pond Ln. I13
Ute Ln. I14
Virgil Ave. G13
West Gate Ave. H15
Westview Dr. I13
White Oak Ct. G13
White Pine Pl. H14
Willow Wood Dr. H16
Winnebago Rd. I14
Worth St. (135th St.) I15
Wyandot Dr. H15
66th Ct. K15
68th Ct. H15
69th Ave. H15
69th Ct. H15
70th Ave. H15
70th Ct. H15
70th Ct. S. I15
71st Ave S. I15
71st Ave. H15
71st Ct. H14
71st Ct. S. I14
72nd Ct. H14
73rd Ave. H14
73rd Ct. H14
74th Ave. H14
75th Ave. H14
76th Ave. H14
77th Pl. I14
78th Ct. I14
79th S. I13
82nd Ave., S. I13
117th St. G13
119th Pl. G14
120th St. G14
121st St. G14
122nd St. H14,15
123rd Pl. H14
123rd St. H14,15
124th Pl. H14,16
124th St. H14-16
125th Ct. H15
125th Pl. H16
125th St. H14,16
126th Pl. H15
126th St. H14
127th St. H14
128th St. H14
130th St. I15
131st St., W. I14
133rd St. I13
135th St. I15
137th St. J15
143rd St. J15

CEMETERIES

Bachelor Grove Cem. K16

FOREST PRESERVES

Bachelor Grove J15
Burr Oak Woods J15
Elizabeth A. Conkey F.P. I16
Rubio Woods J16
Tinley Creek Woods J15

GOLF COURSES

Oak Hills G.C. I14
Westgate Valley C.C. I15

PARKS

Crawford Park I14
Palmer Park G14

SCHOOLS

Arrowhead Sch. H15
Chicago Christian H.S. G15
Independence Jr. H.S. I15
Navajo Hts. Sch. H15
Palos East Sch. H14
Palos Heights Sch. H15
Palos Lutheran Sch. H15
Palos South Jr. H.S. I13
St. Alexander Sch. H15
Stone Church Christian Acad. H16
Trinity Christian College H15

SHOPPING CENTERS

Indian Trails Shopping Center H15
Shopping District H14

MISCELLANEOUS

Camps Falcon & Sullivan K15
City Hall G14
Hospital G14
Library H14
Palos Community Hospital H13

PALOS HILLS

Page 34

STREETS

Alta Dr. E13
Arrowhead Dr. D12
Aspen Dr. E12
Avon Ct. F12
Bennett Dr. F12
Boulder Ct. F12
Breckenridge Dr. E13
Broadmoor Dr. E12
Brook Lodge Ln. E13
Cambridge Ct. D12
Carlton Dr. F12
Catherine Dr. F13
Center Rd. F12
Chamonieux Dr. E13
Charles Ave. E13
Cherry Ct. F13
Chestnut Dr. F13
Christa Ct. F13
Cinnamon Creek Dr. D12
Circle Ct. F13
Circle Dr. F13
Cobblestone Ct. F12
Cork Rd. D12
Cottonwood Dr. F13
Cour Caravelle F12
Cour D'Alene F12
Cour De LaReine F12
Cour Deauville F12
Cour LaSalle F12
Cour LeRoux F12
Cour Madeleine F12
Cour Marquis F12
Cour Masson G12
Cour Michele F12
Cour Monnet F12
Cour Montreal G12
Cour St. Tropez F12
Cour Versaille F12
Dartmouth Rd. E12
Deerpath Ln. F12
Del Prado Dr. D12
Doric Cir. E13
East Rd. F12
Eastwood Dr. F14
Eleanor Ave. E13
Erin Dr. D13
Gladys Ln. D13
Granada Ct. E12
Green Valley Dr. E12
Gruener Ct. F13
Harlem Ave. G14
Helena Dr. F12
Heritage Dr. F12
Hickory Crest Ct. D12
Holly Ct. F13
Interlochen Ct. E13
Interlochen Dr. E12
Juniper Ct. F13
Kathy Ct. E14
Kean Ave. F12
Kingsbury Ct. D12
Lori Ln. E13
Los Palos Ln. D12
Loveland Ln. E12
Lucas Dr. F12
Maple Crest Ct. D12
Meadow Ln. F13
Meryton Ct. D12
Michael Dr. E14
Mill Stone Ct. F13
Moraine Dr. F13
Mulberry Ln. F13
North Rd. F12
Northwest Rd. F12
O'Gorman F12
Oak Crest Ct. D12
Oconto Ct. F13,14
Olympia Cir. F13
Palos Dr. F13
Palos Pl. E13
Peak Dr. F13
Pebble Ct. F13
Pemberly Ct. D12
Poplar Ln. F13
Possum Dr. F12
Roberta Rd. F13
Sheffield Dr. E13
Sierra Ln. D12
South Hill E12
South Rd. H12
Southwest Hwy. F14
Spathis F12
Stone Bridge Ct. F12
Stoney Creek Dr. F13
Stowe Ct. E12
Stratford Ln. D12
Sun Valley Ct. E12
Sun Valley Dr. E12
Surry Park D12
Sycamore Ln. F13
Taos E12
Terry Dr. E14
Theresa Cir. F13
Tod Dr. E13
Tuttle Ct. F12
Vail Dr. E12
Valley Ct. F13
Valley Dr. F13
Vicky Ln. E13
Walnut Terr. F13
Westwood Dr. E13
Willow F13
Windsor Dr. D12
Winter Park Dr. E12
Wood Ln. D13
Wooded Path Dr. D12
Zermatt Dr. E12
73rd Ave. E14
73rd Ct. E14
74th Ave. E14
75th Ave. E14
75th Ct. E14
76th Ave. E,F14
78th Ave. F14
80th (Roberts Rd.) Ave. D13
80th Ct. E13
81st Ave. D13
81st Ct. D13
81st St. E13
82nd Ave. D13
82nd Ct. E13
83rd Ave. E13
83rd Ct. E13
84th Ave. E,F13
84th Terr. E13
85th Ave. E13
86th Ave. E,F12
86th Ct. E12
86th St. F12
86th Terr. E13
87th Ave. E12
87th Ct. D,E12
88th Ave. F12
89th Ave. D12
90th Ave. E12
96th Pl. D12
96th St. D12
97th Ave. D12
97th Pl. D12
97th St. D12,13
98th Pl. D12
98th St. D12,13
99th Pl. D12,13
99th St. D12
99th Terr. D12
100th Pl. D13,E12
100th St. D12,13
100th Terr. D12
101st Pl. E12,13
101st St. E12,13
101st Terr. E12
102nd Pl. E12
102nd St. E12,13
102nd Terr. W. E12
103rd Pl. E12
103rd St. E12
103rd Terr. E12
104th Pl. E12,13
104th St. E13
105th St. E12-14
106th St. E13
107th St. E12
108th St. F13
111th Pl. F13
111th St. F11
112th Pl. F13
112th St. F13
113th Pl. F13
113th St. F13

CEMETERIES

Calvary Memorial Cem. F13

GOLF COURSES

Palos Hills G.C. E14

PARKS

Aspen Park E12
Atman Park G14
Calvary Park F13
Holerding Park G15
Indiana Woods D13
Krasowski Park E13
Loveland Park E13
Michael Dr. Park E14
Penny Park G15
Senior Park E12
Smile Park F15
Stanick Park F15
Volunteer Park D12

SCHOOLS

Amos Alonzo Stagg H.S. F13
Moraine Valley Comm. College F12
Oak Ridge Sch. E12
Quinn Sch. E13
Worth Main Sch. F15

MISCELLANEOUS

Charles Christianson Center G14
City Hall E12
Fire Department E13
Village Hall F15

PALOS PARK

Pages 36,37

STREETS

Algoma Dr. H12
Algonquin Rd. H13
Alpine Ave. G13
Autobahn Dr. G13
Black Forest Ln. G13
Black Walnut Tr. I11
Brand Ave. H13
Brook Ln. H13
Calumet Sag Rd. G12
Cherokee Rd. H12
Commons Dr. H13
Danmar Tr. H9
Deer Cr. G13
Edelweiss Dr. G13
Edgewater Ln. H11
Eldridge Ave. G12
Elm St. H12
Forest Glen Blvd. H12
Forestview Ln. G13
Fox Ln., N. H9
Fox Ln., S. H9
Highwood Dr. G13
Hillcrest Ln. H12
Hillside Cir. H13
Hillside Dr. H13
Hobart Ave. H11
Holmes Ave. G13
Huntleigh Rd. H9
Iroquois Rd. H13
Kean Ave. G12
Kimber Ln. G13
Kinvarra Dr. H11
Knollwood Dr. G13
Lakewood Ave. G12
Laurie Ave. G12
McCarthy Rd. H8
McKinley Ave. H11
Meadow Rd. H8
Mill Rd. I11
Mohawk Rd. H13
Oak Ln. H8
Oak Ridge Dr. H13
Old Creek Rd. H8
Old Prague Path G13
Old Timber Ln. H9
Palos Ave. G13
Parklane Dr. H10
Partridge Ln. H8
Pawnee Rd. H12
Post Rd. H9
Rail Ln. H9
Ramsgate Dr. H8
Regina Ln. H13
Ridge Ave. H12
Roberts Rd. G12
Roma Rd. H12
Romiga Ln. H9
Rosewood Ave. H12
Seminole Rd. H13
Somerset Ln. H11
South St. G12
Spring Dr. H12
Sunnyslope Rd. H9
Timber Ln. G,H13
Vienna Ave. G13
Walnut Ridge G13
Wild Cherry Ln. H11
Wildwood Tr. H9
Windsor Dr. H11
Winslow Rd. G13
Wolf Rd. K9
Woodland Trail, N. H13
Woodland Trail, S. H13
79th Ave. H13
80th Ave. H13
81st Ave. H13
81st Ct. I13
82nd Ave. S. G13
82nd Ct. G13
82nd Ct. S. G13
83rd Ave. S. G,H13
84th Ave. G,H13
85th Ave. G13
86th Ave. G12,H13
87th Ave. H12
88th Ave. H12
89th Ave. H12
89th Ave. W. H12
89th Ct. W. G12
90th Ave. G12
90th Ct. G,H12
91st Ave. H12
92nd Ave. H12
93rd Ave. H11
94th Ave. G12
100th Ave. H10
108th Ave. H9
109th Ave. H9
114th Ave. H8
115th Ave. G13,H8
116th St. G13
117th St. G13
118th St. G12
119th Pl. G12
119th St. G11
120th St. G11-13
121st St. G11,12
122nd St. H11,12
123rd Pl. H8
123rd St. H11
124th St. H12,13
125th St. H12,13
126th St. H10,12,13
127th St. H10-12
128th Pl. I13
129th St. I13
131st St. I11

CEMETERIES

Palos Oak Hill Cem. I12

FOREST PRESERVES

Forty Acres Woods G11
Paddock Woods G12
Palos Park Woods G12
Swallow Cliff Woods G11
Swallow Cliffs G10

SCHOOLS

Palos School G12

MISCELLANEOUS

Library H12
Village Hall H12
Winter Sports Area G11

PALOS TOWNSHIP

Pages 33,34,36,37

STREETS

Adist Rd. Pg.36 I10
Arlington Ct. Pg.36 I10
Bayberry Ct. Pg.36 H10
Bernice Dr. Pg.36 I10
Birchwood Dr. Pg.36 H10
Bishop Ct. Pg.36 I10
Bloomfield Dr. Pg.36 I10
Blue Heron Dr. Pg.36 I9
Brian Pl. Pg.36 I11
Brittany Dr. Pg.36 I9
Brodt Dr. Pg.36 I10
Calumet Sag Rd. Pg.34 F10
Carriage House Ln. Pg.36 J9
Charlotte Ct. Pg.36 I9
Cherrywood Dr. Pg.36 H10
Circle Pkwy. Pg.36 I11
Cornell Ln. Pg.37 I13
Country Manor Ln. Pg.36 I9
Creek Rd. Pg.36 I11
Deerwood Dr. Pg.37 H13
Edgewater Ln. Pg.36 H11
Elridge Ave. Pg.37 G12
Farmhill Ave. Pg.37 I13
Farmhill Ln. Pg.37 H13
Fitzsimmons Dr. Pg.36 I10
Flavin Rd. Pg.33 C10
Ford Rd. Pg.36 G8
Frances Ct. Pg.36 I9
Georgetown Dr. Pg.36 I9
Glen Rd. Pg.36 G8
Grandview Pg.36 H10
Haas Dr. Pg.36 H9
Hampton Ct. Pg.36 I9
Hampton Rd. Pg.36 I9
Hillcrest Dr. Pg.36 I13,J10
Holmes Ave. Pg.37 G13
Indian Trail Dr. Pg.36 H10
Joseph Dr., W. Pg.36 H10
Kean Ave. Pg.37 G12
Kindling Ct. Pg.36 I10
Laflin Ct. Pg.36 I10
Lake Trail Dr. Pg.36 H10
Lakeland Dr. Pg.36 H10
Lakeview Ct. Pg.36 I10
Longwood Ct. Pg.37 I13
Lucille Ln. Pg.36 H10
Maple Ave. Pg.33 C8
McCarthy Rd. Pg.36 H8
Meadowlark Dr. Pg.37 I13
Mill Rd. Pg.36 I11
Mission Dr. Pg.36 H10
Misty Harbour Ln. Pg.36 I10
Newport Dr. Pg.36 I10
Northbridge Ct. Pg.36 J9
Northbridge Dr. Pg.36 J9
Oak Grove Pg.33 C8
Oakwood Dr. Pg.36 H10
Old Tamarack Ln. Pg.36 K9
Paloma Dr. Pg.37 I13
Palos West Dr. Pg.36 H9
Parkside Dr. Pg.36 I10
Parkview Dr. Pg.36 H10
Pauline Ct. Pg.37 I13
Peace Memorial Dr. (Pvt.) Pg.36 I10
Pebble Dr. Pg.36 H11
Poloma Dr. Pg.37 I13
Powell Rd. Pg.36 H10
Prairie View Dr. Pg.36 H10
Public St. Pg.33 C9
Railroad Ave. (91st St.) Pg.33 C8
Richmond Ct. Pg.36 I9
Ridgewood Dr. Pg.36 I10
Sandberg Ct. Pg.36 I10
Sedwick Dr. Pg.36 H9
Sheffield Ct. Pg.36 H9
Southwest Hwy. Pg.37 I12
St. Joseph Dr. Pg.36 I10
Stephen Dr. Pg.36 I10
Suffield Dr. Pg.36 G9
Surrey Ct. Pg.36 I11
Tanglewood Cir., E. Pg.36 I10
Tanglewood Cir., W. Pg.36 I10
Tanglewood Ct. Pg.36 I10
Timber Edge Ln. Pg.36 H10
W. Joseph Dr. Pg.36 H10
Walter Dr. Pg.36 I10
Westport Dr. Pg.36 I10
Whispering Lake Dr. Pg.36 H10
Wildwood Dr. Pg.36 H10
Will-Cook Rd. Pg.36 K8
Windward Tr. Pg.37 I13
Wisteria Ct. Pg.36 H10
Wolf Rd. Pg.36 I9
76th Ave. Pg.37 I14
80th Ave. (Roberts Rd.) Pg.37 H13
80th Ct. Pg.37 I13
81st Ct. Pg.37 I13
82nd Ave., S. Pg.37 I13
82nd Ct. Pg.37 I13
83rd Ave., S. Pg.37 I13
83rd Ct. Pg.37 I13
84th Ave., S. Pg.37 I13
84th Ct. Pg.37 I13
84th St. Pg.37 I13
85th Ave. Pg.37 I13
85th Ave., S. Pg.37 I13
85th Ct. Pg.37 I12
86th St. Pg.37 I12
87th Ave. Pg.37 H12
88th Ave. Pg.37 I12
91st St. Pg.33 C8
92nd St. Pg.37 H12
95th St. Pg.33 D9
96th Ave. Pg.34 I11
104th Ave. Pg.36 F,I10
107th St. Pg.33 E8
108th Ave. Pg.36 I,J9
111th St. Pg.33,34. F8,11
114th Ave. Pg.33 C8
116th St. Pg.37 G13
117th St. Pg.37 G13
118th St. Pg.36 G8
119th St. Pg.37 G11
125th St. Pg.36 H10

127th St. ..... Pg.37 .. H11,12
128th Pl. ..... Pg.37 ..... I13
129th Pl. ..... Pg.37 ... I12,13
129th St. ..... Pg.37 ... I12,13
130th St. Pg.36 I10,12,13
131st Pl., W. .. Pg.37 ..... I12
131st St. ..... Pg.36 ...... I9
132nd St. ..... Pg.37 ..... I13
133rd St. ..... Pg.37 .... I9,13
134th St. ..... Pg.36 ..... I10
135th St. ..... Pg.36 ...... J9

CEMETERIES
Willow Hills Memorial Park ..... Pg.33 ...... D9

FOREST PRESERVES
Cherry Cliff Woods ..... Pg.36 .... G10
Country Lane Woods ..... Pg.33 .... D11
Detony Woods Pg.33 ...... D8
Forty Acres Woods ..... Pg.37 .... G11
Hidden Pond Woods ..... Pg.33 .... D11
McMahon Woods ..... Pg.33 ..... F10
Paddock Woods Pg.37 ..... G12
Palos Park Woods ..... Pg.37 .... G12
Paw Paw Woods Pg.33 ..... C9
Pioneer Woods Pg.33 ..... E10
Red Cats Woods Pg.33 ..... D8
Spears Woods . Pg.33 ..... C11
Swallow Cliff Woods ..... Pg.36 ..... G10
Teasons Woods Pg.36 .... G10
White Oak Woods ..... Pg.33 ..... E11
Willow Springs Woods ..... Pg.33 ..... C10

GOLF COURSES
Oak Hill G.C. .. Pg.37 ..... I14
Palos C.C. .... Pg.37 ..... I11

SCHOOLS
Carl Sandburg H.S. ..... Pg.36 ..... I11
Kennedy Sch. for Exceptional Children ... Pg.36 ...... H9
Palos Sch. .... Pg.37 .... G12
Palos South Jr. H.S. ..... Pg.37 ..... I13
Palos West Sch. Pg.36 .... H10

MISCELLANEOUS
Kiwanis Scout Camp ..... Pg.33 .... D10
Little Red School House ..... Pg.33 ..... E10
Winter Sports Area ..... Pg.33 .... G11

PARK FOREST

Pages 47,48

STREETS
Algonquin St. V22
Allegheny Ct. V23
Allegheny St. V22
Antietam St. V21
Antioch Pl. V22
Apache St. V23
Apple Ct. W21
Apple Ln. W21
Arbor Tr. V21
Arcadia St. V22
Arrowhead Ct. V23
Arrowhead St. V22
Ash St. V22
Bailey Rd. V22
Bay View Dr. V17
Bender Rd. V22
Berry St. U21
Bertoldo Rd. V22
Bigelow Rd. V22
Birch St. V22
Blackhawk Dr. W20
Blair St. U20
Brook Ave. V17
Cedar St. W22
Central Park Ave. W20
Chase St. U20
Cheer Skill Way U21
Cherry St. W21
Chestnut Ct. W22
Chestnut St. W22
Choate Rd. V22
Cromwell Rd. W22
Davis St. U20
Dogwood St. W22
Douglas St. U21
Dunham Rd. W22
Dunlap Rd. W22
Early St. U21
Elm St. V21
Farragut St. U21
Fir St. V21
Forest Blvd. V21
Garman Rd. W22
Gentry St. U21
Gerstung Rd. V22
Gettysburg St. U20
Gibson Rd. V22
Gold St. V21
Grant St. U21
Green St. U21
Hamlin St. U21
Hay St. U21
Hemlock St. W22
Herndon St. U21
Hickory Ct. U20
Hickory St. U20
Homan Ave. U20
Homan Cir. U20
Huron St. W20
Illinois Ct. U21
Illinois St. U21
Indiana St. U21
Iroquois St. W21
Jackson St. U20
Juniper St. V21
Kentucky Ct. U21
Kentucky St. U21
Krotiak Rd. V21
Lakewood Blvd. V21
Lakewood Ct. V20
Larue St. U21
Lee St. U21
Leims Rd. W21
Lester Rd. W21
Manitowac St. W21
Mantua Ct. W20
Mantua St. W21
Marquette Pl. W21
Marquette St. W20
McCarthy Rd. W22
McGarity Rd. W22
Meadow Lake Ct. V17
Meadow Lake Dr. V17
Meota St. W21
Merrimac St. W21
Miami St. W20
Michael Rd. W22
Minocqua Ct. W21
Minocqua St. W20
Mohawk St. W21
Monee Rd. W20
Monitor St. U21
Nashua St. W20
Nassau Ct. W21
Nassau St. W21
Neloa St. W21
Neptune Ln. V17
New Salem St. U21
Niagara St. W21
Nokomis St. W21
North St. U21
Norwood Blvd. V21
Oak Ln. W22
Oakwood St. W21
Onarga St. W21
Orchard Dr. X21
Orchard Dr., N. W21
Orchard Dr., S. W21
Osage St. W21
Oswego St. W21
Ottawa St. W21
Park St. V21
Peach St. W21
Plaza St. V21
Rich Ct. V20
Rich Rd. V20
Rocket Cir., E. W21
Rocket Cir., W. W21
Ruthledge St. U22
Saginaw Pl. W20
Sandburg St. U21
Sangamon Ct. W20
Sangamon St. W20
Sassabee St. W20
Sauganash St. W20
Saugatuck St. W20
Sauk Ct. W21
Sauk Trail W21
Seminole St. W20
Seneca St. W20
Seward St. U21
Shabonna Dr. W20
Shawnee St. W20
Sheridan St. U21
Sherman St. U21
Sioux St. W20
Somonauk Ct. W20
Somonauk St. W20
South St. U21
Spring Ln. V17
Springfield St. U21
Stanton St. U21
Stuenkel Rd. V22
Suwanee St. W20
Sycamore Rd. V22
Thomas St. U21
Todd St. U22
Topeka St. X20
Victory Blvd. V22
Waldmann Dr. V20
Walnut St. V20
Warwick Ct. V21
Warwick St. V21
Washington Ct. V20
Washington St. V20
Water St. V21
Watseka St. V20
Waverly Ct. V20
Waverly St. V20
Wayne Ct. V20
Wayne St. V20
Well Ct. V21
Well St. V21
Western Ave. V,X22
Westgate Dr. V20
Westwood Ct. V21
Westwood Dr. W21
Wildwood Dr. V20
Willow St. V21
Wilshire St. V20
Wilson Ct. V20
Wilson St. V20
Windsor St. V20
Winnebago St. V20
Winnemac St. V20
Winona St. V20
Winslow St. V21

CEMETERY
Calvary Cem. W22
St. Annes Cem. W20

PARKS
Algonquin Park V22
Apache Park V22
Cedar Park V22
Central Park V21
Eastgate Park V22
Illinois Park U21
Indiana Park U21
Juniper Park V21
Keokuk Park W20
Krotiak Park V21
Logan Park U21
Marquette Park W21
Murphy Park W22
Onarga Park W20
Somonauk Park W20
Veterans Park V21
Wayne Park V20
Wildwood Park V21
Winnebago Park V21

SCHOOLS
Algonquin Sch. V22
Blackhawk Jr. High School . W21
Dogwood Sch. V22
Hickory Hills Sch. W22
Hope School W20
Illinois Sch. U21
Indiana Sch. U21
Lakewood Sch. V21
Mohawk Sch. W20
Rich Twp. H.S. East W21
Sauk Trail Sch. W21
St. Irenaeus Sch. W21
Westwood Jr. H.S. V21
Westwood Sch. V20
Wildwood Sch. V21

SHOPPING CENTERS
Central Court Plaza V20
Lincolnwood S.C. U21
Lincolnwood West S.C. U20
Norwood Plaza V22
Plaza West S.C. W21
The Center S.C. V21
Tower S.C. W21

MISCELLANEOUS
Aqua Center V21
Library V21
Ludeman Mental Rehab. Ctr. U21
Park Forest Tennis Club ... W21
Thorn Creek Woods Nature Center W22
Village Hall V21

PARK RIDGE

Pages 28,29

STREETS
Ascot N3
Ashbury Cir. M3
Ashland Ave. K3,M5
Astoria Way M3
Austin Ave. L5
Austin St. L4
Avondale Ave. M3-4
Babetta Ave. M3
Berry Pkwy. M5
Birch St. L3
Boardwalk M3
Bouterse L3
Broadway Ave. M3
Brookline Ave. L5
Busse Hwy. M4
Carol St. K4
Carolyn Ln. M3
Cedar St. M3-5
Cherry St. M3-5
Chester Ave. L-N4
Clifton Ave. L-N4
Clinton St. M5
Courtland Ave. N4
Crain St. K4
Crescent Ave. M4-5
Cumberland Ave. L-N4
Cuttriss St. L5
Cynthia St. L4
Davis St. J4
Decook Ave. L3
Dee Rd. M3
Delphia Ave. L-M4
Dempster Ct. K3
Des Plaines M3
East Ave. L5
Edgemont Ln. L4-5
Edna Ave. L3
Elliott Ave. K-L2
Ellison L3
Elm St. M3-5
Elmore St. M5
Evergreen Ln. K3
Fairview Ave. L-N4
Farrell Ave. K3
Florence Dr. M3
Forestview Ave. M3
Fortuna Ave. L3
Garden St. M3-4
Glenview Ave. L3
Good Ave. K-L3
Goodwin Dr. M3
Grace Ave. L-M4
Grand Blvd. M4
Grant Pl. M5
Greendale Ave. L3
Greenwood Ave. M-N4
Habberton Ave. L2-3
Habberton St. L3
Halberg Ln. K4
Halien Terr. M3
Hamlin Ave. L-M3
Hansen Pl. M4
Hastings St. M4
Helen Ave. L3
Hoffman Ave. K-L3
Hoffman Rd. L3
Home Ave. K-N3
Irwin Ave. M3
Jonquil L5
Joyce Pl. M5
Kathleen Dr. L5
Knight Ave. L-N4
Lahon St. M3-5
Lake N5
Laverne Ave. L4
Leonard St. M4
Lincoln Ave. M-N4
Lundergan Ave. K-L2
Luther Ln. K3
Main St. M4
Marguerite St. L3
Marlowe M3
Marvin Pkwy. M3
Mary Jane Ln. M3
Mayfield Dr. K3
Meacham Ave. M4
Merrill Ave. M5
Merrill St. L-M5
Michael John Dr. L5
Milton Ave. M3
Morris M4
Murphy Lake Ln. M3
Murphy Lake Rd. M3
Norman Blvd. M3
Northwest Hwy. M5
Oak St. N5
Olmstead N5
Oriole Ave. L-M5
Ottawa Ave. L-M5
Ozark St. M5
Park Ln. M3
Park Pl. M4
Park Plaine Ave. M3
Parkside Ave. K-L4
Parkside Dr. K4
Parkwood Ave. L-M3
Poplar St. L3
Potter Rd. L3
Prairie Ave. M3-4
Prospect Ave. L-M5,N4
Rand Rd. L3
Redfield Ct. M-N4
Renaissance Dr. L2
Richardson Pkwy. M4
Ridge Terr. M5
Root St. M4
Rose Ave. M-N4
Rowe Ave. L3
Saloman Ln. K3
Scottylynne Dr. M3
Seeley Ave. L3
Seminary Ave. M-N3
Shibley Ave. L3
Sibley St. M3-5
Spring St. N5
Summit Ave. M4
Sylviawood Ave. M3
Talcott Rd. L-M2
Thames N3
Tomawadee Dr. L3
Touhy Ave. M2-3
Tyrell Ave. L3
Vernon Ave. K-L3
Virginia St L3
Walnut St. L3
Washington Ave. M5
Weeg Way K3
Wesley Dr. M2
Western Ave. L-N4
Wilkinson Ave. L3
Wilma Pl. L5
Wisner St. M5
Woodland Ave. L3
3rd St. M4
5th St. L4
6th St. L4
7th St. L4

CEMETERIES
Maine Cem. N3

GOLF COURSES
Park Ridge C.C. L4

PARKS
Centennial Park M3
Hinkley Park M4
Maine Park M3
Messiah Park K3
Ni-Ridge Park L4
Northeast Park L5
Northwest Park L3
Woodland Park L3

SCHOOLS
Benjamin Franklin Sch. L3
Carpenter Sch. M3
Eugene Field Sch. L5
Jeanine Schultz Mem. Sch. ... L3
Lincoln Sch. N4
Maine Twp. H.S. East K3
St. Pauls Sch. M5
Washington Sch. N4

MISCELLANEOUS
City Hall M5
Fire Station L4
Lutheran General Hospital ... K3
Post Office M4
YMCA M4
Youth Campus L5

PROSPECT HEIGHTS

Pages 9,10

STREETS
Aberdeen Ln. C15
Alderman Ave. D14-15
Alton Rd. D-E14
Andover Ct. C13
Andover Dr. C13
Anne Ct. C13
Apple Dr. C16
Blossom Ln. C16
Blossom Ln. B12
Bonniebrook Ct. D14
Bonniebrook Dr. D14
Brian Ln. D14
Brook Rd. D13
Burning Bush Ln. C13
Burr Oak Ln. C15
Camp McDonald Rd. D13-15
Carl Ct. C14
Carrbridge Ln. D14
Center Ln. D12
Cherry Creek Ln. B12
Chester Ln. E13
Cider Ln. C16
Circle Ave. D13
Claire Ln. D14
Clarendon St. D12-13
Coldren Dr. D14
Compton Ln. D13
Country Club Dr. D,E14
Countryside Ln. C13
Cove Dr. C-D15
Crabapple Dr. C16
Creek Ct. C13
Crest Hill Dr. B13
Crimson Ct. C16
Delicious Ct. C16
Derbyshire Ct. C13
Derbyshire Ln. C13
Dorset St. D12-13
Drake Ave. B13
Drake Terr. B13
Drury Ln. D12
Duchess Ct. C16
Edinburgh Ln. D14
Edward Cul De Sac D15
Edward Rd. E14
Elaine Cir. D14
Eleanor Dr. B13
Elm St. C-D13
Elmhurst Rd. B-E13
Essex St. C13
Etowah Ave. D13
Euclid Ave. E14-15
Fairway Ct. E14
Fairway Dr. E14
Ferndale Ct. C15
Ferndale Ln. C15
Forrest Ave. D12
Frankie Ct. D12
Gail Ct. N. D12
Gail Ct. S. D12
Galway Dr. D14
Garden Ct. B13
Garden Ln. C13
Glasgow Ln. D14
Glenbrook Dr. B13
Glendale Dr. C14
Golfview Cir. E14
Green Bridge Ln. C15
Greening Ct. C16
Grego Ct. D14
Greystone Ln. D15
Grove Pl. E14
Hawthorne Pl. E13
Highland Dr. B13
Hill Ct. D13
Hillcrest Dr. D13-14
Hillside Ave. D13
Hintz Rd. B13
Jonathan Ct. C16
Kenilworth Ave. C13-14
Kenneth Ave. C13
Kerry Ct. B12,13
Kewaunee Ct. C13
Kingsmill Ln. D15
Lancaster St. D12
Lanford Ln. D14
Leon Ln. D14
Lewis Isle Ln. D15
Linden Rd. N. D12
Linden Rd. S. D12
Loch Lommond Ln. C15
Lonsdale Ln. D13-14
Love Dr. C15
Lynnbrook Dr. B13
Mandel Ln. D15
Manor Ave. D13
Maple Ave. D13
Maple Ln. B,D13
Maple St. C13
Marberry Dr. D13
Margate Ln. C15
Marion Ave. D13-14
Marion St. D12
Mars Pl. D13
McIntosh Ct. C16
Meadow Ridge Ln. B12,13
Milwaukee Ave. D16-17
Minnaqua Dr. C12-13
Mohawk Ln. D15
Nawata Pl. D12
Newcastle Ln. D14
Newgate Ln. D14
North Pkwy. D13
Oak Ave. B13
Oakwood Dr. C13
Old Willow Rd. D15
Olive Ave. D12-14
Olive St. D12,13
Owen Ct. D14
Owen Pl. D-E14
Owen St. D14
Palatine Rd. C12-13
Parkview West C16
Patricia Ln. D14
Pembridge Ln. D14
Phelps Ave. D12
Pin Oak B13
Pine Forest Ln. C15
Pine St. D13
Pinecrest Dr. C15
Piper Cir. C15
Piper Ln. C15
Plaza Dr. C16
Prospect Ct. D13
Prospect Dr. B13
Quaker Ln. C-D15
Rand Rd. D12
Regent Ln. C15
Ridge Ave. C13
Riley Ave. D14
Rob Roy Ln. D,E14
Robert Ave. C13
Roberts Ln. D15
Robyn Ct. D14
Rose Ave. D14
Royal Ct. C13
Schoenbeck Rd. B,D13
School Ln. E13
School St. C-D13
Seminole Ln. D16
Shannon Dr. D14
Shawn Ln. D14
Sherwood Dr. B,C13
South Pkwy. D13
Spruce Dr. C13,14
Stirling Ln. D14
Stonegate Dr. B,C13
Stratford Rd. D12
Sussex Corner Ln. C15
Sutherland Ln. C15
Thierry Ln. D14
Thistle Ln. C15
Tomah Ave. C-D12
Tree Ln. C16
Tully Pl. E13-14
Viola Ln. C13
Walden Ln. B12
Waltz Ct. C14
Waterford Dr. D14
Waterman Ave. D12
Wheeling Rd. D14
Wildwood Dr. B,C13
Williamsburg Ln. D15
Willow Hills Ln. C15
Willow Rd. D13
Wimbledon Cir. C15
Winesap Ct. C16
Wolf Rd. C-D15
Woodview Dr. B12

GOLF COURSES
Rob Roy G.C. E14

PARKS
Claire Ln. Park D14
John Muir Park C14
Kiwanis Park C13
Lyons Park D13
McDonald Field D13
Tully Park E14

SCHOOLS
Eisenhower Sch. C12
Harper Coll. N.E. Center C15
MacArthur Jr. H.S. B13
Muir Sch. B13
Ross Sch. C13
St. Alphonsus Cath. Sch. .. D14
Sullivan Sch. C13

70
PROSPECT HEIGHTS
SAUK VILLAGE

SHOPPING CENTERS
Prospect Crossing S.C. D12

MISCELLANEOUS
Fire Department D13
Post Office D13

RICH TOWNSHIP
Pages 41,42,46-48

STREETS
Birchwood Ln. . Pg.47 ..... T18
Blackstone Ave. Pg.47 ..... S19
Blackthorne Rd. Pg.46 .... U15
Briar Branch Terr. ....
.... Pg.46 ..... U15
Briar Ln. ..... Pg.47 ..... S19
Brushwood Dr. Pg.46 ... U,V15
Burlwood Ct. . . Pg.46 ..... V15
Candlegate Cir. Pg.46 ..... U16
Central Ave. ... Pg.41 ..... U17
Central Park Ave. ....
.... Pg.42 .... R,S20
Chaparal Terr. . Pg.46 ..... V16
Cicero Ave. ... Pg.47 ..... V18
Crawford Ave. . Pg.42 .... R,T19
Dan Ryan Expwy. ....
.... Pg.47 ..... V17
Davis Ave. .... Pg.47 .... W19
Dewey Ave. ... Pg.47 .... W19
Elmwood Ln. . . Pg.47 ..... T18
Flossmoor Rd. . Pg.42 ..... R20
Governors Hwy. Pg.47 . Q21,W19
Greenwards Way ....
.... Pg.46 ..... V16
Hamlin Ave. ... Pg.42 ..... R20
Harlem Ave. ... Pg.47 ..... S15
Heartside Rd. . Pg.46 ..... U15
Heathermeade Rd. ....
.... Pg.46 ..... U15
Hedgewood Ct. Pg.46 ..... V15
Hickory Glen . . Pg.46 ..... V16
Homeland Rd. . Pg.47 ..... T18
Huntsbridge Rd. ....
.... Pg.46 ..... V15
Ivylog Terr. ... Pg.46 ..... V16
Kedzie Ave. ... Pg.42 ..... T21
Keeler Ave. ... Pg.47 ..... T19
Keystone Ave. . Pg.47 ..... S19
Knollwood Cir. . Pg.46 ..... U16
Kostner Ave. . . Pg.47 . T,V,W19
Leclaire Ave. . . Pg.47 ..... Q18
Lincoln Hwy. . . Pg.41 ..... U16
Maple Ave. ... Pg.46,47 ... V19
Maplewood Ln. Pg.47 ..... T18
Moorfield Rd. . Pg.46 ..... U15
Oak Park Ave. . Pg.41 ..... Q15
Orchard Ln. ... Pg.47 ..... S19
Pleasant Terr. . Pg.46 ..... V15
Polk Ave. ..... Pg.47 .... W19
Poplar Ave. ... Pg.47 ..... V19
Richton Sq. ... Pg.47 .... W20
Ridgeland Ave. Pg.41 ..... V16
Sauk Tr. ..... Pg.46,47 ... V16
Sprucewood Ln. ....
.... Pg.47 ..... T18
Steger Rd. .... Pg.47 .... W17
Sunset Rd. ... Pg.47 ..... S19
Tanglewood Terr. ....
.... Pg.46 ..... V16
Thistle Ct. .... Pg.46 ..... U15
Thorntree Terr. . Pg.46 ..... V16
Thornwood Ave. Pg.47 ..... S19
Timber Ridge Rd. ....
.... Pg.46 ..... U16
Tullamore Terr. . Pg.46 ..... U15
Vollmer Rd. ... Pg.46,47 ... S19
Wildwood Terr. Pg.46 ..... U15
Windmere Cir., N. ....
.... Pg.46 ..... U15
Windmere Cir., S. ....
.... Pg.46 ..... U15
Woodbine Terr. Pg.46 ..... V16
66th Ave. .... Pg.41 ..... Q15
183rd St. .... Pg.41 ..... Q17
192nd St. .... Pg.42 ..... R20
194th St. .... Pg.42 ..... R20
196th St. .... Pg.47 ..... R20
198th St. .... Pg.47 ..... S20
203rd Ave. ... Pg.47 ..... S19
204th Ave. ... Pg.47 ..... T19
205th Ave. ... Pg.47 ..... T19
206th Ave. ... Pg.47 ..... T19
207th St. .... Pg.47 ..... T19

FOREST PRESERVES
South Greenbelt F.P. ....
.... Pg.47 ..... Q16

SCHOOLS
Central Sch. ... Pg.41 ..... Q17
Sedan Prairie Sch. ....
.... Pg.46 ..... S16

MISCELLANEOUS
Old Plank Rd. Bike Trail ....
.... Pg.47 ..... U17

RICHTON PARK
Page 47

STREETS
Adams Dr. W18
Amy Dr. W18
Andover Dr. V19
Appleberry Ln. V20
Arlington Dr. V19
Arquilla Dr. W18
Ascot Ct. V19
Balmoral Dr. V19
Belmont Rd. V18
Birchwood Rd. V19,20
Bretz Dr. W19
Brighton Ln. V20
Bruce Dr. W18
Butterfield Dr. V19
Camden Ct. V18,19
Canterbury Ct. V19
Carlborg Ct. V18
Carol Ann Ct. W19
Cedar Rd. V20
Cedar Ridge Ln. W20
Central Park Ave. W20
Cherie Ct. V18
Churchill Dr., E. V19
Churchill Dr., S. V18
Cicero Ave. V18
Clarendon Ave. W18
Clark Dr. V19
Coachway Ln. V19
Crescent Way W19
Cypress Ct. W18
Davis Ave. W20
Dewey Ave. W20
East Dr. W18
Edward Dr. W19
Elm Rd. V20
Euclid Ln. V20
Farmington Ave. W18
Franklin Dr. W18
Governors Hwy. W19
Grant Ave. V20
Greenbrier Ln. V19
Hamilton Dr. W19
Hawthorne Way V18
Heartland Dr. W18
Hillside Dr. V18
Imperial Ct. W17
Imperial Dr. W18
Jackson Ave. W20
Jackson Ct. V20
Jean Ct. W19
Jefferson St. W18
Kara Ln. W17
Karlov Ave. V19
Keenhand Ct. V19
Keith Dr. W18
Kings Ct. W18
Kostner Ave. V19
Lake Shore Dr. W18
Latonia Ct. W18
Latonia Ln. W18
Laurel Dr. V18
Lawndale Ave. W20
Lee Ave. W20
Lee Ct. V18
Lesa Ct. V18
Lincoln Blvd. W19
Linden Rd. V20
Lioncrest Dr. V19
Lorraine Ct. W18
Madison W18
Maple Ave. V19
Michael Sohn Ct. W19
Mill Rd. V19
Millard Ave. V20
Mission Dr. W18
Monroe W18
Monterey Dr. W18
Parkview Dr. W19
Picadilly Ct. V20
Pleasant Dr. W18
Polk Ave. W20
Poplar Ave. V18
Redwood Dr. W18
Regency Dr. W19
Richton Pl. V19
Richton Rd. V19
Richton Sq. W19
Ridgeway Ave. V,W20
Riverside Dr. W18
Roberta Ln. W18
Rockingham Rd. V18
Salem Ct. V18
Saratoga Rd. V18
Sauk Trail Rd. V19
Schaat Ct. V18
Scott Dr. W19
St. Ives Ln. V20
Steger Rd. W20
Taylor Ave. W20
Thomas Ct. V20
Thomas Dr. V18
Tower Dr. V19
Tyler Dr. W19
Valley Dr. W18
Victoria Dr. W19
Washington Ct. W19
Washington Dr. W18
Whitehall V19
Windsor Ct. V19
Woodbine Rd. V19
York Ct. W20

PARKS
Dennis Holt Park W18
Glaeser Park V19
Indian Trail Park V18
Jones Park W19
Klawitter Park W18
Pierce Park W18

SCHOOLS
Armstrong School W18
Immanuel Sch. V18
Rich Twp. H.S., South V18
Richton Sq. Sch. W20
Sauk School V19

MISCELLANEOUS
Fire Department V20
Library V19
R.R. Station V19
Rich Township Hall V19
Richton Crossing Nursing Home
.... V18

ROLLING MEADOWS
Pages 7,8,12,13

STREETS
Adams St. .... Pg.7 .... E7
Alder Ct. ..... Pg.7 .... E6
Alexandria Ct. . Pg.7 .... E7
Algonquin Pkwy. ....
.... Pg.13 ...... G9
Algonquin Rd. . Pg.13 ...... G8
Amanda Ct. ... Pg.7 .... F6
Angeline Ct. ... Pg.7 .... E7
Apollo Ave. ... Pg.13 ...... H8
Applejack Rd. . Pg.7 .... D6
Arbor Dr. ..... Pg.12 ...... G8
Arlingdale Ct. . Pg.7 .... E5
Arlingdale Dr. . Pg.7 .... E5
Arrowwood Ln. Pg.7 .... E6
Ashbury ...... Pg.7 .... F7
Ashland Ave. . . Pg.8 .... E8
Astor Ln. ..... Pg.13 ...... G9
Auburn ...... Pg.7 .... F7
Barker Ave. ... Pg.13 ...... G8
Bent Creek Ct. . Pg.7 .... F6
Berdnick St. ... Pg.8 .... D8
Birch Ln. ..... Pg.13 ...... G9
Blackhawk Dr. . Pg.8 .... D8
Blacktwig Rd. . Pg.7 .... F8
Bluebird Ln. ... Pg.8 .... E9
Bluebird Ln. S. Pg.13 ...... F9
Bobolink Ln. . . Pg.8 .... F8
Bobwhite Ln. . . Pg.13 ...... F8
Brockway St. . . Pg.7 .... E7
Brookmeade Dr. Pg.13 ...... G8
Brookview Ln. . Pg.7 .... F6
Brookwood Dr. Pg.7 .... E7
Bryant Ave. ... Pg.8 .... E8
Burning Trees . Pg.7 .... D6
Butterfield Ct. . Pg.7 .... E6
California Ave. . Pg.7 .... F7
California Ct. . . Pg.7 .... F7
Calvert Dr. .... Pg.13 ...... G9
Campbell St. . . Pg.8 .... E9
Cardinal Dr. ... Pg.8 .... E8
Carnegie St. ... Pg.8 .... D8
Carr St. ...... Pg.13 ...... G9
Carriage Way Dr. ....
.... Pg.13 ...... G9
Castle Ct. ..... Pg.7 .... E6
Cedar Glen Rd. Pg.7 .... D7
Cedar St. ..... Pg.13 ...... G9
Central Rd. ... Pg.13 ..... F8,9
Chas Dr. ...... Pg.7 .... E7
Chateau Dr. ... Pg.13 ...... H9
Chicory Ct. ... Pg.7 .... E6
College Crossing ....
.... Pg.7 .... F6
Corona Dr. N. . . Pg.7 .... E6
Corona Dr. S. . . Pg.7 .... E6
Crane Ct. ..... Pg.13 ...... F9
Creekside Dr. . . Pg.7 ... D7,F7-8
Creekside Ln. . Pg.7 .... F6
Crestwood Ln. . Pg.7 .... D7
Croftwood Ct. . Pg.7 .... E6
Crossing Ct. ... Pg.7 .... E6
Crossroads of Commerce ......
.... Pg.13 ...... G8
Cyndi Ct. ..... Pg.13 ...... F9
Dahlia Ct. ..... Pg.7 .... E6
Davis Ct. ..... Pg.7 .... E7
Dawngate Ct. . . Pg.7 .... F7
Debra Ct. ..... Pg.8 .... F8
Deepwood Ln. . Pg.7 .... F7
Deerfield Ln. . . Pg.7 .... E6
Denny Ct. ..... Pg.7 .... D7
Dogwood Rd. . Pg.7 .... D6
Dove Ct. ..... Pg.8 .... F9
Dove St. ..... Pg.8 ..... E-F9
Duxbury ..... Pg.7 .... E7
Eagle Ln. ..... Pg.13 ...... F9
East Frontage Rd. ....
.... Pg.13 ...... F8
Eastman St. ... Pg.8 .... E9
Edgewood Ct. . Pg.7 .... E6
Edison Pl. .... Pg.8 .... D8
Eleanore Ct. ... Pg.8 .... F8
Elk Grove Rd. . Pg.13 ...... H10
Emerson Ave. . Pg.8 .... E8
Essex Way .... Pg.13 ...... G9
Euclid Ae. .... Pg.7 .... E7
Fairfax Ave. ... Pg.8 .... E8
Falcon Ct. .... Pg.8 .... F8
Falcon Dr. .... Pg.8 .... F8
Farmington Ct. Pg.7 .... E6
Fieldstone .... Pg.7 .... D7
Finch Ct. ..... Pg.8 .... F8
Flicker Ln. .... Pg.8 .... E8
Forest Ave. ... Pg.8 .... E8
Fox Ln. ...... Pg.7 .... F6
Fremont St. ... Pg.8 ..... E8-9
Fulle St. ..... Pg.13 ...... F9
George Ct. .... Pg.8 .... E9
George St. .... Pg.8 .... E9
Gettysburg Dr. . Pg.7 .... D7
Ginger Ct. .... Pg.7 .... E6
Golf Pl. ...... Pg.13 ...... H9
Green Meadow Ct. ....
.... Pg.7 .... E6
Greenwich Ct. . Pg.7 .... F7
Grouse Ct. .... Pg.13 ...... F8
Grouse Ln. ... Pg.13 ...... F8
Grove Rd. .... Pg.7 .... F7
Grove St. ..... Pg.8 .... F9
Groveside Ln. . Pg.7 .... F6
Gull Ct. ...... Pg.13 ...... F9
Hampton Dr., N. Pg.13 ...... G9
Hampton Dr., S. Pg.13 ...... G9
Hawk Ct. ..... Pg.8 .... F9
Hawk Ln. ..... Pg.8 ..... F8-9
Hawthorne Ln. . Pg.13 ...... G8
Heather Ct. ... Pg.7 .... E6
Heron Ct. ..... Pg.8 .... E8
Hicks Rd. ..... Pg.7 .... D7
Highland Dr. .. Pg.7 .... E5
Holly Ln. ..... Pg.8 .... E8
Honeysuckle Ct. Pg.7 .... E6
Honeysuckle Ln. Pg.7 .... E6
Hoover Ct. .... Pg.7 .... E7
Hoover St. .... Pg.7 .... E7
Industrial Ave. . Pg.7 .... D8
Ironwood Ct. . . Pg.7 .... E6
Jasmine Ln. ... Pg.7 .... E6
Jay Ln. ...... Pg.8 .... E9
Jay Ln., S. .... Pg.13 ...... F9
Jessica Ct. .... Pg.7 .... E6
Jill Ct. .... Pg.7 .... D7
Jonquil Ct. .... Pg.7 .... E6
Josephine Ct. . Pg.7 .... E7
Juniper Rd. ... Pg.7 .... D6
Keith Ct. ..... Pg.7 .... E7
Kenilworth Dr. . Pg.13 ...... G8
Kevin Ln. ..... Pg.7 .... E6
Keystone Ct. . . Pg.13 ...... G9
Killarney Ct. ... Pg.8,13 ..... F8
Kimball Hill Dr. Pg.13 ...... G9
Kimberly Ct. .. Pg.7 .... E6
Kingfisher Ln. . Pg.8 .... F8
Kingfisher Ln. E. ....
.... Pg.8 .... F9
Kings Walk Dr. . Pg.7 .... E7
Kirchoff Rd. ... Pg.7 ..... E7,F9
Knoll Dr. ..... Pg.7 .... D6
Lark Ct. ...... Pg.8 .... E8
Lilac Ct. ..... Pg.7 .... E6
Lincoln Ave. .. Pg.7 .... D7
Linden Ln. .... Pg.13 ...... G9
Lisa Ct. ...... Pg.7 .... E6
Lois Dr. ...... Pg.13 ...... H9
Magnolia Dr. . . Pg.13 ...... G8
Mallard Ct. ... Pg.8 .... F8
Mallory ...... Pg.7 .... F6
Maple Ct. .... Pg.13 ...... G9
Maple Ln. .... Pg.13 ...... G9
Martin Ct. .... Pg.8 ..... F8-9
Martin Ln. .... Pg.8 .... F9
Mayberry Ct. . . Pg.7 .... E6
McKone Ct. ... Pg.7 .... F7
Meacham Rd. . Pg.7 .... F7
Meadow Dr. ... Pg.8 .... E9
Meadowbrook Ct. ....
.... Pg.13 ...... G9
Meadowbrook Indus. Ct. ....
.... Pg.13 ...... G9
Melone Dr. .... Pg.7 .... F8
Michael Ct. ... Pg.7 .... E6
Mill Creek Ln. . Pg.7 .... E6
Millstone Ln. . . Pg.7 .... E6
Moraine ...... Pg.13 ...... H9
New Castle Ct. . Pg.7 .... E6
Newport Dr. ... Pg.13 ...... G8
Norwood Ct. .. Pg.7 .... E6
Oak Ln. ...... Pg.13 ...... G9
Oaksbury Ct. .. Pg.7 .... F7
Oakwood Ct. .. Pg.7 .... E7
Old Creek Rd. . Pg.7 .... D7
Old Hickory Rd. Pg.7 .... D7
Old Mill Ln. ... Pg.7 .... E6
Old Plum Grove Rd. ....
.... Pg.7 .... F6
Old Valley Rd. . Pg.7 .... F7
Old Wilke Rd. . Pg.13 ...... F9
Oriole Ln. .... Pg.8 ..... E-F9
Owl Dr. ...... Pg.8 .... F8
Owl Ln. ...... Pg.8 .... E8
Oxford ...... Pg.7 .... E7
Oxford Rd. ... Pg.7 .... F7
Park Ct. ..... Pg.8 .... E9
Park St. ..... Pg.8 .... F9
Peacock Ct. ... Pg.13 ...... F8
Peacock Ln. ... Pg.13 ...... G8
Pebblebrook Ln. Pg.7 .... E6
Pheasant Dr. . . Pg.8 .... F8
Pine Valley .... Pg.7 .... D7
Piper Ct. ..... Pg.13 ...... F8
Plum Blossom Ct. ....
.... Pg.7 .... F6
Plum Grove Dr. Pg.13 ...... G9
Plum Tree Ln. . Pg.7 .... E6
Polk Ave. ..... Pg.7 .... E7
Prairie Ln. .... Pg.7 ..... E5-6
Pride Ct. ..... Pg.7 .... D7
Quail Ct. ..... Pg.13 ...... F9
Quail Ln. ..... Pg.13 ...... F9
Quinten Rd. ... Pg.7 .... C6
Raven Ln. .... Pg.13 ...... F9
Red Hawk Rd. . Pg.8 .... F8
Redbud Rd. ... Pg.7 .... D6
Redwing Ct. ... Pg.13 ...... F8
Rhiannon Ct. . . Pg.7 .... E7
Richnee Ln. ... Pg.7 .... F7
Robin Ln. .... Pg.8 .... E8
Rohlwing Rd. . Pg.8 .... E8
Rosewood Dr. . Pg.7 .... D6
Rywick Dr. .... Pg.8 .... E8
Salt Creek Dr. . Pg.8 .... D8
Salt Creek Ln. . Pg.8 .... D8
School Dr. .... Pg.8 .... E8
Shady Ct. .... Pg.7 .... F7
Shagbark Rd. . Pg.7 .... F8
Sigwalt St. ... Pg.8 ..... E8-9
Silent Brook Ln. Pg.7 .... E6
Smith St. ..... Pg.7 .... E6
South Ct. ..... Pg.8 .... E9
South St. ..... Pg.8 .... E9
Spruce Ct. .... Pg.8 .... E8
Squibb Ave. ... Pg.13 ...... G8
St. James St. . . Pg.8 ..... E8-9
Stacy Ln. ..... Pg.7 .... E7
Starling Ln. ... Pg.13 ...... F8
Stoneridge Rd. Pg.7 .... D6
Stork Ct. ..... Pg.8 .... E8
Sunset Dr. .... Pg.6 .... C3
Swallow Ln. ... Pg.8 .... F8
Swan Ln. ..... Pg.8 .... E8
Sycamore Dr. . . Pg.13 ...... G8
Taft Ave. ..... Pg.7 .... E7
Tall Oaks Ln. . . Pg.7 .... F7
Teal Ct. ...... Pg.13 ...... F8
Tern Ct. ..... Pg.8 .... E8
Theda Ln. .... Pg.8 .... E8
Thorntree Ln. . Pg.13 ...... G8
Thrush Ct. .... Pg.8 .... E8
Thrush Ln. .... Pg.8 .... F8
Tinder .... Pg.13 ...... H9
Tollview Dr. ... Pg.13 ...... G8
Vermont Ave. . . Pg.7 .... E6
Vermont St. ... Pg.7 .... E7
Viola Ct. ..... Pg.7 .... E6
Walnut Ct. .... Pg.7 .... F8
Weber Dr. .... Pg.13 ...... G9
West Frontage Rd. ....
.... Pg.13 ...... F8
Wildwood Dr. . Pg.7 .... D6
Wilke Rd. .... Pg.13 ...... G9
Willow Ln. .... Pg.13 ...... G9
Wilson Ave. ... Pg.7 .... E7
Wing St. ..... Pg.8 .... E9
Woodbine Rd. . Pg.7 .... F7
Woodcliff Ct. . . Pg.7 .... F7
Woodcliff Ln. . . Pg.7 .... F7
Woodland Ct. . Pg.7 .... F7
Woods Chapel Rd. ....
.... Pg.8 .... F8
Wren Ct. ..... Pg.13 ...... F9
Wren Ln. ..... Pg.13 ...... E9
Wren Ln. S. ... Pg.8 .... F9
Yarrow Ct. .... Pg.7 .... E6
Yarrow Ln. .... Pg.7 .... E6

GOLF COURSES
Plum Grove Country Club ......
.... Pg.13 ...... F8

PARKS
Countryside Park ....
.... Pg.7 .... E6
Creekside Woods ....
.... Pg.7 .... F7
Kimball Hill Park ....
.... Pg.8 .... E8
Salk Park ..... Pg.8 .... F8
Waverly Park . . Pg.13 ...... G9

SCHOOLS
Carl Sandburg Jr. H.S. ....
.... Pg.8 .... F9
Central Sch. ... Pg.13 ...... F8
Clearbrook Center ....
.... Pg.13 ...... F8
Kimball Hill Sch. Pg.8 .... E8
Plum Grove Sch. ....
.... Pg.7 .... E7
Rolling Meadows H.S. ....
.... Pg.13 ...... G8
St. Collette Sch. Pg.13 ...... F8
Willow Bend Sch. ....
.... Pg.13 ...... G8

SHOPPING CENTERS
Meadows Town Mall ....
.... Pg.13 ..... H10
Paddock S.C. .. Pg.13 ..... H10
Plum Grove S.C. ....
.... Pg.7 .... E7
Rolling Meadows S.C. ....
.... Pg.8 .... F8
Southland S.C. Pg.13 ...... G9

MISCELLANEOUS
Community Center ....
.... Pg.13 ...... F8
County Court House ....
.... Pg.8 .... E9
Fire Dept. ..... Pg.7,8 .... E7,F8
Sports Complex Pg.8 .... F8
Village Hall ... Pg.8 .... E8

ROSELLE
Page 17

STREETS
Acadia Bay M6
Acadia Ct. M6
Acadia Tr. M6
Albion Ave. M6
Arthur Ave. M6
Bryce Tr. M6
Candle Lyte Ct. M4
Canterbury Ct. M6
Carlsbad Tr. M6
Cedar Bear Bay M5
Chisolm Ct. M6
Chisolm Tr. M6
Club House Dr. M6
Conway Bay M6
Cross Creek Ct. M6
Cross Creek Dr. N. M6
Cross Creek Dr. W. M6
Cumberland Ct. M6
Cumberland Tr. M6
Glacier Bay M6
Glacier Ct. M6
Glacier Tr. M6
Indian Hill Dr. M5
Larson Ln. M5
Logan St. M4
May St. M6
Medinah Rd. M6
Nerge Rd. M6
Oregon Tr. M6
Overland Ct. M6
Overland Tr. M6
Roslyn Rd. M5
Schrieber Ave. M6
Shadow Lake Bay M6
Shawnee Tr. M6
Springwood Ct. M5
Springwood Dr. M5
Williams St. M4
Yosemite Ct. M6
Yosemite Tr. M6

PARKS
Nerge Park M5

SCHOOLS
Nerge Sch. M5

SHOPPING CENTERS
Cross Creek Commons M6
Roselle Towne Square M6

SAUK VILLAGE
Page 50

STREETS
Apache Ave. V28
Astor St. U28
Barry Ln. U28
Blackstone Ave. V27
Brookwood Dr. W29
Burnham Ave. W30
Calhoun Ave. U28
Calumet Expwy. U27
Carol Ave. V28
Carol Ln. V28
Carolina Dr. W27
Chappel V28
Charlotte Ct. U28
Clyde Ave. V28
Clyde Ct. V28
Constance U28
Cottage Grove Ave. V26
Cynthia Ave. V28
East Brook Dr. W28
Eastbrook Ct. W28
Frank Wagner Ave. U28
Gailine Ave. V28
Harper Ave. V27
Jeffrey Ave. V28
Joshua Dr. V27
Kalveage Dr. U29
Katz Corner Rd. V29
Lincoln Hwy. U28
Long Ave. W29
Luella Ct. V28
Main St. U26
Marigold Dr. V29
Merrill Ave. V28
Merrill Ct. V28
Murphy Ave. V29
Navaho Ave. V29
Nichols Dr. W29
Oakbrook Ct. W28
Oakbrook Ln. W28
Olivia Ave. V28
Orion Ln. V28
Paxton Ave. V28
Peach Tree Ave. V29
Peterson Ave. U28
Pomo Ct. V28
Poplar St. U28
Prairie Ave. V28
Prairie Dr. W27
Reichert Ave. W28
Ross Crescent W28
Rush St. U28
Sauk Pointe Dr. V27
Sauk Trail V28
Shirley Ave. V28
Southbrook Dr. W28
Spencer W29
Steger Rd. W28
Stone Ln. U28
Strassburg Ave. W28
Talandis Ave. V28
Theisen Ave. W29
Theodore Ave. W29
Torrence Ave. V29

SAUK VILLAGE

Westbrook Dr. ... W28
Willow Tree Ln. ... V29
Woodlawn Ave. ... V27
Yates Ave. ... V28
22nd St. ... U26
30th St. ... W29
215th Pl. ... U28
216th Ct. ... V28
216th Pl. ... V28
216th St. ... V28
217th Pl. ... V28
217th St. ... V28
218th Pl. ... V28
218th St. ... V28
219th Pl. ... V28
219th St. ... V28
220th St. ... V28
221st St. ... V28
222nd Pl. ... V28
222nd St. ... V28
223rd Pl. ... V28
223rd St. ... V28
224th Ct. ... W27
224th Pl. ... W29
224th St. ... V29
225th Pl. ... W29
225th St. ... W29
226th Pl. ... W29
226th St. ... W29
227th St. ... W27

CEMETERIES
St. James Cem. ... V28

FOREST PRESERVES
Plum Creek F.P. ... W29

SCHOOLS
Cornell Sch. ... V28
Jeffery Sch. ... U28
Rickover Jr. H.S. ... V29
Sauk Village Baptist Sch. ... V28
St. James Sch. ... V29
St. Mark's Sch. ... V29
Strassburg Sch. ... V28
Wagner Elem. Sch. ... U28

SHOPPING CENTERS
Sauk Plaza ... V29

MISCELLANEOUS
Fire Station ... V28
Moose Lodge ... U29
Village Hall ... U29

SCHAUMBURG

Pages 7,11,12,16,17

STREETS

Abbington Pl. .. Pg.16 .. J3
Aberdeen Ct. .. Pg.11,16 .. J1
Academy Ln. .. Pg.11 .. K1
Acorn Ct. .. Pg.17 .. K4
Adler Ct. .. Pg.11 .. J2
Aegean Dr. .. Pg.16 .. L3
Aimee Ln. .. Pg.11 .. K1
Aimtree Pl. .. Pg.16 .. J3
Akron Ct. .. Pg.16 .. K2
Albany Ct. .. Pg.16 .. M2
Albion Ave. .. Pg.16 .. M3
Alden Ln. .. Pg.16 .. J3
Alder Ct. .. Pg.16 .. K4
Alexandria Ct. .. Pg.11 .. L3
Algonquin Rd. .. Pg.12 .. F6
Allcott Ct. .. Pg.16 .. L2
Allison Ln. .. Pg.16 .. J3
Allonby Ln. .. Pg.16 .. J3
Alpine Dr. .. Pg.16 .. J3
Altoona Ct. .. Pg.16 .. L2
Amanda Ln. .. Pg.12 .. G5
Amboy Ct. .. Pg.16 .. L4
American Ln. .. Pg.17 .. H6-7
Amherst Dr. .. Pg.16 .. J2
Andover Ct. .. Pg.11,16 .. H,J1
Andrew Ct. .. Pg.16 .. K4
Andrew Ln. .. Pg.16 .. K4
Andria Ct. .. Pg.16 .. J2
Angus Ct. .. Pg.16 .. J2
Apple Dr. .. Pg.16 .. H2
Arbor Dr. .. Pg.12 .. G7
Arbor Sq. .. Pg.12 .. G7
Ardmore Ct. .. Pg.16 .. L3
Argyll Ln. .. Pg.16 .. J3
Arklow Pl. .. Pg.16 .. K2
Arlen Ct. .. Pg.16 .. K2
Arlington Ln. .. Pg.16 .. K2
Arrowwood Ct. .. Pg.17 .. K7
Arthur Ave. .. Pg.16 .. M4
Asbury Ln. .. Pg.17 .. L6
Ascot Cir. .. Pgs.12,17 .. J6
Ash Ct. .. Pg.16 .. K4
Ashcroft Ln. .. Pg.17 .. J5
Ashley Ln. .. Pg.16 .. L4
Ashton Ct. .. Pg.12 .. K5
Ashwood Ct. .. Pg.16 .. K4
Ashwood Dr. .. Pg.16 .. K4
Aspen Ct. .. Pg.16 .. K2
Aspen Ln. .. Pg.16 .. K2
Aster Dr. .. Pg.16 .. K7
Athena Ct. .. Pg.16 .. K4
Attleboro Ct. .. Pg.16 .. L3
Auburn Ln. .. Pg.11 .. L2
Auburn Ln. .. Pg.16 .. L2
Austin Ln. .. Pg.12 .. G5
Autumn Ave. .. Pg.16 .. M2
Avon Ct. .. Pg.16 .. M2

Avondale Ct. .. Pg.12 .. J6
Avondale Ln. .. Pg.12 .. J6
Azelea Cir. .. Pg.12 .. J7
Bahama Ct. .. Pg.16 .. L4
Bahama Ln. .. Pg.16 .. L4
Balboa Ct. .. Pg.16 .. L4
Baldwin Ct. .. Pg.11,16 .. H1
Balsam Ct. .. Pg.16 .. K4
Banbury Ct. .. Pg.16 .. H1
Bank Dr. .. Pg.17 .. K7
Bar Harbor .. Pg.17 .. K4
Barcliff Ct. .. Pg.16 .. J3
Barcliff Ln. .. Pg.16 .. K3
Bardsey Dr. .. Pg.16 .. K3
Barkwood Rd. .. Pg.12 .. F6
Barnaby Ct. .. Pg.12 .. J6
Barnaby Ln. .. Pg.12 .. J6
Barrett Ln. .. Pg.12 .. K5
Barton Cir. .. Pg.12,17 .. J6
Basswood Rd. .. Pg.12 .. G6
Bates Ct. .. Pg.16 .. L3
Bates Ln. .. Pg.16 .. L2
Bay Dr. .. Pg.7 .. F6
Bayshore Dr. .. Pg.16 .. H3
Bayview Pt. .. Pg.16 .. J6
Beachcomber .. Pg.16 .. L4
Beacon Dr. .. Pg.16 .. L4
Beckett Cir. .. Pg.12 .. J6
Beckett Ln. .. Pg.12,17 .. J6,7
Bedford Ct. .. Pg.16 .. L3
Beech Ct. .. Pg.17 .. K4
Beech Dr. .. Pg.17 .. K5
Beechwood Ct. .. Pg.12,17 .. K6
Bellechase Cir. .. Pg.12 .. J7
Belmont .. Pg.16 .. L3
Bent Tree Ln. .. Pg.12 .. G5
Bentley Ln. .. Pg.17 .. L5
Berkley Ct. .. Pg.17 .. J6
Berkshire Ln. .. Pg.16 .. K6
Berry Ct. .. Pg.16 .. J2
Bershire Ct. .. Pg.17 .. K6
Bershire Ln. .. Pg.17 .. K6
Berwick Ct. .. Pg.12 .. K4
Beverly Ct. .. Pg.12 .. K4
Birch Pl. .. Pg.12 .. G7
Bird Song .. Pg.16 .. H1
Bishop Ct. .. Pg.16 .. J2
Bittersweet Ct. .. Pg.17 .. K4
Blackhawk .. Pg.17 .. L5
Bladon Rd. .. Pg.16 .. H3
Blaine Ct. .. Pg.12 .. F6
Blanford Ct. .. Pg.17 .. J7
Blenheim Ct. .. Pg.16 .. H3
Bode Rd. .. Pg.16 .. J1
Boston Cir. .. Pg.12 .. L5
Boston Harbor .. Pg.17 .. M5
Bourne Ln. .. Pg.16 .. L3
Boxwood Dr. .. Pg.16 .. L4
Bradford Ct. .. Pg.11 .. L3
Bradford Ln. .. Pg.16 .. K3
Braintree Dr. .. Pg.16 .. L3
Bramble Ct. .. Pg.16 .. K4
Bramble Ln. .. Pg.16 .. K4
Branchwood Dr. .. Pg.17 .. K4
Breakers .. Pg.16 .. J6
Brendon Ct. .. Pg.16 .. H-J1
Brent Ct. .. Pg.16 .. J1
Brentwood Ct. .. Pg.16 .. L3
Brewster Ln. .. Pg.16 .. L3
Brian Ave. .. Pg.16 .. J2
Briar Hill Dr. .. Pg.16 .. J1-2
Briarwood Ct. .. Pg.16 .. K4
Bridgeport Dr. .. Pg.17 .. L5
Bridgeview Pt. .. Pg.17 .. J6
Bridle Ln. .. Pg.12 .. J7
Bridlewood Ct. .. Pg.13 .. J8
Bright Ridge Dr. .. Pg.12,17 .. J5
Brighton Ct. .. Pg.16 .. L3
Bristol Ln. .. Pg.11 .. J3
Brittany Ct. .. Pg.16 .. H1
Brixham Pl. .. Pg.16 .. K2
Broadway Ln. .. Pg.11 .. K1
Brockton Ln. .. Pg.16 .. L2
Bromley Ct. .. Pg.16 .. H2
Brookdale Dr. .. Pg.16 .. J2
Brookhill Ct. .. Pg.17 .. L5
Brookstone Ct. .. Pg.17 .. K7
Brown Ct. .. Pg.16 .. L3
Brunswick Cir. .. Pg.12 .. L5
Brunswick Harbor .. Pg.17 .. L5
Bryn Rd. .. Pg.12 .. F6
Bryn Mawr Ct. .. Pg.11 .. K1
Buccanneer Dr. .. Pg.7 .. F6
Buckingham Ct. .. Pg.17 .. K7
Bunbury Cir. .. Pg.12 .. K7
Burberry Ln. .. Pg.17 .. K7
Burgess Ct. .. Pg.16 .. H1
Burke Ct. .. Pg.17 .. K6
Burnley Cir. .. Pg.17 .. K6
Burr Oak Ln. .. Pg.17 .. K5
Buttercup Ln. .. Pg.17 .. J7
Buttonwood Cir. .. Pg.17 .. K7
Cable Ct. .. Pg.16 .. K2
Cabot Ln. .. Pg.16 .. L3
Cambria Ct. .. Pg.17 .. L4
Cambourne Ln. .. Pg.16 .. J2
Cambridge Ln. .. Pg.16 .. L3
Camden Ct. .. Pg.11 .. J1
Camellia Ln. .. Pg.17 .. J7
Cannon Ct. .. Pg.16 .. L2
Canterbury Rd. .. Pg.16 .. H3
Cape Ln. .. Pg.16 .. L2
Capital Ct. .. Pg.16 .. L2
Capri Ln. .. Pg.16 .. L4
Captains Cove .. Pg.7 .. F6

Cardiff Ct. .. Pg.16 .. H2
Cardinal Ln. .. Pg.16 .. J1
Carlisle Ct. .. Pg.16 .. J2
Carlton Ct. .. Pg.16 .. K3
Carlton Ln. .. Pg.11 .. K3
Carmelhead .. Pg.17 .. K5
Carnaby Ct. .. Pg.16 .. J2
Carolina Ct. .. Pg.16 .. M2
Carolina Dr. .. Pg.16 .. L2
Carr Ct. .. Pg.16 .. L2
Carriage Cir. .. Pg.17 .. L5
Carriage Ln. .. Pg.17 .. L5
Carryville Ln. .. Pg.16 .. K1
Carson Ct. .. Pg.16 .. L2
Carver Ln. .. Pg.16 .. K3
Casa Dr. .. Pg.17 .. J6
Case Ct. .. Pg.16 .. L2
Casey Ct. .. Pg.7 .. F6
Cedar Ct. .. Pg.16 .. K4
Cedarcrest Dr. .. Pg.16 .. L4
Center Ct. .. Pg.12 .. G4
Century Ct. .. Pg.16 .. K5
Chalfont Dr. .. Pg.16 .. J3
Champlaine Ct. .. Pg.12 .. L5
Charlene Ln. .. Pg.16 .. K3
Charleston Ct. .. Pg.11 .. K1
Charleston Dr. .. Pg.16 .. K1
Charlotte Ct. .. Pg.11 .. K1
Chartwell Rd. .. Pg.16 .. H3
Chatham Ct. .. Pg.16 .. L2
Chatham Ln. .. Pg.16 .. L2
Chatsworth Cir. .. Pg.12,17 .. J6
Chaucer Ct. .. Pg.16 .. L4
Chelsea Ct. .. Pg.16 .. L3
Chelsea Ln. .. Pg.16 .. L3
Cherry Dr. .. Pg.16 .. J2
Cherrywood Dr. .. Pg.12 .. J6
Chesapeake Ln. .. Pg.16 .. M2
Chestnut Ct. .. Pg.16 .. K3
Cheswick Ct. .. Pg.11,16 .. J1
Chilmark Ct. .. Pg.16 .. K3
Chilmark Ln. .. Pg.16 .. K1
Churchill Rd. .. Pg.16 .. H3
Civic Dr. .. Pg.16 .. K3
Clarendon Springs .. Pg.16 .. J2
Claridge Ct. .. Pg.17 .. L6
Classic Rd. .. Pg.17 .. L4
Clayton Ct. .. Pg.16 .. J1
Clearbrook Ct. .. Pg.12 .. L5
Clearwater Ln. .. Pg.17 .. J6
Cleveland Ct. .. Pg.12 .. K5
Clifton Ct. .. Pg.16 .. L4
Clipper Dr. .. Pg.7 .. F6
Cloud Ct. .. Pg.16 .. L2
Clover Ln. .. Pg.16 .. L2
Cloverdale Ct. .. Pg.16 .. J2
Cloverdale Ln. .. Pg.16 .. J2
Cobbler Ln. .. Pg.12 .. J6
Cobblestone Ct. .. Pg.13 .. J8
Colby Ln. .. Pg.16 .. L2
Cole Ct. .. Pg.16 .. K2
College Dr. .. Pg.7 .. F6
Colony Lake Dr. .. Pg.16 .. H3
Columbia Ct. .. Pg.11 .. K1
Columbine Cir. .. Pg.17 .. J7
Columbine Ct. .. Pg.17 .. J7
Columbus Dr. .. Pg.17 .. F6
Colwyn Ct. .. Pg.16 .. J2
Commadore Ct. .. Pg.16 .. M2
Commadore Ln. .. Pg.16 .. M2
Commerce Dr. .. Pg.12 .. G5
Commons Dr. .. Pg.17 .. H6
Compton Ln. .. Pg.16 .. L2
Concord Ln. .. Pg.16 .. L3
Concordia .. Pg.16 .. L2
Continental Ln. .. Pg.17 .. J2
Cooper Ct. .. Pg.12 .. G6
Copley Ct. .. Pg.12 .. G5
Copperfield Ln. .. Pg.17 .. L4
Coral Ct. .. Pg.16 .. L2
Cornell Ln. .. Pg.16 .. I3
Corporate Crossing .. Pg.12 .. J7
Corsaire Ln. .. Pg.17 .. J7
Cottington Ct. .. Pg.16 .. J2
Cottington Dr. .. Pg.16 .. J2
Cottonwood Ct. .. Pg.12 .. K4
Cottonwood Ln. .. Pg.17 .. K4
Cotuit Ct. .. Pg.16 .. K3
Country Club Ln. .. Pg.16 .. L3
Countryside Dr. .. Pg.16 .. M2
County Farm Ln. .. Pg.11,16 .. H1
Courtenay Ln. .. Pg.17 .. L6
Courtland Ct. .. Pg.16 .. K4
Cove Point .. Pg.17 .. J6
Covehill Ct. .. Pg.16 .. J3
Coventry Rd. .. Pg.16 .. G3
Coveside Ln. .. Pg.16 .. L4
Covinton Pl. .. Pg.16 .. J3
Crabtree Ct. .. Pg.17 .. M4
Creekside Dr. .. Pg.17 .. K4
Creighton Ln. .. Pg.16 .. K5
Crest Ct. E. .. Pg.17 .. M5
Crest St. .. Pg.17 .. M5

Crestwood Ct. .. Pg.12 .. G5
Crooked Creek Rd. .. Pg.12 .. F6
Crown Ct. .. Pg.12 .. L5
Crystal Ct. N. .. Pg.17 .. K6
Crystal Ct. S. .. Pg.17 .. K6
Cumberland Ct. .. Pg.16 .. J2
Cutters Mill Ct. .. Pg.16 .. J3
Cutters Mill Ln. .. Pg.16 .. J2
Cypress Ct. .. Pg.16 .. K4
Dana Ct. .. Pg.17 .. M5
Danbury Ct. .. Pg.16 .. L4
Daniels Ct. .. Pg.16 .. H3
Dansford Dr. .. Pg.12 .. K4
Dante Ct. .. Pg.16 .. L4
Danvers Ct. .. Pg.16 .. L3
Dartford Ln. .. Pg.16 .. K2
Dartmouth Ln. .. Pg.16 .. L2
Deborah Ct. .. Pg.16 .. L5
Dedham Ln. .. Pg.16 .. L2
Deerfield Ct. .. Pg.16 .. J1
Deerpath Ct. .. Pg.17 .. K7
Del Lago Dr. .. Pg.17 .. J6
Denham Pl. .. Pg.16 .. H2
Dennis Ct. .. Pg.16 .. K3
Denton Ct. .. Pg.11 .. K1
Derby Ct. .. Pg.12 .. K5
Derry Ct. .. Pg.17 .. L4
Desmond Dr. .. Pg.16 .. L4
Devonshire Ct. .. Pg.13 .. J8
Dickens Way .. Pg.17 .. L4
Dighton Ln. .. Pg.17 .. H6
Discovery Dr. .. Pg.16 .. H1
Dixie Ct. .. Pg.16 .. M2
Dogwood Ct. .. Pg.16 .. K4
Donna Ct. .. Pg.17 .. L5
Dorchester Ct. .. Pg.16 .. J1
Dorset Ln. .. Pg.17 .. K5
Dover Ct. .. Pg.16 .. L2
Downing Dr. .. Pg.16 .. H3
Dracut Ln. .. Pg.17 .. H6
Drake Cir. .. Pg.12 .. L5
Driftwood Ln. .. Pg.17 .. K7
Drummer Dr. .. Pg.12 .. G7
Dublin Ln. .. Pg.11,16 .. H1
Dumont Ln. .. Pg.16 .. H2
Dunbar Ct. .. Pg.16 .. J2
Dunlap Pl. .. Pg.16 .. J2
Dunsford Ct. .. Pg.16 .. H2
Durham Ct. .. Pg.17 .. L5
Duxbury Ln. .. Pg.16 .. L3
E. Point Dr. .. Pg.17 .. L5
Eagle Ct. .. Pg.16 .. J1
East Wood Ct. .. Pg.12 .. G5
Eastham Ct. .. Pg.16 .. K3
Eastview St. .. Pg.17 .. J6
Eaton Ct. .. Pg.17 .. L6
Ebbtide Pt. .. Pg.17 .. J6
Eden Dr. .. Pg.16 .. G3
Edgelake Pt. .. Pg.13 .. J8
Elgin Ln. .. Pg.12 .. J3
Ellington Dr. .. Pg.16 .. L3
Ellisville Ln. .. Pg.16 .. K3
Elm Ct. .. Pg.16 .. K3
Elmhurst Ln. .. Pg.16 .. J3
Elmont Ct. .. Pg.16 .. L2
Elmwood Ln. .. Pg.17 .. K7
Emerald Dr. .. Pg.17 .. J6
Emerson Dr. .. Pg.16 .. K2
Epping Pl. .. Pg.16 .. J2
Essex Ct. .. Pg.16 .. K2
Estes Ave. .. Pg.16 .. M3
Estes Ln. .. Pg.16 .. M3
Evening Song Ct. .. Pg.16 .. H1
Evergreen Ct. .. Pg.12 .. K4
Exeter Ct. .. Pg.17 .. L4
Exmore Ct. .. Pg.16 .. K2
Fabish Ct. .. Pg.11,16 .. K1
Fairbanks Ct. .. Pg.12 .. J6
Fairfield Ct. .. Pg.17 .. K5
Fairhaven Ct. .. Pg.17 .. J2
Fairhaven Ln. .. Pg.16 .. J2
Fairlane Ct. .. Pg.16 .. M2
Fairlane Dr. .. Pg.16 .. M-L2
Fairview Cir. .. Pg.11 .. L3
Fairview Ct. .. Pg.16 .. L3
Falmouth Ln. .. Pg.16 .. L3
Farm Gate Dr. .. Pg.17 .. K4
Farnham Ct. .. Pg.16 .. H2
Featherstone Ct. .. Pg.11,16 .. J1
Fennel Ct. .. Pg.17 .. K6
Fennel Ln. .. Pg.17 .. K6
Fenwick Ct. .. Pg.16 .. J2
Fenz Rd. .. Pg.16 .. M2
Fermi Ct. .. Pg.16 .. L4
Fern Ct. .. Pg.17 .. K6
Ferndale Ct. .. Pg.16 .. K4
Fieldstone Ct. .. Pg.16 .. H3
Finchley Ct. .. Pg.16 .. H2
Fiskeville Ln. .. Pg.16 .. L3
Flintshire Dr. .. Pg.17 .. J2
Flower Ct. .. Pg.16 .. J1
Forest Ct. .. Pg.11 .. K4
Forest Ln. .. Pg.16 .. K4
Forestdale Ct. .. Pg.16 .. K2
Foxboro Ct. .. Pg.16 .. L3
Foxboro Ln. .. Pg.16 .. L3
Foxwood Ct. .. Pg.16 .. H3
Gallery Ct. .. Pg.7 .. F6
Gareth Ln. .. Pg.17 .. K6
Garnet Ct. .. Pg.17 .. L6
Gary Ave. .. Pg.16 .. M2
Gary Ct. .. Pg.16 .. M2

Gastonbury Cir. .. Pg.16 .. L3
Gayton Ln. .. Pg.17 .. K5
Geneva Ct. .. Pg.16 .. L4
Georgean Ln. .. Pg.16 .. K3
Georgia Ct. .. Pg.16 .. M2
Glasgow Ct. .. Pg.11,16 .. H1
Glasgow Ln. .. Pg.11,16 .. H1
Glastonbury Ln. .. Pg.16 .. L3
Glen Byron Ct. .. Pg.11 .. J1
Glengarry Ct. .. Pg.11,16 .. J1
Glenn Ct. .. Pg.17 .. K5
Glenridge Ln. .. Pg.16 .. K1
Glenview Ct. .. Pg.16 .. K1
Gloucester Cir. .. Pg.12 .. L5
Gloucester Harbor .. Pg.17 .. M5
Golf (Evanston- Elgin) Rd. .. Pg.17 .. H6
Good Speed Ln. .. Pg.16 .. J1
Governors Dr. .. Pg.12 .. K4
Grace Ct. .. Pg.16 .. L4
Grace Ln. .. Pg.16 .. L4
Grand Central Ln. .. Pg.16 .. K3
Green Briar Dr. .. Pg.12 .. K7
Green Bridge Ct. .. Pg.11,16 .. H1
Greenhill Ln. .. Pg.16 .. K5
Greenview Ct. .. Pg.17 .. L5
Gregory Ct. .. Pg.16 .. L4
Gregory Ln. .. Pg.16 .. L4
Greystone Ct. .. Pg.17 .. K7
Groen Ct. .. Pg.17 .. K6
Groen Ln. .. Pg.17 .. K6
Groton Ct. .. Pg.16 .. L3
Grove Ave. .. Pg.16 .. M2
Grovener Dr. .. Pg.17 .. L6
Hackberry Ct. .. Pg.17 .. K4
Hadley Run Ln. .. Pg.12 .. J6
Halifax Ct. .. Pg.16 .. L3
Hamilton Cir. .. Pg.11 .. J1
Hamilton Pl. .. Pg.11 .. J1
Hammond Dr. .. Pg.12 .. F6
Hampshire Ct. .. Pg.17 .. L5
Hampton Harbor .. Pg.17 .. M5
Hampton Ln. .. Pg.16 .. L3
Hanley Ct. .. Pg.16 .. H2
Hanover Ct. .. Pg.12 .. J6
Hanscom Ct. .. Pg.16 .. K1
Harbour Ct. .. Pg.16 .. M2
Harmon Dr. .. Pg.16 .. L3
Hartford Ct. .. Pg.17 .. L5
Hartford Dr. .. Pg.17 .. L5
Hartley Hall .. Pg.17 .. H7
Hartmann Ct. .. Pg.16 .. L2
Harvard Cir. .. Pg.16 .. L2
Harvard Ln. .. Pg.16 .. L2
Harwich Ln. .. Pg.16 .. J3
Hastings Ct. .. Pg.16 .. H2
Haverfordd Ct. .. Pg.13 .. J8
Hawthorne Ln. .. Pg.16 .. K1
Hazel Dr. .. Pg.17 .. K4
Heather Ct. .. Pg.17 .. K7
Heatherstone Ct. .. Pg.12,17 .. J6
Heatherstone Dr. .. Pg.12,17 .. J6
Helene Ln. .. Pg.16 .. K3
Hemlock Pl. .. Pg.12 .. G7
Heron Ave. .. Pg.16 .. M2
Heron Ct. .. Pg.16 .. M2
Hickory Ct. .. Pg.17 .. K4
Hickory Ln. .. Pg.17 .. K4
Higgins Rd. .. Pg.17 .. J6
High Pt. .. Pg.17 .. K6
Highland Ct. .. Pg.11,16 .. H1
Hillcrest Blvd. .. Pg.12 .. G4
Hillcrest Dr. S. .. Pg.17 .. M6
Hillside Ct. .. Pg.17 .. L5
Hilltop Ct. .. Pg.16 .. K4
Hilltop Dr. .. Pg.16 .. K4
Hillwick Ln. .. Pg.17 .. K5
Hingham Ct. .. Pg.11 .. L3
Hingham Ln. .. Pg.16 .. L3
Hinkle Ct. .. Pg.16 .. K4
Hinkle Ln. .. Pg.16 .. K4
Hitching Post Ln. .. Pg.16 .. J2
Holli Ct. .. Pg.16 .. J3
Holliston Cir. .. Pg.16 .. J1
Holliston Ct. .. Pg.16 .. L4
Holmes Way .. Pg.16 .. L4
Holyoke Ct. .. Pg.17 .. L4
Houlton Ct. .. Pg.16 .. L2
Howard St. .. Pg.17 .. M5
Hunterdon Ct. .. Pg.16 .. J1
Hunters Cir. .. Pg.17 .. L4
Hunters Cresent .. Pg.17 .. L5
Huntington Ln. .. Pg.17 .. L5
Huntley Ct. .. Pg.17 .. H1
Huntwyck Ct. .. Pg.13 .. J8
Hyannis Ct. .. Pg.16 .. L3
Hyde Ct. .. Pg.11 .. K1
Idle Wild Ct. .. Pg.12 .. G5
Idleston Ct. .. Pg.16 .. L3
Illinois Ave. .. Pg.17 .. K5
Indian Hill Dr. .. Pg.17 .. K6
Ironwood Ct. .. Pg.16 .. K6
Irving Park Rd. .. Pg.16 .. K1
Islington Dr. .. Pg.16 .. J2
Iverson Ct. .. Pg.16 .. J2
Iverson Ln. .. Pg.16 .. J2
Ivy Ct. .. Pg.16 .. K3
James Ct. .. Pg.16 .. J2

Jamestown Ct. .. Pg.17 .. L5
Janine Ln. .. Pg.16 .. L4
Jeffery Ct. .. Pg.16 .. K3
Jeffery Ln. .. Pg.16 .. K3
John Ct. .. Pg.17 .. K5
John Rolfe Dr. .. Pg.16 .. J1
John Smith Dr. .. Pg.16 .. H1
Jones Rd. .. Pg.16 .. G3
Juli Ct. .. Pg.17 .. L5
Jule Dr. .. Pg.17 .. K5
Juniper Ln. .. Pg.16 .. K4
Kavalier Ct. .. Pg.16 .. J1
Keats Ct. .. Pg.16 .. L4
Kemah Ct. .. Pg.16 .. K4
Kemah Ln. .. Pg.16 .. K4
Kendall Ct. .. Pg.11 .. K1
Kendrick Ct. .. Pg.16 .. K1
Kenilworth Dr. .. Pg.17 .. K5
Kenmore Ct. .. Pg.11,16 .. K1
Kensington Dr. .. Pg.16 .. J1
Kent Ct. .. Pg.16 .. L4
Kerri Ct. .. Pg.12 .. J6
Killarney Ct. .. Pg.17 .. L4
Kimberly Dr. .. Pg.17 .. J7
Kings Mill Ct. .. Pg.17 .. K5
Kingsbury Dr. .. Pg.11 .. L1
Kingsley Dr. .. Pg.16 .. J2
Kingsport Dr. .. Pg.17 .. L6
Kingston Ct. .. Pg.11 .. K2
Kingston Ln. .. Pg.16 .. K2
Kirkwall Ln. .. Pg.17 .. K5
Knights Bridge Ln. .. Pg.11 .. G3
Knollwood Ct. .. Pg.16 .. K6
Knollwood Dr. .. Pg.16 .. H-K1
Knottingham Ct. .. Pg.17 .. L6
Knottingham Dr. .. Pg.17 .. L6
Kristen Cir. .. Pg.12 .. G5
Kristen Dr. .. Pg.12 .. G5
Laconia Ln. .. Pg.16 .. L4
Lakeland Dr. .. Pg.17 .. J6
Lakeview Pt. .. Pg.17 .. J6
Lambert Dr. .. Pg.17 .. K5
Lamorak Ct. .. Pg.17 .. K6
Lamorak Dr. .. Pg.17 .. K6
Lancashire Dr. .. Pg.16 .. K5
Langley Dr. .. Pg.17 .. K5
Largo Ct. .. Pg.16 .. H2
Lauder Ln. .. Pg.17 .. L6
Laurel Ln. .. Pg.17 .. M5
Laurette Ct. .. Pg.16 .. K5
Lawson Rd. .. Pg.16 .. K1
Lear Ct. .. Pg.16 .. J1
Leeds Pass .. Pg.16 .. J3
Lela Ct. .. Pg.16 .. K6
Lela Ln. .. Pg.16 .. K6
Lengl Dr. .. Pg.17 .. K5
Lenox Ct. .. Pg.11,16 .. K1
Leslie Ln. .. Pg.16 .. J2
Lewis Ct. .. Pg.17 .. L5
Lexington Cir. .. Pg.12 .. J7
Lexington Dr. .. Pg.17 .. J7
Liberty Ct. .. Pg.16 .. J1
Library Ln. .. Pg.17 .. L4
Lighthouse .. Pg.16 .. L4
Lilac Ct. .. Pg.16 .. M2
Lily Ct. .. Pg.16 .. L4
Limerick Ln. .. Pg.17 .. L4
Lincoln Meadows Cir. .. Pg.12 .. J7
Lincoln Meadows Dr. .. Pg.12 .. J7
Lincoln St. .. Pg.12 .. J7
Lincolnshire Ct. .. Pg.17 .. K5
Linden Ln. .. Pg.12 .. F7
Linsey Ave. .. Pg.16 .. M2
Linton Ct. .. Pg.16 .. M2
Linwood Ln. .. Pg.16 .. K4
Lippitt Ct. .. Pg.16 .. L3
Locust Pl. .. Pg.12 .. G7
Long Island Dr. .. Pg.17 .. L5
Long Meadow Dr. .. Pg.17 .. L4
Longboat Cir. .. Pg.16 .. H3
Longboat Ln. .. Pg.16 .. H3
Longtree Ct. .. Pg.16 .. G7
Lorelei Dr. .. Pg.16 .. L4
Lorraine Pl. .. Pg.17 .. J7
Lowell Ct. .. Pg.11 .. L3
Lowell Ln. .. Pg.16 .. L3
Lucre Ct. .. Pg.12 .. J6
Lundy Ln. .. Pg.17 .. K5
Lunt Ave. .. Pg.16 .. M3-4
Lynnfield Ln. .. Pg.16 .. K2
Madeline Ct. .. Pg.12 .. J7
Magnolia Ct. .. Pg.17 .. K4
Maidstone Ct. .. Pg.11 .. J1
Malden Ct. .. Pg.17 .. L2
Mall Dr. .. Pg.17 .. J7
Mallard Ct. .. Pg.17 .. L5
Mallard Ln. .. Pg.17 .. L5
Manchester Cir. .. Pg.17 .. L5
Manchester Ct. .. Pg.17 .. L5
Manchester Dr. .. Pg.17 .. L5
Manchester Ln. .. Pg.17 .. M5
Manchester Rd. .. Pg.16 .. L6
Manomet Ct. .. Pg.12,17 .. H6
Manomet Dr. .. Pg.17 .. H6
Manor Cr. .. Pg.16 .. J2
Mansfield Ct. .. Pg.16 .. J2
Maple Pl. .. Pg.12 .. G7
Maplewood Dr. .. Pg.16 .. K7
Marble Hill Ct. .. Pg.17 .. J5
Margate Ct. .. Pg.17 .. J5
Marie Ln. .. Pg.16 .. K3
Mariner Pt. .. Pg.17 .. J6

SCHAUMBURG

SCHAUMBURG

Martingale Rd. . . Pg.17 . . . J7
Mashpee Ln. . . Pg.16 . . . J3
Matfield Ct. . . Pg.16 . . . L3
Mayfair Ln. . . Pg.17 . . . K7
Maywood Ln. . . Pg.16 . . . J2
McConnor Pkwy. . . . . . . Pg.12 . . . G7
Meacham Rd. . . Pg.17 . . . J7
Medford Cir. . . Pg.17 . . . J2
Melody Ct. . . Pg.16 . . . J2
Mendon Ln. . . Pg.16 . . . K2
Mercury Ct. . . Pg.16 . . . L2
Mercury Dr. . . Pg.16 . . . M2
Merlin Dr. . . Pg.17 . . . K6
Mermaid Ct. . . Pg.16 . . . L4
Michelle Cir. . . Pg.16 . . . J7
Michelle Pl. . . Pg.12 . . . J7
Middlebury Ct. . . Pg.17 . . . K7
Milan Ct. . . Pg.16 . . . L4
Milford Ct. . . Pg.16 . . . L4
Millbrook Ct. . . Pg.16 . . . K2
Millbrook Ln. . . Pg.16 . . . K3
Mills Ln. . . Pg.16 . . . K1
Milton Ct. . . Pg.16 . . . L3
Mirage Ln. . . Pg.11 . . . J1
Mistic Harbor Ln. . . . . Pg.16 . . . L4
Mitchell Blvd. . . Pg.16 . . . M4
Mohawk Ct. . . Pg.17 . . . L-M5
Mohegan Ln. . . Pg.16 . . . L3
Monet Ct. . . Pg.16 . . . L4
Monson Ct. . . Pg.7 . . . J7
Montclair Cir. . . Pg.16 . . . J6
Montclair Pl. . . Pg.12 . . . J6
Monterey Ave. . . Pg.16 . . . M5
Moon Raker Dr. . . Pg.7 . . . F6
Mora Ct. . . Pg.16 . . . M2
Morning Song Ct. . . . . Pg.16 . . . H1
Morse Ave. . . Pg.16 . . . M3-4
Mullinger Ct. . . Pg.17 . . . L4
Nantucket Har. . . Pg.17 . . . M5
National Pkwy. . . Pg.12 . . . H6
Natwick Ln. . . Pg.16 . . . K1
Nauset . . Pg.16 . . . K3
Neal Ct. . . Pg.17 . . . K5
New Mills Ct. . . Pg.17 . . . K5
Newbury Ct. . . Pg.12,17 . . . H6
Newbury Ln. . . Pg.12,17 . . . H6
Newgate Ct. . . Pg.17 . . . K5
Newport Harbor Pg.16 . . . M5
Newton Ct. . . Pg.11 . . . K1
Niagara Ave. . . Pg.17 . . . L5
Night Song Ct. . . Pg.16 . . . H1
Norman Ct. . . Pg.17 . . . M5
Normandy Dr. . . Pg.12 . . . J7
Northbury Ct. . . Pg.17 . . . K6
Northwest Tollway . . . . Pg.12 . . . G5-6
Northwind Cir. . . Pg.11 . . . H2
Norwell Ct. . . Pg.16 . . . L3
Norwell Ln. . . Pg.16 . . . L2
Norwood Ln. . . Pg.16 . . . L3
Notis Ct. . . Pg.11 . . . J1
Oak Creek Ln. . . Pg.17 . . . K4
Oak Knoll Ct. . . Pg.17 . . . K7
Oak Lawn Ct. . . Pg.12 . . . G5
Oak Meadow Ct. Pg.17 . . . K7
Oakmont Ln. . . Pg.12,17 . . . J6
Oakview Ct. . . Pg.16 . . . K4
Oakwood Ct. . . Pg.16 . . . L3
Ocean Dr. . . Pg.11 . . . L5
Odlum Dr. . . Pg.11 . . . J1
Old Barn Rd. . . Pg.17 . . . K5
Old Bridge . . Pg.17 . . . K5
Old Kings Ct. . . Pg.17 . . . J1
Old Mill Dr. . . Pg.17 . . . K5
Old Plum Grove Rd. . . . . Pg.7 . . . F6
Old Schaumburg Rd. . . . . Pg.16 . . . K7
Oleander Dr. . . Pg.17 . . . J7
Oliver Ct. . . Pg.17 . . . L4
Omni Dr. . . Pg.12 . . . L5
Onyx Ct. . . Pg.16 . . . J1
Onyx Ct. . . Pg.16 . . . J1
Orchard Ln. . . Pg.16 . . . M2
Orleans Ln. . . Pg.16 . . . K3
Orrington Ct. . . Pg.12 . . . J6
Osage Ln. . . Pg.16 . . . J3
Oxford Ct. . . Pg.16 . . . H2
Oxhill Ct. . . Pg.16 . . . J1
Palace Ct. . . Pg.16 . . . J1
Palisades Pt. . . Pg.16 . . . J6
Palmer Dr. . . Pg.12 . . . F6
Park Dr. . . Pg.16 . . . J2
Park Trail Ct. . . Pg.13 . . . J8
Parker Ct. . . Pg.16 . . . J3
Parker Dr. . . Pg.16 . . . J3
Parkville Rd. . . Pg.16 . . . J2
Partridge Dr. . . Pg.17 . . . L5
Patricia Ct. . . Pg.16 . . . K3
Patricia Dr. . . Pg.16 . . . K3
Patuxet Ct. . . Pg.16 . . . J3
Pauline Cir. . . Pg.16 . . . K2
Paxton Ln. . . Pg.16 . . . K2
Payne Rd. . . Pg.17 . . . H6
Peach Ln. . . Pg.16 . . . H2
Pebble Ct. . . Pg.17 . . . K6
Pembridge Ln. . . Pg.17 . . . K5
Pembroke Ct. . . Pg.16 . . . J1
Pembroke Dr. . . Pg.11,16 . . . K1
Pennsbury Ct. . . Pg.17 . . . K5
Pennview Ct. . . Pg.17 . . . H1
Pennwood Ct. . . Pg.12,17 . . . K6
Penny Ln. . . Pg.12 . . . G6

Penrith Pl. . . Pg.16 . . . J2
Peppertree . . Pg.17 . . . K4
Perimeter Dr. . . Pg.12 . . . H7
Persimmon Ct. . . Pg.16 . . . M2
Perth Ct. . . Pg.16 . . . J3
Petersham Ln. . . Pg.17 . . . J7
Pheasant Walk Dr. . . . . Pg.17 . . . L3
Pickwick Dr. . . Pg.17 . . . L4
Pine Valley Dr. . . Pg.7 . . . F6
Pinehurst Ln. . . Pg.16 . . . L3
Pinetree Ln. . . Pg.17 . . . K7
Pirates Cove . . Pg.7 . . . F6
Plaza Dr. . . Pg.17 . . . H7
Pleasant Dr. . . Pg.17 . . . K4
Plum Grove Rd. . . Pg.17 . . . J6
Plum Tree Ct. . . Pg.17 . . . K6
Plumrose Ct. . . Pg.12 . . . J5
Plumrose Ln. . . Pg.12 . . . J5
Plumwood Ct. . . Pg.12,17 . . . J6
Plumwood Dr. . . Pg.12,17 . . . J6
Plymouth Ln. . . Pg.16 . . . L3
Pocasset Ct. . . Pg.16 . . . K2
Pochet Ct. . . Pg.16 . . . K4
Pochet Ln. . . Pg.16 . . . K4
Point Dr. E. . . Pg.17 . . . L6
Point Dr. N. . . Pg.17 . . . L6
Point Dr. S. . . Pg.17 . . . L6
Point Dr. W. . . Pg.17 . . . L6
Pondview Ct. . . Pg.16 . . . K3
Poplar Pl. . . Pg.12 . . . G7
Port Way . . Pg.17 . . . J2
Portland Dr. . . Pg.16 . . . J2
Portsmouth Ln. . . Pg.16 . . . K2
Post Oak Pl. . . Pg.12 . . . G7
Prairie Sq. . . Pg.12 . . . G7
Prairie Wind Ln. . . Pg.12 . . . G7
Pratt Ave. N. . . Pg.16 . . . M3
Pratt Ave. S. . . Pg.16 . . . M3
Presidio Ct. . . Pg.12 . . . G5
Preston Dr. . . Pg.16 . . . J3
Preston Ln. . . Pg.17 . . . K1
Primrose Ln. . . Pg.16 . . . J1
Prince Charles Ct. . . . . Pg.11 . . . G3
Prince Charles Ln. . . . . Pg.11 . . . G3
Prince Edward Cir. . . . . Pg.17 . . . L5
Prince Edward Dr. . . . . Pg.17 . . . L6
Princeton Ct. . . Pg.16 . . . L2
Princeton Ln. . . Pg.16 . . . L2
Putnam Ln. . . Pg.16 . . . K3
Quanset Ct. . . Pg.16 . . . K4
Queens Ct. . . Pg.17 . . . K5
Quincy Ct. . . Pg.17 . . . L4
Quindel Ave. . . Pg.17 . . . K5
Quonset Ct. . . Pg.16 . . . L3
Radcliffe Ln. . . Pg.16 . . . L3
Radley Ct. . . Pg.17 . . . L4
Raleigh Ct. . . Pg.11 . . . K1
Ramsey Cir. . . Pg.16 . . . L3
Raymond Ct. . . Pg.17 . . . K5
Rebecca Ct. . . Pg.16 . . . K4
Redwood Ln. . . Pg.16 . . . K4
Reedham Pass . . Pg.16 . . . K2
Reflections Way . . . . Pg.11 . . . J2
Regal Ct. . . Pg.16 . . . J2
Regatta Ct. . . Pg.12 . . . J6
Regatta Pt. . . Pg.16 . . . J6
Regency Ct. . . Pg.16 . . . M3
Regency Dr. . . Pg.16 . . . M3
Regent Cir. . . Pg.17 . . . J5
Regent Ct. Ln. . . Pg.17 . . . H5
Remington Ln. . . Pg.12 . . . G5
Remington Rd. . . Pg.17 . . . H6
Republic Ct. . . Pg.12 . . . L5
Revere Ct. . . Pg.16 . . . J2
Richard Ct. . . Pg.17 . . . K5
Richmond Ct. . . Pg.16 . . . K3
Ridge Ct. . . Pg.17 . . . K6
Ridgeway Ct. . . Pg.17 . . . K4
Ripplebrook Ct. . . Pg.13 . . . J8
Rob Roy Ct. . . Pg.11,16 . . . H1
Rochester Ct. . . Pg.11 . . . K1
Rockne Ct. . . Pg.16 . . . J1
Rodenburg Rd. . . Pg.16 . . . M3
Romm Ct. . . Pg.16 . . . J2
Rose Ct. . . Pg.16 . . . J2
Roselle Rd. . . Pg.17 . . . L5
Rosewood Ct. . . Pg.12,17 . . . K6
Roslyn Ct. . . Pg.16 . . . J3
Roslyn Dr. . . Pg.16 . . . J3
Roslyn Rd. . . Pg.17 . . . M5
Rothbury Ct. . . Pg.17 . . . L5
Routh Ct. . . Pg.12 . . . G5
Roxbury Ln. . . Pg.16 . . . J3
Royal Ct. . . Pg.16 . . . K3
Rugby Pl. . . Pg.16 . . . L3
Ruskin Ct. . . Pg.16 . . . L3
Ruskin Ln. . . Pg.16 . . . L3
Russelwood Ct. Pg.11,16 . . . K1
Russet Ct. . . Pg.17 . . . J6
Rutland Ln. . . Pg.17 . . . J7
Sagamore Ct. . . Pg.16 . . . J3
Sagamore Dr. . . Pg.16 . . . J3
Salado Ct. . . Pg.12 . . . G5
Salem Ct. . . Pg.16 . . . K3
Salem Dr. . . Pg.16 . . . H-L3
Salford Ct. . . Pg.17 . . . L6
Samoset Ct. . . Pg.16 . . . K4
Samoset Ln. . . Pg.16 . . . K4
Sandalwood Ct. Pg.17 . . . K7
Sandburg Ct. . . Pg.12 . . . J7

Sandhurst Ct. . . Pg.17 . . . K6
Sandpebble Dr. . . Pg.16 . . . L4
Santuit Ct. . . Pg.16 . . . J3
Sarah Constant Ln. . . . . Pg.16 . . . H1
Sarah's Grove Ln. . . . . Pg.12 . . . K4
Saugus Ln. . . Pg.17 . . . J7
Savannah Ln. . . Pg.16 . . . M2
Savoy Ct. . . Pg.16 . . . K3
Saylesville Ln. . . Pg.16 . . . K4
Scarsdale Ct. . . Pg.17 . . . K7
Schaumburg Ct. Pg.17 . . . K5
Schaumburg Rd. . . . . Pg.16 . . . K3
Schooner Pt. . . Pg.17 . . . J6
Scott Dr. . . Pg.17 . . . L6
Scully Ct. . . Pg.12 . . . K5
Scully Dr. . . Pg.17 . . . K5
Seafarer Ct. . . Pg.16 . . . J6
Seaside Ct. . . Pg.16 . . . L3
Seaton Ln. . . Pg.16 . . . L3
Seaview Ct. . . Pg.16 . . . L4
Seers Ct. . . Pg.16 . . . J6
Seers Dr. . . Pg.17 . . . J6
Selkirk Dr. . . Pg.17 . . . J3
Sequoia Ct. . . Pg.16 . . . L5
Serenade Ct. . . Pg.17 . . . L4
Seven Pines Rd. . . . . Pg.17 . . . K7
Seville Ct. . . Pg.16 . . . M2
Shady Ln. . . Pg.12 . . . J7
Shagbark Ct. . . Pg.17 . . . K4
Shakespeare Ct. Pg.16 . . . K2
Shannock Ct. . . Pg.16 . . . L3
Shannock Ln. . . Pg.16 . . . L3
Sharon Ln. . . Pg.17 . . . L3
Shattuck Ct. . . Pg.17 . . . K3
Shattuck Dr. . . Pg.16 . . . K3
Shattuck Ln. . . Pg.16 . . . K3
Shaw Ct. . . Pg.16 . . . L4
Sherborn Ln. . . Pg.16 . . . K1
Sheridan Ln. . . Pg.16 . . . L4
Sherwood Dr. . . Pg.17 . . . M5
Shore Ct. . . Pg.17 . . . M5
Shore Dr. . . Pg.17 . . . M5
Shoreline Cir. . . Pg.16 . . . J6
Sienna Ct. . . Pg.17 . . . L3
Silhouette Pl. . . Pg.11 . . . J1
Silverwood Ct. . . Pg.17 . . . K7
Sky Water Dr. . . Pg.12 . . . F7
Skyvue Ln. . . Pg.17 . . . K6
Sleepy Hollow Ct. . . . . Pg.12 . . . G5
Slingerland Dr. . . Pg.16 . . . L2
Somerset Ct. . . Pg.16 . . . K3
Somerset Ln. . . Pg.16 . . . K3
Song Sparrow Ct. . . . . Pg.12 . . . G7
Southbridge Ct. . . Pg.11 . . . H2
Southbridge Ln. . . Pg.11 . . . H2
Southbury Ct. . . Pg.17 . . . K6
Southwick Ln. . . Pg.17 . . . J7
Southwind Cir. . . Pg.11 . . . H1
Spinnaker Pt. . . Pg.17 . . . J6
Spring Cove Dr. . . Pg.16 . . . L4
Spring South Rd. . . . . Pg.16 . . . M2
Spring Valley Ct. . . . . Pg.12,17 . . . K6
Springinsguth Rd. . . . . Pg.16 . . . L2
Spruce Ct. . . Pg.16 . . . K4
Spruce Dr. . . Pg.16 . . . K4
Squanto Ct. . . Pg.16 . . . K4
St. Claire Cir. . . Pg.17 . . . J6
St. Claire Pl. . . Pg.12 . . . J7
Staffire Ln. . . Pg.16 . . . K1
Staffmark Ct. . . Pg.16 . . . H2
Stamford Ct. . . Pg.16 . . . K4
Standish Ln. . . Pg.16 . . . K3
Stanley Ct. . . Pg.16 . . . K5
Stanton Ct. . . Pg.17 . . . J5
Starboard Pt. . . Pg.17 . . . J6
State Pkwy. . . Pg.17 . . . J5
Steeplechase Ct. . . . . Pg.13 . . . J8
Stevens Dr. . . Pg.17 . . . K2
Stirling Ln. . . Pg.11,16 . . . H1
Stock Port Ln. . . Pg.17 . . . K5
Stockbridge Ct. . . Pg.16 . . . J2
Stone Circle Ct. . . Pg.12 . . . J2
Stone Gate Ct. . . Pg.17 . . . K5
Stone Hedge . . Pg.16 . . . H3
Stone Hill Ln. . . Pg.17 . . . K5
Stonefield Ct. . . Pg.13 . . . J8
Stonington Ct. . . Pg.16 . . . L3
Stormy Ct. . . Pg.16 . . . M2
Stoughton Ct. . . Pg.17 . . . K4
Stratford Ln. . . Pg.17 . . . L4
Stratham Ct. . . Pg.17 . . . L3
Stratton Pond Ln. . . . . Pg.16 . . . J2
Sturnbridge Ct. . . Pg.12,17 . . . H6
Sturnbridge Ln. . . Pg.17 . . . H6
Sudbury Ct. . . Pg.16 . . . L3
Sue Ln. . . Pg.7 . . . F7
Suffield Terr. . . Pg.17 . . . K2
Sumac Ct. . . Pg.16 . . . K4
Sumac Ln. . . Pg.17 . . . K4
Summer Song Ct. . . . . Pg.16 . . . H1
Summit Ct. . . Pg.17 . . . K5
Summit Ln. . . Pg.17 . . . M5
Sunfish Pt. . . Pg.17 . . . J6
Superior Ct. . . Pg.12 . . . K5

Surfside Pt. . . Pg.17 . . . J6
Surrey Ln. . . Pg.17 . . . L6
Susan Ct. . . Pg.17 . . . K6
Sussex Cir. . . Pg.17 . . . K5
Sutton Ln. . . Pg.16 . . . J2
Swansea Ct. . . Pg.16 . . . L3
Swartmore Ct. . . Pg.16 . . . L2
Sycamore Pl. . . Pg.12 . . . G7
Syracuse Ln. . . Pg.16 . . . K2
Tadmore Ct. . . Pg.16 . . . J2
Tall Timbers Rd. . . Pg.12 . . . F6
Tamworth Pl. . . Pg.16 . . . K2
Tarpon Ct. . . Pg.16 . . . L4
Taunton Ct. . . Pg.16 . . . L3
Teal Ct. . . Pg.16 . . . K6
Tebay Pl. . . Pg.16 . . . J2
Terrace Ct. . . Pg.17 . . . K6
Thacker St. . . Pg.17 . . . J6
Thames Cir. . . Pg.17 . . . L5
Thames Dr. . . Pg.17 . . . L5
Thistle Ct. . . Pg.11,16 . . . J1
Thoreau Ct. . . Pg.16 . . . L2
Thoreau Ln. . . Pg.12 . . . G7
Thorney Lea Terr. . . . . Pg.16 . . . K3
Thornhill Ct. . . Pg.16 . . . J6
Thornton Ct. . . Pg.17 . . . L5
Thornwood Ct. . . Pg.17 . . . M4
Ticknor Ct. . . Pg.16 . . . M2
Tiffany Dr. . . Pg.16 . . . K1
Tillipi Ct. . . Pg.16 . . . K4
Tilipi Ln. . . Pg.16 . . . K4
Timbercrest Ct. . . Pg.16 . . . K4
Timbercrest Dr. . . Pg.16 . . . K4
Timberwood Ct. Pg.12,17 . . . K6
Timothy Ct. . . Pg.17 . . . K5
Tipperary Ct. . . Pg.16 . . . L3
Tisbury Ct. . . Pg.16 . . . L3
Tisbury Ln. . . Pg.16 . . . L3
Tiverton Ct. . . Pg.16 . . . L3
Tobey Ct. . . Pg.16 . . . J3
Tonset . . Pg.16 . . . K2
Tory Ct. . . Pg.12 . . . K2
Tower Rd. . . Pg.12 . . . G6-7
Tracy Ct. . . Pg.17 . . . J6
Trails Dr. . . Pg.16 . . . J6
Tralee Ct. . . Pg.16 . . . L4
Travis Ct. . . Pg.12 . . . G5
Treebark Ct. . . Pg.11 . . . K4
Treebark Pt. . . Pg.16 . . . K4
Trent Ln. . . Pg.17 . . . K4
Trenton Ct. . . Pg.17 . . . K6
Truro Ct. . . Pg.16 . . . J3
Tudor Ln. . . Pg.17 . . . K3
Tulip Ct. . . Pg.11,16 . . . K1
Tullamore Ct. . . Pg.17 . . . L5
Tyburn Dr. . . Pg.16 . . . K5
Tyler Dr. . . Pg.17 . . . M5
Vado Ct. . . Pg.16 . . . M2
Valley Lake Dr. . . Pg.12 . . . G4
Valley View Dr. . . Pg.16 . . . M2
Vassar Ct. . . Pg.16 . . . L2
Vassar Ln. . . Pg.16 . . . L2
Venice Ct. . . Pg.16 . . . L4
Verde Dr. . . Pg.12 . . . J6
Verona Pl. . . Pg.16 . . . M3
Victoria Ln. . . Pg.16 . . . K3
Viola Ct. . . Pg.16 . . . M2
Vista Ct. . . Pg.16 . . . M2
Waban Ct. . . Pg.16 . . . K2
Waban Ln. . . Pg.16 . . . K2
Wainno Ln. . . Pg.16 . . . J3
Wakeby . . Pg.16 . . . K3
Wakefield Ln. . . Pg.16 . . . K3
Walden Ct. . . Pg.16 . . . L2
Walnut Ln. . . Pg.16 . . . H-L2
Walpole Ln. . . Pg.16 . . . L3
Wapocs Ct. . . Pg.16 . . . K2
Wareham Ln. . . Pg.16 . . . K2
Warwick Ct. . . Pg.16 . . . K2
Warwick Ln. . . Pg.16 . . . K1-2
Waterbury Ln. . . Pg.12 . . . K5
Waterford Dr. . . Pg.17 . . . L5
Waterford Rd. . . Pg.17 . . . L5
Waverley Ln. . . Pg.16 . . . K2
Wax Wing Ct. . . Pg.12 . . . G7
Wayland Ct. . . Pg.16 . . . L3
Wayland Ln. . . Pg.16 . . . L3
Weathersfield Way . . . . Pg.16,17 . . . K2-5
Webley Ct. . . Pg.16 . . . K2
Webley Ln. . . Pg.17 . . . K2
Webster Ct. . . Pg.16 . . . K2
Webster Ln. . . Pg.16 . . . K-L2
Wedgewood Ln. Pg.16 . . . K2
Wellesley Ln. . . Pg.16 . . . L2
Westbridge Ln. . . Pg.11 . . . H2
Westbridge Ln. . . Pg.11 . . . H2
Westchester Cir. Pg.12 . . . L5
Westchester Ln. Pg.17 . . . L4
Westchester Rd. Pg.17 . . . M4
Westfield Ln. . . Pg.16 . . . K2
Weston . . Pg.16 . . . K2
Westover Ct. . . Pg.16 . . . L3
Westover Ln. . . Pg.16 . . . K-M2
Weyers Ct. . . Pg.16 . . . L3
Weymouth Ct. . . Pg.16 . . . K2
Weymouth Ln. . . Pg.11 . . . K2
Whalom Ln. . . Pg.17 . . . H6
Whidah Ct. . . Pg.16 . . . K4
White Branch Ct. N. . . . . Pg.11,16 . . . H1
White Branch Ct. S. . . . . Pg.11,16 . . . H1
White Oak Ct. . . Pg.12 . . . G5
White Oak Ln. . . Pg.12 . . . G5

White Pines Dr. . . Pg.12 . . . K4
Whitehall Ct. . . Pg.16 . . . J2
Whitesail Dr. . . Pg.17 . . . J6
Whitman Ct. . . Pg.12 . . . K7
Whitman Dr. . . Pg.12 . . . K7
Whittier Ln. . . Pg.16 . . . K2
Wianno Ln. . . Pg.16 . . . K2
Wickham Dr. . . Pg.16 . . . J3
Wild Flower Ct. . . Pg.12 . . . K7
Wild Flower Ln. . . Pg.16 . . . K7
Wildberry Ct. . . Pg.17 . . . K7
Wiley Rd. . . Pg.12 . . . G6
Wilkening Ct. . . Pg.12 . . . G5
Williams Ct. . . Pg.16 . . . K3
Williams Dr. . . Pg.16 . . . K3
Williamsburg Dr. . . . . Pg.12 . . . J5
Willington Dr. . . Pg.16 . . . J2
Willow Brook Ct. . . . . Pg.12 . . . G5
Willow Ct. . . Pg.11,16 . . . H1
Willow Rd. . . Pg.17 . . . J7
Willowby Ct. . . Pg.13 . . . J8
Wilmette Ct. . . Pg.16 . . . K2
Wilmslow Ln. . . Pg.16 . . . H4
Wilton Ln. . . Pg.16 . . . K2
Winchester Ct. . . Pg.17 . . . K5
Winchester Dr. . . Pg.16 . . . K2
Winchester Ln. . . Pg.16 . . . K2
Wind Mill . . Pg.17 . . . K4
Wind Song Ct. . . Pg.16 . . . H1
Wind Song Dr. . . Pg.16 . . . H1
Windemere Cir. . . Pg.11 . . . H2
Windsor Dr. . . Pg.17 . . . L5
Windward Dr. . . Pg.17 . . . J6
Wingate Dr. . . Pg.17 . . . K6
Winston Ln. . . Pg.16 . . . K2
Winthrop Ct. . . Pg.16 . . . K2
Winthrop Ln. . . Pg.16 . . . K2
Wise Rd. . . Pg.16 . . . L4
Wisteria Ln. . . Pg.17 . . . K4
Withaeger Dr. . . Pg.17 . . . H5
Woburn Ln. . . Pg.17 . . . K4
Wolcott Ct. . . Pg.12 . . . K5
Woodbury Ct. . . Pg.17 . . . K5
Woodcroft Ln. . . Pg.12,17 . . . J6
Woodfield Dr. . . Pg.12 . . . H7
Woodfield Office Ct. . . . . Pg.17 . . . H6
Woodfield Rd. . . Pg.17 . . . H6-7
Woodland Dr. . . Pg.12 . . . K7
Woodside Ct. . . Pg.12,17 . . . K6
Woodville Ln. . . Pg.16 . . . K5
Woonsocket Ct. . . Pg.16 . . . L3
Worcester Ct. . . Pg.16 . . . L4
Wright Blvd. . . Pg.16 . . . M3
Wyoma Ct. . . Pg.16 . . . K4
Yale Ln. . . Pg.16 . . . L2
Yardley Ln. . . Pg.16 . . . K1
Yarmouth . . Pg.16 . . . K3
Yorkshire . . Pg.16 . . . K2

AIRPORTS
Muni. Helistop . . Pg.12 . . . H6
Schaumburg Airport . . . . Pg.16 . . . M3

CEMETERIES
St. Peter's Cem. Pg.17 . . . J5

GOLF COURSES
Schaumburg Golf Club . . . . Pg.12 . . . J5
Walnut Greens G.C. . . . . Pg.11 . . . H2

PARKS
Abrahamson Park . . . . Pg.12,17 . . . K5
Apollo Park . . Pg.12,17 . . . K5
Atcher Park . . Pg.11,16 . . . L2
Bock Park . . Pg.11,16 . . . K3
Brandenburg Park . . . . Pg.16 . . . J1
Campanelli Park Pg.11,16 . . . K2
Cove Park . . Pg.16 . . . L4
Derda Park . . Pg.11,16 . . . L3
Dooley Park . . Pg.11,16 . . . L3
Eagle Park . . Pg.11,16 . . . K2
Fairview Park . . Pg.17 . . . J5
Falk Park . . Pg.11,16 . . . L3
Freedom Park . . Pg.11,16 . . . K3
Grey Farm Park Pg.11,16 . . . K2
Hoover Park . . Pg.11,16 . . . J2
Jaycee Park . . Pg.11,16 . . . L3
Kingsport East Park . . . . Pg.17 . . . L6
Lancer Creek Park . . . . Pg.17 . . . L5
Levitt Park . . Pg.11,16 . . . L4
Munao Park . . Pg.11,16 . . . L4
Roberts Park . . Pg.11,16 . . . L4
Slingerland Park . . . . Pg.12,17 . . . L5
Sunset Park . . Pg.17 . . . M5
Timbercrest Park . . . . Pg.12,17 . . . K5
Vogelei Park . . Pg.11,16 . . . H4
Woodstock Park . . . . Pg.16 . . . K4

SCHOOLS
Acarath Discovery Center . . . . Pg.12 . . . G5
Addams Jr. H.S. Pg.16 . . . L2
Aldrin Sch. . . Pg.16 . . . L4

SCHAUMBURG TOWNSHIP

Blackwell Sch. . . Pg.16 . . . J2
Campanelli Sch. Pg.16 . . . K2
Churchill Sch. . . Pg.11 . . . G3
Collins Sch. . . Pg.17 . . . K5
Dirksen Sch. . . Pg.17 . . . K5
Dooley Sch. . . Pg.16 . . . L3
Enders Salk Sch. . . . . Pg.16 . . . J3
Frost Jr. H.S. . . Pg.17 . . . L4
Hale Sch. . . Pg.16 . . . L3
J. Edgar Hoover Sch. . . . . Pg.16 . . . J2
Keller Jr. H.S. . . Pg.16 . . . H3
Schaumburg Christian Sch. . . . . Pg.12 . . . J5
Schaumburg H.S. . . . . Pg.11 . . . K3
Schaumburg Sch. . . . . Pg.16 . . . K5
St. Peter's Luth. Sch. . . . . Pg.17 . . . K5

SHOPPING CENTERS
Annex Shopping Center . . . . Pg.16 . . . H4
Higgins Golf Shopping Center . . . . Pg.16 . . . H4
K-Mart Shopping Plaza . . . . Pg.16 . . . H5
One Schaumburg Place . . . . Pg.16 . . . K5
Schaumburg Rd. Shopping Plaza . . . . Pg.16 . . . K5
Town Square Shopping Center . . . . Pg.17 . . . K5
Weatherway Shopping Plaza . . . . Pg.17 . . . L5
Wiseway Plaza . . Pg.16 . . . M2
Woodfield Commons Shopping Center . . Pg.17 . . . H7
Woodfield Mall . . Pg.17 . . . H7

MISCELLANEOUS
Circuit Court & Schaumburg Police Department . . Pg.16 . . . K3
Dist. 54 Admin. Bldg . . . . Pg.16 . . . K6
Dist. 54 Nature Center . . . . Pg.17 . . . L4
Fire Department Pg.12 . . . G5
Meineke Park District Adm. . . . . Pg.17 . . . K5
Post Office . . Pg.16 . . . K4
Schaumburg Township Bldg. . . . . Pg.16 . . . K4
School Park Dist. Rec. Center . . . . Pg.17 . . . J2

SCHAUMBURG TOWNSHIP
Pages 12,16,17
STREETS
Albion Ave. . . Pg.17 . . . M4
Algonquin Rd. . . Pg.17 . . . M6
Blackhawk Dr. . . Pg.17 . . . M5
Circle Ct. . . Pg.12 . . . G7
Circle Dr. S. . . Pg.12 . . . G7
Council Ct. . . Pg.17 . . . M5
Crest Ave. . . Pg.16 . . . M2
Crest St. . . Pg.17 . . . M5
Devon . . Pg.16 . . . M5
Elmwood Ln. N. Pg.12 . . . G7
Elmwood Ln. S. Pg.12 . . . G7
Grant St. . . Pg.17 . . . M4
Green Briar Ln. Pg.17 . . . M6
Greenview Ct. . . Pg.17 . . . M5
Half Ln. . . Pg.17 . . . M5
Higgins Rd. . . Pg.12 . . . J6
Hillcrest Dr. . . Pg.17 . . . M5
Illinois St. . . Pg.17 . . . M4
Indian Hill Dr. . . Pg.17 . . . M4
Irving Park Rd. Pg.16 . . . M3
Lang Ave. . . Pg.17 . . . M3
Larson Ln. . . Pg.17 . . . M5
Lincoln St. . . Pg.17 . . . M4
Logan St. . . Pg.17 . . . M4
Marion . . Pg.17 . . . M4
Meadows Ln. . . Pg.17 . . . M2
Mohawk Dr. . . Pg.17 . . . M5
Monterey Ave. . . Pg.17 . . . M4
Morse Ave. . . Pg.17 . . . M4
Nerge Rd. . . Pg.16 . . . M3
North Shore Ave. . . . . Pg.17 . . . M4
Oneida Dr. . . Pg.17 . . . M6
Park Ave. . . Pg.16 . . . M3
Park St. . . Pg.17 . . . M5
Parkview Dr. . . Pg.17 . . . M5
Pleasant Dr. . . Pg.17 . . . M2
Pratt Blvd. . . Pg.17 . . . M3
Rodenburg Rd. Pg.16 . . . M3
Roselle Rd. . . Pg.17 . . . M5
Roslyn Rd. . . Pg.17 . . . M7
Schaumburg Rd. . . . . Pg.17 . . . K7
Seward St. . . Pg.17 . . . M4
Springinsguth Rd. . . . . Pg.16 . . . M2
Summit Dr. . . Pg.17 . . . M5
Sunset Dr. . . Pg.17 . . . M5
Valley View Dr. Pg.16 . . . M2

SCHOOLS
St. John's Sch. Pg.16 . . . M3

SHOPPING CENTERS
Park Plaza Pg.16 L2

SKOKIE
Pages 30,31

STREETS
Arcadia St. J9-12
Avers Ave. J-K11
Babb Ave. L9
Bennett Ave. J-K12
Beverly Dr. H10
Birchwood Ave. M9-11
Bobolink Terr. K10
Brandess Terr. J9
Bronx Ave. H-J9
Brown St. L9
Brummel St. L9-11
Capitol St. K12
Carol Ave. K9-11
Carpenter Rd. M9
Central Ave. H,L-M8
Central Park Ave. J-M11
Chase Ave. M9
Cherry Pkwy. H10
Christiana K12
Church St. J10
Clark St. J11
Cleveland St. L9-12
Clifford Terr. K11
Colfax Pl. H9
Colfax St. H9-11
Concord Ln. K10
Conrad Ave. K9
Coyle Ave. M9
Crain St. K9-12
Crawford Ave. J-11
Culver H9
Dartmouth Pl. H9
Davis St. J9-12
Dempster St. K9
Dobson St. L9-11
Drake Ave. J-K12
East Prairie Ave. K11
Edens Expwy. H9
Elgin Rd. H-J12
Elgin St. H12
Elm St. K9
Elm Terr. K10
Elmwood St. L9
Emerson St. J9-12
Enfield Ave. K9-11
Estes Ave. M9
Ewing Ave. J12
Fairview Ln. M9
Fargo Ave. M9-11
Farwell Ave. M9
Fitch Ave. M9
Floral L9
Forestview Rd. J12
Foster St. J9-11
Four Winds Way J11
Galitz St. L9
George St. L9
Golf Rd. H10
Grant St. H9-11
Greenleaf St. K9-11
Greenwood Ave. J9-12
Gross Point Rd. H10,K9
Grove St. J9-10
Hamilton Dr. K9
Hamlin Ave. J-L11
Harding Ave. J-K11
Harms Rd. K9
Harrison St. H10
Harvard St. L9-11
Harvest Ln. H10
Hipple Terr. J11
Hoffman St. L9
Howard St. L9
Hull St. L8-9-11
Isabel L11
James St. K10
Jarlath Ave. M9
Jarvis Ave. M9-11
Jerome Ave. M9-10
Jerome St. M11
Jonathan Ln. H10
Joneway Terr. L9
Karlov Ave. H-L11
Keating Ave. J-L10
Kedvale Ave. H-L11
Keeler Ave. J-L11
Keeney St. L10
Kenneth Ave. J-L10
Kenneth Terr. K10
Kenton Ave. H-L10
Keystone Ave. H-K11
Kilbourn Ave. J-L10
Kildare Ave. J-L10
Kilpatrick Ave. J-M10
Kimball Ave. K12
Kirk St. L9-10
Klehm Ct. K9
Knox Ave. H-L10
Kolmar Ave. J-L10
Korczak Terr. J11
Kostner Ave. J-L10
Kostner Terr. K10
LaCrosse Ave. H-L10
Lake J12
Lamon Ave. H-M10
Laramie Ave. H-M9
Latrobe Ave. H-M9
Lavergne Ave. J-M9
Lawler J9
Lawndale Ave. J-M11
Le Claire Ave. J-M9
Lee St. K9-12
Lemington Ave. J9
Lewis Terr. J10
Lincoln Ave. K9
Lincoln St. M10
Lincolnwood Dr. J12
Linder Ave. M9
Little Elm Bend K11
Little Oak Path K11
Lockwood Ave. H-M9
Long Ave. J-M9
Lorel Ave. J,L-M9
Lotus Ave. H-J9
Louise St. L9-11
Lowell Ave. J-L10
Lowell Terr. K10
Lunt Ave. M9
Lyons Ave. J9-12
Lyons St. J12
Madison St. K9-10
Main St. K10
Major Ave. H-L8
Mamora Ave. L8
Mango Ave. L8
Manor Ct. J12
Mason L8
McCormick Blvd. K-L12
McDaniel Ave. K12
Menard Ave. L-M8
Monroe St. K9
Monticello Ave. J-M11
Morgan J12
Morse Ave. M9
Mulford St. L9-10
Murphy Ln. J11
New Gross Point Rd. L8
Niles Ave. L9
Niles Center Rd. J10,L9
Oakton St. L9-10
Old Orchard H9
Old Orchard Ct. H10
Palma Pl. J9,H10
Park Ave. L9
Parkside Ave. H-L8
Payne St. H9-11
Peach Pkwy. H10
Pottawattami Dr. J11
Prairie Ave. E. J-M11,12
Railroad Ave. H-J9
Raoul Wallenberg Dr. H8
Ridgeway Ave. J-M11
Ridgeway Terr. K11
Roth Terr. K11
Russet Ln. H10
Salem Cir. J12
Salem Ln. J12
Samoset Blvd. J11
Searle Pkwy. L9
Sherwin Ave. M9
Skokiana Terr. H11
Skokie Blvd. J-L10
Sleeping Bear Rd. J11
Springfield Ave. J-K11
St. Louis Ave. K-M12
Suffield Ct. J9-11
Suffield Terr. J9
Sugarloaf Ln. J11
Tamaroa Terr. J11
Terminal J-K9
Touhy Ave. M9
Tower Cir. H11
Tripp Ave. J-L10
Trumbull Ave. K12
Warren St. L11
Washington St. K10
Weber Ln. H9
White Cloud Dr. J11
Wilder St. K12
Williamsburg Cir. J11
Williamsburg Ct. J11
Williamsburg Ln. J11
Williamsburg Rd. J11
Williamsburg Terr. J11
Wilson Terr. J10
Wright Terr. K9-11

CEMETERIES
Memorial Park H10
St. Paul Cem. K9
St. Peters Cem. K9,L9

GOLF COURSES
Evanston G.C. K10
Weber Park G.C. J10

PARKS
Central Park J11
Coyle Park M9
Devonshire Park J10
Emerson Park J9
Emily Park L10
Frontage Park L9
Garden Park K9
George Park L9
Gleiss Park J11
Grant Park H11
Gross Point Park J9
Hamlin Park L11
Kostner Park L10
Laramie Park M9
Lawler Park H9
Lockwood Park K9
Lorel Park L9
McNally Park K12
Oakton Park L10
Searle Park K10
Sequoya Park J9
Shabanee Park H11
Shawnee Park K11
Terminal Park J10
Timber Ridge Park J11
Weber Park J9-10
West Lauth Park L11
Winnebago Park K10
Wright Park K10

SCHOOLS
Cheder Lubavitch Sch. M9
College Hill Sch. J12
Devonshire Sch. J10
East Prairie Sch. L11
Fairview S. Sch. M9
Hebrew Theological College M9
Highland Sch. H11
Joan Stensen Sch. J9
Kenton Sch. K10
Lincoln Park Sch. L9
Madison Sch. K9
McCracken Middle Sch. L11
Middleton Sch. K12
Niles Twp. H.S. North H9
Niles Twp. H.S. West L8
Old Orchard Jr. H.S. J10
Orchard Sch. K9
Solomon Schechter Day Sch. J10
St. Joan of Arc Sch. J11
St. Lambert Sch. K11
St. Peters Sch. L9
Timber Ridge Sch. J11
Walker Sch. J12

SHOPPING CENTERS
Old Orchard S.C. H10

MISCELLANEOUS
Fire Departments J9,K11,M9
Library L9
Little League Park L12
Police Department K9
Post Office K9
Rush North Shore Med. Ctr. H10
Village Hall L9

SOUTH BARRINGTON
Pages 6,11

STREETS
Algonquin Rd. Pg.6 D1
Avon Ln. Pg.6 D3
Barrington Rd. Pg.6 F1
Brackley Pg.6 C2
Bridlewood Tr. Pg.6 D1
Buckthorn Rd. Pg.6 E1
Canterbury Ct. Pg.6 E3
Chipping Campden Pg.6 C2
Corey Dr. Pg.6 F1
Covered Bridge Rd. Pg.6 E1
Deveaux Ct. Pg.6 D1
Eton Ct. Pg.6 D3
Forest Ln. Pg.6 D2
Huntington Blvd. Pg.6 E2
Knoll Ct. Pg.6 D2
Korey Ln. Pg.6 E1
McGlashen Ln. Pg.6 E1
Mohawk Ct. Pg.6 E2
Mohawk Dr. Pg.6 E2
Mundhank Rd. Pg.6 E1
Old Barrington Rd. Pg.11 F1
Overbrook Rd. Pg.6 E1
Palatine Rd. Pg.6 C-1
Pembury Way Pg.6 D2
Polo Dr. Pg.6 E1
Rose Blvd. Pg.6 F1
Shademaster Locust Dr. Pg.6 F1
Shademaster Locust Ln. Pg.6 F1
Shirebrook Way Pg.6 D1
Somerset Ct. Pg.6 E3
Squire Ct. Pg.6 D1
Stannington Way Pg.6 D1
Sunburst Locust Dr. Pg.11 F1
Taynton Ln. Pg.6 C2
Tewkesbury Ln. Pg.6 C2
Wescott Dr. Pg.6 F1
Willowmere Dr. Pg.6 D1
Windmere Ln. Pg.6 D3
Wychwood Ln. Pg.6 C2

SOUTH CHICAGO HEIGHTS
Pages 48,49

STREETS
Aberdeen Ave. V24
Benton Ave. W24
Butler Ave. W24
Campbell Ave. W23
Cappelletti Ln. V23
Cherry Ln. V23
Chestnut Ave. W23
Chicago Pl. W24
Chicago Rd. V24
Commercial Ave. V24
Crescent Dr. V23
Dixie Hwy. W24
Dornell Dr. W24
East End Ave. V24
Enterprise Pk. Ave. V24
Euclid Ave. V23
Fairview Ave. W24
Forest Dr. W23
Forest Preserve Dr. V23
Helred Rd. W23
Holeman Ave. W25
Interocean Ave. V24
Jackson Ave. V24
Lawrence Ave. W23
Lynwood Dr. W23
Magnolia V23
Maple Ave. W23
Michigan Ave. W25
Miller Ave. V24
Miller Rd. W25
Pagoria Dr. W24
Park Terr. W23
Paulsen St. V24
Plaza St. V23
Rennie Smith Dr. W25
Sauk Trail Rd.(32nd St.) W23
State St. W25
Willow Rd. W23
27th Pl. V24
27th St. V24
28th Pl. V24
28th St. V24
29th Pl. V24
29th St. V24
30th Pl. V24
30th St. V24,26
31st St. W24
32nd St. W23
33rd St. W24
34th St. W24

SCHOOLS
Grant Sch. V24
Saukview Sch. W24

STEGER
Pages 48,49

STREETS
Adair Rd. W26
Butler Ave. W24
Calumet Expy. W27
Carpenter St. W23
Chicago Rd. W24
Cottage Grove Ave. W26
Dixie Hwy. W24
Dorchester Ave. W27
Emerald Ave. W24
Florence Ave. W24
Frederick Rd. W26
George St. W26
Green St. W24
Halsted St. W25
Hoffman Ave. W24
Hopkins Ave. W24
Keeney Ave. W25
Lahon Rd. W26
Lewis Ave. W25
Lisa Ln. W26
Lovelock Ave. W25
Mach Dr. W26
Michigan Ave. W25
Miller Rd. W25
Morgan St. W23
Oakland Dr. W26
Patricia Rd. W26
Peoria St. W24
Phillips Ave. W24
Sangamon St. W24
Sherman Rd. W26
State St. W25
Steger Rd. W26
Stewart W25
Union Ave. W24
Wallace Ave. W24
Wentworth Ave. W25
Woodlawn Ave. W27
30th Pl., E. W24
30th Pl., W. W24
30th St. W27
31st Pl., E. W24
31st Pl., W. W24
31st St., E. W24
31st St., W. W24
32nd Pl., W. W24
32nd St., E. W24,27
32nd St., W. W26
33rd Pl., E. W24
33rd St., E. W24
33rd St., W. W24
34th Pl. W25
34th St. W25

SCHOOLS
Bloom Township H.S. V26
Central Jr. H.S. W24
East View Sch. W24
Sauk Trail Sch. V26

THORNTON
Pages 43,44

STREETS
Anne Ct. O25
Apache Dr. O26
Arapaho Dr. O26
Arrowhead O26
Blackhawk Dr. O26
Blackstone St. P26
Bonnie Ct. O25
Brown Derby Rd. P24
Brownell P26
Canal St. N24
Cherry Ln. P26
Chicago Rd. O26
Chippewa Dr. O26
Clark St. N25
Cora Ct. O25
Dorie Ln. O26
Eleanor St. P25
Forest Ln. P26
Francis St. P25
Harriet St. P25
Highland O25
Hubbard St. P25
Hunter St. P25
Indiana Ave. O25
Indianwood Dr. O26
Julian St. P25
Julliette St. P25
Kinzie Pl. O25
Kinzie St. P25
La Salle St. N25
Laura Ln. O25
Leavenworth St. P25
Leverett St. P26
Mallette Ave. P26
Maple Ln. P26
Margaret St. P24,25
Maria P25,26
Marion St. (175th St.) O25
Michigan Ave. N25
Mohawk O26
Park Ave. O26
Parnell Ave. P24
Pawnee Dr. O26
Queens Ln. O25
Ridge Rd. P24
Schwab St. P25
Sunnyside Ave. O26
Tahoe St. O26
Thorncreek Rd. P26
Thornton Lansing Rd. P26
Tri-State Tollway O25
Vincennes Rd. P25
Wabash Ave. N25
Water St. P26
Wentworth N25
Westview Ave. N24
William St. P25
Wolcott St. P25
170th (Armory Dr.) N25
171st St. N25,O26
172nd St. O25
175th St. O25
183rd St. Q25

CEMETERIES
Mt. Forest Cem. O26
Oak Lawn Cem. P24

FOREST PRESERVES
Brownell Woods P26
Wampum Lake Woods F.P. O26

SCHOOLS
Parkside Sch. O25
Wolcott Sch. P25

MISCELLANEOUS
Thornton Ball Fields P25
Village Hall P25

THORNTON TOWNSHIP
Pages 42,43,44,45

STREETS
Artesian Ave. Pg.42 M21
Beaubien St. Pg.44 P27
Blackstone Ave. Pg.44 P27
Blitz St. Pg.44 P27
Bock Rd. Pg.44 P28
Calumet Expwy. Pg.45 P27
Chappel Ave. Pg.44 M,P28
Claremont St. Pg.43 M22
Clyde Ave. Pg.44 L,P28
Cornell Ave. Pg.44 P27
Cottage Grove Ave. Pg.44 P26
Dante Pg.44 P27
Dixie Hwy. Pg.43 M22
East End Ave. Pg.44 L,P28
Elmdale Ave. Pg.42 M21
Eustace St. Pg.44 P27
Fern St. Pg.44 P28
Forest Hills Pg.45 M30
Forest Ln. Pg.45 Q27
Greenwood Ave. Pg.44 M27
Hamilton Pl. Pg.43 M22
Harper Ave. Pg.44 P27
Indiana Ave. Pg.44 P28
Irving Pg.43 M22
Jeffery Ave. Pg.44 L28
Keegan St. Pg.44 O27,28
Leavitt St. Pg.43 M22
Locust Pg.44 P28
Oakley Ave. Pg.43 M22
Paxton Pg.44 M,P28
Poplar Ave. Pg.42 M21
Ridgeland Ave. Pg.44 P28
River Oaks Dr. Pg.44 M28
Rosewood Pg.44 O28
St. Andrews St. Pg.44 P27
Stony Island Ave. Pg.44 P27
Thorncreek Rd. Pg.44 P26
Thorndale Ave. Pg.42 M21
Thornton Lansing Rd. Pg.44 P28
Volbrecht Rd. Pg.44 P27
Wentworth Ave. Pg.45 M30
Whitman Ln. Pg.45 P28
159th Ct. Pg.42 M22
159th St. Pg.43 M22
160th Pl. Pg.43 M22
160th St. Pg.43 M22
161st St. Pg.43 M22
162nd St. Pg.42 M21
177th Pl. Pg.44 O28
177th St. Pg.44 O28,P27
178th St. Pg.44 P27
179th St. Pg.44 P28
183rd St. Pg.44 Q27
186th St. Pg.44 Q27

CEMETERIES
Oakridge Cem. Pg.44 P28

FOREST PRESERVES
Jurgensen Woods Pg.44 Q27

GOLF COURSES
Calumet C.C. Pg.43 O22

TINLEY PARK
Pages 40,41,46

STREETS
Achilles Ct. S16
Aegina Ct. R16
Aegina Dr. R16
Alexandria Dr. M13
Almond Ln. P12
Amherst Ln. O14
Andres Ave. N16
Anne Marie Ave. N16
Anvil Pl. N13
Apache Trail P13
Apollo Ct. S16
Apple Ln. M13
Arcadia Dr. N16
Arlington St. M13
Ash St. P12
Ashley Ln. M13
Aspen Ln. M13
Aster Ln. O13
Athenia Ct. R16
Autumn Dr. O16
Avon Ln. O12
Barbara Ave. N16
Barbara Ln. O16
Bayberry Ln. P11
Bedford Ln. O14
Belle Rive Ct. O14
Bethany Ln. O12
Beverly Ave. N16
Birchwoode Ct. N15
Blossom Ln. N13
Blue Spruce Ct. M13
Bluebird Dr. P12
Bormet Dr. M,N13
Brementowne Dr. N15
Bementowne Rd. N15
Briar Dr. O11
Bridlewood Ln. O12
Bristol Ln. N14
Bristolwood Dr. P14
Brittney Ln. N16
Budingen Ln. O13
Cambridge Pl. O12
Cardinal Ln. P12
Carlsbad Dr. N16
Carriage Ln. O13
Cartier Ave. P14
Castle Dr. O13
Catalpa Ct. O12
Cedar Ln. O14
Centennial Cir. M15
Centennial Dr. M15
Centerway Walk M14
Champlain Ave. P14
Charnswood Ct. N15
Charnswood Dr. N15
Chelsea Dr. N15
Cherokee Trail O13
Cherry Creek Ave. O13
Cherry Hill Ave. N13
Cherry Stone Pl. N13
Chestnut Dr. O12
Chippewa Trail O13
Christopher Ct. N16
Circle Dr. O13
Claremont Dr. N14
Clark Ln. N15
Clover Ave. N13
Cloverview Dr. P13
Coachwood Tr. N15
Cobbler Ct. N13
Cobblestone Ct. N15
Corinth Ct. R16
Corinth Dr. R16
Cottage Ct. O13
Cranberry Ct. N12
Creekmont Ct. M12
Creekside Ave. O13

TINLEY PARK

- Crescent Ave. N13
- Crown Ln. N15
- Current Ave. N13
- Cynthia Ct. N13
- Cypress Ct. O12
- DeSoto Ave. P14
- Debra Ave. O16
- Dee Ct. O12
- Deland Ct. M13
- Delphi Ct. S15
- Derwent Ln. O13
- Desiree Dr. N13
- Dooneen Ave. O14
- Dorothy Ln. N14
- Drummond Dr. O11
- Duvan Dr. O14
- Eagle Ct. P15
- Eagle Dr. P15
- Eagle Ridge Dr. M13
- Edgewood Ct. O12
- Elm Lane N15
- Elmwood Dr. P12
- Elysian Dr. R16
- Everdon Dr. M14
- Evergreen Dr. N13
- Fairfax Ct. N15
- Farmview Ct. N13
- Flamingo Dr. P12
- Forestview Dr. N16
- Fox Grove Ln. O13
- Gaynelle Rd. N16
- Gentry Ln. N16
- George Brennan Hwy. R15
- Glenview Dr. N15
- Golden Pheasant Dr. P12
- Graphics Dr. Q14
- Greenwood Dr. P12
- Grissom Dr. O13
- Hamilton Ave. M13
- Hanover Dr. O14
- Harlem Ave. N,P15
- Heather Ct. P13
- Heather Ln. O13
- Helen Sandidge Ct. N16
- Henry Ln. N13
- Hickory St. O15
- Highland Ave. P16
- Hillcrest Dr. N13
- Hillcrest Ln. N13
- Hillside Pl. N16
- Holly Ct. P12
- Honey Ln. N16
- Horseshoe Dr. N13
- Hubbard Ln. N15
- Humber Ln. O12
- Hummingbird Ln. P12
- Hunter Tr. N15
- Iliad Dr. S15
- Interstate 80 Q14
- Inverness Dr. O12
- Ironwood Dr. N13
- Iroquois Trace P13
- Ithaca Ct. S16
- Jacquelyn Ct. N16
- Jean Ln. N15
- Jeannette Ct. P16
- Jennifer Ave. N16
- Jeremy Ln. O12
- Jessica Ln. O13
- Joliet Dr. P14
- Juniper Ct. O12
- Justin Ct. M13
- Kamp Ct. O13
- Kathleen Ln. O12
- Kensington Ave. M14
- Kildare Ct. N14
- Kingston Ct. N15
- Kingston Rd. N15
- La Grange Rd. O11
- Lake Bluff Dr. N16
- Lake Villa Ave. M14
- Lakeside Pl. N16,R14
- Lakeview Cir. Q16
- Lakeview Terr. R14
- Lakewood Dr. N16
- Laura Ln. N16
- Laverne Ln. N15
- Lexington Ct. M15
- Lilac Ln. P13
- Linden Dr. P12
- Lismore Ct. N14
- Live Oak Ct. P15
- Locust Ave. O12
- Magnolia Ln. O12
- Mallard Rd. P12
- Manchester St. N15
- Mannheim Rd. P11
- Maple Creek Dr. Q14
- Maple Ln. N15
- Maplewoode Ct. N15
- Margaret Ln. O12
- Marilyn Dr. O13
- Market St. O16
- Marquette Dr. P14
- Martin Frances Cir. P15
- Meadow Ct. N13
- Meadow Ln. N13
- Meadowlark Dr. P12
- Messina Ct. R16
- Michelle Ln. N13
- Milford Ave. O14
- Mockingbird Ln. P12
- Mulberry Ave. O12
- Music Center North Rd. Q16
- Music Center South Rd. R16
- Navajo Trace O13
- New England Ave. N15
- Normandy Dr. N16
- North Creek Dr. Q14
- North St. O15
- Nottingham Ct. N14
- Nottingham Dr. N14
- Nottingham Rd. N13
- Oak Forest Ave. O16
- Oak Park Ave. M15
- Oakwood Dr. O12
- Oconto Ave. N,O14,O16
- Odell Ave. N,O14
- Odyssey Dr. S15
- Oketo Ave. N,O14
- Olcott Ave. N,O14
- Olcott Ct. O14
- Old Barn Ct. N13
- Olde Gatehouse Rd. N15
- Oleander Ave. N,O14
- Olympus Dr. S16
- Orchard Ct. N13
- Oriole Ave. O14
- Osceola Ave. O14
- Ottawa Ave. O14
- Overhill Ave. N,O14
- Oxford Dr. N15
- Ozark Ave. N,O14
- Park Central Dr. P14
- Parkside Dr. N15
- Parkview Ave. N13
- Parliament Ave. N14
- Paxton Ave. N14
- Peacock Ln. P11
- Pecan Ln. P12
- Pelican Ln. P12
- Pembroke Ave. O14
- Pheasant Dr. P11
- Pheasant Lake Dr. P12
- Pin Oak Ct. P15
- Pine Cone Dr. Q15
- Pine Dr. M13
- Pine Lake Dr. Q16
- Pine Point Dr. O15
- Pine Wood Ct. P16
- Pine Wood Ln. Q15
- Piute Trail P13
- Plum Ct. O13
- Plymouth Ct. M15
- Poplar St. P12
- Pottawattomi Trail P13
- Prairie Ct. N13
- Prairie Dr. N13
- Prestwick Dr. O14
- Princess Elizabeth Ct. P12
- Princeton Ave. N13
- Quail Crossing O11
- Quail Tr. O11
- Queen Ann Ln. P13
- Queen Elizabeth Ln. O13
- Queen Mary Ln. O13
- Queen Victoria Ln. O13
- Raintree Rd. O12
- Ravina Dr. O15
- Redwood Ln. O12
- Richards Ct. N13
- Richards Dr. N,O13
- Ridgeland Ave. N,P,R16
- Rita Rd. P15
- Riverside Dr. N15,16
- Rochelle Ln. O12
- Rosewood Ln. P12
- Royal Oak Ct. P15
- Salem Ct. O14
- Sandalwood Dr. O14
- Sandy Ln. N14
- Sayre Ave. N,P15
- Scotch Pine Dr. R16
- Scott Ct. N16
- Shannon Ct. N13
- Shannon Dr. O13
- Shetland Dr. O12
- Shoshone Trail P13
- Skyline Dr. N16
- South St. O,R15
- Spring Creek Dr. Q14
- Spruce Ln. O12
- Steeple Ln. O13
- Steven Pl. N13
- Surrey Dr. N13
- Sussex Rd. N15
- Sutton Pl. P11
- Sycamore Ct. O12
- Tamar Ln. O13
- Tanbark Dr. N13
- Tayside Ln. O12
- Teakwood Dr. O11
- Terrace Dr. N15
- Thersea Ln. N15
- Thornwood Dr. O11
- Timber Ct. O12
- Timber Rd.(Pvt.) P14
- Tinley Park Dr. N15
- Tower Ct. N13
- Trent Ct. O12
- Tudor Ln. N13
- Tulip Ln. P13
- Turnberry Ln. O12
- Valley Dr. O13
- Valley Forge Dr. O13
- Valley View Ct. O13
- Valley View Dr. O13
- Vogt St. O16
- Vollmer Rd. S15
- Walnut Ln. O12
- Waterford Dr. N13
- Westberry Ln. M13
- Westway Walk M14
- Westwind Ct. N15
- Westwind Dr. N15
- Wexford Ct. N14
- White Tailed Ln. P15
- Whittington Dr. M13
- Willow Ln. N16
- Windsor Pkwy. O12
- Winston Dr. N15
- Witham Ct. O13
- Woodland Dr. N13
- Woodstock Ave. O14
- 62nd Ave. P16
- 64th Ct. N-P16
- 65th Ave. N,P16
- 65th Ct. N,P15
- 66th Ave. N-P15
- 66th Ct. N-P15
- 67th Ave. O16,P15
- 67th Ct. N-P15
- 68th Ct. O,P15
- 69th Ave. O15
- 70th Ave. O,P15
- 70th Ct. P15
- 71st Ave. O,P15
- 71st Ct. O,P15
- 76th Ave. N,O14
- 78th Ave. M14
- 79th Ave. O14
- 80th Ave. M,S13
- 81st Ave. N13
- 81st Ct. N,O13
- 82nd Ave. O13
- 83rd Ct. O13
- 84th Ave. N13
- 84th Ct. M,N13
- 84th Pl. M13
- 85th Ave. M,N13
- 85th Ct. M13
- 87th Ct. O12
- 88th Ave. O,S12
- 92nd Ave. O,P12
- 94th Ave. P11
- 159th Pl. M14
- 159th St. M14
- 160th Ct. M14
- 160th Pl. M13,14
- 160th St. M13,14
- 161st Pl. M13,14
- 161st St. M13,14
- 162nd Pl. M14,N13
- 162nd St. M14
- 163rd Pl. N14,15
- 163rd St. N13,14,M15
- 164th Ave. N16
- 164th Ct. N13
- 164th Pl. N14,15
- 164th St. N13,15
- 165th Pl. N13-15
- 165th St. N13-15
- 166th Pl. N13,14
- 166th St. N14,16
- 167th Pl. N13
- 167th St. N13
- 168th Pl. N13,15
- 168th St. N15
- 168th Ct. N13
- 169th Pl. O13
- 169th St. N13,15
- 170th Pl. N14,O13
- 170th St. N14,O13,15
- 171st Pl. O13
- 171st St. O15
- 172nd Pl. O14
- 172nd St. O12,15
- 173rd Pl. O12,14,15
- 173rd St. O14,15
- 174th Pl. O13-15
- 174th St. O12-15
- 175th Pl. O14,15
- 175th St. O12,13,16
- 176th Pl. O15
- 176th St. P12,O15
- 177th Pl. P15
- 177th St. P15
- 178th St. P11,12,15
- 179th Pl. P15
- 179th St. P10,15
- 180th Pl. P16
- 180th St. P15
- 181st Pl. P16
- 181st St. P15
- 182nd Pl. P16
- 182nd St. P16
- 183rd St. P11,14
- 185th St. Q13
- 194th St. R15
- 196th St. R14

CEMETERIES

- Lutheran Cem. M15
- Orland/Tinley Park Cem. O13

GOLF COURSES

- Odyssey G.C. R15

PARKS

- Bettenhausen Park N14
- Bicentennial Park M15
- Buedingen Park N13
- Commissioners Park N13
- Filson Rec. Area N14
- German Park N14
- Hirsch Park P16
- Jaycee Park N13
- John Bannes Park N13
- Lancaster Woods N16
- Lewis Park N16
- McCarthy Park N14
- Memorial Park N14,O16
- Paxton Lot N14
- Pottawattomie Park P12
- Rauhoff Park P15
- Richard M. Gory Park N13
- St. Boniface Park N15
- Sundale Park O14
- Veterans Park M14
- Vogt Woods O16
- Volunteer Park O13

SCHOOLS

- Andrews H.S. O12
- Bannes School N14
- Central Jr. High O15
- Christa McAuliffe Sch. O12
- Fulton Sch. O16
- Helen Sandidge Sch. N15
- Hellen Keller School M14
- Kirby Sch. O14
- Memorial Sch. P15
- Prairie View Jr. H.S. O13
- S.W. Christian Sch. O13
- St. George Sch. O15
- Tinley Park H.S. O16
- Virgil Grissom Jr. High O13

SHOPPING CENTERS

- Bayberry Plaza O13
- Brementowne Mall M15
- Brementowne Manor N15
- Brementowne Mini Mall M14
- Park Center Plaza M14
- South S.C. N15
- Tinley Downs S.C. O13
- Tinley Park S.C. M15

MISCELLANEOUS

- Commuter Station P13
- Crisis Center for South Suburbia P14
- Fire Station N14
- Ingalls Family Care Center M15
- Midwest Christian Center Q12
- Post Office O15
- R.R. Sta. O15
- Tinley Downs O14
- Tinley Park Mental Health Ctr. P14
- Village Hall M15
- William A. Howe Developmental Ctr. P14
- World Music Theater R16

VERNON TOWNSHIP

Page 5

STREETS

- Arlington Heights Rd. X11
- Ash St. X14
- Aspen Ct. X14
- Birch St. X14
- Bluebird Ln. X13
- Bluebird St. X13
- Carmen Dr. X13
- Catalpa St. X14
- Catbird Ln. X14
- Celia Ave. X12
- Checker Rd. X10
- Chevy Chase Ave. E. X14
- Clarice Ave. X13
- Columbus Pkwy X14
- Dogwood St. X14
- Driftwood Pl. X12
- East Chevy Chase Ave. X14
- Elizabeth Ave. X13
- Eugene Ave. X13
- Florence Ave. X13
- Frank Ave. X13
- Frontenac X14
- Garden Ct. X13
- Goshawk Ln. X14
- Grouse Ct. X13
- Grouse Ln. X13
- Horatio Blvd. X13
- Hummingbird Ct. X14
- Hummingbird Ln. X14
- Inverray Ln. X14
- James Cir. X14
- Juneway Ave. X13
- Kildeer Ln. X14
- Lake-Cook Rd. X10
- Linden Ave. X14
- Lita X13
- Long Beach Dr. X14
- Loyola Ave. X14
- Mallard Dr. X13
- Mallard Ln. X13
- Maple Ct. X13
- Margaret Ave. X13
- Marie Ave. X13
- Marquette Pl. X14
- Martin Ln. X14
- Mercier Ave. X14
- Milwaukee Ave. A14
- Partridge Ln. X14
- Pauline Ave. X12
- Pekara Dr. X14
- Penguin Dr. X13
- Pheasant Ln. X14
- Pintail Ln. X14
- Pintail St. X12
- Pope Blvd. X13
- Pope Blvd. W. X13
- Raphael Ave. X13
- Redwing Dr. X14
- Sandpiper Ln. X14
- Schaeffer Rd. X10
- Skylark Ln. X14
- Swallow Ct. X13
- Swallow Ln. X13
- Swallow St. X13
- Swan Blvd. X13
- Swan Ct. X13
- Swan Ln. X13
- Tanager Ct. X14
- Walnut Dr. X13
- William Ave. X13
- Winston Dr. X14
- Wren Ln. X14

WHEELING

Pages 4,5,9,10

STREETS

- Abbott Dr. Pg.9 C14
- Acco Plaza Dr. Pg.9 B15
- Acorn Ct. Pg.4 A12
- Albert Terr. Pg.9 A13
- Alder Dr. Pg.10 B14
- Alderman Ave. Pg.9 D15
- Aldgate Ct. Pg.4 A12
- Alice St. Pg.9 B14
- Allen Ct. Pg.10 B15
- Allendale Dr. Pg.4 A13
- Alpine Ct. Pg.4 A12
- Amy Ct. Pg.4 A12
- Ande Ave. Pg.9 B15
- Anita Pl. Pg.10 A15
- Anne Terr. Pg.9 A13
- Anthony Rd. Pg.9 A12-13
- Apache Pg.9 B11
- Arlene Ct. Pg.10 B15
- Arlington Dr. Pg.4 A12
- Arrow Tr. Pg.9 B12
- Ash Ln. Pg.9 C12
- Ashford Cir. Pg.9 A12
- Ashton Ct. Pg.4 A12
- Auborndale Ct. Pg.9 B12
- Audrey Ct. Pg.9 B13
- Baldwin Ct. Pg.4 A12
- Barberry Ln. Pg.9 B13
- Barnaby Pl. Pg.5 A13
- Bayside Ct. Pg.9 C12
- Bayside Dr. Pg.9 C12
- Bayside Ln. Pg.9 C12
- Beech Dr. Pg.10 B14
- Berkshire Dr. Pg.5 A13
- Bernice Ct. Pg.9 A13
- Beverly Dr. Pg.5 A13
- Bina Ct. Pg.10 A15
- Birch Tr. Pg.9 A13
- Blackfoot Ct. Pg.9 B11
- Blackhawk Tr. Pg.9 B11
- Blaze Tr. Pg.9 B13
- Bow Tr. Pg.9 B12
- Boxwood Ct. Pg.4 A12
- Braeburn Ct. Pg.4 A12
- Brandon Pl. Pg.4 A13
- Braver Ct. Pg.4 A12
- Brian Ln. Pg.9 A15
- Briarwood Dr. Pg.9 B13
- Bridgeport Pl. Pg.5 A13
- Bridget Pl. Pg.9 A14
- Bridgeview Ct. Pg.9 B13
- Bridle Tr. Pg.9 C14
- Brighton Pl. Pg.5 A13
- Bristol Ct. Pg.9 B12
- Brittany Ct. Pg.9 A12
- Broadway Ct. Pg.4 A12
- Brougham Dr. Pg.5 A13
- Buckboard Dr. Pg.4 A13
- Buckeye Dr. Pg.10 B14
- Buckingham Ct. Pg.5 A13
- Buffalo Grove Rd. Pg.9 A,B12
- Buffalo Tr. Pg.9 B11
- Buxton Ct. Pg.9 B12
- Cambridge Pl. Pg.5 A13
- Camden Ct. Pg.4 A12
- Canbury Ct. Pg.4 A12
- Candlewood Ct. Pg.9 C12
- Capitol Dr. Pg.9 C15
- Capri Terr. Pg.5 A14
- Captains Ln. Pg.9 B13
- Cardinal Ct. Pg.4 A12
- Carpenter Ave. Pg.9 B14
- Carriage Hill Rd. Pg.5 A13
- Catherine Ct. Pg.9 A14
- Cedar Dr. Pg.9 A13
- Cedar Run Dr. Pg.4 A12
- Cedarwood Ln. Pg.9 B13
- Center Ave. Pg.9 A15
- Century Dr. Pg.9 B15
- Chaddick Dr. Pg.9 B15
- Charbanc Ln. Pg.4 A13
- Chariot Ct. Pg.5 A13
- Chariot Ln. Pg.5 A13
- Chariot Rd. Pg.5 A13
- Chelsea Dr. Pg.5 A13
- Cherrywood Dr. Pg.9 B13
- Chestnut Ln. Pg.5 A13
- Cheswick Ct. Pg.4 A12
- Chippewa Tr. Pg.9 B12
- Chukker Ct. Pg.9 C14
- Cindy Ln. Pg.9 A13
- Clearwater Ct. Pg.9 B13
- Clearwater Dr. Pg.9 B13
- Clearwater Ln. Pg.9 B13
- Cleo Ct. Pg.5 A13
- Coach Rd. Pg.5 A13
- Cobbler Ln. Pg.4 A12
- Colonial Dr. Pg.5 A13
- Commanche Tr. Pg.9 B11
- Coral Ln. Pg.5 A13
- Corey Ln. Pg.9 B12
- Cornell Ave. Pg.9 B12
- Cottonwood Ct. Pg.9 B12
- Courtesy Ln. Pg.10 B15
- Coventry Pl. Pg.5 A13
- Creekside Ct. Pg.9 B12
- Crescent Dr. Pg.9 A15
- Crimson Dr. Pg.9 B13
- Curricle Rd. Pg.4 A13
- Custer Ct. Pg.9 B11
- Cypress Dr. Pg.4 A12
- Cyrilla St. Pg.5 A14
- Dakota Tr. Pg.9 A13
- Dean Ave. Pg.9 B15
- Deborah Ln. Pg.5 A14
- Debra Ln. Pg.9 B15
- Deerpath Ct. Pg.5 A13
- Delaware Tr. Pg.9 B11
- Dennis Rd. Pg.9 A13
- Denniston Ct. Pg.9 A14
- Denoyer Tr. Pg.5 A13
- Derby St. Pg.9 C14
- Diens Dr. Pg.4 A13
- Donna Ct. Pg.9 B15
- Dorset Cir. Pg.4 A13
- Dorset Ct. Pg.4 A13
- Dover Pl. Pg.5 A13
- Drae Ct. Pg.5 A13
- Driftwood Ct. Pg.5 A13
- Dundee Rd. Pg.5 A14
- E. Jeffrey Ave. Pg.10 A15
- Eagle Grove Ct. Pg.4 A12
- East Dr. Pg.9 B13
- Eastchester Rd. Pg.9 B14
- Easton Ct. Pg.4 A12
- Edgewood Dr. Pg.5 A13
- Edward St. Pg.9 B13
- Egidi Dr. Pg.5 A14
- Elden Ct. Pg.5 A13
- Elizabeth Ct. Pg.9 B12
- Elizabeth Ln. Pg.9 B12
- Elm Dr. Pg.10 B14
- Elmhurst Rd. Pg.9 B-C13
- Elmwood Ln. Pg.4 A12
- Ely Ct. Pg.5 A13
- Equestrian Dr. Pg.9 C14
- Exchange Ct. Pg.9 B14
- Exeter Ct. Pg.4 A12
- Fairfield Ct. Pg.4 A12
- Fairview Dr. Pg.5 A13
- Fairway View Dr. Pg.5 A13
- Fall Ct. Pg.5 A13
- Ferndale Ct. Pg.5 A13
- Ferne Dr. Pg.10 B14
- Fletcher Dr. Pg.9 A13
- Fore Ct. Pg.4 A12
- Forestway Ln. Pg.5 A15
- Forums Ct. Pg.9 B14
- Foster Ave. Pg.9 D15
- Foxboro Dr. Pg.9 B15
- Garden Ln. Pg.9 B13
- Garth Rd. Pg.9 B14
- Gayle Ct. Pg.10 B15
- Gee Ct. Pg.5 A13
- George Rd. Pg.9 A14
- Gilman Ave. Pg.9 C14
- Glendale St. Pg.5 A14
- Glengary Ct. Pg.4 A12
- Glengary Ln. Pg.4 A13
- Glenn Ave. Pg.9 B14
- Gray Ct. Pg.5 A13
- Green Dr. Pg.9 A13
- Gregor Ln. Pg.9 B13
- Greystone Ln. Pg.5 A13
- Haben Ln. Pg.4 A13
- Hadley Ct. Pg.4 A12
- Hale Ct. Pg.5 A13
- Hansom Ct. Pg.5 A13
- Hansom Dr. Pg.4 A13
- Harbour Ct. Pg.9 B12
- Harbour Dr. Pg.9 B13
- Harmony Dr. Pg.10 B14
- Harms Ct. Pg.5 A13
- Harvester Ct. Pg.9 B14
- Hastings Ct. Pg.9 B13
- Hastings Rd. Pg.9 B13
- Hawthorne Ct. Pg.5 A13
- Henley Ct. Pg.4 A12
- Hickory Dr. Pg.10 B14
- Highgoal Dr. Pg.9 C14
- Highland Ave. Pg.10 A15
- Hintz Ln. Pg.9 B12
- Hintz Rd. Pg.9 B15
- Holbrook Dr. Pg.9 C14
- Holly Ct. Pg.5 A13
- Honey Locust Dr. Pg.10 B14-15
- Honeysuckle Dr. Pg.9 B14
- Hopi Tr. Pg.9 B12
- Hunter Dr. Pg.9 B12
- Huntington Ct. Pg.4 A12
- Huntington Ln. Pg.9 A12
- Inwood Dr. Pg.9 C14
- Iota Ct. Pg.4 A12
- Ironwood Ct. Pg.5 A13
- Irvine Ct. Pg.9 A12
- Isa Dr. Pg.9 B13
- Ivy Ct. Pg.9 B13
- Jackson Dr. Pg.9 B12

WHEELING

Janice Ct. . . . . Pg.9 . . . . C14
Jaspen Ct. . . . . Pg.5 . . . . A13
Jeanne Terr. . . . Pg.9 . . . . A14
Jefferson Ct. . . . Pg.9 . . . . C14
Jeffery Ave. . . . Pg.9 . . . . A14
Jeffery Ln. . . . . Pg.9 . . . . A14
Jenkins Ct. . . . . Pg.9 . . . . A13
Jerome Pl. . . . . Pg.10 . . . A15
Kenilworth Dr. . . Pg.5 . . . . A13
Kerry Ln. . . . . . Pg.9 . . . . B15
King Ct. . . . . . . Pg.9 . . . . A13
Kingsport Dr. . . . Pg.9 . . . . B13
Kingswood Ln. . . Pg.5 . . . . A15
Knottingham Ct. . . . .
. . . . Pg.4 . . . . A12
Kristy Ln. . . . . . Pg.9 . . . . B13
Laguna Ct. . . . . Pg.9 . . . . B12
Lake-Cook Rd. . . Pg.5 . . . . A14
Lakeland Ct. . . . Pg.9 . . . . B12
Lakeside Dr. . . . Pg.9 . . . . B12
Lakeview Dr. . . . Pg.9 . . . . B11
Landau . . . . . . Pg.5 . . . . A13
Larkin Dr. . . . . . Pg.9 . . . . A15
Laurel Ct. . . . . . Pg.9 . . . . A13
Laurel Tr. . . . . . Pg.9 . . . . A13
Lee St. . . . . . . Pg.9 . . . . A13
Lenox Ct. . . . . . Pg.4 . . . . A13
Leslie Ln. . . . . . Pg.9 . . . . A14
Lexington Dr. . . . Pg.4 . . . . A12
Lilac Ln. . . . . . Pg.9 . . . . A15
Lincoln Rd. . . . . Pg.10 . . . A15
Linda Terr. . . . . Pg.9 . . . . A13
Linden Ln. . . . . Pg.9 . . . . A15
Locust Dr. . . . . Pg.4 . . . . A12
London Pl. . . . . Pg.5 . . . . A13
Longacre Ln. . . . Pg.9 . . . . C14
Longbow Ct. . . . Pg.9 . . . . A12
Longtree Dr. . . . Pg.9 . . . . B13
Lotus Ct. . . . . . Pg.5 . . . . A13
Lynn Ln. . . . . . Pg.9 . . . . B15
Mae Ct. . . . . . . Pg.5 . . . . A13
Mallard Ln. . . . . Pg.9 . . . . A13
Manchester Dr. . . Pg.10 . A14-15
Manda Dr. . . . . Pg.4 . . . . A13
Manda Ln. . . . . Pg.5 . . . . A13
Maple Dr. . . . . . Pg.10 . . . B14
Marcy Ln. . . . . . Pg.9 . . . . A13
Marion Ct. . . . . Pg.9 . . . . A13
Mark Ln. . . . . . Pg.9 . . . . B12
Marquardt Dr. . . Pg.9,10 . . B15
Marvin Pl. . . . . . Pg.10 . . . A13
Maureen Ct. . . . Pg.9 . . . . A13
Mayer Ave. . . . . Pg.5 . . . . A14
Meadow Ln. . . . Pg.5 . . . . A14
Meadowbrook Ln. . . . .
. . . . Pg.5 . . . . A13
Melvin Pl. . . . . . Pg.9 . . . . A14
Mors Ave. . . . . Pg.10 . . . A15
Muriel Ct. . . . . . Pg.9 . . . . C14
Nancy Ln. . . . . . Pg.9 . . . . A14
Newburn Ct. . . . Pg.4 . . . . A12
Noel Ave. . . . . . Pg.9 . . . . B14
Norman Ln. . . . . Pg.9 . . . . A13
Northbury Ln. . . . Pg.5 . . . . A13
Northgate Pkwy. . . . .
. . . . Pg.9 . . . . A14
Nottingham Ct. . . Pg.9 . . . . A12
Nova Ct. . . . . . Pg.9 . . . . A13
Oak Creek Dr. . . Pg.9 . . . . C14
Oak Dr. . . . . . . Pg.5 . . . . A13
Oakmeadow Ct. . Pg.4 . . . . A13
Oakmont Ln. . . . Pg.5 . . . . A13
Oakwood Ln. . . . Pg.5 . . . . A15
Oboe Ct. . . . . . Pg.5 . . . . A13
Old McHenry Rd. . . . .
. . . . Pg.4 . . . . A13
Orrington Ct. . . . Pg.4 . . . . A12
Osage Tr. . . . . . Pg.9 . . . . B13
Ottawa Ct. . . . . Pg.9 . . . . B11
Oxford Pl. . . . . . Pg.5 . . . . A13
Oxley Ct. . . . . . Pg.9 . . . . A12
Pacific Ct. . . . . . Pg.9 . . . . B13
Paddock Dr. . . . Pg.9 . . . . C14
Palatine Rd. . . . Pg.9 . . . . C14
Palm Dr. . . . . . Pg.9 . . . . A13
Palwaukee Dr. . . Pg.9 . . . . B14
Pam Ct. . . . . . . Pg.5 . . . . A13
Park Ave. . . . . . Pg.10 . . . A15
Partridge Ln. . . . Pg.9 . . . . A15
Peace Dr. . . . . . Pg.9 . . . . A13
Pear Tree Ln. . . . Pg.9 . . . . B14
Pebble Dr. . . . . Pg.5 . . . . B15
Peggy Ct. . . . . . Pg.9 . . . . B15
Pensbury Ct. . . . Pg.4 . . . . A13
Peterson Dr. . . . Pg.9 . . . . C14
Phaeton Dr. . . . Pg.5 . . . . A13
Pleasant Run Dr. . . . .
. . . . Pg.9 . . . . C14
Plumtree Ct. . . . Pg.4 . . . . A12
Poplar Dr. . . . . . Pg.10 . . . B14
Portsmouth Pl. . . Pg.5 . . . . A13
Pueblo Tr. . . . . . Pg.9 . . . . B11
Quad Ct. . . . . . Pg.5 . . . . A13
Quail Hollow Rd. . . . .
. . . . Pg.4 . . . . A13
Queens Ct. . . . . Pg.4 . . . . A12
Quincy Ct. . . . . Pg.4 . . . . A12

Railroad Ave. . . . Pg.9 . . . . A14
Redwood Terr. . . Pg.5 . . . . A13
Regent Ln. . . . . Pg.5 . . . . A15
Renee Terr. . . . . Pg.5 . . . . A13
Ridgefield Ln. . . . Pg.9 . . . . B14
Robert Ave. . . . . Pg.9 . . . . A13
Rose Ln. . . . . . Pg.9 . . . . B13
Roth Ct. . . . . . . Pg.4 . . . . A12
Russetwood Ct. . Pg.9 . . . . B13
Rustic Ct. . . . . . Pg.10 . . . B14
S. Crow Tr. . . . . Pg.9 . . . . C12
S. Kiowa Dr. . . . Pg.9 . . . . C12
S. Navajo Tr. . . . Pg.9 . . . . C12
Salvington Pl. . . . Pg.9 . . . . A12
Sander Ct. . . . . Pg.9 . . . . C14
Sandpebble Dr. . . Pg.9 . . . . C14
Sandra Ln. . . . . Pg.9 . . . . C14
Sandstone Dr. . . Pg.9 . . . . C14
Sarah Ct. . . . . . Pg.9 . . . . A13
Sarasota Dr. . . . Pg.5 . . . . A13
Scanlon Dr. . . . Pg.5 . . . . A13
Schoenbeck Rd. . Pg.9 . . . . B13
Scott St. . . . . . . Pg.9 . . . . A12
Seton Ct. . . . . . Pg.9 . . . . B14
Seville Ct. . . . . . Pg.4 . . . . A12
Shadow Bend Dr. . . . .
. . . . Pg.5 . . . . A15
Shady Tree Ln. . . Pg.9 . . . . B14
Shawn Ct. . . . . Pg.9 . . . . C14
Shay Ct. . . . . . . Pg.5 . . . . A13
Shay Rd. . . . . . Pg.9 . . . . A13
Sheldrake Dr. . . . Pg.9 . . . . B12
Shelly Ct. . . . . . Pg.10 . . . B15
Sheppard Ave. . . Pg.9 . . . . B14
Sheridan Ct. . . . Pg.4 . . . . A12
Shore Ct. . . . . . Pg.9 . . . . A12
Shoshone Tr. . . . Pg.9 . . . . B11
Silverwood Ct. . . Pg.5 . . . . A13
South Dr. . . . . . Pg.5 . . . . B13
Southbury Ln. . . Pg.9 . . . . A15
Springview Ct. . . Pg.9 . . . . B11
Spruce Dr. . . . . Pg.4,5 . A12-13
Spur Ct. . . . . . . Pg.4 . . . . A12
St. Armand Ct. . . Pg.5 . . . . A13
St. Armand Ln. . . Pg.5 . . . . A13
Stafford Dr. . . . . Pg.5 . . . . A15
Stafford Ln. . . . . Pg.5 . . . . A15
Stone Pl. . . . . . Pg.5 . . . . A15
Stonehedge Ct. . Pg.9 . . . . A14
Stratford Ct. . . . Pg.4 . . . . A12
Strong Ave. . . . . Pg.5 . . . . A14
Sumac Ln. . . . . Pg.10 . . . B15
Summerhill Ln. . . Pg.5 . . . . A15
Sunrise Dr. . . . . Pg.9 . . . . A15
Sunset Ln. . . . . Pg.9 . . . . A14
Surf Ct. . . . . . . Pg.9 . . . . B12
Surrey Rd. . . . . Pg.5 . . . . A13
Sutton Ct. . . . . . Pg.4 . . . . A13
Sutton Ct. . . . . . Pg.4 . . . . A13
Sycamore Ln. . . . Pg.9 . . . . B13
Tahoe Cir. Dr. . . . Pg.9 . . . . B11
Tanglewood Dr. . Pg.9 . . . . B14
Teal Ln. . . . . . . Pg.9 . . . . B12
Thelma Ct. . . . . Pg.9 . . . . A13
Thorndale Ct. . . . Pg.5 . . . . A13
Thornhill Ln. . . . Pg.4 . . . . A12
Thyne Ct. . . . . . Pg.5 . . . . A13
Tilbury Ln. . . . . Pg.4 . . . . A13
Town St. . . . . . . Pg.9 . . . . A13
Tulip Ct. . . . . . . Pg.4 . . . . A12
Twilight Ln. . . . . Pg.9 . . . . B13
Union Ct. . . . . . Pg.5 . . . . A13
Vail Ct. . . . . Pg.5 . . . . A13
Valley Stream Dr. . . . .
. . . . Pg.9 . . . . A13
Vera Ln. . . . . . . Pg.9 . . . . B13
Virginia Pl. . . . . Pg.10 . . . A15
Vita Dr. . . . . . . Pg.10 . . . B14
Walnut Ave. . . . . Pg.10 . . . A15
Waltz Dr. . . . . . Pg.9 . . . . B15
Warwick Dr. . . . . Pg.4 . . . . A12
Wayne Pl. . . . . . Pg.9 . . . . A13
Weeping Willow Dr. . . . .
. . . . Pg.9 . . . . B14
Weiland Rd. . . . . Pg.4 . . . A-X12
West Lodge Tr. . . Pg.9 . . . . B11
Westwood Ct. . . Pg.9 . . . . A13
Wetumka Ct. . . . Pg.9 . . . . C12
Wheeling Ave. . . Pg.9 . . . . A15
Wheeling Rd. . . . Pg.9 . . B-C14
Whipple Tree Dr. . . . .
. . . . Pg.5 . . . . A13
Whitehall Ct. . . . Pg.4 . . . . A13
Widgeon Dr. . . . Pg.9 . . . . B12
Wildberry Ct. . . . Pg.9 . . . . A13
Wille Ave. . . . . . Pg.9 . . . . A15
Williamsburg Ct. . . . .
. . . . Pg.5 . . . . A13
Willis Ave. . . . . . Pg.9 . . . . B14
Willow Rd. . . . . Pg.9 . . . . D15
Willow Terr. . . . . Pg.9 . . . . F15
Willowbrook Dr. . Pg.9 . . . . B14
Wilshire Dr. . . . . Pg.9 . . . . A13
Wolf Rd. . . . . . . Pg.10 . A14,D15
Woodbury Ln. . . Pg.4 . . . . A13
Woodcreek Dr. . . Pg.9 . . . . C14
Wooddock Dr. . . Pg.9 . . . . B12
Wooddock Ln. . . Pg.9 . . . . B13
Woodland Dr. . . . Pg.5 . . . . A13
Woodmere Ln. . . Pg.5 . . . . A15
Wye Ct. . . . . . . Pg.4 . . . . A12
Wynn Ct. . . . . . Pg.5 . . . . A13
Yorkshire Pl. . . . Pg.5 . . . . A13
Zee Ct. . . . . . . Pg.4 . . . . A13
1st St. . . . . Pg.5 . . . . A14
2nd St. . . . . Pg.5 . . . . A14

3rd St. . . . . Pg.5 . . . . A14
5th St. . . . . Pg.5 . . . . A14
6th St. . . . . Pg.5 . . . . A14
7th St. . . . . Pg.5 . . . . A14
8th St. . . . . Pg.5 . . . . A14
9th St. . . . . Pg.5 . . . . A14
10th St. . . . . . . Pg.5 . . . . A14
11th St. . . . . . . Pg.5 . . . . A14
12th St. . . . . . . Pg.5 . . . . A14

PARKS
Chamber Park . . Pg.5 . . . . A15
Childerly Park . . Pg.4 . . . . A13
Heritage Park . . Pg.9 . . . . A13
Horizon Park . . . Pg.5 . . . . A13
Husky Park . . . . Pg.9 . . . . A13

SCHOOLS
Eugene Field Sch. . . . .
. . . . Pg.5 . . . . A13
Jack London Jr. H.S. . . . .
. . . . Pg.9 . . . . A13
Mark Twain Sch. . Pg.9 . . . . B14
Nathaniel Hawthorne Sch. . . . .
. . . . Pg.4 . . . . A14
O.W. Holmes Jr. H.S. . . . .
. . . . Pg.5 . . . . A15
Sandburg Elem. Sch. . . . .
. . . . Pg.9 . . . . A13
Tarkington Jr. H.S. . . . .
. . . . Pg.5 . . . . A13
Walt Whitman Sch. . . . .
. . . . Pg.10 . . . A15
Wheeling H.S. . . Pg.9 . . . . B13

SHOPPING CENTERS
Center Plaza . . . Pg.5 . . . . A14
Dundee Plaza . . Pg.5 . . . . A14
Dunhurst Shopping Ctr. . . . . . .
. . . . Pg.9 . . . . A13
Gaslight Shopping Ctr. . . . . . .
. . . . Pg.5 . . . . A13
Lexington Plaza . Pg.5 . . . . A13
Riverside Shopping Ctr. . . . . . .
. . . . Pg.10 . . . A15
South Point Shopping Ctr. . . . .
. . . . Pg.10 . . . D15
Wheeling Shopping Ctr. . . . . . .
. . . . Pg.10 . . . A15

MISCELLANEOUS
Fire Dept. . . . . . Pg.9 . . . . B14
Indian Trails Library . . . .
. . . . Pg.9 . . . . A13
Pal-Waukee Airport . . . .
. . . . Pg.10 . . . C15
Post Office . . . . Pg.9 . . . . A14
Wheeling Muni. Complex . . . . .
. . . . Pg.9 . . . . A14

WHEELING TOWNSHIP
Pages 3-5,8-10,13

STREETS
Anita Ave. . . . . Pg.10 . E15-16
Apple Dr. . . . . . Pg.21 . . . D1
Bonnie Brae Ave. . . . .
. . . . Pg.10 . F15-16
Brookfield Ave. . . Pg.10 . F15-16
Camp McDonald Rd. . . . .
. . . . Pg.21 . . . D1
Carol Ave. . . . . Pg.10 . . . B15
Cayuga Ln. . . . . Pg.21 . . . E1
Chicago Ave. . . . Pg.8 . . . . D9
Chinkapin Oak Dr. . . . .
. . . . Pg.24 . . . F1
Cider . . . . Pg.21 . . . D1
Cindy Ln. . . . . . Pg.9 . . . . B15
Cove Ln. . . . . . Pg.21 . . . D1
Crab Apple Dr. . . Pg.21 . . . D1
Crimson . . . . . . Pg.21 . . . D1
Dean Ave. . . . . Pg.10 . . . B15
Des Plaines River Rd. . . . .
. . . . Pg.10 . . . E16
Dundee Rd. . . . . Pg.4 . . A11-12
Edward St. . . . . Pg.8,9 . A13,B10
Forest View Dr. . Pg.21 . . . A1
Graylynn Dr. . . . Pg.10 . . . F16
Gregory St. . . . . Pg.10 . F15-16
Hill St. . . . . Pg.10 . F15-16
Industrial Ln. . . . Pg.10 . . . B15
Inland Dr. . . . . . Pg.10 . . . B15
Ivy Ln. . . . . Pg.24 . . . F1
Jackson Dr. . . . . Pg.9 . . . . B13
Johnathon . . . . Pg.21 . . . D1
Kerry Ln. . . . . . Pg.9 . . . . C12
Lake-Cook Rd. . . Pg.4,5 . A13-14
Lama Ln. . . . . . Pg.21 . . . F1
Lee St. . . . . Pg.21 . . . F15
Lillian Ave. . . . . Pg.8,9 . C9,11
Lynwood Ave. . . Pg.8 . . . . D13
Maude Ave. . . . . Pg.8 . . . . C9
McIntosh Ct. . . . Pg.21 . . . D1
Milwaukee Ave. . Pg.21 . . . D1
Moki Ln. . . . . . . Pg.24 . . . F1
Morrison Ave. . . Pg.10 . F15-16
Mura Ln. . . . . . Pg.21 . . . D1
Park Dr. . . . . . . Pg.21 . . . E1
Pinoak Dr. . . . . Pg.21 . . . D1
Piper Dr. . . . . . Pg.21 . . . D1
Plant Rd. . . . . . Pg.10 . . . B15
Plum Creek Dr. . Pg.10 . . . B15
Portwine Rd. . . . Pg.5 . . . . A15

Quaker Ln. . . . . Pg.21 . . . E1
Rolling Ln. . . . . Pg.9 . . . . E12
Russell St. . . . . Pg.9 . . . . B13
Sauk Ln. . . . . . Pg.21 . . . E1
Seminole Ln. . . . Pg.21 . . . E1
Seneca Ln. . . . . Pg.21 . . . E1
South St. . . . . . Pg.9 . . . . B13
Stavros Rd. . . . . Pg.10 . . . B15
Thomas Ave. . . . Pg.8 . . . . D9
Tree . . . . Pg.21 . . . D1
Vera Ln. . . . . . . Pg.9 . . . . B13
Verde Ave. . . . . Pg.8 . . . C9-10
Wilkie Rd. . . . . . Pg.13 . . . F9
Winesap . . . . . Pg.21 . . . D1
Wintergreen . . . Pg.21 . . . E1
Wolf Rd. . . . . . . Pg.5,10 . A14,B15
Woodland Dr. . . Pg.10 . . . F16
Woodview Dr. . . Pg.21 . . . E1
Yale Ave. . . . . . Pg.8 . . . . C9
Yale Ct. . . . . . . Pg.8 . . . . C9
Yuma . . . . Pg.21 . . . E1

FOREST PRESERVES
Allison Woods . . Pg.10 . . . D16
Lake Ave. Woods . . . .
. . . . Pg.10 . . . E16
Potawatomi Woods . . . .
. . . . Pg.5 . . . . A15

WILLOW SPRINGS
Pages 33,34

STREETS
Abbott St. C10
Archer Ave. C9
Arizona Tr. C8
Beech St. C10
Beverly Ln. B11
Blackstone Ave. B10
Buck Ln. B9
Buckingham Ct. B9
Candlelight Dr. E. B9
Candlelight Dr. W. B9
Cedar St. B11
Charlton Ave. B9
Chaucer Dr. B9
Chelsea Ln. B9
Cliff St. C10
Colonel Ave. B10
Columbia Woods Dr. C9
Crescent Ct. B8
Crestview Dr. B8
Crown Ct. B9
Doogan Ave. C9
Dunbar St. C10
Elm St. B11
Fieldcrest Ave. B8
Flag Ave. B8
Forest Ave. B11
German Church Rd. B8
Glenwood St. B10
Hess Ave. B9
High St. C10
Hill St. B11
Hilton St. B11
Independence Dr. B8
Kazewell St. B9
Lake St. B10
Liberty Grove Dr. C9
Louis Dr. B11
Maple Ave. C10
Market St. B10
Mona St. B10
Mound St. B11
Nolton Ave. B10
Nueport Ct. B8
Nueport Dr. B8
Oakwood Ave. B10
Orlack Dr. B8
Park St. B10
Pearl St. B10
Pine St. B11
Pleasantview B8
Poston Rd. B11
Price St. C10
Prospect Ave. C10
Province Ct. B9
Rainford C10
Ravine Ave. B11
Regency Ct. B9
Rosemere Ct. B9
Rust St. B10
Rust Trail B8
Scenic Ct. B8
School Ave. B10
Sherwood St. B10
Spring St. B,C10
Stratford Dr. B9
Tech Air Dr. (Pvt.) B11
Tower Rd. F9-13
Tri-State Tollway A10
Tudor Ct. B9
Union St. B11
Ursala Dr. C9
Vana Dr. B11
Vinewood Ave. B10
Wadsworth Rd. B9
Walnut St. C10
Wentworth St. C10
Willow Springs Rd. B9
Willow St. C10
Willow West Dr. B9
Wolf Rd. B9
84th Pl. B8
85th St. B8
86th St. C8

87th St. C10

SCHOOLS
Grace Sch. B11
Willow Springs Sch. B11

MISCELLANEOUS
Fire Department B9
Post Office B10
Village Hall B10

WILMETTE
Pages 26,27

STREETS
Alison Ln. G10
Alpine Ln. G11
Amhurst Ln. F11
Apple Tree Ln. G10
Ashland Ave. F12
Avondale Ln. G11
Barclay Ct. G9
Beech Ave. G9
Beechwood Ave. F11
Beverly Dr. G10
Big Tree Ln. G10
Birchwood Ave. G9-11
Birchwood Ct. G9
Birchwood Ln. G10
Blackhawk Rd. G11
Briar Dr. G9
Brookside Dr. F8
Bunker Ln. F8
Cambridge Ln. F11
Canterbury Ct. G14
Cardinal Ln. G10
Carriage Way H10
Catalpa Pl. G12
Cedar Ln. G11
Central Ave. G9,11-13
Central Park Ave. G12
Cherokee Rd. F11
Chestnut Ave. F11-12
Chilton Ln. G10
Chippewa F10
Cleveland G10
Colgate F11
Columbus St. G10
Concord Ln. G10
Cornell St. F-G11
Country Ln. F9
Cove Ln. G11
Crabtree Ln. G9
Cranston Ct. F9
Crescent Pl. G13
Crestview Ln. G11
Dartmouth F10
Dupee Pl. G9
Edgewood Ln. F9
Elmwood G9
Elmwood Ave. F11-13
Fairway Dr. G9
Forest F9
Forest Ave. F11-13
Glendening Rd. F12
Glenview Rd. G8-9
Golf Terr. F10
Grant St. F10
Green Bay Rd. F10
Greenleaf Ave. G9,10,12,13
Greenwood Ave. F9-12
Gregory Ave. G9,12-13
Hartzell St. H9
Harvard Ln. F,G11
Hawthorn Ln. G10
Heather Ln. G9
Hibbard St. G10
Highcrest Dr. G11
Highland Ave. G9-12
Hill Ln. G9
Hill St. G9
Hollywood Ct. G10
Hunter Ct. G11
Hunter Rd. G11
Illinois Rd. F10
Indianwood Rd. F10
Iroquois Rd. F10-11
Isabella Ln. G11
Isabella St. G13
Karey Ct. G10
Kenilworth Ave. F10-11
Kilpatrick Ave. G9
Kin Ct. G10
Knoll Ln. F-G12
Knox F-G10
Koerper Ct. G9
La Crosse Ave. G9
La Crosse St. G9
LaPorte Ave. G9
Lake Ave. F9-13
Lamon Ave. G9
Laramie Ave. F-G9
Laurel Ave. G13-14
Laurel Ln. G10
Lavergne Ave. G9
Lawler Ave. G9
Lawndale Ave. G11
Leamington Ave. G9
Leclaire Ave. G9
Leyden Ln. G10
Lilac Ln. G10
Lincoln Ln. G10
Linden Ave. F11,G12-14
Lockerbie Ln. G9
Locust Rd. G10
Manor Dr. F9

Maple Ave. G12-13
Marian Ln. G10
Meadow Dr. E. G10
Meadow Dr. N. G10
Meadow Dr. W. G10
Meadow Dr.S. G10
Melrose Ct. F9
Miami Rd. F10
Michigan Ave. F13
Middlebury Ln. F10
Millbrook Ln. G9
Mohawk Rd. F10
New Trier Ct. F9
Nina Ave. G9
North Branch Rd. F9
Oak Cir. G12
Oakwood Ave. G12
Old Glenview Rd. G9-11
Orchard Ln. F10
Osage F10
Ottawa F10
Ouilmette Ln. G11
Oxford Ln. F11
Pamona Ln. G10
Park Ave. G12
Parkview Ct. G11
Pawnee Rd. F10
Pine G10
Pine Manor Ln. G11
Pinecrest Ln. G11
Pioneer Ln. G11
Plum Tree Ln. H9
Pontiac Rd. G12
Prairie Ave. G12
Princeton Pl. G12
Railroad G12
Redbud Ln. G12
Richmond Ln. F12
Ridge Rd. F,G11
Riverside Dr. F9
Romona Ct. F10
Romona Rd. F,G10
Sandy Ln. G11
Schiller Ave. G11
Seger St. G9
Seminole Rd. F10
Seneca Rd. F10
Shabona F10
Sheridan Rd. F13
Skokie Blvd. H-J10
Skokie Ct. G10
Spanish Ct. G9
Spencer Ave. G12
Sprucewood Ln. F9
Sprucewood Rd. F9
Sterling Ln. G11
Sunset Dr. G10
Temple Ln. G9
Thelin Ct. G10
Thornwood F9
Thornwood Ave. F11
Timber Ln. F11
Valley View Dr. G10
Valleyview Ct. G10
Vine Ct. G10
Vine St. G10
Virginia Ln. F9
Vista Ct. G10
Vista Dr. G10
Walden Ln. F9
Walnut F9
Walnut Ave. F11
Washington Ave. G9-12
Westerfield Dr. F12
Westmoreland Dr. G10
Westwood Ln. G9
Wilmette Ave. G9-12
Wilshire Dr. E. G10
Wilshire Dr. W. G10
Wood Ct. G12
Yale St. F11
3rd St. G13
4th St. G13
5th St. G13
6th St. F12,G13
7th St. F-G13
8th St. F-G13
9th St. F-G13
10th St. F12
11th St. F-G12
12th St. F12
13th St. F-G12
14th St. G12
15th St. F-G12
16th St. F,G12
17th St. F11
18th St. G11
20th St. G11
23rd St. F11
36th Pl. G11

GOLF COURSES
Westmoreland C.C. G10
Wilmette G.C. F8

PARKS
Centennial Park G11
Gillson Park F14
Maple Ave. Park G13
Roemer Park G10
Thornwood Park F10
Vattman Park F12

SCHOOLS
Avoco Jr. H.S. East F9
Bell Sch. G10

WILMETTE

Beth Hillel Hebrew Sch. G9
Central Sch. G13
Harper Sch. F10
Highcrest Sch. G10
Howard Sch. G11
Locust Jr. H.S. G10
Logan Sch. F12
Loyola Academy F9
Marie Murray Jr. H.S. F10
McKenzie Sch. G12
National College G14
Regina H.S. G10
Romona Sch. G10
Ronald Knox Montessori Sch. F11
St. Francis Sch. F11
St. Josephs Sch. F11

SHOPPING CENTERS
Edens S.C. F9
Plaza del Lago S.C. F13

MISCELLANEOUS
Bahai Temple G14
Mahoney Farm Preserve F12
Maria Immaculata Convent . . F11
Village Recreation Center . . . G13

WINNETKA

Pages 23,27

STREETS
Alles Rd. . . . Pg.23 . . . . E10
Apple Tree Rd. . . Pg.23 . . . . E10
Arbor Viate . . Pg.23 . . . . D11
Ardsley Rd. . . Pg.23 . . . . C9
Asbury Ave. . . Pg.23 . . . . C9
Asbury Ct. . . . Pg.23 . . . . C9
Asbury Ln. . . . Pg.23 . . . . C9
Ash St. . . . Pg.23 . . D10-11
Auburn Rd. . . Pg.23 . . . C-E9
Bell Ln. . . . . Pg.23 . . . . C9
Berkeley . . . . Pg.23 . . . . E10
Bertling Ln. . . Pg.23 . . . . E11
Birch St. . . . Pg.23 . . . . E10
Blackthorn Rd. . Pg.23 . . . . D10
Boal Pkwy. . . Pg.23 . . . . D9
Briar Ln. . . . Pg.23 . . . . D11
Broadmeadow Rd. . . . .
. . . . Pg.23 . . . . E10
Bryant Ave. . . Pg.23 . . . . D11
Burr . . . . . . Pg.23 . . . . D10
Cedar . . . . . Pg.23 . . . . D11
Chatfield Rd. . . Pg.23 . . . . E10
Cherry St. . . . Pg.23 . . D10-11
Chestnut . . . . Pg.23 . . D-E10
Church Rd. . . . Pg.23 . . . . E11
Crescent Ln. . . Pg.23,27 . . . . .
. . . . C10,E11
De Windt Rd. . . Pg.23 . . . . E10
Dinsmore Rd. . . Pg.23 . . . . D10

Edgewood Ln. . . Pg.23 . . . . . C9
Elder Ln. . . . Pg.23 . . . . E11
Eldorado St. . . Pg.23 . . . . D10
Elm St. . . . Pg.23 . . D10-11
Fairview . . . . Pg.23 . . . . E11
Fisher Ln. . . . Pg.23 . . . . C10
Forest . . . . . Pg.23 . . . . E11
Forest Glen Dr. E. . . . .
. . . . Pg.23 . . . . . C9
Forest Glen Dr. N. . . . .
. . . . Pg.23 . . . . . C9
Forest Glen Dr. S. . . . .
. . . . Pg.23 . . . . . C9
Forest Glen Dr. W. . . . .
. . . . Pg.23 . . . . . C9
Forest Way . . . Pg.23 . . . . . D9
Foxdale Ave. . . Pg.23 . . . . C10
Fuller Ln. . . . Pg.27 . . . . E12
Gage . . . . . . Pg.23 . . . . C10
Garland Ave. . . Pg.23 . . . . E11
Glen Oak Dr. . . Pg.23 . . . . C10
Glendale Ave. . . Pg.23 . . D-E10
Golf Rd. . . . . Pg.23 . . . . E11
Gordon Terr. . . Pg.23 . . . . C10
Green Bay Rd. . . Pg.23 . . . . D11
Greenwood . . . Pg.23 . . . . . C9
Grove . . . . . Pg.23 . . . . . C9
Hackberry Ln. . . Pg.23 . . . . . D9
Hamptondale . . . Pg.23 . . . . D10
Hawthorne Ln. . . Pg.23 . . . . E11
Hazel Ln. . . . Pg.23 . . . . . D9
Heather Ln. . . Pg.23 . . . . . D9
Hibbard St. . . Pg.23 . . . . . D9
Hickory Ln. . . Pg.23 . . . . . C9
Higginson Ln. . . Pg.23 . . . . E11
High St. . . . . Pg.23 . . . . E11
Hill Rd. . . . . Pg.23 . . . . E11
Hill Terr. . . . Pg.23 . . . . E11
Holly Ln. . . . Pg.23 . . . . . D9
Hoyt Ln. . . . . Pg.23 . . . . D11
Hubbard Pl. . . Pg.23 . . . . D10
Humboldt . . . . Pg.23 . . . . D10
Indian Hill Rd. . . Pg.23 . . . . E11
Kent Rd. . . . . Pg.23 . . . . . D9
Lake Ln. . . . . Pg.27 . . . . E11
Lamson Dr. . . . Pg.23 . . . . C10
Laurel . . . . . Pg.23 . . . . D10
Lincoln Ave. . . Pg.23 . . D10-11
Linden . . . . . Pg.23 . . . . D10
Lindenwood . . . Pg.23 . . . . D10
Lloyd Pl. . . . Pg.23 . . . . D10
Locust . . . . . Pg.23 . . D-E10
Maple . . . . . Pg.23 . . . . D11
Meadow Ln. . . Pg.23 . . . . C10
Meadow Rd. . . Pg.23 . . . . C10
Merrill Pl. . . . Pg.23 . . . . C10
Mews . . . . . Pg.23 . . . . D10
Michigan Blvd. . . Pg.23 . . . . . E9
Mt. Pleasant . . Pg.23 . . . E9,10
Myrtle . . . . . Pg.23 . . . . E11

Oak . . . . . . Pg.23 . . D10-11
Oakley . . . . . Pg.23 . . . . C10
Orchard Ln. . . Pg.23 . . . . E11
Park Ln. . . . . Pg.23 . . . . D11
Pelham Rd. . . Pg.23 . . . . D10
Pine Ln. . . . . Pg.23 . . . . D10
Pine St. . . . . Pg.23 . . D10-11
Pine Tree Ln. . . Pg.23 . . . . . C9
Plum Tree Ln. . . Pg.23 . . . . . C9
Poplar . . . . . Pg.23 . . . . E11
Prospect Ave. . . Pg.23 . . . . D10
Provident Ave. . . Pg.23 . . . . D10
Ravine Rd. . . . Pg.23 . . . . C10
Ridge Rd. . . . Pg.23 . . . . E11
Rosewood Ave. . . Pg.23 . . . . D10
Scott Ave. . . . Pg.23 . . . . . C9
Sheridan Rd. . . Pg.23,27 . . D-E11
Smith St. . . . Pg.23 . . . . . E9
Spring Ln. . . . Pg.23 . . . . E11
Spruce . . . . . Pg.23 . . D10-11
Starr Rd. . . . Pg.23 . . . . D10
Sumac Ln. . . . Pg.23 . . . . . D9
Summit . . . . . Pg.23 . . . . D10
Sunset Rd. . . . Pg.23 . . E10-11
Sunview Ln. . . Pg.23 . . . . . D9
Taylorsport Ln. . . Pg.23 . . . . C10
Thorn Tree Ln. . . Pg.23 . . . . E10
Tower Manor Dr. . . . .
. . . . Pg.23 . . . . C10
Tower Rd. . . . Pg.23 . . . . D11
Trapp Ln. . . . Pg.23 . . . . . D9
Vernon Ave. . . Pg.23 . . . . . C9
Vine . . . . . . Pg.23 . . . . D10
Walden Rd. . . Pg.23 . . . . D10
Walnut St. . . . Pg.23 . . . . E11
Warwick Ave. . . Pg.27 . . . . E11
Westmoor Rd. . . Pg.23 . . . . E10
Westmoor Trail . . Pg.23 . . . . . D9
Westview . . . . Pg.23 . . . . . E9
White Oak Ln. . . Pg.23 . . . . E10
Whitebridge Ln. . . Pg.23 . . . . C10
Willow Rd. . . . Pg.23 . . E10-11
Wilson . . . . . Pg.23 . . . . D11
Winnetka Ave. . . Pg.23 . . E10-11
Woodland Ave. . . Pg.27 . . . . E11

GOLF COURSES
Indian Hill G.C. . Pg.23 . . . . E10
Skokie Playfield G.C. . . . .
. . . . Pg.23 . . . . . D9
Winnetka G.C. . . Pg.23 . . . . . D9

PARKS
Crow Island Park . . . .
. . . . Pg.23 . . . . E10
Dwyer Park . . . Pg.23 . . . . D10
Edgewood Park . . Pg.23 . . . . . C9
Elder Lane Park . . Pg.27 . . . . E12
Lake Front Park . . Pg.23 . . . . D11
Lloyd Park . . . Pg.23 . . . . D11

Tower Rd. Park Pg.23 . . . . C11
Village Green Park . . . .
. . . . Pg.23 . . . . D11
W. Elm St. Park Pg.23 . . . . D10
Winnetka Park . Pg.23 . . . . E11

SCHOOLS
Cove School . . Pg.23 . . . . D10
Crow Island Sch. . . . .
. . . . Pg.23 . . . . E10
Hubbard Woods Sch. . . . .
. . . . Pg.23 . . . . D10
New Trier H.S., E. . . . .
. . . . Pg.27 . . . . E12
North Shore County Day Sch. . . .
. . . . Pg.23 . . . . E11
Sacred Heart Sch. . . . .
. . . . Pg.23 . . . . C10
Sammuel Greenley Sch. . . . . . .
. . . . Pg.27 . . . . E11
School of Saints Pg.23 . . . . E11
Washburn Jr. H.S. . . . .
. . . . Pg.23 . . . . . D9

MISCELLANEOUS
Community House . . . .
. . . . Pg.23 . . . . D11
Fire Department . . . .
. . . . Pg.23 . . . . D11
Ice Arena . . . Pg.23 . . . . . D9
Police Dept. . . Pg.23 . . . . D11
Post Office . . . Pg.23 . . . . C10
Tennis Neilsen Center . . . .
. . . . Pg.23 . . . . . D9
Village Hall . . . Pg.23 . . . . D11

WORTH

Pages 34,35,38

STREETS
Autullo Dr. . . . Pg.34 . . . . F14
Beloit Ave. . . . Pg.34 . . . F,G14
Columbus Ave. . . Pg.34 . . . . F14
Crandall Ave. . . Pg.35 . . . . F15
Depot St. . . . Pg.34 . . . . F15
Harlem Ave. . . Pg.34 . . . . G14
Highland Ave. . . Pg.35 . . . . E15
Home Ave. . . . Pg.38 . . . . G15
Lloyd Dr. . . . . Pg.35 . . . . F15
Lode Dr. . . . . Pg.35 . . . . E15
Nagle Ave. . . . Pg.35,38. . . F,G15
Nashville Ave. . . Pg.34 . . . . G15
Natchez Ave. . . Pg.34,38. . . F,G15
Natoma Ave. . . Pg.35 . . . . F15
Neenah Ave. . . Pg.35,38 . . F,G15
New England Ave. . . . .
. . . . Pg.35 . . . F,G15
Nordica Ave. . . Pg.35 . . . . F15
Normandy Ave. . . Pg.35 . . . . F15

Oak Park Ave. . . Pg.35 . . . . G15
Oak Tree . . . . Pg.34 . . . . E14
Oconto Ct. . . . Pg.34 . . . . F14
Octavia Ave. . . Pg.34 . . . . F14
Odell Ct. . . . . Pg.34 . . . . F14
Oketo Ave. . . . Pg.34 . . . . F14
Pacific Dr. . . . Pg.34 . . . . F14
Plahm Ct. . . . Pg.35 . . . . E15
Preller St. . . . Pg.34 . . . . F14
Ridgeland Ave. . . Pg.35,38. . . F15
Rutherford Ave. . . Pg.35 . . . . F15
Southwest Hwy. . . . .
. . . . Pg.35 . . . . E15
Wabash Ave. . . Pg.35 . . . . E15
Wood Ave. . . . Pg.38 . . . . G15
Worth Ave. . . . Pg.35 . . . F,G15
71st Ct. . . . . Pg.34 . . . . F14
76th Ave. . . . Pg.34 . . . . F14
76th Ct., W. . . Pg.34 . . . . F14
105th Pl. . . . Pg.35 . . . . E15
106th Pl. . . . Pg.35 . . . . E15
107th Pl. . . . Pg.35 . . . . E15
107th St. . . . Pg.34 . . . . E14
108th Pl. . . . Pg.35 . . . . E15
108th St. . . . Pg.34 . . . . E14
109th Pl. . . . Pg.35 . . . . F15
109th St. . . . Pg.34 . . . F14,15
110th Pl. . . . Pg.34 . . . . F15
110th St. . . . Pg.34 . . . . F14
111th Pl. . . . Pg.34,35 . . F14,15
111th St. . . . Pg.34,35 . . F14,15
112th Pl. . . . Pg.34,35 . . F14,15
112th St. . . . Pg.34,35 . . F14,15
113th Pl. . . . Pg.34 . . . . F14
113th St. . . . Pg.34,35 . . F14,15
114th Pl. . . . Pg.34,35. . . F
114th St. . . . Pg.34,35 . . F14,15
115th Pl. . . . Pg.34,35. . . G14
115th St. . . . Pg.34,35. . . G14
116th St. . . . Pg.34,38 G14,15

PARKS
Peak's Park . . . Pg.35 . . . . F15

SCHOOLS
Libra Sch. . . . Pg.34 . . . . F14
Worth Jr. H.S. . . Pg.35 . . . . F15
Worthridge Sch. . Pg.35 . . . . F16
Worthwoods Sch. . . . .
. . . . Pg.34 . . . . F14

MISCELLANEOUS
Library . . . . . Pg.35 . . . . F15

WORTH TOWNSHIP

Page 35,38

STREETS
Austin Ave. . . . Pg.38 . . . . H16

WORTH TOWNSHIP

Calumet Sag Rd. . . . .
. . . . Pg.38 . . . . H16
Central Ave. . . Pg.38 . . . . H17
Circle Ave., W. . Pg.38 . . . . I17
Le Claire Ave. . . Pg.38 . . . . H17
Major Ave. S. . . Pg.38 . . . . H17
Mason Ave. S. . . Pg.38 . . . . H16
Massasoit Ave. S. . . . .
. . . . Pg.38 . . . . H16
McVicker Ave. . . Pg.38 . . . H,I16
Meade Ave. . . . Pg.38 . . . H,I16
Melvina Ave. . . Pg.38 . . . . I16
Menard Ave. S. . . Pg.38 . . . . H16
Mobile Ave. . . Pg.38 . . . . I17
Monitor Ave. S. . . Pg.38 . . . . I16
Moody Ave. . . Pg.38 . . . H,I16
Parkside Ave. S. . . . .
. . . . Pg.38 . . . . H17
Ridgeland . . . . Pg.38 . . . . G16
123rd St. . . . Pg.38 . . . . H16
124th St. . . . Pg.38 . . . . H16
125th St. W. . . Pg.38 . . . . H16
126th St. . . . Pg.38 . . . H17,20
127th Pl. . . . Pg.38 . . . . H16
127th St. . . . Pg.38 . . . . H16
128th Pl. . . . Pg.38 . . . . H16
128th St. . . . Pg.38 . . . . H16
129th Pl. . . . Pg.38 . . . . I16
129th St. . . . Pg.38 . . . . I16
130th Pl. . . . Pg.38 . . . . I20
130th St. . . . Pg.38 . . . . I16
13lst St. . . . Pg.38 . . . . I20
135th St. . . . Pg.38 . . . . I16
174th Pl. . . . Pg.38 . . . . I18

CEMETERIES
Burr Oak Cem. . . Pg.38 . . . . H18
Chapel Hills Garden South Cem. .
. . . . Pg.35 . . . . F17
Hazelgreen Cem. . . . .
. . . . Pg.35 . . . . G17
Holy Sepulchre Cem. . . . .
. . . . Pg.35 . . . . F16
Rest Vale Cem. . Pg.38 . . . . G17
St. Casimir Cem. Pg.35 . . . . F19

FOREST PRESERVES
Elizabeth A. Conkey Forest . . . . .
. . . . Pg.38 . . . . I16

GOLF CLUBS
Westgate Valley C.C. . . . .
. . . . Pg.38 . . . . I15

SCHOOLS
Chippewa Sch. . . Pg.38 . . . . H16
Indian Hills Sch. . . . .
. . . . Pg.38 . . . . I16
Shepard H.S. . . Pg.38 . . . . I16

ELGIN AND VICINITY
SECTION 5

LEGEND

90	INTERSTATE HIGHWAY		FOREST PRESERVE
20	U.S. HIGHWAY		PARK
31	STATE HIGHWAY		GOLF COURSE
	OTHER PRIMARY THRU ROADS		CEMETERY
	ALL OTHER ROADS		INSTITUTIONAL
+++++	RAILROAD		RIVER OR LAKE
·	SCHOOL		
	FIRE STATION		
▪	POINTS OF INTEREST		

TURN PAGE FOR ORIENTATION MAP

SECTION 5
ORIENTATION MAP

Information on this page is to be used for general reference only.
For definitive listings of all information, see index at end of this section.

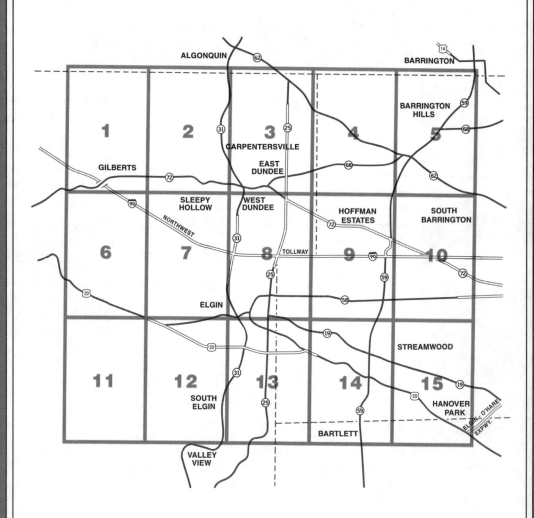

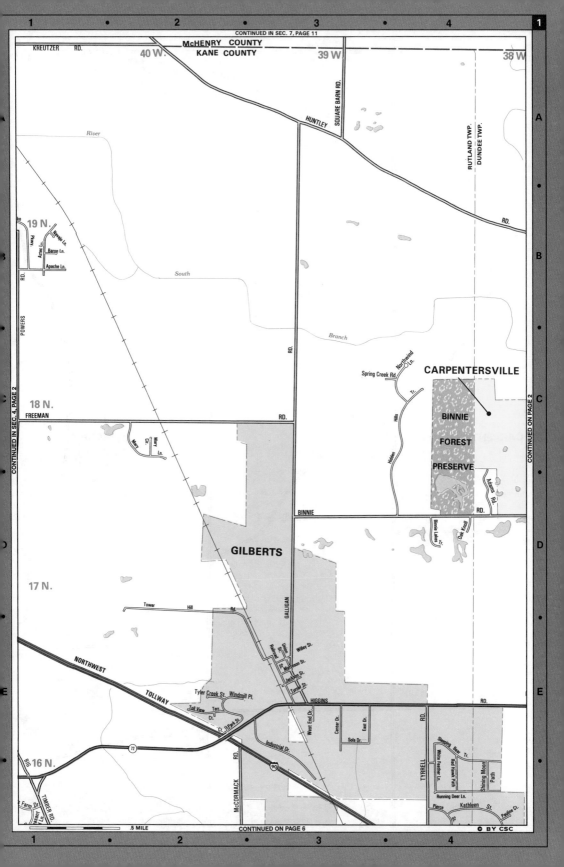

CONTINUED IN SEC. 7, PAGE 11

McHENRY   COUNTY
KANE   COUNTY

KREUTZER   RD.

40 W.

39 W.

38 W.

SQUARE BARN RD.

HUNTLEY

A

RUTLAND TWP.

DUNDEE TWP.

River

RD.

19 N.

Navajo Ln.

Aztec Ln.

Baron Ln.

Apache Ln.

POWERS

PWY.

RD.

South

B

Branch

Northwind
Ln.

Spring Creek Rd.

CARPENTERSVILLE

Tr.

CONTINUED ON PAGE 2

Hills

Holden

C

BINNIE

FOREST

PRESERVE

Adams Rd.

RD.

CONTINUED IN SEC. 4, PAGE 2

18 N.

FREEMAN

RD.

Mary Cr.

Mary St.

BINNIE

Binnie Lakes Tr.

Oak Knoll

CONTINUED ON PAGE 2

GILBERTS

GALLIGAN

D

17 N.

Tower   Hill   Rd.

Toll View

Ct.

Railroad St.

Union St.

Wiley St.

Mattison St.

Jackson St.

Turtle St.

RD.

NORTHWEST

TOLLWAY

Tyler Creek St.   Windmill Pl.

Terr.

Park St.

HIGGINS

West End Dr.

Center Dr.

East Dr.

Sola Dr.

RD.

E

Industrial Dr.

72

16 N.

Farm Dr.

TIMBER RD.

McCORMACK

RD.

90

TYRELL

Sleeping Bear Tr.

White Feather Ln.

Red Hawk Path

Shining Moon Path

Running Deer Ln.

Pierce St.

Kathleen   St.

Pauline Ct.

© BY CSC

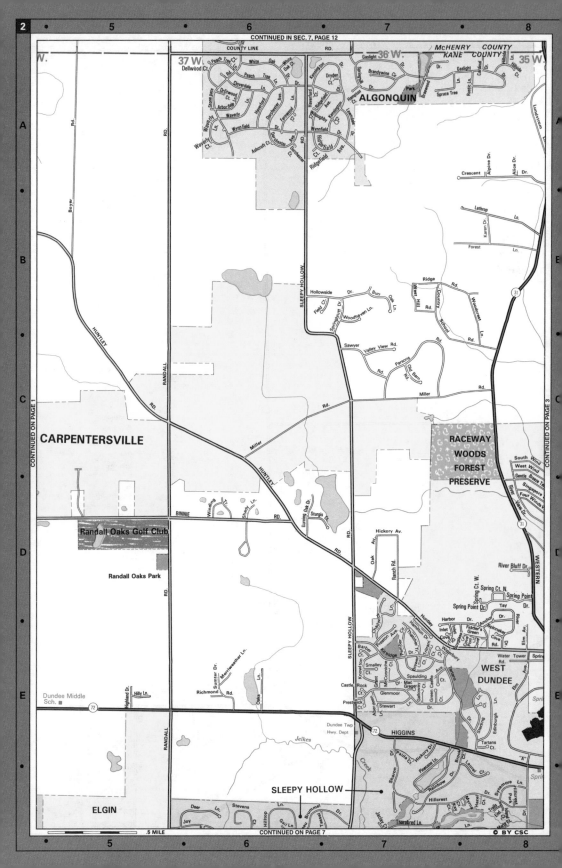

CONTINUED IN SEC. 7, PAGE 12

McHENRY COUNTY
KANE COUNTY

COUNTY LINE RD.

37 W.

36 W.

35 W.

ALGONQUIN

A

B

CONTINUED ON PAGE 1

CONTINUED ON PAGE 3

CARPENTERSVILLE

C

RACEWAY
WOODS
FOREST
PRESERVE

Randall Oaks Golf Club

BINNIE

Randall Oaks Park

D

River Bluff Dr.

WEST
DUNDEE

WESTERN

Dundee Middle
Sch.

Richmond Rd.

E

HIGGINS

Dundee Twp
Hwy. Dept

72

ELGIN

SLEEPY HOLLOW

Thorobred Ln.

CONTINUED ON PAGE 7

.5 MILE

© BY CSC

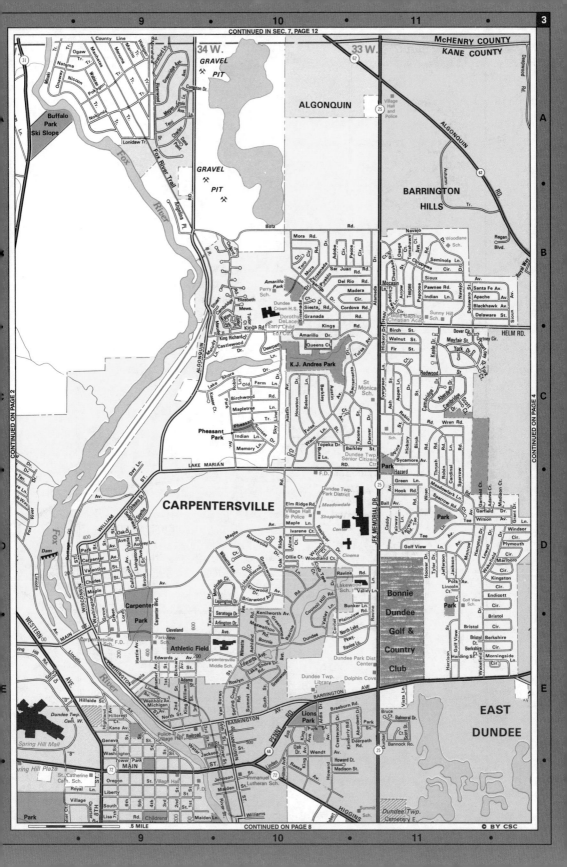

McHENRY COUNTY
KANE COUNTY

34 W.

GRAVEL PIT

33 W.

ALGONQUIN

Village Hall and Police

BARRINGTON
HILLS

GRAVEL PIT

Buffalo Park Ski Slope

Fox River Trail

Fox River

Navajo

Woodlane Sch.

Regan Blvd.

Seminole Ln.

Mora Rd.

Rd.

Adobe Cir.

Pecos

Chippewa

Sioux

Santa Fe Av.

Sunny Hill Sch.

Pawnee Rd.

Apache

Blackhawk Av.

Indian

Delaware St.

Amarillo Park

Perry Sch.

San Juan

Del Rio Rd.

Madera Rd.

Dundee Crown H.S.

Dorothy DeLacey Early Child Ed Ctr.

Siesta Rd.

Cordova Rd.

Granada Rd.

Bible Baptist Christian Aca.

Birch St.

Dover Cir.

Cortney Cir.

HELM RD.

Kings Rd.

Amarillo Dr.

Kings

Walnut St.

Fir St.

Mayfair Cir.

Keele Dr.

York Dr.

Queens Ct.

Deerpath Ln.

K.J. Andres Park

Redwood

Aspen Ln.

Robin

Cambridge

Aberdeen Dr.

Scott

Lake Shore Dr.

Old Farm Ln.

St Monica Sch.

Wren Rd.

Birchwood Ct.

Mapletree Ln.

Meadowlark Sch.

Pine Rd.

Hickory Rd.

Birch

Thrush

Pheasant Park

Pheasant Tr.

Indian Ln.

Memory Ln.

Sky Line Rd.

Topeka Dr.

Barkley St.

Dundee Twp. Senior Citizens Ctr.

Sycamore Av.

Hazard

Green Ln.

Meadowlark Ln.

Sparrow

LAKE MARIAN

F.D.

Park

Hook Rd.

Wren

Sparrow Rd.

Park

Dundee Twp. Park District

Windsor

CARPENTERSVILLE

Elm Ridge Rd.

Meadowdale

Village Hall & Police

Maple Ln.

Shopping Center

JFK MEMORIAL DR.

Ball Av.

Golf View

Plymouth Cir.

Marlboro Cir.

William

Oak Dr.

Audrey Ln.

Ivarene Ct.

Rosewood Dr.

Ridge

Cinema

Hoover Dr.

Tyler Dr.

Jefferson

Jackson

Montrose

Kingston Cir.

Carpenter

Valentine St.

Charles

Maple

Ollie Ct.

Woodland Dr.

Ravine

Lakewood Sch.

Valley Ln.

Endicott Cir.

Carpenter Park

Tamarac Dr.

Saratoga Dr.

Arlington Dr.

Lexington Dr.

Kenilworth Av.

Briarwood Av.

Council Hill Rd.

Bunker Ln.

Bonnie Dundee Golf & Country Club

Golf View Sch.

Bristol Cir.

Cleveland

Parkview Sch.

Athletic Field

Carpentersville Middle Sch.

Edwards Av.

Lake Shore Ln.

North Lake

Pkwy.

Dundee Park Dist Center

Park

Bristol

Berkshire

Morningside

Carpentersville F.D.

Hattie St.

Edwards

Roslyn

Dundee Twp. Library

Dolphin Cove

Harding St.

Wakefield

Dundee Twp. Cem. W.

Hillside Ln.

Hillcrest

Kane Av.

Geneva

Michigan

North

BARRINGTON AVE.

Bruce Ct.

Balmoral Dr.

EAST

DUNDEE

Spring Hill Mall

Police Village Hall

Railroad

Lions Park

Braeburn Rd.

Aldis

Crestwood

Deerpath Rd.

Dunbar

Bannock Rd.

Spring Hill Plaza

St. Catherine Cath. Sch.

Tower Park

MAIN

Oregon

Royal Ln.

Liberty

St. Immanuel Lutheran Sch.

Oak Dr.

Wendt

Howard Ct.

Madison St.

Village

Lisa

Childrens

Williams

Summit

HIGGINS

Dundee Twp. Cemetery E.

CONTINUED ON PAGE 2

CONTINUED ON PAGE 4

CONTINUED ON PAGE 8

.5 MILE

© BY CSC

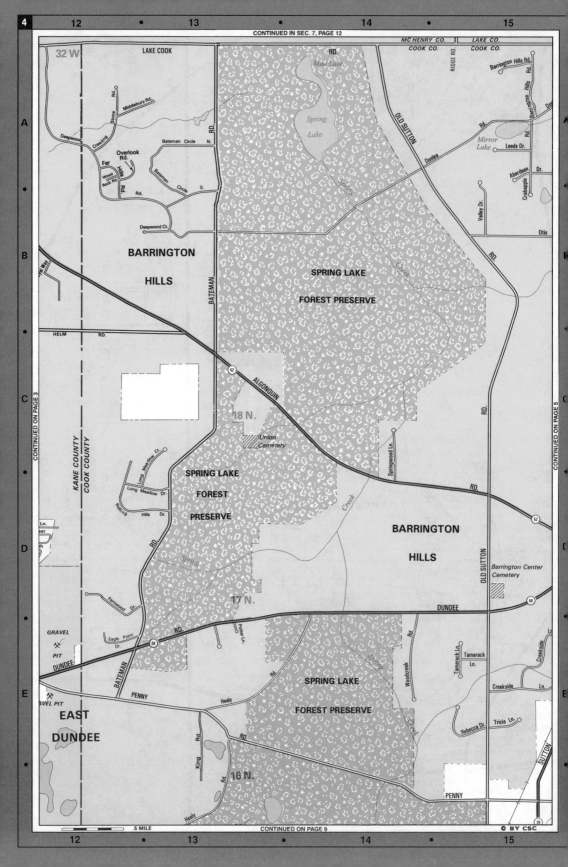

32 W

LAKE COOK

MC HENRY CO. | LAKE CO.
COOK CO. | COOK CO.

RIDGE RD.

RD.
Mud Lake

Barrington Hills Rd.

Middlebury Rd.
Stone Rd.
Crewling

Deepwood

Overlook Rd.
Far
Wood
Rock Rd.
Hills Rd.
Rd.

Bateman Circle N.

Bateman Circle S.

Deepwood Ct.

Spring Lake

OLD SUTTON

Donlea

Mirror Lake

Leeds Dr.

Aberdeen Dr.

Crabapple

Valley Dr.

Barrington Hills Rd.

Otis

BARRINGTON

HILLS

BATEMAN RD.

SPRING LAKE

FOREST PRESERVE

RD.

HELM RD.

62

ALGONQUIN RD.

18 N.

Union Cemetery

Springwood Ln.

CONTINUED ON PAGE 3

KANE COUNTY
COOK COUNTY

Long Meadow Ct.

Long Meadow Dr.

Rolling Hills Dr.

SPRING LAKE

FOREST

PRESERVE

Spring

Creek

RD.

BARRINGTON

HILLS

62

OLD SUTTON RD.

Barrington Center Cemetery

CONTINUED ON PAGE 5

Ln.

sor

h

Farmwood Dr.

17 N.

DUNDEE

68

GRAVEL

PIT

Eagle Point Dr.

68

RD.

Potter Ln.

Rd.

Woodcreek Rd.

Tamarack Ln.

Tamarack Ln.

DUNDEE

Creekside Ln.

GRAVEL PIT

BATEMAN RD.

PENNY

Healy

SPRING LAKE

FOREST PRESERVE

Creekside Ln.

Rebecca Dr.

Tricia Ln.

EAST

DUNDEE

King Rd.

RD.

Spring Creek

SUTTON

16 N.

PENNY

Healy

59

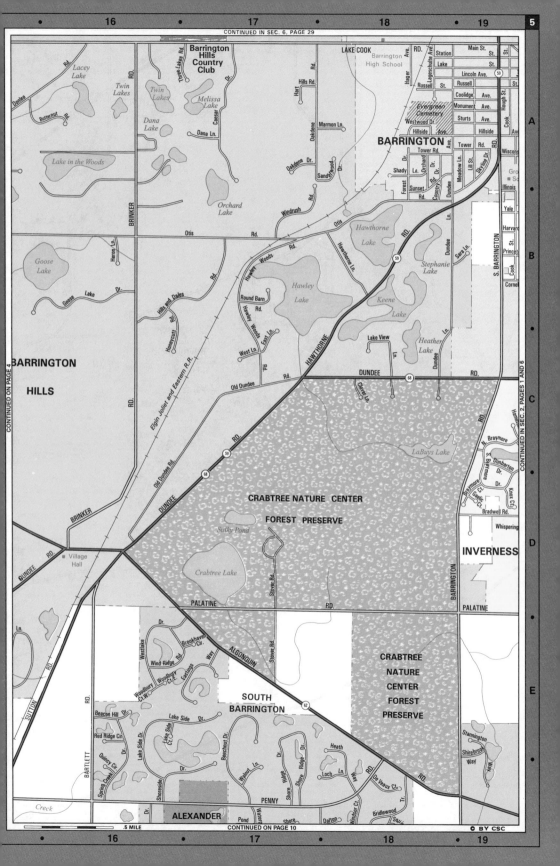

CONTINUED IN SEC. 6, PAGE 29

5

LAKE COOK

Barrington High School

Main St.   St.

Station

Lake

Lincoln Ave.

Russell   St.

Coolidge   Ave.

Monument   Ave.

Sturts   Ave.

Evergreen Cemetery

Westwood Dr.

Hillside   Ave.

Hillside

BARRINGTON

Tower Rd.

Shady   Ln.

Forest

Sunset

Orchard   Dr.

Country   Rd.

Dundee

Meadow Ln.

Tower

Ln.

Illinois

Yale

Harvard   St.

Princeton

Cornell

Wisconsin

S. BARRINGTON

Lacey Lake

Twin Lakes

Donlea

Butternut

Dana Lake

Twin Lakes

Melissa Lake

Caesar

Dana Ln.

Lake in the Woods

Three Lakes Rd.

Barrington Hills Country Club

Dr.

Hart

Hills Rd.

Rd.

Marmon Ln.

Oakdene

Oakdene Dr.

Sands Woods Dr.

Orchard Lake

Windrush

Rd.

Otis   Rd.

Otis

BRINKER

RD.

Hawthorne Lake

Hawthorne Ln.

Rd.

59

Dundee

Sara Ln.

Stephanie Lake

Goose Lake

Heron Ln.

Goose   Lake   Dr.

Hawley Woods

Round Barn Rd.

Hawley Woods East Ln.

Hawley Lake

Keene Lake

Hills and Dales

Hunnycutt Rd.

West Ln.

Old Dundee

Hawthorne

Lake View

Heather Lake

Ln.

CONTINUED ON PAGE 4

BARRINGTON

HILLS

Elgin, Joliet and Eastern R.R.

Old Dundee Rd.

RD.

DUNDEE

Rd.

68

59

DUNDEE   RD.

Village Hall

BRINKER

68

59

DUNDEE

Clover Ln.

LaBuys Lake

CRABTREE NATURE CENTER

FOREST PRESERVE

Sulky Pond

Crabtree Lake

Stover Rd.

PALATINE   RD.

Braymore

S. Braymore Dr.

Dunbarton Dr.

Braymore Ct.

Gaelic Ct.

Knox Ct.

Bradwell Rd.

Whispering

INVERNESS

PALATINE

CONTINUED IN SEC. 2, PAGES 1 AND 6

BARRINGTON   RD.

SUTTON   RD.

BARTLETT   RD.

Westlake Dr.

Wind Ridge Rd.

Woodbury Ct.

Woodbury Ct.W.

Beacon Hill

Red Ridge Cir.

Quincy Cir.

Spring Creek

Shoreside

Lake Side Dr.

Lake Side Ct.

Brookhaven Cir.

Eastings

Way

ALGONQUIN

Stover Rd.

62

SOUTH

BARRINGTON

Beechnut Dr.

Walnut Ln.

Shore Ridge Dr.

Shore Ridge Dr.

Heath

Loch Ln.

Way

RD.

De Veaux Ct.

CRABTREE

NATURE

CENTER

FOREST

PRESERVE

Stannington

Shirebrook Way

Creek

ALEXANDER

Dr.

PENNY

Pond

Shore

Dalton

Windsor Ct.

Bridlewood

Squi

.5 MILE

CONTINUED ON PAGE 10

© BY CSC

A   B   C   D   E

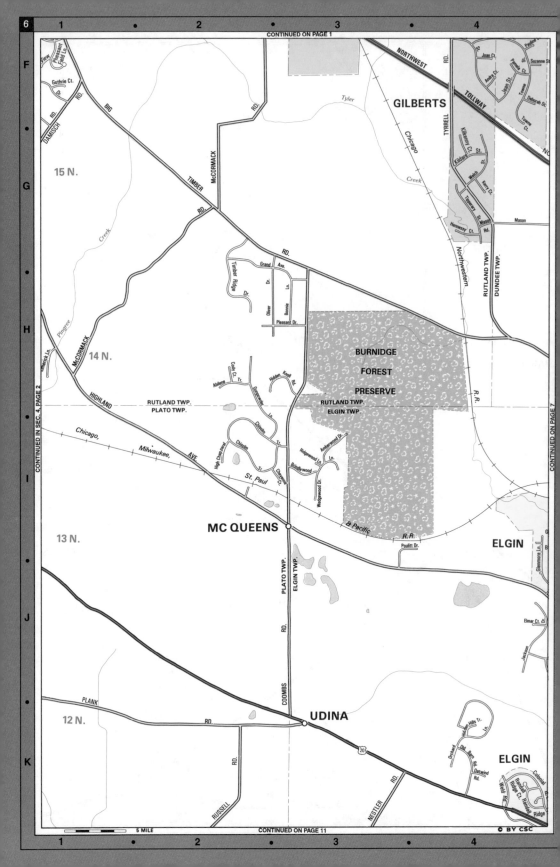

CONTINUED ON PAGE 1

1 • **2** • **3** • **4**

F

GILBERTS

Joan Ct.
Patrick Ct.
Suzanne St.
Andy Ct.
Joan St.
Towne
Deborah St.

NORTHWEST RD.

TOLLWAY

Pleasant
Field Ln.

Guthrie Ct.
Dr.

DAMISCH RD.

McCORMACK RD.

BIG

Tyler

Chicago

TYRRELL RD.

G

15 N.

TIMBER RD.

McCORMACK

Creek

Creek

Northwestern

Kilkenny Ct.
St.
Kilkenny
Dr.
Welch
Kerry Ct.
Tammany St.

Mason
Ct.
Rd.

Hennessy Ct.
Mason

Ridge

RUTLAND TWP.

DUNDEE TWP.

H

Pingree

Smerick Ln.

McCORMACK

14 N.

HIGHLAND

RD.

Timber Ridge
Dr.

Grand Ave.
Oliver Dr.
Ln.
Bonnie
Pleasant Dr.

BURNIDGE
FOREST
PRESERVE

R.R.

CONTINUED IN SEC. 4, PAGE 2

RUTLAND TWP.
PLATO TWP.

Cody Ct.
Tr.
Abilene
Hidden Knoll Rd.
Gunnysacke
Ln.

RUTLAND TWP.
ELGIN TWP.

CONTINUED ON PAGE 7

I

Chicago,

Milwaukee,

AVE.

St. Paul

High Chaparral
Chisolm
Tr.
Chisolm
Tr.
Chisolm
Tr.
Brindlewood Ct.
Brindlewood
Wedgewood Dr.
Ridgewood Ln.
Amberwood Dr.
Ln.

& Pacific

R.R.

Poulitt Dr.

ELGIN

Glenmore Ln.

MC QUEENS

13 N.

PLATO TWP.

ELGIN TWP.

COOMBS RD.

Elmar Ct.

Jackson

J

K

PLANK

12 N.

RD.

RUSSELL RD.

NESTLER RD.

UDINA

20

Holden Hills Tr.
Ln.

Orchard
Old Barn Rd.
Oatwind Rd.
Bartlett Ridge Ct.
Rindale Ridge
Wood Rd.
Colonial

ELGIN

5 MILE

CONTINUED ON PAGE 11

© BY CSC

1 • **2** • **3** • **4**

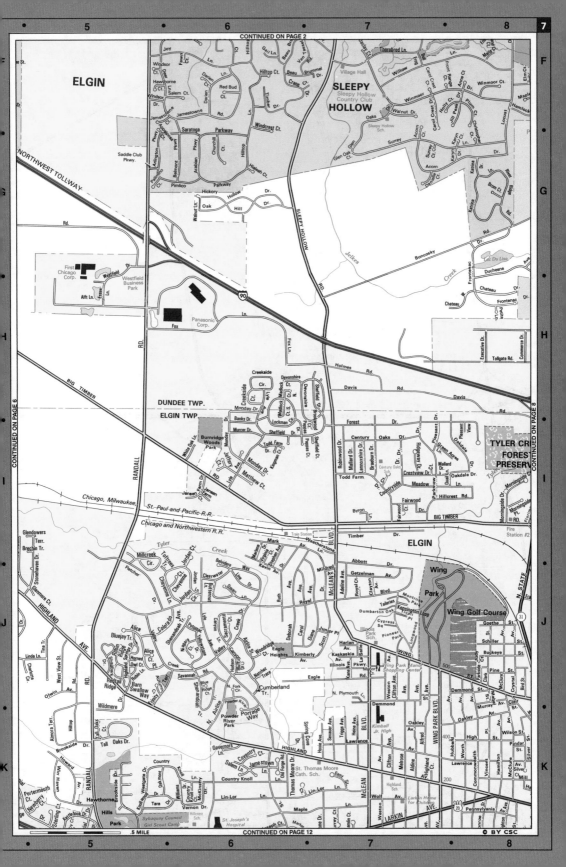

CONTINUED ON PAGE 2

ELGIN

SLEEPY HOLLOW

Sleepy Hollow Country Club

Village Hall

Sleepy Hollow Sch.

NORTHWEST TOLLWAY

Saddle Club Pkwy.

First Chicago Corp.

Westfield

Westfield Business Park

Panasonic Corp.

Fox

CONTINUED ON PAGE 6

CONTINUED ON PAGE 8

DUNDEE TWP.

ELGIN TWP

Burnridge Woods Park

TYLER CREEK FOREST PRESERVE

Century Oaks

Todd Farm

BIG TIMBER

Chicago, Milwaukee,

St. Paul and Pacific R.R.

Chicago and Northwestern R.R.

Train Station

ELGIN

Fire Station #2

RANDALL RD.

HIGHLAND AVE.

Millcreek Cir.

Wing Park

Wing Golf Course

Illinois Park Sch.

Pioneer Park

Eagle Heights

Harlan

Elgin Park Manor Shopping Center

Powder River Park

Kimball Jr. High

Highland Sch.

Larkin Home for Children

RANDALL RD.

Brookside Park

Sybaquay Council Girl Scout Camp

St. Joseph's Hospital

St. Thomas Moore Cath. Sch.

WING PARK BLVD.

HIGHLAND AVE.

LARKIN AVE.

McLEAN

.5 MILE

CONTINUED ON PAGE 12

© BY CSC

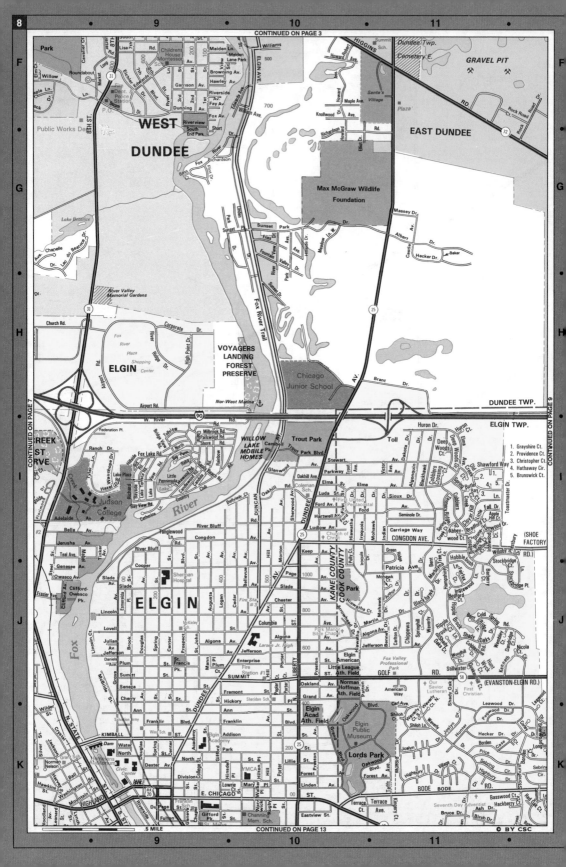

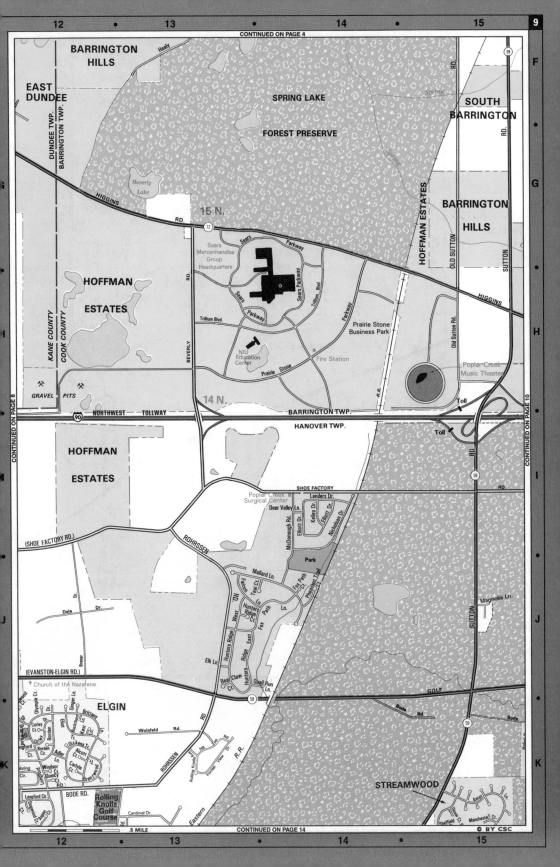

CONTINUED ON PAGE 4

12 • 13 • 14 • 15

F

BARRINGTON
HILLS

Healy

EAST
DUNDEE

SOUTH
BARRINGTON

SPRING LAKE

FOREST PRESERVE

Spring

DUNDEE TWP.
BARRINGTON TWP.

Beverly
Lake

G

HIGGINS

RD.

BARRINGTON

HILLS

15 N.

72

HOFFMAN ESTATES

Sears   Parkway

OLD SUTTON

SUTTON

Sears
Mercahandise
Group
Headquarters

Sears Parkway

Trillium Blvd.

HIGGINS

H

HOFFMAN

ESTATES

Sears   Parkway

Trillium Blvd.

Parkway

Prairie Stone
Business Park

Old Sutton Rd.

KANE COUNTY
COOK COUNTY

BEVERLY   RD.

NIU
Education
Center

Fire Station

Prairie Stone

R. R.

Poplar Creek
Music Theater

GRAVEL   PITS

14 N.

Toll

CONTINUED ON PAGE 8

90   NORTHWEST   TOLLWAY

BARRINGTON TWP.

Toll

CONTINUED ON PAGE 10

HANOVER TWP.

Toll

I

HOFFMAN

ESTATES

SHOE FACTORY

RD.

58

RD.

Shoe Factory

Poplar Creek
Surgical Center

Landers Dr.

Deer Valley

McDonough Rd.

Elliott Dr.

Kelley Dr.

Elliott Dr.

Nicholson Dr.

Magnolia Ln.

(SHOE FACTORY RD.)

ROHRSSEN

Park

SUTTON

Mallard Ln.

Fox Ct.

Pheasant Trail

Dr.

Dale   Dr.

Fox Ct.

Fields

Ln.

Fox Path

Ct.

Ln.

J

Breier

West

Hunters
Ridge
East

Fox   Path

Ridge

Elk Ln.

Hunters

GOLF

(EVANSTON-ELGIN RD.)

Bear Claw
Ct.

Quail Run
Ln.

Bode   Rd.

Bode

Church of the Nazarene

58

59

ELGIN

Wolsfeld   Rd.

RD.

Rolling Knolls

Forest View

Dr.

Rd.

R. R.

Halpin

Olympia Ct.
Ginger Ln.

Brittany

Corley
Ct.

Dickens Tr.

Kent
Ct.

Alcott

Borden
Ct.

Buckthorn
Ct.

Adler

Ct.

Carlyle
Ct.

Brentwood

ROHRSSEN

K

Windsor
Cir.

Quincy
Ct.

Longford Cir.

BODE RD.

Rolling
Knolls
Golf
Course

Cardinal Dr.

Eastern

STREAMWOOD

Shelfield

Manchester Ct.

© BY CSC

12 • 13 • 14 • 15

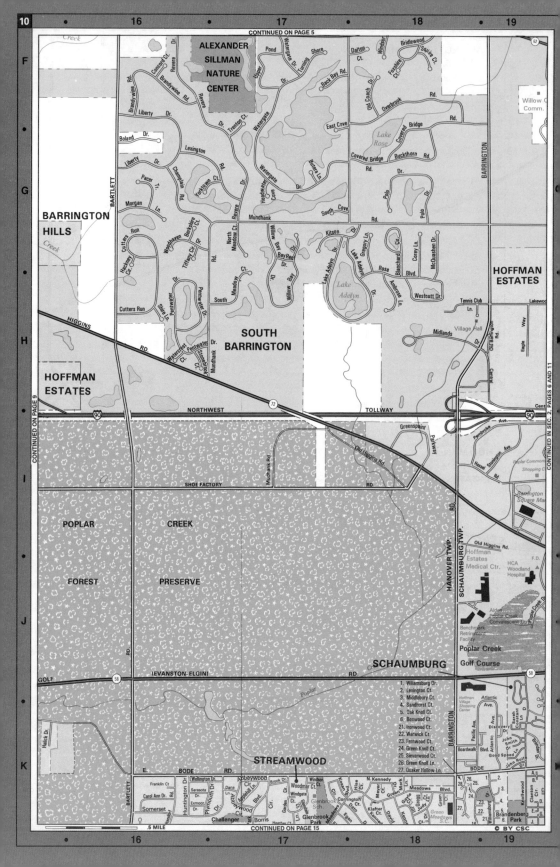

CONTINUED ON PAGE 6

1　　2　　3　　4

RUSSELL
11 N.

Fitchie

RD.

WATER

Creek

RD.

WATER

Cliff Dr.
Romeo Cir. Dr.
Juliet Dr.
Cir.
Senden Dr.
Capulet
Verona Dr.
Capulet Ct. Cir.
Haley Dr.
Capulet
Central Dr.
Romeo

Weld Rd.
Ridge
Reback Ct.
Mary-hill Ln.
Williams burg
Dr.
Johnstown
Lamont
Rd.
Ct.
Stratford Ln.
York
Oxford Ln.
Williamsburg Dr.
Newport Ct.
Burgess Dr.
Jaguar
Ct.
Williamsburg Dr.
Manchester Ln.

EL
Cou
Clu

Creek

Otter

WATER RD.

Red Cloud Ln.
Hogan Hill
Hopi Ln. Tr.
Koshare Cir.
Hogan Hill
Naperville Trail
Hill
Santa Fe Tr.
Lori Ln.
Pueblo Peak
Adobe
Koshare
Koshare
Arrowshaker
Pass
Pass
Nokomis Ln.
Thunder Gap
W. Lori Ln.

Trails End
N. Leland Ct.
S. Leland Ct.
Beckman
Tr.
Beckman
Tr.
Beckman Park Path
Beckman
Ln.
Tipi Tr.
Tipi Tr.

Fitchie

BOWES
NESTLER
RD.

Bowes
Oak Tree Ln.
Sunflower Ln.
CORRON
RD.

Nestler Rd.

Whispering Ln.
Stirling

BOWES

Illinois

Savanna Creek Ct.
Savanna Lakes Dr.
Cross Creek Ct.
Savanna Lakes Ct.

Creek

Central

Gulf Creek

BOWES

RD.

RD.

Creek
Way
Sturbridge
Briarfield Ct.

Creek

Stony

Hopps
NOLAN

HOPPS

RD.
Richard Ln.
Kristen
Dr.
Lisa
Stevens Ln.
Willow Ln.
Acorn Ln.
Wildwood
Dr.
Shady
Running Deer Tr.

Bittersweet
Ln.
Passer. Pt.
Two's Pl.
Gingerwood Ln.

R.F.

RD.

Creek

8 N.
McDONALD

PLATO TWP.
ELGIN TWP.

Sunvale Ct.
Heatherfield Dr.

STEVENS

Heatherfield East Dr.
Peppertree Ct.
Peppertree Ln.

RD.

Citation Ct.

RD.

PLATO TWP.
CAMPTON TWP.

ELGIN TWP.
ST. CHARLES TWP.

Harry Ct.
Summertset Ct.
Eagles Nest Ct.
Chesterfield Brittany Dr.
Calvert field
Fielding Ct.
Felicons Tr.
Johns way
Northern Ln.
Duncan Ln.
Phar. Lap Dr.
Whittney Dr.
Cir.

Oak Dr.
Dogwood Ln.
Sycamore Rd.
Lilac Ln.
Pine Rd.
CRANE
RD.
Otter

Ridge
Northern Ct.

CONTINUED IN SEC. 4, PAGES 2 AND 5
CONTINUED ON PAGE 12

L

M

N

O

P

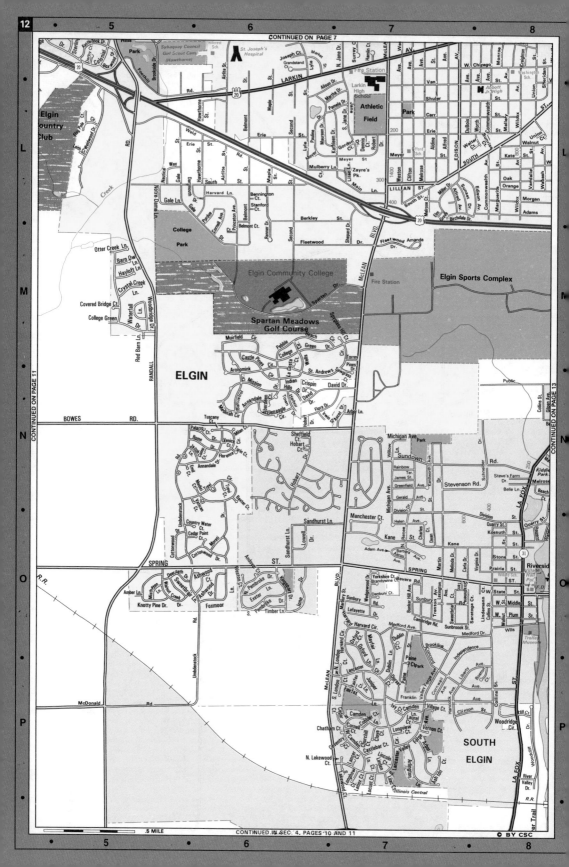

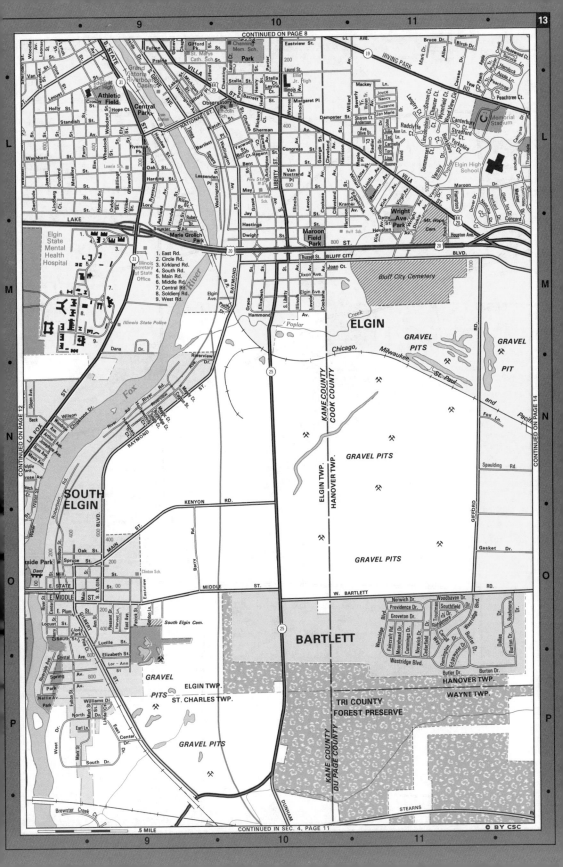

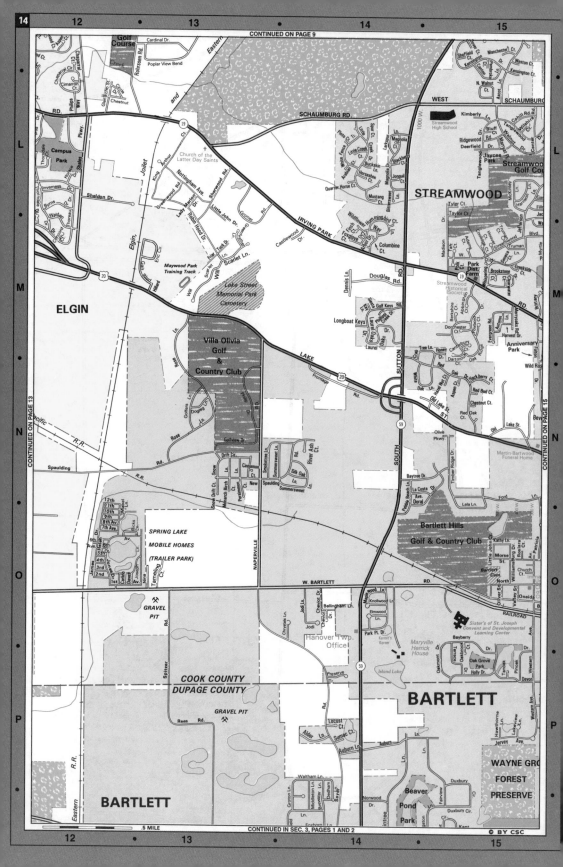

CONTINUED ON PAGE 9

STREAMWOOD

ELGIN

CONTINUED ON PAGE 13

CONTINUED ON PAGE 15

COOK COUNTY
DUPAGE COUNTY

BARTLETT

WAYNE GROVE
FOREST
PRESERVE

.5 MILE

CONTINUED IN SEC. 3, PAGES 1 AND 2

© BY CSC

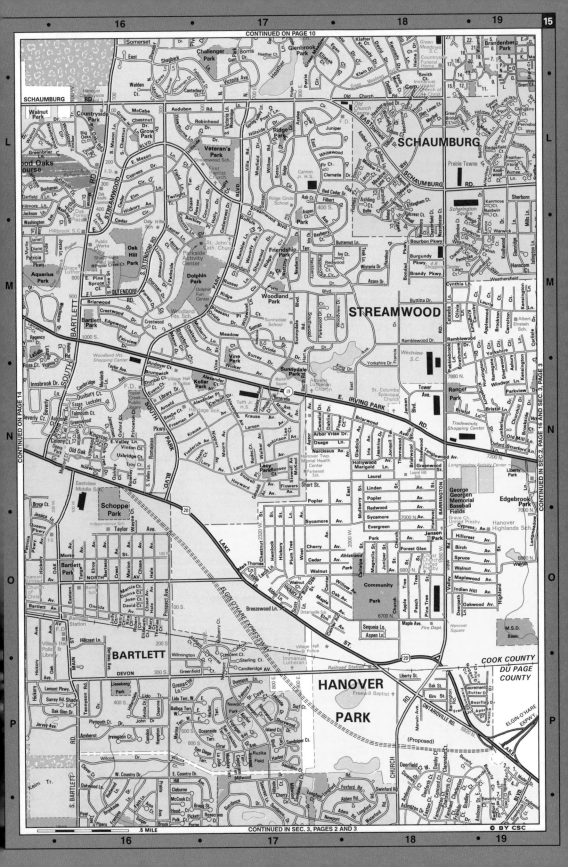

INDEX TO ELGIN AND VICINITY

ALGONQUIN

Pages 2,3

STREETS

Angelica Pl. B9
Arbordale Ln. A6
Ashcroft Ct. A6
Birch Tree Ln. A6
Braewood Dr. A7
Brandywine Cir. A7
Cardinal Dr. A8
Charles Dr. A9
Cloverdale Ln. A9
Compton Ct. A9
Dana Pt. A9
Dellwood Ct. A6
Dorchester Ln. A6
Dorchester Ct. A6
Driftwood Ct. A6
Dryden Ct. A6
Fernwood Ct. A6
Fernwood Ln. A6
Gaslight Dr. A7,8
Greenridge Ave. A9
Hampton Ln. A7
Haverford Ct. A6
Haverford Dr. A6
Hillside Ct. A8
Hillside Ln. A8
Kensington Ct. A7
Kensington Dr. A6
Lawndale Dr. A7
Lonidaw Tr. A9
Louis Ave. A9
Megan Ave. A9
Peach Tree Ln. A6
Peachtree Ct. A6
Ridgefield Ave. A7
Ridgefield Ct. A7
Riverwood Dr. A9
Rustic Ln. A8
Springhill Dr. A7
Sprucetree Ln. A7
Stonegate Ln. A6
Stratford Ln. A9
Terri Ln. A6
Waverly Ct. A6
Waverly Ln. A6
White Oak Ave. A6
White Oak Dr. A6
Willoughby Ct. A7
Wynnfield Dr. A6

BARRINGTON

Page 5

STREETS

Barrington Rd. A19
Cook St. A19
Coolidge Ave. A18
Cornell Ave. B19
Dundee Ave. A19
Forest Dr. A19
Grove Ave. A19
Hager Ave. A18
Hillside Ave. A19
Hough St. A19
Illinois Ave. A19
Lageschulte Ave. A18
Lake Cook Rd. A18
Lake St. A18
Lill St. A18
Lincoln Ave. A18
Main St. A18
Meadow Ln. A19
Monument Ave. A18
Orchard Dr. A18
Otis Rd. A19
Russel St. A18
Shady Ln. A18
Skyline Dr. A19
Station St. A18
Sturts Ave. A18
Sunset Rd. A19
Tower Rd. A18
Westwood Dr. A18
Wisconsin Ave. A19

CEMETERIES

Evergreen Cemetery A18

SCHOOLS

Grove Sch. A19

BARRINGTON HILLS

Pages 3,4,5,9

STREETS

Aberdeen Dr. .. Pg.4 ...... A15
Algonquin Rd. . Pg.4 .... A11,C13
Autumn Tr. .... Pg.3 ...... A11
Barrington Hills Rd. ....
.... Pg.4 ...... A15
Barrington Rd. B19
Bateman Cir. N. Pg.4 ...... A13
Bateman Cir. S. Pg.4 ...... A13
Bateman Rd. ... Pg.4 ...... B13
Brinker Rd. ... Pg.5 ..... B-D16
Butternut Rd. . Pg.5 ...... A16
Caesar Dr. .... Pg.5 ...... A17
Clover Ln. .... Pg.5 ...... C18
Crabapple Rd. . Pg.4 ...... A15
Crawling Stone Rd. ....
.... Pg.4 ...... A12
Creekside Ln. . Pg.4 ...... E15
Dana Ln. ...... Pg.5 ...... A17

Deepwood Ct. .. Pg.4 ...... B13
Deepwood Rd. .. Pg.4 .... A,B12
Donalea Rd. ... Pg.4 ...... A15
Dundee Ln. .... Pg.5 ...... C18
Dundee Rd. .... Pg.4 ... D16,E12
Eagle Point Dr. Pg.4 ...... E12
East Ln. ...... Pg.5 ...... C17
Far Hills Rd. . Pg.4 ...... A12
Fernwood Dr. .. Pg.4 ...... D12
Goose Lake Dr. Pg.5 ...... B16
Hart Hill Rd. . Pg.5 ...... A17
Hawley Woods Rd. ....
.... Pg.5 ...... B17
Hawthorne Ln. . Pg.5 ...... A18
Hawthorne Rd. . Pg.5 ...... C17
Healy Rd. ..... Pg.4 .... E,F13
Helm Rd. ...... Pg.4 ...... C12
Heron Ln. ..... Pg.5 ...... B16
Hills and Dale Rd. ....
.... Pg.5 ...... B16
Honey Cut Rd. . Pg.5 ...... C16
King Rd. ...... Pg.4 ...... E13
Lake View Ln. . Pg.5 ...... B18
Lake-Cook Rd. . Pg.5 ...... A16
Leeds Dr. ..... Pg.4 ...... A15
Long Meadow Ln. ....
.... Pg.4 ...... D12
Long Meadow Dr. ....
.... Pg.4 ...... D12
Marmon Ln. .... Pg.5 ...... A18
Middlebury Rd. Pg.4 ...... A12
Oakdene Dr. ... Pg.5 ...... A17
Oakdene Rd. ... Pg.5 ...... A17
Old Dundee Rd. Pg.5 ...... D16
Old Sutton Rd. Pg.4 ... A14,D15
Otis Rd. ...... Pg.4 ... B15,18
Overlook Rd. .. Pg.4 ...... A12
Palatine Rd. .. Pg.5 ...... D17
Penny Rd. ..... Pg.5 ...... A18
Potter Ln. .... Pg.4 ...... E13
Rebecca Dr. ... Pg.4 ...... E13
Regan Blvd. ... Pg.3 ...... B12
Ridge Rd. ..... Pg.4 ...... A15
Rolling Hills Dr. Pg.4 .... D12
Round Barn Rd. Pg.5 ...... B17
Royal Way ..... Pg.3 ...... B12
Sandalwood Dr. Pg.5 ...... A17
Sara Ln. ...... Pg.5 ...... B12
Springwood Ln. Pg.4 ...... C14
Tamarack Ln. .. Pg.4 ...... A15
Three Lakes Rd. Pg.5 ..... A17
Tricia Ln. .... Pg.4 ...... E15
Valley Dr. .... Pg.4 ...... B15
West Ln. ...... Pg.5 ...... C17
Windrush Rd. .. Pg.5 ...... B17
Wood Rock Rd. . Pg.4 ...... A12
Woodcreek Rd. . Pg.4 ...... E14

CEMETERIES

Barrington Center Cemetery ......
.... Pg.4 ...... D15
Union Cemetery . Pg.4 ..... C13

FOREST PRESERVES

Spring Lake Forest Pres. ....
.... Pg.4 ...... B14

GOLF COURSES

Barrington Hills Country Club ....
.... Pg.5 ...... A17

MISCELLANEOUS

Crabtree Nature Center ....
.... Pg.5 ...... D17
Village Hall .. Pg.5 ...... D16

BARRINGTON TOWNSHIP

Page 5,10

STREETS

Barrington Rd. . Pg.5 ..... B19
Bartlett Rd. .. Pg.10 ..... G16
Boland Dr. .... Pg.10 ..... G16
Higgins Rd. ... Pg.10 ..... H16
Stover Rd. .... Pg.5 ...... E17
Sutton Rd. .... Pg.5 ...... E15

BARTLETT

Pages 13-15

STREETS

Acorn Ct. ..... Pg.15 ..... P17
Adare Rd. ..... Pg.15 ..... P18
Alda Ln. ...... Pg.14 ..... P14
Amhurst Dr. ... Pg.15 ..... P16
Anchor .... Pg.15 ..... P17
Anita Dr. ..... Pg.15 ..... P16
Aspen Ct. ..... Pg.14 ..... N15
Auburn Ln. .... Pg.14 ..... P14
Balboa Terr. .. Pg.15 ..... P16
Bartlett Ave. . Pg.15 ..... O15
Bartlett Rd. .. Pg.15 ..... N16
Bartlett R. E. Pg.15 ..... O16
Bartlett R. W. Pg.15 ..... O14
Bay St. .... Pg.15 ..... P17
Bayberry Dr. .. Pg.15 ..... O15
Baytree Dr. ... Pg.14 ..... N14
Bellingham Ln. Pg.14 ..... O14
Berteau Ave. .. Pg.15 .... O,P16
Betty Ct. ..... Pg.15 ..... O15
Bryce Ct. ..... Pg.15 ..... N15
Camdon Ct. .... Pg.15 ..... P16
Candleridge Ct. Pg.15 .... P17
Capistrano Terr. Pg.15 ... P17
Carlino Ct. ... Pg.14 ..... O12

Chase Ave. .... Pg.15 ..... O16
Chestnut Ct. .. Pg.14 ..... N15
Cheviot Dr. ... Pg.14 ..... O14
Chrystals Ln. . Pg.14 ..... O13
Church Ct. .... Pg.15 ..... O15
Cleburne ...... Pg.15 ..... P16
Clover Ct. .... Pg.15 ..... P16
Coral Ave. .... Pg.15 ..... P17
Costa Ave. .... Pg.14 ..... N14
Country Dr. E. Pg.15 ..... P16
Country Dr. W. Pg.15 ..... P16
Cove Ct. ...... Pg.15 ..... P17
Crab Tree Ln. . Pg.14 ..... N14
Crescent Ct. .. Pg.15 ..... P17
Crest Ave. .... Pg.15 ..... O16
Cutlass Ave. .. Pg.15 ..... O16
David Ct. ..... Pg.15 ..... O16
Davies .... Pg.14 ..... O12
Deanne Dr. .... Pg.15 ..... P16
Devon Ave. .... Pg.15 ..... P15
Dogleg Ln. .... Pg.14 ..... N13
Donna Ct. ..... Pg.15 ..... O16
Doral Dr. ..... Pg.14 ..... N14
Dunmore Ln. ... Pg.15 ..... P16
Duxbury Cir. .. Pg.14 ..... P15
Eastern Ave. .. Pg.15 ..... O16
Elizabeth Ct. . Pg.15 ..... O16
Elmwood Ln. ... Pg.14 ..... O14
Elroy Ave. .... Pg.15 ..... O16
Falmore Dr. ... Pg.14 ..... P17
Ford Ln. ...... Pg.14 ..... N15
Frontage Rd. .. Pg.14 ..... N14
Golfers Ln. ... Pg.14 ..... N13
Greenfield Ct. Pg.15 ..... P16
Hackberry Ct. . Pg.14 ..... N15
Hale Ave. ..... Pg.15 ..... O16
Hampton Cir. .. Pg.15 ..... P16
Harbor Terr. .. Pg.15 ..... P17
Hawthorne Ln. . Pg.15 ..... P15
Hazel Nut Ct. . Pg.14 ..... N15
Helen Dr. ..... Pg.15 ..... O12
Hill Ave. ..... Pg.15 ..... O16
Hillandale Dr. Pg.15 ..... P16
Hillcrest Ln. . Pg.15 ..... O16
Holly Dr. ..... Pg.15 ..... P16
Honey Ct. ..... Pg.14 ..... M15
Irvington Ct. . Pg.14 ..... P16
Island .... Pg.14 ..... P17
James Dr. ..... Pg.15 ..... P15
Jervey Ln. .... Pg.14 ..... P15
Jessica Ln. ... Pg.15 ..... P15
Joan Ct. ...... Pg.15 ..... O16
Jodi Ln. ...... Pg.14 ..... O16
John Dr. ...... Pg.15 ..... P16
Joseph Dr. .... Pg.14 ..... O12
Judy Ct. ...... Pg.15 ..... O15
Kathy Ln. ..... Pg.15 ..... O15
Knollwood Ln. . Pg.14 ..... O14
La Jolla Terr. Pg.15 ..... P16
Lake St. ...... Pg.14 ..... N14
Lakeside ...... Pg.15 ..... P17
Lakeview Ln. .. Pg.14 ..... P15
Lamont St. .... Pg.15 ..... P16
Laurie Ln. .... Pg.15 ..... O12
Lela Ln. ...... Pg.15 ..... O16
Lido Terr. .... Pg.15 ..... P16
Little Hale Ct. Pg.15 .... O15
Locust Ct. .... Pg.14 ..... P14
Longford Rd. .. Pg.15 ... P17,18
Mabel Ln. ..... Pg.14 ..... O12
Main St. ...... Pg.15 ..... P16
Mallard Ct. ... Pg.15 ..... P17
Maplewood Ln. . Pg.14 ..... O14
Marcia Ct. .... Pg.15 ..... O16
Marina Terr. .. Pg.15 ..... P16
Marion Ave. ... Pg.15 ..... O16
Mary Ct. ...... Pg.15 ..... P17
Millwood Dr. .. Pg.15 ..... P16
Molobay Terr. . Pg.15 ... O15,16
Morse Ave. .... Pg.15 ..... O16
Mulberry Ct. .. Pg.15 ..... P17
Naperville Rd. Pg.15 ..... O13
Newport Ln. ... Pg.14 ..... P17
North Ave. .... Pg.15 ... O15,16
Oak Ave. ...... Pg.15 .... O,P15
Oak Glen Dr. .. Pg.15 ..... P15
Oakbrook Ct. .. Pg.14 ..... P15
Oakmont Dr. ... Pg.14 ..... P15
Oakwood Ln. ... Pg.15 ..... P16
Oceanside Ct. . Pg.15 ..... P17
Old Lake St. .. Pg.14 ..... N15
Olive Pkwy. ... Pg.14 ..... N15
Oliver St. .... Pg.15 ..... O15
Oneida Ave. ... Pg.15 ..... O16
Park Place Dr. Pg.15 ..... O14
Patricia Pkwy. Pg.15 ..... O15
Pebble Beach Ln. Pg.15 ... P15
Phillip Dr. ... Pg.14 ..... N13
Pinoak Dr. .... Pg.14 ..... P15
Plymouth Ct. .. Pg.15 ..... P16
Preserve Tr. .. Pg.15 ..... M15
Prospect Ave. . Pg.15 ..... O15
Queens Pkwy. .. Pg.15 ..... O15
Red Bud Ct. ... Pg.14 ..... N15
Red Oak Dr. ... Pg.14 ..... N15
Redwood Ln. ... Pg.15 ..... P16
Rees Rd. ...... Pg.14 ..... N14
Rick's Ln. .... Pg.15 ..... O12
Ridge Ln. ..... Pg.14 ..... M13
Rita Ct. ...... Pg.15 ..... O16
River Ash Ct. . Pg.14 ..... N14
Robert Ct. .... Pg.15 ..... O15
Rose Ln. ...... Pg.14 ..... N13
Roslara Ct. ... Pg.15 ..... P17
San Diego Terr. Pg.15 .... P17

Sandpiper Ct. . Pg.15 ..... P17
Sausalito Ct. . Pg.15 ..... P17
Shady Ln. ..... Pg.15 ..... P16
Shorewood Ct. . Pg.15 ..... P17
Spitzer Rd. ... Pg.14 ..... P13
Sterling Ct. .. Pg.15 ..... P17
Sumac Ct. ..... Pg.14 ..... P14
Surf Ct. ...... Pg.15 ..... P17
Surrey Rd. .... Pg.15 ..... P15
Tanoak .... Pg.14 ..... P15
Tatge Ave. .... Pg.15 ..... O16
Taylor Ave. ... Pg.15 ..... O16
Tennyson Rd. .. Pg.15 ..... P16
Terrace Dr. ... Pg.14 ..... P15
Thomas Ct. .... Pg.15 ..... D10
Thorntree Ct. . Pg.15 ..... P17
Timberidge Dr. Pg.15 ..... P16
Valley St. .... Pg.14 ..... O15
Voyager Terr. . Pg.15 ..... P17
Waltham Ln. ... Pg.14 ..... P14
Wayne Ct. ..... Pg.15 ..... O16
Western Ave. .. Pg.15 ..... P15
White Oak Ln. . Pg.14 ..... N14
Williamsburg Dr. Pg.15 ... O15
Wilmington Ct. Pg.15 ..... P17
Wilmington Dr. Pg.15 ..... P17
1st Ave. ...... Pg.14 ..... O12
2nd Ave. ...... Pg.14 ..... O12
3rd Ave. ...... Pg.14 ..... O12
4th Ave. ...... Pg.14 ..... O12
5th Ave. ...... Pg.14 ..... O12
6th Ave. ...... Pg.14 ..... O12
6th Ct. .... Pg.14 ..... O12
7th Ave. ...... Pg.14 ..... O12
8th Ave. ...... Pg.14 ..... O12
9th Ave. ...... Pg.14 ..... O12
10th Ave. ..... Pg.14 ..... O12
11th Ave. ..... Pg.14 ..... O12
12th Ave. ..... Pg.14 ..... O12

CEMETERIES

Bartlett Cem. . Pg.14 ..... O15

FOREST PRESERVES

Wayne Grove Forest Pres. ....
.... Pg.14 ...... P15

GOLF COURSES

Bartlett Hills Golf & C.C. ......
.... Pg.14 ...... O15

PARKS

Bartlett Park . Pg.15 ..... O16
Leiseberg Park . Pg.15 .... P16
Newport Park . Pg.15 ..... P17
Oak Grove Park Pg.14 ..... P15
Ruzika Field . Pg.15 ..... N16
Schoppe Park . Pg.15 ..... N16

SCHOOLS

Bartlett Sch. . Pg.15 ..... O16
East View Middle Sch. ....
.... Pg.15 ...... N16
Independence Sch. ....
.... Pg.15 ...... O16
Maryville Herrick House ....
.... Pg.14 ...... O14

MISCELLANEOUS

Fire Department Pg.15 ..... O16
Hanover Township Office ....
.... Pg.14 ...... O14
Public Library Pg.15 ..... O16
Railroad Station Pg.15 .... O16
Village Hall & Police ....
.... Pg.15 ...... O16

BOWES

Page 11...N2

CAMPTON TOWNSHIP

Page 11

STREETS

Brittany Ct. P3
Cloverfield Cir. P2
Cloverfield Dr. P2
Fielding Ct. P3
Johnsway P2
Northern Dancer Ln. P2
Phar Lap Dr. P2
Whirlway Dr. P2

CARPENTERSVILLE

Pages 2,3

STREETS

Aberdeen Dr. C11
Adams Ct. D12
Adobe Cir. B10
Alameda Dr. C11
Algonquin Rd. C9
Allison E8
Alma Ct. D10
Amarillo Ct. D10
Amarillo Dr. D10
Anchor Dr. E8
Apache Ave. B11
Arlington Dr. E10
Arrow St. C11
Ash St. C11
Aspen Ln. C11
Audrey Ln. D9
Austin Ave. C11
Ball Ave. D11

Berkley St. C10,11
Berkshire Cir. E12
Berkshire Ct. E11
Besinger Dr. D10
Birch St. C11
Birchwood Rd. C10
Bismark Ave. E9
Blackhawk Ave. B11
Bolz Rd. B10
Bramer Ave. E9
Briarwood Ave. D10
Bristol Cir. E12
Bristol Ct. E11
Brook St. D9
Bunker Ln. D11
Butte Ln. C10
Caddy Ave. D11
California Ave. D9
Cambridge Dr. C11
Cardinal Ln. D11
Carpenter Ave. D9
Carpenter Blvd. E9
Center Dr. E10
Charles St. D9
Cherokee Ct. B11
Cherokee Rd. D11
Chippewa Ct. B11
Cleveland Ave. E9
Cordova Rd. B11
Cottage Ave. D8
Country School Rd. B7
Courtney Dr. C11
Cove E8
Cove Port E8
Crab Tree Ct. D10
Crescent Dr. A8
D St. E8
Day Ln. D9
Del Rio Rd. B10
Delaware St. B,C11
Denver Dr. C11
E St. E8
Eaton B10
Edwards Ave. E9
Elizabeth Mews B10
Esmeralda Ln. B10
Esmeralda Dr. B10
Evergreen Ln. C11
Fairway Ln. D11
Fairway Rd. C11
Fiddler's Green E8
First St. C11
Four Winds Way D8
Fox River Dr. D8
Garfield Ct. D11
Garfield Dr. D11
Gentle Breeze Terr. D8
Goethe St. D9
Golf View Ln. D11
Granada Rd. B10
Grant Dr. D12
Green Ln. D11
Greenwood Ave. D10
Greenwood Ct. D10
Grove St. E9
Hampton Dr. D11
Harbor Dr. E8
Harding St. E11
Harrison St. E11
Hartke Ln. E9
Hawthorne Ct. D10
Hawthorne Ln. D10
Hazzard Rd. C11
Hickory Ave. D7
Hickory Ct. C11
Hickory Dr. C11
Hillside St. E9
Hook Rd. D11
Hoover Dr. D11
Hopi Ln. B11
Houston Dr. C10
Huntley Rd. E8
Illinois St. E8
Indian Ln. B11,C10
Inlet Cove E8
Inlet Dr. E8
Ivarene Ct. D10
Jackson Ave. D11
Jefferson Ave. D11
Keele Dr. C11
Kings Rd. C10
Kingston Dr. D12
Lake Marian Rd. C9
Lake Shore Dr. C10
Lexington Dr. D10
Lincoln Ave. D,E8
Lincoln Ct. D11
Livingston Ave. D9
Lord St. E9
Lowell Dr. D11
Madera Ct. B11
Madison Ct. D12
Main St. E8
Maple Ave. D9,10
Maple Ln. D10
Marlboro Dr. C11
Maude D10
Mayfair St. C11
Meadowdale Dr. D10
Meadowlark Ln. D11
Miller Rd. C7
Mocasin Ln. B11
Monroe Ave. D11
Monticello Cir. D10

Mora Rd. B10
Morningside Cir. E12
Morningside Ln. E12
Navajo Dr. D11
North Lake Pkwy. E10
Oak Ave. D9
Oak Ridge Rd. D10
Ollie Ct. D10
Orleans St. B11
Osage Ct. B11
Oxford Dr. C10
Papoose Rd. B11
Park Ave. D9
Pawnee Rd. B11
Pecos Cir. B11
Pine St. C11
Plainview Rd. E10
Plymouth Cir. D12
Polk Ave. D11
Pueblo Rd. B10
Queens Ct. C10
Ranch Rd. D7
Ravine Rd. D10,E11
Redwood St. C11
Ridge Rd. B7
Ring Rd. E8
River Bluff Dr. D8
Riverview Dr. D8
Robin Rd. D,E11
Rosewood Ct. D10
Rosewood Dr. D10
Sacramento Ct. C10
Sacramento Dr. C11
Salem Ln. C10
San Juan Rd. B10
Santa Fe Ave. B11
Saratoga Dr. E10
Sedgewick St. D9
Seminole Ln. B11
Siesta Ct. B10
Siesta Rd. B10
Singapore Ln. D8
Sioux Ave. B11,12
South Wind Dr. C8
Sparrow Ct. D11
Sparrow Rd. D11
Spinnaker Cove E8
Spring Ct. D8
Spring Hill Rd. E8
Spring Point Dr. D8
Spruce Dr. E8
Spyglass E8
Stuart B10
Sycamore Ave. C11
Tacoma St. C11
Tamarac Dr. D11
Tay River Dr. D8
Tee Ln. D11
Tee Rd. D11
Tepee Ave. B11
Thrush Rd. D11
Tomahawk Ct. B11
Topeka Dr. C10
Toro Ct. B10
Tudor Ct. B10
Tulsa Ave. C11
Tulsa Ct. C10
Tyler Dr. D11
Valentine St. D9
Valley Ln. D11
Varia St. D9
Vista Ln. E11
Waco Ln. C10
Wakefield Dr. C11
Walnut St. C11
Washington St. E9
Waverly Ct. D10
West Hill Rd. B7
West Wind Dr. C8
Western Ave. D8
William St. D9
Wilmette Ave. D10
Wilson Ave. D11
Windsor Dr. D12
Wisconsin St. D10
Woodcrest Ln. B8
Woodland Ct. D10
Wren Rd. C,D11
York Dr. C11
1st St. E9

FOREST PRESERVES

Raceway Woods C8

GOLF COURSES

Bonnie Dundee Golf & C.C. ... D11

PARKS

Amarillo Park B10
Carpenter Park D9
Dolphins Cove E11
K. J. Andres Park C10
Pheasant Park C10

SCHOOLS

Carpentersville Middle Sch. .. E10
Carpentersville Sch. C10
Dundee Crown H.S. E9
Golf View Sch. D11
Lakewood Jr. H.S. D11
Meadowdale Sch. C11
Parkview Sch. E9
Perry Sch. B10
St. Monica School C11
Sunny Hill Sch. B11

CARPENTERSVILLE

Woodlane Sch.	B11

SHOPPING CENTERS

Meadowdale Shopping Center	D10
Spring Hill Mall	E8

MISCELLANEOUS

Bible Bapt. Christian Acad.	B11
DeLacey Early Child Ed. Center	C10
Dundee Twp. Park Dist.	E11
Dundee Twp. Sr. Citizens Ctr.	D11
Fire Department	C10
Fire Station	E9
Village Hall & Police	D10

DUNDEE TOWNSHIP

Pages 1-3,6-8

STREETS

Albert Dr.	Pg.8	G11
Algonquin Rd.	Pg.3	C9
Alice Dr.	Pg.2	A8
Alpine Dr.	Pg.2	A8
Baker	Pg.8	G11
Bass Ct.	Pg.8	G9
Big Timber Rd.	Pg.7	H5
Binnie Rd.	Pg.2	D5
Birchwood Rd.	Pg.3	C10
Bolz Rd.	Pg.3	B10
Boncosky Rd.	Pg.7	G7
Boyer Rd.	Pg.2	B5
Burning Oak Dr.	Pg.2	D6
Burr Oak Ln.	Pg.2	B7
Castle Ave.	Pg.8	G11
Castlewood Dr.	Pg.3	C10
Chapelle	Pg.8	G8
Chateau Dr.	Pg.7	H8
Chateau Dr., W.	Pg.7	H8
Country Line Rd.	Pg.3	A9
Country School Rd.	Pg.2	B7
Crescent Dr.	Pg.2	A8
Deerpath Ln.	Pg.3	C10
Duchesne Dr.	Pg.7	G8
Duncan Ave.	Pg.8	G10
Dundee Ave. (Rte.25)	Pg.8	G10
Elliot Dr.	Pg.8	G10
Elm Ave.	Pg.2	D7
Field Ct.	Pg.2	B7
Forest Ln.	Pg.2	B8
Fountain Valley Dr	Pg.8	G10
Fox River Dr.	Pg.8	G9
Fries Ave.	Pg.8	G10
Frontenac Dr.	Pg.7	G8
Hecker Dr.	Pg.8	G11
Hickory Ave.	Pg.2	D7
Hickory Hill Dr.	Pg.7	G6
Hickory Hollow Dr	Pg.7	G6
Highland Dr.	Pg.2	E5
Hillside Dr.	Pg.8	G10
Hilly Ln.	Pg.2	E5
Hollowside Dr.	Pg.2	B7
Hopi Ln.	Pg.3	B11
Howard Ave.	Pg.8	F10
Howard Dr.	Pg.8	F10
Indian Ln.	Pg.3	C9
Karen Dr.	Pg.2	B8
Kasser Ct.	Pg.3	C10
King Richard	Pg.3	C10
Kings Rd.	Pg.3	C10
Knollwood Ave.	Pg.8	F10
Lac Du Beatrice Dr.	Pg.8	G8
Lake Marian Rd.	Pg.3	C9
Lake Shore Dr.	Pg.3	C10
Lathrop Ln.	Pg.2	B8
Linden Dr.	Pg.8	G10
Lundaw Tr.	Pg.3	A9
Lundstrom Ln.	Pg.2	A8
Manhatas Tr.	Pg.3	A9
Manito Tr.	Pg.3	A9
Maple Ave.	Pg.8	F10
Mapletree Ln.	Pg.3	C10
Mary Dr.	Pg.2	D6
Mason Rd.	Pg.6	G5
Massey Dr.	Pg.8	G11
Meadow Ln. W.	Pg.8	G10
Melody Ln.	Pg.3	C10
Memory Ln.	Pg.3	C10
Menoma Tr.	Pg.3	A9
Merriweather Ln.	Pg.2	E6
Miller Rd.	Pg.2	C7,8
Minaki Tr.	Pg.3	A8,9
Natoma Tr.	Pg.3	A8
Niccon Tr.	Pg.3	A9
Nokomis Tr.	Pg.3	A9
Northwest Tollway (I-90)	Pg.7	G5
Oak Ave.	Pg.2	D7
Oak Hill Dr.	Pg.7	G6
Oak Hollow Dr.	Pg.7	G6
Oaks Ln.	Pg.2	E6
Ogaw Tr.	Pg.3	A9
Old Barn Rd.	Pg.2	C7
Old Farm Ln.	Pg.3	C10
Onaway Tr.	Pg.3	A8
Park Ave.	Pg.8	G10
Park Dr.	Pg.8	G9
Parsons Rd.	Pg.2	C7
Petite Ln.	Pg.7	H8
Pheasant Tr.	Pg.3	C10
Pokagon Tr.	Pg.3	A9
Randall Rd.	Pg.2	C,E5
Richardson Dr.	Pg.8	G9
Richardson Rd.	Pg.8	G10
Richmond Rd.	Pg.2	E6
Ridge Rd.	Pg.2	B7
River View Dr.	Pg.8	G10
Riverwood Rd.	Pg.3	A9
Robert	Pg.8	F10
Robin Ln.	Pg.3	C10
Sawyer Rd.	Pg.2	C7
Shady Ln.	Pg.2	D6
Sky Line Dr.	Pg.3	C10
Sleepy Hollow Rd.	Pg.2,7	B6,E,G7
Springbluff Dr.	Pg.2	B7
Sturgis Ct.	Pg.2	D7
Sumter Dr.	Pg.2	E6
Sunset Dr.	Pg.3	C10
Sunset Park Dr.	Pg.8	G10
Vadican Tr.	Pg.3	A9
Valley View Rd.	Pg.2	C7
Wakigan Tr.	Pg.3	A9
Walnut Ln.	Pg.7	G6
West Hill Rd.	Pg.2	B7
Winding Tr.	Pg.2	D6
Wood Heaven Ln.	Pg.2	B7
Woodcrest Ln.	Pg.3	B8

CEMETERIES

Dundee Twp. Cem. E.	Pg.3	F11
Dundee Twp. Cem. W.	Pg.3	E9
River Valley Memorial Gardens	Pg.3	E8

FOREST PRESERVES

Max McGraw Wildlife Foundation	Pg.8	G10

GOLF COURSES

Randall Oaks C.C.	Pg.2	D5

PARKS

Buffalo Park Ski Slope	Pg.3	A8
Randall Oaks Park	Pg.2	D5

SCHOOLS

Chicago Jr. Sch.	Pg.8	F8

EAST DUNDEE

Pages 3,4,8

STREETS

Aberdeen Dr.	Pg.3	E11
Adams St.	Pg.3	E9
Aldis Dr.	Pg.3	E10
Ashland Rd.	Pg.3	E10
Balmoral Ct.	Pg.3	E11
Balmoral Dr.	Pg.3	E11
Bannock Rd.	Pg.3	E11
Barrington Ave.	Pg.3	E10
Braeburn Rd.	Pg.3	E10
Bramer Ave.	Pg.3	E9
Bruce Ct.	Pg.3	E11
Center Dr.	Pg.3	E10
Council Hill Rd.	Pg.3	D10
Crab Tree Ct.	Pg.3	D10
Crestwood Dr.	Pg.3	E10
Dawn Ct.	Pg.3	E11
Deerpath Rd.	Pg.3	E11
Dunbar Ct.	Pg.3	E11
Dundee Rd.	Pg.3	E10
Edwards Ave.	Pg.8	F10
Elgin Ave.	Pg.8	F10
Greenwood Ave.	Pg.3	E10
Guth St.	Pg.3	E10
Hawthorne Ln.	Pg.3	D10
Higgins Rd.	Pg.3	F10
Hill Ave.	Pg.3	E10
Hill St.	Pg.3	E10
Hilton Ave.	Pg.3	F10
Howard Ave.	Pg.3	F10
Howard Ct.	Pg.3	F10
Jackson St.	Pg.3	E9
Johnson St.	Pg.3	F10
Kenilworth Ave.	Pg.3	D10
Kimberly Rd.	Pg.3	E10
King Ave.	Pg.3	F10
King William St.	Pg.3	E9
Lake Shore Dr.	Pg.3	E10
Lincoln Ave.	Pg.3	E9
Linder Ave.	Pg.3	E10
Madison St.	Pg.3	F7
Maiden St.	Pg.3	F10
Main St.	Pg.3	F9
Maxwellton Rd.	Pg.3	E10
Michigan Ave.	Pg.3	E9
North Lake Pkwy.	Pg.3	E10
North St.	Pg.3	E9
Oak Dr.	Pg.3	F10
Park St.	Pg.3	E10,11
Penny Ave.	Pg.3	E10
Penny Rd.	Pg.4	E12
Railroad St.	Pg.3	E9
Ravine Rd.	Pg.3	D,E10
Reese Ave.	Pg.3	F10
River St.	Pg.3	E,F10
Rock Road Ct.	Pg.8	F12
Rock Road Dr.	Pg.8	F12
Roslyn Rd.	Pg.3	E10
Scott St.	Pg.3	E11
South St.	Pg.3	E10
Spring Crest Rd.	Pg.3	E10
Summit Ave.	Pg.3	E10
Valley Ln.	Pg.3	E10
Van Buren St.	Pg.3	E10
Washington St.	Pg.3	E9
Water St.	Pg.3	E9
Wendt Ave.	Pg.3	E10
Wenholz Ave.	Pg.3	E9
Williams	Pg.3	F10
Wilmette Ave.	Pg.3	E10
1st St.	Pg.3	E9
2nd St.	Pg.3	E9
3rd St.	Pg.3	E9
4th St.	Pg.3	E10

CEMETERIES

Dundee Twp. Cem. E.	Pg.3	F11

PARKS

Lions Park	Pg.3	E10

SCHOOLS

Immanuel Lutheran Sch.	Pg.3	F10
Summit Sch.	Pg.8	F11

MISCELLANEOUS

Dundee Twp. Library	Pg.3	E10
Fire Department	Pg.3	E9
Frontier Museum	Pg.8	G11
Santa's Village	Pg.8	F11
Village Hall & Police	Pg.3	E9

ELGIN

Pages 6-9,12-14

STREETS

Abbeywood Ct.	Pg.8	I11
Abbot Dr.	Pg.7	J7
Academy Pl.	Pg.8	K9
Adams St.	Pg.12	L8
Addison St.	Pg.8	K10
Adelaide Ave.	Pg.8	I8
Adeline Ave.	Pg.7	J7
Adler Ct.	Pg.9	K12
Airlite St.	Pg.12	L6
Airlite St. N.	Pg.7	K6
Airport Rd.	Pg.8	H9
Alcott Ct.	Pg.9	K12
Alder Ln.	Pg.9	K12
Aldine St.	Pg.7	J,K7
Alfred Ave.	Pg.7	K,L7
Alft Dr.	Pg.12	O5
Algona Ave.	Pg.8	J9,10
Algonquin Rd.	Pg.8	I11
Alice	Pg.7	J5
Alice Ct.	Pg.7	J5
Alice Pl.	Pg.7	J5
Alison Dr.	Pg.12	L7
Allen Dr.	Pg.13	K11
Aller St.	Pg.13	L11
Amanda Cir.	Pg.12	M7
Amber Ln.	Pg.12	O5
American Way	Pg.8	J11
Anderson Ave.	Pg.13	L11
Andrews Cir.	Pg.12	M7
Ann Ct.	Pg.7	J6
Ann St.	Pg.8	K9
Annandale Dr.	Pg.12	N6
Apple Hill Ct.	Pg.8	I11
Apple Ln.	Pg.13	L11
Arlington Ave.	Pg.13	L10
Aronomink Cir.	Pg.12	M6
Arrowhead Dr.	Pg.8	J10
Arthur Dr.	Pg.8	J11
Ash Dr.	Pg.8	K11
Ashland Ave.	Pg.13	M9
Ashwood Ct.	Pg.12	O6
Ashwood Dr.	Pg.12	O6
Aspen Ct.	Pg.9	K12
Augusta Ave.	Pg.8	J9
Autumn Ct.	Pg.7	J5
Ball St.	Pg.8	K8
Baltustrol Dr.	Pg.12	M,N6
Banks Dr.	Pg.7	I6
Barberry Ct.	Pg.8	J11
Barn Owl Ln.	Pg.12	M5
Barn Swallow Way	Pg.7	J6
Barrett St.	Pg.13	L10
Bartlett Pl.	Pg.13	L9
Baxter Ct.	Pg.12	N6
Bayside Rd.	Pg.8	I9
Bayview Rd.	Pg.8	I9
Bedford Ct.	Pg.8	J11
Bel Aire Ct.	Pg.12	N6
Bel-Aire Rd.	Pg.8	I9
Belle Ave.	Pg.8	I8
Bellevue Ave.	Pg.8	J10
Belmont St.	Pg.12	L6
Belvidere Line Dr.	Pg.7	J6
Bennet Dr.	Pg.8	J11
Bennington Ct.	Pg.12	L6
Bent Ridge Ln.	Pg.8	J11
Bent St.	Pg.13	L10
Bent Tree Ct.	Pg.8	J11
Berkley St.	Pg.12	L6
Berkshire Ct.	Pg.13	L11
Billings St.	Pg.13	L9
Birch Dr.	Pg.8	K11
Birchdale Dr.	Pg.12	L7
Bird St.	Pg.7	J8
Blackhawk Dr.	Pg.8	I,J11
Blue Ridge Ct.	Pg.7	J6
Bluff City Blvd.	Pg.13	M10
Bode Rd.	Pg.8	K11,12
Booth Ct.	Pg.13	L10
Borden Cir.	Pg.9	K12
Borden Dr.	Pg.9	K12
Bowen Ct.	Pg.13	L10
Bowes Rd.	Pg.12	N5
Boxwood Dr.	Pg.12	K5
Bradford Ct.	Pg.8	I11
Braeburn	Pg.7	I7
Braeburn Dr.	Pg.7	I7
Brant Dr.	Pg.8	H11
Brechin Tr.	Pg.7	I5
Brener Dr.	Pg.9	J12
Brentwood Tr.	Pg.8	K12
Briarwood Ct.	Pg.9	K12
Brittany Tr.	Pg.9	K12
Brook St.	Pg.8	J9
Brookline Ct.	Pg.12	N6
Brookwood Ct.	Pg.7	I7
Bruce Dr.	Pg.8	K11
Buckeye St.	Pg.7	J8
Burning Tree Ln.	Pg.12	M7
Burns Dr.	Pg.14	L12
Butler Bay Dr.	Pg.8	I11
Butternut Ln.	Pg.7	J6
Byron Ln.	Pg.7	I7
Campus Dr.	Pg.13	L12
Candida Rd.	Pg.8	I9
Candlewood Rd.	Pg.8	I9
Canyon Ln.	Pg.7	J6
Capital	Pg.12	O5
Carl Ave.	Pg.8	K11
Carlton Dr.	Pg.8	J11
Carlyle Ct.	Pg.9	K12
Carmella Ln.	Pg.13	L11
Carnoustie Ct.	Pg.12	M6
Carol Ave.	Pg.7	J6
Carr St.	Pg.12	L7
Carriage Way	Pg.8	I11
Case Dr.	Pg.8	K11
Casper Ct.	Pg.12	M7
Castle Pines Cir.	Pg.12	M6
Catherine Ln.	Pg.8	I9
Cedar Ave.	Pg.8	J10
Cedar Point Ct.	Pg.12	O6
Center St.	Pg.8	J,K9
Century Oaks Dr.	Pg.7	I7
Ceresa Dr.	Pg.13	L11
Channing St.	Pg.13	L10
Chaparral Cir.	Pg.14	L12
Chaparral Ct.	Pg.14	L12
Chapel St.	Pg.8	K9
Charlotte Ct.	Pg.7	J5
Chaucer Ct.	Pg.13	L11
Cherry St.	Pg.8	J9
Chester Ave.	Pg.8	J10
Chestnut St.	Pg.14	L12
Chicago St. E.	Pg.8	K9
Chicago St. W.	Pg.12	K8
Chippewa Dr.	Pg.8	J11
Church Dr.	Pg.12	M5
Church Rd.	Pg.8	H8
Cimarron Ct.	Pg.14	L12
Circle Dr.	Pg.14	L12
Clair St.	Pg.7	K8
Clark St.	Pg.7	J8
Clayton Ave.	Pg.7	J7
Clayton Dr.	Pg.8	J11
Clearwater Way	Pg.7	J6
Cleveland Ave.	Pg.13	L10
Clifford Ave.	Pg.8	J8
Clifton Ave.	Pg.7	J-L7
Clover Hill Ln.	Pg.8	I11
Cobblers Crossing	Pg.8	I11
Cobblestone Ct.	Pg.8	J11
Cold Spring Rd.	Pg.8	J11
Coleman Dr.	Pg.13	L11
College Green Dr.	Pg.12	M5,6
College St.	Pg.8	K9
Colonial Dr.	Pg.6	K5
Colorado	Pg.7	J6
Columbia Ave.	Pg.8	J10
Commerce Dr.	Pg.7	H8
Commonwealth Ave.	Pg.8	K,L8
Como Ct.	Pg.12	N6
Congdon Ave.	Pg.8	I9
Congdon Rd.	Pg.8	I11
Congress St.	Pg.13	L10
Cookane Ave.	Pg.13	L,M10
Cooper Ave.	Pg.8	J9
Corley Ct.	Pg.9	K12
Corley Dr.	Pg.9	K12
Cornell Ave.	Pg.12	M6
Corporate Dr.	Pg.8	H9
Cottonwood Dr.	Pg.12	O6
Country Club Rd.	Pg.8	I9
Country Knoll Ct.	Pg.7	K6
Country Knoll Ln.	Pg.7	K6
Country Water Ct.	Pg.12	O6
Countryside Ct.	Pg.7	I7
Countryside Dr.	Pg.7	I7
Coventry Ct.	Pg.7	K6
Covered Bridge Ct.	Pg.12	M5
Covered Bridge Dr.	Pg.12	M5
Creekside Cir.	Pg.7	H6
Creekside Ct.	Pg.7	H6
Creighton Ave.	Pg.12	K8
Crescent St.	Pg.13	L8
Crestview Ct.	Pg.7	I7
Crestview Dr.	Pg.7	I7
Crispin Dr.	Pg.12	N7
Crosby St.	Pg.13	L9
Crystal Ave.	Pg.8	K8
Crystal Creek Ln.	Pg.12	M5
Cumberland Tr.	Pg.7	J6
Cypress Sq.	Pg.7	J7
Dakota Dr.	Pg.8	I11
Dale Dr.	Pg.9	J12
Dandridge Ct.	Pg.8	J12
Daniels Ave.	Pg.8	J9
Dartmouth Dr.	Pg.12	L6
David Dr.	Pg.13	L11
Davis Rd.	Pg.7	H7,8
Deborah Ave.	Pg.7	J6
Deer Woods Dr.	Pg.8	I11
Deerpath Dr.	Pg.12	O5
Demert Ct.	Pg.12	N6
Demmond St.	Pg.7	J8
Dempster St.	Pg.13	L10
Dennis Ct.	Pg.12	L7
Derby Ct.	Pg.12	K5
Devonshire Cir.	Pg.7	H6
Devonshire Ct.	Pg.7	H6
Dexter Ave.	Pg.8	K9
Diane Ave.	Pg.7	J7
Dickens Tr.	Pg.9	K12
Dickie Ave.	Pg.13	M11
Division St.	Pg.8	K9
Dixon Ave.	Pg.13	M10
Dogwood Ct.	Pg.9	K12
Douglas Ave.	Pg.8	J,K9
Du Bois Ave.	Pg.12	L7
Du Page St.	Pg.8	K9
Dumbarton Oak	Pg.7	J7
Duncan Ave.	Pg.8	I10
Dundee Ave.	Pg.8	K9,I10
Dwight St.	Pg.13	M10
Eagle Rd.	Pg.7	J7
Eastview St.	Pg.8	K10
Easy St.	Pg.7	K7
Edgebrook Tr.	Pg.13	L10
Edison Ave.	Pg.12	L7
Elgin Ave.	Pg.13	M10
Eliot Tr.	Pg.9	K12
Elizabeth St.	Pg.13	M10
Elm Grove Ct.	Pg.12	L7
Elm St.	Pg.13	L9
Elma Ave.	Pg.8	I10
Elma Dr.	Pg.8	I11
Elma St.	Pg.8	I10
Elmar Ct.	Pg.7	J5
Ely St.	Pg.13	L9
Emil Ct.	Pg.12	N6
Enterprise St.	Pg.8	J10
Eric Cir.	Pg.14	M13
Erie St.	Pg.12	L6,7
Esmerelda Pl.	Pg.8	J9
Essex Ln.	Pg.7	H5
Executive Dr.	Pg.7	H8
Fairfax Ct.	Pg.8	J11
Fairwood Ct.	Pg.7	I7
Fairwood Dr.	Pg.7	I7
Federation Pl.	Pg.8	I9
Fieldstone Ct.	Pg.8	I11
First St.	Pg.8	I10
Flag Pole Cir.	Pg.12	L5
Flag Pole Ct.	Pg.12	L5
Fleetwood Dr.	Pg.12	M6,7
Fletcher Dr.	Pg.7	I5
Flora Dr.	Pg.12	N7
Florence Cir.	Pg.12	N6
Florimond Dr.	Pg.8	I8
Foothill Rd.	Pg.12	K5
Ford Ave.	Pg.8	I10
Ford Ct.	Pg.8	I10
Forest Ave.	Pg.8	K10
Forest Dr.	Pg.7	I7
Fork Cir. N.	Pg.7	J6
Fox Ln.	Pg.12	O6
Foxmoor Ln.	Pg.12	O6
Franklin Blvd.	Pg.8	K9
Frazier Ave.	Pg.8	J8
Fremont St.	Pg.8	J10
Frontage Rd.	Pg.8	H9
Fulton St.	Pg.8	K9
Gale Ln.	Pg.10	L5
Gale St.	Pg.12	L5,6
Galt Blvd.	Pg.14	M13
Garden Crescent Dr.	Pg.7	J7
Gasket Dr.	Pg.13	O11
Genesee Ave.	Pg.8	J8
Geneva St.	Pg.8	K9
George St.	Pg.13	L10
Gertrude St.	Pg.13	L8
Getty St.	Pg.13	M11
Getzelman Ave.	Pg.7	J7
Gifford Pl.	Pg.13	L9
Gifford Rd.	Pg.13	O11
Gifford St.	Pg.8	K9
Ginger Ln.	Pg.9	K12
Glen Ivy Dr.	Pg.13	L12
Glendowers Terr.	Pg.7	I5
Gleneagle Cir.	Pg.12	N6
Glenmore Ct.	Pg.7	J5
Glenmore Ln.	Pg.6	J4
Glenwood Ave.	Pg.8	I10
Goethe St.	Pg.7	J8
Golf (Evanston- Elgin) Rd.	Pg.8	J11
Gordon Ct.	Pg.12	L7
Governors Ln.	Pg.7	K6
Grace St.	Pg.13	L10
Grand Ave.	Pg.8	J10
Grand Blvd.	Pg.8	K10
Grandstand Ct.	Pg.12	K6
Green Acres Ln.	Pg.7	I7
Green Ridge Cir.	Pg.8	J11
Griswold St.	Pg.13	L9
Grove Ave.	Pg.13	L9
Hamilton Ave.	Pg.7	K8
Hamlin Ct.	Pg.12	K7
Hammond Ave.	Pg.13	M10
Hampshire Ln.	Pg.8	J11
Harbor Town Dr.	Pg.12	N6
Harding St.	Pg.13	L9
Harlan Ave.	Pg.7	J7
Harrison St.	Pg.13	L10
Hartwell Ave.	Pg.8	I10
Harvey St.	Pg.8	K8
Hawkins St.	Pg.8	K8
Hawthorne St.	Pg.12	L6
Hayloft Ln.	Pg.12	M5
Hazel Dr.	Pg.8	I9
Healy St.	Pg.13	L10
Hecker Ct.	Pg.8	K12
Hecker Dr.	Pg.8	K11
Heine Ave.	Pg.7	K7
Hemlock Ln.	Pg.13	L12
Hendee St.	Pg.13	L9
Henry St.	Pg.13	L10
Hiawatha Ct.	Pg.8	J10
Hiawatha Dr.	Pg.8	I,J10
Hickory Pl.	Pg.8	K10
High Point Dr.	Pg.8	H9
High St.	Pg.7	K8
Highbury Ct.	Pg.8	K11
Highbury Dr.	Pg.8	K11
Highland Ave.	Pg.7	J5,K6,8
Hill Ave.	Pg.8	J,K10
Hillcrest Rd.	Pg.7	I8
Hillside Rd.	Pg.8	I9
Hilton Pl.	Pg.8	K10
Hinsdell Pl.	Pg.8	K10
Hobart Dr.	Pg.12	N6
Hobble Bush Ln.	Pg.8	J11
Holly St.	Pg.13	L8
Holmes Rd.	Pg.7	H6,7
Homer St.	Pg.13	L9
Hope Ct.	Pg.13	L9
Horace Dr.	Pg.14	L12
Houston Ave.	Pg.13	M11
Howard Ave.	Pg.7	K5
Hoxie Ave.	Pg.7	K7
Hubbard Ave.	Pg.7	K8
Hudson Bluff Dr.	Pg.7	J6
Hunter Dr.	Pg.8	K11
Huntwyck Ct.	Pg.8	J11
Huron Dr.	Pg.8	I11
Illinois Ave.	Pg.13	L,M10
Illinois Pkwy.	Pg.7	J7
Indian Dr.	Pg.8	I11
Indian Wells Cir.	Pg.12	M6
Inglewood Ln.	Pg.8	J11
Inverness Ct.	Pg.12	N6
Inverness Dr.	Pg.14	L12
Ironwood Ct.	Pg.8	I11
Ironwood Dr.	Pg.8	I11
Iroquois Dr.	Pg.8	I10
Irving Park Rd.	Pg.13	K11,M12
Irwin Dr.	Pg.12	N7
Jackson Dr.	Pg.7	J5
Jackson St.	Pg.8	K8
Jacob Ln.	Pg.12	N6
Jamestown Ln.	Pg.7	K6
Jan Marie Ln.	Pg.13	L11
Jane Dr.	Pg.12	K,L7
Jansen Farm Ct.	Pg.7	I6
Jansen Farm Dr.	Pg.7	I6
Jay St.	Pg.13	M10
Jefferson Ave.	Pg.8	J9,10
Jeffery Ct.	Pg.7	I6
Jerusha Ave.	Pg.8	I8
Jewett St.	Pg.13	L8
Joan Ct.	Pg.13	M10
John Dr.	Pg.13	L11
Johnston Rd.	Pg.12	L5
Jordan Cir.	Pg.7	J6
Jordan Ct.	Pg.7	I6
Jordan Ln.	Pg.7	J6
Joseph Ct.	Pg.12	K6
Joslyn Dr.	Pg.8	K11
Joyce Ln.	Pg.13	L11
Judy Ct.	Pg.7	J8
Julian Ave.	Pg.8	J9
Julie Ann Ln.	Pg.13	L11
Junior Pl.	Pg.7	J7
Kane Ave.	Pg.7	J7
Kaskaskia Ave.	Pg.7	J7
Kate St.	Pg.12	L8
Kathleen Dr.	Pg.12	L7
Keep Ave.	Pg.8	I10
Kenneth Cir.	Pg.8	J11
Kensington Loop	Pg.7	J7
Kent Ln.	Pg.9	K12
Kettlehook Dr.	Pg.12	K5
Kevin Ave.	Pg.7	J6
Kimball St.	Pg.8	K9
Kimberly Ave.	Pg.7	J7
Kinds Riverview Ct.	Pg.8	K9
Kingman Ct.	Pg.7	I6
Kirk Ave.	Pg.13	L,M11
Knollwood Dr.	Pg.7	K5
Knotty Pine Dr.	Pg.12	O5
Kramer Ave.	Pg.13	L10
LaCosta Ct.	Pg.12	N6
LaSalle Ave.	Pg.7	J7
Lake St.(US-20)	Pg.13	M8
Lake Ter. Rd.	Pg.8	I9
Lake View Rd.	Pg.8	I9
Lakewood Rd.	Pg.8	I9
Lamont Ct.	Pg.12	L5
Langtry Ct.	Pg.13	L11
Larkin Ave.	Pg.12	L6
Laurel St.	Pg.13	L10
Laurel Valley Ct.	Pg.12	N6
Lavoie Ave.	Pg.13	L,M10
Lawrence Ave.	Pg.7	K7,8
Leawood Ct.	Pg.8	K12
Leawood Dr.	Pg.8	K11,12
Leith Ct.	Pg.12	L5
Lenoxshire Dr.	Pg.7	I7
Leonard St.	Pg.8	K8
Lessenden Pl.	Pg.13	L9
Levine Ct.	Pg.13	L10
Liberty St., N.	Pg.8	K,M10
Liberty St., S.	Pg.13	M10
Lilac Ln.	Pg.12	L7
Lillian St.	Pg.12	L7
Lillie St.	Pg.8	K10
Lin-Lor Ct.	Pg.7	K6
Lin-Lor Ln.	Pg.7	K6,7
Lincoln Ave.	Pg.8	J9
Lincoln Ct.	Pg.8	J9
Lincolnshire Ct.	Pg.13	L11
Linda Ln.	Pg.7	J5
Lindberg Ct.	Pg.13	L8
Linden Ave.	Pg.8	K10
Lisa	Pg.13	L11
Little Fall Dr.	Pg.8	I11
Little Pen Rd.	Pg.8	I9

ELGIN

Lockman Cir. ... Pg.7 ... I6
Locust St. ... Pg.13 ... L8
Logan Ave. ... Pg.8 ... J9
Longford Cir. ... Pg.9 ... K12
Longford Dr. ... Pg.9 ... K12
Longwood ... Pg.7 ... I8
Lord St. ... Pg.13 ... L9
Lovell St. ... Pg.8 ... J9
Lovers Ln. ... Pg.7 ... H6
Lucille Ave. ... Pg.13 ... L11
Lucille Ct. ... Pg.13 ... L11
Luda St. ... Pg.7 ... I10
Ludlow Ave. ... Pg.8 ... I10
Ludlow Pl. ... Pg.13 ... M11
Lyle Ave. ... Pg.1 ... I,P6
Lyle St. ... Pg.12 ... K,L6
Lynch St. ... Pg.7 ... K8
Mabel St. ... Pg.7 ... J8
Mackey Ln. ... Pg.13 ... L11
Madlock St. N. ... Pg.7 ... H6
Madlock Ct. S. ... Pg.7 ... H6
Main Ln. ... Pg.12 ... L7
Mallard Dr. ... Pg.7 ... I7
Mallery Ave. ... Pg.12 ... L8
Mann Pl. ... Pg.8 ... J11
Manor Ct. ... Pg.7 ... J7
Maple Ln. ... Pg.7 ... K6
Maple Pl. ... Pg.13 ... L9
Maple St. ... Pg.12 ... L6
Marbilynn Dr. ... Pg.8 ... J11
Margaret Pl. ... Pg.13 ... L10
Marguerite St. ... Pg.12 ... L9
Mariner Dr. ... Pg.13 ... L12
Mark Ave. ... Pg.7 ... I6
Mark Dr. ... Pg.13 ... L8
Market St. ... Pg.7 ... K6
Marlene Dr. ... Pg.7 ... I6
Maroon Dr. ... Pg.13 ... L11,12
Martha Dr. ... Pg.7 ... L7
Mary Pl. ... Pg.8 ... J11
Maryhill Ln. ... Pg.12 ... L5
Matthew Ct. ... Pg.12 ... L7
Maureen Dr. ... Pg.7 ... L7
May St. ... Pg.13 ... L9
McBride St. ... Pg.8 ... J9
McClure Ave. ... Pg.7 ... J,K8
McKinstry Dr. ... Pg.7 ... K6
McLean Blvd. ... Pg.7 ... J,K,M7
Meadow Ln. ... Pg.7 ... I7
Medici Ct. ... Pg.12 ... N6
Medinah Cir. ... Pg.12 ... N6
Melbrook Rd. ... Pg.8 ... I9
Melrose Ave. ... Pg.12 ... K,L7
Melrose St. ... Pg.12 ... L7
Meyer St. ... Pg.7 ... J8
Michigan St. ... Pg.12 ... L9
Milan Ct. ... Pg.12 ... N6
Mildred Ave. ... Pg.7 ... J7
Mill St. ... Pg.7 ... K8
Millcreek Ct. ... Pg.7 ... J6
Miller Dr. ... Pg.7 ... L7
Mohawk Dr. ... Pg.8 ... I,J11
Monday Dr. ... Pg.7 ... H,I6
Monroe St. ... Pg.7 ... K8
Monterey Ct. ... Pg.12 ... N6
Montrose Park ... Pg.7 ... J7
Moreti Dr. ... Pg.12 ... O6
Morgan St. ... Pg.7 ... I8
Morningside Ct. ... Pg.7 ... I8
Morningside Pl. ... Pg.7 ... I8
Morningside Pt. ... Pg.7 ... I8
Morton Ave. ... Pg.8 ... I10
Moseley St. ... Pg.7 ... K10
Mountain St. ... Pg.8 ... J9
Muirfield Cir. ... Pg.12 ... M6
Mulberry Ct. ... Pg.12 ... L7
Mulberry Ln. ... Pg.12 ... L7
Mulford Dr. ... Pg.8 ... K11
Murcer Dr. ... Pg.7 ... J8
Murray Ave. ... Pg.7 ... K8
Nancy Ln. ... Pg.13 ... L11
Natchez Trace ... Pg.7 ... J7
National St. ... Pg.13 ... L9
Newberry Ct. ... Pg.6 ... K4
Niagra Ct. ... Pg.7 ... J6
Nicola Dr. ... Pg.7 ... J12
Norman Nelson ... Pg.12 ... K12
North Shore Rd. ... Pg.8 ... I9
North St. ... Pg.7 ... K9
Northwest Tollway ... Pg.8 ... I11
Notre Dame Ln. ... Pg.7 ... J7
Oak St. ... Pg.12 ... L8
Oakdale Ave. ... Pg.8 ... I10
Oakdale Pr. ... Pg.7 ... I8
Oakhill Rd. ... Pg.8 ... I10
Oakland Ave. ... Pg.8 ... J11
Oakwood Blvd. ... Pg.8 ... K11
Olive St. ... Pg.13 ... L11
Old Forge Rd. ... Pg.7 ... K6
Olympia Ct. ... Pg.9 ... K12
Orange St. ... Pg.12 ... L8
Orchard St. ... Pg.8 ... I10
Otter Creek Ln. ... Pg.12 ... M5
Owasco Ave. ... Pg.7 ... J6
Oxford St. ... Pg.13 ... L9
Page Ave. ... Pg.8 ... J10
Palazzo Ct. ... Pg.12 ... N6
Palazzo Dr. ... Pg.12 ... N6
Palmer Circle ... Pg.12 ... M7
Pamela Dr. ... Pg.12 ... L7
Pappas Ct. ... Pg.7 ... J8
Pappas Dr. ... Pg.7 ... J8
Park Ln. ... Pg.8 ... I9
Park St. ... Pg.8 ... J9
Parkside St. ... Pg.7 ... J8
Parkview Dr. ... Pg.7 ... I7
Parkway Ave. ... Pg.8 ... I10
Parkwood Rd. ... Pg.7 ... I9
Patricia Ave. ... Pg.8 ... J11

Patton Dr. ... Pg.8 ... J10
Pauline Ct. ... Pg.12 ... L6
Pauline Dr. ... Pg.12 ... L6
Peach Tree Ct. ... Pg.13 ... L11
Peach Tree Ln. ... Pg.13 ... L11
Pebble Beach Cir. ... Pg.12 ... M6,7
Pegwood Dr. ... Pg.8 ... K11
Pennsylvania Ave. ... Pg.7 ... K8
Percy St. ... Pg.13 ... L10
Perry St. ... Pg.13 ... L9
Philips Way ... Pg.14 ... L12
Pindar St. ... Pg.7 ... K8
Pine St. ... Pg.7 ... J8
Pinehurst Dr. ... Pg.12 ... N6
Pioneer Park Pl. ... Pg.7 ... J7
Player Circle ... Pg.12 ... M6
Pleasant Dr. ... Pg.7 ... I7
Pleasant View ... Pg.7 ... I8
Plum Ct. ... Pg.8 ... J9
Plum St. ... Pg.8 ... J9
Plymouth Ln. N. ... Pg.7 ... J7
Polly Ct. ... Pg.8 ... J10
Poplar Creek Dr. ... Pg.13 ... L11
Poplar Ct. ... Pg.8 ... J10
Portage Way ... Pg.7 ... J6
Porter St. ... Pg.7 ... J,K10
Portsmouth Ct. ... Pg.6 ... K4
Potomac ... Pg.7 ... J6
Powder River ... Pg.7 ... J6
Prairie St. ... Pg.13 ... K9
Presbury Dr. ... Pg.13 ... L11
Preston Ave. ... Pg.7 ... J,K10
Price Dr. ... Pg.8 ... K11
Princeton Ave. ... Pg.7 ... K6
Princeton Ct. ... Pg.12 ... M6
Prospect Blvd. ... Pg.8 ... J9
Purdue Ln. ... Pg.12 ... L5
Purify Dr. ... Pg.13 ... M10
Quail Ln. ... Pg.7 ... I8
Quakerhill Ct. ... Pg.8 ... J11
Quincy Ct. ... Pg.9 ... K12
Radclyffe Ct. ... Pg.13 ... L11
Raleigh Ct. ... Pg.12 ... L5
Ramona Ave. ... Pg.13 ... L11
Ranch Dr. ... Pg.8 ... I9
Randall Rd. ... Pg.7 ... I,K,L5
Randall Ridge ... Pg.6 ... K4
Randall Ridge Ct. ... Pg.6 ... K4
Raymond St. ... Pg.13 ... M10
Red Barn Ln. ... Pg.12 ... M5
Red Oak Ct. ... Pg.8 ... K12
Red Tail Ridge ... Pg.7 ... J6
Regent St. ... Pg.13 ... L10
Renner Dr. ... Pg.12 ... M6
Rickert Ct. ... Pg.13 ... L10
Ridge Ln. ... Pg.14 ... M13
Ridgeway Dr. ... Pg.7 ... I7
Riley St. ... Pg.13 ... L9
Ripplebrook Ln. ... Pg.8 ... J11
River Bluff Rd. ... Pg.8 ... I9
River Rd. W. ... Pg.8 ... I9
River Ridge Rd. ... Pg.8 ... H9
Riverside Dr. ... Pg.8 ... K9
Robert Dr. ... Pg.12 ... L7
Robey St. ... Pg.13 ... M9
Robin Ridge ... Pg.7 ... J6
Robinhood Dr. ... Pg.7 ... I7
Rodney St. ... Pg.13 ... L10
Rosewood Ct. ... Pg.13 ... K12
Royal Blvd. ... Pg.7 ... J6
Royal Ct. ... Pg.7 ... J7
Rugby Pl. ... Pg.7 ... K10
Russell Rd. ... Pg.13 ... M10
Ruth Dr. ... Pg.7 ... J6
Ryerson Ave. ... Pg.13 ... L9
Sacramento Ct. ... Pg.7 ... J6
Sadler Ave. ... Pg.13 ... L11
Salem Rd. ... Pg.12 ... K6
Sandra ... Pg.13 ... L11
Savanna Rd. ... Pg.7 ... J6
Sawgr Ct. ... Pg.12 ... M7
Saxon Ct. ... Pg.13 ... L11
Schiller St. ... Pg.7 ... J8
Scott Dr. ... Pg.7 ... J7
Sebring Dr. ... Pg.8 ... K11
Second St. ... Pg.12 ... L,M6
Seminole St. ... Pg.8 ... I11
Seneca St. ... Pg.8 ... J9
Sexauer Ave. ... Pg.7 ... K7
Shady Oak Dr. ... Pg.8 ... J11
Shady Oaks Ct. ... Pg.8 ... J11
Shagbark Dr. ... Pg.7 ... J5
Sharon Ct. ... Pg.13 ... L11
Sharon Dr. ... Pg.13 ... L11
Sharon St. ... Pg.8 ... I9
Sheffield Ct. ... Pg.7 ... I7
Sheffield Dr. ... Pg.7 ... H7
Sheldon Dr. ... Pg.14 ... L12
Shenandoah ... Pg.7 ... J5
Shepard Dr. ... Pg.12 ... M7
Sheridan St. ... Pg.12 ... L8
Sherman Ave. ... Pg.13 ... L8
Sherwood Ave. ... Pg.8 ... I10
Shiloh Ct. ... Pg.8 ... K11
Shiloh Ln. ... Pg.8 ... K11
Shoe Factory Rd. ... Pg.8 ... I11
Shuler St. ... Pg.12 ... L7
Silver Ct. ... Pg.7 ... K8
Silver St. ... Pg.7 ... K8
Sioux Dr. ... Pg.8 ... I11
Slade Ave. ... Pg.8 ... J10
Sleepy Hollow Rd. ... Pg.7 ... I7
Sommerfield Ct. ... Pg.13 ... L11
Souster Ave. ... Pg.13 ... M9
South Plymouth Ln. ... Pg.7 ...
South St. ... Pg.12 ... L6,7
Spartan Ct. ... Pg.12 ... M6
Spaulding Rd. ... Pg.13 ... N12

Spring Cove Dr. ... Pg.7 ... K6
Spring Creek Ct. ... Pg.7 ... J5
Spring Creek Dr. ... Pg.8 ... I11
Spring St. ... Pg.8 ... J,K9
Springhill Ct. ... Pg.8 ... J11
Spruce Ln. ... Pg.13 ... K12
Spyglass Hill Ct. ... Pg.12 ... M7
St. Andrews Ct. ... Pg.12 ... N6
St. Charles Ave. ... Pg.13 ... L10
St. John St. ... Pg.8 ... J9
Standish St. ... Pg.13 ... L8
Stanford Ct. ... Pg.12 ... L6
State St. N. ... Pg.8 ... J,K8
State St. S. ... Pg.13 ... L8
Steel St. ... Pg.8 ... J8
Stella St. ... Pg.13 ... L10
Stella St. ... Pg.13 ... L10
Stephan Ave. ... Pg.7 ... J8
Sterling Ct. ... Pg.7 ... K5
Stewart Ave. ... Pg.8 ... I10
Stillwater Rd. ... Pg.8 ... J11
Stockbridge Ct. ... Pg.8 ... J11
Stockbridge Pl. ... Pg.8 ... J11
Stone Ridge Dr. ... Pg.8 ... I11
Stonehaven Dr. ... Pg.7 ... J5
Stonehurst Dr. ... Pg.8 ... K12
Stuart Warner ... Pg.8 ... K12
Sumac Ln. ... Pg.13 ... K12
Summit St. ... Pg.8 ... J9
Sunrise Ct. ... Pg.12 ... L8
Sunshine Dr. ... Pg.12 ... L7
Surrey Dr. ... Pg.12 ... K7
Susanne Ln. ... Pg.13 ... L11
Swan Ln. ... Pg.7 ... J6
Sweetbriar Ln. ... Pg.12 ... O6
Tanney Ridge ... Pg.8 ... I11
Tara Dr. ... Pg.7 ... J6
Teal Ave. ... Pg.7 ... I9
Ted Ln. ... Pg.13 ... L11
Teft Ave. ... Pg.8 ... K11
Terrace Ave. ... Pg.8 ... K11
Terrace Ct. ... Pg.8 ... K10
Thomas Moore Dr. ... Pg.7 ... K6
Thoreau St. ... Pg.14 ... L12
Thorndale Ct. ... Pg.14 ... L12
Thorndale Dr. ... Pg.14 ... L12
Thunderbird ... Pg.12 ... N7
Timber Dr. ... Pg.7 ... J7
Tina Tr. ... Pg.7 ... J5
Tinker Ave. ... Pg.8 ... I9
Tivoli Pl. ... Pg.7 ... J7
Toastmaster Dr. ... Pg.8 ... I11
Todd Farm Ct. ... Pg.7 ... I7
Todd Farm Dr. ... Pg.7 ... I7
Toftress Tr. ... Pg.7 ... J6
Toll Gate Rd. ... Pg.7 ... H8
Tori ... Pg.13 ... L11
Torrey Pines Dr. ... Pg.12 ... M7
Tower Ct. ... Pg.12 ... L6
Trevi Ct. ... Pg.12 ... N6
Trevi Dr. ... Pg.12 ... N6
Triggs Ave. ... Pg.7 ... K7
Trinity Terr. ... Pg.7 ... J6
Trout Ave. ... Pg.8 ... I10
Trout Park Blvd. ... Pg.8 ... I10
Tuileries ... Pg.12 ... J7
Turnberry Ct. ... Pg.12 ... N6
Tuscany Ct. ... Pg.12 ... N6
Understock Rd. ... Pg.12 ... O5
Union Ct. ... Pg.12 ... L8
Union St. ... Pg.12 ... L8
Valley Creek Dr. ... Pg.7 ... J5
Van Nostrand Pl. ... Pg.13 ... L10
Van St. ... Pg.12 ... L7,8
Vandalia St. ... Pg.12 ... L8
Varsity Dr. ... Pg.13 ... L11
Vatican Ct. ... Pg.12 ... N6
Venice Ct. ... Pg.12 ... N6
Vernon Dr. ... Pg.7 ... K6
Victor Ave. ... Pg.8 ... I11
Villa St. ... Pg.13 ... L11
Vincent Pl. ... Pg.7 ... K8
Vine St. ... Pg.13 ... L11
Virgil Ave. ... Pg.13 ... L11
Virginia Ct. ... Pg.7 ... I6
Virivan Tr. ... Pg.12 ... L11
Wabash Ave. ... Pg.12 ... L8
Walden Dr. ... Pg.14 ... M12
Walker Pl. ... Pg.8 ... K10
Walnut Ave. ... Pg.12 ... L8
Walnut Creek Ct. ... Pg.12 ... O5
Walter Ct. ... Pg.12 ... L8
Warwick Pl. ... Pg.8 ... K10
Washburn St. ... Pg.12 ... L8
Watch St. ... Pg.7 ... K9
Waterfall Ln. ... Pg.12 ... M5
Watres Ave. ... Pg.13 ... L10
Watson Ave. ... Pg.12 ... L8
Wauchope Dr. ... Pg.8 ... J9
Waverly Ct. N. ... Pg.8 ... K11
Waverly Ct. S. ... Pg.8 ... K11
Waverly Dr. ... Pg.8 ... J,K11
Weatherstone Ln. ... Pg.7 ... I7
Weld Rd. ... Pg.7 ... K4
Weldowood Dr. ... Pg.12 ... L5
Wellington Ave. ... Pg.13 ... L10
Wellington St. ... Pg.13 ... L9
Westfield Ct. ... Pg.7 ... H5
Westhaven Ln. ... Pg.8 ...
Weston Ave. ... Pg.7 ... J-L7
Wheelock St. ... Pg.13 ... L9
Wilber St. ... Pg.13 ... L9
Wilcox Ave. ... Pg.12 ... L8
Wilder St. ... Pg.8 ... K8
Willard Ave. ... Pg.13 ... L10
Williams Dr. ... Pg.7 ... K6

Williamsburg Dr. ... Pg.12 ... L5
Willis St. ... Pg.13 ... M9
Willow Dr. ... Pg.8 ... I11
Willow Lake Rd. ... Pg.8 ... I9
Willow Ln. Dr. ... Pg.8 ... I9
Wilson St. ... Pg.7 ... K8
Win Haven ... Pg.7 ... K5
Windsor Ct. ... Pg.9 ... K12
Wing Park Blvd. ... Pg.7 ... K7
Wing St. ... Pg.7 ... J7
Wolf Ave. ... Pg.7 ... K7
Woodbridge Dr. ... Pg.7 ... J6
Woodbridge Dr. ... Pg.12 ... M5
Woodhill Ct. ... Pg.8 ... J11
Woodland Ave. ... Pg.8 ... K8
Woodridge Ct. ... Pg.7 ... J6
Woodward St. ... Pg.13 ... L9
Worth Ave. ... Pg.7 ... K,L8
Wright Ave. ... Pg.13 ... M11
Wynnfield Ct. ... Pg.13 ... L11
Yale Ln. ... Pg.12 ... L6
Yarwood St. ... Pg.13 ... L10
Yellowstone Dr. ... Pg.7 ... J6
Yew Ct. ... Pg.13 ... L11

CEMETERIES

Bluff City Cem. ... Pg.13 ... M11
Lake St. Memorial Park ... Pg.14 ... M13
Mt. Hope Cem. ... Pg.13 ... L11
River Valley Mem. Gardens ... Pg.8 ... H9

FOREST PRESERVES

Tyler Creek Forest Pres. ... Pg.7 ... I8

GOLF COURSES

Elgin Country Club ... Pg.12 ... L5
Municipal Golf Course ... Pg.12 ... M6
Rolling Knolls Golf Club ... Pg.9 ... K12
Spartan Meadows Golf Courses ... Pg.12 ... M6
Wing Golf Course ... Pg.7 ... J8

PARKS

Burnridge Woods Park ... Pg.7 ... I6
Campus Park ... Pg.14 ... L12
Central Park ... Pg.13 ... L9
Clifford-Owasco Park ... Pg.7 ... J8
College Park ... Pg.12 ... M5
Eagle Heights Park ... Pg.7 ... K9
Gifford Park ... Pg.7 ... K8
Hawthorne Hills Park ... Pg.7 ... J5
Illinois Park ... Pg.7 ... J7
Lords Park ... Pg.8 ... K10
Marie Grolich Park ... Pg.7 ... L9
Maroon Field Park ... Pg.13 ... M10
Observatory Park ... Pg.7 ... L10
Powder River Park ... Pg.7 ... J6
St. Francis Park ... Pg.8 ... J8
Trout Park ... Pg.8 ... I10
Wing Ave. Park ... Pg.13 ... L11

SCHOOLS

Abbott Jr. H.S. ... Pg.12 ... L8
Central Jr. H.S. ... Pg.8 ... K9
Century Oaks Sch. ... Pg.7 ... I7
Channing Mem.Sch. ... Pg.8 ... K10
Chicago Junior Sch. ... Pg.8 ... H10
Coleman Sch. ... Pg.8 ... I10
Columbia Sch. ... Pg.8 ... J10
Elgin Academy ... Pg.8 ... K9
Elgin Community College ... Pg.12 ... M6
Elgin H.S. ... Pg.13 ... L11
Ellis Jr. H.S. ... Pg.13 ... L10
Franklin Sch. ... Pg.8 ... K9
Garfield Sch. ... Pg.12 ... L7
Gifford Sch. ... Pg.12 ... L7
Grant Sch. ... Pg.8 ... K8
Highland Sch. ... Pg.7 ... K7
Hillcrest Sch. ... Pg.7 ... K6
Huff Sch. ... Pg.12 ... L10
Judson College ... Pg.8 ... I9
Kimball Jr. H.S. ... Pg.7 ... K7
Larkin H.S. ... Pg.12 ... L7
Larsen Jr. H.S. ... Pg.8 ... J10
Lincoln Sch. ... Pg.13 ... L8
Lowrie Sch. ... Pg.13 ... L8
McKinley Sch. ... Pg.13 ... L9
Sheridan Sch. ... Pg.13 ... L8
St. Edwards Sr. H.S. ... Pg.12 ... L7
St. Laurence Cath. Sch. ... Pg.13 ... L9
St. Mary's Cath. Sch. ... Pg.7 ...
St. Thomas Moore Cath. Sch. ... Pg.7 ... K7
Washington Sch. ... Pg.12 ... L9
Wayne Sch. ... Pg.8 ...

SHOPPING CENTERS

Fox Valley Plaza ... Pg.13 ... O9
Wing Park Manor S.C. ... Pg.7 ... J7

MISCELLANEOUS

Civic Center ... Pg.8 ... K9
Elgin Little League Fld. ... Pg.7 ...
Elgin Public Museum ... Pg.8 ... K10
Elgin Sports Complex ... Pg.12 ... M8
Elgin State Hospital ... Pg.13 ... M8
Fire Station ... Pg.12 ... M7
First Chicago Corp. ... Pg.7 ... G5
Fox Valley Professional Park ... Pg.8 ... J11
Grand Victoria Riverboat Casino ... Pg.13 ... L9
Hemmens Auditorium ... Pg.8 ... K9
Illinois Sec. of State Office ... Pg.13 ... M9
Illinois State Police ... Pg.13 ... M9
Memorial Stadium ... Pg.13 ... L11
Norman Hoffman Ath. Fld. ... Pg.8 ... J10
Panasonic Corp. ... Pg.7 ... H6
Sherman Hospital ... Pg.8 ... J9
St. Joseph's Hospital ... Pg.7 ... K6
Sybaquay Council Girl Scout Camp ... Pg.7 ... K5
Westfield Business Park ... Pg.7 ... H5

ELGIN TOWNSHIP

Pages 6-8,11-13

STREETS

Acorn Ln. ... Pg.11 ... O4
Airlite St. ... Pg.12 ... L6
Almora Terr. ... Pg.7 ... K5
Amberwood Dr. ... Pg.6 ... I3
Arrowmaker Pass ... Pg.11 ... N3
Barry Rd. ... Pg.13 ... O9
Beckman Tr. ... Pg.11 ... M3
Belmont St. ... Pg.12 ... L6
Bittersweet Ln. ... Pg.11 ... O3
Bowes Rd. ... Pg.11 ... N4
Brindlewood Ln. ... Pg.6 ... I3
Brookside Dr. ... Pg.7 ... K5
Burgess Dr. ... Pg.11 ... L4
Center Dr. ... Pg.13 ... P9
Charlotte Ct. ... Pg.7 ... J5
Crispin Dr. ... Pg.12 ... N7
Cross Creek Ct. ... Pg.11 ... N3
David Dr. ... Pg.12 ... N6
Eagle Rd. ... Pg.7 ... J5
Elmar Ct. ... Pg.6 ... J4
Erie St. ... Pg.12 ... L6
Flagpole Ct. ... Pg.12 ... L5
Fletcher Dr. ... Pg.7 ... I5
Flora Dr. ... Pg.12 ... N7
Frontage Rd. ... Pg.7 ... K5,L6
Gale St. ... Pg.12 ... L5
Gingerwood Ln. ... Pg.11 ... O3
Gordon Ln. ... Pg.13 ... O9
Hawthorne St. ... Pg.12 ... L6
Heatherfield Dr. ... Pg.11 ... P3
Heatherfield East Dr. ... Pg.11 ... P4
Highland Ave. ... Pg.7 ... J5
Hidden Hills Tr. ... Pg.6 ... K4
Hill Ct. ... Pg.12 ... P8
Hilltop Rd. ... Pg.7 ... J,K5
Hobart Dr. ... Pg.12 ... L6
Hopi Tr. ... Pg.11 ... M3
Hopps Rd. ... Pg.11 ... O3-6
Howard Ave. ... Pg.7 ... K7
Hoxie Ave. ... Pg.12 ... L5
Illinois 25 ... Pg.13 ... N10
Irwin Dr. ... Pg.7 ... I5
Jackson Dr. ... Pg.6 ... J4
Jaguar Ct. ... Pg.11 ... L4
Johnstown Rd. ... Pg.12 ... L5
Kenyon Rd. ... Pg.13 ... N9
Kingsman Ct. ... Pg.12 ... P8
Koshare Ct. ... Pg.11 ... M3
Koshare Tr. ... Pg.11 ... N3
Kristen Dr. ... Pg.11 ... O3
Leith ... Pg.12 ... L5
Leland Ct. N. ... Pg.11 ... M3
Leland Ct. S. ... Pg.11 ... M3
Linda Ln. ... Pg.7 ... J5
Lisa Ln. ... Pg.11 ... O4
Manchester Ln. ... Pg.11 ... M4
Maple St. ... Pg.12 ... L5
McDonald Rd. ... Pg.12 ... P5
McLean Blvd. ... Pg.12 ... P7
Middle St. ... Pg.7 ... O10
Nestler Rd. W. ... Pg.6 ... K3
Newport Ct. ... Pg.11 ... L4
Nokomis Ln. ... Pg.11 ... N3
Nolan Rd. ... Pg.11 ... N,O3
Northwest Tollway ... Pg.7 ... H7
Oatwind Rd. ... Pg.6 ... K4
Old Barn Rd. ... Pg.6 ... K4
Olwin Ave. ... Pg.11 ... L5
Orchard Ln. ... Pg.6 ... K4
Oxford Ln. ... Pg.2 ... F7
Park Path ... Pg.11 ... N3
Pasec Pl. ... Pg.11 ... O3
Peppertree Ct. ... Pg.11 ... P4
Peppertree Ln. ... Pg.11 ... P4
Poulitt Dr. ... Pg.6 ... I3
Raleigh Ct. ... Pg.11 ... O4
Randall Rd. ... Pg.7,12 ... I,M5
Richard Dr. ... Pg.11 ... O3
Ridgewood Ln. ... Pg.6 ... I3
River Valley Dr. ... Pg.12 ... P8
Running Deer Tr. ... Pg.11 ... O4
Sandhurst Ln. ... Pg.12 ... O6
Savanna Lakes Ct. ... Pg.11 ... N3
Savanna Lakes Dr. ... Pg.11 ... N3
Shady Ln. ... Pg.13 ... O4
South St. ... Pg.12 ... L5
Stevens Ln. ... Pg.11 ... P3
Sunvale Ct. ... Pg.11 ... P3
Sunvale Dr. ... Pg.11 ... P3
Taos Pl. ... Pg.11 ... N3
Thunder Gap ... Pg.11 ... N3
Tina Tr. ... Pg.7 ... J5
Tipi Ln. ... Pg.11 ... N3
Trails End ... Pg.11 ... M3
Umdenstock Rd. ... Pg.12 ... P6
Water Rd. ... Pg.11 ... M3,N4
Wedgewood Dr. ... Pg.6 ... I3
Weld Rd. ... Pg.12 ... L6
Weldwood Dr. ... Pg.12 ... L5
West River Rd. ... Pg.12 ... I9
West View St. ... Pg.7 ... P3
Wildwood Dr. ... Pg.11 ... O4
Williamsborg Dr. ... Pg.12 ... L5
Willow Ln. ... Pg.11 ... O4
Win Haven Dr. ... Pg.7 ... K5
Windmere Dr. ... Pg.11 ... K5
Woodcliff Dr. ... Pg.12 ... M3
York Ln. ... Pg.3 ... F7

GILBERTS

Pages 1,6

STREETS

Andra Ct. ... Pg.6 ... F4
Center Dr. ... Pg.1 ... E3
Deborah St. ... Pg.6 ... F4
East Dr. ... Pg.1 ... E3
Freeman Rd. ... Pg.1 ... E3
Galligan Rd. ... Pg.1 ... D3
Hennessy Ct. ... Pg.6 ... F4
Higgins Rd. ... Pg.1 ... E3
Industrial Dr. ... Pg.1 ... E3
Jackson St. ... Pg.1 ... E3
Jean St. ... Pg.6 ... F4
Joan Ct. ... Pg.6 ... F4
Kathleen St. ... Pg.6 ... F4
Kerry Ct. ... Pg.6 ... F4
Kildare St. ... Pg.6 ... G4
Kilkenny Ct. ... Pg.6 ... G4
Mason Rd. ... Pg.6 ... G4
Matteson St. ... Pg.1 ... E3
McCormack Rd. ... Pg.1 ... F2
Northwest Toll Rd. ... Pg.1 ... E1
Pamela Ln. ... Pg.6 ... F4
Park St. ... Pg.1 ... E2
Pauline Ct. ... Pg.1 ... E2
Pierce St. ... Pg.1 ... E2
Railroad St. ... Pg.1 ... E3
Red Hawk Path ... Pg.6 ... F4
Running Deer Ln. ... Pg.6 ... F4
Shining Moon Path ... Pg.6 ... F4
Sleeping Bear Tr. ... Pg.6 ... F4
Sola Dr. ... Pg.6 ... F4
Suzanne St. ... Pg.6 ... F4
Tipperary St. ... Pg.6 ... G4
Tollview Ct. ... Pg.1 ... E2
Tollview Terr. ... Pg.1 ... D2
Tower Hill Rd. ... Pg.1 ... F3
Towne Ct. ... Pg.6 ... F4
Towne St. ... Pg.6 ... F4
Turner St. ... Pg.1 ... E3
Tyler Creek Ct. ... Pg.6 ... F4
Tyrrell Rd. ... Pg.1 ... E3
Union St. ... Pg.1 ... E3
Welch St. ... Pg.6 ... G4
West End Dr. ... Pg.1 ... E3
White Feather Ln. ... Pg.6 ... F4
Willey St. ... Pg.1 ... E3
Windmill Pl. ... Pg.1 ... E2

HANOVER PARK

Page 15

STREETS

Alden Ln. ... Pg.1 ... O17
Apple Tree St. ... Pg.1 ... O18
Arbor Vitae Dr. ... Pg.1 ... N17
Argyle Rd. ... Pg.1 ... P18
Aspen Ln. ... Pg.1 ... O18
Astor Ave. ... Pg.1 ... N17
Barrington Rd. ... Pg.1 ... P18
Bartels Rd. ... Pg.1 ... M17
Bearflag Dr. ... Pg.1 ... P18
Birch Ave. ... Pg.1 ...
Brairwood Ave. ... Pg.1 ... N18
Breezewood Ln. ... Pg.1 ... O17
Briar St. ... Pg.1 ... N18
Briarwood St. ... Pg.1 ... N18
Burr Oak St. ... Pg.1 ... O17
Camelia Dr. ... Pg.1 ... O17
Catalpa St. ... Pg.1 ... O18
Catawba Ln. ... Pg.1 ... M18
Cedar Ave. ... Pg.1 ... O17
Center Ave. ... Pg.1 ... O17
Cherry Ave. ... Pg.1 ... O17
Chestnut St. ... Pg.1 ... O17

HANOVER PARK

Church St. O18
Clarendon Ct. P18
Curtis Ln. R17
Cynthia Ln. M18
Cypress Ave. O18
Dahlia Dr. N17
Danby Ct. P18
Danforth Ct. P18
Deerfield Ct. P18
Deerpath Ln. O18
Devon Ave. P16
Downey Ct. P18
East Ave. N18
Elm Ave. O17
Elm St. P18
Evergreen Ave. O18
Flower Ct. N18
Forest Glen O18
Fremont Dr. P18
Fremont Jct. P18
Gladiola Ave. N18
Gold Cir. P18
Greenwood St. N18
Hanover St. O18
Hemlock St. O17
Hickory St. O17
Hillcrest Ave. O18
Hollywood Ave. N18
Huntington Cir. N19
Indian Hill Ave. O18
Iris Ave. N18
Irving Park Rd. N18
Jasmine Dr. N18
Jonquil Terr. N18
Juniper St. O18
Larch Ln. O17
Laurel Ave. N18
Lemon St. R18
Leslie Ln. O17
Liberty St. (Ontarioville) . P18
Linden Ave. N18
Magnolia St. O18
Maple Ave. O17,18
Maplewood Ave. O18
Marigold Ln. N18
Mark Thomas Ln. N17
Merwin Ave. P18
Mulberry St. O18
Narcissus Ave. N17
Nugget Cir. P18
Oak Ave. O17
Oak St. (Ontarioville) . . . P18
Oakwood Ave. O18
Olivia Ln. M18
Ontarioville Rd. (Ontarioville) . P18
Osage Ln. N17
Park Ave. O18
Peach Tree St. O18
Pebblebrook M18
Pine Tree St. O18
Plum Tree Ln. O17
Poplar Ave. O18
Ramblewood Dr. M18
Redwood Ave. N18
Rosewood N18
Sacramento P18
Scott Ln. O17
Sequoia Ln. N18
Short St. N17
Spruce Ave. O18
Strathmore Ln. M18
Sutter Dr. P18
Sycamore Ave. O18
Tanglewood Ave. N18
Thornwood St. N18
Tower Dr. N18
Valley View Rd. O18
Walnut Ave. O17,18
Walnut Ct. O17
West Ave. O18
Willow Ave. O18

PARKS

Community Park O18
Geo. Georgen Mem. Baseball Fields
. . . . N18
Ranger Park N18

SCHOOLS

Laurel Hill Sch. N18
Ontarioville Sch. O17

SHOPPING CENTERS

Hanover Square N18
Tradewinds Shopping Center . N18

MISCELLANEOUS

Hanover Twp. Mental Health Center
. . . . N17
Railroad Sta. P18
Village Hall & Police O17

HANOVER TOWNSHIP

Pages 8-10,13-14

STREETS

Barrington Rd. . . Pg.10 . . . K18
Bartlett Rd. . . . . Pg.10 . . . I16
Bartlett Rd. W. . . Pg.13 . . . O11
Berner Dr. . . . . . Pg.9 . . . . J12
Beverly Rd. . . . . Pg.9 . . . . I13
Bode Rd. . . . . . . Pg.9 . . . . K16,18
Castlewood Dr. . Pg.14 . . . M14
Chestnut St. . . . Pg.14 . . . L12
Chevoit Ln. . . . . Pg.14 . . . O14
Circle Dr. . . . . . Pg.14 . . . L12
Dale Dr. . . . . . . Pg.9 . . . . J12
Dennis Ln. . . . . Pg.14 . . . M14
Douglas Ln. . . . Pg.14 . . . M14
Forrest View Dr. Pg.14 . . . K13
Friar Tuck Dr. . . Pg.14 . . . M13

Gifford Rd. . . . . Pg.13 . . . O11
Glen Echo St. . . Pg.14 . . . L12
Golf Rd. (Evanston- Elgin) . .
. . . . Pg.9,10 . . J11-15
Golfview Dr. . . . Pg.14 . . . N13
Greenwood Rd. Pg.14 . . . L13
Gromer Rd. . . . . Pg.14 . . . M13
Higgins Rd. . . . . Pg.10 . . . I18
Hill Top Rd. . . . . Pg.9 . . . . K13
Ill. Rt.19 (Irving Pk. Rd.) . .
. . . . Pg.14 . . . L13
Ill. Rt.20 (Lake St.) . . . . . .
. . . . Pg.14 . . . N14
Ill. Rt.58 (Golf Rd.) . . . . . .
. . . . Pg.10 . . . J16
Ill. Rt.59 (Sutton Rd.) . . . . .
. . . . Pg.9 . . . . I15
Irving Park Rd. (Rt.19) . . . .
. . . . Pg.14 . . . M14
King Arthur . . . . Pg.14 . . . L13
Lady Marion Dr. Pg.14 . . . L13
Lake St. . . . . . . Pg.14 . . . M14
Little John Dr. . . Pg.14 . . . L13
Magnolia Ln. . . . Pg.9 . . . . J15
Mudhank Rd. . . . Pg.10 . . . I17
Naperville Rd. . . Pg.14 . . . O13
Northwest Tollway (I-90) . . .
. . . . Pg.9,10 . . I12-16
Nottingham Ln. . Pg.14 . . . L13
Old Higgins Rd. . Pg.10 . . . I18
Old Lake St. . . . Pg.14 . . . N15
Robin Hood Dr. . Pg.14 . . . M13
Rohrssen Rd. . . Pg.9 . . . . J13
Rolling Knolls Ave. . . . . . .
. . . . Pg.9 . . . . K13
Schaumburg Rd. Pg.14,15 . L14-19
Sherwood Rd. . . Pg.14 . . . L13
Shoe Factory Rd. Pg.9 . . . I14,16
Tameling Ct. . . . Pg.14 . . . O13
Will Scarlet Ln. . Pg.14 . . . M13
Wolsfeld Rd. . . . Pg.9 . . . . K13

CEMETERIES

Lake St. Memorial Park . . . .
. . . . Pg.14 . . . M13

FOREST PRESERVES

Poplar Creek Forest Pres. . .
. . . . Pg.10 . . . I16

GOLF COURSES

Rolling Knolls Golf Club . . .
. . . . Pg.9 . . . . K12
Villa Olivia Golf & Country Club
. . . . Pg.14 . . . M13

MISCELLANEOUS

Maywood Park Training Track .
. . . . Pg.14 . . . M13

HOFFMAN ESTATES

Pages 9,10

STREETS

Atlantic Ave. . . Pg.10 . . . H19
Barrington Rd. . Pg.9 . . . . J18
Bear Claw Ct. . . Pg.9 . . . . J13
Beverly Rd. . . . Pg.9 . . . . J18
Boardwalk Blvd. Pg.10 . . . H19
Bode Rd. . . . . . Pg.10 . . . H19
Central Rd. . . . Pg.10 . . . H19
Eagle Way . . . . Pg.10 . . . H19
Falcon Ln. . . . . Pg.9 . . . . J13
Fox Path Ct. . . . Pg.9 . . . . J13
Fox Path Ln. . . . Pg.9 . . . . J13
Golf Rd. (Evanston-Elgin) . .
. . . . Pg.9 . . J15-19
Hassell Rd. . . . Pg.10 . . . I19
Higgins Rd. . . . Pg.9,10 . G12,I19
Hunters Ridge Ct. . . . .
. . . . Pg.9 . . . . J13
Hunters Ridge, E. . . . .
. . . . Pg.9 . . . . J13
Hunters Ridge, W. . . . .
. . . . Pg.9 . . . . J13
Mallard Ln. . . . . Pg.9 . . . . J13
Old Barrington Rd. . . . .
. . . . Pg.10 . . . H19
Old Higgins Rd. . Pg.10 . H18,19
Old South Rd. . . Pg.10 . . . K19
Pacific Ave. . . . Pg.10 . . . K19
Pembroke Ave. . Pg.10 . . . K19
Pheasant Trail Ct. Pg.10 . . J13
Poplar Creek Dr. Pg.10 . . . J19
Prairie Stone Pkwy. . . . . . .
. . . . Pg.9 . . . . H14
Quail Run Ct. . . Pg.9 . . . . J13
Rohrssen Rd. . . Pg.9 . . . . J13
Sears Pkwy. . . . Pg.9 . . . . H14
Shoe Factory Rd. Pg.9 . . . I14
Stonington Ave. Pg.10 . . . I19
Teal Ct. . . . . . . Pg.9 . . . . J13
Trillium Blvd. . . Pg.9 . . . . H13

FOREST PRESERVES

Poplar Creek Forest Pres. . .
. . . . Pg.10 . . . J18

GOLF COURSES

Poplar Creek G.C. Pg.10 . . J19

SCHOOLS

NIU Education Center . . . . .
. . . . Pg.9 . . . . H13

SHOPPING CENTERS

Barrington Sq. Shopping Ctr. .
. . . . Pg.10 . . . I19
Hoffman Village Shopping Ctr. .
. . . . Pg.10 . . . K18

MISCELLANEOUS

Benchmark-Alden Retirement Fac. . .
. . . . Pg.10 . . . J18
Humana Hosp. . Pg.10 . . . J18
Poplar Creek Music Theatre . .
. . . . Pg.9 . . . . H15
Poplar Creek Surgical Ctr. . .
. . . . Pg.9 . . . . J13
Sears Merchandise Group H.Q. .
. . . . Pg.9 . . . . H13

INVERNESS

Page 5

STREETS

Barrington Rd. C19
Bradwell Rd. D19
Braymore Ln. D19
Braymore Dr. C19
Dunbarton Dr. C19
Gaelic Ct. D19
Hamilton Ct. C19
Knox Ct. D19
Palatine Rd. C19

MC QUEENS

Page6...I3

PLATO TOWNSHIP

Pages 6,11

STREETS

Adobe Ridge . . Pg.11 . . . N2
Apache Run . . . Pg.11 . . . M2
Appaloosa Ct. . . Pg.11 . . . O11
Binnfield Dr. . . . Pg.11 . . . N1
Bowes Rd. . . . . Pg.11 . . . L2
Central Dr. . . . . Pg.11 . . . L2
Cheyenne Ct. . . Pg.6 . . . . I3
Chisholm Tr. . . . Pg.6 . . . . I2
Citation Ct. . . . . Pg.11 . . . P2
Cliff Dr. . . . . . . Pg.6 . . . . K2
Coombs Rd. . . . Pg.6 . . . . J3
Corron Rd. . . . . Pg.11 . . . O11
Harty Ct. . . . . . Pg.11 . . . P2
High Chapparel . Pg.6 . . . . I2
Highland Ave. . . Pg.6 . . . . I2
Hogan Hill Trail . Pg.11 . . . N2
Juliet Dr. . . . . . Pg.11 . . . L2
Lori Ln. . . . . . . Pg.11 . . . N2
Lori Ln. W. . . . . Pg.11 . . . N2
McDonald Rd. . . Pg.11 . . . P1
Nestler Rd. . . . . Pg.11 . . . N2
Oak Tree Ln. . . . Pg.11 . . . N1
Plank Rd. . . . . . Pg.6 . . . . K2
Pueblo Peak . . . Pg.11 . . . N2
Red Cloud Ln. . . Pg.11 . . . M2
Romeo Cir. . . . . Pg.11 . . . L2
Romeo Dr. . . . . Pg.11 . . . L2
Russell Rd. . . . . Pg.11 . . . K2
Saindon Dr. . . . Pg.11 . . . N2
Santa Fe Tr. . . . Pg.11 . . . N2
Secretariat Ct. . . Pg.11 . . . P2
Sturbridge Way . Pg.11 . . . O11
Sunflower Ln. . . Pg.11 . . . N1
Verona Dr. . . . . Pg.11 . . . L2
Water Rd. . . . . . Pg.11 . . . M2
Whispering Springs Ln. . . . .
. . . . Pg.11 . . . N1

RUTLAND TOWNSHIP

Pages 1,6

STREETS

Abilene Ct. . . . . Pg.6 . . . . H2
Apache Ln. . . . . Pg.1 . . . . B1
Aztec Ln. . . . . . Pg.1 . . . . B1
Balko Parkway . Pg.1 . . . . B1
Baron Ln. . . . . . Pg.1 . . . . B1
Big Timber Rd. . Pg.6 . . . . G2
Binnie Lakes Tr. Pg.1 . . . . D4
Binnie Rd. . . . . Pg.1 . . . . D3
Bonnie Lane . . . Pg.6 . . . . H3
Cody Ct. . . . . . Pg.6 . . . . H2
Damisch Rd. . . Pg.6 . . . . G1
Freeman Rd. . . Pg.1 . . . . C1
Gary Ln. . . . . . . Pg.1 . . . . B1
Grand Ave. . . . . Pg.6 . . . . G2
Gunpowder Ln. Pg.6 . . . . H2
Guthrie Ct. . . . . Pg.6 . . . . F1
Hidden Hills Trail Pg.1 . . . . C4
Hidden Knoll Rd. Pg.6 . . . . H3
Highland Ave. . . Pg.6 . . . . H1
Huntley Rd. . . . Pg.1 . . . . A3,B4
Mary Cir. . . . . . Pg.1 . . . . C2
Mary Ln. . . . . . Pg.1 . . . . C2
McCormack Rd. Pg.6 . . . . G2
Navajo Ln. . . . . Pg.1 . . . . B1
Northwind Lane Pg.1 . . . . C4
Oak Knoll . . . . . Pg.1 . . . . D4
Oliver Dr. . . . . . Pg.1 . . . . B1
Pheasant Field Ln. . . . .
. . . . Pg.6 . . . . H2
Pleasant Dr. . . . Pg.6 . . . . H3
Powers Rd. . . . Pg.1 . . . . C1
Spring Creek Rd. Pg.1 . . . . C4
Square Barn Rd. Pg.1 . . . . A3
Timber Ridge Dr. Pg.6 . . . . H2

FOREST PRESERVES

Binnie Forest Pres. . . . .
. . . . Pg.1 . . . . C4
Burnidge Forest Pres. . . . . .
. . . . Pg.6 . . . . H3

SCHAUMBURG

Page 10,15

STREETS

Adams Ct. . . . . Pg.15 . . . L18
Amber Ct. . . . . Pg.15 . . . L18
Andover Ct. . . . Pg.10 . . . J18

Ashburn Ct. . . . Pg.15 . . . L18
Ashling Ct. . . . . Pg.15 . . . L18
Barrington Rd. . Pg.15 . . . L18
Beechmont Ct. . Pg.15 . . . L18
Belle Ln. . . . . . Pg.15 . . . M18
Charleston Dr. . Pg.15 . . . M18
Charlotte Ct. . . Pg.15 . . . M18
Chesterfield Ct. Pg.15 . . . M18
Columbia Ct. . . Pg.15 . . . M18
Crescent Ln. . . Pg.15 . . . M18
Debbie Ln. . . . . Pg.15 . . . L18
Delaware Ct. . . Pg.15 . . . L18
Dorshire Ct. . . . Pg.15 . . . L18
Dublin Ln. . . . . Pg.15 . . . L18
Effingham Ct. . . Pg.15 . . . L18
Fallbrook Ct. . . Pg.15 . . . L18
Fremont Ct. . . . Pg.15 . . . M18
Gilcrest Ct. . . . Pg.15 . . . L18
Glasgow Ct. . . . Pg.15 . . . L18
Glasgow Ln. . . Pg.15 . . . L18
Glen Byron Ct. . Pg.15 . . . L18
Glen Leven Ct. . Pg.15 . . . L18
Green Bridge Ct. Pg.15 . . . L18
Hawk Ct. . . . . . Pg.15 . . . M18
Heatherwood Dr. Pg.15 . . . L18
Holmes Way . . Pg.15 . . . L18
Hunterdon Ct. . Pg.15 . . . L18
Island Ct. . . . . . Pg.15 . . . M18
Larch Ct. . . . . . Pg.15 . . . M18
Maidstone Ct. . Pg.15 . . . L18
Meadow Lane Ct. Pg.15 . . . L18
Meadow Ln. . . . Pg.15 . . . L18
Meribel Ct. . . . . Pg.15 . . . E-G16
Odlum Ct. . . . . Pg.15 . . . M18
Odlum Dr. . . . . Pg.15 . . . L18
Odlum Ln. . . . . Pg.15 . . . L18
Old Church Rd. . Pg.15 . . . M18
Pembroke Ct. . . Pg.15 . . . M18
Raleigh Ct. . . . . Pg.15 . . . M18
Schaumburg Rd. Pg.15 . . . L18
Sheffield Dr. . . . Pg.15 . . . M18
Small Dr. . . . . . Pg.15 . . . M18
Weathersfield Way . . . .
. . . . Pg.10 . . . M18
Westminister Ct. Pg.15 . . . M18
Winnsboro Ct. . Pg.15 . . . M18

SLEEPY HOLLOW

Pages 2,7,8

STREETS

Acorn Ct. . . . . . Pg.7 . . . . G7
Acorn Dr. . . . . . Pg.7 . . . . G7,8
Appaloosa Ct. . . Pg.7 . . . . F6
Arabian Pwy . . . Pg.7 . . . . G6
Arlington Pkwy. . Pg.7 . . . . G6
Beau Brummel Dr. . . . .
. . . . Pg.7 . . . . F6
Belmont Pwy . . Pg.7 . . . . F6
Brom Ct. . . . . . Pg.7 . . . . G8
Brook Ct. . . . . . Pg.2 . . . . E8
Bull Frog . . . . . Pg.7 . . . . F8
Carol Crest Ct. . Pg.7 . . . . F8
Christopher Ct. . Pg.7 . . . . G8
Churchill Pwy. . . Pg.7 . . . . F8
Crane Ct. . . . . . Pg.7 . . . . F6
Crane Dr. . . . . . Pg.7 . . . . F6
Danielle Ct. . . . Pg.7 . . . . G7
Darien Ct. . . . . Pg.7 . . . . F6
Darien Ln. . . . . Pg.7 . . . . F6
Deer Ln. . . . . . . Pg.7 . . . . F6
Elm Ct. . . . . . . Pg.8 . . . . F8
Fawn Ct. . . . . . Pg.7 . . . . F8
Front Range Ct. Pg.7 . . . . F8
Gail Ln. . . . . . . Pg.7 . . . . F8
Glen Oak Ct. . . Pg.7 . . . . G7
Glen Oak Dr. . . Pg.7 . . . . G7
Hawthorne Ct. . Pg.7 . . . . F6
Hazel Ct. . . . . . Pg.2 . . . . F8
Hemlock Dr. . . . Pg.7 . . . . F8
Hialeah Ct. . . . . Pg.7 . . . . G6
Hickory Dr. . . . . Pg.2 . . . . E7
Higgins Rd. . . . Pg.2 . . . . E7
Hillcrest Dr. . . . Pg.7 . . . . F7
Hillcrest Park . . Pg.7 . . . . F7
Hilltop Ct. . . . . . Pg.7 . . . . F6
Hilltop East . . . Pg.7 . . . . F6
Hilltop Ln. . . . . Pg.2,7 . . . F6
Holly Ct. . . . . . Pg.7 . . . . F6
Island Ct. . . . . . Pg.2 . . . . F8
Jamestowne Ct. Pg.7 . . . . F6
Jamestowne Ln. Pg.7 . . . . F6
Jill Peak Dr. . . . Pg.7 . . . . F6
Joy Ln. . . . . . . Pg.7 . . . . F7
Karyn Ct. . . . . . Pg.7 . . . . G8
Karyn Dr. . . . . . Pg.7 . . . . G8
Katrina Ct. . . . . Pg.7 . . . . G8
Katrina Ln. . . . . Pg.7 . . . . G8
Kay Ct. . . . . . . Pg.2 . . . . F7
Laurel Ct. . . . . Pg.2 . . . . F8
Locust Dr. . . . . Pg.7 . . . . F8
Maple Ln. . . . . Pg.8 . . . . F8
Maria Ct. . . . . . Pg.7 . . . . G8
Mason Rd. . . . . Pg.7 . . . . G8
Myrna Ct. . . . . Pg.7 . . . . F7
Palomino Ct. . . Pg.7 . . . . G6
Paula Ct. . . . . . Pg.2 . . . . E7
Pimlico Pwy . . . Pg.7 . . . . G6
Pinecone Ln. . . Pg.7 . . . . F7
Plum Ct. . . . . . Pg.2 . . . . F8
Rainbow Dr. . . . Pg.7 . . . . F7
Red Bud Ct. . . . Pg.7 . . . . F7
River Ridge Rd. Pg.7 . . . . G8
Saddle Club Pkwy. . . . .
. . . . Pg.7 . . . . F6
Salem Ct. . . . . Pg.7 . . . . F6
Saratoga Pwy . Pg.7 . . . . G6
Sharon Dr. . . . . Pg.2 . . . . F7
Sleepy Hollow Rd. . . . .
. . . . Pg.7 . . . . G6
Stevens Ct. . . . Pg.2 . . . . F6

Surrey Ct. . . . . Pg.7 . . . . G7
Surrey Ln. . . . . Pg.7 . . . . G7
Sycamore Ln. . Pg.2 . . . . F8
Thorobred Ln. . Pg.7 . . . . F7
Timber Dr. . . . . Pg.7 . . . . F6
Trails End . . . . Pg.2 . . . . F8
Van Tassel Rd. . Pg.7 . . . . F7
Walnut Dr. . . . . Pg.7 . . . . F7
Whitney Rd. . . . Pg.7 . . . . G6
Willow Ln. . . . . Pg.8 . . . . F7
Windcrest Ct. . . Pg.7 . . . . F6
Windsor Ct. . . . Pg.7 . . . . F7
Winmoor Ct. . . Pg.7 . . . . F8
Winmoor Dr. . . Pg.7 . . . . F8
Woodbury Dr. . Pg.7 . . . . G6

GOLF COURSES

Sleepy Hollow Country Club . .
. . . . Pg.7 . . . . F7

SCHOOLS

Sleepy Hollow Sch. . . . .
. . . . Pg.7 . . . . F7
Village Hall . . . Pg.7 . . . . F7

SOUTH BARRINGTON

Pages 5,10

STREETS

Algonquin Rd. . Pg.5 . . . . E17
Back Bay Rd. . . Pg.10 . . . F17
Bartlett Rd. . . . Pg.5 . . E-G16
Bay Reef Dr. . . Pg.10 . . . G17
Beachnut Dr. . . Pg.5 . . . . E17
Beacon Hill Dr. Pg.5 . . . . E16
Berkshire Ct. . . Pg.10 . . . G16
Blanchard Cir. . Pg.10 . . . G18
Brandywine Rd. Pg.10 . . . F16
Bridlewood Tr. . Pg.5 . . . . F18
Brookhaven Ct. Pg.5 . . . . E17
Buckthorn Rd. . Pg.10 . . . G18
Butera Ln. . . . . Pg.10 . . . G18
Central Rd. . . . Pg.10 . . . G18
Champlain Rd. . Pg.10 . . . G16
Concord Ct. . . . Pg.10 . . . F16
Corey Ln. . . . . Pg.10 . . . G18
Covered Bridge Rd. . . . .
. . . . Pg.10 . . . G18
Cutters Run . . . Pg.10 . . . H16
Dalton Ct. . . . . Pg.10 . . . F18
De Veaux Ct. . . Pg.5 . . . . F18
East Cove . . . . Pg.5 . . . . E17
Eastings Way . . Pg.5 . . . . F17
Foxshire Ct. . . . Pg.10 . . . F18
Gregory Ln. . . . Pg.10 . . . G16
Hackney Cir. . . Pg.10 . . . G16
Headwater Cove Pg.10 . . . G17
Heath Way . . . Pg.5 . . . . E18
Higgins Rd. . . . Pg.10 . . . H16
Kitson Dr. . . . . Pg.10 . . . G17
Lake Adalyn Dr. Pg.10 . . . G18
Lakeside Ct. . . Pg.5 . . . . E16
Lakeside Dr. . . Pg.5 . . . . E16
Lexington Rd. . Pg.10 . . . G16
Liberty Dr. . . . . Pg.10 . . . G16
Loch Ln. . . . . . Pg.5 . . . . F18
McQuashen Dr. Pg.10 . . . G18
Midlands Dr. . . Pg.10 . . . H18
Morgan Ln. . . . Pg.10 . . . G16
Mundhank Rd. . Pg.10 . . G,H17
North Meadow Ct. . . . .
. . . . Pg.10 . . . G18
Northwest Tollway . . . .
. . . . Pg.10 . . . H17
Old Barrington Rd. . . . .
. . . . Pg.10 . . . H18
Old Coach Dr. . Pg.10 . . . F18
Old Sutton Rd. . Pg.9 . . . . F15
Overbrook Rd. . Pg.10 . . . F18
Pacer Tr. . . . . . Pg.10 . . . G16
Palatine Rd. . . . Pg.5 . . . . E17
Penny Rd. . . . . Pg.5 . . . . F17
Pentwater Dr. . Pg.10 . . . H16
Polo Dr. . . . . . Pg.10 . . . G18
Quincy Ct. . . . . Pg.5 . . . . F16
Red Ridge Cir. . Pg.5 . . . . F16
Revere Dr. . . . . Pg.10 . . F16,G17
Rose Blvd. . . . . Pg.10 . . . G18
Shire Ln. . . . . . Pg.10 . . . F16
Shirebrook Way Pg.5 . . . . E19
Shore Ridge Dr. Pg.5 . . . . F17
Shoreside Dr. . . Pg.10 . . . F16
South Cove . . . Pg.5 . . . . E17
South Meadow Ct. . . . .
. . . . Pg.10 . . . H17
Spring Creek Dr. Pg.10 . . . F16
Squire Ct. . . . . Pg.10 . . . G18
Stannington Way Pg.5 . . . . E19
Sutton Rd. . . . . Pg.5 . . . . H15
Tennis Club Dr. Pg.10 . . . F18
Tiffany Cir. . . . . Pg.10 . . . G16
Trenton Ct. . . . Pg.10 . . . F17
Turning Shore . Pg.10 . . . F17
Upper Pond . . . Pg.10 . . . F18
Walnut Ln. . . . . Pg.5 . . . . F18
Watercrest Ct. . Pg.10 . . . H16
Watergate Dr. . Pg.10 . . F,G17
Westlake Dr. . . Pg.5 . . . . E16
Willow Bay Dr. . Pg.10 . . . G17
Wind Ridge Rd. Pg.5 . . . . E16
Windsor Ct. . . . Pg.5 . . . . F18
Woodbury Ct. . Pg.5 . . . . E16
Woodbury Ct. W. Pg.5 . . . . E16
Woodhaven Dr. Pg.10 . . . G16
Yorktown Ct. . . Pg.10 . . . G16

MISCELLANEOUS

Alexander Sillman Nature Ctr. .
. . . . Pg.10 . . . F17

Crabtree Nautre Pres. . . . . . .
. . . . Pg.5 . . . . E18

SOUTH ELGIN

Page 12,13

STREETS

Aaron Ave. O7
Adam Ave. O7
Andover Ct. O6
Ann St. O9
Arbor Ln. P7
Arlington Cir. P7
Arlington Cir. E. P7
Arlington Cir. W. P7
Arlington Ct. P7
Arthur Ave. N8
Ashton Ct. P7
Barbara Ave. O7
Beach Ct. N8
Beck Ave. N8
Belle Ln. N8
Boston Ct. P8
Brandywine Ct. O7
Brookline O7
Bunker Hill Ave. O7
Burnidge Rd. N9
Cambridge Rd. P7
Camden Ct. P7
Camden Ln. P7
Carla Dr. O7
Carlton St. N9
Castlebar Ct. P7
Cedar Ct. P7
Center St. P9
Charles Ct. O7
Cherry St. O8
Chipstone Dr. N8
Churchill Ct. P7
Clinton St. P7,8
Clove Ct. P7
Cobbler Ct. P7
Collins St. N,O8
Concord Ave. O7
Concord St. P7
Cornell Ct. P7
Cornwall Ave. P7
Coventry Ct. P7
Crystal Ave. P8
Danbury Ct. O7
Dean St. O7
Division St. O8
East Ln. P8
East Ave. O9
East Dr. P9
East State St. O8
Eastview P9
Elizabeth St. P9
Exeter Ln. O6
Fairfax Dr. P7
Fairfax Ln. P7
Franklin Ave. P8
Fulton St. P8
Gerald Ave. O7
Gilbert St. O9
Gilpin Ave. N8
Gordon Ln. O9
Greenfield Ave. N7
Hancock Ave. P7
Hartman Ct. N9
Harvest Ln. O9
Helen Ave. O7
Hill Ct. P8
Hobart St. N6
Hobart Dr. N6
Hollywood Ct. N9
Hopp Rd. O6
Independence Ave. O8
Ione Dr. O8
Ivy Ln. P7
James St. N7
Josephine Ave. N8
Juniper Ln. P7
Kane St. O7
Kenilworth Ave. N7
Kingsport Dr. O6
Kossuth St. O8
La Fox St. N8
Lafayette Dr. O7
Lakewood Ct. P7
Lancaster Cir. N. P7
Lancaster Ct. S. P7
Lancer Ct. P7
Laurel Dr. P7
Laurel Ln. P7
Lenox Ct. P7
Lexington Ave. P7
Liberty Ave. P8
Lilac Ct. P7
Lincoln St. P7
Linda Ct. P7
Lindemann Ct. O8
Linden Ct. P7
Locust St. P7
Locust St. O8
Longbow Ct. P7
Longview Ct. P7
Lor-Ann St. P9
Lucile St. P7
Main St. O8
Manchester Rd. O7
Marbury St. P7
Mark St. P8
Martin Dr. P7
Mavis Ave. N8
McLean Blvd. O7
Medford Ave. O7
Medford Dr. P7
Melinda Dr. O7
Melrose Ave. N8
Mestic Ct. N9

SOUTH ELGIN

Michigan Ave. N7
Middle St. O9
Mill St. O8
Moody Ct. N9
Nellie Ave. P8
North Dr. P8
Oak St. O8
Paine Ct. P7
Paine St. P7
Park Ave. P8
Patrick St. O9
Pembroke, N. O9
Pleasant Dr. O9
Plum St. O8
Prairie St. N8
Public Rd. N8
Quarry St. O8
Rainbow Terr. N7
Raymond St. N9
Red Gate Ct. R5
Regent St. O8
Renee Dr. N. O7
Revere Rd. O7
River Rd. N9
River St. N8
River Valley Dr. P8
Riverside Ave. N9
Riverview Dr. N9
Robertson Rd. N8
Ross Ave. O8
Saratoga Ct. O8
Schneider Rd. N8
Sheffield Ct. N6
Smith Ct. N9
South Dr. P9
South Elgin Blvd. O9
South London Ct. P7
Spring Ave. P8
Spring St. O7
Spruce St. O8
State St. E. N8
State St. W. N8
Steve's Farm Dr. N8
Stevenson Rd. N8
Stone St. O8
Strathmore Terr. O7
Sunbrook St. O8
Sunbury Rd. O7
Sundown Rd. N7
Sweetbriar Ct. O7
Trenton Ave. O7
Valley Forge Ave. P7
Valley Forge Ct. P7
Vernon Ct. P7
Village Ct. P7
Virginia Dr. O7
Walnut St. O8
Water St. O8
Wedgewood Dr. O7
West Dr. P8
Weston Ct. O6
Whispering Ct. P9
Williams Dr. P9
Willow Ln. N7
Wills St. O8
Wilson Ave. N8
Woodbury St. O8
Woodcliff Dr. P8
Woodridge Cir. P8
Woodrow Ave. N8
Yorkshire Ct. O7

CEMETERIES
South Elgin Cem. O9

PARKS
Lions Park O8
Riverside Park O8

SCHOOLS
Clinton Sch. O9
Pioneer Sch. O8
Willard Sch. O8

MISCELLANEOUS
Fire Department O8
Trolley Museum O8
Village Hall and Police O8

ST. CHARLES TOWNSHIP
Pages 11-13
STREETS
Crane Rd. .... Pg.11 .... P4
Dogwood Ln. .... Pg.11 .... P3
Eagles Nest Ct. .... Pg.11 .... P3
East Dr. .... Pg.13 .... P9
Falcons Tr. .... Pg.11 .... P3
Hill Ct. .... Pg.12 .... P8
Lilac Ln. .... Pg.11 .... P4
Northern Ct. .... Pg.11 .... Q3
Oak Dr. .... Pg.11 .... P3
Pine Rd. .... Pg.11 .... P3
River Valley Dr. .... Pg.12 .... P9
South Dr. .... Pg.13 .... P9
Sycamore Ave. .... Pg.11 .... P4
West Dr. .... Pg.13 .... P8
Woodcliff Dr. .... Pg.12 .... P9

STREAMWOOD
Pages 9,10,14,15
STREETS
Abbeywood Cir. .... Pg.10 .... K17
Abbington Ct. .... Pg.14 .... M15
Acorn Dr. .... Pg.15 .... M18
Adams Ct. .... Pg.14 .... M15
Alexander Ave. .... Pg.15 .... N17
Alexander Dr. .... Pg.15 .... N17
Alexander Pl. .... Pg.15 .... N17
Andover Ct. .... Pg.15 .... N16
Apple Hill Ln. .... Pg.10 .... K17
Arabian Ct. .... Pg.14 .... L14
Arbor Ct. .... Pg.14 .... M14
Arbor Dr. .... Pg.14 .... M14
Arnold Ave. .... Pg.15 .... N16
Arrowwood Ct. .... Pg.10 .... K17
Arthur Ct. .... Pg.15 .... L16
Ascot Ln. .... Pg.9 .... K15
Ash Ct. .... Pg.15 .... L17
Ashton Ct. .... Pg.15 .... N16
Aspen Ct. .... Pg.15 .... M17
Audubon Rd. .... Pg.15 .... L16
Autumn Ln. .... Pg.14 .... M15
Azalea Cir. .... Pg.15 .... L17
Barrington Rd. .... Pg.15 .... L18
Bartlett Ct. .... Pg.15 .... N16
Bartlett Rd. S. .... Pg.15 .... O16
Bayberry Ct. .... Pg.15 .... M17
Beaver Dr. .... Pg.15 .... L17
Beebe Ct. .... Pg.15 .... N16
Berkley Pl. .... Pg.15 .... M16
Berkshire Ct. .... Pg.14 .... M17
Beverly Ct. .... Pg.15 .... N15
Beverly Ln. .... Pg.15 .... N15
Big Oaks Ct. .... Pg.15 .... L16
Big Oaks Rd. .... Pg.15 .... L16
Birchwood Ct. .... Pg.10 .... K18
Bittersweet Ln. .... Pg.14 .... L14
Blackberry Ct., W. ....
Bluff Ct. .... Pg.14 .... L14
Bode Rd., E. .... Pg.10 .... K16
Bonded Pkwy. .... Pg.15 .... M18
Borris Cir. .... Pg.15 .... K17
Bourbon Pkwy. .... Pg.15 .... M18
Boxwood Ct. .... Pg.10 .... K18
Brandy Pkwy. .... Pg.15 .... M18
Briarwood Dr. .... Pg.15 .... M16
Bristol Ct. .... Pg.15 .... N16
Brittany Dr. .... Pg.14 .... M15
Brook Dr. .... Pg.10 .... K17
Brookstone Ct. .... Pg.14 .... M15
Brookstone Dr. .... Pg.14 .... M15
Brunswick Ct. .... Pg.15 .... N16
Buchanan Dr. .... Pg.15 .... L15
Buckskin Ln. .... Pg.14 .... L14
Burgundy Pkwy. .... Pg.15 .... M18
Bussey Ct. .... Pg.15 .... N17
Butternut Ln. .... Pg.15 .... M18
Cahill Rd. .... Pg.15 .... L18
Cambridge Ave. .... Pg.15 .... N16
Canterbury Ct. .... Pg.14 .... M15
Carey Ln. .... Pg.15 .... L16
Carlson Dr. .... Pg.15 .... N17
Carol Ann Dr. .... Pg.10 .... K16
Cedar Cir. .... Pg.15 .... L16
Cedar Circle Ct. .... Pg.15 .... L16
Cedarcrest Dr. .... Pg.15 .... M17
Center Rd. .... Pg.14 .... L15
Chase Ct. .... Pg.15 .... L15
Chase Terr. .... Pg.15 .... L16
Chaucer Ln. .... Pg.15 .... L16
Cherry Ln. .... Pg.15 .... M16
Chestnut Dr. E. .... Pg.15 .... L16
Chestnut Dr. S. .... Pg.15 .... L16
Chrisman Rd. .... Pg.15 .... L16
Clairidge Ct. .... Pg.10 .... K17
Clearwater Ct. .... Pg.14 .... M15
Clematis Ct. .... Pg.15 .... L17
Club Tree Dr. .... Pg.15 .... N16
Colony Ct. .... Pg.15 .... N16
Columbine Ct. .... Pg.14 .... M14
Concord Dr. .... Pg.15 .... L18
Coolidge Ct. .... Pg.14 .... M15
Corrington Ct. .... Pg.10 .... K18
Creekside Ct. .... Pg.14 .... M15
Crestwood Ct. .... Pg.15 .... M16
Crestwood Dr. .... Pg.15 .... M16
Cypress Dr. .... Pg.15 .... L16
Dana Ln. .... Pg.10 .... K17
Dartmouth Ct. .... Pg.14 .... M15
Dato Ct. .... Pg.15 .... K18
Dato Dr. .... Pg.15 .... K18
David Dr. .... Pg.15 .... L17
Debbie Ln. .... Pg.15 .... L18
Deerfield Dr. .... Pg.14 .... L15
Diane Dr. .... Pg.15 .... M15
Dogwood Ct. .... Pg.15 .... K18
Dorchester Ct. .... Pg.14 .... M16
Dorman Dr. .... Pg.15 .... M16
Dover Ct. .... Pg.9 .... K15
Driftwood Ct. .... Pg.10 .... K17
Dunbar Ct. .... Pg.15 .... N16
Duxbury Ct. .... Pg.15 .... N16
East Ave. .... Pg.15 .... L,M17
Edgewood Dr. .... Pg.15 .... M16
Egan Ct. .... Pg.15 .... K18
Egan Dr. .... Pg.15 .... K18
Eliasek Ct. .... Pg.10 .... K17
Elm Ln. .... Pg.15 .... L16
Essex Ct. .... Pg.15 .... N16
Evans Ct. .... Pg.14 .... L15
Evergreen Dr. .... Pg.14 .... M15
Exmoor Dr. .... Pg.10 .... K16
Fairview Dr. .... Pg.15 .... M16
Fallstone Ct. .... Pg.15 .... L17
Falmouth Ct. .... Pg.15 .... N16
Fernwood Ct. .... Pg.15 .... K18
Field Ln. .... Pg.15 .... L16
Filbert Ln. .... Pg.15 .... L17
Fillmore Ln. .... Pg.15 .... L15
Finch Ct. .... Pg.14 .... M14
Fir Ct. .... Pg.15 .... L17
Flowers Ave. .... Pg.15 .... N17
Forest Dr. .... Pg.15 .... M16
Foxboro Ct. .... Pg.14 .... M15
Foxglove Ct. .... Pg.14 .... M14
Francis Dr. .... Pg.15 .... M18
Franklin Ct. .... Pg.10 .... K16
Frederick Ave. .... Pg.15 .... N17
Freeman Ave. .... Pg.15 .... N16
Fulton Dr. .... Pg.14 .... M15
Gant Ct. .... Pg.15 .... K17
Garfield Ln. .... Pg.15 .... L15
Garfield Ct. .... Pg.15 .... L15
Genualdi Ave. .... Pg.15 .... N17
Glendale Ct. .... Pg.10 .... K17
Green Ct. .... Pg.15 .... K18
Green Knoll Ln. .... Pg.10 .... K18
Green Meadows Blvd. ....
Greenbriar Ln. .... Pg.15 .... K18
Greenwood Ct. .... Pg.15 .... N16
Gregg Ct. .... Pg.15 .... K18
Greystone Ct. .... Pg.15 .... K18
Grow Ln. .... Pg.15 .... L16
Gulf Keys Rd. .... Pg.14 .... M14
Hackberry Dr. .... Pg.15 .... M17
Halick Dr. .... Pg.15 .... K16
Hampton Ct. .... Pg.15 .... N16
Harrison Ln. .... Pg.15 .... L16
Hartwood Dr. .... Pg.15 .... M17
Harvest Dr. .... Pg.14 .... M15
Hastings Mill Rd. .... Pg.10 .... K18
Hawthorne Ln. .... Pg.15 .... L16
Hayward Ave. .... Pg.15 .... N17
Hazelnut Dr. .... Pg.15 .... M18
Heath Ct. .... Pg.15 .... N17
Heather Ct. .... Pg.15 .... L17
Heather Ln. .... Pg.15 .... L17
Hecht Rd. .... Pg.15 .... K18
Heine Ct. .... Pg.15 .... K18
Heine Dr. .... Pg.15 .... K18
Helen Ct. .... Pg.15 .... M16
Hickory Ave. .... Pg.15 .... L17
Hillside Ct. .... Pg.15 .... L17
Hillside Dr. .... Pg.15 .... L17
Hise Ct. .... Pg.15 .... K18
Holly Ct. .... Pg.15 .... L17
Holly Dr. .... Pg.15 .... L17
Hoover Ct. .... Pg.15 .... M15
Horseshoe Ct. .... Pg.14 .... L14
Hummingbird Ct. .... Pg.14 .... M14
Hummingbird Ln. ....
Huntington Dr. .... Pg.14 .... L14
Innisbrook Dr. .... Pg.15 .... L17
Iris Dr. .... Pg.15 .... M17
Ironwood Ct. .... Pg.15 .... K18
Irving Park Rd. E. ....
 .... Pg.15 .... N18
Ivy Ct. .... Pg.15 .... M18
Jackson Ln. .... Pg.15 .... L15
Jamestown Ct. .... Pg.15 .... N16
Janet Ave. .... Pg.15 .... M15
Jefferson Ct. .... Pg.15 .... L15
Jefferson Ln. .... Pg.15 .... L15
Jill Ln. .... Pg.15 .... L16
Jonquil Ct. W. .... Pg.14 .... L14
Joyce Ln. .... Pg.15 .... L16
Judy Ln. .... Pg.15 .... K18
Juniper Ct. .... Pg.15 .... L17
Juniper Pl. .... Pg.15 .... L17
Kennedy Ct. .... Pg.15 .... L17
Kennedy Dr. N. .... Pg.10 .... K18
Kennedy Dr. S. .... Pg.10 .... K18
Kennedy Dr. W. .... Pg.10 .... K18
Kensington Ct. .... Pg.14 .... M15
Kensington Dr. .... Pg.14 .... K15
Kevin Morris Ct. .... Pg.15 .... L18
Kimberly Ln. .... Pg.14 .... M15
King Dr. .... Pg.15 .... N18
Kingston Ct. .... Pg.15 .... N16
Klafter Ct. .... Pg.15 .... M16
Klein Dr. .... Pg.15 .... L18
Kosan Cir. .... Pg.15 .... N16
Krause Ave. .... Pg.15 .... N16
La Salle Ct. .... Pg.15 .... M15
La Salle Rd. .... Pg.15 .... M15
Lacy Ln. .... Pg.15 .... N17
Lake St. .... Pg.15 .... O17
Lancaster Ct. .... Pg.15 .... N17
Larkspur Ln. W. .... Pg.14 .... L14
Larsen Ave. .... Pg.15 .... N17
Laurel Ct. .... Pg.15 .... L16
Laurel Ln. .... Pg.15 .... L16
Laurel Oaks Dr. .... Pg.15 .... M17
Lee Ct. .... Pg.15 .... N17
Lexington St. .... Pg.15 .... N16
Library Dr. .... Pg.15 .... N16
Lincoln Ave. .... Pg.15 .... N16
Lincoln Ct. .... Pg.15 .... M16
Lincolnwood Dr. .... Pg.15 .... M16
Linda Ln. .... Pg.15 .... K18
Lisa Ln. .... Pg.15 .... M15
Little Creek Ct. .... Pg.14 .... L14
Little Creek Dr. .... Pg.14 .... L14
Locksley Dr. .... Pg.15 .... L16
Longboat Key Ln. ....
 .... Pg.14 .... M14
Lynnwood Ct. .... Pg.15 .... N16
Madison Dr. .... Pg.15 .... M15
Magnolia Ct. .... Pg.14 .... L14
Magnolia Dr. W. .... Pg.15 .... L14
Manchester Ct. .... Pg.9 .... K15
Manor Dr. .... Pg.15 .... K16
Marion Ln. .... Pg.15 .... L16
Mark Ln. .... Pg.10 .... K18
Marryat Pl. .... Pg.14 .... L15
Maxon Ln. E. .... Pg.15 .... L16
Maxon Ln. S. .... Pg.15 .... L16
Mayfield Dr. .... Pg.15 .... L17
McCabe Ct. .... Pg.15 .... L16
McKinley Ln. .... Pg.14 .... L15
McKool Ave. .... Pg.15 .... N17
Meadow Ct. .... Pg.15 .... M17
Meadow Ln. .... Pg.15 .... M17
Medford Ct. .... Pg.15 .... M17
Merideth Ln. .... Pg.15 .... N16
Merryoaks Rd. .... Pg.14 .... M15
Meyer Ct. .... Pg.15 .... K18
Middlebury Ct. .... Pg.10 .... K17
Miller Ave. .... Pg.15 .... L18
Monroe Ct. .... Pg.15 .... L16
Moore Ave. .... Pg.15 .... N16
Mulberry Ln. .... Pg.15 .... M17
Mustang Ct. .... Pg.14 .... M14
Myrtle Ln. .... Pg.15 .... M15
Newberry Dr. .... Pg.15 .... M17
Nippert Ave. .... Pg.15 .... N16
North Ave. .... Pg.15 .... O16
Norwood Ct. .... Pg.15 .... N16
Oak Knoll Ct. .... Pg.10 .... K17
Oak Meadow Ct. .... Pg.10 .... K17
Oak Ridge Dr. .... Pg.15 .... M15
Oakland Dr. .... Pg.15 .... K17
Oakmont Ct. .... Pg.10 .... K17
Old Church Rd. .... Pg.15 .... L18
Old Oak Ct. .... Pg.15 .... N16
Old Oak Ln. .... Pg.15 .... N16
Oltendorf Rd., E. .... Pg.15 .... N16
Oltendorf Rd., N. .... Pg.15 .... L16
Oltendorf Rd., S. .... Pg.15 .... N16
Oriole Dr. .... Pg.14 .... M14
Oxford Dr. .... Pg.15 .... N16
Park Blvd., N. .... Pg.10 .... K16
Park Blvd., S. .... Pg.15 .... N16
Parkside Cir. .... Pg.15 .... M16
Parkwood Ct. .... Pg.15 .... M17
Parkwood Dr. .... Pg.15 .... M17
Patricia Pkwy. .... Pg.15 .... M15
Pembroke Ct. .... Pg.14 .... L15
Pepperidge Cir. .... Pg.15 .... M17
Petrie Cir. .... Pg.15 .... N17
Phillips Cir. Dr. .... Pg.14 .... M14
Pine St. E. .... Pg.15 .... M16
Pine St. S. .... Pg.15 .... M16
Pinto Ct. .... Pg.14 .... L14
Pleasant Pl. .... Pg.15 .... M17
Plum Tree Ct. .... Pg.10 .... K17
Plymouth Dr. .... Pg.10 .... K16
Polk Ct. .... Pg.15 .... M15
Poplar Creek Ct. .... Pg.15 .... M16
Post Ct. .... Pg.15 .... L17
Post Ln. .... Pg.15 .... L17
Princeton Ct. .... Pg.15 .... N16
Quaker Hollow Ct. ....
 .... Pg.10 .... K18
Quaker Hollow Rd. ....
 .... Pg.10 .... K18
Quarter Horse Ct. .... Pg.14 .... L14
Quincy Ct. .... Pg.15 .... N16
Rambler Ct. .... Pg.15 .... M17
Rambler Ln. .... Pg.15 .... M17
Ramblewood Dr. .... Pg.15 .... M18
Red Cedar Dr. .... Pg.15 .... L17,18
Redwood Ct. .... Pg.15 .... L17
Regency Ct. .... Pg.15 .... M15
Ridge Ct. .... Pg.15 .... M17
Ridge Ct., N. .... Pg.15 .... L17
Ridgewood Ct. .... Pg.14 .... L15
Robinhood Ct. .... Pg.15 .... L17
Robinhood Dr. .... Pg.15 .... L17
Robinson Ave. .... Pg.15 .... N17
Roder Ct. .... Pg.15 .... N17
Roma Jean Pkwy. ....
 .... Pg.15 .... N16
Rowley Ct. .... Pg.15 .... N16
Russel Ln. .... Pg.15 .... M17
Sandalwood Ct. .... Pg.10 .... K17
Sandhurst Ct. .... Pg.15 .... M17
Sarasota Dr. .... Pg.15 .... K16
Saybrook Ct. .... Pg.15 .... N16
Schaumburg Rd., E. ....
 .... Pg.15 .... L18
Schaumburg Rd., W. ....
 .... Pg.15 .... L17
Seneca Ct. .... Pg.15 .... M15
Seton Ct. .... Pg.15 .... N16
Seton Pl. .... Pg.15 .... L17
Shadywood Ln. .... Pg.15 .... L15
Shagbark Ln., E. .... Pg.10 .... K17
Sheffield Ct. .... Pg.15 .... K15
Sherwood Dr. .... Pg.15 .... M17
Shirley Ave. .... Pg.15 .... N17
Siesta Key Ln. .... Pg.14 .... M14
Sieverwood Ct. .... Pg.10 .... K18
Smith Ct. .... Pg.15 .... L18
Somerset Dr. .... Pg.15 .... K17
Southbury Ct. .... Pg.15 .... N16
Southwood Ct. .... Pg.15 .... M17
Spring Valley Ln. .... Pg.15 .... M17
Spruce Dr. .... Pg.15 .... M16
Spur Ct. .... Pg.14 .... L14
Stowell Pl. .... Pg.15 .... M16
Stowell Rd. .... Pg.15 .... N17
Stratford Ct. .... Pg.15 .... M16
Stratford Ct., S. .... Pg.15 .... M16
Streamwood Blvd., E. ....
 .... Pg.15 .... N16
Streamwood Blvd., W. ....
 .... Pg.15 .... M17
Suffolk Ct. .... Pg.15 .... M17
Suffolk Pl. .... Pg.15 .... M17
Sumac Dr. .... Pg.15 .... M17
Sunnydale Blvd. .... Pg.15 .... M17
Sunset Ct. .... Pg.15 .... L17
Surrey Ct. .... Pg.15 .... M17
Surrey Dr. .... Pg.15 .... M17
Sutton Rd., S. .... Pg.14 .... M14
Taft Ct. .... Pg.14 .... M15
Tall Tree Rd. .... Pg.15 .... N16
Tanglewood Dr. .... Pg.15 .... L15
Taylor Ct. .... Pg.15 .... L15
Teak Ln. .... Pg.15 .... M18
Thorndale Ct. .... Pg.15 .... L15
Timber Ct. .... Pg.15 .... L16
Timber Tr. .... Pg.15 .... L16
Tinnerella Ave. .... Pg.15 .... N17
Troy Ct. .... Pg.15 .... N16
Truman Ct. .... Pg.14 .... M15
Truman Ln. .... Pg.15 .... M15
Twilight Terr. .... Pg.15 .... L16
Tyler Ct. .... Pg.15 .... L15
Uxbridge Ct. .... Pg.15 .... N16
Valley Ln. E. .... Pg.15 .... N16
Valley Ln. S. .... Pg.15 .... N16
Victoria Ln., N. .... Pg.15 .... L17
Villa Rd. .... Pg.15 .... L17
Vine St. .... Pg.15 .... N17
Vinton Ct. .... Pg.15 .... N16
Virginia Ct. .... Pg.15 .... M17
Walden Tr. .... Pg.15 .... L16
Walker Ave. .... Pg.15 .... N16
Walnut Ct., N. .... Pg.14 .... L15
Walnut Dr. .... Pg.15 .... L16
Warwick Ct. .... Pg.10 .... K18
Washington Ave. .... Pg.15 .... M15
Washington Ct. .... Pg.15 .... L16
Waverly Ave. .... Pg.15 .... M17
Wellington Dr. .... Pg.15 .... K16
Westgate Ct. .... Pg.15 .... M15
Westgate Terr. .... Pg.15 .... M15
Weston Ct. .... Pg.14 .... K15
Whispering Ct. .... Pg.14 .... M15
Whispering Dr. .... Pg.15 .... M15
White Fence Tr. .... Pg.14 .... L14
White Hall Ct. .... Pg.15 .... L18
Whitewood Dr. .... Pg.15 .... L17
Wicker Ave. .... Pg.15 .... N17
Wild Rose Ct. .... Pg.14 .... N15
Wildflower Way .... Pg.14 .... M14
Wildwood Ct. .... Pg.15 .... M17
Wildwood Ln. .... Pg.15 .... M17
Williamsburg Dr. .... Pg.10 .... K17
Willow Ct. .... Pg.15 .... L17
Willow Rd. .... Pg.15 .... L17
Wilshire Ct. .... Pg.15 .... L17
Winchester Dr. .... Pg.15 .... M16
Windgate Ct. .... Pg.10 .... K17
Winding Run Ln. .... Pg.10 .... K18
Windsor Ct. .... Pg.10 .... K17
Wisteria Dr. .... Pg.15 .... L18
Woodbury Ct. .... Pg.10 .... K18
Woodcrest Cir. .... Pg.15 .... L16
Woodland Hts. Blvd ....
 .... Pg.15 .... M17
Woodland Hts. Ct. ....
 .... Pg.15 .... M17
Woodmar Ct. .... Pg.10 .... K17
Woodridge Ln. .... Pg.15 .... L17
Woodview Ct. .... Pg.15 .... M17
Woodview Dr. .... Pg.15 .... M17
Yorkshire Dr. .... Pg.15 .... N18

GOLF COURSES
Streamwood Oaks G.C. ....
 .... Pg.14 .... L15

PARKS
Anniversary Park .... Pg.14 .... M15
Aquarius Park .... Pg.15 .... M17
Challenger Park .... Pg.10 .... K17
Countryside Park .... Pg.15 .... L16
Dolphin Park .... Pg.15 .... M16
Friendship Park .... Pg.15 .... M17
Glenbrook Park .... Pg.10 .... K17
Jaycee Park .... Pg.14 .... L15
Kollar Park .... Pg.15 .... N17
Lacy Park .... Pg.15 .... N17
Oakhill Park .... Pg.15 .... N17
Ridge Park .... Pg.15 .... L17
Sunnydale Park .... Pg.15 .... M17
Veteran's Park .... Pg.15 .... L17
Vine Park .... Pg.15 .... N17
Walnut Park .... Pg.15 .... L15

SCHOOLS
Canton Jr. H.S. .... Pg.15 .... L17
Glenbrook Sch. .... Pg.10 .... K17
Hanover Countryside Sch. ....
 .... Pg.15 .... N16
Heritage Sch. .... Pg.15 .... N16
Oakhill Sch. .... Pg.15 .... N17
Parkwood Sch. .... Pg.15 .... N17
Ridge Circle Sch. .... Pg.15 .... L17
Streamwood H.S. 4 Pg.14 .... L15
Streamwood Sch. ....
 .... Pg.15 .... M17
Sunnydale Sch. .... Pg.15 .... M17
Tefft Jr. H.S. .... Pg.15 .... N17
Woodland Hts. Sch. ....
 .... Pg.15 .... M16

SHOPPING CENTERS
Hillbrook S.C. .... Pg.15 .... L16
Market Square .... Pg.15 .... N17
Oak Forest Plaza .... Pg.15 .... M17
Oak Knolls Commons ....
 .... Pg.15 .... L16
Streamwood S.C. .... Pg.15 .... L16

WEST DUNDEE

Westview Ctr. .... Pg.15 .... M18
Woodland Hts. Shopping Center ....
 .... Pg.15 .... N16

MISCELLANEOUS
Fire Dept. .... Pg.15 .... L18
Public Works .... Pg.15 .... M16

UDINA
Page6...K3

WEST DUNDEE
Pages 2,3,8
STREETS
A St. .... Pg.2 .... E8
Aberdeen Ln. .... Pg.2 .... E7
B St. .... Pg.2 .... E8
Barber Ct. .... Pg.2 .... E7
Bass Ct. .... Pg.8 .... G9
Brewer Ct. .... Pg.2 .... E7
Browning Ave. .... Pg.8 .... F9
Castle Ct. .... Pg.2 .... E7
Castle Rock Ct. .... Pg.8 .... F9
Cavalier Ct. .... Pg.8 .... F8
Chadwick Ln. .... Pg.2 .... E7
Dunning Ave. .... Pg.8 .... F9
Edinburgh Ln. .... Pg.2 .... E8
Edwards Ave. .... Pg.8 .... F9
Eichler Dr. .... Pg.8 .... F9
Fay Ave. .... Pg.8 .... F9
Flint Dr. .... Pg.8 .... G9
Fox Ave. .... Pg.8 .... F9
Galloway Ct. .... Pg.2 .... E7
Garrison Ave. .... Pg.8 .... F9
Geneva St. .... Pg.3 .... E9
Glenmoor Dr. .... Pg.2 .... E7
Grant St. .... Pg.2 .... E7
Green Castle Ct. .... Pg.2 .... E7
Green Ct. .... Pg.2 .... E7
Hamilton Dr. .... Pg.2 .... E7
Hawley Ave. .... Pg.8 .... F9
Highland Ave. .... Pg.3 .... E9
Hillcrest Ct. .... Pg.8 .... F9
Kane Ave. .... Pg.8 .... F9
Kittridge Dr. .... Pg.2 .... E7
Knowlton Dr. .... Pg.2 .... E7
Liberty St. .... Pg.3 .... E9
Lincoln Ave. .... Pg.3 .... E9
Lisa Rd. .... Pg.3 .... F9
MacGregor .... Pg.2 .... E7
Maiden Ln. .... Pg.2 .... E7
Main St. .... Pg.2 .... F9
Market Loop .... Pg.2 .... E9
McConniche Ct. .... Pg.2 .... F9
Oregon St. .... Pg.2 .... F9
Pember Cir. .... Pg.2 .... F9
Preston Ave. .... Pg.2 .... E7
Prestwick Ct. .... Pg.2 .... E7
Richardson .... Pg.8 .... G9
Riverside Ave. .... Pg.8 .... F9
Riverview St. .... Pg.8 .... F9
Roundabout .... Pg.8 .... F8
Royal Ln. .... Pg.2 .... E9
Ryan Ln. .... Pg.2 .... F9
Short St. .... Pg.8 .... F9
Smalley Ct. .... Pg.2 .... E7
South St. .... Pg.2 .... E7
Spaulding Ave. .... Pg.2 .... E7
Spring Hill Ring Rd. ....
 .... Pg.3 .... F9
Sterling Dr. .... Pg.3 .... E8
Sterling Ln. .... Pg.2 .... E8
Stewart Ln. .... Pg.2 .... E7
Strom Dr. .... Pg.2 .... E8
Tartans Ct. .... Pg.3 .... E8
Tartans Dr. .... Pg.2 .... E8
Thatcher Tr. .... Pg.2 .... E7
Tritram Ct. .... Pg.2 .... E7
Village Quarter Rd. ....
 .... Pg.3 .... F9
Washington St. .... Pg.3 .... E9
Water Tower Rd. .... Pg.2 .... E8
Waterbury Ct. .... Pg.2 .... E7
Western Ave. .... Pg.3 .... F9
1st St. .... Pg.3 .... E9
2nd St. .... Pg.3 .... E9
3rd St. .... Pg.3 .... E9
4th St. .... Pg.3 .... E9
5th St. .... Pg.3 .... E9
6th St. .... Pg.3 .... E9
7th St. .... Pg.3 .... E9
8th St. .... Pg.3 .... E9

CEMETERIES
Dundee Twp. Cem. West ....
 .... Pg.3 .... E8

PARKS
Tower Park .... Pg.3 .... E8

SCHOOLS
Childrens House Mont. Sch. ....
 .... Pg.8 .... F9
St. Catherine's Sch. ....
 .... Pg.3 .... F9

SHOPPING CENTERS
Spring Hill Mall .... Pg.3 .... E8

MISCELLANEOUS
Fire Dept. .... Pg.3 .... F9
Public Library .... Pg.3 .... E9
Spring Hill Plaza .... Pg.3 .... E9
Village Hall & Police Dept. ....
 .... Pg.3 .... F9